The English Church 1066–1154

The English Church 1066-1154

Frank Barlow

Longman
London and New York

Longman Group Limited London

*Associated companies, branches and representatives
throughout the world*

*Published in the United States of America
by Longman Inc., New York*

© Longman Group Limited 1979

First published 1979

ISBN 0 582 50236 5

British Library Cataloguing in Publication Data

Barlow, Frank
  The English Church, 1066-1154.
  1. England – Church history
  2. Church history – Middle ages, 600-1500
  I. Title
  274.2   BR750   78-40458

ISBN 0–582–50236–5

Printed in Great Britain by Richard Clay (The Chaucer Press) Ltd, Bungay, Suffolk

Contents

Preface

When I wrote *The English Church, 1000–1066* in the early 1960s I hoped 'to continue the constitutional history of the *ecclesia anglicana* in other volumes'. My progress has been slower than I expected; and this second volume is a little different in scope and treatment from the other. Although the plan is still determined by an interest in structure, function, and activity, the greater richness of the sources allowed most of the subjects to be given more human and social features, and I came to think that the sub-title which the first volume originally carried, 'A Constitutional History', was too limiting. It has therefore been dropped. Even so I have not ventured into the realms of intellectual history or *spiritualité*; nor have I been much concerned with buildings or their furnishings.

I would like to thank my former secretary, Sheilagh Edmonds (now Banner), for typing the manuscript, George W. Greenaway and Timothy Reuter for reading and criticizing the book in draft, and all those others who directly or indirectly have helped me. The writer of a book like this incurs many debts; I only wish I could pay them all in full.

Middle Court Hall, Kenton, Exeter   Frank Barlow
5 September 1978

Abbreviated References

AB	*Analecta Bollandiana* (Brussels 1882–)
Acta Lanfranci	in John Earle *Two of the Saxon Chronicles Parallel* (1865) 271
Acta Sanctorum	ed. J. Bolland, Henschenius, Papebroch, etc. (1734–)
Adami de Domerham historia	ed. Tho. Hearne (1727)
AEp	see Anselm *Ep*
Anglia Sacra	ed. Henry Wharton (2 vols, 1691)
Annales monastici	ed. H. R. Luard (Rolls ser. 5 vols, 1864–9)
Anselm *Ep*	in *Anselmi Opera Omnia*, ed. F. S. Schmitt (1946–52) vols 3–5.
ASS	see *Acta Sanctorum*
Barlow *English Church 1000—1066*	Frank B. *The English Church 1000—1066* (1963)
Bede	*Bede's Ecclesiastical History of the English People*, ed. B. Colgrave and R. A. B. Mynors (Oxford Med. Texts 1969)
B.M. MS Harl.	British Museum, Harleian Manuscript
Böhmer *Die Fälschungen*	Heinrich B., *Die Fälschungen Erzbishof Lanfranks von Canterbury* (Studien zur Geschichte der Theologie und der Kirche, Leipzig 1902)
Böhmer *KuS*	*Kirche und Staat in England und in der Normandie im XI. und XII. Jahrhundert* (Leipzig 1899)
Cahiers de Civ. Méd.	*Cahiers de Civilisation Médiévale, Xe—XIIe siècles* (Université de Poitiers)
CambHJ	*Cambridge Historical Journal*
CCM	*Corpus consuetudinum monasticarum*, ed. K. Hallinger (Sieburg)
Chron.	*The Anglo-Saxon Chronicle*, a revised trans., ed. Dorothy Whitelock, David C. Douglas, and Susie I. Tucker (1961)
Chron. Abingdon	*Chronicon monasterii de Abingdon*, ed. J. Stevenson (Rolls ser. 1858)

Chron. Evesham	*Chronicon abbatiae de Evesham,* ed. W. D. Macray (Rolls ser. 1863)
Davies *Episcopal Acts*	J. Conway Davies, *Episcopal Acts Relating to Welsh Dioceses, 1066—1272* (Hist. Soc. of the church in Wales, 2 vols, 1946–8)
DB	*Domesday Book seu Liber Censualis Willelmi primi . . .* (1783–1816)
De injusta vexatione	in Simeon of Durham (q.v.) *Opera* i
Diceto *Abbrev. chron.*	in *Opera,* ed. W. Stubbs (Rolls ser.) i (1876)
Diceto *Ymagines*	*ibid.*
DNB	*Dictionary of National Biography,* ed. Leslie Stephen and Sidney Lee
Eadmer *HN*	*Historia Novorum in Anglia,* ed. Martin Rule (Rolls ser. 1884)
Eadmer *VA*	*The Life of St Anselm . . . by Eadmer,* ed. R. W. Southern (Nelson's Med. Texts 1962)
EHD	*English Historical Documents, 1042—1189,* ed. D. C. Douglas and G. W. Greenaway (1953)
EHR	*English Historical Review*
English Church 1000—1066	see Barlow
Epistola de contemptu mundi	see HH
Ep., Epp.	*Epistola/ae*
Florence	F. of Worcester, *Chronicon ex chronicis,* ed. B. Thorpe (Eng. Hist. Soc. 1848–9)
Foreville	Raymonde Foreville, *Latran I, II, III, IV,* Histoire des conciles œcuméniques, ed. Gervais Dumeige, VI (Paris 1965)
Fröhlich	Walter Fröhlich, 'Die bischoflichen Kollegen Erzbishof Anselms von Canterbury' (Doctoral diss., philos. fac., University of Munich, 1970)
Geoffrey of Coldingham	*Liber de statu ecclesiae Dunhelmensis* in *Historiae Dunelmensis scriptores tres,* ed. J. Raine (Surtees Soc. ix, 1839)
Gerald of Wales	see Giraldus Cambrensis
Gervase	*G. of Canterbury: historical works,* ed. W. Stubbs (Rolls ser. 1879–80)
GG	*Histoire de Guillaume le Conquérant (Gesta Guillelmi ducis Normannorum et regis Anglorum),* ed. Raymonde Foreville (Paris 1952)
Giraldus Cambrensis *Opera*	ed. J. S. Brewer (vols i–iv), J. F. Dimock (vols v–vii), G. F. Warner (vol. viii) (Rolls ser. 1861–91)

Giraldus Cambrensis *Vita S. Remigii*	in *Opera* vol. vii.
GP	see William of Malmesbury
GR	see William of Malmesbury
GSteph	*Gesta Stephani*, ed. K. R. Potter (Nelson's Med. Texts 1955)
H and S	*Councils and Ecclesiastical Documents Relating to Great Britain and Ireland*, ed. A. W. Haddan and W. Stubbs, i (1869)
HA	see *HH*
Hardy *Catalogue*	*Catalogue of Materials Relating to the History of Great Britain and Ireland*, ed. T. D. Hardy (Rolls ser. 1862–71)
HCY	*Historians of the Church of York*, ed. J. Raine (Rolls ser. 1879–94)
HDE	see Simeon
HEp	*Epistolae Herberti de Losinga, Osberti de Clara, et Elmeri*, ed. R. Anstruther (Brussels 1846)
HH	*Henrici Huntendunensis historia Anglorum*, ed. T. Arnold (Rolls ser. 1879)
HH *De contemptu mundi*	*ibid.*
Hist. Nov.	see William of Malmesbury
Hist. Pont.	see John of Salisbury
Historiola	*A Brief History of the Bishoprick of Somerset* in *Ecclesiastical Documents*, ed. Joseph Hunter, Camden soc. (1890)
HJ	*Historische Jahrbuch*
H-L	C. J. Hefele, *Histoire des conciles*, trans. H. Leclercq (Paris 1907–)
HN	see Eadmer
Howden	*Chronica Rogeri de Hovedene*, ed. W. Stubbs (Rolls ser. 1868–71)
Howell	Margaret E. Howell, 'The King's Government and Episcopal Vacancies in England eleventh to fourteenth Century (unpublished London PhD thesis, 1955); published as *Regalian Right in Medieval England* (1962).
HR	see Simeon of Durham
Hugh *HCY*	*Hugh the Chantor: the history of the church of York, 1066—1127*, ed. and trans. Charles Johnson (Nelson's Med. Texts 1961)
HZ	*Historische Zeitschrift*
Jaffé-Wattenbach	*Regesta Pontificum Romanorum*, ed. P. Jaffé and G. Wattenbach (2 vols, Leipzig 1885–8)
JEH	*Journal of Ecclesiastical History*

John of Hexham	continuation of *HR*: see Simeon of Durham
John of Salisbury *Hist. Pont.*	*The Historia Pontificalis of John of Salisbury*, ed. Marjorie Chibnall (Nelson's Med. Texts 1956)
John of Salisbury *Metalogicon*	*Iohannis Saresberiensis episcopi Carnotensis Metalogicon*, ed. Clement C. J. Webb (1929)
John of Salisbury *Policraticus*	*Iohannis Saresberiensis episcopi Carnotensis Policraticus*, ed. Clement C. J. Webb (1909)
John of Schalby	in Giraldus Cambrensis *Opera* (q.v.) vii
John of Worcester	*The Chronicle of John of Worcester 1118—1140*, ed. J. R. H. Weaver (Anecdota Oxoniensia 1908)
JTS	*Journal of Theological Studies*
J-W	see Jaffé-Wattenbach
Knowles *Episcopal Colleagues*	David K., *The Episcopal Colleagues of Archbishop Thomas Becket* (1951)
Knowles *Monastic Order*	David K., *The Monastic Order in England 943—1216* (1949)
KuS	see Böhmer
Lanfranc *ep.*	in *Opera*, ed. L. Dachery (Paris 1648)
LEp	see Lanfranc
Liber Eliensis	ed. E. O. Blake, Camden 3rd. ser. RHistSoc xcii (1962)
Liebermann *Gesetze*	F. L., *Die Gesetze der Angelsachsen* (Halle 1903)
Liebermann *Ungedruckte*	*Ungedruckte Anglo-normannische Geschichtsquellen*, ed. F. L. (Strassburg 1879)
Lœwenfeld	*Epistolae Pontificum Romanorum Ineditae*, ed. S. L. (1885)
Malmesbury	*see* William of Malmesbury
Manitius	Max Manitius and Paul Lehmann, *Geschichte der lateinischen Literatur des Mittelalters* iii (Munich 1931)
Mansi	J. D. M., *Sacrorum conciliorum nova et amplissima collecto* (1759–, reprinted 1960–1)
MARS	*Mediaeval and Renaissance Studies*, ed. Richard Hunt and Raymond Klibansky
Mayr-Harting *Acta*	*The Acta of the Bishops of Chichester, 1075—1207*, ed. H. M–H., Canterbury and York soc. lvi (1964)
MB	*Materials for the history of Thomas Becket*, ed. J. C. Robertson (vols i-vi), J. B. Sheppard (vol. vii) (Rolls ser. 1875–85)
MGH	*Monumenta Germaniae Historica*
Monasticon	*Monasticon Anglicanum*, ed. W. Dugdale, revised by Caley, Ellis, and Bandinel (1817–30)

Vita Gundulfi	in *Anglia Sacra* (q.v.) ii
Vita Herluini	in J. Armitage Robinson, *Gilbert Crispin abbot of Westminster* (Notes and Docs. relating to Westminster Abbey 3, 1911)
Vita S. Remigii	see Giraldus Cambrensis
Vita S. Willelmi Norwic.	A. Jesop and M. R. James, *The Life and miracles of St William of Norwich* (1896)
Vita Wulfstani	The *V. W. of William of Malmesbury,* ed. R. R. Darlington, Camden 3rd ser. xl (1928)
William of Malmesbury *GP*	*De gestis pontificum Anglorum,* ed. N. E. S. A. Hamilton (Rolls ser. 1870)
William of Malmesbury *GR*	*De gestis regum,* ed. W. Stubbs (Rolls ser. 1887–9)
William of Malmesbury *Hist. Nov.*	*Historia Novella,* ed. K. R. Potter (Nelson's Med. Texts 1955)
William of Malmesbury *Vita Wulfstani*	q.v.
William of Newburgh	*Historia rerum anglicarum* in *Chronicles of the Reigns of Stephen, Henry II and Richard I,* ed. R. Howlett (Rolls ser.) i (1885)
Wilkins	David W., *Concilia Magnae Britanniae et Hiberniae* (1737)

Introduction

The hundred years from the mid-eleventh to the mid-twelfth century were one of the most lucrative periods in the history of western civilization.[1] In the first millennium after the birth of Christ the western world, as generation after generation of ecclesiastical writers recognized, decomposed. The great economic and cultural achievements of the Greco-Latin empire were lost; and the most distinguished new culture which arose out of its ruins, the Muslim or Arabic, was too remote – and too advanced – to have much effect before the end of the eleventh century. The few epochs of artistic activity, such as the Northumbrian in the seventh century and the Carolingian in the ninth, did no more than recover a very small part of what had been lost. It was the survival of monasticism, often seemingly extinct, but as often revived, which carried through its libraries a tenuous tradition from the ancient world into the new. And it was the various monastic reform movements in the tenth century which prepared the way for the several, sometimes unconnected, religious and intellectual advances which followed. No doubt there were economic factors. Ecclesiastical reform, with its building programme, its demand for costly furnishings, its stimulation of pilgrimage, and its capitalist enterprises, may even have set the economy in motion and helped to keep it moving.[2] But the key to most of the cultural advances was education, with its cumulative improvement and effects. Men began to become thirsty for the basic arts subjects, grammar, rhetoric, and dialectic or logic; and in that arid climate those beverages were heady. When men acknowledged that with Lanfranc of Pavia *Latinitas* was renewed,[3] they were recognizing that the real heralds of the new world were the schoolmasters.

---

1.   C. H. Haskins popularized in Anglo-American circles the term 'Twelfth-century Renaissance' for the period 1000–1250 through his book *The Renaissance of the Twelfth Century* (Cambridge, Mass. 1928). There was, however, in the 1940s and 50s some discussion of the concept, and it seems to be falling out of favour. Cf. William A. Nitze, 'The so-called twelfth-century Renaissance', *Speculum* xxiii (1948) 464; Eva Matthews Sanford, 'The twelfth century – Renaissance or Proto-Renaissance', *ibid.* xxvi (1951) 635; Urban T. Holmes, jr, 'The idea of a twelfth-century Renaissance', *ibid.* 643.

2.   Cf. Noreen Hunt, 'Cluniac monasticism', in *Cluniac Monasticism in the Central Middle Ages,* ed. Noreen Hunt (1971), 5 ff., referring to the Marxist interpretations of Ernst Werner and B. Töpfer. At the end of the eleventh century Prior Turgot of Durham had a great bell cast at London for his new church. The difficulties of transporting it to Durham by cart are vividly described in 'De miraculis et translationibus S. Cuthberti', Simeon, *Historical Works,* ii. 356–9.

3.   Gilbert Crispin, *Vita Herluini* 95, in J. Armitage Robinson, *Gilbert Crispin Abbot of Westminster* (Notes and Documents relating to Westminster Abbey, no. 3, 1911).

By any standards the period under consideration was revolution-ary.[4] The church was radically reformed. Fundamental to the reform move-ment was the re-establishment of the authentic canonical tradition, the true law of the church.[5] This could serve as a springboard for both the war on abuses and the cultivation of a new spirituality. Through the application of canonical laws, old, resharpened, or new, the marriage of priests was invalidated, their children bastardized, and hereditary succession to benefices denounced;[6] the people were debarred from active participation in church government, and the investi-ture of the clergy with their spiritual offices by the laity was abolished; while the bishop of Rome acquired and exercised an uncontested primacy in the Western church. The constitutional changes which took place between Popes Leo IX (1048–54) and Alexander III (1159–81) transformed the status and almost the nature of the church as an institution. Church government was made more effective. The traditional ultimate coercive power, available to most of its ministers, the sentence of excommunication, the exclusion of named Christians from the fellowship of the faithful, was turned from a moral and defensive weapon almost into a warrant for the excommunicate's arrest by the lay power and his delivery to the church for punishment.[7] But without precedent in Christian history, although foreshadowed by Gregory VII's visionary projects,[8] was the First Crusade preached in 1095 at Clermont, a step with unforeseen but dire consequences.[9]

It was perhaps one of the most religious periods of all time. A transfer of land on an exceptional scale from the laity to the church through private gifts[10] provided the material resources for the church's novel activity in so many different directions and also provoked a new evangelical movement within its two great communal orders, the canonical and the monastic. All claimed to be restoring the *vita apostolica*, a life of apostolic poverty, and the

4. The standard textbook is *Handbook of Church History: iii The Church in the Age of Feudalism* (1969), by Friedrich Kempf, Hans-Georg Beck, Eugen Ewig, and Josef Andreas Jungmann, trans. by Anselm Biggs. The volume covers the period *c.* 700–1122 (Concordat of Worms). There are useful bibliographies listing publications up to at least 1965. For the historiography of the Gregorian reforms, see also Norman F. Cantor, *Church, Kingship, and Lay Investiture in England 1089–1135* (Princeton 1958) 3ff.

5. A good introduction and an interesting contribution to this subject is J. Joseph Ryan, *Saint Peter Damiani and his canonical sources* (Toronto: Pontifical Institute of Medieval Studies: studies and texts ii, 1956). See further, Horst Fuhrmann, *Einfluss und Verbreitung der pseudoisidorischen Fälschungen* (Stuttgart 1972–74).

6. It was, of course, at the time only an unenforceable programme. For the position in Henry II's reign, see Mary G. Cheney, 'Pope Alexander III and Roger, bishop of Worcester, 1164–1179: the exchange of ideas', *Monumenta iuris canonici,* ser. C: subsidia, v (Vatican City 1976) 211 ff.

7. Formulae in *Textus Roffensis*, ed. T. Hearne (1720) 55 ff.

8. But see also Augustin Fliche, 'Les origines de l'action de la papauté en vue de la Croisade', *RHE* xxxiv (1938) 765; Carl Erdmann, *Die Entstehung des Kreuzzugsgedankens* (Stuttgart 1935); H. E. Mayer, trans. John Gillingham, *The Crusades* (1965: 1972).

9. It should, however, be noticed that in the twelfth century Crusades were considered merely an ephemeral ecclesiastical institution and lacked both appropriate laws and a technical vocabulary. Kenneth Pennington, 'The rite for taking the Cross in the twelfth century', *Traditio* xxx (1974) 429; Marjorie Chibnall, OV, v. p. xiii; J. A. Brundage, *Medieval Canon Law and the Crusader* (Madison 1969).

10. Cf. G. Duby, 'Le budget de l'abbaye de Cluny entre 1080 et 1155', in *Annales: économies — sociétés – civilisations* vii (1952) 155; *La Société aux XIe et XIIe siècles dans la région mâconnaise* (Paris 1953).

canons expressed a new sense of responsibility for moral education by teaching as well as example.[11] There were also significant shifts in the objects of popular worship. Awe of God the Father was almost replaced by a christocentric piety, strongly reinforced by a cult of the Blessed Virgin Mary.[12] Christ ceased to be depicted on the cross as the triumphant god, eyes open, serene, without pain. Instead he became the dying and suffering lord, a piteous creature. At the same time the position adopted by worshippers in prayer started to change. Originally Christians had prayed standing, with arms raised high to heaven. Now they began to assume the posture taken by feudal vassals when performing fealty to their lord, on their knees with hands joined together before their bowed heads. In the autumn of 1109 a knight, Gerard of Crécy-sur-Serre, when praying in the crypt of Laon cathedral, on his knees, his cloak opened and thrown back, and the palms of his hands joined together before his breast, was assassinated by Rorigo, the brother of the bishop, Waldric, King Henry I's former chancellor, on the bishop's orders.[13] It was possible to improvise. In the 1120s Gilbert of Sempringham, when a clerk of Bishop Alexander of Lincoln, so disturbed one of his master's guests, another bishop who also lodged in their chamber, by rising during the night to pray by his bed-side, and repeatedly throwing up his arms and going down on his knees, that in the morning the visitor complained to Alexander of the antics of his dancing boy.[14] In these ways the religious drama was recast and transformed. And the emergence in the Isle de France between 1135 and 1154 of an entirely different style of ecclesiastical architecture, the 'gothic', in which all values were changed, showed that the new-fashioned play needed a new stage. An outburst of lyric poetry[15] and a greater respect for women are signs of gentler social attitudes.

---

11.   There was much interest in the 1940s and 50s in the origins of eleventh-twelfth century 'monastic' reform. An invaluable review article, which considers the origins of and provides a bibliography for Cîteaux, Prémontré, the Templars, the Grande Chartreuse, Grandmont, and canons regular, is Charles Dereine, 'La spiritualité "apostolique" des premiers fondateurs d'Affligem (1083–1100)', *RHE* liv (1959) 41. For Cîteaux and the articles of J.-A. Lefèvre, see also David Knowles, 'The primitive Cistercian documents', *Great Historical Enterprises and Problems in Monastic History* (n.d. ? 1963) 198–222. Cf. also Charles Dereine, 'Vie commune, Règle de Saint Augustin, et Chanoines réguliers au XIe siècle', *RHE* xli (1946) 365; 'Les origines de Prémontré', *RHE* xlii (1947) 352; 'L'élaboration du statut canonique des chanoines réguliers spécialement sous Urbain II', *RHE* xlvi (1951) 534; M. D. Chenu, 'Moins, Clercs, Laïcs au Carrefour de la vie évangélique (XIIe siècle)', *RHE* xlix (1954) 59; Alain d'Herblai, 'Le problème des origines Cisterciennes', *RHE* l (1955) 158; Jean Leclercq, 'The monastic crisis of the eleventh and twelfth centuries' [1958], translated in *Cluniac Monasticism in the Central Middle Ages,* ed. Noreen Hunt (1971); Caroline W. Bynum, 'The spirituality of Regular canons in the twelfth century: a new approach', *Medievalia et Humanistica* iv (1973) 3; M. O. Garrigues, 'A qui faut-il attribuer le *De vita vere apostolica*?', *Le Moyen Age* lxxix (1973) 421. See also below 199 ff.

12.   Cf. Sandro Sticca, 'Drama and spirituality in the Middle Ages', *Medievalia et Humanistica* iv (1973) 69, especially section iv. For the cult of the BVM see below 195.

13.   Guibert of Nogent, *De vita sua libri tres,* in *PL* clvi. 917, *De Miraculis S. M. Laudun.* 964.

14.   *Vita S. Gileberti* in *Monasticon* vi. 2, p. vii*.

15.   Philip W. Damon, 'Style and meaning in the medieval Latin nature lyric', *Speculum* xxviii (1953) 516. Wolfram von den Steinen, 'Les sujets d'inspiration chez les poètes latins du XIIe siècle', *Cahiers de Civilisation Médiévale X–XII sièecles* ix (1966) 165–75. Peter Dronke, *The Medieval Lyric* (Hutchinson University Library 1968), argues that all kinds of lyric poetry had a long history in Europe. Cf. p. 30, 'we can conclude that already around the year 1100 practically all the basic types of medieval and Renaissance lyric had evolved'. But no doubt some periods were more productive than others.

Abelard wrote love songs (both words and music) to Heloise, and later hymns for her monastery.[16] Chivalry and *courtoisie* were not far away.[17]

Intellectual advances were remarkable. The revival of the study of Roman law,[18] the growing acceptance of Greco-Arabic science through translations, the courageous application of logic in most speculative fields, contributed to a transformation of the attitudes of thinking men. Characteristic of this intellectual ferment are the cathedral schools when ruled by inspiring teachers; and for them and other places of education knowledge in all its branches was turned into school subjects, given a form in which the authorities could be learned, questioned, and then used as the basis for new advances.[19] Almost inevitably, therefore, as a result of the intrusion of dialectic into theology, the greatest intellectual problem in the schools was the relation between faith and reason. This debate, although sometimes painful, especially for the boldest thinkers and the most public teachers, was not disgraced by extreme intolerance,[20] and contributed to an important advance in metaphysics. Another result of this rationalizing tendency[21] was that the world was no longer regarded as incoherent but as an organic, regularly structured whole which could be explored and explained.[22] The enormous romanesque churches

16. For love songs, Abelard *Historia calamitatum, PL* clxxviii. 128, Heloise, ep. 2, *ibid.* 185–6, 188. For hymns, *ibid.* 1759 ff. and see below 166.

17. Robert W. Hanning, 'The social significance of twelfth-century chivalric romance', *Medievalia et Humanistica* iii (1972) 3; Francis L. Utley, 'Must we abandon the concept of Courtly love?', *ibid.* 299. Not all observers would accept that there was in any sense a liberation of women from male domination: putting women on a pedestal degrades them even further.

18. See H. F. Jolowicz, 'Revivals of Roman law', *Journal of the Warburg and Courtauld Institutes* xv (1952) 88. Also below 253 ff.

19. Cf. Berthe Widmer, 'Thierry von Chartres, ein Gelehrtenschicksal des 12. Jahrhunderts', *HZ* cc (1965) 553. John R. Williams, 'The twelfth-century theological "Questiones" of Carpentias MS 110', *Medieval Studies* xxviii (1966) 300, where there is a useful bibliography on the *quaestio* and *disputatio*. J. O. Ward, 'The date of the commentary on Cicero's *De Inventione* by Thierry of Chartres and the Cornifician attack on the Liberal Arts', *Viator* iii (1972) 219–73. Daniel D. McGarry, 'Educational theory in the *Metalogicon* of John of Salisbury', *Speculum* xxiii (1948) 659. George Makdisi, 'The scholastic method in medieval education: An inquiry into its origins in law and theology', *ibid.* xlix (1974) 640. Two of the great encyclopedic manuals of the period are Thierry of Chartres's still unpublished *Heptateucon* and Hugh of St Victor's *Didascalion* (*c.* 1127) (*PL* clxxvi). One of the most famous of the new textbooks is Peter Comestor's *Historia scolastica* (*PL* cxcviii), produced about 1173, a Christian history to be used in the schools in place of the historical books of the Bible. For the format of the books, see M. B. Parkes, 'The influence of the concepts of *Ordinatio* and *Compilatio* on the development of the book', *Medieval Learning and Literature: essays presented to R. W. Hunt* (1976) 115.

20. There was no conception of 'academic freedom' or 'freedom of speech'. See Herbert Grundmann, 'Freiheit als religiöses, politisches und persönliches Postulat im Mittelalter', *HZ* clxxxiii (1957) 23. But there was Christian charity. Cf. Arno Borst, 'Abälard und Bernhard', *HZ* clxxxvi (1958) 497.

21. This eleventh- and twelfth-century rationalism was in no way secularist; it was not sceptical in the modern sense; and it did not imply any criticism of, or hostility to the church and its beliefs. Reason (logic) was applied by some thinkers to theology in order better to understand, and display, the teaching of the church. Abelard was as unquestioning a believer as Bernard. St Anselm's 'fides quaerens intellectum' (faith seeking understanding or a rational explanation) is the key text. Cf. G. Paré, A. Brunet, P. Tremblay, *La Renaissance du XIIe siècle: les écoles et l'enseignement* (publ. de l'Institut d'Études médiévales d'Ottawa III, Paris and Ottawa 1933) 277 ff.

22. M. D. Chenu, 'Moins, clercs, laïcs au carrefour de la vie évangélique (XIIe siècle)', *RHE* xlix (1954), on William of Conches and Bernard Silvestris. F. J. E. Raby, '*Nuda natura* and twelfth

which were built, and the statuary with which they were adorned, reveal a confidence and optimism without equal since the fall of the Roman empire.

A few names from that century show how rich it was in great men. Berengar of Tours, Lanfranc, Anselm of Laon, and Peter Abelard were influential teachers. Irnerius started the systematic exposition of Roman law at Bologna, where Gratian made the definitive codification of the old canon law. There were the poet Hildebert of Lavardin, the historian Guibert of Nogent, and the historical novelist Geoffrey of Monmouth, the father of the chivalric romance. Among the masters of spirituality were Peter Damian and Bernard, among the theologians Anselm of Aosta, Gilbert of la Porrée, Hugh of St Victor, and Peter Lombard. Hugh of Cluny and Suger of St Denis were outstanding abbots. Gregory VII is the pope who best exemplifies in the sphere of government the enthusiastic idealism of the eleventh-century renaissance. Thomas Becket, archdeacon of Canterbury in 1154, was to become one of the most popular medieval saints. Arnold of Brescia was one of the earliest puritanical and revolutionary demagogues produced by an Italian city.

None of these names would have sounded strange in England about 1100. Most of them are to be found in the early twelfth-century lists of Winchester burgesses, from which we also learn that in 1148 Heloise lived next door to Gawain in what is now Upper Brook Street, while not far away, in Lower Brook Street, lived Brunnhildr Pricklouse. In the south-west quarter of the city were the houses of Turpin and Alexander son of the donkey driver; and Arthur, who drew a rent from High Street, had a property outside the South Gate.[23] A few of the most distinguished clerks of the period were Englishmen of a kind. Of the three archbishops of Canterbury in the roll of honour, Lanfranc, a Lombard, and Anselm of Aosta, a Burgundian, were *novi Angli,* while Thomas, although born of Norman parents, was 'of London', and was commonly so called before he became archbishop. In a longer list of *emeriti,* room could be found for Adelard of Bath, the translator and popularizer of Arabic science, Robert Pullen, the theologian and first English cardinal, Nicholas Breakspear, the only Englishman ever to be made pope (Adrian IV), and John of Salisbury, an Englishman who became bishop of Chartres. The Anglo-Norman historian, William of Malmesbury, when he turned to the European scene, was quick to identify a compatriot. In his *Gesta Regum* (1118–25), after recounting how William Rufus met his death, he prefaced an interlude with an account of Harding, an Englishman with an English name, originally a monk of Sherborne, who 'founded the Cistercian order'.[24]

Some brilliant foreigners came to England and some promising Englishmen went abroad. These migrations are an important feature of the period. Men travelled around to find the best teachers and the most generous

century cosmology', *Speculum* xliii (1968) 72; Richard C. Dales, 'Marius "On the elements" and the twelfth-century science of matter', *Viator* iii (1972) 218.

23.   Survey II (1148); Arthur (items 112, 767), Gawain (576), Heloise (575, 577, 1055), Brunnhildr Prick-louse (645), Alexander, son of the donkey-driver (1079), Turpin (885). Frank Barlow, Martin Biddle, Olof von Feilitzen, and D. J. Keene, *Winchester in the Early Middle Ages* (Winchester Studies I, ed. Martin Biddle, 1976).

24.   *GR* 308–5. Cf. Jean-A. Lefèvre, 'Saint Robert de Molesme dans l'opinion monastique du XIIe et du XIIIe siècle', *AB* lxxiv (1956) 70–2.

patrons. They also sometimes moved later in their careers into relatively backward areas where their skills would be most appreciated.[25] Edward the Confessor attracted many foreigners to his court.[26] So did Henry II.[27] In between, the Norman kings were, naturally, rather more provincial. They had Normans and Bretons and men from Maine to reward. There was not much, although always something, left for the real outsider. Yet, even if they wished to protect their dominions from interference and defend their *Eigenkirchen*,[28] they could not isolate the English and Norman churches from the new ideas. Owing to the Norman Conquest, the English church between 1066 and 1154 is usually seen by English historians as the creation of the Norman conquerors. And in an obvious sense this was so. But it is doubtful whether the English church would have evolved all that much differently had Harold won the battle of Hastings and the Anglo-Danish dynasty remained on the throne.[29] Most of the superficial changes after 1066 were due to the impact of French culture rather than to any local variety of it; and most of the deeper changes were part of the general transformation of Europe. It was not the Norman conquest which led to an investiture quarrel in England or caused the introduction of Augustinian priories and Cistercian abbeys, or even introduced the Burgundian romanesque style of architecture which we call 'Norman', although the existence of a French-speaking aristocracy certainly favoured the importation of novelties from the romance areas and hindered it from the Teutonic. Between 1070 and 1100 the English church was given a new stamp by the new prelates. The bishops, for example, mostly sat in new churches in different places. But never was it other than the *ecclesia anglicana,* which traced its history back to the mission of Augustine by Pope Gregory I. It had been created and influenced by many foreigners. The Normans were only the latest.

Most of the great changes which occurred during this century in Europe, and which affected the English church, can be seen at their best in the kingdom of France.[30] The council of Rheims (1049) marks an early step towards stronger papal leadership and papally directed reform. The council of Clermont (1095) not only completed the first age of Gregorian reform but also

---

25. For example Lanfranc to Burgundy and Normandy; see Frank Barlow, 'A view of Archbishop Lanfranc', *JEH* xvi (1965) 167.

26. Frank Barlow, *Edward the Confessor* (1970) 190–2.

27. W. Stubbs, 'Learning and literature at the court of Henry II', *Seventeen Lectures on the Study of Medieval and Modern History* (1886) 115 ff.

28. *Die Eigenkirche* (pl. *die Eigenkirchen*), the term used by German historians to translate the Latin *ecclesia propria,* is used also by most English historians, although 'proprietary church' is sometimes found. Almost all churches – episcopal, monastic, collegiate, or manorial – had in this period an owner, whether ecclesiastical or secular, and hence were *Eigenkirchen.* The most accessible work of Ulrich Stutz, one of the greatest authorities on this institution, is 'The proprietary church as an element of medieval Germanic ecclesiastical law', in *Studies in Medieval History: Medieval Germany 911–1250,* ed. Geoffrey Barraclough (1938) ii. 35–70. See also Heinrich Böhmer, 'Das Eigenkirchentum in England', in *Texte und Forschungen zur englischen Kulturgeschichte, Festgabe für Felix Liebermann zum 20 Juli 1921* (Halle 1921).

29. For the contrary view, see, e.g. Jürgen Petersohn, 'Normannische Bildungsreform in Hochmittelalterlichen England', *HZ* ccxiii (1971) 265.

30. George Sarton, *Introduction to the History of Science,* ii (1931) 151, considered that in Western Christendom in the period 1100–50 one hundred scholars were mainly responsible for the intellectual progress; of these 40 were French, 24 Italian, 11 German, 11 English, 4 Spanish, etc.

inaugurated the Crusades. The Benedictine monastic reform movement which began in Burgundy at Cluny in 909 was renewed towards the end of the eleventh century at Muret-Grandmont, Cîteaux, and Savigny, and given a new direction by Bruno, the former schoolmaster at Rheims, at the Grande Chartreuse near Grenoble. It was in the forest of Voix near Laon (Prémontré) that the itinerant preacher Norbert of Gennep, the former canon of Xanten, in 1120 at the persuasion of the bishop formed a community of his disciples to live an eremitical life according to the canonical rule of St Augustine.[31] In the evolution of ecclesiastical architecture Cluny III (begun 1085–86 and dedicated 1130),[32] Sens (built 1124–28), and St Denis, Paris (dedicated 1144) are important milestones. The Gothic style was a French invention. The schools of Rheims, Chartres,[33] Orleans, Laon, and Paris were in their different ways among the most distinguished centres of the new learning. The greatest exponents of the new theology and philosophy were mainly French. France was the home of the various kinds of lyric poetry which flourished towards the end of the eleventh century. The nobility of northern France were the staunchest supporters of the Crusades. Culturally France led the way in the West.

Germany had its own traditions which were not easily influenced by the new movements.[34] Normandy and England, although keen observers of the French and Italian scenes, were at the flotsam edge of all these currents. And their geographical isolation was reinforced by the policies of the rulers. None of the king-dukes stressed his position as a vassal of the king of France or wanted to play any role at the court or in the company of the Capetians. None wished to open his dominions to papal influence. None encouraged his vassals to take part in foreign adventures[35] or Crusades. None visited Paris, Rome, Palermo, or indeed any place outside his borders, except for Henry I's solitary visit to Chartres, the home of a nephew, on 13 January 1131 in order to meet the fugitive Innocent II. Characteristically, Henry, after his terrifying nightmare in 1130, vowed in expiation of his sins to go on a pilgrimage to the shrine of St Edmund, king and martyr, at Bury. No St James of Compostela or Saint-Gilles for him.[36]

---

31. Charles Dereine, 'Les origines de Prémontré, *RHE* xlii (1947) 352–78.

32. The dating of Cluny III is controversial; see René Crozet, 'A propos de Cluny', *Cahiers de Civilisation Médiévale X–XII siècles* xiii (1970) 149.

33. The cathedral school at Chartres had only two known masters of the first rank, Fulbert in the early eleventh century and Bernard in the early twelfth century. The latter was remembered, when John of Salisbury studied at Paris (1136–47), as a great, if old-fashioned, teacher of grammar. The importance of the school of Chartres has been grossly inflated according to R. W. Southern, 'Humanism and the School of Chartres', in *Medieval Humanism* (1970). But J. O. Ward, 'The date of the commentary on Cicero's *De Inventione* by Thierry of Chartres and the Cornifician attack on the liberal arts', *Viator* iii (1972) 221 n., disagrees.

34. The strongest expression of this view is in Kassius Hallinger, *Gorze-Kluny: Studien zu den monastischen Lebensformen und Gegensätzen im Hochmittelalter* (Rome 1950; reissued Graz 1971).

35. Cf. William I's treatment of his half-brother, Odo bishop of Bayeux, when the prelate proposed to intervene in Italy, possibly with a view to becoming pope: below 281.

36. Suger, *Vie de Louis VI*, ed. H. Waquet (Paris 1929; 1964) 260. John of Worcester 34 and below 91. Botilda, the wife of Gerard, the monks' cook at Norwich, travelled with a party of prilgrims to Arles (St Giles) and Santiago (St James) in 1150; *Vita S. Willelmi Norwic.* 178.

The Normans had a reputation for hospitality.[37] But after 1070 foreign immigration was on a limited scale. When Henry I, after much deliberation, proposed that his Italian doctor, Faricius, abbot of Abingdon, should succeed Anselm at Canterbury, there was lively and successful opposition from the highest clergy and laity. It was about time, they said, that someone speaking the mother tongue (and by this they meant French) was given the archbishopric, for example Ralf d'Escures, bishop of Rochester.[38] Ralf, the son of a Norman baron, brother of Siegfried, abbot of Glastonbury, had been monk and abbot of Sées and possessed many admirable virtues. But he was hardly the equal of Lanfranc in learning and Anselm in piety as his supporters are said to have claimed. Even the effect of schooling in France, mainly at Laon, which was beginning for the sons of the great and ambitious, was muted in England. Anselm of Laon was a conservative, and English clerks do not seem to have had revolutionary ideas. The most they aimed at was a reformed church with a free and influential position within the *respublica*.

This Anglo-Norman isolationism did not go with a general backwardness. Since the Normans were a very gifted and also adaptable people they could be according to the circumstances both inventive and conservative. The conquest of England was a remarkable achievement which posed all manner of problems, gave new opportunities, and stretched the conquerors' ingenuity to the full. Several precocious advances were the result. The military occupation of England encouraged a rapid improvement in castle building. Motte and bailey castles and other ring defences, which had been used as little more than temporary field defences in Normandy, were employed in England as permanent strongholds, and so were quickly improved in design. And almost from the beginning great stone keeps were built, such as Bishop Gundulf of Rochester's tower of London (1078), which were quite outstanding. Similarly, the Norman 'conquest' of the church led to a rebuilding programme which stimulated technical innovation. The ribbed vaults of Durham cathedral (1093) were at least a decade in advance of anything under construction in the north of France. The removal of several bishops' sees and the destruction of some old cathedrals raised the problem of the authenticity of relics and the validity of traditional claims to sanctity. Not only the ancient calendars, but the old constitutions and rituals came under scrutiny. The intellectual advances caused by these reappraisals may not have been spectacular, but they encouraged that pragmatic adjustment to changed circumstances which seems to have been a characteristic ability of the Normans.

Settlement in an old-fashioned country may also in time have reinforced the conservative streak in the Normans. Some of the new developments seem soon to have lost momentum. For example, in ecclesiastical architecture the innovations at Durham were almost the point at which development stopped. After the death of Henry I there was even retrogression. The stonework, instead of being reduced to a skeleton, remained thick and ponderous. The new gothic style which developed in the Isle de France after 1135 and spread rapidly through Normandy and other adjoining areas, made no real

37.   *GR* 306.
38.   *GP* 126; cf. 332.

impact on England before the 1160s; and Canterbury (1174–78) was the first great church to break with conservative insular tradition.[39]

In some ways the Normans remained very French. Independence of the French monarchy did not weaken their attachment to the French language. These *novi Franci* would not stoop to conquer, and even though many soon became bilingual in England, French remained the badge of their superiority.[40] It was the language of polite society. England, therefore, which had produced a unique body of vernacular literature in the Old English period, now led the way with compositions in French.[41] In the twelfth century Anglo-Norman writers were pioneers in two fields: they used French instead of Latin for historical and religious compositions before that happened in France, and they composed romance and drama in their own vernacular before the English writers did so in theirs.

There was also the success in government. Norman kings, barons, bishops, and abbots found little difficulty in striking a compromise between insular and French customs and in producing systems which worked. The more autocratic the king, the more pragmatic. Almost as soon as 'lay investiture' and the homage of the clergy became a matter of great concern to the papacy, Henry I made in 1106 the earliest negotiated settlement, antedating the Concordat of Worms by sixteen years. What is more, the whole kingdom, in its cohesion, its consistency and its orderliness, and in the elaboration and effectiveness of its administration, was a model for other more slowly evolving national states. Able kings, driven by their insatiable need for money, created a polity out of a tamed feudalism and the skills of the church. Ranulf Flambard, *procurator regis,* prostituted all the ecclesiastical arts in the service of the monarchy and was widely hated, especially by monks, although not by his own. His case illustrates the dynamic empiricism and even unconventionality which conservative kings, certain of their ends but unsure of the means, encouraged in their servants.

The Anglo-Norman church can be studied from its own records – its historical writings, professional literature, and business documents – and other remains, its buildings and ecclesiastical furnishings. All these things it deliberately left for posterity, and for a didactic purpose. It produced little which had no practical use and refashioned anything which was found to be unserviceable or indecorous. The materials it used – cut and carved stone, metals and jewels, parchment, pigments and gold leaf – were expensive; labour was cheap. Hence there was always the temptation to re-employ materials, to over-elaborate, to

39. Jean Bony, 'French influence on the origins of English Gothic architecture', *Journal of the Warburg and Courtauld Institutes* xii (1949) 1–15.

40. The concurrence of the three languages (Latin, English, and French) is shown very clearly by the happenings after the cure of a deaf mute at St Swithun's tomb at Winchester in Bishop Walkelin's time (1070–98). The boy who had been cured 'loquebatur omnibus linguis ad omnem quae sibi fiebat interrogacionem, latine videlicet interrogacioni per latinam, per anglicam anglice, per romanam romane respondens', *Translatio S. Swithuni* in *AB* lviii (1940) 196; see also below 133, 211.

41. Mary Dominica Legge, *Anglo-Norman Literature and its Background* (1963), 'La précocité de la littérature anglo-normande', *Cahiers de Civilisation Médiévale Xe–XIIe siècles* viii (1965) 327. See also Ruth J. Dean, 'The fair field of Anglo-Norman: recent cultivation', *Medievalia et Humanistica* iii (1972) 279.

copy and repeat, a temptation which only a few puritans, like St Bernard, could resist. Monastic authors were under strict supervision.[42] Everything was against the hoarding of the ephemeral. The trivialities of the cloisters and schools were wiped off the wax writing tablets,[43] and as a result the period appears more solemn than it really was. But it has bequeathed the image it wanted to be remembered by. The church operated, not only through its institutions but also through the universal habit of vigilance and denunciation, a most effective censorship.

The church can be studied only from its own productions. There was no secular literature in this period,[44] and the few non-Christians in western Christendom – almost exclusively Jews – although their beliefs were a standing, and sometimes disturbing, challenge to Christian theology, for they had the Old Testament in common, were in no position to record and transmit their thoughts about the Christian scene. A further limitation is that the literary sources are mainly monastic, for the Benedictine culture had its distinct characteristics,[45] habits of thought which were to be increasingly abandoned, and to some extent derided, by the clerks educated in non-monastic schools. The first secular clerk in England in this period to write a history was Henry, archdeacon of Huntingdon in the diocese of Lincoln, the son of his predecessor, whose own son, grandson, and great-grandson held church benefices.[46] Although his differs in no obvious way from the other compilations, it is more likely that he was unable to escape from the dominant literary conventions than that married archdeacons thought like monks.[47] What is more, some of the most influential historical writings were the work of a special class of men, the English and Anglo-Normans. Eadmer, John of Worcester, and Simeon of Durham were natives, Orderic Vitalis and William of Malmesbury were the offspring of mixed marriages. Even the surviving documents (mostly in copies) are almost entirely from monastic *scriptoria*; and as one of the occupations of these offices was the construction of ancient deeds, it is likely that English monks were also much engaged in this. Historical curiosity was especially aroused in this segment of society. It was no doubt the conscious or unconscious protest of the conquered against the parvenus, against masters without a respectable history. English men of letters were immediately after the Conquest much distressed by the barbarism of the conquerors. This feeling was expressed by a stranger who

42. Cf. the Rule of St Gilbert of Sempringham, *c*. 1148, 'Nullus de nostris praesumat libros aliquos, vel etiam orationes vel meditationes scribere, vel scribi facere, sine assensu prioris domus, vel scriptores conducere et retinere in ecclesiis monialium', *Monasticon* vi. 2, p. 1*.

43. For Bishop Herbert Losinga of Norwich and the trivialities which the monk Felix was copying, see below 243.

44. Although Peter Dronke, *The Medieval Lyric* 30, would allow the influence of vernacular and secular songs on clerical verse.

45. See the writings of Dom Jean Leclercq. A useful work is 'The love of Learning and the Desire for God', trans. Catharine Misrahi (Mentor Omega 1962).

46. Charles Clay, 'Master Aristotle', *EHR* lxxvi (1961) 303.

47. He reveals a dislike of legislation against married priests more obviously than any monk would have done. Roger D. Ray, 'Orderic Vitalis and William of Poitiers: a monastic reinterpretation of William the Conqueror', *Revue Belge de philologie et d'histoire* 1 (1972) 1116–27, shows how the Benedictine monk refashioned the work of the archdeacon (William of Poitiers) – turned panegyric into a moral story.

made his home in England, the hagiographer Goscelin of St Bertin. 'A victim of reptilian envy and stepfatherly barbarity', he was expelled from Salisbury when Osmund (the future saint) replaced Herman as bishop in 1078, and in his *Liber confortatorius* wrote bitterly of the ignorant newcomers who derided and despised the learned and forbade scholarship on the grounds that it led to pride, and of the barbarous pride and bragging of these undisciplined ignoramuses who seemed to think that illiteracy was a sign of secular wisdom or holiness of life.[48] But within a generation, except for military boasting,[49] the Norman prelates had accepted the English past.

A common culture did not, however, produce a placid society. The tone of its products is far from peaceful and reflects a world in turmoil. The sharp exchanges between the Latin and Greek churches came close to questioning the foundations on which each was built. The claim of the canons regular that they were restoring the *vita apostolica,* modelling themselves on the most primitive Christianity, provoked a quarrel with the monastic order and an investigation into the lawfulness of some Benedictine customs, such as the exercise of the cure of souls, the right to baptize and to preach, and the possession of tithe. The establishment of new, more ascetic, orders within the *ordo monasticus* itself produced much heart-searching in the older communities.[50] The application of some of these evangelical ideals to the lower clergy, especially the attempt to tear them out of lay society and deny them the comfort of ordinary family life, was the sending of a sword into their world. It was a tenet of the Gregorian reformers that custom was no defence against the true law; and many eleventh-century practices when put on trial were found to be corrupt. The popes' willingness to hear appeals from the courts of the local ordinaries made it more difficult for national churches to maintain their traditional way of life.

Important matters of principle, great issues, were in debate. And the clergy were a bad-tempered lot. Most of their written works, the documents and literature, are contentious. Even the Lives of the Saints were often written to defend property and privileges against rivals.[51] Hardly an author finished his preface without an appeal to his patron to protect him from the barks and bites of the envious. And the constant attack on worldliness in all its ramifications could include much satire and some pornography. Those members of the clergy who renounced marriage, especially those who relinquished private ownership of goods as well, were professional dissenters, radicals of a sort. Even the

---

48. 'The *Liber confortatorius* of Goscelin of Saint Bertin', *Studia Anselmiana,* fasc. xxxviii = *Analecta Monastica,* 3rd ser. (Rome 1955), ed. C. H. Talbot, 29, 82.

49.   Ralf Novel bishop of the Orkneys, suffragan bishop in the province of York, in his address to the troops before the Battle of the Standard in 1138, according to Henry of Huntingdon, reminded the Norman soldiers of their feats in France, and their conquest of England, Apulia, Jerusalem, and Antioch. It was now the turn of Scotland: HH 262.

50.   It should, however, be noticed that in the diocese of Durham in the mid-twelfth century there were excellent relations between Benedictines, Cistercians, and canons, witness many anecdotes in Reginald of Durham *St Godric.* Cf. also *Vita S. Roberti Novi Monasterii in Anglia abbatis,* cap. 8, ed. Paul Grosjean, *AB* lvi (1938) 353.

51.   Cf. Baudouin de Gaiffier, 'Les revendications de biens dans quelques documents hagiographiques du XIe siècle', *AB* l (1932) 123.

gossipy, snobbish chronicler Orderic Vitalis was saved from utter worldliness in his view of Norman society, ecclesiastical as well as lay, by his monastic separateness, his professional standards which required him to judge by right and wrong, and to censure sinners, even if they were the great men of the world. But the radicalism did not usually get out of hand. The family with wife and children was normally replaced by some male group, and, except for hermits, private needs were amply supplied by official or communal property. All the clergy, including the anchorites, had an accepted place in society. And, on the whole, with reservations, they accepted that society. When Pope Paschal II agreed in 1111, as a solution of the investiture dispute, that the German bishops should relinquish their *regalia* (those secular possessions for which homage was due)[52] the protest was so great that the plan had to be abandoned at once. The clergy also accepted in the main their own traditions. There was some theological frivolity here and there. When the schools began to develop a life of their own in the twelfth century, clever men were sometimes tempted to outrageous speculation. But so confident were the church leaders that they were usually indulgent. Nor was imprudence confined to the clergy – laymen could mock. King William Rufus even enjoyed a theological dispute between Jews and Christians. It was not taken too seriously; it was regarded more as an eccentricity. Such deviations were the extravagances of a society which was changing fast, faster than it realized, but which believed that there were limits which only the fool or the sinner overstepped.

The remains of the Anglo-Norman church which make the greatest impact are the stone churches, and, since they are also the most familiar relics of the period, they have contributed much to the accepted view of that church: its leaders were builders, administrators, men of ambition.[53] Although the design of the new churches and much of the ornamentation was strictly functional,[54] contempt for the Anglo-Saxon style of romanesque and the smallness of the buildings (in 1066 often about a century old), and rivalry between the new bishops and abbots led to great projects and initially to technical improvements. The Normans were not at first bound up with the English past, and although some native idiom persisted there was a sharp break in style and a new beginning. They erected buildings typical of conquerors: churches with dungeons, vaulted corridors, great halls, and lofty towers. The simple geometry of the design and the massive construction make a powerful impression. The

52.   M. J. Wilks, '*Ecclesiastica* and *Regalia*: papal investiture policy from the council of Guastalla to the First Lateran Council, 1106–23', *Studies in Church History*, ed. G. J. Cuming and Derek Baker vii (1971) 69. Better, Johannes Fried, 'Der Regalienbegriff im 77. und 12. Jahrhundert', *Deutsches Archiv* xxix (1973) 450, where there is a comprehensive discussion.

53.   The following bishops started the rebuilding of their cathedrals: Lanfranc (1070–89) Anselm (1093–1109) Canterbury, Wulfstan (1062–95) Worcester, Thomas I (1070–1100) York, Walkelin (1070–98) Winchester, William of St Calais (1081–96) Durham, Gundulf (1077–1108) Rochester, Osmund (1078–99) (Old) Salisbury, Maurice (1086–1107) London, Remigius (1086–92) Lincoln, John (1090–1127) Bath, and Herbert Losinga (1095–1119) Norwich. For the three churches at Canterbury, see R. W. Southern, *St Anselm and his Biographer* 260 ff. Canterbury II (Lanfranc) was based on St Stephen's, Caen; Canterbury III (Anselm) on Cluny III (dedicated 1095).

54.   Some Marxist historians explain the whole development of romanesque architecture in terms of the veneration of relics, a cult fostered by the church in the tenth and eleventh centuries in order to bring the lower classes under control. See Noreen Hunt, *loc. cit.*

carved decoration, starkly geometrical, monotonously repeated from building to building across the length and breadth of the kingdom, even beyond its political frontiers, although sometimes rather dull, contributes to the effect. Occasionally some bizarre pattern, like the incisions on the columns at Durham cathedral or the beaked heads which cluster round doorways, recalls the barbarous origins of the Normans. But, on the whole, the builders achieved the true romanesque aims of order and harmony in buildings of great size and weight. The change in style was not a deliberate proclamation that a new variety of religion had been introduced or that a moral crusade was about to be launched, but it did probably follow in part from changes in the ritual and different ceremonial requirements as well as from the desire of new prelates, who had come into great wealth, to commission the best buildings that money could buy. They wanted to have churches in the height of fashion. Similar feelings inspired the lay owners of village churches to make improvements. The English church had come under new management.

Rebuilding usually preceded the manufacture of historical memorials. And there was sometimes a connexion. The destruction of ancient tombs stimulated an interest, often at first critical, in the lives of the local saints. William of Malmesbury in his guide to the English church often laments the absence of legends of the saints even at the place where they were honoured. At Tavistock, he observed, Rumon, reputed a bishop and saint, had a beautiful shrine, but there were no writings in support of the cult. 'And this you will find not only there but in many other places in England: all records of their deeds have perished, I think as a result of the wars. All you get are the bare names of the saints even though present day miracles suggest that there is much that could be known.'[55] He himself worshipped, after God, Aldhelm, abbot of Malmesbury and first bishop of Sherborne, to whom Faricius, abbot of Abingdon, in the *Vita* he had composed, had not done full justice. William tells us that Aldhelm's chasuble, which he hung on a sunbeam in the Lateran palace, and the Bible he bought from the French sailors at Dover after he had worked a miracle, were still preserved in the abbey. Also the white marble altar, which was broken when the camel carrying it fell in the Alps, and which Aldhelm gave to King Ine on his safe return, could still be seen in the church at Bruton (Somerset). At Doulting, where Aldhelm died, was to be found the stone on which he sat, and the crosses which marked the route of the funeral procession still stood.[56] It was, indeed, William of Malmesbury, continuing the work of Goscelin of St Bertin, who rescued so much of England's hagiographical past and helped to transmit, and even refurbish, traditional cults. Moreover the rehousing of the archives after rebuilding led at least to a physical evaluation of the title deeds. And the building costs made the church authorities very aware of the need to exploit every profitable right to which they had a claim. So chronicles, saints' lives, and title deeds were created. These were *munimenta*, muniments, weapons with which the church could be defended by its servants, present and to come.[57]

55. *GP* 202.
56. *GP* 330 ff., 365, 373–4, 377–8, 383–4; cf. 421.
57. Cf. John of Salisbury, *Hist. Pont.* 3.

History was not part of the medieval scholastic curriculum, and in the twelfth century was not written by any of the great schoolmasters or polymaths. The intellectual giants were interested in dialectics and its application to theology. History was principally a monastic occupation; there was little fame to be had from its writing; and from the evidence of library catalogues and the survival of manuscripts history was not much read.[58] Although forgery was a popular medieval activity, it was condemned by moralists and lawyers, and some of this opprobrium may have brushed off on historians, for much of the early history of the church and of most individual churches was apocryphal. Indeed few historians drew a sharp line between history and fiction.[59] In its use to establish and defend rights it was tainted with spuriousness and in its chronicling of the worldly scene it smelt of triviality, flattery, and similar curial passions.

All histories were chapters in the history of the world, continuations of the Book of Genesis, which would end with Doomsday.[60] The earliest chapters, even if omitted, were taken for granted, and the very nature of the work, with its preoccupation with death and disaster, kept the Last Judgment firmly in mind. In practice, however, for the twelfth-century English historian the Anglo-Saxon Chronicle, whether in the vernacular or in some Latin version, provided the bulk of the introductory material. And the Day of Judgment was inevitably always postponed. Indeed, the chronicler Henry, archdeacon of Huntingdon, quoted the opinion of Herbert Losinga, bishop of Norwich, that the world might easily last for another millennium.[61] The chronicler was very much the dwarf perched on the shoulders of the giants of the past.[62] And however much monastic chroniclers were driven by interest in history to offer their own instalment of the story of God's Great Design, they were reluctant to make an abrupt personal intervention. Occasionally the very act of copying some other work may have inspired a monk to take the story further. He rarely signed his contribution. Most sets of annals are anonymous, and a change of scribe is often easier to detect than a change in the authorship. Because of the habit of continuation, histories were transferred from centre to centre, and in their final form may be likened to a rope, made out of several shorter pieces, all of different colours and textures, spliced together. Such geographical dislocations, often camouflaged by later insertions and a final revision and copying out, make the analysis of the Anglo-Saxon Chronicle and its various manuscripts difficult.[63] Sometimes the joins are easy to see (see diagram, p. 318, for

---

58. James Stuart Beddie, 'Libraries in the twelfth century: their catalogues and contents', *Anniversary Essays in Medieval History by Students of Charles Homer Haskins* (Boston and New York 1929) 18–19. For the motives of medieval historians, see Gertrud Simon, 'Untersuchungen zur Topik der Widmungsbriefe mittelalterlicher Geschichtsschreiber bis zum Ende des 12. Jahrhunderts', *Archiv für Diplomatik* iv (1959) 52, v/vi (1959–60) 73.

59. Cf. the paper and discussion on medieval forgery, Duisberg 1962, Horst Fuhrmann, 'Die Fälschungen im Mittelalter', *HZ* cxcvii (1963) 529.

60. Cf. John of Salisbury, *Hist. Pont.* prologue.

61. HH p. xix.

62. Bernard of Chartres on the teachers of the liberal arts, as reported by John of Salisbury, *Metalogicon* III, 4 (ed. Webb) 136.

63. We lack modern first-class editions of most of the Anglo-Norman historians, and in their absence a definitive study of their interrelationship cannot be attempted. The basic work on the

the literary relationship between some of the sources). The Worcester chronicle called 'Florence' was started by interpolating and continuing the world chronicle written c. 1060–73 by the Irish monk, Marianus Scotus, at the German monastery of Fulda. It is thought that Robert bishop of Hereford passed a copy of the foreign work after 1082 (the date of Marianus's death) to his friend and neighbour, Wulfstan bishop of Worcester, who set some of his monks to work upon it.[64]

Although clerks wrote the histories, and these were eschatological in tone, not all the accounts were strictly ecclesiastical. The anonymous Anglo-Saxon Chronicle had had from the beginning a secular purpose – the glorification of Alfred and the commemoration of his wars against the heathen Danes – and even at its most jejune, retained a national coverage. This national character was retained by most of the chronicles and histories based on it,[65] such as William of Malmesbury's *Gesta Regum,* Florence's *Chronica e Chronicis* and Henry of Huntingdon's *Historia Anglorum.* William of Malmesbury wrote two complementary histories, the deeds of the kings and *Gesta Pontificum,* the deeds of the bishops, and in the introduction to the latter complained that whereas the Chronicle had been of great use when he had been writing about the kings, it had failed to provide him with the basis for an ecclesiastical history.

At Worcester when Marianus was continued the horizons closed in. The monks Florence and John, although they never lost sight of great events in the Western church, were more interested in happenings closer at hand. At Durham the viewpoint was different. The Durham monk who compiled the chronicle known as Simeon's *Historia Regum,* after copying Florence until 1119, and selecting mostly notices of secular affairs, suddenly changed course and wrote a history of his own times, 1119–29, which has a very strong northern ecclesiastical interest. At St Evroul the horizons widened. Orderic Vitalis started to write the history of his own monastery in the south of Normandy and enlarged his plan to include, among other extensions, not only the ecclesiastical but also the secular history of the Normans. And although he intended to keep the various topics separate, he was always running from one to another. At the other extreme are the humbler, domestic histories of religious communities, for this period usually charter chronicles, accounts of benefactions and losses

Anglo-Saxon Chronicle was done by Charles Plummer in the introduction to vol. ii. of Plummer and Earle, *Two of the Saxon Chronicles Parallel* (1899). Attempted revisions in the light of later contributions are to be found in the *EHD* edition (Dorothy Whitelock) and Sten Körner, *The Battle of Hastings, England and Europe, 1035–1066* (Lund 1964). For *Chron. E* see also *The Peterborough chronicle (The Bodleian manuscript Laud Misc. 636)* ed. Dorothy Whitelock (Early English manuscripts in facsimile, iv, Copenhagen 1954). R. R. Darlington gave his view of the historical value of some of these writers in his inaugural lecture at Birkbeck College, University of London, 20 May 1947, *Anglo-Norman Historians.*

64.   OV (Chibnall) ii. 186–9; *GP* 301; cf. W. H. Stevenson, 'A contemporary description of the Domesday survey', *EHR* xxii (1907) 72.

65.   They are what German historians call 'Volksgeschichten'. Cf. Karl Schnith, 'Von Symeon von Durham zu Wilhelm von Newburgh', in *Speculum historiale* (Festschrift für Johannes Spörl, Munich 1965) 242.

either based on charters or linking the documents into a story. Many of these were assembled in the first half of the twelfth century.[66]

The centres of historical writing after the Conquest were those churches where the old traditions were not completely broken, where Englishmen remained and were still recruited. Canterbury was important. In St Augustine's abbey, colonized from Christ Church after 1089, the Anglo-Saxon Chronicle was maintained; and at Christ Church Eadmer wrote the profoundly influential *Historia Novorum,* a history of his own times. At Worcester, where Bishop Wulfstan spanned the Conquest, and at Peterborough, a centre of nationalism, chronicles were written. At Malmesbury William devoted himself to recovering and presenting attractively the history of the English people. Winchester is not to be counted here. Demoralized under Stigand and then Walkelin, its annals are thin. In the north at York and even more at Durham historical studies flourished. None of the new episcopal sees, like Salisbury, Chichester, Chester, Bath, or Norwich, although some were monastic, produced anything at all. Two literary events determined the continuity and then the flowering of English historical scholarship: the maintenance of the vernacular annals, and Eadmer's production of a Latin history in which an Englishman explained the Conquest and paid tribute to two foreign archbishops. The first secured the transmission of a great body of historical fact; the second inspired others to employ this material in Latin compositions. Only very restricted use was made in England of the Norman historians.[67]

Despite William of Malmesbury's strictures, the vernacular annals, the Anglo-Saxon chronicle, is of great use to the ecclesiastical historian. Its purpose was to record, without much comment, the interesting events of each year. So it includes the obits of bishops and abbots, sometimes appointments, occasionally other ecclesiastical happenings, such as the dedication of an important church, conflagrations, the visit of a papal legate, the holding of a council. Although there are chronological dislocations and confusions, it usually presents events in their proper order.

Several different versions of the *Chronicle* exist for the period up to 1066. But the *C* manuscript ends in that year, and *D,* put into its present shape after 1100, breaks off in 1079. One manuscript alone, the twelfth-century Bodleian Library, Oxford, Laud Misc. 636 (*E*) goes on until 1154. This is a Peterborough abbey continuation, from 1122, of an earlier set of annals. After 1031 a copy of the northern version of the Chronicle (δε, the prototype of DE), kept probably at York, reached St Augustine's abbey, Canterbury, and was continued there until 1066 and probably until 1121. Although no manuscript of the version which ended in 1121 has survived,[68] it was, no doubt because of its home at Canterbury,[69] a most influential work, for it was used as a source by

66. See below 170.

67. Cf. Liebermann *Ungedruckte* 31 ff., especially on the *Annales Rotomagenses* (Rouen).

68. The bilingual chronicle *F,* which ends imperfectly in the middle of the annal for 1058, was compiled at Christ Church, Canterbury, probably from ε, at the end of the eleventh century or the beginning of the twelfth.

69. At Christ Church, Canterbury, in the eleventh century were also the *B* version, which ends in 977, and the *A* version, which peters out after 975 and which was possibly transferred from

many twelfth-century English historians. Peterborough abbey borrowed it after 1121, possibly because of the loss of its library in the fire of 1116, copied it out at one go, while interpolating it with Peterborough material, and then maintained it spasmodically from 1122 until 1131 as a Peterborough chronicle. Finally, the section 1132–54 was put together rather carelessly at Peterborough after King Stephen's death, and the work was abandoned. It was a confused ending to a great annalistic tradition.[70] The existence of only a single version of the *Chronicle* for 1080–1154 deprives us of that conflict of views which aids the historian's understanding and which shows how prejudiced even the most laconic annals can be. Nor are the vernacular annals at their best in the Anglo-Norman period. There are a few literary insertions of the old kind, notably the obituary of the Conqueror and the lamentation on Stephen's reign; but these are not often inspired by purely ecclesiastical themes.

Most twelfth-century Latin chronicles are heavily dependent on the vernacular annals for the period from 1066 until somewhere in Henry I's reign. The point at which each becomes independent is not easy to see because for the twelfth century they not only begin to use each other but also come into their own times. It is generally true to say that whenever they could copy they did so. Henry of Huntingdon, at the end of Book VII and the death of the Conqueror, wrote that although up to that point he had been dependent on what he found in books or folklore, henceforth he intended to rely on what he himself and others had themselves seen. But in fact he continued to use the *Chronicle,* and there is no discernible break at 1121. No one seems to have used the Peterborough chronicle (*E*) 1122–54; but it is likely that there were other continuations, like *H,* of which only a fragment (for 1113–14) has survived, on which the Latin writers could rely.

One of the earliest to draw upon the *Chronicle* was William of Malmesbury for his *Gesta Regum* and *Gesta Pontificum,* both of which were composed between 1118 and 1125.[71] William, who wrote these histories 'in his greener years' – he was well under thirty when he started[72] – had literary ambitions. In the former work he claimed, with justification, to be the first since Bede to write a history of the English people in Latin. He made disparaging remarks about the *Chronicle,* although he used ε extensively, and flattering remarks about Eadmer, on whose history he also drew. In his *Gesta Regum,* which effectively closes in 1120, he did not really free himself from the annalistic form: he merely disguised it by his often extensive insertions into his translation of most of the Anglo-Saxon Chronicle and by devoting a separate

Winchester to Canterbury by Archbishop Stigand who held both sees together 1052–70. These incomplete versions were naturally of less interest to twelfth-century historians.

70.   This is probably a simplified story. It does not account for the close relationship between *D* and *E* 1057–79, or for *E* sharing a common entry with Florence in 1130. But these problems are at present insoluble.

71.   For William as an historian and scholar see, as well as Stubbs's introductions to *GR*, Marie Schütt, 'The literary form of William of Malmesbury's "Gesta Regum"', *EHR* xlvi (1931) 255; Hugh Farmer, 'William of Malmesbury's Life and Works', *JEH* xiii (1962) 39. But neither considers William's moral purpose.

72.   As he states in the prologue to his commentary on Lamentations, written on his fortieth birthday (or ? in his forties), *GR* i, p. cxxii.

book to each of the Norman kings. But with the *Gesta Pontificum* he was forced to make his own plan. Starting with Canterbury and Kent, he made a circuit of the dioceses, according to the ancient kingdoms to which they had belonged, and for each gave an account of its bishops, monasteries, and other interesting features.

William had some useful talents. He could read Old English and had an outstanding skill in one form of literary Latin. He had a good historical curiosity, some interest in archaeology; and he could often use documents quite intelligently as a source for a narrative account.[73] He was aware that the historian's task was to criticize discordant stories in order to establish the truth, and he was as fairminded as his strong prejudices would allow. He had also a sense of importance which, with his pessimism and malice, gave him a mastery over the characters he depicted. But he was alive to the dangers of writing contemporary history[74] and seldom devoted a setpiece to any bishop alive at the time of publication. For example, he finished his history of the diocese of Salisbury with the death of Osmund in 1099 and omitted an account of the pontificate of the great Roger, 1107–39. He also preferred to cut most of the more unkind remarks about prelates out of the later editions of his book, although this robbed the work of some of its interest and weakened its purpose.[75] William, using all his resources of irony, sarcasm, and invective, castigated the post-Conquest bishops, especially those whom he believed to have been unfavourable to monks, or those whom, although monks, the episcopal office had corrupted.

Clearly he was a writer of the new age, like Eadmer and Orderic Vitalis interested in the particular, in individual characteristics. For example in his *Gesta Regum* he gives a brilliant physical description of William Rufus. But to the modern mind his histories are unsuccessful as histories. He could have told so much more. He could have been the English counterpart to Orderic Vitalis. It seems that he was too bookish and cared little for oral tradition or even the living witness. It is possible that he was frightened of his caustic pen. It may be that he had no literary fluency. Indeed, his style was too artificial to be suited to extended narrative. He tried to write in a more classical style than had been usual, and his conciseness and peculiar vocabulary not only sometimes made his meaning far from clear but also did not encourage the excursions of the scribbler. It is revealing that he himself should have begged in the introduction to *Gesta Regum* that divine aid would carry him safely past the rocks of a fractured vocabulary, on which Ethelwerd (the tenth-century Latin chronicler), when he chased after resounding and borrowed words, was miserably wrecked.

Far less lively, but providing more factual information, is the Worcester chronicle commonly known as 'Florence' from its supposed compiler,

---

73. He used them well in his *De antiquitate Glastoniensis ecclesiae,* in Adam of Domerham, *Historia de rebus gestis Glastoniensibus,* ed. T. Hearne (1727) i. 1–122. He was less successful with his account of the Canterbury–York dispute, *GP* 39–132, which degenerates into an undigested collection of documents.

74. Cf. *GR* 357.

75. In the Rolls ser. edition, Thomas Arnold followed the unhelpful policy of printing the revised version. The suppressed passages are to be found in the footnotes.

the monk of the cathedral church who died in 1118. Although the work was probably started between 1082 and 1095, the annals for 1095–1121 were written after 1125; the chronicle continues without a perceptible break until 1141; and it seems likely that most of the work was done by a younger monk, an Englishman named John, who used some material collected or translated by Florence.[76] For the earlier period the Worcester chronicle relies much on the Anglo-Saxon Chronicle, using both *D* and ϵ for the period 1066–79, and continuing to use the latter possibly until it finished in 1121, although by the end of Rufus's reign it becomes so independent that the relationship goes out of sight. The Worcester compiler also drew on all other sources available to him, and for this period certainly used Eadmer's *Historia Novorum* and probably William of Malmesbury's works.[77] From these and local sources, and probably also from oral testimony and personal knowledge, the chronicler interpolated into his translation or version of the *Chronicle* additional detail, local items, and general ecclesiastical material; and as he approached his own time he very much made his own pattern. Florence is journeyman's work, but is all the better for that.

Similar to Florence are the Durham chronicle, *Historia Regum,* attributed to the monk Simeon, which runs from 616 to 1129, and Henry of Huntingdon's *Historia Anglorum,* which runs from Caesar's first invasion of Britain likewise until 1129, but was extended by Henry himself successively to 1139, 1145, and 1154. Simeon's work was continued by John, prior of Hexham, until 1153. These coincidences, however, seem to be without significance. The *HR,* from the middle of the ninth century until 1119, consists largely of extracts from Florence,[78] although Simeon also drew directly on Eadmer and William of Malmesbury and some others. The *HA* is indebted primarily to the *Chronicle* but also probably to the other English historians. Both chroniclers as they approached the time of composition introduced more and more material of their own; but neither escaped from the annalistic form. These several annals

76.   A critical edition of the Worcester chronicle is sadly lacking; J. R. H. Weaver published the section 1118–40 separately, under the title *The Chronicle of John of Worcester.* For a discussion of the authorship, see Darlington, *op. cit.* 13 ff. Orderic Vitalis's evidence is crucial: OV (Chibnall), ii. 186–9. Simeon of Durham in his *HR* made little if any use of Florence after 1119; but this may have been due to a change of plan. In any case he copies from the annals 1118–19, which must have been written after Florence's death. In order to indicate here the edition cited, the annals up to 1118 are referred to in the apparatus as Florence and thereafter as John of Worcester.

77.   Opinion is divided over who was the borrower, and until a critical edition of Florence is available no case can be proved. Most discussion of the problem has been bedevilled by the view that all the chronicle's entries before 1118 must have been written before that year because it was then that Florence died. Stubbs, *GR* ii. p. cxxviii, pointed out that, as William does not acknowledge any debt to Florence, the presumption must be that he did not use it, and since Florence could not have used William, and there clearly was a relationship, it was likely that they used a common source. But if Florence was not completed as a whole before 1141 the common source can be eliminated and John of Worcester made the borrower. There may, however, have been earlier editions of the Worcester chronicle. It is unlikely, although not impossible, that Simeon of Durham, who copied whole stretches of Florence into *HR,* was working as late as 1141 (see also next note). Nevertheless the case for William of Malmesbury being one of Florence's sources seems the stronger, and Darlington, *op. cit.* 14–15, adduces evidence in support.

78.   Stubbs *GR* ii, p. cxxviii, wondered whether there was a Latin version of the Chronicle which was used by both Florence and Simeon.

written in Henry I's and Stephen's reign were to serve in their turn as bases for the histories written later in the century.

A contemporary of John of Worcester, and one who saw him at work in the twelfth century, was Orderic Vitalis. Born in the Welsh marches near Shrewsbury in 1075, put as a boy into the monastery of St Evroul in the marches of Normandy and Maine, and taught by John, who had been a pupil and master at Rheims and a younger contemporary of Bruno (founder of the Grande Chartreuse),[79] he wrote in a thumping monastic style, richly rhymed, a loosely constructed, discursive history of great length, which is for the most part completely free from the annalistic bonds.[80] Indeed, the few dates he gives when his narrative is in full flood are often wrong. He had a lively curiosity, a retentive, but not very accurate, memory, and every opportunity to gain information about the Norman aristocracy which was the real subject of his book. The volumes which are concerned with the period 1087 to 1141, when he laid down his pen, are based largely on his own recollections and the information which came from friends and acquaintances and the connexions of his brother monks. Although immersed in the contemporary scene and Proustian in his exploration of it, like Proust he was not entirely at home in his *milieu*. He was always conscious of his Englishness and aware that the Normans had conquered his people. And he was a priest and monk. Orderic is without rival in his description of the feudal world, physical and moral. Although his style can pall, the imaginary conversations which he introduces to give heightened dramatic effect to the great events never fail to delight and instruct. Now it is William the Conqueror on his deathbed, confessing his many crimes; now the conspirators of 1088 give their views on the Norman empire and the law of succession; now Rufus and Helias of la Flèche exchange challenges and taunts. Orderic describes their persons, analyses their motives. It may be that the actors always talk in the terms of his maturity rather than of his youth: but there is no doubt that they speak like stylized, perhaps idealized, twelfth-century kings and nobles. He saw the men and women he described as characters in a historical drama, and by looking at them anew in different situations portrayed them in the round. In one context Odo of Bayeux is a worldly prelate, in another a patron of the arts, in another a wicked conspirator. Orderic knew right from wrong; he could distinguish law and custom; but he was not censorious.

The monk of St Evroul wrote on such a vast scale that he is without rival. But civil war in Stephen's reign not only inspired William of Malmesbury to take up his pen again but also persuaded an unknown clerk to write a history of the king's military campaigns. William's *Historia Novella,* in which he starts with Henry I's nomination of his daughter Matilda as his heir and continues the story of the disputed succession until 1142, when the author may have died, is scrappy, incomplete, and unpolished; but it is written more freely than his other

79.   John R. Williams, 'The cathedral school of Rheims in the eleventh century', *Speculum* xxix (1954) 669.

80.   For Orderic we have the advantage of a new edition (in progress) by Marjorie Chibnall; see also Hans Wolter, *Ordericus Vitalis: ein Beitrag zur Kluniazensischen Geschichtsschreibung* (Weisbaden 1955).

histories and includes some excellent accounts of ecclesiastical councils, one of which he had attended, of politics, and, as usual, of the character of the actors. William was able to discuss events with men as great as Roger bishop of Salisbury and, presumably, Robert earl of Gloucester, to whom he dedicated the history. He retained a sharp eye, a good understanding, and the ability to convey his meaning in few words.[81]

The *Gesta Stephani,* an anonymous history running from Henry I's death to Henry II's coronation, was planned and partly written when Stephen's victory in the war of succession seemed inevitable, and completed in 1154–55, when his failure was known. Despite the author's attempt to trim his sails to the new wind and his introduction of Henry, 'the lawful heir', the work was naturally unpopular and pointless after the triumph of the Angevins, and survived the Middle Ages in only a mutilated copy. Although the author was a well educated and pious clerk, very partial to moral observations, and believing that God intervened constantly to punish sin with defeat and reward virtue with victory – in 1153 God changed sides – no chronicle more secular in content was written in the Norman period. The anonymous work is less a biography of the king than an account of the civil war. The author had an excellent knowledge of military matters and of feudal politics, and a delight in the movement and hazards of warfare. He brings sieges, ambushes, and battles alive because he knew what he was talking about. (His scenes can be compared with the wooden and classical battle pieces of Henry of Huntingdon.)[82] Naturally he drew the reader's attention to the destruction of sacred buildings, the tribulations of the church, and the ill-treatment of bishops and clerks, for these explained the fortunes of the combatants; but ecclesiastical affairs always remained subordinate to his main purpose. If, as has been suggested,[83] this history was indeed written by Robert bishop of Bath, a former Cluniac monk of Lewes, it is proof of the way in which warfare could corrupt others besides Roger of Salisbury and his kin and Henry of Blois and his. Robert of Bath cut a sorry figure in the only military action he saw (in 1138); but he may none the less have been fascinated by the soldier's world.

Likewise incomplete and anonymous, but firmly attributed to John of Salisbury, are brief memoirs of the papal court 1148–52, worked up probably in 1164, when he was in exile. This *Historia pontificalis,* as it has been called, thrown together by one of the most intelligent and best educated men of

---

81. An attack on his reliability by Robert B. Patterson, 'William of Malmesbury's Robert of Gloucester: a re-evaluation of the *Historia Novella*', *American Hist. Rev.* lxx (1965) 983; 'Stephen's Shaftesbury charter: another case against William of Malmesbury', *Speculum* xliii (1968) 487, seems to be misconceived.

82. Antonia Grandsen, 'Realistic observation in twelfth-century England', *Speculum* xlvii (1972) 42, notices the author's interest in the exact topography of castles.

83. R. H. C. Davis, 'The authorship of the *Gesta Stephani*', *EHR* lxxvii (1962) 209–32. Davis's case rests, persuasively, on the geographical setting and the author's sympathies; he does not, however, notice the writer's knowledge of and interest in warfare, which ill suits a pious Cluniac monk. Davis adduces evidence of a rather general kind to prove that the author was a bishop. One bit of evidence, however, points in the other direction: under the year 1143 he condemns the bishops for doing nothing to protect the church, and the bishops are *illi,* not *nos.* He was not very sympathetic to Stephen's military actions in the neighbourhood of Salisbury in 1149. A canon of Salisbury with political views opposed to his bishop is at least as likely a candidate.

his age, is in quite a different class.[84] Its account of St Bernard's attack on the orthodoxy of Gilbert of la Porrée's teaching on the Trinity is acute, fair, and compassionate; but as this episode, with John's exposition of his old teacher's views, occupies about a third of the work as it stands, it will be seen that John was not much concerned with the plan of his essay or, indeed, with historical writings as such. For the historian of the English church this fragment is particularly useful for the view it conveys of Stephen's government from the standpoint of Archbishop Theobald and the papal curia – a view also coloured by John's experiences, culminating in exile, in the world of Henry II and Becket. John moved in the highest intellectual and governmental circles and, while he could be respectful, was completely without awe.

In general, however, the writing of history remained very much a monastic occupation, and it spread to the Augustinian priories of the north. At Hexham (Northumberland) Prior Richard (1142 – c. 1170) and his successor, John, were both interested in history. The latter wrote after 1162 a continuation of Simeon's *Historia Regum* from 1130 to 1153, a northern chronicle about events many of which he had witnessed at first hand. He was remarkably detached from the various rivalries. He supported the English, but greatly preferred David of Scots to Stephen. He was not involved in the Durham–York dispute or much concerned by the struggle between York and Canterbury. He had an independent religious point of view, but was neither bigoted nor completely unworldly. At Newburgh (Yorks) the canon William, who had been born in 1135–36 at Bridlington, wrote at the end of the century a history of the period 1066–1198 in five books.[85] He too supported an independent attitude with a sharp critical sense. History writing was also spreading to parsons. The precedent set by Henry of Huntingdon was continued by Ralf (of Diceto), son of Ulfketel, hereditary parson of Diss (Norfolk),[86] and Roger (of Hoveden), hereditary parson of Howden (Yorks).[87]

Associated with monastic history was hagiography. Although there was a reflorescence of hagiographical writing in England after the Conquest, the two professionals most concerned, both immigrants from St Bertin at St Omer, Folcard and Goscelin,[88] were not commissioned to write the lives of any contemporary or near-contemporary prelate. Indeed, there was almost no autobiographical and little biographical composition in the Anglo-Norman period. Goscelin wrote the partly autobiographical *Liber Confortatorius* for Eve, the girl he had loved at Wilton; but it lags far behind Abelard's *Liber calamitatum,* and had no imitators. Letters, which were written in great quan-

84.   See Heinrich Hohenleutner, 'Johannes von Salisbury in der Literatur der letzen zehn Jahre' *HJ* lxxvii (1958) 493–500, where Marjorie Chibnall's edition is rather roughly handled; Johannes Spörl, *Grundformen hochmittelalterlicher Geschichtsanschauung* (Münschen 1935); Walter Freund, *Modernus und andere Zeitbegriffe des Mittelalters* (Köln-Graz 1957).

85.   Cf. Rudolf Jahncke, *Guillelmus Neubrigensis: ein pragmatischer Geschichtsschreiber* (Bonn 1912).

86.   Charles Duggan, *Twelfth-century Decretal Collections and their Importance in English History* (1963) 10–11.

87.   Cf. Frank Barlow, 'Roger of Howden', *EHR* lxv (1950) 352; Doris M. Stenton, 'Roger of Howden and Benedict', *ibid.* lxviii (1953) 574.

88.   Cf. Frank Barlow, *VEdR* pp. xliv ff., 91 ff.

tity, were the usual vehicle for news and anecdote, and the commonest outlet for the emotions. The two leading biographers were Englishmen. Coleman, monk of Worcester, a chaplain of Bishop Wulfstan, wrote his master's life in Old English shortly after his death in 1095. William of Malmesbury translated it into Latin. And Eadmer, monk of Christ Church, Canterbury, wrote two works in Latin on his abbot, Archbishop Anselm, the *Historia Novorum,* which is essentially an account of Anselm's pontificate, and the *Vita,* a more personal story.[89] Both Coleman's and Eadmer's biographies are eye-witness accounts by admirers. The former is a worthy work, but uninspired. Eadmer wrote, largely from diaries he had kept and his collection of documents, a loving and partisan account of his hero, designed to defend him against criticism as much from his own monks and the church at large as from the royalist clerks and prelates. He wrote the life of a man he thought was a saint, not in the conventional terms of the traditional *vitae,* nor in the homiletic style of Coleman, but as a friend evoking for other friends the memory of a man they loved. More typical are a short Latin life of the saintly Gundulf bishop of Rochester,[90] and for its time a very old-fashioned Life and Miracles of Robert of Béthune, prior of Llanthony and bishop of Hereford (1131–48).[91] Two somewhat later accounts of twelfth-century hermits, John of Ford's Life of Wulfric of Haselbury and a Life of Theodora of Huntingdon (Christina of Markyate) by an anonymous monk of St Albans, exemplify respectively the traditional religious stereotype and the more directly observed historical biography which was beginning to edge its way in.[92]

The art of writing Latin verse was taught as part of grammar, and the art of letter writing, later called *dictamen,* as part of rhetoric. Although by and large the former was a monastic predilection, the latter clerical, the few large English collections of correspondence of this period are all the work of monks. Among the prelates Archbishop Anselm with almost 500 letters is followed at a considerable distance by Lanfranc and Herbert Losinga with sixty apiece. At the end of our period the Cluniac Gilbert Foliot abbot of Gloucester, bishop of Hereford and then of London, took his place with Bishop Arnulf of Lisieux, Abbots Bernard of Clairvaux and Peter of Celle, and other influential letter writers of the French world. It will be noticed that the great managerial figures of the English church, men like Ranulf Flambard, Roger of Salisbury, and Henry of Winchester, are not represented. And Theobald of Bec archbishop of Canterbury can only appear because he employed John of Salisbury as his clerk. Letter writing was too time consuming for busy men. From clergy beneath the rank of prelate the only collections are those of Elmer prior of Canterbury (died 1137), and of the slightly later Osbert of Clare prior of Westminister.[93] It was not until the second half of the twelfth century that the

---

89.   Cf. R. W. Southern, *St Anselm and his Biographer* (1963).

90.   *Anglia Sacra* ii. 273.

91.   *Ibid.* ii. 295.

92.   John abbot of Ford, *Wulfric of Haselbury,* ed. Maurice Bell, Somerset record soc. xlvii (1933); *The Life of Christina of Markyate,* ed. and trans. C. H. Talbot (1959).

93.   *Anselmi opera omnia,* ed. F. S. Schmitt (1946–52), vols ii–v; *Epistolae Herberti de Losinga, Osberti de Clara, et Elmeri,* ed. R. Anstruther (Brussels 1846); *The Letters and Charters of Gilbert*

publication of editions of elegant and interesting letters became all the rage. Elaboration of composition and the fashion of collecting and publishing went hand in hand.

The general documentary situation showed similar features. In the Western church as a whole the trickle of business papers became a flood with the pontificate of Alexander III (1159–81), the canonist and former papal chancellor, Roland Bandinelli. Before then papal and episcopal privileges and papal decretals were relatively few, and before the introduction of the bishop's register in the course of the thirteenth century episcopal *acta* survive only in handfuls.[94] Alexander himself did not cause the change. The pressure was coming from below. Most documents, whether papal, episcopal, or royal, were issued at the request of the petitioner, were based on his petition, and conceal the background and initiative. They give, therefore, a false impression of purposeful, centralized government. Much of the growing documentary habit was simply part of the collecting mania. Churches gathered in charters from every available source as well as relics and other precious or useful objects. And as with most collections the genuine, the damaged, the doctored, and the spurious were jumbled together.

Between 1070 and 1154 the clergy had done quite well for themselves. Most sections had become wealthier, some spectacularly so, through the generosity of the laity and the improvement in the general economic situation. The only class which may have become poorer was the village priests, and this was because the corporations, by means of impropriation, became richer at their expense. The church used its larger revenue not only to increase the number of its ministers and improve the services, but also to give itself better accommodation and a better standard of living, better education, and a much more professional and cultured tone. Moreover wealth and improved techniques of government had given the church greater authority. It was organizing itself as a corporate body which, besides controlling its own affairs, disciplined the laity for breaches of the moral code. It had not, however, advanced confidently on a broad front. Its success had been partly dependent on an internal moral reform, preached by some great leaders, which had only in part found a response within the clergy as a whole. And, indeed, when there were orders in the church, like the monastic, expressly committed to chastity, it was perhaps unnecessarily heroic to demand the same of village priests. Moreover,

Foliot, ed. Z. N. Brooke, A. Morey, and C. N. L. Brooke (1976); *The Letters of John of Salisbury*, i, *The early letters*, ed. W. J. Millor, H. E. Butler, C. N. L. Brooke (Nelson's Medieval Texts 1955) and *PL* cxc.

94. An increase in papal correspondence with Italy, France, and to some extent Spain had started in 1124 with Honorius II. Germany and England lagged behind. For papal documents see R. L. Poole, *Lectures on the History of the Papal Chancery* (1915), Jaffé-Wattenbach, Loewenfeld, and *PU*. Cf. Christopher R. Cheney, 'Some features of surviving original papal letters in England', *Annali della scuola speciale per archivisti e bibliotecari dell' università di Roma'*, Anno XII – 1–2 – Gennaio-Dicembre 1972 (Turin 1973) 1. For decretals cf. Duggan, *Decretal collections* 21; Mary G. Cheney, 'Pope Alexander III and Roger, Bishop of Worcester, 1164–1179: the exchange of ideas', *loc. cit.* For episcopal acta cf. F. M. Stenton, 'Acta episcoporum', *The Cambridge Historical Journal* iii (1929) 1; C. R. Cheney, *English Bishops' Chanceries, 1100—1250* (1950). The British Academy has plans to publish, diocese by diocese, all acta before the beginning of episcopal registers.

the very acquisition of great corporate wealth created recurrent crises of conscience in a clergy which taught the virtues of poverty and renunciation. Nevertheless, all scruples were overcome; and in the thirteenth century the church built proudly on the foundations laid in the eleventh and twelfth.

In one sense the church relied entirely on the cooperation and generosity of the laity to the clergy. The ecclesiastical services were maintained by the people as a means to their salvation – put crudely, to avoid the pains of hell. These things can properly be expressed crudely, for it was in such terms that they were expressed at the time. Orderic Vitalis devoted Books V and VI of his *Ecclesiastical History* particularly to the domestic affairs of his monastery, an interlude of charter-chronicle within the great design. He ended Book V with words:

> I have given a very lengthy account of the properties donated to the church of St Evroul, but I have by no means been able to include everything in this present book. For the properties are small, and have been wrung from men of modest fortune, sometimes by persuasion, sometimes by force or purchase or in some other way, and are scattered widely through several dioceses. On them as many monks as the property can support are established, and these serve the Lord daily in hymns and prayers and abstinence of life for the good of their benefactors. The remaining properties shall be gathered together in the next book and recorded for the information of the monks who will labour in the Lord's field after us.[95]

The two services most regularly 'sold' in return for land were the acceptance of a boy as an oblate monk and of a dying man or woman into the community *ad succurrendum*.[96] But a monastery would accept anything of value. Orderic's religion was unashamedly commercial, and he believed that St Evroul gave good value for money. Salvation had its price and the monks were there to exact the entrance fee and to secure for the purchaser his due reward. The large number of small gifts made to monasteries proves that it was widely believed that the services of monks were worth acquiring. The attitude of the laity to the secular church cannot be stated so simply. In effect the churches, through tithe, mortuaries, and other dues and fees, taxed the people; and tax gatherers are never popular. Famous shrines, miraculous relics, effective preaching, could earn special rewards; but the ease with which the people could forego the services and sacraments during an interdict suggests that although religion and its ministers were taken for granted, indeed were considered indispensable, they were also associated with oppression. An interdict was a sort of holiday.

What in fact did the church do for the people in return for the revenues it enjoyed? It interceded with God for humanity at large and benefactors in particular. It offered through its sacraments the only road to salvation. It provided beautiful places for corporate worship, a satisfying ritual, and a comforting message. In the village priest it supplied a schoolmaster and a local leader who could help his flock in the various ways open to an educated man.

---

95. OV (Chibnall) iii. 210. Cf. my review in *Medium Ævum* xlii (1973) 156.
96. Good examples of both can be found in *Textus Roffensis*, ed. T. Hearne (1720).

With the monasteries it provided refuges for many injured, whether physically or spiritually, in the world, and alms for the poor and medical treatment for the sick. To society in general and especially to the *respublica* it contributed an educated class of the utmost value as clerks and administrators. The very poor were undoubted gainers. Only at the monastic gate could they be sure of some distribution of food. Those engaged in the direct farming of land probably suffered from the economic burden of maintaining the church; but whether they felt the cost worth while cannot be answered with assurance, mainly because they did not look at it in quite that way. The church and its taxes were inescapable except by fraud and evasion, and the extent to which recourse was had to those depended on individual piety. The attitudes of the rich are easier to see. Most of the clergy were their social inferiors and often under their power or patronage. Each party, therefore, regarded the other with a mixture of deference and authority, in proportions which varied according to the persons and the occasion.

Generally speaking noble soldiers of this period despised clerks. The lower clergy rode mares or mules and were hypocrites. They also, as William the Marshal observed a century later, shaved the dying too close.[97] They made unreasonable demands, such as the return of everything that had been acquired unjustly. Since most men waited until their deathbed before making a full confession and seeking total absolution, and were prepared to take the not uncommon risk of a violent and unexpected end, the church made much of death. No one of this time surpassed Orderic Vitalis as a mounter of set pieces, and his reconstruction in 1133 of the passing of William I is one of his masterpieces. He has the Conqueror confess, one after the other, the many injustices he had committed. 'O my friends', he said,

> 'I am weighed down with the burden of my sins and tremble, for I must soon face the terrible judgment of God, and do not know what I shall do. From childhood I was bred to arms and am deeply stained with all the blood I have shed. The evil deeds that I have done in the sixty-four years I have passed in this troubled life cannot be numbered; and for them I must soon render account before the most just Judge.

And so on for some seven pages in the latest edition.[98] William grovelled. And his dutiful heir in England, Rufus, distributed his father's treasure to the church and the poor for the salvation of the dead man's soul.

It is one of the oddities of Rufus's spiritual life that he expressed total contrition and made full amends in 1093, when he did not die, and was unable to utter a word when killed seven years later – and also was succeeded by the more hard-hearted of his brothers (Henry I), who would not waste a penny on the dead man's soul – throwing good money after bad, he thought. In 1093 the bishops suggested that Rufus should open all his prisons and release all the prisoners, pardon all debtors, and appoint pastors to all vacant churches,

97. *William, earl of Pembroke, Knight-Marshal of the King's House. L'Histoire de Guillaume le maréchal*, ed. Paul Meyer, Soc. de l'hist. de France (Paris 1891–1901), lines 18476–502.
98. OV (Chibnall) iv. 80 ff.

especially Canterbury, and restore the church's liberty. And then Abbot Anselm added that first the king should make a complete confession of all his sins and crimes against God, and promise that if he recovered he would honestly correct them. Next he must give immediate effect to his earlier undertakings by issuing orders to his servants in writing. Anselm was nobody's fool: Rufus was in no position to demur, and obeyed. The clergy were not so understanding at a deathbed as before. The roles were reversed. But Rufus recovered, protested that no man could keep all his promises, and that he would pay God back for his bad turn. The roles had been reversed again.[99]

Rufus was a coarse man, with little more than a robber's interest in the church. But he did concern himself with the correct behaviour of soldiers of noble birth; he practised what he preached, and helped to develop a code of chivalry. This in its origins owed little or nothing to Christian teaching. The church was not the exclusive provider of answers to men's needs and aspirations. But it soon managed to take chivalry under its care. And so it usually was. Whenever possible the church assimilated the social customs of the age. If, when with leaders who neglected their duty to instruct, it could be regarded by that stern censor of prelates, William of Malmesbury, as the ostrich in the wilderness (Lamentations 4:3), which has wings but cannot fly,[100] seen from a distance it looks more like the giant roc of Arabian tales whose outspread wings covered the whole vault of heaven. Some things it seized in its beak or grasped with its talons, while others, like Sindbad the Sailor, could hang on to its legs.

99. Eadmer *HN* 30 ff. *Chron. E.* OV (Chibnall) iv. 176.
100. W. Stubbs, introduction to *GR* i, pp. xii-xiv, Hugh Farmer, *op. cit.* 51.

Chapter I

Structure

All were agreed in the eleventh and twelfth centuries, popes as well as kings, that northern Christendom was composed of national churches. In the papal chamber was kept a Register or *Provinciale,* a list of the churches subject to Rome, arranged as far as possible according to the regions (e.g. *Gallia, Britannia*) and provinces of the Roman Empire. As it was based on a variety of earlier administrative lists, some secular, the presentation is not uniform; and as it was haphazardly revised, there are many discrepancies between the cities and churches listed and the numerical summaries. The earliest of these lists to have survived is one which may have been made about 1165 by Cardinal Boso, a chamberlain of Popes Adrian IV and Alexander III, who was possibly an Englishman. But this no doubt merely updated an earlier catalogue, and itself, as transmitted by Cardinal Albinus in 1188–89, contains some later additions.[1]

In the Register Gaul is divided into sixteen provinces. In *Lugdunensis secunda* are the metropolitan city of Rouen and the cities of Bayeux, Avranches, Evreux, Sées, Lisieux, and Coutances. In *Lugdunensis tertia* are the metropolitan city of Tours and, among others, Le Mans and the Breton cities.[2] Britain, in the preliminary material,[3] is divided into five provinces according to the fourth-century scheme: *Britannia prima, Britannia secunda, Flavia, Maxima,* and *Valentina* (Brittany). But when it came to listing the episcopal cities in the kingdom of England those divisions had perforce to be ignored, and no provinces are assigned to it; otherwise the arrangement is as with Gaul. The metropolitan city of Canterbury is credited with the following subject cities: London, Rochester, Chichester, Chester, Exeter, Winchester, Salisbury, Hereford, Worcester, Bath, Lincoln, Norwich, and Ely. After this occurs the entry: 'There are also (*vero*) in Wales St David's, Bangor, Llandaff, and St Asaph.' The total is given as eighteen. To the metropolitan city of York, in similar fashion, is ascribed Durham, followed by the entry, 'Scotland has these bishops: St Andrews, Glasgow, Galloway, Dunkeld, Dunblane, Brechin, Aberdeen, Moray, Ross, Caithness, and Argyll.' The total is given as eleven.[4] Carlisle, which is omitted, can possibly be left out of account as it was in

---

1. *Le Liber Censuum de l'Eglise romaine,* ed. P. Fabre and L. Duchesne (Paris 1910) ii. 68 ff.; for the sources i, introduction. Cf. also R. L. Poole, *Lectures on the History of the Papal Chancery* (1915) 150–1, 193–6. For Boso see below 266 and n.

2. ii. 97b.

3. ii. 96a.

4. ii. 100. The editors, i. 44, assumed that the last figure referred to the Scottish sees, of which eleven are indeed listed. But on the analogy of Canterbury it more likely refers to all the cities in the northern province or to all the suffragans of York. The totals are frequently wrong.

abeyance between 1157 and 1203. And one or two of the Scottish bishoprics, Argyll and possibly Dunblane, may be additions to the original list. Finally, after the kingdoms of Norway, Denmark, and Sweden, with the obvious intention of detaching it completely from the churches in *Britannia* (or the kingdom of England), the Irish church occurs with the explanation: 'In Ireland are 4 provinces. In the time of Pope Eugenius III all Ireland was divided into 4 metropolitan divisions (*metropoles*) by John Paparo, cardinal-priest of St Laurence *in Damaso,* legate of the apostolic see, in this wise.' It is then laid out on the standard pattern.[5]

From this arrangement there can be no real doubt, although in 1199–1200 Gerald of Wales was to argue the contrary,[6] that in the mid-twelfth century the papal chamber regarded the Welsh churches as subject to Canterbury and the Scottish as subject to York, and thought it necessary to emphasize the contrasting independence of Ireland. This interpretation is supported by a significant change in the arrangement of a new register, the *Liber Censuum,* drawn up in 1192 by the chamberlain, Cardinal Censio Savelli, later Pope Honorius III. Here Scotland has been shifted to join Ireland after the Scandinavian kingdoms, a move explained by the note that (since 1192) all the Scottish bishops are subject directly to the pope.[7]

The order in which the English bishoprics are given in these *Provincialia* (and there are slight differences between the two) seems to be roughly geographical, although the priority of London and Rochester may have some significance.[8] William of Malmesbury in his *Gesta Pontificum,* by describing the English church according to the ancient Anglo-Saxon kingdoms, produced an even more logical order in the bishoprics. And his scheme lies behind the information given by a mid-twelfth-century writer, perhaps a canon of the priory of Hexham in the diocese of Durham, who composed some useful historical and geographical tables.[9] English Britain, this man observed, was an island in the ocean. Far removed from the world, situated almost at the furthest extent of the western climate, placed in the cold region of the north, set almost on the very rim of the earth, it was of all the islands the biggest and best. Since it was surrounded by the ocean it was called by some 'the second world' (*alter orbis*).[10] England was, he thought, 800 miles long from Lands End (*Penwithstert*), which was fifteen leagues beyond St Michael's Mount, to Caithness at the top of Scotland (*Scotia*). It was 300 miles wide from St David's to Dover. It had two metropolitan and fifteen episcopal sees, which he identified correctly.

Although the writer considered that England for some purposes included Wales and Scotland, he, no more than William of Malmesbury, listed the Welsh and Scottish sees; and he made no mention at all of Ireland. On the

5. ii. 101b.

6. *De jure et statu Menevensis ecclesiae* in *Opera* iii. 165–6. Cf. Poole 150–1.

7. i. 230.

8. Below 47.

9. Simeon, appendix III, ii. 389–93.

10. Cf. C. Erdmann, *Forschungen zur politischen Ideenwelt des Frühmittelalters* (1951) 8–11, 38–43; Eric John, ' "Orbis Britanniae" and the Anglo-Saxon kings', *Orbis Britanniae and other studies* (1966) 1–63. See also 46.

whole he thought that the English church was coterminous with the shired area; and, deliberately leaving out Cumberland, Cornwall (with its seven small shires), Scotland, Wales (*Bretland*), and the Isle of Wight (in fact all territories west of the Tamar and the Welsh marcher earldoms and north of the Ribble and Tyne), he listed thirty-two English shires, divided between the West-Saxon Law, the Danelaw, and Mercian Law. These, had he wished, he could have assigned to the several bishoprics. But although the English bishops ruled over one or more shires, or viscounties,[11] owing to amalgamations it was more difficult than in the tenth century to call them after these. The bishop of Wiltshire, for example, had become the ruler also of Berkshire and Dorset, and it was easier to style him bishop 'of Salisbury'. Perversely, the most English of the Welsh sees, Llandaff, was frequently called Glamorgan by English writers. All the same, half the bishops had their see in the borough after which one of their shires was named.

The ecclesiastical geography of England was almost entirely shaped by secular units and political history. But the organization was purely ecclesiastical. The church had made use of a secular framework for its own purposes. Moreover, the ecclesiastical structure was so stable that, at least in the higher tiers, it could successfully withstand the pressures exerted by secular lordship. The duke-kings at the height of their power controlled Maine and Brittany and dominated Wales and Scotland. Rufus could send Hildebert bishop of Le Mans into exile in England.[12] Henry I could appoint to all the Welsh bishoprics. And William I had had the Scottish church placed under the metropolitan authority of York. Irish bishops came to Canterbury for consecration. But Le Mans and the Breton bishops were under the archbishop of Tours and so could not be annexed to the Norman church. Conversely, Sées, although it was sometimes controlled by the count of Bellême, could not be subtracted from the Norman church because it was subject to the archbishop of Rouen. In contrast, in Britain there was a large Celtic fringe which was not organized into territorial dioceses and ecclesiastical provinces, indeed was considered by both the English and the Roman church irregular and unsatisfactory. It was an area to be penetrated, subdued, and reformed.

Canterbury's claim to a primacy was directed almost exclusively to its attempt to subdue York; but, since it came to be based on texts from Bede's *Historia Ecclesiastica*,[13] took the form of a primacy over the whole of Britain, and so could be used against Wales, Scotland, and Ireland. Metropolitan and primatial claims fared best when they accorded with the political situation or were supported by secular imperialism. The Norman rulers, as inheritors of English pretensions, could regard themselves as kings of the whole of Britain and also hope to extend the limits of England. Wales was under the most pressure; and in the twelfth century the conquerors appointed, or secured the appointment of, bishops who took an oath of fealty to the English king, made

11.   According to Archdeacon Herman, writing at the end of the eleventh century, Herfast bishop of Elmham was, 'duorum Estengle vicecomitatuum episcopus', *Mirac. S. Eadmundi* in Liebermann *Ungedruckte* 248.

12.   Hildebert's poem on his exile is *Carmina minora*, ed. A. B. Scott (Teubner) no. 22.

13.   Especially Pope Gregory to Augustine, i. 27, cap. 7 (pp. 86–8), i. 29 (pp. 104–6); cf. also ii. 2 (pp. 134 ff.) ii. 4 (p. 146). Cf. R. W. Southern, *Saint Anselm and his Biographer* 127 ff.

their profession to the archbishop of Canterbury before consecration, and not only created see-towns, cathedrals, and dioceses on the English pattern, but also invented the past history of their creations.[14] Llandaff was founded by Urban after 1107, St David's by Bernard after 1115, and Bangor by David after 1120. St Asaph, to which Geoffrey of Monmouth (the main inventor of Welsh history) was consecrated in 1152, remained outside English control. The bishops of Llandaff and St David's also thought that they could base claims to metropolitan status on the legends they appropriated and the history they thought up. But, except when dreaming dreams, they, with the bishop of Bangor, behaved as though they were part of the English church. Even Gerald of Wales, strong advocate of the claim of St David's to be independent of Canterbury though he was, when arguing his case before Innocent III in 1199–1200 insisted that Wales was not a kingdom of itself, but merely a part of the English kingdom.[15]

A similar, but less successful, pressure was exerted on Scotland, with the ecclesiastical position complicated by the extension of York's metropolitan authority to that area as part of the compromise of 1072. In 1125–26 the archbishop of York argued before the pope against the Scottish bishops that Scotland was part of the kingdom of England: the king of Scots was the vassal of the king of England for Scotland.[16] That argument had little future with regard to Scotland, for national churches were resistant to political annexation. But the boundary between England and Scotland remained uncertain. In Stephen's reign King David tried to control the bishopric of Durham; and it was always on the cards that the English monarchy might regain at least Lothian.

Ireland, on the other hand, had never been subject to England, and barely tempted Norman cupidity. If all the bishops of Dublin from 1074 to 1152 and the bishop of Waterford in 1097 went to Canterbury for ordination and acknowledged their subjection in writing, it was not because they were compelled by either ecclesiastical or secular force, nor because they wanted to make themselves an ordinary and integral part of the English church. Canterbury under its great archbishops attracted and was convenient. The overtures came from Ireland, but, as Eadmer perceived, the subjection of Irish as well as Welsh bishops was useful supporting evidence for Canterbury's primacy over the whole of Britain, and so *a fortiori* over York.[17]

Within the national churches were normally provinces and bishoprics, although in the eleventh century it was more usual to write of metropolitan and episcopal sees or churches. The bishops' dioceses contained a number of lesser churches, which were usually grouped into archdeaconries, with these divided into (rural) deaneries. A scattering of franchises, often now called peculiars, complicated the pattern, and the various monastic orders were in varying degrees resistant to episcopal authority. From the earliest times the basic ministers in the Christian church were the bishop (*episcopus*) and the

---

14. Cf. Christopher Brooke, 'The archbishops of St David's, Llandaff and Caerleon-on-Usk' in *Studies in the Early British Church*, ed. Nora K. Chadwick (1958) 201 ff.

15. It suited his argument about the significance of the rubric *Wallia* in the cameral *provinciale*: 'De jure et statu Menevensis ecclesiae' in *Opera* iii. 166.

16. Hugh *HCY* 126.

17. Cf. below 45–6.

priest (*presbiter* or *sacerdos*). By the eleventh century the law and theology pertaining to their offices had become confused. The Norman Anonymous of *c.* 1100 favoured the patristic use of *sacerdos* for a bishop.[18] In the twelfth century the canon lawyers championed the view that episcopacy was a separate order against the theologians who argued that it was a dignity added to the presbyteral order.[19] But, whatever the theory, in practice the position of the bishops was unassailable. Because some of their functions were considered indispensable, and hardly to be delegated, bishops had survived in even the most anarchical areas of the church in the period of general governmental collapse.

Associated with the eleventh-century reform movement was the urge to establish a purely ecclesiastical administration independent of the lay powers, and so a hierarchical government with a chain of command. There was resistance to this among metropolitans and bishops, especially in Germany, and the Norman Anonymous was a strong defender of the equality of all bishops, and an opponent of any attempt to mediatize them.[20] But in England after the Conquest the principle was laid down distinctly. In 1088, when Archbishop Lanfranc took profession from Bishop Godfrey of Chichester, he declared in the instrument, 'Whoever requires obedience from his subjects should obey his own superiors (*prelati*). He is justly damned who disobeys or rebels against the spiritual commands of his pastor.' And Godrey promised obedience and service to the archbishop and his successors.[21] Lanfranc required similar written submission from all his suffragan bishops and also, as primate, from the archbishop of York. This produced a sort of 'feudal' pyramid.

In the time of Lanfranc's successor Gilbert, the first incumbent of the Norse-Irish bishopric of Limerick, and, as papal legate in Ireland, the first to begin the reorganization of the Irish church on the standard hierarchical pattern (council of Rathbreasail, 1111), wrote, probably between 1107 and 1111 and in preparation for the reform, a short tract, *De statu ecclesiae,* in order to instruct the native clergy in the common administrative law of the Western church.[22] Gilbert's background and ordination are unknown. But, presumably a Norman, he had met Anselm at Rouen, and was in friendly communication with him. He described the church in geometrical terms, as an accompanying diagram, constructed out of isosceles triangles, made plain. The two basic pyramids in the church were the parish under its priest and the monastery under its abbot. Subject to the priest were the six clerical grades (doorkeeper to deacon) and the three orders of the laity, those engaged in prayer, the farmers, and the soldiers.[23] The next tier of pyramids, the bishops' dioceses, were constructed out of from ten to a thousand of the two basic units. The archie-

18.   See below 292 ff.

19.   Robert P. Stenger, 'The Episcopacy as an Ordo according to the medieval canonists', *Medieval Studies* xxix (1967) 66.

20.   See below 293.

21.   Mayr-Harting *Acta,* no.2.

22.   Gilbertus Lunicensis, *Liber de statu ecclesiae* in *PL* clix, 995. Diagram in A. B. Mynors, *Durham Cathedral Manuscripts to the End of the Twelfth Century* (1939) pl. 32. For Gilbert, J. A. Watt, *The Church and the Two Nations in Medieval Ireland* (1970) 9 ff.

23.   It is difficult to see who these lay *oratores* are, unless hermits, or even monks.

piscopal pyramids were formed out of from three to twenty bishoprics. In the primatial (or, in the East, patriarchal) pyramids were from one to six archbishoprics. And, finally, above the primates and at the apex of the whole structure, was the pope, who was not only the one supreme governor but also ordained by all the rest, for it was with the consent of the whole church that the Romans made the appointment.

Gilbert's scheme is clear enough. But, although metropolitans, patriarchs, and the pope had ancient offices, the exact additional powers enjoyed by these superior bishops were not obvious to either canon lawyers or theologians.[24] It was never seriously suggested that any of them had a distinct and higher *ordo*. Dignity could only be defined in terms of precedence and powers. And the inherent or ordinary powers attached to these titles or appointments were by no means clear. In fact any historical investigation would show that they had varied considerably from place to place and from time to time. Even more uncertain was the status of those primacies which were equated with Roman provinces by the fabricators of the Pseudo-Isidorian decretals in the ninth century. All these superiorities, however, became of special interest to their claimants in the eleventh and twelfth centuries, when ecclesiastical government began to quicken. But once the reformed papacy saw monarchical powers within its grasp, it ceased to be interested in steps intermediate between it and the bishops. It could be indulgent to its supporters, such as the archbishop of Lyons, but in general it strove to confine primacies to titles of honour. At the same time, with the development of legations the pope was able arbitrarily for the time being to change the patterns of subordination. For example, papal legates in Ireland from 1101 helped to destroy Canterbury's influence there.[25] But any interference with the traditional pattern was usually unwelcome to the lay ruler: when Gregory VII in 1079 subordinated the metropolitan sees of Rouen, Sens, and Tours to the primacy of Lyons (an episcopal see in Burgundy outside the kingdom of France), he aroused the Conqueror's anger.[26] And English kings were normally hostile to papal legates sent from Rome.

Once William I had established Lanfranc's claim to a primacy over York and perhaps over the whole of Britain, and after the bishops had created archdeaconries, the English church had acquired a logical structure quite separate from its secular counterpart, and, despite the peculiars, remarkably simple. It was not, however, without its weaknesses. Its greatest flaw was that it was not based as firmly on its original founder's plan, with subsequent authorized modifications, as William I and Lanfranc had believed. And the gulf between claims and the documentary evidence produced some most vexatious

24.   It hardly simplified matters when popes, especially in the eleventh century, held on to their previous episcopal appointment. Werner Goez, 'Papa qui et episcopus. Zum Selbstverständnis der Reformpapsttums im 11. Jahrhundert', *Archivum Historiae Pontificiae* viii (1970) 27.

25.   Watt, *The Church and the Two Nations in Medieval Ireland* 10.

26.   Reg. VI, 34; *MGH* ep. sel. 2, 1, ed. E. Caspar, 447–9. Gregory on 25 March rebuked Lanfranc for not visiting him, *ibid.* VI, 30; 443; and on 20 April included Rouen among the four provinces of Lyons. The four provinces were to render to the archbishop condign obedience and honour. See also *KuS* 184 ff. For the primacy of Rheims, see Horst Fuhrmann, *Studien zur Geschichte der mittelalterlichen Patriarchate 3*, in *Zeitschrift der Savigny Stiftung für Rechtsgeschichte*, Kan. Abt. xli (1955) 111–14.

and well-nigh insoluble conflicts. The struggle between Canterbury and York, the ambitions of the Welsh and Scottish churches, the claim of St Augustine's, Canterbury, to be exempt from the archbishop, were not only disruptive, time-consuming, and scandalous, they also from the very start led to appeals to Rome which hindered William's attempt to make the *Landeskirche* his *Eigenkirche*.

However deceptive the theoretical simplicity of the church organization may have been, the ecclesiastical structure was even in practice simpler than its secular counterpart in the kingdom. A reversal of the old order had occurred. In the Anglo-Danish state the king had governed through, on the one side, the earls, and on the other, the bishops. With the disappearance of the great earls, the secular hierarchy had become very complicated; but with the creation of a primacy, the re-establishment of the metropolitans, and the stimulation to the bishops to govern their dioceses, and through archdeacons, coherence had returned to the church. In practice the ecclesiastical structure remained decentralized. Power was in the hands of the bishops, not the archbishops. That is why, despite the plan, the king remained the real governor of the church. He, much more effectively than the archbishops, could give orders and see that they were carried out. The easiest way for an archbishop to discipline a subordinate was probably to ask the king to show his displeasure. And across the ecclesiastical hierarchy lay the pattern of royal patronage. There were always some bishops in the special confidence and employment of the king. Lanfranc had the problem of Odo of Bayeux and Geoffrey of Coutances, Henry I's archbishops the problem of the chief justiciar, Roger bishop of Salisbury. Theobald of Bec had to contend with Henry of Blois, bishop of Winchester and the king's brother. It was William I's attempt to make the *ecclesia anglicana* legally and administratively a single unit, while in practice following a policy of checks and balances, which created the tensions which in the end destroyed much of its autonomy.

Anglo-Saxon as well as Roman geography had determined the creation of two provinces in the English church, one for the south- and one for the north-Humbrians. And the perpetuation of this plan had produced two provinces of unusual size, Canterbury remaining one of the largest in Christendom. Gregory the Great had instructed Augustine that the two metropolitan sees should be in London and York.[27] But Augustine and his successors had not moved from Canterbury; and although long before 1066 the claim of St Salvator's (Christ Church) Canterbury to be the mother church of the southern province and, in a sense, of the whole English church was incontestable, when Canterbury, by claiming more, provoked opposition, it was embarrassing for the Canterbury lawyers that this displacement had to be explained away. A proposal to substitute London for Canterbury was indeed made by King Cenwulf of Mercia in 797, when he abandoned an earlier Mercian scheme in favour of Lichfield.[28] And the church of St Paul's, mindful of Gregory's letter,

---

27. Bede i. 29. For Arch-abbot Suso Brechter's views of Augustine's see, refer to Henry Mayr-Harting, *The Coming of Christianity to Anglo-Saxon England* (1972) 265–6.

28. Dorothy Whitelock, *Some Anglo-Saxon Bishops of London* (The Chambers memorial lecture 1974, 1975) 14.

from time to time claimed a pallium for its bishop. Richard of Beaumais I asked for one in 1108,[29] and later Gilbert Foliot (1163–87), because of his hatred of Archbishop Thomas Becket, tried once more.[30] Lichfield's metropolitan status, created by authentic papal action in 787, may have been intended to lead to the formation of a third province. But the plan once dropped was never taken up again. Lichfield was usually a rather obscure and uninfluential bishopric. The only plans for a new English province to emerge in the Norman period were the schemes of Henry bishop of Winchester. He was believed to have asked his friend Pope Innocent II (1130–43) to make Winchester an archbishopric and Hyde abbey a bishopric, and also subject the bishopric of Chichester to him. Later he suggested to Pope Lucius II (1144–45) that he should have seven bishops subject to him, presumably London, Chichester, Salisbury, Wells, Exeter, Worcester, and Hereford, a kind of West-Saxon province. And it seems that Lucius even sent a pallium. But Lucius's successor, the Cistercian Eugenius III, would have none of it.[31]

Gregory I had put all the British bishops under Augustine,[32] and familiarity with Bede engendered not a little support for the view that Augustine's successors had some sort of authority, either primatial or metropolitan, over the Celtic bishops. But when the 'patriarchate' over the British Isles created by Lanfranc of Canterbury started to collapse in the twelfth century, new provinces began to be planned in the West and North. In 1111 the council of Rathbreasail divided Ireland on the English pattern into a northern (Armagh) and a southern (Cashel) province, and each metropolitan was, as with Gregory's scheme for England, to have twelve suffragans.[33] In 1152 the papal legate, John Paparo, arrived with four pallia, and the council of Kells-Mellifont divided the north between Armagh and Tuam and the south between Cashel and Dublin. The primacy was awarded to Armagh.[34] Neither the king of England nor the archbishop of Canterbury had much interest in Ireland and there is nothing to suggest that they tried to hinder this development. But it was otherwise in Wales. The new-type bishops of Llandaff and St David's, possibly harnessing Welsh nationalism to their own ambitions, claimed that they had archbishops among their predecessors, and then tried to exploit to their advantage the ambiguous and mischievous Romano-British history created by Geoffrey of Monmouth. A Norman, Bernard, bishop of St David's 1115–48, came close to obtaining from the papacy an independent Welsh province and a metropolitan church. But the hostility of Canterbury, the jealousy of the other Welsh sees, the ambivalent attitude of the Welsh bishops, and papal indifference defeated the scheme.[35]

29. Anselm, *ep.* 451. When the pope replied to Anselm on 12 October 1108 (*ibid.* no. 452) he ignored the subject.
30. David Knowles, *The Episcopal Colleagues of Archbishop Thomas Becket* (1951), appendix III.
31. Winchester annals in *Annales Monastici* ii. 53. Diceto *Abbrev. Chron.* 255; *Hist. Pont.* 78–9.
32. Bede i. 29; cf. i. 27, cap. 7.
33. Watt 15–19.
34. Watt 28–31.
35. I. P. Shaw, 'Giraldus Cambrensis and the primacy of Canterbury', *Church Quarterly Review* cxlviii (1949) 82. Schafer Williams, 'Geoffrey of Monmouth and the canon law', *Speculum* xxvii

In Scotland the desire of the bishops to escape from English control was even greater and their geographical position much more favourable. But Henry I exerted considerable influence over the Scottish kingdom, and the ambitions of his nephew, King David I (1124–53), were not necessarily towards independence of England. In 1126 John bishop of Glasgow, who had denied York's authority, claimed at Rome that Scotland was not part of England and wanted a pallium for St Andrew's.[36] In the summer of 1151 the papal legate, John Paparo, on his way to Ireland, in order to avoid Stephen travelled through Scotland. He was given a great welcome there and promised that he would persuade the pope to grant the pallium to the bishop of St Andrew's and make it the metropolitan see for Scotland, Orkney, and the other islands.[37] In fact in 1152, while Nicholas Breakspear was papal legate to Norway and Sweden, Trondheim was given metropolitan status and the bishop of Orkney was subordinated to him.[38] In 1189 Richard I released William the Lion from the feudal dependency imposed on him by the Treaty of Falaise (1174) and on 13 March 1192 Pope Celestine III made the ten Scottish bishops immediately subject to the apostolic see, and so created an abnormal situation.[39]

The usual claim of the archbishops of Canterbury and York was that they ruled a metropolitan church and had metropolitan powers. The outward sign of this was that they had been given a pallium by the pope, a gift which the Norman Anonymous, in the untechnical fashion of his time, calls a sacrament,[40] and which recognized that the recipient was in a special relationship to the pontiff and invested with some of his powers, especially authority over suffragan bishops. But although the authority was delegated, the claim to it was perpetual. Canterbury and York had always been metropolitan churches. It is doubtful whether an archbishop could exercise metropolitan authority without a pallium, but the archbishops only stressed their relationship with the pope as a last resort when under attack by other powers. Anselm regarded the pope as his protector against tyrannical kings. And York developed this idea in its struggle against Canterbury. It was one of the northern archbishop's constant arguments against Canterbury's primacy that, as he had sworn fealty to both the king and pope, it was unreasonable and uncanonical to subject him to another metropolitan. Metropolitans owed profession to the Roman pontiff

---

(1952) 184. David Knowles *loc. cit.* M. Richter, 'Professions of obedience and the metropolitan claim of St David's', *Journal of National Library of Wales* xv (1967–8) 197; 'Giraldus Cambrensis', *ibid.* xvi (1969–70) 193, 293; xvii (1971–72) 1; 'Canterbury's primacy in Wales and the first stage of Bishop Bernard's opposition', *JTS* xxii (1971) 177; 'Gerald of Wales: a reassessment on the 750th anniversary of his death', *Traditio* xxix (1973) 379; Christopher Brooke, 'Geoffrey of Monmouth as a historian', *Church and Government in the Middle Ages: essays presented to C. R. Cheney* (1976) 77. A large collection of extracts and documents (unfortunately translated into English) with useful historical introductions is in Davies, *Episcopal Acts.*

36.   Hugh *HCY* 119–28.

37.   *Hist. Pont.* 72. Tillmann 52.

38.   Helmut Gleber, *Papst Eugen III., 1145–1153* (Jena 1936) 168–70. Cf. H and S, ii. 1, 229.

39.   For the circumstances, see R. K. Hannay, 'The date of the *Filia Specialis* bull', *Scottish Historical Review* xxiii (1926) 171.

40.   *NA,* J 29, p. 219.

alone.[41] York developed the theme of his direct relationship with the pope and the special position conferred by the pallium in a way which was prejudical to the autonomy of the English church.

Three of the five archbishops of Canterbury, Lanfranc (1071), William of Corbeil (1123), and Theobald (1139), went to Rome for the pallium. The pope sent it to Anselm (1095) and Ralf d'Escures (1115). Five of the six archbishops of York received their pallia abroad, Thomas I (1071), Gerard (1001–02), Thurstin (1119, council of Rheims), Henry Murdac (probably at Trier in 1147), and William fitzHerbert (1154). The last was sent a pallium in 1145, but did not take it, and then went unsuccessfully to Rome in 1146. Thomas II received his pallium in England.[42] Since Anselm would certainly have gone to Rome had the king allowed, a personal visit to the pope was the accepted custom.

The usual way of describing the ambit of a metropolitan's authority was to list the episcopal sees subject to him.[43] The archbishop of Canterbury normally consecrated the bishops in Wales. In Ireland he consecrated between 1070 and 1139 four or five bishops of Dublin, one of Waterford, and one of Limerick, and some of these men were English monks.[44] In Scotland Archbishops Lanfranc and Anselm had a considerable personal influence, and there can be no doubt that the Scottish bishops, if they had to submit to an English metropolitan, would have preferred Canterbury to York. It had higher repute and offered less threat. Eadmer, monk of Christ Church and Anselm's biographer, who was elected to St Andrew's in 1120, withdrew because he would not accept consecration from York.[45] In England there was a boundary dispute between Canterbury and York which developed quickly after both sees had been given Norman prelates. Because the archbishops of York since the late tenth century had usually held also the bishopric of Worcester, Thomas I claimed that church for his province as well as Lichfield and Lindsey (Lincoln), part of the diocese of Dorchester. The case was referred by the pope to an English council, and in 1072 it was decided that the authority of York did not extend south of the Humber.[46] York's claim to Lindsey was revived when

---

41.   Cf. Hugh *HCY* 39.

42.   *Canterbury*: Lanfranc, Florence *s.a.* 1071; Anselm, *Chron. E,* Florence, *HN* 70 ff., *GP* 91; Ralf, *Chron. E;* William, *ibid.*; Theobald, John of Hexham 300. *York*: Thomas I, Florence *s.a.* 1071; Gerard, *GP* 259, Hugh *HCY* 13; Thomas II, Florence, *GP* 262, Hugh *HCY* 23, 30; Thurstin, Hugh *HCY* 75; William fitzHerbert, John of Hexham 317–18, Gervase 157–8; Henry Murdac, John of Hexham 320–1.

43.   It was still possible in the eleventh and twelfth centuries, as with the bishops of Bamberg and Pavia, to receive a pallium from the pope as a mark of special favour without achieving metropolitan status. But it was discussed before Eugenius III *c.* 1151, in connexion with Hugh archbishop elect of Palermo, whether a bishop could properly have the title of archbishop and a pallium and yet have no suffragans. John of Salisbury, *Hist. Pont.* 67–8.

44.   Watt 6–8. William of Malmesbury *GR* 353, in the context of the Canterbury–York settlement of 1072, wrote that Canterbury had the bishops of Ireland and Wales subject to him.

45.   R. W. Southern, *Saint Anselm and his Biographer* (1966) 236.

46.   *HN* 252–4; *GR* ii. 349–52; T. A. M. Bishop and P. Chaplais, *Facsimiles of English Royal Writs to A. D. 1100* (1957), pl. xxix; R. W. Southern 'The Canterbury forgeries', *EHR* lxxiii (1958) 198–201; R. R. Darlington, *Vita Wulfstani* pp. xxviii–xxix. For York's disclaimer, Lanfranc *Epp.* 11–12.

Bishop Remigius removed his see from Dorchester to Lincoln,[47] and in 1094 Thomas sought to prevent Anselm, who was in disgrace with the king, from ordaining the royal clerk, Robert Bloet, to the new see. But when Robert tried to evade making profession, Rufus came to Anselm's (or rather, perhaps, Robert's) aid.[48] This seems to have been the end of the matter. In 1125 it was proposed that Canterbury, in return for York's recognition of its primacy, should cede to the northern metropolitan the dioceses of Chester (=Lichfield), St Asaph, and Bangor. However this sensible plan came to nothing.[49]

In 1072 York was granted, in compensation for its 'loss' of southern dioceses, metropolitan authority over Scotland. Successive popes backed York strongly in this direction,[50] and York was able to consecrate some bishops to St Andrew's, Glasgow, Galloway, Sodor, and Orkney.[51] But there was general reluctance to go to York, and the archbishops did not venture into Scotland. By 1123 the Scottish bishops, led by John of Glasgow, who had been consecrated by Pope Paschal II, were fighting to throw off York's authority.[52] York got a second English suffragan in 1133, when the see of Carlisle was created for Cumbria. But Durham was often unfilial. According to the Durham chronicler, Archbishop Thomas did not take a profession when he consecrated William of St Calais in 1081 and Ranulf Flambard in 1099.[53] Then in Stephen's reign Durham was almost wrenched from York's control by Scottish violence.

Even more contentious and protracted was the matter of Canterbury's primacy over the metropolitan see of York. Lanfranc was consecrated archbishop of Canterbury by almost all the English bishops on 29 August 1070. The king's intention was that he should then consecrate Thomas (I) as archbishop of York. But when Lanfranc required Thomas to make a profession of obedience to him and claimed a primacy, Thomas refused consecration on those terms, saying that they were contrary to the rights of his church. So began a dispute which was not to subside before 1125.[54]

---

47. Florence *s.a.* 1092. Most recently, Margaret Gibson, *Lanfranc of Bec* (1978) 118 ff.

48. *HN* 47–8: Hugh *HCY* 8; Winchester annals in *Annales Monastici* ii. 37.

49. See below 44.

50. The evidence is conveniently displayed in H and S, ii, 1: Pope Paschal II (1101), p. 167; Calixtus II (1119, 1122), pp. 192, 193, 205; Honorius II (1125), p. 211; Innocent II (1131), p. 217; Adrian IV (1155), p. 231.

51. *St Andrews:* Turgot (1109), Robert (1127); *Glasgow:* Michael (1109 x 14); *Galloway:* Gilla-Aldan (1133 x 40); *the Isles:* John (*c.* 1151), Gamaliel (1154 x 61); *Orkney:* Ralf (1073), Roger (1101 x 8), Ralf Nowell (1109 x 14), Hugh *HCY* 31–2. Margaret Gibson, *op. cit.* 125 ff.

52. Hugh *HCY* 119, 122, 126–7, 129; John of Salisbury *Hist. Pont.* 72. In 1120 Nicholas, monk of Worcester, wrote to his friend Eadmer, Anselm's biographer, elect of St Andrew's, a sophistical 'proof' that York had no primacy over Scotland – which was not the point at issue: *Anglia Sacra* ii. 234.

53. Simeon Cont. I, *HDE* 138.

54. This dispute dominates Hugh *HCY*, is featured in Eadmer *HN*, destroys the balance of William of Malmesbury *GP*, and finds a place in all the English chronicles of the period. It has been treated by Margarete Dueball (born Telle), *Der Suprematstreit zwischen dem Erzdiözesen Canterbury und York, 1070—1126: ein Beitrag zur Geschichte der englischen Kirche im Zeitalter des Gregorianismus* (Historische Studien vol. clxxxiv, Berlin 1929). Cf. also Kurt-Ulrich Jäschke, 'Frühmittelalterliche Festkrönungen? Überlegungen zu Terminologie und Methode', *HZ* ccxi (1970) 556.

Primacies were much rarer and on the whole of far less importance than metropolitan rights. The most famous primacy, although not usually expressed in this form, was that of Rome. Most national churches had one bishopric with a (not always uncontested) claim to be the first in honour. But none of these seems to have claimed juridical authority over the other churches. Indeed it is not certain why Lanfranc should have made this claim in 1070. There may have been some immediate personal and political reasons. Thomas elect of York was the protégé of Lanfranc's rival, Odo of Bayeux. And as Lanfranc intended to reform the English church he may have thought a primacy would facilitate his measures. Both sides probably produced political arguments for the king. Contemporaries believed that Lanfranc drew attention to the danger of Northumbrian separatism.[55] A generation later Archbishop Thurstin of York shrewdly pointed out to Henry that if a king quarrelled with his archbishop of Canterbury, an archbishop of York who had made profession to Canterbury might feel obliged to support his ecclesiastical superior against the king.[56] William I's own feelings are unknown. York believed that he was surprised by Lanfranc's action but was persuaded to support it.[57] And it is unlikely that the Conqueror, who was inclined to a domestic policy of checks and balances, was unreservedly enthusiastic about a primacy. On the other hand, it probably suited him for the time being: Lanfranc was his devoted servant and there was no overwhelming reason why he should not be indulged.

Lanfranc can hardly have made his demand without a strong belief that the claim was well-founded. He was a stranger to England and must have been briefed by his cathedral chapter. Canterbury was undisputedly the first and mother church in England, founded directly by Rome and its missionaries. Moreover, the monks of Christ Church from their knowledge of English history may reasonably enough have thought that, until the recent reversals caused by Archbishop Stigand's irregular position, Canterbury had always had a primacy of honour. In most royal charters of all dates (and great quantities of these documents were possessed by churches in 1070) the archbishop of Canterbury signed after the royal family and before York. It was also evident that, with very few exceptions, the archbishops of Canterbury had been the more distinguished and the more prominent in history. There was at least a *prima facie* case. And, the monks probably thought, it was up to Lanfranc to recover what Stigand had lost. If Harold and William had indeed been crowned by Ealdred of York, then it was imperative that Lanfranc should reaffirm Canterbury's primacy.

Canterbury had undoubtedly usually enjoyed a *de facto* primacy.[58] York had no claims to one, and could aspire to no more than equality; it tended to argue against primacies in general: it was wrong to subject one metropolitan to another. Canterbury's difficulties started when Lanfranc's claim was denied by York and evidence useful in a court of law had to be assembled. It needed a papal letter expressly granting or confirming to Canterbury a primacy over

---

55. Hugh *HCY* 3.
56. *Ibid.* 34.
57. *Ibid.* 2–3.
58. *English Church 1000—1066*, 232–6.

York. This it did not have, and until 1122 archbishops chose to make the best and most plausible use of such genuine documentary evidence as they could find. It was difficult satisfactorily to base Canterbury's claim on Gregory I's letter to Augustine as transmitted by Bede. The pope made the metropolitans of London and York of equal status, with precedence, after Augustine's death, depending on seniority of consecration.[59] That Canterbury did not come into it was awkward and always a complication. Other papal letters issued before the northern metropolitan was established and confirming Canterbury's primacy over the English or British bishops were useful, though not unanswerable. When the case based on this evidence finally collapsed in 1120, Christ Church at last produced the sort of proof required. This was forged, and was probably generally recognized as such.[60]

The primacy that Lanfranc and his successors claimed was not much more than a higher dignity and precedence, and since it was almost exclusively a matter of prestige, Canterbury could not abandon its claim, and York, conscious of its inferiority in wealth and number of suffragans, could not graciously submit. Both principals were pushed into fighting attitudes by their cathedral chapters who obviously enjoyed the struggle, especially as it was one of clerks against monks. A settlement could only be imposed by a superior authority. The English kings after William I had no special interest in Canterbury's primacy, and both Rufus and Henry I were at loggerheads with Anselm. They also found the quarrel inconvenient and embarrassing. Since they were usually obliged to appoint an independent man of high repute to Canterbury, they used York as the plum for their greatest clerical friend. But as the southern metropolitan had the king's ear, and all the bishops, with the doubtful exception of Durham, supported Canterbury in this matter, the king was always tempted to force York to give way, usually by offering some face-saving formula. Not all archbishops of York were totally averse to forced submission. Most were lucky to get the preferment[61] and had little interest in the North, and all were going to spend much of their time at the king's court in company with the southern bishops and did not want to be shunned. In 1122–23 the bishops

59. Bede i. 29, 'in posterum ista distinctio, ut ipse prior habeatur, qui prius fuerit ordinatus'. There was to be a revolving primacy of honour.

60. See below 44. In 1902 Heinrich Böhmer established that a series of the Canterbury proofs was forged, and attributed the forgery to Lanfranc in 1072: *Die Fälschungen Erzbischof Lanfranks von Canterbury*, Studien zur Geschichte der Theologie und der Kirche (Leipzig 1902). In 1926, in an appendix to his *Lanfranc*, 271 ff., A. J. Macdonald reconsidered the evidence and suggested that the forgeries were not published before 1120 and had then only recently been concocted, possibly by Eadmer. In 1929 Margarete Dueball came to Böhmer's support: *Der Suprematstreit*. In 1958 R. W. Southern, without reference to Mrs Dueball, restated most of Macdonald's arguments, except that he exonerated Eadmer: 'The Canterbury Forgeries', *EHR* lxxiii (1958) 193–226. Josef Deér, 'Der Anspruch der Herrscher des 12. Jahrhunderts auf die apostolische Legation', *Arch. Hist. Pont.* ii (1964) 173 ff., relying on Anselm, *ep.* 214, claims (on this evidence probably mistakenly) that the forgeries were already in existence by 1099. Margaret Gibson, *Lanfranc of Bec* 231 ff. argues successfully against Southern (and Macdonald) that the monks started forging the bulls immediately after 1070, and gradually assembled a dossier which was not directed solely against York. Her main suspect in this enterprize is Osbern the precentor.

61. As the king normally appointed one of his clerks to York, there was usually some serious impediment to consecration. Thomas I, for example, was the son of a priest. The need to get a dispensation and Canterbury's support for this, was an initial handicap.

told Thurstin of York, who had not made profession, that they did not regard him as one of them and they objected to his taking part in the election of the archbishop of Canterbury.[62]

The dispute was also an embarrassment to the popes. They did not like primacies and had no interest at all in Canterbury's claim. They could see that on the evidence York had the better case and were not deceived by the Canterbury forgeries. But they were most reluctant to give a verdict against such luminaries as Lanfranc and Anselm or go against the express wishes of the king. There were nine different holders of the office in the half century between the death of Urban II (1099) and the accession of Adrian IV (1154), and one of the longest in power, Innocent II (1130–43), had a rival. Nevertheless, not even Anselm could get a confirmation of the primacy in satisfactory form,[63] and later archbishops of Canterbury, less distinguished, were much less favoured. The general result was that although there were many complaints to Rome, many legations, much seeking of papal bulls and much manoeuvring behind the scenes, the case was never put formally before the curia and the pope was never required to give a formal decision. Normally, like the king, he looked for some way out for the time being.

Both churches started on equal terms, for Canterbury's muniments were lost when the cathedral was burned in 1066, York's when the city was sacked in 1069. The dispute began, therefore, with both protagonists, strangers in their churches, unprepared and for a time without useful briefing. In 1070 Thomas I, after some hesitation, under general pressure made a profession of obedience to Lanfranc. No doubt partly because various formulae were proposed between 1070 and 1072 there was later dispute over what form had been used. Canterbury maintained that Thomas had submitted unconditionally. York claimed that he had made no more than a personal submission to Lanfranc which, of course, lapsed on Lanfranc's death.[64] However that might be, during the avoidance of Canterbury (1089–93) Thomas recovered some ground, for he was the only metropolitan in Britain, and it seems that he performed all those functions, whether metropolitan or primatial, which usually were Canterbury's.

When, however, Anselm was appointed to Canterbury, it had to be decided to what office Thomas and the bishops were to consecrate him.[65] The situation was not helped by an initial 'blunder' by Canterbury in describing

---

62. Hugh *HCY* 109.

63. *Epp.* 222, 303, 304, confirmation 'as possessed by your predecessors'.

64. Scriptum Lanfranci de primatu: London BL Cotton Nero A vii; *Chron. A,* Eadmer *HN* 10; Hugh *HCY* 4 ff., 8. Margaret Gibson *op. cit.* 116 ff., 231 ff.

65. Hugh *HCY* 7–8, 16–17; *HN* 42–3. Early in 1073 Thomas wrote to Lanfranc asking him to send him two bishops to York to enable him to consecrate a clerk [Ralf] to the bishopric of Orkney. He addressed Lanfranc as 'Piissimo et sanctissimo Cantuariorum archiepiscopo, totius quoque Britanniae summo pastori Lanfranco, Thomas fidelis suus et, nisi praesumptuosum sanctitati suae videatur, Eboracensis ecclesiae archiepiscopus.' He described himself as Lanfranc's son and his church as Lanfranc's daughter, and also disclaimed any intention of using this occasion in attempting to get the subjection of the bishops of Worcester and Dorchester. Lanfranc ordered the bishops of Worcester and Chester to go to York and sent them copies of York's disclaimer. Lanfranc *Epp* 11–12. If the date is indeed 1073, the title of Chester is an anachronism. Perhaps the headings to these letters must be treated with caution.

Anselm in the documents as 'metropolitan of the whole of Britain'.[66] When this had been corrected to 'primate of all Britain', Thomas, according to Eadmer, was content and performed the consecration. But, according to Hugh the Chanter, Thomas consecrated him only as 'metropolitan of Canterbury'. Again there may have been subterfuges and reservations, and doubtless subsequent lying. As it does not appear that Thomas was required to renew his profession to Anselm, there is much to be said for the Canterbury version of the event both in 1070 and 1093.[67] Thomas I's successor in 1101 was Gerard, bishop of Hereford, who in that capacity had made his profession to Anselm in 1096. The king found a compromise solution by requiring Gerard to give an undertaking that he would maintain in force his earlier profession.[68] Anselm was not a great champion of Canterbury's dignity and, according to the York story, at the council he summoned to Westminster in 1102 Gerard kicked over the lower chair which the monks had provided for him, and would not take his place until he was given one as high as Anselm's.[69] This was too much even for Anselm and he caused Paschal II on 12 December 1102 to order Gerard to make his profession.[70] But owing to Anselm's renewed exile Gerard was able to avoid compliance until the council of London in 1107, when he was almost at the end of his life.[71] The replacement of the unpopular Gerard in 1108 by Thomas II, the son of Samson bishop of Worcester, the brother of Richard bishop of Bayeux, and the nephew of Thomas I, reopened the matter.[72] This Thomas had been educated in the chapter of York and was fully committed to its cause. The dispute over his profession had already reached alarming proportions when Anselm died (21 April 1109), and the cause devolved on the monks of Christ Church and the southern suffragans. With Anselm's death, Henry had less interest in York's position. Enormous pressure was put on Thomas by the king and the elect's kinsmen, and before his consecration on 27 June he made, according to the northern story, a personal submission to an unnamable archbishop, saving his obedience to the pope and fealty to the king and saving the rights of the church of York. Also the king agreed that Thomas had yielded to the royal command and will, and not to the lawful judgment of a court.

Canterbury was still vacant when Thurstin, a clerk and friend of the king, succeeded Thomas II in 1114.[73] Thurstin, unlike his predecessor, was prepared to be a martyr, and Henry, presumably because he had not expected this of his friend, became determined to fight it out. Rather than make the

---

66. This expression was, however, current at Canterbury: cf. 'aecclesia domini Salvatoris quae in Cantuaria totius Angliae metropoli sita est', a variant of 'quae mater est omnium aecclesiarum per Angliam constructarum'. A tract, probably by Eadmer, edited A. Wilmart, 'Les Reliques de Saint Ouen à Cantorbéry, *AB* li (1933) 291, 289. See also below pp. 45–6.

67. Dueball, *Der Suprematstreit* 21–2, 45 favours Hugh's version; cf. Southern, 'The Canterbury forgeries', 207, where he suggests that here Canterbury suffered its first defeat.

68. *GP* 259.

69. Hugh *HCY* 13.

70. *Ep.* 283. J–W 5930. Böhmer *KuS* 191 ff., especially 195, argued that NA's Tract 29 was written in answer to this.

71. Florence *s.a.*

72. Hugh *HCY* 15 ff. Fröhlich 174–7.

73. Hugh *HCY* 33 ff.

required profession, Thurstin resigned the see and went into exile. In 1119, before the meeting of the council of Rheims, Calixtus II defiantly consecrated him archbishop and gave him the pallium; later he offered to make him his legate in England, a dignity which Thurstin prudently declined. After Henry's misfortune in 1120 the two were reconciled and Thurstin returned to England and was enthroned at last at York. He was then required to make his profession to Canterbury. While he still resisted, Archbishop Ralf of Canterbury died, and it was decided to punish Thurstin by committing the consecration of the next primate, William of Corbeil, to the bishop of London and the others. The existence, however, of two metropolitans was an opportunity and an inducement to negotiate a settlement. It was about this time that Christ Church Canterbury published for the first time a collection of forged papal privileges concerning the dignity and primacy of their church, and these were examined and ridiculed at Rome in 1123.[74] Nevertheless the new dossier did improve Canterbury's bargaining position, and in the autumn of 1125 a concordat was drawn up in Normandy to which many parties contributed, including the papal legate, John of Crema.[75] Canterbury should surrender to York the bishoprics of Chester, Bangor, and the non-existent diocese of St Asaph; Thurstin should accept Canterbury's primacy verbally; and his successor should make a full submission. But when the two archbishops and the legate reached Rome, and the treaty was discussed with Honorius II, the pope, probably because he did not want to confirm the primacy, persuaded them all that it would be better if Canterbury were to have a papal legation over Britain. This was done: on 25 January 1127 William of Corbeil was made papal vicar and legate within England and Scotland.[76]

Although Archbishop William did not completely abandon hope of getting a profession from Thurstin,[77] the 1125 settlement marks the effective end of the dispute over the primacy in the Norman period. Both archbishops survived into Stephen's reign and after them both sees fell on evil days. Canterbury under Theobald of Bec (1139–61) was at first depressed by the transfer of the papal legation to Henry bishop of Winchester, the king's brother (1 March 1139–24 September 1143), who for that period was the real ruler of the English church. York, owing to disputed elections, had after 1140 a valid archbishop only for the last three years of the reign. In 1154 Roger of Pont l'Evêque, archdeacon of Canterbury, was promoted to York,[78] and in 1162 his rival and successor as archdeacon, Thomas Becket, received Canterbury. With them a new chapter in the history of the dispute began.

Metropolitan status, symbolized by a pallium, was a papal vicariate. In the new age, however, it was subordinated to special papal legations, whether standing or temporary. These were unpopular in England with the

74.   Hugh *HCY* 104–5, 114–15.
75.   *Ibid.* 122 ff.
76.   Florence; *HR* 281; J-W 7284; *PL* clxvi, 1272. See further Denis Bethell, 'William of Corbeil and the Canterbury York dispute', *JEH* xix (1968) 145.
77.   Hugh *HCY* 131.
78.   According to William of Newburgh 95, Roger persuaded Theobald to consecrate him in his capacity as papal legate, not as archbishop of Canterbury.

archbishops, bishops, and abbots, and William I and his sons, pleading the special customs of the kingdom, excluded all papal legations which they had not requested. Indeed it is possible that in 1095–96 and 1119 the pope accepted for the time being and for political reasons this English custom.[79] In the circumstances, and in the context of the primacy struggle with York, it is not surprising that Canterbury should have tried to reinforce the negative right by claiming a standing and autonomous vicariate.[80] Such a position would both keep papal interference at bay and place Canterbury automatically above York.

In 1101 Anselm on his return to England from exile learned that Paschal II had granted a legation over England to Guy, archbishop of Vienne, the future Calixtus II.[81] He wrote to Paschal in protest, pointing out how inconvenient, owing to the distance, such an arrangement was, and claiming that a Roman legation over the kingdom of England had been held by the church of Canterbury from the earliest times up to the present, an arrangement advantageous to both churches. He was sending (unspecified) reasons, and asked that the legation should be restored to him. Paschal, however, was quite unmoved. On 15 April 1102 he confirmed Anselm's primacy in unsatisfactory terms but added as a rather small sweetener the negative privilege that Anselm, so long as he was archbishop, should not be subjected to the jurisdiction of a papal legate.[82] In 1125–26 king and pope made reciprocal concessions. First Henry, in return for a papal service, allowed John of Crema to perform novel legatine duties in England. Then on 25 January 1127, as we have seen, Honorius II granted a personal legation over England and Scotland to Archbishop William of Corbeil.[83] But when the papal legation was granted to the bishop of Winchester in 1139, Canterbury found this formulation of its superiority as unsatisfactory as the others. The aberration, however, proved to be exceptional. After Henry of Blois lost his legation on the death of Innocent II (24 September 1143), Theobald of Canterbury began to petition for it. He was rewarded early in 1150 by Eugenius III with a legation over the kingdom of England (but not, apparently, over Scotland), and this was renewed by successive popes up to Theobald's death (1161).[84] Thus in the end Canterbury's unquestionable governmental superiority over York depended on papal grant, and lapsed automatically whenever the archbishop or pope died.

Eadmer in his histories gave Canterbury and Archbishops Lanfranc and Anselm magniloquent titles. Lanfranc was 'primate of the whole of Britain'.[85] On his death Rufus confiscated 'the mother church of the whole of England, Scotland, Ireland, and the neighbouring isles'.[86] At Rockingham in 1095 the bishops say to the king, 'Anselm is primate not only of this kingdom

79. Deér (above 41, n. 60) 172 ff.
80. Cf. R. W. Southern, *Saint Anselm and his Biographer* 130–2.
81. *Ep.* 214; *GP* 68, 128.
82. *Ep.* 222.
83. John of Worcester 20–2; J-W 7284; *PL* clxvi. 1272.
84. Avrom Saltman, *Theobald archbishop of Canterbury* (1956) 30–3.
85. *HN* 12.
86. *HN* 26.

but also of Scotland, Ireland, and the neighbouring isles'.[87] From this we see that Eadmer regarded Wales as part of the kingdom of England and Canterbury's authority throughout the British Isles as primatial. He avoided the term 'metropolitan', presumably because it could also be applied to York. Yet Alexander II referred to Canterbury as 'the metropolis of the whole of Britain.'[88] In 1098, according to Eadmer, Urban II called Anselm, 'almost our equal, since he is pope and patriarch of the second world (*alterius orbis*)'.[89] All these are courtesy titles. However, they suggest that in Canterbury circles little technical distinction was made between archiepiscopal, metropolitan, and primatial rights. Since the archbishops had not established a professional chancery, equipped with formularies, the terminology was fluid. Even at the end of our period Archbishop Theobald's own clerks, and when drafting official *acta,* used a variety of styles to describe their master's position.[90] This absence of legalism, indeed the failure of the archbishops to publish their exact claims, did not help matters with York.

The Norman Anonymous, although he wrote tracts in defence of the metropolitan churches of Rouen and York against primates and the pope, and in some contexts understandably identified the church with the province,[91] in general showed no interest in metropolitan powers. For him the national or royal church was composed of bishoprics, essentially equal in authority.[92] This view was not far from the facts. The bishop or archbishop in his own diocese was the true ordinary. The church rested on the bishops.

The old Anglo-Saxon dioceses, in some acceptable conjunctions,[93] continued after the Conquest with boundaries unaltered until Henry I made additions. The diocese of Dorchester=Lincoln was obviously too large, and the ecclesiastical allegiance of the territory west of the Pennines and north of the Ribble was uncertain. The former situation was ameliorated accidentally. The abbey of Ely claimed to be exempt from the jurisdiction of the bishops of Lincoln. The high-born abbot Richard (1100–02, ?1103–07) tried to turn it into a bishopric,[94] and after his death Henry, with the purchased connivance of the bishop of Lincoln and papal agreement, pushed the scheme through in favour of his clerk, Hervey, the fugitive bishop of Bangor. Cambridgeshire (part of an archdeaconry), containing two other monasteries, Thorney and Chatteris, was made into a diocese, and the abbey church into its see.[95] In 1133 Henry made Carlisle, where a house of canons regular had been established, a bishop's see for Cumbria (Cumberland and Westmorland), Rufus's acquisi-

87. *HN* 63.

88. *HN* 20. Cf. also above 43, n. 66.

89. *VA* 105.

90. Saltman 192 ff.

91. J 2, p. 9.

92. Cf. J 23, 29.

93. Cornwall and Devon (Exeter); Ramsbury and Sherborne (Sherborne = Salisbury).

94. *Liber Eliensis* 225–6, 237.

95. For the circumstances and negotiations and papal bulls and royal charters, see *ibid.* 245 ff. See also HH *De contemptu mundi* 302, Diceto *Ymagines* 201–2, Giraldus Cambrensis *Vita S. Remigii* 32, John of Schalby *ibid.* 196.

tion, removing it from the archdeaconry of Richmond.[96] The king of Scots did not immediately accept this innovation,[97] and after the death of the first bishop the see remained vacant for 32 years. With these additions there were seventeen dioceses in England and four in Wales.

Lanfranc at his second general council (London 1075) asked the senior bishops (five of the Confessor's bishops were present, including London) what was the traditional order of seating. After consultation they replied on the following day that Canterbury should have York on his right, then Winchester, and London on his left. If either Canterbury or York was absent, the presiding archbishop should have London on his right and Winchester on his left. The rest of the bishops sat according to seniority of ordination.[98] London had his position of honour because of his claim to be dean of the church of Canterbury and the archbishop's second-in-command in the province, a claim which, although seemingly uncontested, has obscure antecedents and justification. Winchester is found acting as London's surrogate or as sub-dean; but again the background to the right is unknown.[99] In 1108, according to Eadmer, Anselm, after consulting his suffragans, decided to send two bishops with a message to the archbishop of York – London, because he was dean of the church of Canterbury, and Rochester, because he was acknowledged to be the archbishop's very own and domestic vicar.[100] Rochester, the second see in Kent, although again there is little Anglo-Saxon evidence, may well have been normally under the ecclesiastical and secular lordship of the archbishop. Certainly after the Conquest the archbishops appointed to the see, took homage and fealty from the elect, and invested him with ring and staff.[101] The bishop normally acted as the archbishop's vicar-general in the diocese of Canterbury, *sede plena* as well as *sede vacante,* and it is surprising that he was allowed no special seat at councils, not even the last.

The foreign bishops were accustomed to the see being in a Roman city and found many of the English see-towns unsatisfactory. Some of them cast their eyes covetously on richer churches, usually monasteries, which, if taken over, would raise their income. The reorganization, already begun in Edward's reign by Leofric's migration from Crediton to Exeter (1050) and Herman's from Ramsbury to Sherborne (1058) and in William I's by Herfast's move from Elmham to Thetford, while attempting to enter the monastery of St

96. John of Hexham 285; H and S ii. 1, 26–7; cf. Pope Innocent III on the subject in 1201, Howden iv. 178.

97. John of Hexham 298. David died in 1153 at Carlisle, where he seems to have established his headquarters in Stephen's reign: *ibid.* 330.

98. *GP* 67; *Vita S. Lanfranci* c. 12. Cf. Florence i. 280. Mansi xx. 451. William of Malmesbury, *GR* 353, attributes both the discussion and the decree to Winchester (1072). This seems to be just a slip.

99. For both these offices, see below 142.

100. *HN* 204, cf. Hugh *HCY* 210.

101. *English Church 1000—1066,* 221; H. A. L. Smith, 'The place of Gundulf in the Anglo-Norman church', in *Collected Papers,* ed. David Knowles (1947) 88–91. For appointments, see *Acta Lanfranci* 272, *Vita Gundulfi* in *Anglia Sacra* ii. 279–80, *PL* clix. 820, Gervase i. 132–3 (election of Bishop Walter in 1148); for homage and fealty, *HN* 196–7; for investiture, *HN* 2.

Edmunds,[102] was probably encouraged by the decree of a general council held at Windsor (?1072) ordering the bishops to have fixed sees.[103] At the general council of London (1075) it was decreed 'by royal benevolence and synodal authority' that, in accordance with the ancient decretals and canons, permission was given to Herman to move from Sherborne to (Old) Salisbury, Stigand from Selsey to Chichester, and Peter from Lichfield to Chester. Some other cases were left over for discussion with the king on his return from the war in France, possibly the controversial moves of Herfast to Bury and Remigius from Dorchester to Lincoln.[104] The former did not take place, the latter had been effected by 1086.[105] One of the removals sanctioned by the council proved unsatisfactory: Robert of Limesey left Chester for Coventry abbey about 1087;[106] and in Rufus's reign John moved from Wells into the monastery of Bath (about 1090)[107] and Herbert Losinga abandoned Herfast's plans and in 1095 started building a great cathedral at Norwich.[108] These changes in the second half of the eleventh century were the last before the Reformation of the sixteenth century.

Although there were archdeacons in the Old English church, it is doubtful whether, except possibly in the diocese of York, there were territorial archdeaconries.[109] These were, however, a feature of the Norman church. The archdeacon's right to his archdeaconry was proclaimed by Archbishop Mauger

102. *Heremanni archidiaconi mirac. S. Eadmundi* in Liebermann *Ungedruckte* 251–3; V. H. Galbraith, 'The East Anglian see and the abbey of Bury St Edmunds', *EHR* xl. (1925) 222; Barbara Dodwell, 'The foundation of Norwich cathedral', *TRHistS* 5th ser. vii (1957) 1–18. All the same, according to the *Acta Lanfranci,* the primate in his sixteenth year [25 December 1086] consecrated William [of Beaufai] to Elmham. This document, however, was drawn up after Anselm's consecration, December 1093, and cannot wholly be trusted in such matters.

103. As the canon continued, 'and not to conspire against the prince', the main target was probably *episcopi vagantes,* such as the bishop of Durham. Wilkins i. 365 (dated 1076); Mansi xx. 459–60.

104. Can. 3, Wilkins i. 363; Mansi xx. 449–54. The report has been tampered with and is misleading. It contains an introductory list of bishops attending and a final list of bishops attesting. Of the six bishops who had moved or were to move their sees four are given in the first list their original titles: Herman of Sherborne, Giso of Wells, Stigand of Selsey, and Peter of Lichfield. Remigius, however, is styled of Dorchester or Lincoln and Herfast of Elmham or Norwich. This process is carried even further in the subscriptions, where Herman is of Salisbury, Remigius of Lincoln, Herfast of Norwich, Stigand of Chichester, and Peter of Chester. Clearly the manuscript has been updated, and it is reasonable to think that only Herfast of the six bishops had in fact changed his title by 1075. For Salisbury, see *Annales IV* in Liebermann *Ungedruckte* 19: *VCH Wilts* ii. 121; *VEdR* 95. For Chichester, see *Annales IV* 18–19; *GP* 204–5. For Chester, see James Tait, 'An alleged Charter of William the Conqueror', *Essays in History presented to Reginald Lane Poole,* ed. H. W. C. Davis (1927) 154–9.

105. *DB* i. 336; *Annales IV, loc. cit.* 18; Giraldus Cambrensis, *Vita S. Remigii* 18–21; John of Schalby, *ibid.* 193–5; *VCH Lincs* ii. 9.

106. *GR* 385, 388–9. *LEp* 29.

107. *Historiola* 21; *Annales IV, loc. cit.* 19; *Reg.* 314–15, 326, 544, 988, 1573.

108. *Annales S. Edmundi* in Liebermann *Ungedruckte* 130; Barbara Dodwell, 'The foundation of Norwich cathedral', *loc. cit.*

109. *English Church 1000–1066,* 247–9. In addition to the examples cited there, an Archdeacon Aluric held property in Winchester before the Conquest, Frank Barlow, Martin Biddle, Olof von Feilitzen, D. J. Keene, *Winchester in the Early Middle Ages* (Winchester Studies, ed. Biddle, 1) 58 (no. 176).

of Rouen's council of *ante* 1046,[110] the sale of archdeaconries was prohibited by Archbishop John's council of Rouen (1074),[111] and archidiaconal visitations were enjoined and regulated by the council of Lillebonne (1080).[112] The system was introduced into England. At what may have been Lanfranc's first general council (Winchester–Windsor, ?1072) bishops were ordered to appoint archdeacons and other clerical servants in their churches.[113] There was no need to repeat this injunction. All the evidence points to a rapid subdivision of the dioceses into archdeaconries. Canterbury and Rochester were small and did not need more than one archdeacon apiece. But in the larger dioceses often each shire was made an archdeaconry. In Yorkshire the ridings were used.[114] Remigius, who had the largest diocese, Dorchester=Lincoln, created seven archdeaconries for seven provinces,[115] Lincolnshire, Cambridgeshire with Huntingdonshire and Hertfordshire, Northampton, Leicester, Oxford, Buckingham, and Bedford. Henry of Huntingdon, archdeacon of the second province, lists all their holders. In the diocese of Durham there was one archdeacon for Durham and one for Northumberland,[116] in Salisbury two for Wiltshire and one each for Berkshire and Dorset.[117] Conservative Exeter seems to have persevered with one archdeacon until well into William Warelwast's pontificate (1107–37), and it appears that it was not until just before the consecration of the new cathedral church in 1133 that Cornwall was split off and the eastern shire divided into three: Exeter, Barnstaple in the north, and Totnes in the south, all sites of important castles.[118] By 1120 archdeacons had secured an established and important place in the English church, but they seem never to have been enfeoffed by their bishop with the archdeaconry or to have taken an oath of fealty to him, as was sometimes the case in Normandy,[119] and we notice that archdeaconries were not units in Gilbert of Limerick's hierarchical scheme. They were still the bishop's domestic arrangements.

Archdeaconries were subdivided into rural deaneries.[120] The process is obscured by the co-existence of many different officials with the title of dean, and cannot be distinguished. It may be that in most places the ancient parochial groupings were simply renamed: the old minsters with their superior parochial rights were called deaneries. Hence the rural deaneries usually

---

110.   Cap. 11, Mansi xix. 751; H-L iv. 993. See below 123.

111.   Cap. 1, Mansi xx. 397; H-L v. 112.

112.   Cap. 6, Mansi xx. 556; OV (Chibnall) iii. 28.

113.   Cap. 5, Wilkins i. 324 (dated 1076); Mansi xx. 459.

114.   Charles T. Clay, 'Notes on the chronology of the early archdeacons of the church of York', *Yorks. Arch. Journ.* xxxvi (1944–47) 269–87, 409–34.

115.   HH *De contemptu mundi* 302–3.

116.   Frank Barlow, *Durham Jurisdictional Peculiars* (1950) 153 ff.

117.   Edward J. Kealey, *Roger of Salisbury* (1972) 96.

118.   Adrian Morey, *Bartholomew of Exeter* (1937), appendix 1; David W. Blake, 'The Church of Exeter in the Norman period' (unpublished Exeter MA thesis 1970) 167–72; 'Bishop William Warelwast', *Trans. Devonshire Association* civ (1972) 26.

119.   Cf. OV (Chibnall) ii. 152; *LEp* 17.

120.   Cf. A. Hamilton Thompson, 'Diocesan organization in the Middle Ages: archdeacons and rural deans', *Proc. of the Brit. Academy* xxix (1943) 167; Pierre Andrieu-Guitrancourt, *Essai sur l'évolution du décanat rural en Angleterre d'après les conciles des XIIe, XIIIe, et XIVe siècles* (1935); William Dansey, *Horae decanicae rurales* (2nd ed. 1844).

corresponded to hundreds or similar secular units.[121] This operation seems to have been completed by 1108, when deans were associated with archdeacons in the duty of enforcing the decrees against unchaste priests. Deans who were remiss were to lose their deaneries.[122] Although deans acted as agents of their archdeacon, they were not archidiaconal but episcopal servants. Early in Stephen's reign Roger bishop of Salisbury, the royal justiciar, addressed a writ composed in chancery style in favour of Reading abbey to the archdeacon of Berkshire and all deans and the whole clergy of Berkshire.[123] And about 1113 he issued an ecclesiastical precept which, if disregarded (*nisi feceritis*), would be enforced by Ilbert the dean, probably a rural dean in Berkshire.[124]

Cutting across this organization were the various franchises, irregularities caused usually by the influence of rank or special position.[125] Monastic congregations crossed diocesan boundaries, and, although there were no totally exempt orders nor even completely and undisputedly exempt individual houses in England before 1154, monasteries had a special standing and controlled subordinate priories and churches.[126] More widespread were claims made by important persons or corporations for their *Eigenkirchen*. A bishop's estates and churches in his own diocese were usually separately administered, in other dioceses allowed a privileged position.[127] Similar claims were made for the estates and churches of cathedral chapters and other monasteries.[128] The king advanced claims in respect of the chapels royal.[129] All these demands proceded from a conception of private ownership and re-presented deep-rooted attitudes of the sort that the Gregorian reformers were trying to extirpate; they also were based on how the church had been governed in the days before the bishop's office was re-activated and were a response to the creation of archdeaconries and deaneries. When they were advanced by important ecclesiastical persons they were not inherently objectionable, and, moreover, such owners could redefine their claims in legal terms acceptable to the age. After 1070 there were two counter movements. On the one side the hopeful immunists tried to make their liberties effective and establish a title to them. They strove to break the independence of their *Eigenkirchen* by rooting out the hereditary parsons and impropriating the endowments. And they

121. *English Church 1000—1066,* 184 ff.

122. General Council of London, 1108, Florence ii. 59.

123. Most recently printed by Kealey, *Roger of Salisbury* 258.

124. *Ibid.* 230.

125. J. -F. Lemarignier, *Etude sur les privilèges d'exemption et de juridiction ecclésiastique des abbayes normandes depuis les origines jusqu'en 1140,* Archives de la France monastique (1937); David Knowles, *The Monastic Order* (1940) chapters 32 and 34, 'Essays in monastic history: vi – parish organization', *Downside Review* li (1933) 501–22; Barlow, *Durham Jurisdictional Peculiars* (1950), especially the Introduction and Conclusion; C. R. Cheney, *From Becket to Langton, English Church Government 1170–1213* (1956) 121–2.

126. Cf. J. H. Denton, *English Royal Free Chapels 1100—1300,* 15–16.

127. For Canterbury peculiars, see *HN* 45–7.

128. For example, Robert of Chesney bishop of Lincoln (1148–66), granted to the prebends the *jura episcopalia* and complete exemption from archidiaconal jurisdiction and the same liberties in their prebends as possessed by the canons of Salisbury, *The Registrum antiquissimum of the cathedral church of Lincoln* i, ed. C. W. Foster, Lincoln record soc. xxvii (1931) no. 287.

129. Denton 23 ff.

endeavoured to justify their control of them either by showing peaceful possession or by acquiring or manufacturing legal documents. On the other side, the
bishops, and sometimes the archdeacons, especially when the church began to
administer a common law, tried to impose a uniform system and destroy
irregularities. The die became loaded against franchisal claimants and prescription.

 Each franchise had its individual history. But some general tendencies can be seen. Episcopal claims fared the best. Bishops were usually tolerant
of each other's peculiars. The king, although a late starter, did surprisingly well.
Elsewhere bishops were in general the winners and only the most plausible
claims to privilege survived. In the eleventh and twelfth centuries the immunists usually claimed to possess *episcopalia,* the episcopal customs, various
financial rights which bishops enjoyed in their diocese. Nevertheless, these
claims, even when vindicated, seldom (except in the hands of bishops) produced episcopal franchises, that is to say areas from which the local ordinary
was completely excluded. For by the time an immunist substantiated his claim
to the episcopal customs, he found that they had been debased to archidiaconal
rights. Similar *episcopalia* had been entrusted to the archdeacons. And so most
capitular and monastic parochial franchises, and these were the commonest to
survive, were in the later twelfth century considered archidiaconal peculiars,
that is to say private archdeaconries (corresponding to private hundreds), or
something less. Also in the course of establishing the liberty it had changed
from a personal, movable franchise, consisting of all churches belonging at any
time to the immunist, to an established list, a definite geographical area. These
peculiars had their secular counterparts, were unremarkable in a world which
believed in privilege, and did little more than slightly complicate the church's
administration.

 The broad basis of the ecclesiastical organization consisted of the
village and urban churches ('parish churches') which were grouped into the
archdeaconries, deaneries, and peculiars. These *Eigenkirchen* usually
belonged to the lords on whose lands they stood and whose ancestors had built
them, although sometimes they had been alienated, especially to monasteries.
Their incumbents, in the eleventh and twelfth centuries usually hereditary
parsons, married priests who passed on the churches to their sons, were a kind
of ecclesiastical vassal of their lord, holding a benefice in return for service.
Hereditary succession, however, made them resistant to seigneurial exploitation and reduced almost to nothing rights of appointment to them (advowson),
custody during vacancy, or induction of a new incumbent.[130] The parsons were
usually burdened with a money pension, and could be heavily burdened,
although the council of Winchester (1076) decreed that no clerk, whether in a
borough or the countryside (*civilis vel rusticus*), should be required to perform
more service for his ecclesiastical benefice than was rendered in King Edward's
day.[131] Lay lords were thus hampered. But ecclesiastical owners, bishops,
cathedral chapters, and particularly monasteries, could attempt a profitable

130. Barlow, *Durham Jurisdictional Peculiars,* 17–19, 33 ff., 88–9, 132 ff. 146, 148; Cheney,
From Becket to Langton, 126 ff.

131. Wilkins i. 367; Mansi xx. 462. Cf. also Cheney 129.

radical reorganization. Monasteries and other corporations, if they could get rid of the parson, could serve the church out of their own members and take all the profits. Or the revenues could be shared with a humbler incumbent, either a stipendiary priest or a chaplain who farmed the church, that is to say paid the owner an agreed fixed rent for it.

By such expedients the village church could be appropriated to an ecclesiastical corporation. But first the parson (and his heir) had to be prised out. A change could sometimes be made when he died, but such disinheritances upset local society. A better opportunity was offered by Anselm's draconian decrees against married priests at the council of Westminster, 1102. Anselm in his letters to puzzled correspondents enjoined that the expelled parsons should be replaced with celibate priests; if none could be found, monks could hold services for the parishioners and the sacramental capacities of clerks and even laymen could be used.[132] He himself was accused by the opposition of allowing reprobate clerks to invade and devastate Canterbury churches and of giving churches to laymen. He answered that his actions had been misunderstood. He had given his manors, not his churches, at farm to laymen. The farmers had been instructed to act as custodians of the churches and do nothing about their priests except through him, his archdeacon, or, in the case of Christ Church manors, the prior.[133] But clearly the measures not only aroused considerable ill will but also caused irregularity and confusion. Some married parsons tried to avoid the ban by employing vicars, who seem to have been mere hirelings.[134] Not much later we find Archbishop Thomas II or Thurstin of York (1109–14 or 1119–40), when granting four churches to the priory of Holy Trinity, York, making provision for the assignment of 'a competent vicarage' to those serving the churches.[135] These look like the perpetual vicarages, permanent and episcopally supervised provision for the vicar, usually the assignment of the altarage (gifts on the altar) and lesser tithes, which were thereafter to be created in such large numbers.[136] Perpetual vicars had to be presented to the bishop for institution and once instituted had security of tenure.

The parish churches served by parsons (later called rectors) or vicars competed with the mother church and each other for the various parochial rights.[137] They were not all on an absolutely equal footing, but normally they had a right to some tithe, offerings on the altar, baptism, and burial. The proof of the last two were a font and a graveyard. Ministers were usually entitled as well to church-scot and some other customary payments. Much less privileged and endowed were the little urban churches and the 'field chapels' founded within the greater parishes for the convenience of special or

132. Anselm *Epp.* 254.

133. *Ibid.* 327.

134. Cf. General Council of London 1108, Florence ii. 59.

135. *Early Yorkshire Charters*, ed. C. T. Clay, vi. 82–4; Cheney 133–4.

136. Cheney 131 ff. 182 ff., revising R. A. R. Hartridge, *History of vicarages in the Middle Ages* (1930). For Durham D. and C. impropriations, *Durham Annals and Documents of the thirteenth century,* ed. Frank Barlow (Surtees Soc. clv, 1945) 145 ff.; for the diocese of Chichester, Mayr-Harting *Acta* 57–8; for Winchester, Lena Voss, *Heinrich von Blois Bischof von Winchester* (Berlin 1932) 97–9.

137. Barlow *English Church 1000–1066*, 183 ff.

remote communites. In English cities and boroughs, unlike the continental, the religious life of the people centred not on the great minsters, old or new, but on the large number (in London, scores) of tiny box-like churches,[138] built on a street, often at a cross roads, by the owner of the estate, or even the neighbour-hood, to serve the local population and also attract offertories from passers by. The rural chapels, too, were often humble edifices. Reginald of Durham, when recording the miracles of St Cuthbert, mentions a roofless stone chapel dedi-cated to that saint at Slitrig in Teviotdale (Northumberland), an area overrun by wolves. Nevertheless it had a parson with the aristocratic name of Dolfin.[139] In a hamlet of the village of *Lixtune,* probably in Lancashire, was a field chapel dedicated to St Cuthbert. It was despised because it was built of rough branches and thatched with osiers and hay, and it was in such a bad condition that a youth who climbed up to rob a crow's nest on the roof by kicking footholds in the walls and roof, fell through the rotten structure to the ground. This church had a baptismal font, and was rebult in stone by a rich man, whose son endowed it with lands.[140] Thriving communities were ambitious to get a permanent minis-ter and parochial rights, especially a font and cemetery, for their chapel. The subdivision of parishes was a feature of colonization and economic growth.

The aim of the church leaders in the eleventh and twelfth centuries was to apply the law of the church to all these ecclesiastical properties and societies, to release them from secular lordship, and reorganize them according to ecclesiastical principles. In the purely professional and administrative fields the church was most successful. New standards were set for, and to some extent imposed on, the clergy. A visible and workable governmental system, inspired and controlled by canon law, came into existence. And the church acquired greater independence and a higher status. At the same time it had been forced to abandon its most radical claims, and compromise with the world. Temporal lordship, whether exercised by the clergy or laity, had had to be accepted, although in less objectionable forms. Secular participation in appointments had to be tolerated; it was agreed that ownership of temporalities, especially regalities, carried temporal duties; and political pressures were a feature of everyday life. Moreover the church favoured strong and beneficent secular rule, all the more since it could not automatically take advantage of the weakness of the prince. While Stephen floundered, the archbishop of Canter-bury, even though ably served by lawyers and scholars, saw his own govern-ment disintegrate. Nevertheless, the success of the church in articulating and animating the *sacerdotium,* in advancing roughly step by step with the *regnum* in organizing a government, is truly remarkable in this period.

138. Cf. Christopher Brooke and Gillian Keir, *London 800–1216* (1975) 122 ff. See Map 2, below 320.
139. Reginald of Durham, *St Cuthbert,* c. 136.
140. *Ibid.* cc. 68–9.

Chapter II

The Men and Main Events:
an outline history

1. The Norman Settlement

The English church supported King Harold, Earl Godwin's son, until his death in the battle of Hastings on 14 October 1066. When Edward died on 4 or 5 January, if choice of successor was to be limited to the immediate royal family, Harold was the only possible candidate.[1] The bishops and abbots knew him well; and, although his Christianity was distinctly Danish in flavour, he had refounded a minster and probably made a pilgrimage to Rome.[2] The church helped him to get effective control of the kingdom, made no contact with the invaders, and sent its contingents to the royal army. It was with the same realism that the church, after Harold's death and William's recovery from the sickness which almost robbed him of his victory, submitted to the Conqueror and served him just as faithfully. The prelates had no alternative. Moreover, since Harold had not had time to make any changes in the church, they probably felt no great anxiety and expected the newcomer, as with Cnut fifty years before, to turn to them for help and advice.

Not only the Norman conquest but also William's character and purpose had an important effect on the English church. The simplest view of William is that he was an excellent and renowned soldier, *miles*. And not unfittingly, he died by an accident of war. His panegyrist, William of Poitiers, stresses his courage and power of discipline.[3] He was also a religious man. The sincerity of his belief is proved as much by his actions as by the exaggerated claims of his biographer.[4] Although William of Poitiers does not claim that William was chaste, no bastards are recorded and there are signs that he could be puritanical. His obvious hostility towards married clergy suggests that the irregularity of his own birth had produced a rancour against sexual licence. He was orthodox, superstitious, and observant of religious duties. But it was very much a soldier's religion, the search for aid and advantage amid the perils of diplomacy and war, the quest for salvation despite the sins necessary for achieving worldly success.

William, although not an evil man, had some evil passions, and his lust for power, his ferocity, and his avarice were hardly subdued by religion. Yet he was not without restraint. The discipline which he imposed on his army, his barons, his sons, and on his church flowed from a man who had partly

1. Barlow *Edward the Confessor* 240 ff.
2. *English Church 1000–1066*, 58–60.
3. *GG* 12–14, 156 ff. etc.
4. *Ibid.* 14, 114 ff. etc.

disciplined himself, whom men could respect and trust as a lord. The concepts of justice and equity, which William of Poitiers would apply to all his actions, were indeed understood by him in a sense. He had a strong grasp of the importance of order, and so of law, and, when he himself took the offensive, preferred to have a case which could be pleaded as just. William, however, is credited with few of the ordinary Christian virtues, such as mercy, magnanimity, humility, or alms-giving. There is no suggestion that he was often light-hearted or ever much loved. Saddened though he may have been by the slaughter at Hastings, he would not let Gytha even buy the corpse of her son; Harold, the perjured vassal, should not be allowed Christian burial.[5] William had suffered from his kin, and he threw Odo, his half-brother, into prison. Charm had little power over him: he discarded Archbishop Stigand when convenient and had Earl Waltheof executed for a doubtful crime. William's religion may sometimes have modified his ambition, or coloured his expression of it, sometimes checked a move, but never in a decisive way. He probably thought that the monasteries he had encouraged and built[6] and the church he had protected and fostered would surely be weighed against the occasional enormity forced on him by circumstances or by the passions within. Like many gloomy men he was probably obsessed by a lively vision of Hell.[7]

According to William of Poitiers,[8] the Conqueror provided carefully for the Christian education of his children. One daughter, Cecilia, became abbess of Holy Trinity at Caen and her sisters were well regarded by the church.[9] William's third son, and his successor in England, William Rufus, was educated in Archbishop Lanfranc's household.[10] The fourth son, Henry, may even have been given some parts of a literary education.[11]

William's record in ecclesiastical affairs was, by the standards of his age, almost entirely good. It is perhaps true that he used the church rather than had a disinterested love of its aims. He would not be thwarted by ecclesiastical censure. He married his wife despite the papal ban and then made the necessary amends. He was rude to Gregory VII whenever he felt that his royal dignity was slighted. If the pope would depose the English bishops whom he was determined to get rid of, well and good. But he would imprison a bishop, even if only as an earl, whether the papacy liked it or not. William may well have held the see of Rome in respect. Alexander II, by confirming his conquest of England, had clearly done him a good turn. Collaboration could sometimes

---

5. *The Carmen de Hastingae proelio,* ed. Catherine Morton and Hope Muntz (Oxford Medieval Texts 1972) 36–9; cf. *GG* 204. The matter has most recently been discussed by Kurt-Ulrich Jäschke, *Wilhelm der Eroberer, sein doppelter Herrschaftsantritt im Jahre 1066* (Sigmaringen 1977).

6. Raymonde Foreville, *GG* 122–3, for a list of these. William did not usually waste his own resources. He considered that he made a large personal contribution by allowing a baron to alienate land to the church.

7. OV (Chibnall) iv. 81 ff., imaginatively reconstructs the deathbed scene for us.

8. *GG* 120.

9. Cf. Baudri de Bourgueil, poems 196–7, 198, *Les oeuvres poétiques,* ed. Phyllis Abrahams (Paris 1926); *GG* 142 and 143 n.

10. *GR* 360.

11. Below 222, n. 27.

be mutually advantageous. Even Gregory VII could be helpful.[12] But there is not a shred of evidence that William looked to Rome for advice or as a rule accepted its counsel when offered.

The churches under his power he treated as far as he could like a just lord. He was anxious for their wellbeing. He was innocent of simony but not of nepotism;[13] he attracted and rewarded learned men, especially foreign monks, and gave a measure of trust to church leaders whose services he had tried. He knew some of the church's aims and furthered them. It can hardly be doubted that he encouraged the drive to greater administrative efficiency and the crusade to purify the church of its grossest failing, its worldliness. His calling of ecclesiastical councils and presidency of them were more than conventional gestures.[14] He was as interested in the *militia Christi* as in the *militia ducis*. But he was sympathetic only so long as the church was respectful and amenable. When he was opposed or unheeded his anger knew no bounds. His brush with Lanfranc, about 1053, cost Bec the destruction of one of its villages by fire.[15] When the bishops became slack in their measures against married clerks, he treated them roughly at Lillebonne in 1080.[16] He was a stern master, and harsher perhaps to his ecclesiastical than to his lay vassals because with the church he was really out of his depth. Despite William of Poitiers's words about William's interest in ecclesiastical matters it is hard to believe that the duke was much moved by the artistic manifestations of religion or was other than coarse-grained in his spiritual life. He would attend church councils, for that was a world which he could understand and direct; on the other hand, although in Normandy, he was not present at the dedication of the new church at Bec in 1077, a ceremony which lay close to the heart of many of the most distinguished prelates and monks of his realm, a ceremony which no one truly concerned with the spiritual life of his country would have missed. Queen Matilda, likewise unable to attend, at least sent a gift.[17]

William, it will be seen, was one of the last great lay patrons of the church in the descent through Charlemagne and the German emperors from Constantine, one of the last of the benevolent despots. The contribution of men such as the Emperor Henry III and William to the church was enormous. Their motives may have been impure and their domination could be resented, but their drastic reform both of administration and morals produced the conditions in which the church could develop its own ideals and plans. William could be an old-fashioned lay reformer because he was operating in one of the more sheltered corners of Europe. Even if he could have read the signs of change, it is unlikely that he would have acted otherwise than he did: his religious policy was little more than the exercise of his power within a particular sphere. It

12.   Cf. H. E. J. Cowdrey, 'Pope Gregory VII and the Anglo-Norman church and kingdom', *Studi Gregoriani* ix (1972) 77.

13.   See Raymonde Foreville's notes (especially pp. 136–7) on *GG* 128.

14.   *GG* 124–5.

15.   *Vita Herluini* 97 = *Vita Lanfranci* in *Opera* (ed. D'Achery) cap. 3. Margaret Gibson, *Lanfranc of Bec* 31 (with a wrong page reference to *VH*), ascribes this business not to William's matrimonial affairs but to his siege of the rebel Guy of Burgundy in Brionne (1047–50).

16.   Mansi xx. 555, cap. 3. Below 120 ff.

17.   *Vita Herluini* 106.

seems that he viewed the new currents of 'Gregorian' reform merely as sporadic outrageous moves, exploratory threats from afar that could never touch his shield.

After his coronation on Christmas Day 1066 William showed his rough side immediately by robbing the churches, especially the monasteries, of much of their treasure in order to embellish a victory parade through Normandy and reward his own churches for their successful prayers on his behalf.[18] But once the rebellions broke out in England he moderated his harshness towards the church, gave Archbishop Stigand an honourable place at court, entrusted great administrative commands to Archbishop Ealdred of York in the north and Abbot Æthelwig of Evesham in the west,[19] and with their help managed to survive. His gratitude, however, was limited; he was under great pressure from future beneficiaries to make changes in the personnel of the English church,[20] and when Ealdred died in September 1069, the one restraint was removed. It would have been disgraceful and probably impossible to depose Ealdred.[21] Stigand, with his invalid pallium and irregular entry into Canterbury, was not only defenceless but also unable to protect his subordinates. In 1070 Pope Alexander II was persuaded to legitimise the conquest. He sent papal legates to England, who deposed 'unworthy' bishops, held a reforming council, crowned William anew, and imposed penances on the invaders.[22] It was a comprehensive act of settlement. But for the native church it was the start of its humiliation.

Since William when replacing the deposed bishops or filling later vacancies chose none but foreigners, the episcopal bench was quickly but not totally Normanized. In 1073 there were one Italian, two English, four Lotharingian, and eight Norman bishops. Six of these had been promoted by King Edward and a further two had been his clerks. At William's death the Normans had increased to eleven, and the English were reduced to one and the Lotharingians to two, while only three of the fifteen had served Edward. In the monastic order, although foreigners were soon appointed to the more important abbacies, the general replacement of the English was even slower. If we turn to the professional background of the bishops, although William did not particularly favour the elevation of monks, in this he was only conforming to a trend which had already set in. At the time of Cnut's death ten of the sixteen bishops were monks, in 1066 seven of the fourteen,[23] and in 1087 five of the fifteen. More drastic changes in the traditional pattern occurred later (see

18. *GG* 242 ff.

19. *Chron. Evesham* 90–1; R. R. Darlington, 'Æthelwig, abbot of Evesham', *EHR* xlviii (1933) 10 ff.

20. Cf. the nice story in the Winchester annals *s.a.* 1086, in which Bishop Walkelin refers to royal clerks and chaplains queueing up for bishoprics: *Annales Monastici* ii. 34–5.

21. William of Poitiers had a very high opinion of him because he served the king faithfully, *GG* 220, 271. On the last page what looks like the beginning of a panegyric has been lost, owing to the truncation of the MS, and was not taken up by OV (Chibnall) ii. 208.

22. For the penances *EHD* ii. 606, translated from Wilkins i. 366. An important article is Catherine Morton, 'Pope Alexander II and the Norman Conquest', *Latomus: Revue d'études Latines* xxxiv (1975) 362.

23. Barlow, *English Church 1000–1066*, 63.

diagram, p. 318). William appointed Remigius, monk of Fécamp, to Dorchester in 1067, Lanfranc, abbot of Caen, to Canterbury in 1070, and William of St Calais, abbot of St Vincent, to Durham in 1081. As Lanfranc appointed monks to Rochester and two of Edward's monk-bishops were left undisturbed, usually one-third of the bishops were monks.[24]

The rest of the bishops were mostly royal clerks, men rewarded because of their service in the king's court. They had usually been educated in one of the Norman episcopal churches and had sometimes held an office in the chapter before transferring to royal service. The church of Bayeux under the Conqueror's half-brother, Odo, raised a notable crop. There were the brothers, Thomas I archbishop of York (1070–1100) and Samson bishop of Worcester (1096–1112), and Samson's sons, Thomas II of York (1109–14) and Richard II bishop of Bayeux (c. 1108–33); William of St Calais bishop of Durham (1081–96) and his successor, Ranulf Flambard (1099–1128); the brothers Thurstin, who held York after Thomas II (1119–40), and Ouen bishop of Evreux (1113–39); and Theulf, who succeeded Samson at Worcester (1115–23). There were also Thurstin, the unsatisfactory abbot of Glastonbury (c. 1077–?1096), and William of Rots, the excellent abbot of Fécamp (1082–1107). Clearly William I relied much on Odo for the recruitment of clerical servants.[25] A comparable situation occurred in Stephen's reign, when his brother was bishop of Winchester.

The Conqueror's foreign bishops introduced foreigners into their chapters and monasteries and preferred compatriots when they appointed to dignities and offices. Archdeacons were mainly of Norman extraction. But within the secular and monastic communities some natives remained. Edward, archdeacon of London, who became a monk at Christ Church, Canterbury, was clearly a thorn in Lanfranc's flesh.[26] Eadmer, in the same monastery, became the historian of the changes. At a lower level the parish clergy were hardly disturbed. One of the immediate effects of the 'Normanization' of the prelacy was to increase the gap which already existed between the princes of the church and the village priests. A bishop like Wulfstan of Worcester, who regularly perambulated his diocese, must have known most of the lower clergy. The new men were cut off from their subordinates by the barrier of language.[27] In the case of the laity this change made little difference. A man needed the services of a bishop only once in his lifetime, for confirmation, and this was, even for good bishops, a hurried ceremony.[28] The homily was probably left to the village priest.

The individuals whom William rewarded with bishoprics in England reveal the different claims on his gratitude, his policy, and the flexibility of his conscience in ecclesiastical matters. Undoubtedly his first requirement was loyalty. He was not averse to some military talent. He preferred celibate or at

---

24. The composition and origins of the episcopate during Anselm's tenure of Canterbury (1093–1109) are analysed by Fröhlich 31 ff.

25. Cf. David R. Bates, 'The character and career of Odo, bishop of Bayeux (1049/50–1097)', *Speculum* l (1975) 13.

26. See below 190 f.

27. See below 133 f.

28. Cf. *Vita Wulfstani* 36–7.

least respectable prelates. He drew a distinction between the qualities required of an archbishop and those of a simple diocesan. And he normally balanced all powers. The one exception to this last policy was his securing a primacy for Canterbury over York. York's hostility remained; and Lanfranc was also checked by William's half-brother, Odo bishop of Bayeux, who had been made earl of Kent, and by the military and administrative commands given in England to Geoffrey bishop of Coutances.[29]

It may be that Odo hoped to get Canterbury. But William had suffered from the ambition of his uncle, Mauger, archbishop of Rouen; he wanted an entirely reliable man at Canterbury; and it is likely that Alexander II, whose services the king was using, pressed for Lanfranc abbot of Caen. In 1070 Lanfranc was about fifty-five, with an adventurous career behind him.[30] The son of a 'lawman' of Pavia, that staging post famous for its market in relics and the welcome it gave its visitors – *'Quis in igne positus/igne non uratur?/Quis Papiae demorans/castus habeatur,/ubi Venus digito/iuvenes venatur,/oculis illaqueat,/facie praedatur?'*, as the Archpoet wrote about 1165 – Lanfranc at an early age renounced his father's profession and left Pavia in order to study the arts in other Italian cities. In 1072 William of Poitiers in the final portion of his panegyric of the Conqueror, now lost and recoverable only in part from the use made of it by Orderic Vitalis,[31] turned his praises to the new archbishop of Canterbury and recounted his youthful triumphs as a pleader in the law courts. This improbable story from an unreliable writer is often given far more weight than it deserves.[32] Lanfranc abandoned Lombard law as soon as he could. He became a wandering scholar – 'a clerk and scholar', as he told his future abbot[33] – about 1030 crossing the Alps with some companions in search of knowledge and the keys to understanding. He studied in the metropolitan city of Tours under Berengar,[34] visited Burgundy, and entered Normandy because he had heard that owing to the low standard of education there the prospects of a teacher were bright. He became the schoolmaster in the ruined episcopal city of Avranches, perhaps under the aegis of Mont St Michel. He was, of course, a teacher of the arts, probably the quadrivium as well as the trivium,[35] and was particularly remembered as a dialectician. Although at the start he may have

---

29. For Odo, see *inter alia* Bates, *op. cit.*; for Geoffrey, see E. A. Pigeon, *La diocèse d'Avranches* (Coutances 1887–88).

30. A. J. Macdonald, *Lanfranc* (1926) has now been superseded in part by Margaret Gibson, *Lanfranc of Bec* (1978); cf. also Frank Barlow, 'A view of Archbishop Lanfranc', *JEH* xvi (1965) 163.

31. Marjorie Chibnall suggests the relationship for this passage, OV ii, pp. xvi ff., but seems then to complicate the position unnecessarily.

32. Marjorie Chibnall, OV ii, pp. xix-xxi, 248 and n.; but cf. Heinrich Boehmer, *Die Fälschungen Erzbischof Lanfranks von Canterbury*: Studien zur Geschichte der Theologie und der Kirche, viii, pt. 1 (Leipzig 1902) 135–7, and Margaret Gibson pp. 4 ff.

33. *Miracula S. Nicolai*, in *Catalogus Codicum Hagiograph. in Bibl. Nat. Parisiensi* (Brussels 1890) 410.

34. *Ibid.* 409. An episode often censored from the story. Cf. also Robert Somerville, 'The case against Berengar of Tours – a new text', *Studi Gregoriani* ix (1972) 53.

35. It was not an age of specialization in the *artes*. Cf. Richard Hunt, 'Studies on Priscian in the eleventh and twelfth centuries', *MARS* i (1943) 223. Lanfranc lectured on *Rhetorica ad Herennium, ibid.* 207–8.

been outclassed by the brilliance of Berengar, later his pupils and admirers recalled that he was the greatest master of the liberal arts in the Latin world, the brilliant star that God had given to lighten Europe's darkness.[36]

About 1042 Lanfranc had a religious conversion. By becoming a monk at Bec, then in its humble and rustic beginnings, he publicly dissociated himself from the 'heretical' wing of the scholars and renounced literary education, human reason, and worldly success. After a great struggle, and with the sympathetic help of his abbot Herlwin, a retired knight, he became a good monk; and when he was encouraged to open an external school, he was able to apply his talents to his new vocation. He studied and lectured on the Bible (his commentaries on the Psalms and St Paul were in some respects original and were undoubtedly influential), disputed with his old teacher, Berengar, on the eucharist,[37] made a collection of canon law, and attracted to Bec some excellent pupils, including his successor at Canterbury, Anselm of Aosta. About 1044 Herlwin made him prior and in 1063 the duke removed him to become first abbot of his penitential foundation at Caen.

Although out of the world, Lanfranc was not isolated. In 1049 he had attended Leo IX's council at Rheims, and thereafter was frequently at the papal court and councils. He knew the persons, programme, and politics of the reform party well; and he was in complete sympathy with their moral aims: the abolition of simony and clerical marriage, and, more generally, the spiritualization of the church. It was probably because of his contacts and his talent for diplomacy that the duke granted him his favour; and Lanfranc could respond because William, despite his acts of violence, could be persuaded to advance ecclesiastical reform. Nevertheless, Lanfranc, ageing and sick, resisted his translation to Canterbury and shrank from the prelacy which was forced on him. But unlike his successor, Anselm, he not only yielded gracefully to authority, but also met every requirement with complete success. He had the advantages of a high academic and moral reputation, of wide experience of men and affairs, and of a large circle of friends. All noted his ability and wisdom. Simple administration caused him no trouble. And he possessed that reciprocal humility and authority possessed by soldiers and monks. He had excellent manners and a dislike for extremes.

As archbishop he supported the Conqueror and then his son through thick and thin. His first care was his own church, Canterbury, which he reformed and rebuilt; and he took the whole English monastic order under his protection. He could not control the king's appointments to abbeys and bishoprics; but he set before the church, through councils and letters, ideal Norman conditions as the model, and urged the bishops to attain them. With

36.   Guitmund, *De corporis et sanguinis Christi veritate in Eucharistia, PL* cxlix. 1428; Pope Clement III in F. Liebermann, 'Lanfranc and the Antipope', *EHR* xvi (1901) 331; Gilbert Crispin, *Vita Herluini*, 95.

37.   Although Lanfranc has no modern reputation as a theologian, it should be noticed that one of the books John of Salisbury left to his cathedral church was *Lamfrancus de Eucaristia contra Berengarium* (presumably his *Liber de corpore et sanguine domini*), C. J. J. Webb, 'Note on books bequeathed by John of Salisbury to the cathedral library of Chartres', *MARS* i (1943) 128. For his lectures on the Psalms (lost) and on St Paul, and his place in the pre-history of the Gloss, see Beryl Smalley, *Richerches de théologie ancienne et médiévale* ix (1937) 374 ff.

the king's consent he gave the bishops the powers they required, encouraged them to create the necessary administrative machinery, and made the execution of the policy their responsibility. His lack of enthusiasm for Gregory VII's more unusual claims helped towards the re-establishment of the *ecclesia anglicana* as a royal church of the traditional type. Only in one direction did he allow Canterbury's ambition to outstep the bounds of moderation. By persuading William to support his claim to primacy over York he unwittingly prepared the way for a harmful feud within the English church. By Rufus's reign this restless searcher after the true road had become a figure of great authority, the strong ox of Anselm's rural metaphor.[38] But more discerning is the story told by William of Malmesbury of Lanfranc on his deathbed, begging God to allow him to die, lest his memory be disturbed or his speech confused.[39] He retained until the end the fastidiousness of a scholar.

William had already appointed Remigius to Dorchester, Thomas I to York, and Walkelin to Winchester. Remigius, monk of Fécamp, had been present at the battle of Hastings and was accused of having bought his bishopric by his contribution to the campaign.[40] He, like Herbert Losinga later, had served under Abbot John of Ravenna, and so inherited the Italian cultural legacy which had been handed on by William of Volpiano.[41] When he moved his see to Lincoln he built a new church which he constituted on the model of Rouen and in which he established the new learning.[42] The historian Henry, archdeacon of Huntingdon, whose father had been one of the bishop's first appointments, listed with admiration some of the members of Remigius's chapter;[43] and towards the end of the twelfth century there was an attempt at Lincoln to get him canonized.[44]

Thomas I of York was an outstanding bishop by any standards and earned encomia from both William of Malmesbury and Hugh, precentor of York.[45] The son of a priest, who founded a distinguished clerical dynasty, he represented the best non-monastic tradition. A canon and treasurer of Bayeux under Odo, and educated in the cathedral school and probably at Liège, his attitude and interests were complementary to Lanfranc's. A strong, handsome man, charming, generous and kind-hearted, a person of the utmost elegance, yet with an unspotted reputation for chastity and integrity, he, like Remigius, was a great patron of scholars and useful clerks. Music was his special love. He had a good voice, composed hymns, and would turn any popular song sung in

38. See below 287 f.

39. *GP* 73.

40. For his life and career, see *GP* 65–6, 312–13; HH 212, 300–2; Giraldus Cambensis, *Vita S. Remigii* 3 ff; John of Schalby's *Vita, ibid.* 193–5.

41. See below 180 ff., 240.

42. The move, which took place 1072–75, is described by Gerald of Wales 18–19 and John of Schalby.

43. *De contemptu mundi,* HH 300 ff.

44. *Vita S. Remigii* 6. Gerald of Wales relates seven 'ancient' post-mortem and about as many recent miracles.

45. For his life and career, see *GP* 257–8; Hugh *HCY* 2–12; Simeon *HDE* 133; OV (Chibnall) iv. 118. Fröhlich 49–53.

his presence immediately into a hymn of praise.[46] In his church he insisted on vigorous rather than effeminate chanting. He found his cathedral church destroyed, his chapter dispersed, and his diocese ravaged by war. He more than restored York's ancient glory. He was, indeed, a fitting successor to Ealdred.

The king's chaplain Walkelin, a former canon of Rouen, was consecrated bishop of Winchester by the papal legate immediately after Stigand's deposition; and in 1070 and the following quinquennium the king gave Lanfranc a further six colleagues. Walkelin, once he had learned to tolerate and then love the monks of his cathedral, earned a high reputation. He was a builder and good administrator and was trusted by Rufus as well as by the Conqueror. He also appointed the learned and holy Godfrey from Cambrai as prior of St Swithun's, a man whom William of Malmesbury singled out for special praise.[47]

Two other royal chaplains promoted in 1070 were less satisfactory. Stigand of Selsey, who moved his see to Chichester, received little notice[48] and Herfast, William's chancellor, who changed his see from Elmham to Thetford, was, according to his detractors, not only unintelligent, badly educated for his office, and immoral, but also an old enemy of Lanfranc's. The *prognosticon* at his consecration was 'Not this man, but Barabbas' (John 18: 40).[49] Much superior to this pair, but hardly more successful as bishop, was the Lotharingian clerk, Walker, appointed to Durham in 1071.[50] He was remembered as a good and well-educated man who encouraged the re-establishment of monasticism in his diocese and planned to introduce monks into his own cathedral church. But in this outpost in an untamed region, entrusted by the king with the earldom of Northumberland, he failed to control the illegalities of his kinsmen and vassals, and in 1080 was murdered in a feud.

In 1072 it was the turn of two royal clerks, both of whom had probably started their careers at Edward's court. Osbern, the brother of William's steward and friend, William fitzOsbern, was appointed to succeed Leofric at Exeter.[51] Completely anglicized, he continued modestly and blamelessly in the ways of his predecessor. Peter, promoted to Lichfield in place of the married monk Leofwine, moved his see to Chester, and into oblivion.[52] Hugh of Orival, perhaps another royal chaplain, was given London in 1075. Attacked by leprosy, he underwent the drastic cure of castration, but without effect on the disease.[53]

---

46. Cf. J. D. A. Ogilvy, '*Mimi, Scurrae, Histriones*: Entertainers of the early Middle Ages', *Speculum* xxxviii (1963) 603.

47. For Walkelin, see Winchester annals in *Annales Monastici* ii, 39; *GR* 329; *GP* 71–2, 172, *HN* 18–19, 42, 75, 81–2. Fröhlich 43–6. For Godfrey, see *GR* 516; *GP* 172–3; Manitius iii. 769–71; Hardy *Catalogue* ii. 100.

48. Florence *s.a.* 1070; *GP* 205.

49. *GP* 150–2. Hermann *Mirac. S. Eadmundi* in Liebermann *Ungedruckte* 248. For Herfast's sons, who held in 1086 the church of St Mary Thetford, *DB* ii. 118 b.

50. Florence *s.a.* 1072, 1080; *GR* 330–1; *GP* 271–2; *HDE* 105–17; *HR* 195–201.

51. *GP* 201–2. David W. Blake, 'The church of Exeter in the Norman period' (unpublished Exeter University MA thesis, 1970) 66–87. Fröhlich 41–3.

52. *GP* 66, 308. It may, however, have been him, and not his successor (the MS reads *P* not *R*, as printed), who raided St Peter's, Coventry, and earned a rebuke from Lanfranc: *LEp* 29.

53. *GP* 145.

These men, together with the surviving Edwardian bishops of Rochester, Sherborne, Wells, Worcester, and Hereford, were Lanfranc's colleagues in the six years in which he held his three reforming councils: Winchester (?1072), London (1075), and Winchester (1076). We have a full list of the attendance at the second of these:[54] of the twelve bishops present, although only one was an Englishman, five had been appointed by Edward, two had been Edward's clerks, and one (Remigius) had been consecrated by Archbishop Stigand. Most of the twenty-one abbots were natives. The attitude of these survivors into the Norman period can only be guessed. Edward's foreign bishops are likely to have had an ambivalent attitude both to the past and to the future. Some measure of criticism of the state of the English church was no doubt called for, and could have been readily obtained. But they are unlikely to have crawled abjectly before their new colleagues. Monks may well have been restrained critics of some aspects of the Edwardian church and would cooperate easily with Lanfranc in furthering traditional reform. But all these prelates, familiar with the impressive royal legislation and abundance of homiletic literature of the English church, who knew what had already been accomplished, could not have failed to explain the position to the newcomers and to have been on the defensive against ill-founded criticism and sweeping change. It should not be overlooked that if Lanfranc's meagre legislation was issued at a time when English control over the church was weakening, it was still confined to the era in which English influence was present in strength.

In the next decade, as a result of deaths, William nominated six bishops, three in 1078–80 and three at Christmas 1085, near the close of his reign. The first group was one of the more distinguished, the second among the least worthy of his appointments. Osmund a royal chaplain, perhaps William's chancellor, was selected to succeed Herman of Sherborne in 1078, and completed his predecessor's plans to move his see into the borough of (Old) Salisbury.[55] Osmund, like Thomas I at York and Remigius at Lincoln, created a learned chapter in his new church. He was a distinguished liturgist and assembled and manufactured an important library, even copying and binding books himself. Although celebrated for chastity, his carefulness with money, his harshness as a confessor, and a suspicion that his ill-health was punishment for some worldly faults darkened his reputation. He expelled from his church Goscelin of St Bertin, the hagiographer. Nevertheless he was canonized by Calixtus III on 1 January 1457. In 1079 the Conqueror made what was for him a rather unusual appointment, preferring the Lotharingian scholar, Robert, to Hereford.[56] Robert, a mathematician, computist and astronomer, and a very religious man, not only introduced Ottonian scientific learning into his diocese, but also joined it to surviving Old English scholarship as professed at Hereford

---

54. Mansi xx. 452–3.

55. *HN* 72; 'De injusta vexatione', Simeon *HDE* i. 193; *GR* 372–5; *GP* 183–4, 424–5, 428–31; 'Goscelin of St Bertin', *VEdR* 101. Fröhlich 46–9. For Old Sarum, see Christopher N. L. Brooke and Gillian Keir, *London 800–1216* (1975) 7–9 and pl.

56. *HN* 72; Florence *s.a.* 1079, 1095; *GP* 300–3, 313; *Vita Wulfstani* 60–3; Hardy *Catalogue* ii. 46, 75; omitted from G. Sarton, *Introduction to the History of Science*. Fröhlich 53–5. Alfred Cordoliani, 'L' activité computistique de Robert, évêque de Hereford', in *Mélanges offerts à René Crozet* (Poitiers 1966) 333.

and in the neighbouring diocese of Worcester. He and Wulfstan became great spiritual friends.

The last appointment in this group was again unusual, as it concerned a monk. In 1080 William appointed William (monk and prior) of St Calais, abbot of St Vincent-des-Prés, also in the diocese of Le Mans, to replace the murdered Walker at Durham.[57] He was another who had started his clerical career in Odo's chapter at Bayeux, but owed his promotion probably to his fame as a counsellor and diplomatist and his diplomatic services for the king in Maine, Anjou, and France. He was regarded at Durham as a paragon of all monastic virtues: well-educated, most intelligent, eloquent, and supremely wise; yet at the same time sober, chaste, and a true father to his church and monks. He introduced monks into his cathedral church, associated them with his ministry and government, started to rebuild the cathedral, and by his gifts of books and ornaments prepared the way for its magnificence. Undoubtedly a great bishop of Durham, his adventures in politics, particularly his involvement in the rebellion of 1088 and then in Rufus's schemes against Anselm, were less reputable. But he died well, and it was Anselm who comforted him and heard his confession.

At Christmas 1085 William made his last nominations to the bench, appointing three of his chaplains, Maurice to London, Robert of Limesey to 'Lichfield', and William of Beaufai to Thetford. Maurice, who had been archdeacon of Le Mans and royal chancellor, was the most distinguished of these.[58] He started the rebuilding of St Paul's on an extravagant scale and left the great cost to his successors. Among the clerks was the lecher, Ranulf Flambard; his own addiction to women he excused on medical grounds. Robert of Limesey moved his see about 1087 from Chester into the abbey of Coventry, and so incurred the hostility of the monks and earned a prejudiced notice from William of Malmesbury.[59] William of Beaufai only ruled for five years and was overshadowed by his successor. It is believed that he was married and had a son who became archdeacon of Norwich.[60]

It is clear from the kind of men appointed by the Conqueror that Lanfranc can have had little influence over this section of the royal patronage. Where the archbishop could make his own choice, at Rochester, he appointed monks of Bec, first Arnost in 1076 and then, on his untimely death, Gundulf.[61] The latter, another Italian and perhaps related to Anselm of Aosta, when a clerk of Archbishop Maurilius of Rouen, before 1057, had gone on a pilgrimage to Jerusalem with his archdeacon, William de Bonne Ame, and was

57. HN 40, 59–62; HR 211–21; HDE 119–35; 'De injusta vexatione' HDE 170 ff.; 'De Mirac. et translat. S. Cuthberti', Simeon Historical Works ii. 340–1; Florence s.a. 1081; GR 331; GP 88, 272–3; Hildebert, Carmina Minora (Teubner) no. 1. Fröhlich 60–7.

58. GP 145; Regesta i. 147. OV (Chibnall) vi. 144 gives a sympathetic obituary notice. Fröhlich 67–9. Brooke and Keir, London 800–1216, 340–2.

59. GR 388–9; GP 107, 309–10; Hugh HCY 35. Fröhlich 69–72.

60. Chron. E, Florence; HEp no. 54 and n.

61. Vita Gundulfi in Anglia Sacra ii. 273, also The Life of Gundulf bishop of Rochester, ed. Rodney Thomson (Toronto Medieval Latin Texts vii, 1977); HN 2; Florence s.a. 1070; GP 136–7. R. A. L. Smith, 'The place of Gundulf in the Anglo-Norman church', EHR lviii (1943) 257–72; Barlow, Edward the Confessor 268; Fröhlich 55–60.

celebrated for being both Martha and Mary. He not only created a fine monastic community at Rochester, acted as a sort of vicar-general for Lanfranc and Anselm, became a specialist in the exhumation and translation of saints (because of his own immaculate chastity), but also shone as an architect.[62] Nor could Lanfranc have controlled even the royal monastic appointments.[63] William colonized his own foundation at Battle with monks from Marmoutier on the Loire and chose his abbots mainly from the ducal monasteries in Normandy. In this field William looked essentially for pious men, and most of his choices were worthy; but at least two, Turold of Fécamp, who ruled over Malmesbury and then Peterborough, and Thurstin of Caen at Glastonbury, were unwise appointments.

Goscelin of St Bertin, the hagiographer, who was expelled from Sherborne about 1079 and then toured the East Anglian monasteries in search of commissions, considered the newcomers barbarians. They were ignorant men incapable of appreciating the Old-English cultural achievement.[64] Eadmer, an English monk at Canterbury, praised the new conditions. Much depended on the persons, the place, and the time; most changes, even those for the better, are initially painful.

After the purge of the episcopate in 1070–72 and the reforming councils of 1072–76, a new looking English church evolved. Episcopal rights were strengthened in the dioceses; cathedral chapters and monasteries were reformed; sees were moved and cathedrals rebuilt; customs were changed. Only two events aroused much general interest. The first was the king's arrest, trial, and imprisonment of his half-brother, Odo bishop of Bayeux, in 1082.[65] Odo's crime was, apparently, desertion of his post in England and recruitment of troops for an expedition to Italy, possibly in order to seize the papal throne. This event demonstrated William's ruthlessness and also became an important legal precedent for royal jurisdiction over bishops.[66] In the following year Abbot Thurstin of Glastonbury used armed force against his rebel monks and killed some of them. The king had him sent back to Caen in disgrace.[67] The breach with the papacy went almost unnoticed. In 1084 the Emperor Henry IV occupied Rome and drove out Gregory VII. For William and Lanfranc Gregory and his belated successor disappeared from the reckoning. They made cautious answers to the overtures of Wibert (Clement III), the anti-pope,[68] but were not anxious to substitute one meddler for the other. When William died in Normandy in 1087, the Anglo-Saxon chronicler, a monk probably of St Augustine's, Canterbury, looked back on his rule and pointed to things both good and bad. In ecclesiastical matters William had fostered monasticism in England and

62. Cf. Brooke and Keir, *London 800—1216*, 31.

63. For the monasteries, see below, ch. v.

64. 'Goscelin of St Bertin', *VEdR* 99 ff.

65. David R. Bates, 'Odo bishop of Bayeux 1049–1097' (unpublished Exeter PhD thesis, 1970) 247 ff., 'The character and career of Odo', *Speculum* l (1975) 15 ff.

66. See below 281 ff.

67. *Chron. E.*; *GR* 329–30; *GP* 196–8.

68. F. Liebermann, 'Lanfranc and the anti-pope', *EHR* xvi (1901) 328; P. Kehr, *Zur Geschichte Wiberts von Ravenna: Clemens II* in Abh. d. Preuss. Akad. d. Wiss. Phil.-hist. Kl. 1921, 355–68.

kept good peace, but he had been a harsh master, expelling bishops and abbots from their churches, taxing the land extortionately, and imposing the cruel forest laws. Most clerical observers of the reign left the auditing of William's balance sheet to God.[69]

Because of the Conqueror's great power, his death was unsettling, and his decision to divide his dominions between his two eldest sons, Robert and William Rufus, added to the unrest. With most barons holding lands on both sides of the Channel, sharing a common culture and interest, the division was unpopular with everyone except the enemies of the dynasty, and for twenty years, until the issue was settled for the time by the battle of Tinchebrai, the church was involved in the succession question. In some ways the church had a difficult decision to make, for neither Robert nor Rufus was the sort of ruler it wanted. Robert, a wastrel whose only redeeming feature was a love of adventure, not only failed to control the anarchy in Normandy but also introduced simony into the church. Rufus, a notorious homosexual and irreligious soldier, likewise guilty of simony, was a strong but harsh ruler and all too ready to make the church pay for his schemes and wars. In fact both churches favoured Rufus and then, with greater zeal, Henry against Robert. They preferred a king to a duke, and tyrants to a bungler.

Lanfranc executed the Conqueror's last will in respect of England and confirmed Rufus on the throne. Rufus, always a dutiful son, distributed the generous alms his father had bequeathed in aid of his soul. It is not known for what reason the king promptly filled the vacant see of Chichester with a clerk, Godfrey, about whom we have little information because he died within a year.[70] It was probably in memory of his father that he granted the bishopric of Wells, as soon as it became vacant in 1088 by the death of Edward's old bishop, Giso, to John of Villula, one of the Conqueror's chaplains and doctors.[71] John, a native of Tours, seems to have been an interesting man. But because he bought the abbey and then the city of Bath from Rufus, and moved his see into the abbey, he was traduced by William of Malmesbury. And because he destroyed the canonical community at Wells, established by his predecessor, he was blamed by a member of that society. If we make allowance for William's bias, we have the portrait of a skilful doctor, who had learned from practice rather than from theory, and, although self-indulgent and a hard drinker, enjoyed good health and lived to a great age. He may have lacked eloquence and episcopal polish, but he took pleasure in the company of well-read men and seems to have been a reformer. His initial harshness at Bath may indeed have been caused, as he claimed, by the slackness and barbarity of the community. And after he had brought in better monks and scholars he rebuilt on a great scale, adorned the church, and gave it a new library. Although after his reforms he loved his chapter more, he kept most of the monastic estates in his own

---

69. Cf. Roger D. Ray, 'Orderic Vitalis and William of Poitiers: a monastic reinterpretation of William the Conqueror', *Revue Belge de Philologie et d'Histoire* 1 (1972) 1116–27.

70. Profession in Mayr-Harting *Acta*, no. 2; *Ann. Cicestrenses* in Liebermann *Ungedruckte* 92. William of Malmesbury, *GP* 205, called him William and wrote nothing about him.

71. *GR* 387–8; *GP* 194–6; Simeon *HR* 268; Florence *s.a.* 1122; *OV* (Chibnall) v. 204; *Historiola* 21–2. R. A. L. Smith, 'John of Tours, bishop of Bath', reprinted from the *Downside Review* lxx (1942) 132 in *Collected Papers by R. A. L. Smith* (1947) 74; Fröhlich 74–8.

hands – a 'bad example' which William of Malmesbury also condemned at Norwich.

At the beginning of Rufus's reign Lanfranc was the power behind the throne, and William of St Calais bishop of Durham, was the king's chosen counsellor. In the rebellion of 1088 in favour of Rufus's elder brother, Robert, the only bishops in England to support the duke were Odo of Bayeux, Geoffrey of Coutances, and William of Durham. The king's decisive victory led to the expulsion of his uncle Odo, the taming of Geoffrey, and the famous trial of the bishop of Durham.[72] Thereafter England remained at peace. In 1091, in return for a service in Normandy, Rufus forgave William of Durham,[73] and the bishop, possibly because he aspired to Canterbury,[74] supported the king without reservation and became a most useful adviser against Anselm.

Rufus was a slightly more polished version of his father, although by no means as smooth as his younger brother, Henry.[75] He was one of the most famous knights of his time, respected for his knightly word as well as for his martial skill. With social equals he was very much a gentleman. Despite his exotic oath, 'By the holy face of Lucca',[76] he did not share his father's or his brothers' piety. It is nowhere stated that he did not take part in church services, and no churchman, not even Anselm, shunned his company. But, although an adventurer, he was completely unmoved by the challenge of the First Crusade; and, although no intellectual, he showed some interest in Jews and the conflict of religions.[77] It is possible that he grew tired of admonition, especially from Anselm, to abandon his homosexual practices, and revenged himself on the more serious prelates by coarse humour and profanity. No general church council was held in his reign of thirteen years, although Anselm begged for permission. No pope was recognized until he found it convenient. The key to his favour was money, and even Anselm almost became involved in what would have looked like a simoniacal transaction.[78]

William I normally kept bishoprics vacant after the death of the incumbent for less than a year. The ten vacancies in the period 1070–87 average ten months in length. Rufus's eight vacancies average just over two years. But if we subtract three long vacancies, the other five were each a year or

---

72. See below 281 ff.

73. Simeon *HDE* 128; 'De injusta vexatione', 195; *HR* 218; 'De mirac. et translat. S. Cuthberti', Simeon *Historical Works* ii. 338–41. H. H. E. Craster, 'A contemporary record of the pontificate of Ranulf Flambard', *Archaeologia Æliana* 4th ser. vii (1930) 35.

74. *GP* 273.

75. Most contemporary or near-contemporary writers give basically similar descriptions of Rufus, and he comes alive in the pages of OV, Eadmer, and William of Malmesbury; OV, who is generally favourable to him, gives the most elaborate analysis of his character: cf. OV (Chibnall) iv. 110, 178, v. 200–2, 214, 238, 244, 293. The most elaborate, but now old-fashioned, account of Rufus's reign is Edward A. Freeman *The Reign of William Rufus and the Accession of Henry I*, 2 vols (1882).

76. Eadmer seems to be the ultimate authority for his oath, 'Per sanctum vultum de Luca': see *HN* 101, *VA* 39; cf. *GR* 364, *GP* 273. But *De injusta vexatione* 186 is probably independent. For the *Saint Voult*, see René Herval, 'En marge de la légende du Précieux–Sang–Lucques–Fécamp-Glastonbury', *L'abbaye Bénédictine de Fécamp* (1959) 108 ff.

77. *HN* 99–101; *GR* 371; *GP* 104 n. Cf. Brooke and Keir, *London 800–1216*, 179, 223–4.

78. *HN* 43 ff.; *VA* 67.

a little more, although two were unavoidably undetermined at the king's death. It seems that, as in so many things, Rufus acknowledged, but sometimes broke, his father's rule, and real change came only with Henry I. Nor can it be said that Rufus's appointments to bishoprics, even if simoniacal, were inferior to his father's – indeed it could be argued that they were better.

Godfrey of Chichester died in 1088, Lanfranc in 1089, William of Thetford in 1091, Remigius of Lincoln in 1092, Wulfstan of Worcester and Robert of Hereford in 1095, and William of Durham in 1096. All these, with the possible exception of Godfrey, were excellent bishops. In 1090–91 Rufus appointed his friend and chaplain, Ralf Luffa, to Chichester and another friend, Herbert Losinga abbot of Ramsey, to Thetford, and in 1092 his Breton clerk, Hervey, to Bangor.

Ralf had learned from his royal master not vice but courage, and William of Malmesbury, usually hostile to non-monastic bishops, gave Ralf one of his best notices.[79] The bishop opposed all the iniquities of both Rufus and Henry I, but managed to keep their respect. He toured his small diocese three times a year in order to preach to the people, and he took no more than free-will offerings from his parishioners. After his church was burned down he restored it worthily. He died like a true Christian (the historian probably meant 'monk'), having given all his goods to the poor, even his underwear and bedding. William of Malmesbury suggests that men such as Ralf, who were prepared to defend the church against secular oppression, were let down by Anselm's failure to provide them with leadership. In contrast, the Malmesbury monk felt some contempt for Herbert Losinga:[80] he was a monk who betrayed their principles. Even if Ralf Luffa got his preferment free, Herbert in the same year had to pay Rufus 1,000 marks for the abbey of Winchester (Newminster) for his father, Robert, and the bishopric of Thetford for himself.[81] The simony was notorious, and he never lived it down; but he soon repented. The *prognosticon* at his consecration was, 'Friend [Judas] wherefore art thou come?' (Matt. 26: 50); and, possibly urged by Anselm, he went to Rome at the end of 1093 to make amends, only then to fall foul of Rufus who had not recognized Urban II as pope. Otherwise Herbert seems to have been an exemplary bishop. Like Remigius of Lincoln, a monk of Fécamp and educated under the great ultramontane John of Ravenna, he transferred his see to Norwich, where he created a monastery and took a great interest in the education of the monks.[82] His letters and some sermons were collected and preserved, but no verses have survived. He seems to have been an active and, except for the one lapse, blameless bishop, respected for his learning and useful to the king. Although William of Malmesbury also charged him with maintaining the monks at Norwich by money payments instead of endowing them with land, Herbert reappeared in visions for some years after his death, and must have been

79. *GP* 265–7; OV (Chibnall) v. 204. For a monastic deathbed, *Vita Gundulfi* 290–1.

80. *GR* 369, 385–7; *GP* 151–2. *Epistolae Herberti de Losinga, Osberti de Clara, et Elmeri prioris Cantuariensis,* ed. R. Anstruther (Brussels 1846); E. M. Goulburn and H. Symonds, *The Life, Letters, and Sermons of Bishop Herbert de Losinga* (1878). J. W. Alexander, 'Herbert of Norwich', *Studies in Medieval and Renaissance History* vi (1969) 115; Fröhlich 82–9.

81. Florence, *s.a.* 1094.

82. See below 240 ff.

remembered as a better pastor than his successors, Everard and William Turbe.[83]

As a consequence of the Norman advance into Gwynneth, Rufus appointed the first French bishop in Wales in 1092.[84] With Canterbury vacant, Hervey's consecrator was Thomas I of York. The Breton clerk, like many of his compatriots a man of some intellectual interests, also, characteristically, had a troubled career. After he had been driven from Bangor by the natives, Henry I tried to get him the bishopric of Lisieux before creating him the first bishop of Ely.

Rufus left Canterbury vacant for almost five years after Lanfranc's death, probably not only to exploit the revenues but also to avoid religious interference in his affairs. A conspiracy among the bishops and some of the barons to get the king to nominate Anselm abbot of Bec, succeeded when Rufus fell seriously ill in 1093. Anselm resisted the translation with some stubbornness, although his biographer, Eadmer, perhaps over-emphasized the reluctance in order to exonerate his hero from blame for the disasters which followed. Anselm was a failure as bishop, metropolitan, primate and even as abbot of Christ Church, but he was one of the best men ever to occupy St Augustine's chair.[85] A nobleman from Aosta in Burgundy, he, like Lanfranc, travelled in search of knowledge, and after he had studied under Lanfranc at Bec, he became a monk there, succeeding his master as prior and Herlwin as abbot. Gentle yet courageous, sweet-tempered but inflexible on principle, he was conspicuously honest, simple and good. He became the centre of a wide circle of spiritual friends.

It has been claimed that as a speculative theologian Anselm was without equal in the West between St Augustine of Hippo and St Thomas Aquinas.[86] His celebrated phrase, *fides quaerens intellectum,* 'faith seeking understanding', or 'what should the intelligent Christian believe?', is the real clue to his purpose and method. A firm believer and a humble monk, he nevertheless applied human reason remorselessly to a series of the most difficult theological problems: the Trinity, theodicy, free will and grace, the fall and original sin, the incarnation and redemption, and proof of the existence of God. He wrote for a monastic audience a series of monographs, in which the conjunction of loving mysticism and rigorous logic produced quite original

---

83. *Vita S. Willelmi Norwic.* 83 ff., 116 ff.

84. *GP* 325–6; Hugh *HCY* 7; *Lib. El.* 238 ff.; OV (Le Prévost) iv. 312–3. The earlier transfer of the see of Lichfield to Chester was, of course, a move in this direction.

85. Works: *Anselmi Opera Omnia,* ed. F. S. Schmitt OSB (6 vols 1946–61); *Memorials of Saint Anselm,* ed. R. W. Southern and F. S. Schmitt (Auctores Britannici Medii Aevi – i, 1969). Contemporary lives: Eadmer *HN* and *VA.* No comprehensive biography of Anselm has been written in English since R. W. Church, *Saint Anselm, Archbishop of Canterbury* (1913). But in recent years there has been mounting interest in Anselm's thought and theology. For the historiography, Fröhlich 3 ff. Cf. also *inter alia* J. de Ghellinck, *Le Mouvement théologique du XIIe siècle* (Bruges, 2nd ed 1948) 78–86, *L'Essor de la littérature latine au XIIe siècle* (Paris 1946) 36–41, with bibliography; R. W. Southern, *Saint Anselm and his Biographer* (1963); S. Vanni Rovighi, 'Notes sur l'influence de Saint Anselme au XIIe siècle, '*Cahiers de Civ. Méd.* vii (1964) 423. C. A. Volz, *Honorius Augustodunensis, A twelfth-century enigma* (New York 1966). For Anselm's relations with Kings William II and Henry I, see below 287 ff.

86. J. de Ghellinck, *Le Mouvement théologique, loc. cit.*

results. But both the monastic setting and the originality deprived his works of wide influence before the thirteenth century. Nor does it seem that his writings strengthened his position against his critics and enemies. Most English bishops had no patience with him: he would not operate within the conditions. Anselm is the best known of all the bishops of this period, for not only have his works and letters been preserved, but his admirer Eadmer wrote two books about him.

Rufus was not an impossible king to deal with: he welcomed courage and had some respect for goodness. Many bishops, including the religious William of St Calais, served him devotedly; Ralf Luffa kept his good will; and the saintly Gundulf of Rochester, who had to act for Anselm during his exiles, managed to cope with Rufus's outbursts. Gundulf once told the king that he should continue to behave religiously even though he had recovered from his illness, and Rufus shouted, 'By the holy face of Lucca, I will not repay God with good for the evil he has done to me'.[87] Intimates learned to live with these sallies. But Anselm, although because of his high birth and faith entirely fearless, could infuriate men less violent than Rufus by his unworldliness and lack of tact. He drove a hard bargain with Rufus before he would accept Canterbury and then handled the matter of a money payment to the king for the Norman campaign extremely clumsily. He pestered Rufus in 1094 for permission to hold a reforming church council and correct the evil-living at court. And when Rufus asked him what vices he had particularly in mind, he answered, 'sodomy and incest'. When the king returned from Normandy in 1095 Anselm asked for permission to go to Urban II for his pallium. Although Anselm could not have done otherwise, for he had already as abbot 'in another kingdom' recognized Urban, knowing as he did that Rufus had not himself acknowledged Urban, he could have approached the matter more cautiously. As it was he had to stand by while Rufus tried to bargain recognition of Urban in return for his deposition. And although the king was out-manoeuvred and had to accept both Urban and Anselm, he did apparently secure from the pope a recognition of his royal rights in the English church.[88] Even Anselm was chagrined when in 1097 he was accused of neglecting his feudal obligations and was forced to offend the barons as well as the prelates by the irresponsible stand he felt obliged to take. That he welcomed the exile the king imposed shows how escape from his duties had become for him the only solution.

Rufus, when in fear of death in 1093, appointed not only Anselm to Canterbury but also his chancellor, Robert Bloet, to Lincoln,[89] which had been vacant for less than a year, and so completed the episcopal bench. They represented two completely different types of bishop. Robert, a member of the Norman baronial family of Ivry and related to Hugh bishop of Bayeux

87. *HN* 39. He is, of course, inverting Rom. 12: 17. For Gundulf's excellent relations with Rufus, *Vita Gundulfi*, 283 ff.

88. Joseph Deér, 'Der Anspruch der Herrscher des 12. Jahrhunderts auf die apostolische Legation', *Arch. Hist. Pont.* ii (1964) 168 ff.

89. *Chron. E. s.a.* 1093, 1123; Florence; *HN* 47–8, 82; *GP* 313–14; OV (Chibnall) v. 202; *HH* 216–17, 244, 299–300, 304–5; Giraldus Cambrensis, *Vita S. Remigii* 31–3; John of Schalby, *ibid.* 195–6. Fröhlich 89–93. For his Norman kin, see Raymonde Foreville in *Studia Anselmiana* xli (Rome 1957) = *Analecta Monastica* 4, 21 n., and *GG* 137 n.

(1015–49) and his brother John bishop of Avranches (1060–67) and arch-bishop of Rouen (1067–87), had served in the Conqueror's chapel and had accompanied Rufus to England. He was an exceedingly worldly prelate, a great man in royal affairs, a justiciar and, when necessary, a soldier, who lived in ostentatious splendour surrounded by knights and noble youths. He appointed his son Simon dean of Lincoln and does not seem to have changed his ways at all when he took major orders and a bishopric. Henry of Huntingdon, who was educated in his household, considered no one more handsome, more cheerful, or more affable; but also used him as an example of the mutability of human fortune and as a warning against excessive love of the world. Robert was remembered at Lincoln as a great patron who had enriched and adorned his predecessor's church and doubled the number of canons. But it was also remembered that he had settled the dispute with York over Lindsey and Lincoln at too great a cost and surrendered Ely for a new diocese without sufficient compensation. William of Malmesbury denounced him as a hater of monks who moved the convent from nearby Stow to distant Eynsham and conspired with Roger of Salisbury in 1123 to break the monastic hold on Canterbury. It is possible that Robert became too great and proud, and in 1109 was too resentful at being deprived of Ely, for he lost Henry I's favour. His sudden death in 1123 at Woodstock, when riding with the king and Bishop Roger in the deerpark, made a great impression on contemporaries. He col-lapsed into Henry's arms and died of apoplexy in the king's chamber, speech-less, uncomforted and unshriven. Most men assumed that he went to hell.

Five bishoprics fell vacant in the later part of the reign, and Rufus filled up Winchester and Hereford reasonably quickly. He could not effectively appoint to Winchester (1098) or Salisbury (1099) because of Anselm's exile, but he could appoint to Durham, which fell vacant in 1096, because the archbishop of York was the consecrator. Rufus continued to reward clerks from the chapel royal. Anselm was the only monk he preferred.

To Worcester, vacant since 18 January 1095 by the death of (St) Wulfstan, the last survivor on the bench from the reign of the Confessor, Rufus appointed about a year later Samson, brother of Thomas I archbishop of York and father of the future Thomas II of York and Richard II of Bayeux.[90] Educated like others of his family under Odo at Bayeux, where he rose to be dean, and at Liège and Angers, he became one of the Conqueror's men of business and was much concerned with the Domesday survey, being perhaps even the master mind who produced the final reports.[91] He had refused the bishopric of Le Mans in 1081 and was still in minor orders, and free to marry, in 1096; but the appointment of a married clerk to a famous monastic see shows how little Rufus cared for ecclesiastical tradition. William of Malmesbury considered Samson adequately educated for the post, and allowed that he did not ill treat the monks. But he was a slave to lust and gluttony, and died badly,

90. *HN* 74; *GP* 289–90; OV (Chibnall) ii. 300, iv. 118, v. 211. Fröhlich 108–18.

91. V. H. Galbraith, 'Notes on the career of Samson, bishop of Worcester (1096–1112)', *EHR* lxxxii (1967) 86. I do not find all Galbraith's arguments convincing and do not accept that the recipient of Lanfranc's letter is Samson rather than Svein of Essex.

unanointed. It would seem that Samson was a rather old-fashioned, liberal and worldly bishop, sinful, but not actively hostile to the good.

Gerard, appointed to Hereford at the same time as Samson to Worcester, likewise came from an important ecclesiastical family. He was the nephew of Walkelin bishop of Winchester (1070–98) and of Simeon abbot of Ely (1082–94), and may have been precentor of Rouen.[92] A royal clerk, he had served William I and Rufus as chancellor. He seems to have been better educated than most of the curials, and, although William of Malmesbury considered him a windbag, was used by both Rufus and Henry I as an ambassador to Rome, proof that he spoke Latin and had diplomatic graces. He is often found in association with Herbert Losinga bishop of Norwich. At Hereford he took up some of his predecessor's interests in science and perhaps the occult. The author of the *Quadripartitus* and of the *Leges Henrici Primi,* law books produced in the royal court, was associated with him, and he has been considered to have had some connexion with the collection of tractates now attributed to the Norman Anonymous. William of Malmesbury accused him of sorcery and lust, and was doubly prejudiced against him, for in 1101 the bishop was translated to York and became involved in the intrigues against Anselm. But Gerard had no great wish to quarrel with the primate and in 1105 made his peace with him. Since the chapter at York had wanted the immediate succession of Thomas II, it is not surprising that the canons cared little for him and, when he died, refused to bury his corpse in the cathedral. That there were flaws in his character is obvious, but he seems to have suffered unduly from prejudice and to have been a better than average bishop.

Except from the standpoint of an observer such as William of Malmesbury, who was not only a fanatical champion of his own monastic order but also a severe censor of prelates, Rufus's eight appointments to bishoprics in the first decade of his reign were rather better than might have been expected. They were mostly royal clerks of a rather worldly type, but, consequently, educated men of proved administrative ability. In 1099 Rufus allowed his faithful servant, Ranulf Flambard, to buy for £1,000 the bishopric of Durham which had been vacant for three and a half years.[93] And when Rufus died a year later several annalists took the opportunity to denounce both master and servant, who had been in an unholy alliance to oppress and despoil the church, corrupt morals and impede the religious life of the kingdom.

92. *HN* 68–9, 74; *GP* 107, 258–60, 303; Hugh *HCY* 12; *AEp* 214; OV (Chibnall) v. 204; Walter Map, *De Nugis curialium* V, vi. V. H. Galbraith, 'Gerard the chancellor', *EHR* xlvi (1931) 77. L. J. Downer, *Leges Henrici Primi* (1972); G. H. Williams, *The Norman Anonymous of 1100 A. D.* (1951) 88 ff. Fröhlich 118–25. See also below 257, 259.

93. *Chron. s.a.* 1099, 1100, 1101, 1128; Florence *s.a.* 1099, 1100; *HN* 41; *GR* 274, 470–1, 517; *GP* 273–5; *AEp* 214; Simeon *HDE* 135–41; *HR* 260; Reginald of Durham *St Cuthbert* 101, 205; 'De mirac. et translat. S. Cuthberti', Simeon *Historical Works* i 248 ff; Durham obituary in *Liber Vitae ecclesiae Dunelmensis,* ed. J. Stevenson, Surtees Soc. xiii (1841); *Lib. El.* 219 ff.; OV (Chibnall) iv. 170–7, v. 202, 204, 250, 310–14, 320–2; John of Hexham 312; Hugh *HCY* 5–6, 26, 29–30, 74; H.H.E. Craster, 'A contemporary record of the pontificate of Ranulf Flambard', *Archaeologia Æliana,* 4th ser. vii (1930) 33; F. Barlow, *Durham Jurisdictional Peculiars* (1950) 12–16, 153–5; R. W. Southern, 'Ranulf Flambard', *Medieval Humanism and other Studies* (1970) 183–205; Fröhlich 135–44; C. Warren Hollister, 'The Anglo-Norman civil war: 1101', *EHR* lxxxviii (1973) 315; Brooke and Keir, *London 800–1216,* 163, 311, 345.

Ranulf Flambard and his brother Fulcher were sons of a parish priest in the diocese of Bayeux, who at the end of his life became a monk of St Augustine's Canterbury; and Ranulf is said to have been educated among the hangers-on at Bishop Odo's court. He found a new patron in Maurice, archdeacon of Le Mans and bishop of London, settling himself and his family firmly in the chapter of St Paul's and serving as keeper of the king's seal when Maurice was chancellor. But after a quarrel he transferred to royal service and under Rufus acquired great power. Although no scholar, he was adequately educated and able to use his outstanding physical and mental qualities to achieve his exceptional ambitions. Strong, healthy, active, and courageous, he impressed with his quick mind and readiness of tongue, although some found his volatile temperament and his habit of saying serious things in a jesting manner disconcerting. His wife or mistress before he was bishop was an English woman, Ælfgifu, a burgess of Huntingdon, who bore him children; in 1114, on one of his later visits, he attempted to seduce her niece, Theodora, the future Christina of Markyate.[94] No doubt such events were a feature of the age. Loyal and generous to his own people, he was haughty and overbearing when acting for the king. What is most remarkable about his career is how master and servant trusted each other: Rufus gave Ranulf a free hand and paid no attention at all to complaints against his behaviour, and Ranulf acted with complete confidence that the king would support him against his enemies.

Ranulf as Rufus's clerk or chaplain seems to have held no other established office, but to have been the king's financial agent, responsible for squeezing as much money out of royal rights in England as he could. He is perhaps best regarded as the king's *procurator*, or steward. Besides imposing geld, he had some control over the courts, and administered vacant ecclesiastical benefices. Except that he lacked Becket's military interests, and Becket was chaste, there are similarities in their pre-episcopal careers. It was Ranulf's farming of the widowed bishoprics and abbeys and the accumulation of a private fortune which made him so hated in certain areas of the church. He had some strange adventures. In Rufus's reign he was kidnapped on the Thames and taken out to sea by his captors, who intended to kill him, but he gained a mastery over the ruffians; and Henry I on his accession imprisoned him in the Tower of London, from which he managed to escape by means of a rope. In Normandy he held for a time the bishopric of Lisieux, before passing it on to his brother and then to his sons, and he most capably managed Duke Robert's invasion of England. Although after the Treaty of Alton he was reconciled to Henry, he never gained that king's complete favour, and consequently gave fruitful attention to his church and city.

Ranulf was respected by his monks. He was a magnificent builder at Durham, translated in a famous ceremony the body of St Cuthbert to a new tomb, and made Durham a great provincial capital in the north. On the whole he was a loyal suffragan of York. There was a price to pay: Ranulf could not live with Prior Turgot or accept all the convent's claim to privileges, and he had his carnal family to endow. One nephew, Osbern, became sheriff of Durham, a second, Ranulf, archdeacon, and after their uncle's death proved to be staunch

94. Below 202.

supporters of the church and city against the Scots. Another nephew, Richard, was given one of the cathedral's churches. One of the bishop's sons, Elias, became a canon of Lincoln, another, Thomas, he made for a time bishop of Lisieux. But Ranulf was religious. He was a friend and patron of the hermit St Godric and was noted for his alms to the poor. In the end, despite Anselm's contempt and bewilderment, the adventurer achieved respectability; it is a testimonial to his household that one of his clerks, William of Corbeil, became archbishop of Canterbury in 1123.

In November 1095 Pope Urban II preached what became known later as 'the First Crusade' in the gloomy cathedral church at Clermont Ferrand in the Auvergne. The project did not pass unnoticed in England, for an account of the expedition is given under the year 1096 in the English Chronicle and by Florence of Worcester. William of Malmesbury devoted to it a chapter in his *Gesta Regum* derived from one of the several French accounts, and Orderic Vitalis, writing in 1135, included in his work a complete book (IX) taken from Baudry of Bourgueil's *Historia Ierosolimitana,* itself derived from the anonymous *Gesta Francorum.*[95] Robert Curthose, duke of Normandy, went with the counts of Flanders, Blois, and Boulogne; and his pawning of his duchy to Rufus had important consequences, both ecclesiastical and political, for England. Rufus, however, was completely uninterested, and he must have discouraged his vassals from leaving. A few Englishmen are said to have taken part, but the only known adventurer is the 'English knight', Robert fitzGodwin, who accompanied Edgar Ætheling from troubled Scotland, and when captured died a martyr to his faith.[96]

Nor was England much involved in later events. In 1128 one of the founders of the Templars, Hugh, approached Henry I in Normandy and was allowed to go on a preaching and recruiting tour of England and Scotland. According to the English chronicler he raised great sums of money and also attracted a large number of people to go out to fight. But these were completely disillusioned when they got there, because there was no fighting.[97] There was again some small English contribution to the main operations of the Second Crusade of 1147. Arnulf bishop of Lisieux took the Cross at Vézelay in Burgundy in 1146 and had some authority over the Anglo-Norman contingent which joined the French army.[98] Henry of Huntingdon believed that the Franco-German expeditions failed so ignominiously because of the sins of the Crusaders. And he presented as an antithesis to the large and well-equipped aristocratic enterprizes a humble naval expedition which was victorious against all the odds because it was led not by the mighty of this world but by Almighty God.[99] An account of the events between May and November 1147 was written by one of its members, an unidentifiable clerk, R. from East Anglia.[100] In May a

95.   *Chron.,* Florence, *s.a.* 1096; *GR* 390 ff; OV (Chibnall) ii, pp. xiii ff; 4 ff.

96.   *GR* 310, 449.

97.   *Chron. s.a.* 1128.

98.   Cf. Barlow, *The Letters of Arnulf of Lisieux* (1939) pp. xxv–xxvii.

99.   HH 280–1.

100.   *De expugnatione Lyxbonensi* in *Chronicles and Memorials of the Reign of Richard I,* ed. W. Stubbs (Rolls ser. 1864) i, p. cxlii ff. C. W. David, 'The authorship of the *De Expugnatione*

fleet of 164 vessels, drawn from the Empire (Cologne), Flanders, Boulogne, East Anglia, Kent, London, and the rest of England (a priest of Bristol is mentioned), assembled at Dartmouth in Devon, and on the 23rd set sail for Spain. Lisbon fell in October after a seventeen-week siege, and an Englishman, Gilbert of Hastings, was elected bishop of the city. Dissention between the allied nations had already developed (R. had a low opinion of the Germans and Flemings), and the squadron divided. Some crews remained to fight the Moors in Spain and took part in the siege of Tortosa, July-December 1148; some went on to Syria and engaged in the siege of Damascus in July. It may be that these naval crusaders were less sinful than the soldiers; but their behaviour does not make pretty reading. Warfare against pagans usually brought out the worst in christians.

Before the Conquest the English had been interested in the holy places of the East;[101] and it is possible, as the entries in the chronicles and the events of 1128 and 1147–48 suggest, that a popular interest in the Holy Land remained. But it could not find an effective outlet because both Rufus and Henry I, on account of their political and military difficulties, took care to keep their vassals at home, and in Stephen's reign, when there was less effective control, most English barons dared not abandon their fiefs. For this tradition that great conqueror, William I, followed by Rufus, one of the noblest and most famous captains of his day, were mostly responsible.

Another irony of Rufus's life is that his premature death was the result of a domestic hunting accident; he departed burdened with all his sins and with the English church in sad disarray. In August 1100 Archbishop Anselm was in exile, Winchester and Salisbury were vacant, and Ranulf had just bought Durham. No church council of any moment had been held since 1076. At least ten of the fourteen bishops were former royal clerks. William of Malmesbury, at the end of Book IV of the *Gesta Regum* devoted to Rufus's reign, after a disapproving account of how three bishops (Herbert Losinga, John of Tours, and Robert of Limesey) had moved their sees into monasteries, and an appreciative report on Goscelin of St Bertin and his Lives of the Saints (works of great use to William), promised that since he had been forced to write some disparaging things about certain bishops in the previous pages he would make amends at the close of the next book, which would be devoted to the deeds of Henry I. He would introduce some bishops who were not only quite different in their behaviour from those he had censured but also, since they were contemporaries, would demonstrate that, although their own age had not produced a saint, it was by no means without zeal. But when in 1125 he came to that point, he was unable to carry out his promise.[102] This general pessimism of the historian puts the matter into perspective. The Normans had made great changes in the church. They had reserved to themselves the higher positions; they had rebuilt their churches and reformed the administration; but they had only transformed one corrupt church into another. The faults, even if different,

Lyxbonensi', *Speculum* vii (1932) 50, corrected by C. R. Cheney, *ibid*. 395. Giles Constable, 'A note on the route of the Anglo-Flemish crusaders of 1147', *ibid*. xxviii (1953) 525.

101.   *English Church 1000–1066*, 21–2.

102.   See below 78 f.

were just as heinous. Worldliness was the besetting sin; and the unworldly, like
Anselm, were almost worse than useless. The moralist was here taking over
from the historian. In more genial moods William could appreciate the new
liveliness and capability which he believed the Normans had brought into
England.[103]

2. The new age

Henry I was in the beginning well regarded by the church.[104] He was seen to be
a true son of his father: a man of grave faults but religiously inclined and more
than willing that the church should exercise a pastoral ministry. That he rid the
court of parasites and perverts was counted very much in his favour, and
reduced censure of his own heterosexual excesses. No English king, it seems,
has had more bastards than Henry. His avoidance of the grosser forms of
simony also distinguished him from both his brothers. Like his father and Rufus
he stood on his ecclesiastical rights, and although he was better educated and
more attuned to new and progressive movements than they, he strongly
resisted novelties which threatened his power. His experiences with Anselm at
the beginning of his reign inclined him towards safe and worldly appointments.
Although he had close connexions with Cluny and Fleury,[105] he seems at first to
have shared the fashionable slighting of Benedictine monasticism and
approved the queen's interest in Austin canons. From 15 March 1124 until 12
April 1125 no Benedictine monk held an English bishopric, a situation without
parallel since the early tenth century. But that was the turning point. Henry's
desire for God's help after his son and heir was drowned in November 1120
clearly had an effect on his patronage; and by the end of the reign the
composition of the English episcopate was much changed. Henry gives the
impression of having been less provincial than his predecessors. With his grasp
of diplomacy and his eye for useful servants, he moved easily into the new age.
He refined the Conqueror's cunning into calculation and Rufus's strength into
firmness, sharpened, when necessary, by ferocity.

　　　　When Henry seized the throne after Rufus had been killed in a
hunting accident he was in an extremely weak position. His eldest brother, now
a famous Crusader, was this time prepared to invade, and soon had the services

---

103.　*GR* ii. 306.

104.　An interesting essay on Henry's character and fate is in HH *De contemptu mundi* 311–13.
Hildebert of Le Mans naturally regarded him as a great improvement on Rufus: *Carmina Minora*
(Teubner) no. 37. For more recent views see R. W. Southern, 'King Henry I', *Medieval Humanism*
(1970) 206; Everett U. Crosby, 'The organization of the English episcopate under Henry I',
Studies in Medieval and Renaissance History iv (1967) 1. Martin Brett, *The English church under
Henry I* (1975).

105.　For Henry and Cluny, see below 193. Hugh monk of Fleury dedicated his earliest surviving
work, *De regia potestate et sacerdotali dignitate,* to Henry, his *Historia Ecclesiastica* (1109–10) to
Henry's sister, Adela countess of Blois, and his *Modernorum regum Francorum liber* (1114) to
Henry's daughter, Matilda 'the Empress'. For Hugh, see Manitius iii. 518 and Hubert Jedin, 'Zur
widmungsepistel der "Historia Ecclesiastica" Hugos von Fleury', in *Speculum Historiale*
(Festschrift für Johannes Spörl, Munich 1965) 559.

of Ranulf Flambard who had escaped from Henry's prison.[106] The whole church, however, regarded Rufus's untimely death as God's punishment for his sins and rallied to Henry's support. In his coronation charter Henry renounced his brother's illegalities and promised that the church should be free. But he was disconcerted when Anselm, on his welcome return from exile, refused to do homage for Canterbury and gave notice that he was required to enforce in England the conciliar decrees against lay investiture.[107] In this matter Henry thought that Anselm was objecting to the good customs of his father rather than the illegalities of his brother. In all other directions Anselm was helpful enough. He allowed Henry to make a political marriage with Edith, daughter of Malcolm Canmore of Scots and (St) Margaret, despite general knowledge that she had been a nun,[108] and aided him during Robert's invasion in 1101. In return he received permission to hold a great reforming council at Westminster in the following year, at which severe laws were passed against married and unchaste clergy.[109] In 1102 Henry astutely had Gerard translated from Hereford to York, which had fallen vacant by the death of Thomas I. In this case consecration was not required, and Gerard even avoided making a new profession of obedience to Anselm. Henry was attempting, although with little success, to threaten the primate with a rival. The quarrel over investitures dragged on for another five years. Anselm returned to the Continent in 1103, and it was not until 1107 that the compromise which Henry had reached with Paschal II in the previous year was ratified at London. It was then possible to fill five vacant bishoprics according to the new formula.

Henry made, or influenced, thirty episcopal appointments in his reign of thirty-five and a half years. Vacancies occurred regularly and after 1107 were filled without excessive delay. The average voidance was two years four months. If we subtract the four vacancies totalling twenty-seven years, which were not his fault, we get an average of eighteen months, rather longer than Rufus's norm but not of a different order. The longest vacancies were at Canterbury after Anselm's death (five years) and at York after the death of Thomas II (five years eight months). This record is worse than Rufus's, and it is also possible to consider that the quality of Henry's appointments was inferior to those of his father and brother. It would be difficult to maintain that they were distinctly better. It was in 1124, when Henry had made twenty-two appointments, that William of Malmesbury, reluctantly and evasively, honoured his promise to praise the bishops of his own time.[110] 'Lest it should seem', he wrote, 'that England was still without good men, let us not forget Serlo abbot of Gloucester, Lanzo monk of Cluny and prior of Lewes, and Godfrey prior of Winchester.' No doubt these three Benedictine monks were, indeed, saintly and learned men, but none was a bishop and the last was a bishop's second-in-command.

106. C. Warren Hollister, 'The Anglo-Norman civil war: 1101', *EHR* lxxxviii (1973) 315.
107. See below 297 ff.
108. For this amazing affair, see R. W. Southern, *St Anselm and his biographer*, 182 ff., and below 169 ff.
109. *Chron.*; Florence; *GP* 118, Hugh *HCY* 13; Mansi xx. 1149. See also below 100 f.
110. *GR* 512 ff.

The historian added in an irrelevant and discursive way that there were in fact at that time in England many men distinguished by their learning and famous for their piety. And their excellence was all the more remarkable in that it grew in strength while the century grew old (William was thinking of the late eleventh century). If there had, indeed, been prelates who seemed to have fallen short of the holiness of the ancients by their activity in worldly affairs and their sloth in spiritual matters, such men had tried to conceal their errors by adorning their churches in a sumptuous manner. William gives as an example of this type of degenerate bishop the hated Ranulf Flambard, who built monastic offices at Durham and translated St Cuthbert. This reminded him of the translation of St Etheldreda at Ely and allowed him to make an unflattering reference to Hervey, the first bishop of that new see. And he finishes by mentioning the unedifying struggle between the metropolitans of Canterbury and York. In his heart of hearts he held most *episcopi moderni* in contempt.

Henry usually appointed to bishoprics clerks out of his chapel. He seems to have gone out of his way to secure the election of mediocrities to Canterbury, and in 1123 even broke the Benedictine tradition. He was no more attracted to monk-bishops than his predecessors had been, but he did promote three monks of noble birth: the brothers Siegfried and Ralf d'Escures, scions of a Norman baronial family, and his nephew, Henry of Blois. Signs of change are the preferment of Augustinian canons, archdeacons, and clerks who had been educated in a cathedral school abroad. But only one of Henry's nominees, Gilbert the Universal, had any reputation as a divine or scholar. It may be that in a more educated age achievements which had once been memorable were now taken for granted. But it is clear that the English church again lacked any distinction. On the other hand, Henry was not afraid of ability in his servants. Two of his creations used their talents to build up their baronial power in England, and were destined to play important parts in Stephen's reign: Roger of Salisbury and Stephen's brother, Henry of Blois. It was, however, the changed conditions under Stephen which allowed these men to become exceptionally prominent.

In 1106, as a result of Robert's defeat and capture at Tinchebrai, Henry also became ruler of Normandy. The reunion of the Norman dominions allowed an easier movement of persons and ideas between the two. But, except in the person of the king and his household, there was no real integration of goverment. Henry organized a resident administration for each part under a body of justiciars sitting at the exchequer courts; and the two churches, unlike the Anglo-Welsh, but like the Anglo-Scottish and Anglo-Irish situations, remained quite separate. English bishops went only exceptionally to Normandy and then to see the king on business; and Norman bishops rarely visited England. This may well have been Henry's policy. He could remain master of an island church and feared contamination from the more exposed Norman body. The ancestral customs had become less effective in the homeland than in the colony.

On 11 August 1107 Anselm consecrated William Giffard to Winchester, Roger to Salisbury, Rainald to Hereford, William Warelwast to Exeter, and Urban to Llandaff. William Giffard, a member of an important baronial family, who had been dean of Rouen and William I's chaplain and

Rufus's chancellor, was given immediate promotion by Henry in 1100, doubt-less in order to steady the administration behind the new king.[111] But he got caught up in the investiture quarrel, refused to accept consecration from Gerard of York in 1102, and was despoiled by Henry and driven into exile. After his eventual enthronement he seems to have played no great part in public affairs but applied himself primarily to his diocese and city, where he was a great builder. Roger was the clerk whom Henry advanced to replace Rufus's men.

Roger, a priest from the Avranchin, who had been Henry's man of affairs (*procurator*) in Normandy, was appointed by the king to succeed Wil-liam Giffard as chancellor and then, after Roger had in turn become bishop, justiciar of the whole of England and vicegerent.[112] He took the place in the English government formerly held by Ranulf Flambard, and his and the king's achievement was to institutionalize the position and make it acceptable to the kingdom. He and Robert count of Meulan were Henry's principal advisers, and when Henry was out of England Roger governed the kingdom for him. He was involved in, and must have been partly responsible for, the improvements in the techniques of government noticeable in this reign.[113] He managed, in an old-fashioned way, to combine the roles of bishop, royal justiciar and baron without, it seems, any problem of conscience or any great affront to public morals. He carried out his episcopal duties efficiently, was a great builder, educated his children and *nipoti* well, maintained Salisbury's reputation as a place of learning, and patronized the Augustinian priory of St Frideswide at Oxford. He also, less worthily, administered for a time the abbeys of Malmes-bury and Abbotsbury. He was considered hostile to monks and was one of those who secured the election of William of Corbeil to Canterbury in 1123. As justiciar he had all the English moneyers deprived of their right hands and castrated at Christmas 1124 (a popular act), and managed to accumulate a great fortune. As a magnate he built castles and walls and lived in great state. Naturally he advanced his sons and nephews and his wife's relatives in the church and royal service. A nephew, Alexander, whom he appointed his archdeacon at Salisbury, got the see of Lincoln in 1123; another nephew, Nigel, the king's treasurer, got Ely in 1133; one son, Roger, became Stephen's chancellor and another, Adelelm, his treasurer. Nor did the dynasty end there, for Nigel's son, Richard fitzNeal (bishop of London) and Richard's kinsman, William of Ely, also acted as royal treasurers in their turn. Stephen's blow in 1139 against this family, which he believed was about to desert him in favour of

111.   *Chron. s.a.* 1100, 1103, 1129; Florence *s.a.* 1103; *GP* 109–10, 132 n., 192; Winchester annals in *Annales Monastici* ii. 46–9. C. H. Haskins, *Norman Institutions* (1948) 79. George H. Williams, *The Norman Anonymous of 1100 A.D.* (Cambridge, Mass. 1951) 90–5. Fröhlich 144–52. Cf. J. H. Round, 'Walter Tirel and his wife', *Feudal England* (1895) 468; C. Warren Hollister, 'The strange death of William Rufus', *Speculum* xlix (1973) 637.

112.   *Chron.;* Florence; *GR* 483–4, *GP* 109–10, 117, 132 n., 316; John of Worcester 27, 57–8; John of Hexham 302; HH 245, 256; *Hist. Nov.* 5, 25–7, 37–9; *GSteph* 48 ff.; Wm of Newburgh 35–8; *Dialogus de Scaccario,* ed. Charles Johnson, 42. Fröhlich 156–9. Edward J. Kealey, *Roger of Salisbury Viceroy of England* (1972).

113.   Among his greatest admirers are H. G. Richardson and G. O. Sayles, *The Governance of Medieval England* (1963) 156 ff.

Matilda, and which led to Roger's death of grief, was not widely popular. Stephen's brother, Henry of Winchester, regarded it as an outrage.[114]

When Gerard of Hereford was translated to York, Henry first substituted his larderer, Roger, who died almost immediately[115] and inaugurated a series of short tenures. He next nominated the queen's chancellor, Rainald,[116] another whom Anselm refused to consecrate and who, like William Giffard and Roger of Salisbury, declined to accept consecration from Gerard of York. Rainald resigned the see; but, like William, was pardoned and shared in the reconciliation of 1107. According to William of Malmesbury he was a good and modest man, although less hospitable than he should have been; he died eight years later of gout.

To Exeter, vacant in 1103 by the death of the aged and blind Osbern, Edward the Confessor's old clerk, Henry appointed in July 1107 William Warelwast,[117] one of Rufus's most trusted agents, and, exceptionally, on that account acceptable to Henry, for he had undertaken diplomatic missions at the papal curia against Anselm and in 1097 had searched Anselm's baggage at Dover as the primate went into exile. Henry wanted both to insult Anselm and also to make use of William's experience. It was William, in company with Anselm's clerk, Baldwin of Tournai, who negotiated the settlement of the investiture question in 1106 at Rome; and he was used later by Henry in diplomacy with the pope over the Canterbury–York dispute. William of Malmesbury believed that he went blind as divine punishment for his attempt to oust his blind predecessor from Exeter and that the clerk was uneducated. But this denigration is largely the result of Eadmer's bias. William went on at least eight missions to the pope and attended papal councils. He must have been well versed in Latin. He acted as a royal judge in both reigns. He was primarily a royal servant, but valued by the pope and not despised by Anselm. As bishop he rebuilt his cathedral (dedicated in 1133) and improved the organization of his chapter. In his diocese he founded three houses of canons regular, Plympton, Bodmin, and Launceston. The evidence suggests that he was interested in the education and efficient administration of his large and remote parish.

The fifth bishop consecrated in 1107 was Urban of Glamorgan, or Llandaff, 'in Wales'.[118] This was the first real success of the Norman conquerors west of Hereford, for Urban, although a kinsman and the archdeacon of his predecessor Herewald, and a member of the Llancarfan family which regarded

114.   See below 305 f.

115.   *GP* 303; Florence *s.a.* 1102. Fröhlich 153–4.

116.   Also spelled Regenhelm and Reinhelm. Florence *s.a.* 1102, 1107, 1115; *GP* 109–10, 117, 303–4. Fröhlich 154–6.

117.   *Ann. Plympton.* in Liebermann *Ungedruckte* 27; *HN* 68–9, 88, 110–11; *VA* 97–8, 113; *GR* 492; *GP* 111–14, 117, 202; Florence; OV (Chibnall) v. 204; Hugh *HCY* 47, 68, 73–5, 85. Fröhlich 159–66. D. W. Blake, 'Bishop William Warelwast', *Trans. Devonshire Assoc.* civ (1972) 15. Cf. R. W. Southern, *St Anselm and his Biographer* 172.

118.   Florence; *GP* 117; HH 253. J. E. Lloyd, *A History of Wales* (1939) ii. 450–1. Christopher Brooke, 'The Archbishops of St David's, Llandaff and Caerleon-on-Usk' in *Studies in the Early British Church*, ed. Nora K. Chadwick (1958) 201 ff. Davies *Episcopal Acts* ii. 515 ff. J. W. James, 'The book of Llan Dav and the diocesan boundaries disputes *c.* 960–1133', *Journal Nat. Library of Wales* xvi (1969–70) 332 ff.

that monastery and the bishopric as its hereditary estate, was imbued with Norman ideals and created the first see and diocese on the Anglo-Norman pattern in Wales. He was often to be found at the king's or primate's court, behaving just like an English bishop. In his attempt to define the boundaries of his diocese he pushed against both Hereford and, after 1115, the new diocese of St Davids; and it was while litigating against the latter that he died in 1134 at Rome. The see then remained vacant for six years, and early in the avoidance the *Book of Llandaff,* an historical dossier designed to prove Llandaff's antiquity, importance, size, and metropolitan status, and Urban's efforts on its behalf – and mostly forged – was put together, possibly by Caradoc of Llancarfan.

Three bishoprics fell vacant in the last two years of Anselm's life and all were promptly filled in a rather old-fashioned way. Henry first thought of his chaplain Thomas when Maurice of London died in September 1107, but on Gerard of York's death in May 1108 agreed that Thomas should become archbishop,[119] and that Richard of Beaumais (I), Rufus, should have London. Richard, an honorial baron of the Montgomeries,[120] had become Henry's trusted agent on the Welsh march when the Montgomeries, in the person of Robert of Bellême, were expelled from Shropshire in 1102;[121] and, although he had a reputation for knowledge of law, it was his military and administrative skill which earned him preferment. His transformation from sheriff to bishop gave him new opportunities which he was not slow to take. On the one hand, he used the offices and endowments of St Paul's to provide for his son, nephews, and other relatives, and, on the other, he became a great benefactor of his church and a patron of learning and of learned clerks. He carried on with the rebuilding of his cathedral; he encouraged the cathedral school; and he founded the Augustinian canonry of St Osyth's at Chich near Colchester in Essex, to which he appointed as first prior his clerk, William of Corbeil, who had once been in Ranulf Flambard's service.[122] On 9 August 1108 Richard assisted Anselm in the consecration of Ralf d'Escures as bishop of Rochester. Ralf was to succeed Anselm as archbishop of Canterbury, and William of Corbeil to succeed Ralf.

Ralf, the son of a Norman baron, Siegfried d'Escures, and with a half-brother who was likewise to make a career in the English church, had the same social background as Richard of Beaumais but a completely different education.[123] A child oblate in the monastery of Sées, which was under the lordship of the Montgomeries, he had risen to be abbot when he fell foul of Robert of Bellême, on the earl's expulsion from England, and fled to Henry's

119. Hugh *HCY* 15.

120. *HN* 197–8; *GP* 146, 262; OV (Chibnall) vi. 144. R. W. Eyton, *Antiquities of Shropshire* ii (1855) 192 ff. W. Stubbs, *Radulfi de Diceto Opera* (RS 1876) i, pp. xxi ff. Fröhlich 167–70. Brooke and Keir, *London 800–1216,* 134–7.

121. Leland's notes from William de Vere's Life of St Osyth, *Itinerary,* ed. Lucy Toulmin Smith (1910) v. 168–9. See also Denis Bethell, 'The lives of St Osyth of Essex and St Osyth of Aylesbury', *AB* lxxxviii (1970) 91.

122. William de Vere *op. cit.,* 169.

123. *Chron.*; Florence; *GR* 472, 517; *GP* 125–132, 138, 265, 275; OV (Chibnall) iv. 168–71, vi. 46, 319; *Vita Gundulfi* in *Anglia Sacra* ii. 290–2; Gervase i. 10–11; Fröhlich 170–2.

court. On 24 August 1104, at the invitation of Ranulf Flambard, he took an important part in the translation of St Cuthbert at Durham; and Anselm, when he returned from exile, went to live with his old acquaintance. A monk of blameless life, well educated, and with a reputation for eloquence and light-hearted humour (although William of Malmesbury thought that this verged on frivolity), he was *persona grata* to both the archbishop and the king.

Anselm died on 21 April 1109. Except on this latest occasion he had had no influence on the appointment to bishoprics, and, although highly respected by many of his brethren, had been forced by his attitudes to operate outside the mainstream of English ecclesiastical life. His policies had always been too extreme for general acceptance. On his death Henry appointed to York and left Canterbury vacant, filling the latter only when Thomas II of York died. It seems that at this time he wanted to have but one archbishop.

The promotion to York of Thomas, provost of Beverley, the son of Bishop Samson of Worcester, brother of Richard bishop of Bayeux and nephew of Archbishop Thomas I, and probably a disappointed candidate on his uncle's death nine years before,[124] raised the usual problems, particularly since Thomas had been educated in the chapter and was expected loyally to withstand the claims of Canterbury. But, although Thomas resisted the dying Anselm, he then, at the king's command and persuaded by the bishops, abandoned his chapter's case.[125] Renowned for his sexual purity, but addicted to gluttony, and so fat that he could hardly move, he died as a young man through overeating, after only four years as archbishop.[126] Eilaf, the last hereditary parson of Hexham, made a sour jest when his four year old son, Ailred, the future Cistercian saint, 'miraculously' announced the archbishop's death.[127]

The subsequent Canterbury election is the best documented of this period, presumably because of the debate among the magnates on the qualities required of the primate and the successful challenge to the king's wishes.[128] At a council at Windsor in 1114, four years after the death of Anselm, Henry proposed the election of his Italian doctor, Abbot Faricius of Abingdon. The magnates wanted a Norman, one of themselves, and suggested Ralf d'Escures of Rochester, and in the end Henry agreed. Ralf substituted at Rochester the aged Ernulf abbot of Peterborough, a Frenchman and former monk at St Symphorien, Beauvais, who had studied under Ivo of Chartres at Beauvais and Lanfranc at Bec, and later joined Lanfranc at Canterbury to take the post of schoolmaster. Under Anselm he rose to be prior.[129] A great builder at Canter-

124.   Above 77.

125.   Above 43.

126.   *Chron.*; Florence; *GP* 260–3; Hugh *HCY* 29–33; *Vita S. Oswaldi* in Simeon *Historical Works* i. 370. Fröhlich 172–7.

127.   'Vere ille obiit qui male vivit', Walter Daniel, *Epistola ad Mauricium* in *Walter Daniel's Life of Ailred*, ed. and trans. F. M. Powicke (Nelson's Medieval Classics 1950) 72.

128.   *GP* 125 ff.

129.   *Chron.*; Florence; *GP* 137–8; *Vita Gundulfi* in *Anglia Sacra* ii. 292; HH 245. *Textus Roffensis*, ed. T. H. Hearne (1720), *Early English Manuscripts in Facsimile:* vii and xi: *TR*, pts 1 and 2, ed. Peter Sawyer (1957, 1962). F. Liebermann, 'Notes on the Textus Roffensis', *Archaeologia Cantiana* xxiii (1898) 101. For his theological essays, d'Achery, *Spicilegium*, iii. 464

bury and Peterborough and a notable reformer, he had less scope at Rochester. But by compiling there the *Textus Roffensis* he preserved a corpus of legal and historical texts of the utmost importance. He was generally considered a very good man and an excellent prelate.

Ralf's decline was faster than Ernulf's. Ill-health made him irascible and a peevish defender of his rights. On 16 August 1114 Henry appointed his friend Thurstin to York, and, unexpectedly and to everyone's dismay, a new struggle broke out between the metropolitans, fiercer, more protracted, and with greater consequences than ever before.[130] Thurstin, another from Bayeux, once Rufus's clerk, was Henry's almoner, possibly in charge of the privy purse. A canon of St Paul's he was well educated and a good lawyer, and had the reputation of being an excellent civil and military administrator. As archbishop he earned golden opinions in the north (John of Hexham was an enthusiastic admirer); and before his edifying death he became a Cluniac monk at Ponte-fract. But, like another royal favourite half a century later, he espoused the cause of his church more fanatically than any of his predecessors, was prepared to break with the king and the English bishops, and eagerly used papal author-ity to further his own ends. After his belated enthronement in 1121, possibly because he had no friends in the south, he became an important figure in the north, the first and last archbishop in this period to act as a true metropolitan beyond the Humber. In 1138 he organized the defence of Yorkshire against the Scots which led to the battle of the Standard.[131] Thurstin's brother Ouen, bishop of Evreux since 1113, seems often to have been in England and sometimes in company with his brother. He died in 1139, just before Thurstin, having taken the habit of the canons regular at Merton.[132]

Less favourably mentioned by monastic chronicles was Theulf, appointed to Worcester at Christmas 1113.[133] Like his predecessor, Samson, he was a canon of Bayeux and a royal clerk, but William of Malmesbury claimed that although he had as big a belly as Samson he was less hospitable and generous and also became increasingly oppressive to the monks. Too late – on his unedifying deathbed – Theulf lamented the simony with which he had acquired the bishopric. In 1115 it was the turn of another royal clerk, Geoffrey of Clive, at neighbouring Hereford.[134] He was dead within five years and was remembered as an austere man who was not over-generous to the poor. Also in 1115 Henry gave St David's to Bernard, the queen's chancellor, a clerk whom he used as an ambassador, principally in the defence of Canterbury at Rome.[135] This was the Normans' second success in Wales; and Bernard not only estab-

(a matrimonial question), 471 (a christological question). Cf. also R. W. Southern, *St Anselm and his biographer* 269–70, and see below 168 f.

130.   *Chron.*; Florence; *GP* 262–6; *HR* 254; John of Hexham 285–305; Wm of Newburgh 49–50. Above 43 f. D. Nicholl, *Thurstan, Archbishop of York (1114–40)* (1964).

131.   Ailred of Rievaulx, *De Bello Standardii* in *PL* cxcv, 701.

132.   John of Hexham 301; OV (Chibnall) vi. 530.

133.   *Chron.*; Florence; *GP* 290.

134.   John of Worcester 14; *GP* 304.

135.   *Chron.*; Florence; *HR* 269; *Hist. Nov.* 11, 51; Hugh *HCY* 90, 112, 114, 121. Lloyd, *History of Wales,* ii. 452–4. Brooke, 'The Archbishops of St David's, Llandaff and Caerleon-on-Usk', 215 ff.

lished a see and diocese according to Anglo-Norman customs, but also, like Urban of Llandaff, accepted his church's mythical past. Taking advantage of the political disorder which followed Henry I's death, he almost succeeded in making St David's a metropolitan church. He died when about to press his claims once more at the council of Rheims in 1148.

In the last fifteen years of the reign Henry made sixteen appointments to sees. Because of the truce in the Canterbury–York dispute and Henry's greater piety after the death of his only legitimate son in November 1120 vacancies were generally short. Moreover, there was a slight shift in the king's policy. Although royal clerks still got their share of the bishoprics, and he even went as low as the keeper of his seal, more room was found for episcopal clerks and members of the religious orders. The promotion of canons regular and archdeacons was a sign of a new age.

Henry's four appointments in the year April 1120-March 1121 were, however, on the old pattern. The first was of Henry's clerk and ambassador, David the Scot, probably a Welshman, to Bangor, with the necessary agreement of Gruffydd ap Cynan and the local church.[136] The power of the Normans was reaching into North Wales, but not as effectively as in the south. David, who had accompanied Henry's daughter to Germany in 1110 and had written a now lost panegyric of the Emperor's Italian campaign of 1111 and his treatment of the pope, played a full part in the life of the English church and apparently entrusted his diocesan duties to a holy archdeacon, Simeon. In the following year, 1121, the king rewarded three more of his clerks, giving Richard *de Capella,* keeper of the royal seal, Hereford,[137] Everard of Montgomery, a former archdeacon of Salisbury, Norwich,[138] and Robert Peche, an obscure person, Chester.[139] None of these cut much of a figure in the church. But their being in office when William of Malmesbury wrote his *Gesta Pontificum* saved their reputations. William did reproach the last for following in his diocese the hated policies of the infamous Robert of Limesey, but allowed that he was an agreeable, hospitable man, who started great buildings at Lichfield. Robert's son, Richard Peche, obtained the see in 1161. Everard was deposed in 1145 'for cruelty'.[140] As a result of these appointments in 1121–22 fifteen of the eighteen bishops were former royal clerks, the highest proportion since the Conquest and perhaps in the whole history of the English church. The greater recruitment of talented clerks into the royal service may have contributed to the situation. But the opportunities for advancement in a purely ecclesiastical career which were opening up at the same time, and for the same reasons, produced another set of claimants to bishoprics which the king could not entirely overlook.

136.   *HN* 259; John of Worcester 58; *GR* 498–9, 502. Lloyd, *History of Wales,* ii. 454–5. Davies *Episcopal Acts* ii. 550 ff. F. Hausmann, *Reichskanzlei und Hofkapelle unter Heinrich V. und Konrad III* (Schriften der MGH xiv, Stuttgart 1956); cf Karl Leyser, 'England and the Empire in the early twelfth century', *TRHistS.* 5th ser. x (1960) 61.

137.   *HN* 290; *GP* 304; *HR* 259.

138.   *HN* 293; *GP* 429. Edward J. Kealey, *Roger of Salisbury* 101, includes him among the relatives of that great nepotist.

139.   *Chron.*; *HN* 290; *GP* 310–11; *HR* 259.

140.   HH *De contemptu mundi* 316.

On 20 October 1122 the archbishop of Canterbury, Ralf d'Escures, died, and Henry immediately concerned himself with his replacement. As in 1114 there were divided counsels. On the last occasion the prelates and magnates had combined to prevent the king appointing an unworthy monk. This time there was a powerful party among the bishops, led by Roger of Salisbury, who wanted to prevent the election of any monk at all. In the end there was a general compromise: the monks of Christ Church with reluctance elected the least offensive of the bishops' candidates, William of Corbeil, a canon regular, prior of St Osyth's, Chich, in Essex. William had had an interesting career.[141] A clerk of Ranulf Flambard bishop of Durham, and then of Richard of Beaumais bishop of London, he became a canon of St Martin's, Dover, and later first prior of St Osyth's. He had studied under Master Anselm of Laon, had been friendly with Anselm of Canterbury, and was acknowledged to be both a good man and an excellent scholar. But he was austere, perhaps avaricious, and certainly a reformer; and his policies were not popular in all quarters. Within a few years, because of the changed conditions – Thurstin's age and isolation, the Canterbury forgeries, and new administrative development in the church at large – a working solution was found to the fifty-year-old controversy between Canterbury and York.[142] And in 1125 he appointed his archdeacon John, the nephew of Ralf d'Escures, to Rochester, a man who had protested at the council of Rheims in 1119 against the pope's intention to consecrate Thurstin before he had made his profession to Canterbury. The appointment of a clerk to Rochester was a significant break with tradition.[143] But it was the important legatine councils held at Westminster in 1125, 1127, and 1129, the first summoned by a papal legate, John of Crema, the others by the archbishop, which severely jolted the church.[144] The definition of simony was extended and many traditional fees were condemned. Clerical marriage and unchastity (and archdeacons were named) and the hereditary descent of benefices were prohibited. Except among the religious orders these laws were widely unpopular, and usually evaded.

No less important for the archbishop's reputation and fateful for the future of the English church was the council assembled by the king on 29 April 1128 to secure from his magnates recognition of his daughter Matilda as his heiress and successor.[145] Roger of Salisbury was the master of ceremonies. First the archbishops swore, then the bishops. The abbots were called last, after the lay magnates from the king of Scots and the queen of England to the sheriffs and the more noble of the knights. Anselm abbot of Bury St Edmunds (Archbishop Anselm's nephew) in the name of all the abbots protested against this order of precedence. But the king would have none of it. Ecclesiastical law and custom did not run in the royal court. In 1135 William of Corbeil crowned

141.   *Chron.*; John of Worcester 17; *GP* 146; Simeon *De Mirac. et Translat. S. Cuthberti* in *HDE* 258; *HR* 268–73; John of Hexham 287–8; HH 256; *Hist. Nov.* 11; Gervase i. 10, 96–9; *HCY* 109. Denis Bethell, 'William of Corbeil and the Canterbury York dispute', *JEH* xix (1968) 145, 'The Lives of St Osyth of Essex and St Osyth of Aylesbury', *AB* lxxxviii (1970) 75.

142.   Above 44.

143.   John of Worcester 19; *GP* 265; HH 245; Gervase i. 100.

144.   Below 129.

145.   John of Worcester 26–8.

Matilda's supplanter, Stephen, and all the bishops forswore their oaths. It can easily be understood how Henry, hereditary archdeacon of Huntingdon, came to regard William as the only archbishop of Canterbury since the Conquest unworthy of the post.[146]

Henry's four appointments in the period 1123–25 were of the usual type. Lincoln, after Robert Bloet's death, was given to Roger of Salisbury's nephew and archdeacon, Alexander, another who had been educated at Laon.[147] Although the promotion of archdeacons was a new departure, it was inevitable when bishops began appointing their nephews (or sons) to that post. Brought up in luxury, Alexander lived a life of ostentation which caused hardship to his subordinates. He rebuilt his cathedral church which had been destroyed by fire, founded four monasteries, and built three castles. He preferred a brother and a nephew to archdeaconries in his church. His archdeacon of Huntingdon, Henry, when dedicating to him his *Historia Anglbrum,* hailed him as the chief ornament of the English kingdom and people. By Stephen's reign he was emulating Henry of Blois as a prince-bishop; but, more weakly based and with less resources, he suffered even greater vicissitudes of fortune.[148] Also in 1123 the bishopric of Bath was filled by the new queen's chancellor, Godfrey, a native of Louvain, who had accompanied her from that county.[149] In 1125 the noble-born Siegfried d'Escures, also called Pelochin, abbot of Glastonbury, a half brother of the recently deceased archbishop of Canterbury, was promoted to the secular see of Chichester.[150] He was deposed in 1145 because, according to Henry of Huntingdon, he was a 'parasite' (*gnatonicus* = Gnatho: Terence *Eunuchus*). A better choice in 1125 was Simon, who had succeeded Godfrey as Queen Adela's chancellor.[151] He was given the monastic see of Worcester, and although a clerk, both John of Worcester and William of Malmesbury thought well of him. He was pious, upright, pleasant, and generous.

Henry's last seven appointments to the bench show how eclectic he could be. Besides his own nephew, royal clerks, and episcopal nephews and archdeacons, he patronized one foreign scholar of European fame, and two Augustinian priors. Gilbert the Universal, appointed to London in 1128, had a dazzling reputation for learning.[152] A Breton and relation of Bishop Hervey of Bangor, a pupil of Anselm of Laon, a commentator on the Old Testament and a contributor to the *Glossa Ordinaria,* he became the schoolmaster at Auxerre, perhaps also at Nevers, and a canon of Lyons. Retained by Thurstin of York in

146. HH *De contemptu mundi* 314.

147. *Chron.*; John of Worcester 17; HH 245–80; *De contemptu mundi,* 302–3, 316; *Hist. Nov.* 51; *GSteph* 48, 104; Giraldus Cambrensis *Vita S. Remigii* 33; John of Schalby, *ibid.* 197–8. Below 249.

148. Below 95 ff.

149. *Chron.*; John of Worcester 17–18; *HR* 269; HH 245; *Historiola* 22–3.

150. The name is sometimes rendered 'Seffrid'. *Ann. Cicestrenses* in Liebermann *Ungedruckte* 94–5, *s.a.* 1125, 1145, 1150; John of Worcester 17–19; *GP* 265; HH 245.

151. John of Worcester 18–19; *GP* 290–1; HH 245; John of Hexham 300; Gervase i. 138.

152. John of Worcester 26; HH 307, 247, 253, 307–8; *Hist. Pont.* 19; Hugh *HCY* 127; *Liber Eliensis* 279. Beryl Smalley, 'Gilbertus Universalis bishop of London (1128–34) and the problem of the *Glossa Ordinaria',* *Recherches de théologie ancienne et médiévale* vii (1935) 235; viii (1936) 24; ix (1937) 365; *The Study of the Bible* (1952) 60–1. Brooke and Keir, *London 800–1216,* 356.

1126 to plead his case at Rome, he changed sides, and, presumably in consequence, earned this reward from Archbishop William and the king. An old man with many nephews, he only lasted seven more years, and the unexpected riches of a bishopric turned him, it seems, into an avaricious miser. No less suspect was the appointment to Chester in 1129. Geoffrey de Clinton, one of Henry's most important servants, is said to have promised the king three thousand marks for the promotion of his nephew, Roger, archdeacon of Buckingham. Little is known about this bishop.[153] He was blamed, with Henry of Winchester and Alexander of Lincoln, by the author of *Gesta Stephani* for being too involved in military affairs in Stephen's reign; but as he was with Arnulf archdeacon of Sées in the successful legation sent by Stephen to Rome in 1139 to defend him against the charges of the Angevins, he must also have been considered an able and suitably educated clerk.

Henry, the fourth son of Stephen I, count of Blois, and Adela, the Conqueror's daughter, was educated at Cluny as an oblate, rose to the office of prior, and in 1126 was brought to England by his uncle and given the abbey of Glastonbury when Siegfried d'Escures was promoted to Chichester.[154] He retained Glastonbury after his elevation to rich Winchester in 1129, and in 1139 added the deanery of St Martin le Grand, London, and at an unknown date the deanery of Holy Cross, Waltham, pluralism which brought him great wealth. Henry held the bishopric for almost forty-two years, was papal legate in England from 1139 to 1143, and was undoubtedly the greatest figure in the English church between Anselm and Thomas Becket, whom he survived. A prince by birth and inclination, endowed with intelligence, educated for high office, and with an appetite for power, the only surprise is that he was content with the English provincial scene. But his behaviour could arouse strong opposition, and his greatest ambitions even in England, such as the archbishopric of Canterbury or alternatively a new western province, were thwarted.

No exception could be taken to Henry's morals, religion, learning, or attention to business. His private life was pure; he was a devoted son of Cluny and the patron of monasteries and hospitals in his diocese; and although not a creative scholar, he was an eloquent speaker, a man of taste, and a patron of other scholars. He bought heathen statues in Rome to adorn his buildings in Winchester. He was a careful administrator, surveyed his episcopal city, and improved the economy of all his possessions. He was quite fearless in his behaviour, whether defending the rights of the church or those of his family. But his ability to treat kings and archbishops as equals and his belief that he could through influence and money manipulate Rome, sometimes led to his discomfiture when his back was turned. It is possible that he planned his brother's seizure of the throne in 1135, and it is likely that if he could have

---

153.   John of Worcester 29; *HR* 283; HH 303; *GSteph* 104; *Hist. Pont.* 83. For Geoffrey 'who had been raised from the dust' by Henry – OV (Le Prévost) iv. 164 – see especially H. G. Richardson and G. O. Sayles, *The Governance of Medieval England,* 175–7, 219–20 etc.

154.   The standard work on Henry is Lena Voss, *Heinrich von Blois, Bischof von Winchester (1129–71): Historische Studien* ccx (Berlin 1932). See also Knowles *Episcopal Colleagues* 33–7. An interesting *Libellus,* with autobiographical material, compiled by Henry, is in *Adami de Domerham historia* ii. 305.

retained his influence over Stephen the inevitable changes in the English church after the end of a great but severe reign would have been more orderly and the king's government more successful. But with Stephen determined to go his own erratic way and Henry forced to fight both for the freedom of the church as he saw it and also for his own position, an incoherent period opened in which developments bad as well as good took place. Typically, although the church became more independent of the king, Henry filled it with his and Stephen's kinsmen. In a way Henry's position in the English church became more like that of a king than of a prince bishop.

King Henry I in his last five years made four appointments. In 1131 he moved the Augustinian prior, Robert of Béthune, from Llanthony to neighbouring Hereford.[155] Robert, for whom we have a *vita* written by one of the canons, but unfortunately rather short of biographical detail, turned from the liberal arts to theology, studying in France under William of Champeaux and Anselm of Laon, before entering the Welsh priory as a canon. It was believed that as bishop he lived a holy life, behaved with perfect propriety during the civil war, and was fearless against local evil-doers, such as the powerful Miles of Gloucester. Although he was a trusted agent of the papal curia, his canons considered him a candidate for sanctity.

In 1133 Henry made three bishops. To Ely he sent his treasurer, Nigel, a nephew of Roger of Salisbury, the brother of Alexander of Lincoln, and the father of Richard fitzNeal, Henry II's treasurer and author of the *Dialogus de Scaccario.*[156] He, like his brother was educated at Laon, no doubt studied mathematics there and picked up the latest arithmetical ideas. Ely welcomed his appointment; but with the rest of his kinsmen he became involved in the royal succession business, favoured the Angevin cause, and brought great hardship to his church and diocese. Henry had founded the diocese of Ely in 1109. In 1133 he made Carlisle the cathedral for a new diocese, covering Cumberland and Westmorland, hitherto in the archdeaconry of York, and to it appointed the Augustinian prior of Nostell (Yorks), Aldulf, a man with an English name.[157] At the same time, he gave Durham, vacant since Ranulf Flambard's death in 1128, to his chancellor, Geoffrey Rufus.[158] Geoffrey had been a clerk of the former chancellor, Ranulf, and himself trained William Cumin, who became chancellor to David king of Scots and in 1141 conspired to succeed Geoffrey at Durham. Geoffrey was more fortunate than his colleague at Carlisle, who seems always to have found it difficult, owing to Scottish hostility, to occupy his see. Durham's troubles came after Geoffrey's death. Geoffrey, like Ranulf Flambard, was a married clerk (a daughter is mentioned) with the usual nephews; and episcopal nepotism at Durham com-

155. John of Worcester 31; *GP* 304–5; John of Hexham 284, 298, 321; *Hist. Nov.* 51; *GSteph* 104, 106; *Vita* printed without the miracles in *Anglia Sacra* ii. 293. For his education, see below 229, 249 f.

156. *Hist. Nov.* 51; *GSteph* 48, 52, 65–7; Wm of Newburgh 36–7; *Lib. El.* 283 ff. and Appendix E; *Dialogus de Scaccario,* ed. Charles Johnson, 50. Knowles, *Episcopal Colleagues* 9–12.

157. *Adulfus,* often given as 'Adelulf'. John of Hexham 285, 298, 320, 322; HH 253; *Hist. Nov.* 27.

158. *HDE,* cont. I, 141–3, cont. II, 164; John of Hexham 285, 309, 316–17; HH 253. J. H. Round, 'Bernard the king's Scribe', *EHR* xiv (1899) 418.

plicated a disturbed situation. At the start he fell foul of his cathedral monks; but later he allowed them their privileges, and it was in his time that the building of the chapterhouse was completed. The pontificates of Archbishop Thurstin and Geoffrey Rufus were the last period of ecclesiastical order in the North before the accession of Henry II.

When Henry died in 1135 the number of sees in England and Wales had been raised from sixteen to twenty, and of the eighteen bishops nine were former royal clerks, five were monks, and four cathedral clergy. This mixture was the effect of new trends which had started in 1122 and kept steadily on course. And it was their persistence throughout Stephen's reign, rather than any novel policies, which was to produce by 1154 the complete reversal of the earlier position. (See diagram, p. 318.)

Henry of Huntingdon, in his *Epistola de contemptu mundi,* composed in the year of Henry I's death and revised about a decade later, after Stephen's restoration to power, passed under review all the English bishops who had died in his time, as an illustration of the transitoriness of human life and fame.[159] Apart from omitting the see of Hereford and the Welsh dioceses entirely and forgetting a few very early post-Conquest bishops, he gives fairly complete and accurate lists for 1066–1145, a total of forty-nine bishops. Henry as an archdeacon must have been accustomed to the seamier side of life, and he had been in the household of two bishops of Lincoln, Robert Bloet and Alexander, who were among the most worldly of the age, and he notices both of them kindly. Although his Epistle was a call to penitence and humility, he is not likely to have been unnecessarily severe in his judgments. He names twenty-seven bishops without comment and gives five a neutral epithet. Six bishops are noticed unfavourably, eleven favourably. In the last category four are scholars – five if John 'the doctor', bishop of Bath, is included. These figures can be interpreted as meaning that Henry considered two-thirds of the bishops to have been of satisfactory standard and the episcopal bench as a whole respectable.

He admired four out of the five archbishops of Canterbury: Lanfranc was a philosopher and a far-seeing man, Anselm a philosopher and a most saintly man, Ralf d'Escures was thought to be worthy of so high an office, and the present incumbent, Theobald of Bec, was entirely praiseworthy. Only William of Corbeil could not be praised, 'because there is nothing to praise'. In contrast, only one of the four archbishops of York, Thurstin, got a good notice: he was entirely praiseworthy. Of the three bishops of Lincoln, Robert Bloet was a most merciful man and Alexander was faithful and munificent. At Winchester William Giffard was most noble (a reference to his rank), but Henry of Blois was a new sort of monster, half monk half knight. Gilbert the Universal of London was a great philosopher; his successor (in 1141), Robert *de Sigillo,* was magnanimous. Of the Worcester bishops Samson was the most famous. At Norwich Herbert Losinga was a kindly and learned man whose writings still survived; but his successor, Everard of Montgomery, was deposed for cruelty. Roger of Salisbury was a man important in worldly affairs. At Chichester Pelochin (Siegfried d'Escures) was deposed for sodomy. Finally, among the bishops of Durham was Ranulf Flambard, a robber who set all

159. HH 314–16.

England on fire. Because Henry's judgments are casual and superficial they are of special value. They tell us what a well-informed man who had studied English history thought about the bishops he had recorded. What particularly impressed the archdeacon was that so many bishops had died.[160] But he also pointed the moral that few of those important men were remembered for anything, either good or bad.

The English bishops may well have been mediocre. But the English church had not remained isolated from western Christendom and was changing fast. The standard of education among the clergy had risen appreciably, and a good number of English clerks were going to northern France for more advanced studies. Bishops and their subordinates were more active in government, as the emergence of the archdeacon to importance proves. In Henry I's reign two archbishops of Canterbury, Anselm and William of Corbeil, had begun an effective drive to get an unmarried priesthood and emphasize the distinction between an ecclesiastical benefice and a lay fief.

Although it was not an age of great abbots, the old Benedictine houses in England flourished as religious and cultural centres. But public favour was turning towards more active orders, such as the Austin canons, or those, like the Cistercians, which practised more rigorously the apostolic life. Queen Edith and the court patronized the canons regular. She founded in London the priory of Holy Trinity, Aldgate (1107–08) and the leper hospital of St Giles 'in the Fields' of Holborn; Henry founded Cirencester and several smaller priories.[161] Augustinian houses, with their emphasis on an instructional ministry among the laity, usually in towns, appealed to men of business and even to monk-bishops as dissimilar as Anselm and Henry of Blois. But the king, who was helping to rebuild Cluny, where his nephew was a monk, still hankered after that aristocratic monasticism, and after the death of Edith in 1118 placed the convent he was building at Reading under Cluny's care and appointed as its first abbot Hugh of Amiens prior of Lewes.[162] Hugh, a pupil of Anselm of Laon and a distinguished theologian, was made archbishop of Rouen in 1130. He saw Henry I out of this world in 1135 and played a part in English history during Stephen's reign.

The landed aristocracy, especially in the north of England, looked with favour on the Cistercians, all the more since their houses were cheap to establish. Waverley was founded in Surrey in 1128 and its offshoot, Garendon in Leicestershire, in 1133. In the wilder areas Tintern was founded in 1131 and Rievaulx and Fountains in 1132. Stephen of Blois brought in 1124 the first Saviniac monks to Tulketh near Preston, and during his reign occurred one of the greatest monastic movements in the history of the English church.[163] The fashion of founding a religious community of some kind, from a great Cistercian abbey to a little home for the poor, swept through the high nobility, the

160. Cf. Peter Damiani, *De brevitate vitae pontificum Romanorum et divina providentia* in *PL* cxlv 471.

161. Brooke and Keir *London 800–1216,* 312 ff. Below 206 ff.

162. *Hist. Nov.* 12–13. Hardy *Catalogue* ii. 290–1. J. de Ghellinck *Le mouvement théologique du XIIe siècle 120–1, 183, L'Essor de la littérature latine au XIIe siècle* 193–4, bibliog. 190 n.

163. In a famous passage, William of Newburgh 53, associated the frantic building of castles and monasteries (God's fortresses) in this weak reign.

royal officials, and the bourgeoisie. Most of the orders favoured had their headquarters abroad. It is evident that the relative isolation of England from continental movements was rapidly coming to an end, not because there was anywhere a conscious drive to break down the barriers, but because England was joined to Normandy, which was part of France. The spread of ideas proceeded unhindered. Henry I, as much as Archbishop William of Corbeil, Bishop Henry of Blois, or Abbot Hugh of Reading, was a man of the new age. But, no more than his father, did he allow private piety to weaken his government.

At his accession in 1100 Henry had promised the church its freedom. Thirty years later, one night in Normandy, he had in succession three most frightening dreams.[164] First he was attacked by a crowd of rustics brandishing their farm implements; then by a squadron of knights armed cap-à-pie; and finally by a concourse of archbishops, bishops, abbots, deans, and priors, who in search of the lost possessions of their churches threatened him with the spikes of their pastoral staves. Grimbald, the king's doctor, who had noticed the nightmares, asked him about them in the morning, and then expounded them as Daniel did to King Nebuchadnezzar (Dan. 2), advising him to atone for his sins with alms. What the church most resented about his rule is revealed by the concessions his successor was forced to make. Basically Stephen promised the church restoration of all the property it had possessed in 1087, together with subsequent benefactions, and complete control over its own lands, movables, and persons.[165] The church felt strongly that not only Rufus but also Henry had deprived it of its proper rights, had treated it as 'dominical', as part of the royal demesne, when it should have been a separate order, self-sufficient and self-directing. It wanted the king to be the protector, not the destroyer, of its abundant liberties.

On 22 December 1135, three weeks after Henry's death, William of Corbeil, with the assistance of Henry of Winchester and Roger of Salisbury, crowned Stephen king.[166] No abbots and few nobles were present. Henry guaranteed Stephen's promise that he would restore and preserve the freedom of the church, and after Easter 1136 all the bishops swore fealty to the king for as long as he should preserve the liberty of the church and enforce ecclesiastical discipline. Stephen then gave the largely ecclesiastical charter of liberties which has already been mentioned; in it he was given a title which described his election and confirmation in terms more suited to a bishop.[167] The prelates were, no doubt, not only using the opportunity to obtain privileges from a weak prince in his weakest moment, but also salving their consciences, for all had

---

164. John of Worcester 32–3. Henry seems to have suffered from nightmares. In 1118 he dreamt that he was attacked by lions and saved only by the intervention of Petreus, first prior of Bermondsey: Bermondsey annals in *Annales Monastici* iii. 432.

165. See below 303 ff.

166. For the latest views of Stephen, see R. H. C. Davis, *King Stephen* (1967) and H. A. Cronne, *The Reign of Stephen* (1970); neither is particularly sympathetic to the more attractive sides of Stephen's character, for which see Frank Barlow, *The Feudal Kingdom of England* (3rd ed, 1972) 201 ff. Cf. also Isabel Megaw, 'The ecclesiastical policy of Stephen, 1135–39: a reinterpretation', *Essays in British and Irish History in Honour of James Eadie Todd*, ed. H. A. Cronne, T. W. Moody, and D. B. Quinn (1949) 24.

167. Below 304.

sworn in 1128 to receive Matilda as queen. But their rejection of the empress because of her autocratic ways and identification with imperial and anti-papal policies,[168] and of her husband, Geoffrey of Anjou, for many reasons, could be excused if they were to substitute a properly elected and just ruler who would remedy all the kingdom's wrongs. Stephen came from a family renowned for its piety, was himself religious, chivalrous, and generous, with a private life unusually respectable, and he had his clever episcopal brother at his side.

The king, however, quickly disappointed all the church's hopes. He tried to keep the royal rights intact; he soon ceased to take the advice of his brother; he was mistrustful of those who had been most faithful to his uncle; his baronial friends and counsellors had an aristocratic disdain of clerks; and once the civil war began the church was open to spoliation. Few of the combatants, least of all Stephen's mercenaries, respected ecclesiastical rights. Stephen, in the eyes of the church, changed from a model prince-elect into the worst kind of tyrant, the oppressor who could not even protect his victims from the oppression of others. Control of the church passed gradually out of his hands. The dioceses of Worcester, Hereford, Carlisle, and Durham came under the influence of his enemies. Henry of Winchester, when papal legate (1139–43), tried to take the place of his brother in the church.[169] And most churches took advantage of the weakness of royal government to manage their own affairs more independently, even if this often led to division and disorder. The English church was getting liberty of a kind it had not bargained for, to which it was unaccustomed, and which it did not altogether like. And since it always marginally preferred Stephen to Matilda and Geoffrey no quick or easy solution of the problem was possible.

Three episcopal sees were vacant at Stephen's accession, London, Bath, and Llandaff; and there were twenty vacancies in all (as well as four in the Welsh church) in the seventeen English and three Welsh sees during his reign of nineteen years. Three bishops, Henry of Winchester, Nigel of Ely, and Aldulf of Carlisle, went right through the reign; in ten dioceses there was but one change, in three there were two; only York, with four substitutions, was unstable. The average length of the vacancies, helped a little by the quick changes at York, was eighteen months, the traditional figure. In the first phase of the reign, which closed in 1139 with Bishop Henry's papal legation and the Angevin invasion, Stephen made only three appointments, Robert of Lewes to Bath in 1136, Robert I to Exeter in 1138, and Theobald of Bec to Canterbury in 1138. London remained vacant because of disputes within the chapter of St Paul's, the see of Llandaff because it was under the control of Earl Robert of Gloucester.

The choice of a Cluniac monk for Bath was certainly influenced by Henry of Blois, for Henry was at the time employing him as a specialist

168.   Her use of the title 'Empress', when she seems never to have received an imperial coronation, is discussed by Karl Schnith, " 'Kaiserin' Mathilde", *Grossbritannien und Deutschland: Festschrift für John W. P. Bourke* (Munich 1975) 166. Schnith is more sympathetic to her than most English historians, see his *'Regni et pacis inquietatrix*: zur Rolle der Kaiserin Mathilde in der "Anarchie" ', *Journal of Medieval History* ii (1976) 135.

169.   For church appointments influenced by Henry (and Stephen), see G. V. Scammell, *Hugh du Puiset* (1956) 6.

administrator at Glastonbury.[170] Robert, born in England of Flemish parents, was both pious and a man of business. His reorganization of his diocese, his restoration of the former see at Wells, and his rebuilding were much in line with the diocesan interests of his patron. When the civil war began he found himself in the middle of the fighting, and it has been suggested that he was the author of the *Gesta Stephani,* although the military interests of the chronicler do not entirely suit this rather reluctant and unfortunate soldier. He joined the empress when she triumphed in 1141, but was probably as usual following the lead of Henry of Winchester. The two Roberts who held Exeter between 1138 and 1160 have been badly confused.[171] The one appointed in 1138 was probably the nephew and archdeacon of his predecessor, William of Warelwast, and if so the succession probably represents the wishes of the cathedral chapter.

On 21 November 1136 William of Corbeil archbishop of Canterbury died, and once again there were divided counsels.[172] Henry of Winchester wanted to succeed and went abroad the better to negotiate with Pope Innocent II, who, threatened by an antipope, Anacletus, was at Pisa. But all he could obtain was the temporary administration of the diocese of Canterbury. Stephen was faced by serious difficulties in 1138 – Geoffrey of Anjou's invasion of Normandy, Robert of Gloucester's rebellion which removed the Welsh marches and south-west England from his control, and David of Scots' invasion of Yorkshire which was checked by the battle of the Standard on 22 August – but by Christmas he had weathered the storm. Likewise the pope had settled the Anacletus schism, and in the summer of 1138 he sent a legate, Alberic cardinal-bishop of Ostia, to England to investigate the situation and, presumably, watch over the Canterbury election. Alberic summoned a general council of the English church to meet at Westminster in December. Eighteen bishops, about thirty abbots, and a great number of other clergy and laity attended; and with Canterbury vacant and Thurstin of York dying and absent the legate had no rival except Henry of Winchester. At the council three abbots were deposed, and Robert was consecrated bishop of Exeter and Stephen's illegitimate son, Gervase, abbot of Westminster. Some sixteen canons were promulgated, mostly on the themes of the legislation of the last reign, including the prohibition of clerical marriage and illegal charges for services. But the threat to excommunicate usurpers of ecclesiastical movables and immovables struck a topical note.

At the very end of the council, after Henry of Blois had been sent by the legate to perform a ceremony at St Paul's, Theobald abbot of Bec was elected archbishop.[173] The move must have been prepared in advance by the

170.   John of Worcester 38; *Hist Nov.* 51; *GSteph* 39–41, 43; Gervase 138; *Historiola* 23–8. J. Armitage Robinson, *Somerset Historical Essays* (1921) 54–72. Knowles, *Episcopal Colleagues* 30–1. For his itinerary and familia, R. H. C. Davis, 'The authorship of the *Gesta Stephani'*, *EHR* lxxvii (1962) 209–32.

171.   The position is cleared up by D. W. Blake, 'The Church of Exeter in the Norman Period' (unpublished Exeter University MA thesis 1970) 125–6. For Robert I, see *Annal. Plympton.* in Libermann *Ungedruckte* 27; John of Worcester 48, 53; John of Hexham 300; *GSteph* 68; Gervase i. 138.

172.   Diceto 252; HH 265; John of Hexham 299; Gervase i. 109; John of Worcester 53; OV (Chibnall) vi. 478. Lena Voss, *Heinrich von Blois* 20–2. Tillmann 38–9.

173.   For Theobald, see Avrom Saltman, *Theobald Archbishop of Canterbury* (1956).

pope, the legate, the king, and some of the bishops, but had been carefully concealed from Henry. The bishop blamed his brother for this cowardly treachery and thereafter, although not entirely immune from family sentiments, played largely for his own hand. There can be no doubt that Stephen had opposed his brother's election; and the pope must have agreed. What we cannot know is what Innocent would have done if Stephen had pressed Henry's claims. Only the pope could transfer a bishop from one see to another. It may be, since he immediately compensated Henry with a standing papal legation,[174] that he would have agreed to the move.

Theobald, in whom Stephen had no particular interest, was a candidate sufficiently distinguished to cloak the real reason for his choice. (Lanfranc's appointment in 1070 over the head of Odo of Bayeux can be compared.) But the way in which he was appointed ensured that he would have a difficult time. He had to suffer not only the rivalry of Henry, the distrust of those bishops who were opposed to monk-bishops, and the suspicion of all his subjects to whom he was an unknown foreigner, but also the hostility of his new prior and chapter, for Jeremiah and the monks of Christ Church had not been consulted. Moreover, although spared, by York's troubles, the traditional conflict, he had the problem of the Angevin claim to the throne. Because of his Norman background he stood for the maintenance of the cross-Channel empire and after Stephen's loss of Normandy inevitably became an Angevin supporter, in the end negotiating Henry fitzEmpress's succession. And however honourably he behaved towards Stephen, he could not avoid occasionally incurring his displeasure. More serious for the future history of his cathedral church, he could not agree with his monks nor with those of St Augustine's. Changing from an abbot to a bishop, he recruited learned clerks as his advisers and helpers. These *eruditi,* who included his chancellor, John of Salisbury (bishop of Chartres in 1176), Master Vacarius, Roger of Pont l'Evêque, Thomas Becket, and John of Beaumais (bishop of Poitiers in 1163, archbishop of Lyons in 1182), had little sympathy with traditional monasticism. To his archdeaconry Theobald appointed in succession his brother Walter, Roger of Pont l'Evêque (1148), and Thomas Becket (1154). And he took every opportunity to advance his clerks. Even getting into a serious scrape did not debar Roger from one of the highest rewards.[175]

---

174. Tillman 41–50. See also above 44 f. and below 110 f.

175. Thomas Becket's household, fierce and probably unscrupulous enemies of Roger, reminded William archbishop of Sens in 1171–72 that in 1151x53, when he was in England with his uncle Henry of Winchester, Roger, then 'archdevil' of Canterbury, had had his penitent lover, a certain Walter, blinded and then hanged by lay judges whom he had suborned. Becket had persuaded Theobald to listen to Hilary of Chichester and John of Worcester and admit Roger to purgation in the monastic chapter at Canterbury; Roger had then gone to Rome and through the services of Gregory cardinal of St Angelo and much bribery had cleared himself completely. *MB* vii. 527–9. The clerks' claim was that Roger destroyed the man he had debauched because his accomplice had denounced him. Roger obviously maintained that he had been falsely accused. R. L. Poole, 'Two documents concerning Archbishop Roger of York', *Speculum* iii (1928) 84, regarded the story as a fiction; David Knowles, *Episcopal Colleagues* 13–14, considered it 'rash to attach any weight whatsoever to the precise charge of immorality made by the clerks'. Although it seems unlikely that all the circumstantial details of the affair were invented in 1171–72, the account was obviously biased, and stresses the charges which Roger rebutted rather than his repeated exculpation of improper behaviour.

It seems that the pope or his legate had also interfered in the appointment to Rochester, which was traditionally in the archbishop's gift. John (I) of Rochester had died in 1137, during the avoidance of Canterbury, and his successor was another John, who once styled himself as, 'exercising the episcopal office by papal precept'. This man seems to have been 'of Sées', perhaps a monk of that house, but more likely John bishop of Sées, a refugee from Angevin Normandy.[176] It must have been at this time that Robert Pullen was appointed archdeacon of Rochester,[177] and as he went on to Paris to teach theology, perhaps invited and certainly encouraged to stay by St Bernard, his English patron is more likely to have been the bishop of Sées, who had good contacts with the schools of Paris, than an obscure monk. Bishop John II was dead or had left Rochester by 1142.

Stephen followed the victory over his brother with a successful attack on an even better entrenched, but less influential group, Roger bishop of Salisbury and his family.[178] Believing, rightly or wrongly, that they were plotting with the Angevins, he trumped up charges against them at his Oxford court in June 1139 and required the three bishops – Roger, Alexander, and Nigel – to surrender their castles. Although Nigel escaped, the six castles were handed over, and in December Roger died of chagrin. In the meantime Henry of Winchester as papal legate attempted to put his brother on trial for his ill-treatment of the bishops, some revenge for the humiliation he himself had suffered.[179] Stephen, defended by Hugh of Amiens archbishop of Rouen, came through the ordeal unscathed. But that the king-duke could be treated in such a way shows how low the royal dignity had sunk and how high Henry was raising the clerical order.

Hardly was this episode over when Matilda and Robert of Gloucester landed in England and started the civil war. At Lincoln, just before he was captured on 2 February 1141, Stephen made three bishops. Two Welshmen, Uchtred of Llandaff and Maurice or Meurig of Bangor, both local choices, came to the king for confirmation and to Theobald for consecration.[180] Maurice, who arrived with his sponsors Robert of Hereford and Siegfried of Chichester, at first refused to swear fealty to Stephen. He said that he had been forbidden to take the oath by his predecessor's archdeacon, Simeon, a man of great holiness whom he regarded as his spiritual father. But when the other bishops argued that what they had done Maurice could do he gave way. Uchtred, a married archdeacon and another member of the Llancarfan family,

176. J. Thorpe, *Registrum Roffense* (1769) 8. The identity of John (II) has been much discussed. See Wharton, *Anglia Sacra* i. 343 n., R. L. Poole, 'The English bishops at the Lateran council of 1139', *EHR* xxxviii (1923) 62, W. Hunt, *ibid.* 559, A. Saltman, 'John II, bishop of Rochester', *EHR* lxvi (1951) 71. For John of Sées, the brother of Arnulf of Lisieux, see F. Barlow, *The Letters of Arnulf of Lisieux*, R. Hist. Soc. Camden 3rd ser. lxi (1939) pp. xi ff.

177. F. Courtney, *Cardinal Robert Pullen* (Analecta Gregoriana lxiv, Rome 1945) 9–10. For Pullen, see also below 252, 266, 308.

178. Edward J. Kealey, *Roger of Salisbury*, 173 ff.

179. Below 305 ff.

180. John of Worcester, 58, 60. Lloyd, *History of Wales*, ii. 483–5; Davies *Episcopal Acts* ii. 519–21. Maurice was a reformer; for the wicked clerks he expelled and the wickedness of the Welsh in general, see Archbishop Theobald to the pope: *The Letters of John of Salisbury* (Nelson) no 87, (PL) 53.

had taken the bishopric because his predecessor's son, Nicholas, was still too young to succeed.

The third confirmation was that of William fitzHerbert archbishop elect of York.[181] But if Stephen and Henry of Winchester thought that this was the end of the troublesome business they were much mistaken. After the death of Thurstin early in 1140 Henry had persuaded the chapter to elect his and Stephen's nephew, Henry of Sully abbot of Fécamp who, however, withdrew when the pope would not allow him, like his uncle, to hold both offices together. Pressure was then put on the canons through William of Aumale earl of York, to elect their treasurer, William fitzHerbert, another royal nephew and from the highest ministerial circle. Although William was a generous and attractive man, capable of piety, and indeed canonized in 1226, in 1140 he symbolized the old order and, probably, the interference of the South in the North. He had some support from the Benedictines and was entirely acceptable to the English episcopate and baronage, but was bitterly opposed by the archdeacons of his church and by the Cistercian abbots and Augustinian priors of his province who would have preferred Waldef, prior of Kirkham.[182] They pressed a charge of simony against him and eventually procured his deposition by the Cistercian pope, Eugenius III (1147).

After the battle of Lincoln Stephen was in the hands of the Angevins from February until 1 November 1141. Henry of Blois held a legatine council at Winchester in April which recognized Matilda as ruler of England,[183] and in June she entered London for her coronation. But she aroused no enthusiasm. Theobald made, with Stephen's consent, a token submission; but only five bishops, Henry of Winchester, Bernard of St David's, Robert of Hereford, and Nigel of Ely, were in regular attendance on her, and Henry was soon disillusioned by her refusal to rely on his advice. The see of London had been vacant since 1134.[184] Gilbert the Universal's nephew, Arcoid, had tried to secure the election of Anselm abbot of Bury St Edmunds, but the kinsmen of Gilbert's predecessor, Richard of Beaumais (I), still powerful in the chapter, were intent on getting the see for one of themselves. Matilda decided to appoint an old servant of her father's, Robert *de Sigillo,* a former Keeper of the Seal who had become a monk at Reading. Robert had a son, whom he made a canon; but he had put off the old Adam and earned a high reputation as a reforming bishop. Matilda also proposed to invest William Cumin, her uncle David's candidate, with the bishopric of Durham, a much less popular action and one frustrated when she was expelled from London by the citizens.[185]

181.   John of Worcester 61; John of Hexham 306–25; Gervase 123, 135; Wm of Newburgh 55–6; Winchester annals in *Annales Monastici* ii. 54. R. L. Poole, 'The appointment and deprivation of St William, archbishop of York', *EHR* xlv (1930) 273. D. Knowles, 'The case of St William of York', *Camb HJ* v (1936) 162, 212, reprinted *The Historian and Character* (1963) 76. G. V. Scammell, *Hugh du Puiset* (1956) 8 ff. Life and Miracles in B.M. MS Harl. 2, ff. 76–88, from the Austin priory of Thornton-on-Humber, Lincs. The account is not very informative.

182.   Below 210.

183.   Below 306 f.

184.   Florence *cont.* 131; *Hist. Pont.* 46, 88; John of Hexham 309, 324; Diceto *Abbrev. Chron.* 254; Gervase 142; OV (Chibnall) vi. 478. Brooke and Keir *London 800–1216,* 356–7.

185.   *HDE cont.* i. 145.

After Stephen's release from prison Henry of Winchester had him recognized as king again by a church council held at Westminster,[186] and at Christmas Stephen and his queen were crowned by the archbishop at Canterbury. The civil war continued fiercely, but began to abate in 1147 and by 1149 was virtually over. Stephen had lost Normandy to Geoffrey of Anjou, had no control over the western and northern parts of England, and was without great authority in the remainder; but his fortunes were on the mend and his opponents became reconciled to waiting for his death.

No less hampered was the archbishop of Canterbury. In 1142 Theobold nominated to Rochester Ascelin (or Anselm), a former sacristan of Christ Church and prior of Dover (1139–42), and the new bishop so harassed his absentee archdeacon, Robert Pullen, that in 1144 this famous theologian left Paris for Rome and a cardinal's hat.[187] But it was Henry of Blois, still papal legate, who had the greater influence on episcopal elections. In 1142 he got his archdeacon, Jocelin of Bohun, a member of a baronial family, made bishop of Salisbury, a position he held for forty-two years. Jocelin's brother Richard became bishop of Coutances, and his son Reginald, whom he made his archdeacon, bishop of Bath in 1174.[188]

Henry's last success was the election of William of Ste Barbe dean of York, to Durham.[189] Since 1141 William Cumin, the chancellor of King David of Scots, aided by a nephew of the late bishop, supporters in the cathedral and castle, and several local barons, was in control of the city and castle and attempting to become bishop in the interests of the king of the Scots and the Empress. He was resisted locally by a party led by the cathedral prior and Archdeacon Ranulf, the late Bishop Ranulf Flambard's nephew, and, after Stephen's restoration, was opposed by the legate. The loyalists in Durham resisted enormous pressure and endured great hardship before, in the spring of 1143, escaping to York and, on papal authority, electing there Dean William, a man of good reputation. The legate consecrated William in June, after Stephen had given his consent; but it was not until October 1144 that the new bishop could enter his episcopal city. William Cumin had been forced to submit by ecclesiastical censures and dwindling baronial support. He surrendered the castle, did penance, and paid damages.

On the other frontier, despite Welsh political revival, the English church even extended its influence. North Wales (Gwynedd), although usually dominated by Chester (and perhaps for that reason) had hitherto been left in an ecclesiastically ambiguous position. In 1125 it had been proposed to create a

186. Below 307 f.

187. *Annales ecclesiae Roffensis* in *Anglia Sacra* i. 343; Registrum Roffense, ed. J. Thorpe (1769) 39–40. For Robert Pullen, see below 252, 266, 308. F. Courtney, *Cardinal Robert Pullen (Analecta Gregoriana* lxiv, Rome 1945) 11 ff.

188. John of Hexham 302. In 1140 Stephen had attempted to nominate his chancellor, Philip of Harcourt, archdeacon of Evreux; but the chapter, supported by the legate, objected. John of Worcester 60–1 and n; Waverley annals in *Annales Monastici* ii. 228; OV (Chibnall) vi. 536. Philip became in 1142 a distinguished bishop of Bayeux. For Jocelin see especially Knowles *Episcopal Colleagues* 17–22 and appendix II.

189. *HDE* cont. i, 143 ff., cont. ii, 161 ff.; John of Hexham 309, 312 ff., 326, 328; Geoffrey of Coldingham 3. Bernard of Clairvaux interfered: see F. E. Croydon, 'Abbot Laurence of Westminster and Hugh of St Victor', *MARS* ii (1950) 169–70.

diocese for the region, to be awarded with its neighbours, Bangor and Chester, to the province of York;[190] when that scheme fell through nothing was done until 1143, when a certain Gilbert, from his name a Norman but about whom we know nothing, was consecrated by Theobald to St Asaph.[191] It does not seem that Gilbert had much success.

In 1143 Henry of Blois held several legatine councils to deal with the affairs of the church and the kingdom.[192] His aim was to restore orderly government, and he directed that disturbers of the peace and enemies of the church should be excommunicated. Between October 1143, when Henry lost his legation on Innocent II's death, and spring 1150, when Eugenius III granted Theobald a legation, there was an uneasy period in which the archbishop had to rely on his metropolitan and primatial powers and found Henry an awkward subordinate. It is likely, however, that the English church had had enough of strong government – the legate had become King Henry writ large – and welcomed the return to more normal conditions, a view shared by the papal curia, which thought that Henry used his position to further his private policies. Nevertheless, the bishop of Winchester had taken advantage of the collapse of royal power to show what a great church leader could do. Thanks to him the English church acquired many liberties to which its more progressive members had long aspired. It would never be the same again, as Henry fitzEmpress was to discover. But the episode was an aberration. Henry was to have no successors.

Stephen seems to have had little influence on the episcopal elections of 1146–47. First William Turbe, prior of the monastery, was elected bishop of Norwich in 1146. His leadership of the party which claimed that William, the skinner's apprentice, had been martyred by the Jews and his agitation against those 'ritualistic murderers', rendered him offensive to the king, who was committed to protecting the Jewish community. The sheriff of Norwich, it seems, tried to prevent William's election.[193] Then, after William fitzHerbert had been deposed from York, there was again a divided election. The dean, Robert of Ghent, who was also Stephen's chancellor, and the treasurer, Hugh of le Puiset, Stephen's nephew and a close intimate of Henry of Winchester, led a party which favoured Master Hilary, a former clerk of Henry's who had recently been practising as an advocate at the papal court.[194] The bishops of Durham (the former dean of York) and Carlisle (an Austin canon) and the precentor and archdeacons of York supported Henry Murdac, a Yorkshireman whom Bernard abbot of Clairvaux had made abbot of Fountains, and who had reanimated the campaign against Archbishop William. The pope on appeal

190. Above 44.

191. Gervase, i. 126. Lloyd, *History of Wales,* ii. 455–7, 485; Davies *Episcopal Acts* ii. 545. M. Richter, 'Giraldus Cambrensis', *Journ. Nat. Library of Wales* xvi (1969–70) 227, interpreting a letter of the chapter of St David's to Pope Eugenius III, recorded in Gerald's *De Invectionibus,* in *Opera* iii. 58, argues, not entirely convincingly, that Gilbert (in the text 'Richard') was consecrated by Theobald during Stephen's captivity (1141).

192. Below 131.

193. Gervase i. 130; Vita S. Willelmi Norwic. 112. Below 241 ff. Knowles *Episcopal Colleagues* 31–3.

194. John of Hexham 306–25; Gervase i. 123, 135; Wm of Newburgh 56–7.

from the rival parties decided for Henry Murdac, whom he consecrated archbishop at Trier on 7 December 1147. But he ordered Hilary to be compensated
by appointment to Chichester,[195] and he is reported to have remarked after
meeting Gilbert of Sempringham at the general chapter at Cîteaux in September that if only he had met Gilbert earlier he would have made him
archbishop of York.[196] Stephen and his brother were furious at this disregard of
their wishes and interference with their patronage, and on the archbishop's
eventual return to England prevented him from occupying his see. Henry
Murdac excommunicated the earl of York and Hugh of le Puiset, and Hugh
coolly returned the compliment. Henry had to take refuge with his suffragan
bishops.

　　　　　Stephen's cousin and rival, Robert earl of Gloucester, one of the
main pillars of the Angevin cause in England,[197] died on 31 October 1147, and
Stephen became even bolder in ecclesiastical as well as secular affairs. Not only
did he refuse to accept Henry Murdac, he also, by reasserting another traditional royal policy,[198] attempted to control the English representation at
Eugenius's council at Rheims and confine it to three 'safe' bishops. The pope,
however, had summoned all bishops and abbots, and Theobald was determined
to attend. On 14 March the archbishop consecrated his brother and arch-
deacon, Walter, as bishop of Rochester[199] – no doubt the better to look after his
interests in England should his defiance of the king lead to reprisals – and
Nicholas ap Gwrgant, monk of Gloucester, a son of Bishop Urban of the
Llancarfan family, to Llandaff,[200] and then went to the council with Gilbert
Foliot abbot of Gloucester, despite the royal ban. There he joined his clerks,
John of Salisbury, Roger of Pont l'Evêque, and Thomas Becket, and also found
Henry Murdac, still in company with his Cistercian patrons.

　　　　　The diplomatic position was delicately poised. Eugenius was insecure in Italy; his main supporter, Louis VII of France, had left on the Second
Crusade; and the Crusade was going so badly that the pope and Bernard of
Clairvaux were incurring blame.[201] But Geoffrey of Anjou, whom Eugenius
had met at Paris in 1147, had obtained a firm grip on Normandy; his son, Henry
fitzEmpress, was growing up; and the pope felt that he could at least threaten
Stephen with ecclesiastical penalties for his misdeeds. He suspended all the
missing bishops and abbots (Henry of Winchester by name) and would have
excommunicated the king had not Theobald interceded. Stephen answered by
refusing both archbishops permission to return. Theobald waited at St Omer
and placed an interdict on the kingdom. The pope announced that he would

195.　For Hilary, Mayr-Harting *Acta* nos. 19 ff.; John of Hexham 320–1; Gervase i. 135; Diceto,
Abbrev. Chron. 263. Knowles *Episcopal Colleagues* 24–7; Mayr-Harting, 'Hilary bishop of
Chichester (1147–1169) and Henry II', *EHR* lxxviii (1963) 209.

196.　*Vita S. Gileberti confessoris* in *Monasticon*, vi. 2, pp. xi-xii*. Gilbert had travelled to Cîteaux
to persuade the abbot to take the Gilbertines under his care.

197.　For the composition and several aims of the Angevin party, see Karl Schnith, '*Regni et pacis
inquietatrix*' (see above 92, n 168).

198.　See below 111 f.

199.　Gervase i. 132–3. Knowles *Episcopal Colleagues* 16–17.

200.　Lloyd, *History of Wales*, ii. 484–5; Davies *Episcopal Acts* ii. 521 ff.

201.　Eugène Willems, 'Cîteaux et la seconde Croissade', *RHE* xlix (1954) 116.

excommunicate Stephen at Michaelmas. Whereupon with the mediation of Hugh Bigod earl of Norfolk and Bishops Robert of London, Hilary of Chichester, and William of Norwich, king and archbishop were reconciled. It was not, however, until 1151 that Stephen patched up his quarrel with Henry Murdac.

These were futile gestures on the part of Stephen, for he had lost control over the English church. Of the ten bishops made between the council of Rheims and the end of the reign none was a royal clerk. Henry of Winchester was almost as powerless. William fitzHerbert was restored to York in 1153 and Hugh of le Puiset got Durham with great difficulty in the same year. On the other hand Theobald, to whom Eugenius early in 1150 at last granted a legation over the whole of England,[202] influenced at least three of the elections.

Robert of Béthune died at the council of Rheims and his corpse worked miracles on its journey back to Hereford.[203] As that see was under the control of the Angevins, a new bishop was provided in a most irregular manner.[204] It was agreed between Archbishop Theobald, the pope, and the Angevin interest that Gilbert Foliot, Benedictine abbot of Gloucester and a former prior of Cluny, who was at the council, should be elected. Gilbert apparently gave an undertaking that he would not do fealty to Stephen, and Theobald consecrated him on 5 September 1148 at St Omer with the help of the bishops of Amiens and Cambrai, since no English bishop wanted to be involved. The prognosticon at his consecration, 'Sleepest thou? Couldest not thou watch one hour with me?' (Mark 14: 37), was considered fulfilled when, on his return to England, he submitted and did fealty to the king. Gilbert, a very austere, learned, able, and ambitious man, in 1148 hoped to hold his abbey together with the bishopric, but was defeated by the monks. He aspired to Canterbury after Theobald's death in 1161 but only got London. It was probably because he was so self-righteous that it could be suggested that his behaviour was sometimes devious.

Theobald, after his return to England, consecrated two bishops at Canterbury, David fitzGerald to St David's and Robert of Chesney to Lincoln (19 December 1148). The presence of Walter of Rochester, Hilary of Chichester, Gilbert of Hereford, and Patrick of Limerick shows how Theobald was relying on the newer bishops. David, archdeacon of Cardigan and son of the castellan of Pembroke and the famous Welsh princess, Nest, certainly represented local interests. He was the uncle of Gerald of Wales and educated him in his household. But he agreed under oath to abandon his predecessor's ambition to make St David's an archbishopric.[205] Robert of Chesney, Gilbert Foliot's uncle, and connected with both sides in the civil war, was a canon of St George's in Oxford castle, prebendary of Stow, and archdeacon of Leicester,

202.   Avrom Saltman, *Theobald Archbishop of Canterbury* (1956) 32–3.

203.   Brit. Mus. MS Cott. Julius D X, fos. 24v–28.

204.   *Hist. Pont.* 47–9; Gervase, i. 135. Knowles *Episcopal Colleagues* 37–49.

205.   Gervase, i. 138; *Vita Davidis II* in *Anglia Sacra* ii. 652–3. Lloyd, *History of Wales,* ii. 482–3; Davies *Episcopal Acts* ii. 562 ff.

and was presumably freely elected *e gremio*.[206] It was a sign of the times that when Arnulf bishop of Lisieux wrote to congratulate him on his elevation, he asked him to favour, as far as he could honourably do so, the cause of their duke (Henry fitzEmpress) who by hereditary right should also be king of England.[207]

In 1149 the prior of Christ Church, Canterbury, Walter Durdent, a theologian of excellent repute, through Theobald's influence was elected bishop of Chester by the convent of Coventry,[208] and in 1151 Theobald's clerk, John of Pagham, was elected to Worcester. John was the first to give a benefice to another of the archbishop's clerks, Thomas Becket.[209] In February 1152 Theobald consecrated the celebrated romancer Geoffrey of Monmouth to St Asaph, a dubious reward which he held for only two years and an inhospitable see which he probably never visited.[210] London had become vacant in 1150 by the death of Robert *de Sigillo,* some believed by poison.[211] Possibly in order to avoid another long vacancy the pope, on whose initiative is not known, ordered the chapter to elect within three months a man of good morals and learning and 'adorned by the clothing of religion'. When the last phrase had been explained away as having no technical significance, the chapter elected in 1152 the archdeacon of Middlesex, Richard of Beaumais II, the nephew of the earlier bishop of that name and a man generally considered worthy of the office.[212] Theobald consecrated him on 28 September, and Richard's first act was to appoint Ralf of Diss (Diceto), the historian, possibly another member of the clan, to the vacant archdeaconry.

Theobald was by now firmly in the saddle. At mid-Lent 1151 he held by legatine authority a general council in London, at which Stephen, his elder son Eustace, and the English barons were present. According to Henry of Huntingdon this council gnashed its teeth at appeals made from its decisions to the papal audience. This detestable practice of appeal, he claimed, had first come in while Henry of Winchester was legate.[213] Of more concern to Stephen, however, was his scheme to get Eustace acknowledged as his successor. For this he needed the consent of the church, and he began to court its favour. In 1150 he had repulsed, and in 1151 cold-shouldered, John Paparo, the papal legate to Ireland;[214] but in the latter year he reconciled himself to Henry Murdac so that the archbishop could try to persuade his friend the pope to allow Eustace to be

206. HH 281, 302; Diceto *Abbrev. Chron.* 258; Gervase i. 138; John of Hexham 324; Giraldus Cambrensis *Vita S. Remigii* 34–5, John of Schalby, *ibid.* 198. H. E. Salter, 'The family of Chesney', *Cartulary of the Abbey of Eynsham* (Oxford Hist. Soc. xlix, 1906) i. 411 ff. Knowles *Episcopal Colleagues* 15–16.

207. *The Letters of Arnulf of Lisieux,* ed. F. Barlow, R. Hist. Soc. Camden 3rd ser. lxi (1939), no. 4.

208. Gervase i. 44, 141.

209. Gervase i. 142; *MB* iii. 17.

210. Gervase i. 142. For Geoffrey and Welsh ecclesiastical affairs, see Christopher Brooke, 'The Archbishops of St David's, Llandaff and Caerleon-on-Usk', *Studies in the Early British Church,* ed. Nora K. Chadwick (1958).

211. *Hist. Pont.* 88; John of Hexham 324.

212. Diceto *Ymagines* 295–6; Gervase, i. 148; W. Stubbs, Diceto i, pp. xxi ff. Brooke and Keir *London 800–1216,* 357.

213. HH 282.

214. John of Hexham 326–7; *Hist. Pont.* 6, 61–2. Tillmann 52–3.

crowned. Eugenius at Theobald's request, made through Thomas Becket, forbade Theobald to perform the ceremony; and when, after the barons had recognized Eustace as heir to the throne and done him homage at Easter 1152, Stephen required Theobald to consecrate his son, the primate escaped from Stephen's violence by retiring to France.[215] Thereafter, Stephen's fortunes declined. In May 1152 Queen Matilda died, and on 10 August 1153 Eustace also. Stephen had a second son, William, but seems never to have planned to make him king. Although Pope Eugenius also died in July 1153, and Bernard of Clairvaux in August, the short pontificate of Anastasius IV, the former cardinal bishop of Sabina, came too late to bring much relief.

Stephen and Henry of Winchester did have some ecclesiastical success in 1153. The prior and convent of Durham, which remained most loyal to Stephen owing to the Scottish threat, and the archdeacons, apparently with the general support of the clergy of the diocese, on 22 January 1153 elected to the vacant see the king's nephew, Hugh of le Puiset treasurer and archdeacon of York, who, together with the deposed archbishop, William fitzHerbert, was living with their uncle Henry at Winchester.[216] Henry Murdac naturally objected to the promotion of his enemy: he excommunicated the electors and declared the election null. Even before news arrived of Eugenius's death, Hugh set off for Rome. Among his companions was Master Laurence, a Durham man and clerk of the convent, who, when they reached St Albans, turned aside and became a monk. About 1158 Laurence replaced Stephen's son Gervase as abbot of Westminster. Hugh found favour with the new pope and was consecrated bishop by Anastasius IV on 21 December. Meanwhile on Henry Murdac's death (14 October) William fitzHerbert followed his cousin to Rome.[217] Hugh interceded for him, and Anastasius restored him to his see (a rather unusual event) and granted him the pallium. Hugh hastened back to Durham, so as to be enthroned on 24 May 1154, and began a forty-one year tenure of the bishopric. But William, always dilatory, spent Easter with Henry at Winchester before proceeding to York, where he died on 8 June. Although there were rumours of poison the story was categorically denied by William of Newburgh, who investigated the case.[218]

Eugenius's death could not save Stephen. In January 1153 Henry fitzEmpress invaded and was more successful than on previous occasions. Few were now prepared to fight to the death for an ageing king with no acceptable heir. It was the time for a settlement. Theobald together with some of his

215. HH 288; Gervase i. 150–1; Waverley annals in *Annales Monastici* ii. 234.

216. *HDE* cont. II, 167–9; John of Hexham 320 ff.; Wm of Newburgh 78; Gervase i. 157–8; Geoffrey of Coldingham 4 ff. Knowles *Episcopal Colleagues* 14–15. G. V. Scammell, *Hugh du Puiset* (1956).

217. According to the *Vita* several 'miraculous' coincidences occurred. Henry Murdac and the pope died on the same day, and on the very day that the news reached William, apparently by the aid of the Holy Spirit, Henry of Winchester gave him some wonderfully.engraved spurs which had just been sent him from abroad. This was an intimation that he must set off immediately for Rome, where the cardinal who had been his strongest supporter in 1147 had been elected pope. B.M. MS Harl. 2, fos. 78–78v.

218. John of Hexham 319 ff.; Diceto *Ymagines* 297–8; Gervase i. 157–8; Wm of Newburgh 79–81. According to the *Vita,* fo. 80, he died of fever; quite a respectable number of cures took place at his tomb, *ibid.* fo. 80v ff.

bishops started negotiations, and on 6 November a treaty was agreed.[219] Stephen adopted Henry as his son and heir and successor, who in the meantime was to be associated with the king in the government. Henry allowed that after his succession Stephen's son William should hold all his existing honours and also inherit Stephen's, with the exception of those pertaining to the crown. The new heir left England at Easter 1154 to wait on events. There was time for one episcopal appointment during Stephen's last months of power. About Michaelmas Theobald secured the election of his archdeacon, Roger of Pont l'Evêque, to the archbishopric of York,[220] and gave the archdeaconry to another of his clerks, Thomas Becket. On 25 October Stephen died and was buried near his wife and son in the Cluniac monastery they had founded at Faversham. And on 8 December Henry returned to receive his inheritance. The actors in a new drama were taking up their places.

Of the seventeen English and three or four Welsh bishops left by Stephen to his successor only Henry of Winchester and Hugh of Durham were closely tied to the house of Blois. The aged Robert of Bath, Jocelin of Salisbury, and Hilary of Chichester, although originally connected with Henry, had moved on. The continuation of the new trends which had set in during the last thirteen years of Henry I's reign had produced a larger bench of bishops and of a new type. Among the twenty-one was only a single former royal clerk. In 1140 Stephen had failed even to get his chancellor a bishopric.[221] Instead there were eleven former episcopal servants (including nine archdeacons) and six monks and one canon regular. These changes reflect the emergence of the *sacerdotium* and the growing distinction between it and the *regnum*. The English church was at last acquiring some of the liberty – its proper rights – promised it in 1100 and 1135. But when a new and masterful king succeeded in 1154 he thought that the process had gone too far and began to look back to the ancient customs of his grandfather's reign. The new situation, however, was not simply a result of Stephen's incompetence or the ambition of Henry of Winchester. And Henry fitzEmpress, even if he himself had not gone too far, and martyred his primate, could not have put the clock back to 1135, let alone 1100. Times had changed.

219. T. Rymer, *Foedera* (1714) i. 13. Wm of Newburgh 90–1; HH 289; Gervase i. 156.
220. Gervase i. 159; Diceto *Ymagines* 298; Wm of Newburgh 81–2, 94–5. Knowles *Episcopal Colleagues* 12–14.
221. Above 97, n. 188.

Chapter III

Government

In the church all members had some powers. For example, the administration of the sacraments devolved, in the unavoidable absence of ministers, on the laity, and bishops were supposed to be elected by the clergy and people of the city. But long before the eleventh century a magistracy had been acquired by the order of priests, who had become not only the usual celebrants of the Eucharist but also when they had cure of souls, the pre-eminent possessors of the power to bind and loose. They were mediators between the people and God. A few powers, like ordination and consecration, had been retained by the bishops; and these prelates also held governmental offices which among themselves differed in dignity and were graduated in rank. In charge of cities or dioceses were simple bishops; of metropolitan churches archbishops; of provinces primates; and of the whole Roman church, the bishop of Rome, the pope. Within the monastic order the heads of monasteries, abbots, had supreme authority over the monks. The rights and duties of all these servants of God, *servi servorum dei, ministri* or *vicarii dei,* were defined partly by the collections of ancient ecclesiastical law,[1] partly by unwritten custom, whether general or particular, partly by privileges and charters possessed by individual churches, and increasingly by decrees issued by church synods.

There were also 'unlawful' wielders of power in the church, mostly secular rulers, emperors, kings, and lords, who based their claims largely on custom, and whose pretensions and interference had usually to be tolerated by the priesthood with good or bad grace according to the time and circumstances.

The organization of the church in the eleventh century was very loose. In theory, strongly reinforced by the Pseudo-Isidorian decretals, there was a strict hierarchy. In fact there was little active government. The contrast between the ideal and reality was not due to any discord or opposition. The pope and other princes of the church had maintained their claims unabated during the administrative collapse of the ninth and tenth centuries while accepting their impotence without resentment. Even when a worthy pope ruled under the protection of the German emperor or a reformed and independent pontiff drew attention to his powers, distant bishops and archbishops were not prepared to accept him as a master. Similarly archbishops had little authority over their bishops, and one of the purposes of the False Decretals had been to weaken the archbishops by strengthening the phantom relations between the bishops and the pope. In well-organized kingdoms, however, metropolitan power was abetted by the king as a political measure. In Germany Bremen-

1. See below 145.

Hamburg was advanced as the metropolitan of a northern territory which included the Scandinavians, and Mainz over Bohemia, even if the pretensions of Magdeburg over Poland, and Salzburg, Passau, and Regensburg over Hungary failed. Nor, in general, had the bishops much authority over their diocesan clergy.

The ordinary government of the church was carried on concurrently by the parish priests and the diocesan bishops. And the initiative for many, if not most, specific administrative and judicial actions by higher authorities came from below. This is a general feature of the period and applied to *sacerdotium* and *regnum* alike. Authorities acted as a result of complaints made or favours sought, rather than *motu proprio*. Indeed there was a strong feeling among the laity, and expressed in directives by the kings, that it was not for individuals, even when clothed by office, but for bodies of people (often institutionalized as juries), to set processes in motion.[2] In the monastic order reform movements were often from below; in the eleventh and twelfth centuries it was lay piety which fed the monastic fires. And there were also populist movements in theology.

With regard to the general reform of the secular church the position was, at least in the kingdom, rather different. Village priests seem never in England to have urged the bishops to introduce or press on with reform; English bishops and archbishops never urged the pope to take a greater interest in the royal church. There were a few bishops in both Normandy and England who took the initiative in legislating and acting against current abuses, and archbishops and bishops are not to be regarded in this period as simply agents of the papacy even in the field of reform. Nevertheless, by the eleventh century the papacy had adopted a reform programme for the church which it pushed fairly steadily thereafter. It was the papal curia which sketched the grand strategy of the campaign; and on the whole the initiative and the reminders for most of the general changes in the sphere of government came from the top. It is therefore convenient first to consider papal influence on the English church before describing its more routine administration.

The pope, whatever his claims to authority over every part of the church may have been, was in no position to interfere with local government. The papacy had exercised no direct control over the English church since the time of King Offa; the reconstruction after the Scandinavian devastations, the reestablishment of the dioceses, the monastic revival, the general reform of the English church had been a completely domestic affair. Such outside help as had been required had been enlisted through personal contacts, and from centres north of the Loire. Before the eleventh century the pope had no private sources of information, no staff, and minimal interest in the outlying provinces. He knew from Bede's *Ecclesiastical History* that the English church had been founded by Rome and was therefore in a special relationship. He knew from his financial records that England owed him (and usually paid) 299 marks of silver

---

2. Cf. Raoul C. van Caenegen, 'Public prosecution of crime in twelfth-century England' in *Church and Government in the Middle Ages: essays presented to C. R. Cheney* (1976) 41.

a year (Peter's Pence).[3] And he knew that the English archbishops must ask him for their pallium.[4] But he made no attempt to extend this last right. It is possible that Alexander II had some say in Lanfranc's translation to Canterbury in 1070. But in normal circumstances the papacy had no influence over the appointment to English archbishoprics nor, of course, to bishoprics and abbacies. As the eleventh century progressed the papacy tried increasingly to introduce its reform programme into Britain, and Gregory VII even had the startling idea that William I should become his vassal, and so join him in the war against evil and injustice. But the Conqueror, although well disposed, thought this was going too far.[5] In practice the English church in 1087, as in 1066, was self-directing and self-contained.

In the eleventh century the papacy had begun to reestablish lines of communication with the provinces in order to serve its campaign against simony, clerical marriage, and other abuses. It made use of legates *a latere*, and Gregory VII aspired to set up standing vicars in the kingdoms. It encouraged archbishops to visit Rome. And it welcomed – sometimes summoned – bishops to its councils. These moves were rarely welcome to either the kings or their bishops; even Gregory recognized that they were simply means to an end and that their indiscreet employment could be counterproductive.[6] In 1080 his legates to France, Hugh of Die and Amatus of Oleron, summoned the bishops and abbots of Normandy to a council to meet at Saintes in January 1081, and when they did not appear suspended them from office. The Conqueror indignantly pretended that they had been kept away not by disobedience but by fear of the king of France. Gregory accepted the excuse and issued instructions to his legates which established a principle with regard to England which Urban II also was to observe. Although the king of England, he wrote, in some matters does not behave quite as religiously as we could wish, nevertheless in others he behaves much more commendably than the rest. For example, he does not destroy or sell God's churches, he maintains the rule of peace and justice for his subjects, and, although solicited by enemies of the holy see, remains faithful to it. Also he compels priests, even upon oath, to give up their wives, and laymen likewise the tithes they wrongfully detain. It is therefore not improper in return to treat his authority more respectfully and, because of his probity, entirely to bear with the negligent behaviour of his subjects and friends. There were, Gregory assured his legates, divine and papal precedents for such an attitude. Accordingly the legates were immediately to withdraw their sentences on the

---

3.   Albinus, 'In Anglia: De denario B. Petri ccc marcas singulis annis, viz de unaquaque domo l sterling', *Liber Censuum* ii. 121a. Censius, 'Denarius B. Petri colligitur in hunc modum in Anglia: dioc. Canterbury £7.18s., Rochester £5.12s., London £16.10s., Ely £5, Lincoln £42, Chichester £8, Winchester £17.6s.8d., Exeter £9.5s., Worcester £10.5s., Hereford £6, Bath £11.5s., Salisbury £17, Coventry £10.5s., York £11.10s. Summa ccc marcas minus unam marcam', *ibid.* i. 226b. See further Barlow, *English Church 1000–1066*, 295–7.

4.   Barlow, *ibid.* 298 ff. Gilbert of Limerick, *De Statu Ecclesiae* in *PL* clix. 1003, believed that archbishops and primates ought to be ordained by the pope at Rome, and that the pallium was sent and the archbishop consecrated by his fellow bishops only if he was prevented by sickness, age, or war etc. from going to Rome.

5.   Cf. H. E. J. Cowdrey, 'Pope Gregory VII and the Anglo-Norman church and kingdom', *Studi Gregoriani* ix (1972) 89 ff.

6.   *Register* ix. 5: *MGH Ep. sel.* ii. 1, ed. E. Caspar (1955) 579–80.

prelates and in future were not to annoy William in this sort of way without the pope's prior approval, 'For it seems to us that he can be much more successfully won for God and encouraged to lasting love of St Peter by sweet blandishments and reasonableness than by harshness and inflexibility.'

The authority of the king of England, because it operated for the good of the church, was to be treated tenderly. Initially the Conqueror made considerable use of the pope. In 1070 the legates Ermenfrid bishop of Sion (who had visited England in Edward's reign) and the cardinal-priests, Peter and John Minutus, crowned the king, deposed those prelates whom he had marked down, and held a reforming council at Winchester, before leaving for Normandy, where Ermenfrid and the Roman clerk Hubert imposed penance on the Norman army and persuaded Lanfranc to accept Canterbury.[7] But then William and his sons in turn carefully controlled all traffic with Rome. Since there was a schism in the papacy from 1080 to 1100 the king reserved to himself the right of recognizing the true pope, and by licensing the entry of papal legates and the exit of his bishops and abbots protected his church from interference in a way which for a time the papacy was prepared to tolerate. These rules became known as the ancestral customs and were observed, although reluctantly, even by Anselm.[8]

The papacy at times of active government had always used legates, personal representatives or vicars of the pope; and since Leo IX their mission had again become common. On the whole their role was simply diplomatic. They carried letters of credence and recommendation and did their business orally. All the powers in Europe maintained diplomatic relations with the English king, and the appearance of papal legates at Edward the Confessor's court caused little stir.[9] The policy of the English king was to treat them as couriers or at most nuncios, requiring that they approach the king alone and by the shortest route, avoid all unauthorized contacts, and shun all unacceptable business. And since the king was usually in Normandy papal legates did not need to enter the kingdom. Hubert, who had joined the other legates in Normandy in 1070, returned serveral times to England on diplomatic missions. In 1072 he was present at the council of Windsor when the Canterbury-York dispute was heard. In 1079 he summoned the English and Norman bishops to Gregory's Lent synod at Rome in 1080 (they were not allowed to go). In May 1080 he came to collect Peter's Pence and ask William to hold England as a papal fief (he got the money but not the homage). And he then died at Bec, where the abbot, Anselm, was his friend.[10]

At the end of William I's reign and in the first year of his son's there were approaches from the anti-pope, Clement III, and then from Urban II,

---

7.   Helene Tillmann, *Die päpstlichen Legaten in England bis zur Beendigung der Legation Gualas (1218)* (Bonn 1926) 12–15. Catherine Morton, 'Pope Alexander II and the Norman Conquest', *Latomus* xxxiv (1975) 362.

8.   Below 279 f., 289 ff.

9.   *English Church 1000–1066*, 106–7, 301 ff.

10.   Tillmann 15–17.

elected in March 1088.[11] But Rufus had no need of papal services until 1094, when he decided to trade recognition of Urban for the pope's deposition of Anselm. Urban sent Walter cardinal-bishop of Albano, who refused to depose the archbishop but conceded the privilege that no papal legate should be sent to England in Rufus's reign except at the king's request.[12] But Rufus was soon involved in negotiations over Robert's crusade and taking Normandy in pawn; and early in 1096 Abbot Jarento of St Bénigne at Dijon, accompanied by Hugh of Flavigny, who gave an account of the mission in his chronicle, worked out a satisfactory agreement betweeen the brothers.[13]

With the accession of Henry I papal traffic with England increased. The returned Crusader Robert claimed that Henry had usurped his kingdom. Henry was required to give up the investiture of bishops and abbots. Later there was the scandal of his capture and imprisonment of his brother and exclusion of his nephew from Normandy. And there was his almost constant war with Louis VI of France. Paschal II made his intentions clear immediately by appointing in 1100 Guy archbishop of Vienne, the future Calixtus II, legate and vicar in England and Scotland. But the king refused him admission.[14] Henry, however, allowed in John cardinal-bishop of Tusculum, a former monk of Bec, in 1101, and Tiberius, a much more lowly emissary, in 1103 to collect Peter's Pence. John's mission was also concerned with Robert's claims and invasion.[15] In 1109 the cardinal-priest Ulrich brought a pallium for Thomas II of York and had the task of investigating the dispute between the metropolitans. But Anselm died before the case could be heard.[16] After Henry had uncanonically translated Ralf d'Escures from Rochester to Canterbury in 1115, he could hardly refuse Paschal's mission of Anselm abbot of St Sabas in Rome with the pallium and with instructions to investigate the situation, complain about the king's hindrance of traffic with Rome, and demand that there should be a standing vicariate in the kingdom to hear the more important ecclesiastical cases. These charges were rendered less abrasive by the choice of Anselm as the papal envoy, for he was the late archbishop's nephew and had been educated at Canterbury. Next year the pope appointed Anselm papal vicar in England; but Henry kept the abbot with him in Normandy for three years and so frustrated the pope's purpose. All the same some advance was made, for all papal letters dealing with English affairs were channelled through Anselm who also received Peter's Pence.[17]

A new concordat was negotiated on 20 November 1119 when Calixtus and Henry met at Gisors to discuss ending the war with the king of

11.   *Ibid.* 17–18. For the legations and diplomacy between 1086 and 1126 see also Josef Deér, 'Der Anspruch der Herrscher des 12. Jahrhunderts auf die apostolische Legation', *Archivum Historiae Pontificiae* ii (1964) 117, Margaret Gibson, *Lanfranc of Bec* 136 ff.

12.   *Chron.*; *HN* 68 ff. Tillmann 19–21.

13.   *Chronicon Hugonis . . . abbatis Flaviniacensis* ed. G. H. Pertz in *MGH SS* viii (1948) 475–6. Tillmann 21–2.

14.   *GP* 128, where William of Malmesbury mentions also Anselm and Peter Pierleone, all useless and in search of booty. Tillmann 22.

15.   Tillmann 22–3.

16.   Florence; *GP* 262. Tillmann 23–4.

17.   Florence *s.a.* 1116; *GP* 129–31. Tillmann 25.

France. The pope recalled Anselm and promised Henry that he would not again send a legate to England during the king's lifetime except at his request or to deal with a case too important to be settled by the English church.[18] In 1120 Henry had interviews with the papal legate to France and Normandy, Cuno cardinal-bishop of Palestrina, on the frontier to discuss peace with Louis and the admission to England of the exiled archbishop Thurstin of York.[19] But in 1121 the pope, strengthened by his capture of the anti-pope in April and wishing to settle the important case of the archbishop of York, named Peter Pierleone cardinal-priest of St Mary in Trastevere (the future anti-pope Anacletus II) as his vicar for England and his legate in Scotland, Ireland, the islands, and France. Henry allowed him to come to him when on campaign in Wales but only to dismiss him with rich presents.[20] In 1123 Henry abbot of St Jean d'Angely, a son of Duke William VII of Aquitaine, fetched Peter's Pence from England, and so impressed the king that in 1127 Henry gave him Peterborough abbey, a move which turned out badly.[21]

So far Henry had held to his predecessors' policy. In 1124, partly because of his growing piety, partly in order to reward the pope for annulling the marriage between William Clito, the pretender to Normandy, and Sibyl, daughter of the count of Anjou, an alliance which threatened his security,[22] Henry allowed John of Crema cardinal-priest of St Chrysogonus, named legate to England, Scotland, and Normandy, to conduct a general visitation of the major churches in the kingdom, to treat with David king of Scots concerning York's metropolitan powers in Scotland, and to hold, in his absence, a great council at Westminster in 1125.[23] This unprecedented papal activity in England made a great impression on contemporaries.[24] The cardinal was also involved in an imaginative scheme to end the Canterbury–York feud, and on his return to Rome was accompanied by both archbishops. Rather surprisingly a different settlement was made which put Canterbury-York and also Anglo-papal relations on an entirely new basis. It was decided that William of Corbeil archbishop of Canterbury should be papal legate in England and Scotland, and so York's superior but also the pope's vicar. All the same, in 1128 Thurstin made his fourth visit to Rome and obtained an important bundle of privileges for his see.[25]

---

18. *HN* 258; Hugh *HCY* 76–80. Cf. the different account in OV (Chibnall) vi. 282 ff.

19. Tillmann 25–6.

20. *HN* 294–6. Tillmann 26–7.

21. Tillmann 27. *Chron. E.,* because written at Peterborough, is interested in Henry. See also below, 197.

22. Cf. C. Warren Hollister and Thomas K. Keefe, 'The making of the Angevin empire', *The Journal of British Studies* (Trinity Coll., Hartford, Connecticut) xii (1973) 11.

23. *Chron.*; John of Worcester 20–2; *HR* 276–81. Tillmann 27–30.

24. A good story that the legate went to Durham to investigate Ranulf Flambard's morals and was compromised by the bishop's niece is in the Winchester annals in *Annales Monastici,* ii. 47–8. Cf. HH 245–6. Such stories were probably invented by those who opposed his decree against clerical marriage. Gilbert Foliot remembered the legation some forty years later for other reasons, *MB* v. 539.

25. *PU* ii. 147. Cf. Denis Bethel, 'William of Corbeil and the Canterbury York dispute', *JEH* xix (1968) 157.

The archbishop of Canterbury, except for a break when Honorius II died (1130–32), kept the legation until his death on 21 November 1136.[26] Henry of Blois bishop of Winchester was legate 1139–43, and Theobald archbishop of Canterbury from 1150 until his death in 1161. The native standing legate was to become the norm. This was a compromise which, although greatly to the advantage of the pope (for he had at last got his permanent and accepted agent in the kingdom) was not repugnant to the king. Papal government had become such a normal feature by 1126 that it was convenient to have the lines of communication regularized. William of Corbeil was in Henry's power, and the king clearly expected him to act as a sort of royal ecclesiastical justiciar, a counterpart to the other justiciar, Roger bishop of Salisbury.

Standing legations lapsed with the death of either the legate or the pope. At the beginning of Stephen's reign, while Canterbury was still vacant, Innocent II, free at last from the anti-pope Anacletus II, sent Alberic cardinal-bishop of Ostia to England.[27] Like John of Crema thirteen years before, Alberic in 1138 first went on a visitation of the churches, then approached David of Scots, who was besieging Carlisle, with overtures of peace and the demand that he should allow Bishop Aldulf to return to his see, and finally held a council at Westminster. Stephen assisted at this council, which assumed all the functions of the great courts of the early Norman period. Abbots were deposed; bishops and abbots were consecrated and blessed; canons were promulgated; and Theobald was elected archbishop of Canterbury. A new envoy, Peter, had come to summon the prelates to the Lent council of 1139 at Rome (Lateran II); and in mid-January the legates left, to be followed by the English contingent. It was not, however, the new archbishop of Canterbury who was to be appointed papal legate. The king's brother, Henry of Blois, had negotiated with the pope for his translation to Canterbury, and on 1 March 1139 Innocent compensated him with the legation. It was probably a Roman solution, ingenious, opportunistic, and disturbing.

The position of Henry of Blois was not to be that of William of Corbeil.[28] A greater prelate in conjunction with a weaker king, a believer not only in the rights of the aristocracy but also in the freedom of the church from secular interference, he exploited his claims with courage and enthusiasm during his four years' legation. He made himself the effective ruler of the English church, holding councils, deciding cases, and influencing elections, and so brought it into immediate contact with the papacy, for he was, for all his authority, only the papal vicar. Equally important, by sharing or disputing ecclesiastical patronage with his brother the king, and by transforming church councils into national bodies which not only legislated against the country's ills but also attempted to determine its fate, he raised the *sacerdotium* in England to a position it had never had before. Henry gathered together all the movements which had been gaining strength during his uncle's reign and used them

26. Tillmann 30–2.

27. John of Worcester 49, 53; John of Hexham 297–300. Tillmann 38–41.

28. Tillmann 41–50. Lena Voss, *Heinrich von Blois, Bischof von Winchester (1129–71):* Historische Studien ccx (Berlin 1932) 21 ff.

for revolutionary ends. Only one new order stood aloof, the Cistercians; and Henry's clash with the Cistercian abbots over the election of his nephew William fitzHerbert to York was fatal to the continuation of his power. Celestine II did not renew Henry's appointment, and Lucius II and Eugenius III took into account the possible success of the Angevin cause.

Between 1143 and 1150, when Theobald of Canterbury became legate, the uneasy relations of former days returned. Lucius II sent Imar cardinal-bishop of Tusculum in 1144, and Stephen allowed him a free run.[29] Imar, who brought the pallium for William fitzHerbert, heard cases and even, it seems, in 1145 deposed two bishops, Siegfried of Chichester for sodomy and Everard of Norwich for cruelty. This was a quite exceptional action. Imar was also empowered to investigate the metropolitan claims of St David's. But in 1147 Stephen warned off Eugenius III's legates sent to summon the English prelates to the council of Rheims (1148), and, after the council, paid little attention to an invitation delivered by Miles bishop of Thérouanne to appear before the papal court to answer Geoffrey of Anjou's complaint that he had usurped England. Stephen answered that Geoffrey had usurped Normandy and was in illegal occupation of parts of England.[30] After Theobald had become legate Stephen was troubled only by the mission of John Paparo cardinal-deacon of St Adrian to Ireland in 1150 and 1151.[31] The sole effect of Stephen's refusal to cooperate was the use by the legate of the Scottish route and an understanding between him and David king of Scots. John Paparo was accompanied in 1151 by Christian O Conairche bishop of Lismore, a Cistercian, who was to be the native standing legate in Ireland. The church in Great Britain was assuming new forms.

Except for Gregory VII, who tried to make Lanfranc pay him a visit,[32] popes did not venture to summon individual prelates to Rome. The reintroduction of general and provincial councils of the Western church under papal presidency was, however, a feature of this period,[33] and the popes put increasing pressure on the English church to send at least representative delegations to the more important of these. William I sent no contingents to Alexander II's or Gregory VII's councils. English bishops were absent from Clermont (1095) where Urban II preached the first Crusade and issued thirty-two canons. But Anselm in exile attended his important councils at Bari and Rome (1097–98) and was influenced by them when he held his own councils at London in 1102 and 1108. After this some representatives were sent to most papal councils to which English bishops and abbots were summoned. To Calixtus II's council of Rheims (1119) Henry sent the bishops and abbots of Normandy and those English bishops who were with him in the duchy, William Warelwast of Exeter, Ranulf Flambard of Durham, Bernard of St David's, and Urban of Llandaff, all safe men, closely connected with the English court. The

29.   John of Hexham 317–18. Tillmann 50–1. Böhmer *KuS* 387.
30.   Tillmann 51.
31.   John of Hexham 326–7; Diceto *Ymagines* 295; *Hist. Pont.* 70–2. Tillmann 52.
32.   J-W. 5121. Cf. Cowdrey, *op. cit.* (above 106, n. 5) 94.
33.   For a brief account, see Raymonde Foreville, *Latran I, II, III, IV: Histoire des conciles oecuméniques,* ed. Gervais Dumeige, vi (Paris 1965).

archbishop of Canterbury was too ill to go, and the attendance of the elect of York led not only to his unauthorized consecration by the pope but also to his disgrace.[34] There seems to have been no English representative at Calixtus II's Lateran I (1123), possibly because it was arranged during the vacancy of Canterbury; but the council was followed by the mission of the legate, John of Crema, to England (1125). It is possible that English bishops were at Innocent II's councils of Rheims (1131) and Pisa (1135);[35] and to his more famous Lateran II (1139) were sent Archbishop Theobald, Roger of Coventry, Simon of Worcester, Robert I of Exeter, John of Sées, and Reginald abbot of Evesham.[36] To Eugenius III's council of Rheims (1148) Stephen sent Robert of Béthune of Hereford, William Turbe of Norwich, and Hilary of Chichester to present the apologies of the rest. But Theobald attended despite the king, and the pope suspended from office all those who had not attended, specifically naming Henry of Winchester. In the end the pope gave Theobald authority to absolve in England the guilty absentees.[37] The pressure to attend papal councils was becoming more severe.

The purpose of these councils was the reform of the church, and all condemned simony in its various forms, the marriage and concubinage of the clergy in major orders, lay investiture, and secular violence against the church and its ministers. And the Lent council customarily ended with sentences of anathema on the current enemies of the church. Measures which had been revolutionary in the eleventh century had through repetition become so familiar by 1148 that John of Salisbury had to defend the council's prohibition of marriage to bishops and monks which many observers thought absurd.[38] English, Norman, and papal conciliar activity between 1070 and 1148 was closely connected. The main targets of the reformers were attacked at both levels. One English chronicler states expressly that the English delegation returned from Lateran II (1139) bearing the synodal decrees with it, and that these were then disseminated throughout England.[39] But, as we shall see, provincial councils were not just part of the papal machinery of government.

The papal conciliar legislation, although repetitive, was for that very reason influential. But the councils did more than legislate, they were helping to create a European ecclesiastical high society. They were social events of gripping interest not only to the participants but also to the much

34.   Florence *s.a.* 1119; *HN* 255 ff.; *GP* 131. Mansi xxi. 233. Foreville 34 ff.

35.   Foreville 75, 77. William of Malmesbury was very interested in the schism: *Hist. Nov.* 5–10.

36.   John of Worcester 54; John of Hexham 300; *The Life of Christina of Markyate*, ed. and trans. C. H. Talbot (1959) 162. Mansi xxi. 523; Foreville 73 ff., 183 ff. See further, J. H. Round, 'Nigel bishop of Ely', *EHR* viii (1893) 516; R. L. Poole, 'The English bishops at the Lateran Council of 1139', *EHR* xxxviii (1923) 61; William Hunt *ibid.* 557; R. L. Poole, John of Salisbury's *Historia Pontificalis*, app. VI. A. Saltman, 'John II, bishop of Rochester', *EHR* lxvi (1951) 71. The question whether the 'trial' between the rivals, Stephen and Matilda, took place at Pisa in January 1136 or at II Lateran (1139), or at both, remains contentious. Among the latest commentators is Giles Constable, *The Letters of Peter the Venerable* (Cambridge Mass. 1967) ii. 252.

37.   Gervase 134; *Hist. Pont.* 4 ff. Foreville 101 ff. Marvin L. Colker, 'The trial of Gilbert of Poitiers, 1148: a previously unknown record', *Medieval Studies* xxvii (1965) 152. Nicholas M. Haring, 'Notes on the Council and the Consistory of Rheims (1148)', *ibid.* xxviii (1966) 39.

38.   Cf. *Hist. Pont.* 8–9.

39.   Florence 115.

wider circle to whom they told the story. There were the debates, the cases heard, and the general gossip and exchange of news and views. These councils and their acts were reported in the English chronicles. Thanks to the presence of Norman prelates at Rheims (1119) Orderic Vitalis devoted to its proceedings one of his magnificent set-pieces.[40] The special aims of Calixtus II at this council were the establishment of peace in the West and the settlement of the quarrel over investitures with Henry V of Germany.[41] Louis VI of France attended in person, and according to Orderic, who reconstructs (and no doubt in his usual fashion embroiders) his speech, denounced all Henry I's crimes from making war on his overlord, imprisoning his elder brother, disinheriting his nephew William Clito, whom Louis had with him, to arresting Robert of Bellême. A month after the council Calixtus met Henry I at Gisors on the Norman frontier and made peace between the two kings. The investiture dispute could not be settled so quickly. The pope suspended the council while he went to a fruitless meeting with Henry V at Mouzon in the Ardennes, and the council ended with the excommunication of the German king. Among the debates was a heated discussion on how far the prohibition of lay investiture should be extended. And among the interesting cases heard were the Countess of Poitou's complaint against the scandalous conduct of her husband, that celebrated roué William IX,[42] and the attack by the archbishop of Lyons and the bishop of Mâcon on Cluny's privileges of exemption from episcopal authority. The decrees of the council were drafted by Cardinal John of Crema who was to hold a council at Westminster in 1125.

Calixtus settled the investiture dispute with Henry V by the Concordat of Worms (September 1122) and six months later held Lateran I in order to ratify the terms.[43] If English bishops were absent they missed the regrant of metropolitan authority over the whole of Scandinavia to the new archbishop of Hamburg-Bremen, the hearing of several other metropolitan disputes, and the debate on monastic exemptions and the ministry of monks. On 13 January 1131 Henry I met the new pope, Innocent II, at Chartres and agreed to support him against Peter Pierleone, the anti-pope Anacletus II; in the spring Innocent visited Rouen; and there was probably an English representation at Innocent's poorly recorded council of Rheims in October.[44] The new English king, Stephen, immediately recognized Innocent, perhaps at Pisa (May 1135), and, more important, in 1136 Innocent returned the compliment.[45] In 1138 the papal legate, Alberic of Ostia, visited England and held the council of Westminster. And in 1139 a strong delegation was sent from England to Lateran II, a council concerned with the aftermath of the schism, in

40. OV (Chibnall) vi. 252 ff.

41. *Chron.*; *GR* 482; *GP* 265–6; HH 242. Foreville 33 ff. Stanley A. Chodorow, 'Ecclesiastical politics and the ending of the investiture contest: the papal election of 1119 and the negotiations of Mouzon', *Speculum* xlvi (1971) 613.

42. François Villard, 'Guillaume IX d'Aquitaine et le concile de Reims de 1119', *Cahiers de Civilisation Médiévale* xvi (1973) 295.

43. Foreville 44 ff. Below 273.

44. *Hist. Nov.* 6–10; HH 252; Suger, *Vie de Louis VI,* ed. and trans. H. Waquet (Paris 1964) 260, 266, 268; OV (Chibnall) vi. 420. Foreville 73 ff. Below 273.

45. J-W 7804. *SSC* 143.

order to defend Stephen against Angevin charges.[46] Partly because Innocent was more autocratic than his predecessors fewer cases were heard in general sessions; but the affair of the radical demagogue Arnold of Brescia, who was opposed to the church holding property, was in most men's minds. The council also legislated on novel topics, condemning the use of those inhuman weapons, bows and crossbows, in wars against Christians, and the holding of knightly tournaments. At Eugenius III's council of Rheims (1148) the *cause célèbre* was the attack on the orthodoxy of Gilbert of la Porrée bishop of Poitiers by the great abbots Suger of St Denis and Bernard of Clairvaux. Among his accusers were Robert of Melun, Adam of the Little Bridge, and Hugh of Amiens (Reading), theologians of English birth or connexions, who were with the even more famous Peter Lombard, the Master of Sentences.[47] John of Salisbury, because of the attack on his old teacher, discusses the council at length in his *Historia Pontificalis.*[48] He was not only sympathetic to Gilbert, but also excited by the action of this drama. Great men, rather than great issues, were in conflict.

There were at all times English prelates who were well known at Rome and throughout Christendom, like Lanfranc, Anselm, Henry of Blois, and Theobald. In 1139, when Geoffrey de Gorron abbot of St Albans was chosen to be a member of the English delegation to Lateran II, he was at first quite pleased, for he considered himself well-regarded at the curia and welcomed the opportunity to meet old friends again.[49] By 1148 there was even wider integration. Englishmen went to Rheims also from Paris and Rome. The regular calling of councils and the pope's frequent visits to France were creating a sense of collegiality among the higher ranks of the clergy which by 1159 had made a structured government within the church for the first time both feasible and generally welcome.

The papal councils and legates, especially the activities of the standing vicars, also gave rise to increasing business traffic between England and the papal curia. It became usual for bishops and abbots to make use of any visit to the pope to secure papal privileges for themselves and their friends to add to their collection of royal charters. The ecclesiastical documents, however, in this period rarely did more than confirm possessions and rights which the petitioners claimed were already theirs. Seldom were they innovatory. And grants of papal protection were not yet of much legal significance. Even slower to get under way was litigation in the papal court or before judges appointed by the curia. The famous appeals to Rome of this period were more in the nature of diplomatic manoeuvres than of the formal initiation of legal proceedings. The system of appeals, the use by the pope of judges delegate, and the issue of papal decretals (papal decisions of points of law) in vast quantities were all part of the same movement and one which had hardly started by 1154. The earliest surviving collection of papal decretals was made after 1174.[50] Indeed, it is easy

46. Arnulf of Lisieux was among Stephen's attorneys. See Barlow, *The Letters of Arnulf of Lisieux,* p. xix. Foreville 78 ff. 180 ff. Above 112.

47. Foreville 101 ff. Below 251 ff.

48. *Hist. Pont.* 4 ff.

49. *The Life of Christina of Markyate* 162–6.

50. See above 24.

to misunderstand the evidence. Collections of papal documents and letters, whether in contemporary official registers or near-contemporary unofficial editions, or brought together by modern scholars, can give the impression of an originating government with centralizing tendencies. In fact most of the documents were issued by the papal chancery for a fee at the request of the beneficiary and were merely a redrafting of the petition. The curia was a place of resort, a market, not the power house of an active governmental machine; all that it could hope to achieve was the maintenance of standard diplomatic forms and a consistent policy in the face of the diverse wishes of its clientèle.[51]

So even in 1159, when Roland Bandinelli was elected pope, the king rather than the pope was the more effective overlord of the English and Norman churches. Indeed, the way in which Alexander III, who was opposed by an anti-pope, Victor IV, received recognition in the kingdoms of France and England illustrates this well.[52] Although the acknowledgment of Alexander was not quite so brutally at the nod of Henry II as Urban II's recognition had been at Rufus's in 1096, nevertheless, just as the pope had pronounced on the disputed succession to the English crown after 1135, so now Henry pronounced on the disputed succession to the papacy. And no one, including the grateful Alexander, queried his right.

The king's attitude towards the English church was basically proprietary. Not only was the church within his dominions, it had also been endowed by his ancestors. He therefore claimed and exercised powers over it which, although never exactly nor acceptably defined, were acknowledged by all clerics from royal clerks to the pope. The church preferred to stress the king's ministry: he was an anointed ruler who should serve as the church's strong arm; he was not an owner but an advocate. Such considerations could, and did, influence a king's behaviour. Nevertheless, for all the Norman kings the church within the kingdom and duchy was dominical, part of their demesne, and the bishops and royal abbots were vassals. Nor did they allow this authority to be usurped, as in France, by earls or other barons. Their feudal vassals had rights only in the lesser churches, those on their demesnes.

The king never hesitated to interfere in any aspect of church affairs if he felt so inclined or his interest was solicited. But his main concerns were his bishops and abbots, ecclesiastical business which touched the whole kingdom, and developments which affected his own rights, or public order. He also, as we have seen, resented interference in the church from outside.

The basic royal right, the *jus regale* par excellence, was custody of a vacant bishopric or royal abbey during its vacancy; and from this followed logically the confiscation of the personal wealth of a dead prelate (*jus spolii*), the nomination of a new incumbent, the taking of a fee (however disguised) in return, the requirement of homage and fealty, and the investiture with the church, besides jurisdiction over the prelates and their lands. All these rights

51. Cf. E. Pitz, *Papstreskript und Kaiserreskript im Mittelalter* (Tübingen 1971) 281 ff.

52. F. Barlow, 'The English, Norman, and French councils called to deal with the schism of 1159', *EHR* li (1936) 264, *The letters of Arnulf of Lisieux*, R. Hist. Soc. Camden 3rd ser. lxi (1939) p. xl; Mary G. Cheney, 'The recognition of Alexander III: some neglected evidence', *EHR* lxxxiv (1969) 474; T. A. Reuter, 'The papal schism, the Empire and the West, 1159–1169' (unpublished Oxford D Phil thesis 1975).

were based on ancient custom. And although the eleventh-century ecclesiastical reformers liked none of them, they disliked some more than others and, after the heroic period, were prepared to distinguish, negotiate separately on some of the various parts, and also to bow to necessity.

Custody was not surrendered by even the weakest king. The sharpest definition of this regalian right is in Henry II's inquest into the ecclesiastical customs of his grandfather's reign, the Constitutions of Clarendon of 1164. Chapter 12 opens: 'When an archbishopric or bishopric, or an abbey or priory on the royal demesne, shall fall vacant, it shall be taken into the king's hands, and he shall take all its rents and revenues as though it was [royal] demesne.'[53] In 1176 Henry promised the pope that in future he would not keep sees vacant for more than one year unless there was urgent necessity or good reason.[54] But this was the only restriction on his right that he allowed. No less explicit is a writ of William II addressed to the tenants of the bishopric of Worcester after Wulfstan's death (1095): 'Know that on the death of the bishop the honour has returned into my hands.'[55]

Whatever may have been the position before the Conquest – and it is unlikely that Old English kings took no steps to control and protect vacant bishoprics and abbeys – after 1066 Carolingian and Norman custom prevailed: the vacant see or abbey reverted to the king as though it was a feudal benefice or honour.[56] The king appointed custodians whose first duty was to make a survey and inventory (*descriptio*) of the lands and chattels.[57] The use he made of the escheat depended on his character and the circumstances. The Conqueror was notorious for his avarice; but Rufus must have gone much further. It was generally held that he abused his rights by trying to squeeze every possible profit out of the estate. He was accused of selling the custody to the highest bidder, and putting it up to auction annually; of wasting the capital assets by felling woods, taxing the tenants, and enfeoffing his knights on the demesne; and of making the minimum provision for the chapter or priory. His agent in these matters was Ranulf Flambard.[58]

Henry I in his coronation charter renounced his brother's abuses but not his father's rights. And he seems to have been at least as extortionate as Rufus and his minister. From the Pipe Roll of 1130 we see that after Ranulf Flambard's death Henry made from Durham a clear profit of over £1,200 in two years.[59] There were renewed complaints about these practices when Henry died, and Stephen in his turn promised reform.[60] He declared that he would

53. *SSC* 166.

54. Diceto, *Ymagines,* i. 410.

55. *SSC* 109.

56. Margaret E. Howell, 'The king's government and episcopal vacancies in England eleventh to fourteenth century' (unpublished London PhD thesis, 1955) 12 ff.; published as *Regalian right in medieval England* (London Univ. Hist. Studies, IX) (1962); references are to the thesis.

57. An example is *Liber Niger Monasterii S. Petri de Burgo* [1125] in *Chronicon Petroburgense,* ed. Thomas Stapleton, Camden Soc. xlvii (1849) 157.

58. Cf. *HN* 26–7.

59. *SSC* 117; *Pipe Roll 31 H I,* 128–33. Howell 40 ff. According to Simeon *HDE* 135 Rufus only got £300 *p.a.* from Durham during the previous vacancy.

60. *SSC* 144. Howell 56 ff. Below 130, 304.

commit the vacant bishopric to the custody of clerks or honest vassals of the church. This was an important concession. Such domestic custodians would be milder than royal servants.[61] But, since nothing is said about the destination of the revenue, the clause is ambiguous; and the final saving clause, protecting the royal dignity, was also an impediment to radical change. Stephen did not renounce in the charter the taking of the church into his own hands and its eventual grant to the new incumbent. And, although hampered by rival forces, he exercised whenever he could the traditional royal rights.[62] That Henry II could immediately reestablish the old position and hold on to it without difficulty[63] shows that Stephen had not yielded much ground.

Later the church asserted that the king should have custody and profit only of the temporalities, not of the spiritualities.[64] But since Henry II took Peter's Pence, synodals, archidiaconal dues, and revenues from prebends and vacant churches in the bishop's gift,[65] we can assume that the Norman kings hardly recognized the distinction. Custody was lucrative. In Henry II's reign three bishoprics (Canterbury, York, and Winchester), when vacant, yielded to the royal exchequer £1300–1500 a year net, two (Ely and Lincoln) over £800, Durham £600, four (Bath, London, Salisbury, and Worcester) £300–400, three (Chichester, Exeter, and Hereford) over £200, two (Lichfield and Norwich) over £100, and two (Carlisle and St David's) less than £100.[66] But although custody justified or facilitated other royal claims, the twelfth-century church treated the problem realistically. Royal custody at least limited robbery and reduced it to its most inoffensive form. There were radicals in the church who believed that total renunciation of temporalities would solve most of the church's problems, and many practical men appreciated the difficulties for a king and nation created by the unrestricted movement of land into *mortmain*. When Rufus enfeoffed his knights with Canterbury estates *sede vacante* he was not inventing the practice.

Much less indignation was aroused by the *jus spolii*, for even conventional churchmen believed that a bishop should not die rich. Accumulation of wealth was wrong in itself, and the least an avaricious prelate could do was to distribute his movables before he died. He should pass from death into life naked on the bare ground.[67] Since the tenth century kings had not required a mortuary from prelates,[68] but they thought that personal grants of land and undistributed wealth should revert to them. How they behaved on a prelate's death, however, depended on the circumstances. Rufus, according to the Chronicle, wanted to be the heir to every man, clerk and lay.[69] In 1129, on the

---

61. Henry I, when he took Canterbury into his hands in 1103, used men of the archbishopric as his custodians, *GP* 113.

62. As, for example, when he arrested the bishops who would not surrender their castles *sede plena:* below 305.

63. Howell 60 ff.

64. For temporalities and spiritualities, see Barlow *English Church 1000–1066*, 159 ff.

65. Howell 68–9. Cf. above 116, below 130.

66. Howell 484 ff.

67. Cf. the deathbed of Ralf Luffa, bishop of Chichester, in 1123, above 68.

68. Eric John, *Land Tenure in Early England* (1960) 57–8.

69. *Chron. s.a.* 1100.

death of Ranulf Flambard, Henry I confiscated all his money, whether distributed or stored, except that which he had given to some churches and the poor,[70] and in 1135 he took from the vast treasure left by Gilbert the Universal bishop of London greaves decorated with gold and silver.[71] Henry had made no reference to this custom in his coronation charter and it was not mentioned among the catalogue of his misdeeds at the London council of 1136. Nevertheless Stephen in his Oxford charter (1136) allowed that a bishop, abbot, or other ecclesiastical person could make a reasonable distribution of his possessions before his death, or leave them by will. Moreover, if he died before either of these could be done, his goods should be distributed according to the church's advice for the good of his soul.[72] When the disgraced Roger bishop of Salisbury died at the end of 1139, leaving, it was rumoured, about £27,000 in silver coin as well as gold and ornaments of every kind, Stephen at first took it all, but later returned some of the money to relieve the poverty of the canons and pay for the roofing of the cathedral church.[73] There does not seem to have been a general rule.

Since after the death of a prelate the benefice was always in the king's hands, and the king could not be forced to grant it to anyone except by the successful use of excommunication and interdict, even the most ardent champions of ecclesiastical rights allowed the king the right of confirmation of the canonically elected bishop. In practice all the popes and most of the reformers accepted that the king must be allowed some part in the selection of his bishops. But most kings could be influenced in varying degrees by their archbishops and other bishops, by their clerks, and sometimes by the chapters. Elections were often made in great royal courts or national synods, attended by the king and his earls and barons as well as by his archbishops, bishops, and abbots. There was probably the feeling that all interests should be satisfied: that the king should not take all the sees for his own clerks and that he should not make outrageous appointments. Above all he should not sell bishoprics (simony). Under Stephen the church made great strides towards getting episcopal elections under its own control. Both the king's brother, Henry bishop of Winchester, and Theobald archbishop of Canterbury, were committed to the principle of free and canonical elections in the vacant churches by the proper electors.[74] But both in turn, using legatine authority or other powers, made their own appointments or influenced elections.

Until 1107 the king, after taking feudal homage and fealty from the bishop-elect, invested him with his bishopric by ring and staff. By the twelfth century most commentators agreed that although the king was using spiritual symbols he was only granting the temporalities, and that spiritual authority was conferred only when the archbishop, assisted by at least three suffragans, ordained the candidate bishop.[75] The position after 1107 is described (from the

70. Simeon *HDE cont.* 141.
71. HH 308. Cf. OV (Chibnall) vi. 336–40.
72. *SSC* 144.
73. Florence 113–14; *GSteph* 65; *Hist. Nov.* 39.
74. Tillmann 46, n.180.
75. See below 294 ff.

royalist standpoint) in the second part of chapter 12 of the Constitutions of Clarendon:

> And when provision has to be made for the [vacant] church, the king should inform the more important members of that church [? the cathedral chapter] and the election should be made in the chapel of the lord king with the lord king's assent and the counsel of those [? ecclesiastical] persons of the kingdom whom the king has summoned for this purpose. The elect should then, and before he is consecrated, do homage and fealty to the lord king as his liege lord with respect to his life, limbs, and earthly honour, but saving his order.[76]

Henry II was attempting to recover control over the appointment of bishops and abbots. The language is circumspect: to the prelates and chapter is awarded advice, to the king assent. This was an acceptable formula. In any case the Constitutions only described the preliminaries, the necessary secular entanglement. The ordination ceremony, usually at Canterbury, although attended by the laity (but not by the king), was a purely ecclesiastical rite. It was the church which gave the bishop-elect his spiritual authority.

Kings as much as the reformers accepted that simony, the buying and selling of church offices, was a sin, but a sin into which it was easy to fall. Rufus sold blatantly; the others expected some return. And there was plenty of room for equivocation. Even Anselm after his consecration offered Rufus a financial aid, a doubtful action from which he was saved only by the king's greed in demanding a larger sum.[77]

More political and more variable was the king's general supervision over the activities of the church. All the Norman kings controlled in some degree ecclesiastical councils, legislation, and jurisdiction, sometimes encouraging action, as against married priests, sometimes discouraging it, as when it concerned feudal land, sometimes restraining its abuse, as with archidiaconal inquisitions, sometimes protesting angrily, as when it seemed that clerical criminals were not only increasing in number but also escaping proper punishment. Above all, the bishops were in the king's power. If a bishop was guilty of a serious offence against the king's honour he was tried in the *curia regis* and could be sentenced to banishment and forfeiture of his fief.

When we turn from the super-powers to look at the domestic government of the English church we find another monarch. On the purely spiritual side the archbishop of Canterbury was normally accepted as the head of the whole English, if not British church; and the only problem was how to define that authority in terms acceptable primarily to York, but also to the Welsh, Scottish, and Irish bishops. It was not unusual for Canterbury, even when exercising ordinary and basic metropolitan rights, to have York in attendance.[78] And in the Norman period Canterbury apologists tended to confuse metropolitan, primatial, and legatine authority. Eadmer's exalted

76. *SSC* 166 and above 116.
77. *HN* 43 ff.
78. Cf. below 143.

claims for his church were always loosely attributed. And they were vast claims. He thought that the post-Conquest opposition of the non-monastic bishops to the monastic constitution of Canterbury was partly because of the sublimity of the primatial see, which had the right to supervise the management and disciplining of all the churches throughout England through their rectors. And he reports that when the bishops withdrew their friendship from Anselm at Rufus's court at Rockingham in 1095 the archbishop told them that they did wrong to withhold the subjection, fealty, and friendship which they owed him as their primate and spiritual father simply because he himself held to the subjection and fealty he owed to the pope.[79] We can now, therefore, turn our attention to Canterbury's superior governmental powers without attempting their precise attribution. These consisted almost entirely in the right to hold what were usually called by contemporary writers general councils of the English church. Two of the councils held by Lanfranc, Winchester (1072) and London (1075) – those which the author of the *Acta Lanfranci* knew to have issued canons – are thus described.[80] The ordinary meaning of the phrase would be that they were attended by all the prelates in England. The archbishop of York was certainly at these meetings, and Durham sent an apology to London. Yet York was also at Gloucester in 1080 and this council is not awarded the epithet. Nor is it clear by what authority such councils met. Winchester and Windsor (1072), which considered the Canterbury–York disputes, and Winchester (1076), which completed the case against Bishop Æthelric of Selsey, were probably called under papal authority and so can be described as legatine. Lanfranc styled himself 'primate of the whole of the British Isle' in his account of the council of London in 1075. And the untechnical adjective 'general' may have been used by the author of the *Acta Lanfranci* both because he did not know the ecclesiastical standing of those two councils and also because they had issued decrees.

There is also the difficulty that in this period ecclesiastical councils are not easily separated from royal courts. The king's court could deal with both secular and ecclesiastical affairs and could try bishops for feudal offences. Sometimes a court was transformed into an ecclesiastical council, as the great assembly at Gloucester at Christmas 1085, which authorized the Domesday survey and other defence measures. According to the English annalist, after William had held his court for five days, the archbishop and his clerks held a synod for three days. The only ecclesiastical business mentioned is the election of three bishops, all royal clerks, and more likely elected in the court than the synod. Nor was this type of confusion confined to the early Norman period. Some of the great councils called by Henry I and Stephen, especially those concerned with the succession, were of a hybrid nature. The attendance at councils was always mixed. Bishops and abbots were members of the royal court; the king claimed the uncontested right to preside if he so wished over a national council of the church; and the laity were present, even if only as

79.   *HN* 19, 63.

80.   *Acta Lanfranci* in John Earle, *Two of the Saxon Chronicles Parallel* (1865) 271 ff. Cf. C. R. Cheney, 'Legislation of the Medieval English church', *EHR* l (1935) 197–8.

auditors, at such assemblies. It is pedantic, therefore, to draw too sharp a line between royal and ecclesiastical councils.[81]

By the twelfth century, however, the two can be distinguished in theory, if not always in practice. The criteria are the authority by which the council was summoned and its composition. There is no ambiguity when in 1125 Archbishop William of Corbeil, on behalf of the papal legate, John of Crema, summoned the bishops, together with the archdeacons, abbots, and priors of their diocese, to attend a council 'in order to settle ecclesiastical business and to reform and correct those things which the judgment of our convocation shall show ought to be corrected, reformed, or brought to notice'.[82] But it is unlikely that Lanfranc always issued a separate summons when he was going to hold a synod in connexion with a royal court. And there is no reason to think that archdeacons or priors attended before Anselm's council of Westminster (1102). In 1070 the papal legates instructed the bishops to attend a council at Winchester with all the abbots of their diocese.[83] Rockingham (1095) can be used as a test case.[84] After a dispute between Anselm and Rufus over the recognition of the pope, Anselm asked the king to call together the bishops, abbots, and all the other princes of the kingdom, so that they might determine by common assent whether he could, saving the obedience he owed to the holy see, maintain the fealty he owed to the king. The resulting *conventus* met on a Sunday in the church within the castle. William of St Calais, bishop of Durham, was the king's spokesman, and the bishops played the largest part in the proceedings. But there can be no doubt that the assembly was a royal court, investigating what Rufus considered a breach of the royal customs and an affront to his royal dignity. Although Rufus believed himself competent in ecclesiastical matters, Anselm, no more than William of St Calais in 1088, would not have recognized the king's court as an ecclesiastical council.

Nevertheless, the line is not easy to draw. Only a handful of undoubted church synods can be distinguished, either because they were held by the primate in the king's absence or by a papal legate, whether *a latere* or standing, or because they were generally so regarded. Chronologically these fall into three main groups: Lanfranc's councils held under William I, principally between 1072 and 1076; the series in Henry I's reign started by Anselm and continued by his successors and the papal legate, John of Crema; and the more compact group of legatine councils under Stephen, inaugurated by Alberic of Ostia in 1138 and maintained by Henry bishop of Winchester.

No systematic record of the proceedings of these councils was kept.[85] The *Acta Lanfranci,* compiled from Canterbury records after the archbishop's death – most of which are still available to us – gives a sparse account of

---

81. There is a useful list of 'provincial and national councils of the church in England' in *Handbook of British Chronology* 549–60.

82. Summons to Urban of Llandaff in Wilkins i. 408.

83. Printed *Vita Wulfstani* 189–90.

84. *HN* 53 ff.

85. Cf. C. R. Cheney, 'Legislation of the Medieval English Church', 193, 385; C. N. L. Brooke, 'Canons of English church councils in the early decretal collections', *Traditio* xiii (1957) 472; Martin Brett, 'A collection of Anglo-Norman councils', *JEH* xxvi (1975) 305–6.

his conciliar action.[86] We are told that Lanfranc himself was persuaded to write the minutes (*gestio*) of the council of London (1075); and an account survives. We also know something about the *decreta* of the council of London (1102). After the council Anselm explained to enquirers that owing to the hasty conclusion of the proceedings and the ill-considered announcement of the decrees (*sententiae*) he did not want these to be published before they had been scrutinized by all the bishops at their next meeting, for he thought they needed proper revision. To the archbishop of York he would send only the headings (*capitula*) and to the archdeacon of Canterbury a list of the subjects treated (*nomina rerum*). After the revision the decrees would be copied out (*dictatae*) and sent for publication to all the English churches (presumably the episcopal sees).[87] In this matter Anselm showed a strong sense of collegiality. The wording had to be agreed by all the participating bishops, but not, we notice, by the others who had been present, such as abbots, lay magnates, and the king. These, however, had assented to the subject matter of the legislation; and it is unlikely that Anselm was intending here to flout the ancestral custom which gave the king control over ecclesiastical legislation.[88] It is also of interest that not even in 1102 was the drafting of the legislation left to a secretariat.

The record of councils is, therefore, imperfect. Of some assemblies we have no report; and canons have survived only because they were copied by a church into some existing canonical collection or other handy manuscript or because they were incorporated into its chronicle. This lack of documentation is itself a clue to the nature of the meetings. The business was essentially deliberative and the purpose disciplinary. For example, Eadmer relates that at one of Lanfranc's general councils there was a discussion on the status of those English women who had taken the veil to escape the lust of the Normans.[89] It was not unusual for abbots to be deposed,[90] and occasionally bishops were consecrated after their election in the associated royal court.[91] Disputes could be ventilated, if not always settled, for it was the king who could most effectively put an end to quarrels between the prelates. And matters could be raised which led to the issue of legislative or administrative decrees.

The impetus to this conciliar activity came not from Anglo-Danish England but from abroad. In England owing to the spate of royal ecclesiastical legislation between 942 and 1023 there was a lull in Edward the Confessor's reign. The law had been declared.[92] The only bishop known to have issued canons on the eve of the Conquest is Ealdred of York.[93] The movement was reactivated in 1070 by papal legates, but once Lanfranc had been made primate

---

86. Councils are mentioned in years 2 (general council at Winchester), 5 (general council at London, 6 (council at Winchester), 8 (council at London), 11 (council at Gloucester), and 16 (council at Gloucester): *Two of the Saxon Chronicles Parallel* 271–3.

87. *AEp* 253 (to Gerard of York), 257 (to William archdeacon of Canterbury); cf. also 254–6.

88. Below 279 f.

89. *HN* 124.

90. For example, at Lanfranc's councils of Winchester (1072), London (1077–78), and Gloucester (1085), Anselm's council of Westminster (1102), Alberic's at Westminster (1138).

91. For example, at Gloucester (1080) and Gloucester (1085).

92. *English Church 1000–1066.* 137 ff.

93. *Ibid.* 245–6.

the background became the duchy; and in Normandy, where a shattered Carolingian church had been reconstructed by penitent Vikings, the position was very different. Although the most important Norman councils were contemporary with the English post-Conquest activity – and were part of the same movement – there were precedents in the duchy without parallel in the kingdom.[94] Archbishop Mauger's council of Rouen (1037x46; ? before 1042),[95] antedating Pope Clement II's and the Emperor Henry III's council at Rome in January 1047, was exceptionally early; and Maurilius's councils at Rouen (1055x63)[96] and Lisieux (1064)[97] were also ahead of the field. Norman conciliar legislation is impressive. Rouen (1037x46) issued nineteen canons, Lisieux (1064) ten, Rouen (1072)[98] twenty-four, Rouen (1074)[99] fourteen, and Lillebonne (1080)[100] forty-six. Its purpose was the moral and administrative reform of the secular clergy of the province. Mauger legislated comprehensively against all forms of simony. Maurilius started the attack on clerical marriage which his successor, John of Avranches, intensified.

Since the prelates assembled in council were only drawing attention to those parts of the law which at that time needed special enforcement, or applying a principle to a particular problem, or elaborating or clarifying an accepted rule, there were differences of emphasis at different times and places. The Truce of God, to which Norman and papal councils paid much attention, was not introduced into England. The kingdom had no interest in the crusading movements. The prohibition of lay investiture was not promulgated in England until after the concordat with the papacy. Nor in general does it seem that English legislation was simply the belated re-enactment of the decrees of papal councils. But it was not autonomous or dissenting. All ecclesiastical authorities in this period were advancing along the same broad highway and taking note of each other's progress.

The English legislative programme has, therefore, a unity. The reform measures taken by the cardinal-priests John and Peter and Ermenfrid bishop of Sion at Winchester (1070) were completed by Alberic cardinal-bishop of Ostia at Westminster (1138); and all the English ecclesiastical legislation which falls between those two points is inspired by the same, basically eleventh-century ideals: to rid the church of simony, to enforce celibacy on the clergy in major orders and generally free them from worldly entanglements and interests, and to secure a greater observance of Christian

94. Raymonde Foreville, 'The synod of the province of Rouen in the eleventh and twelfth centuries', in *Church and Government in the Middle Ages: essays presented to C. R. Cheney* 19; a useful list is on p. 22.

95. Mansi xix. 751; H-L, iv. 993. Mauger was probably a pupil of William of Dijon's school at Fécamp, Böhmer *KuS* 11.

96. Mansi xix. 841, 1027; H-L, iv. 1233; *PL* cxlvii, 277–8. Böhmer, *KuS* 16, n.3, dates the council 1055 x 63, Raymonde Foreville 1055 (?). But it is not clear whether there was one council or two in this period, and, if two, to which Lisieux (1064) refers.

97. L. Delisle, 'Canons du Concile tenu à Lisieux en 1064', *Journal des Savants* (Paris 1901) 516–21; H-L iv. 1420. Delisle suggested that the MS which contains the canons came from Bec.

98. OV (Chibnall) ii. 284–92; Mansi xx. 33; H-L iv. 1281.

99. Mansi xx. 397; H-L v. 113, where it is claimed, probably mistakenly, that there were two councils at Rouen in this year.

100. OV (Chibnall) iii. 24 ff.; Mansi xx. 555; H-L v. 279; below 148 ff.

rules among the laity. It should be noticed that the archbishops who inspired the legislation were all vowed to chastity, poverty, and obedience, and were not markedly sympathetic to the problems of the secular clergy.

Six sets of English conciliar decrees have survived, mostly in the form of headings or summaries, which can be attributed with some confidence to the period 1070 to 1087.[101] Only two are precisely dated: Lanfranc's own summary of canons issued at London (1075) is extant,[102] and a summary of six decrees dated Winchester, 1 April 1076,[103] must be a report overlooked by the compiler of *Acta Lanfranci*. The exact provenance of the other four is uncertain, and the problem is how to distribute them between the councils held by Ermenfrid bishop of Sion in the spring of 1070 and Lanfranc's five undocumented councils: Winchester (Easter 1072), adjourned to Windsor (Whitsun), London (1077x8), Gloucester (Christmas 1080), and Gloucester again (Christmas 1085).[104] One clue is that all the *acta* seem to be primitive.

It is possible that the headings to sixteen canons issued at Winchester at an unspecified date may be assigned to Ermenfrid's council in 1070.[105] They are, although possibly incomplete, the longest and most miscellaneous of the early Anglo-Norman ecclesiastical codes and must have been produced largely by the survivors of the Old English prelacy under the guidance of the legates. Except for the opening decree – that no one was to hold two bishoprics, an enactment which was never repeated – the legislation has the appearance of what the English church would itself have issued at the time. The two main planks of the reform programme are there: simony is condemned (2), and, almost as an afterthought (15), clerks are enjoined either to live chastely or to surrender their office. The latter, at least in its given summarized form, needed construing. It could be understood as a sweeping injunction applying to the clergy in general (and seems to have been interpreted thus by Bishop Wulfstan of Worcester[106]) or as referring only to canons, members of collegiate bodies. The ambiguity was possibly intentional. Penance for crimes was reserved to the bishop (11). Apostate monks were to be excommunicated (12). Tithe was to be paid by all (14). A number of irregularities in the administration of the sacraments and in liturgical practices were condemned. And, to enforce and continue the reform, bishops were to hold a synod every year (13).

---

101. The problem of sorting out the decrees attributed to Winchester was attempted by Böhmer 62, n.3. As he at least put the various sets in a logical order according to contents, his attributions have been generally accepted. But cf. Tillmann 14, n.8. In 1975 Martin Brett, 'A collection of Anglo-Norman councils', *JEH* xxvi (1975) 301, re-examined the question, and published for the first time a set of 14 canons which he attributed to Winchester (1072). He did not, however, redistribute the 13 canons printed Wilkins i. 365, Mansi xx. 459–60, which Böhmer had assigned to this council. It is clear that Brett's decrees are early, but so it would seem are the set of 13. One possibility, followed here, is to transfer Wilkins's decrees to Windsor (1072). There is little overlap.

102. Wilkins i. 363; Mansi xx. 449–56.

103. Wilkins i. 367; Mansi xx. 462, 459. Böhmer 62, n.2.

104. *Acta Lanfranci:* see above n.86. For Winchester (1072) see also *GR* 349–55, *GP* 42 ff., *Vita Wulfstani* 25–6; *Palaeographical Soc.* iii, pl. 170; P. Chaplais, 'The Anglo-Saxon chancery from the diploma to the writ', *Journ. of the Soc. of Archivists* iii. 4 (1966) 161–2; for London (1075) *GP* 66; for Gloucester (1080) Simeon *HDE* i. 119; for Gloucester (1085) *Chron. E.*

105. Wilkins i. 365; Mansi xx. 400–2, 460.

106. *Vita Wulfstani* 53–4.

Lanfranc's earliest enactments may be represented by a summary of fourteen canons (? Winchester 1072)[107] and thirteen headings supposed to indicate the *acta* of a council held at Windsor at Whitsun (Windsor ? 1072).[108] There is no problem with London (1075) and Winchester (1076). And the remaining set of eight decrees may have been issued by one of Lanfranc's later councils.[109] The degree of error in these allocations is probably not substantial, but since the exact order of the enactments is not certain the precise way in which the reform programme unfolded in England cannot be shown.

Lanfranc had been made abbot of Caen in 1063, and had probably attended Maurilius's councils at Rouen (1055x63) and Lisieux (1064), especially since both declared the Catholic faith against Berengar of Tours, Lanfranc's theological opponent. Thus when Lanfranc went from Caen to Canterbury in 1070 he was familiar with metropolitan action against the main evils of the day, and it is not surprising that post-Conquest reform councils in the two countries should have started almost simultaneously. Indeed, there is almost a suggestion of rivalry in reform between Lanfranc and John of Avranches, Maurilius's successor. The position was delicate, for Lanfranc had been considered for Rouen and had then accepted (although certainly with reluctance) the even greater see of Canterbury.

One of Lanfranc's first purposes seems to have been to secure the loyalty of the English church and people to the Norman king. Winchester (?1072) (9) ordered that bishops should not conspire against the prince, and Windsor (? 1072) enacted that no one was to be a traitor to the king or the land in which he dwelt. Every bishop and priest should excommunicate such traitors in his parish. Each priest should recite three masses for the king and all other orders one psalter, and the laity were to bestow alms seven times. All were to aid the poor with their alms. These measures were probably in part penances for the recent rebellions against Norman rule.

The archbishop's reform programme in England was a repetition of that begun in Normandy. He wanted to impose on England ideal Norman conditions. The two themes which run through all his legislation are the reform of the *vita et conversatio* of the clergy and the need for more orderly diocesan government under the direction of the bishop. In the first category the chastity of the clergy was the most important matter. The subject was probably discussed by Windsor (?1072) (3),[110] and Winchester (1076) (1) gives us the full text of Lanfranc's decree against clerical marriage, which, even if it reveals the lost injunction of the earlier English council, certainly reproduces Lisieux (1064) (2–3), Rouen (1072) (15), and so Rouen (1055x63). The same laws were to run on both sides of the Channel.[111] Separate rules were made for canons and

---

107.   Brett 307–8.

108.   Wilkins i. 365; Mansi xx. 459–60.

109.   Mansi xx. 400. Böhmer *ibid*. In the MS they follow Rouen (1074). Böhmer's specific argument, that chapter 5 – no parish is to be ruled by a monk – is inapplicable to Normandy, is, however, of doubtful cogency. Cf. also Brett 301–2.

110.   'De vita et conversatione eorundem.' The last word has no antecedent and may be a mistake for 'clericorum' or 'canonicorum'. See also the next note.

111.   Lanfranc wrote to John of Rouen (*LEp*. 17); 'immo vestro aliorumque venerabilium patrum exemplo provocatus, per totam Anglicam terram pastorali auctoritate prohibui, ne cuiuslibet

parish priests. Winchester (1076) states baldly that no canon is to have a wife. The Norman decrees distinguish: married canons in minor orders, though not to be deprived of their wives by force were to be urged to dismiss them, but married canons in priest's or deacon's orders were to send them away. Parish priests (the Norman decrees add deacons) who were already married were not to be forced to dismiss their wives, although in future bishops were to ordain only those priests and deacons who would vow that they would not marry. The form of profession of chastity to be taken by ordinands is extant. The Norman decrees simply state that none was to marry or keep a mistress in future.

These injunctions, although a humane application of the revived discipline, were much opposed by those to whom they should have applied, and there is little evidence that they were generally observed. When Rouen (1072) repeated the earlier decree the 'libidinous priests' attacked the archbishop with stones, and as he fled from the church in which the synod was being held, he cried out, 'O God, the heathen are come into thine inheritance: thy holy temple have they defiled' (Ps. 79: 1).[112] In England, except in the diocese of Worcester,[113] trouble did not start until Anselm tried to enforce the law.

The other main target of this reform movement was simony. From Winchester (?1070), through Winchester (?1072) (4) and Windsor (?1072) (1–2), to London (1075) (7), following the decrees of Rouen (1037x46) (2, 6–9) and its successors, the selling of bishoprics and abbeys and the selling of ordination was prohibited. Winchester (?1072) (3) condemned the selling of the Eucharist. Secular pursuits also were condemned. Clerks were not to be gamesters or hunters, or be the reeve of anyone but a bishop (Winchester ?1072) (7, 10) or to bear arms (Windsor, ?1072) (12); nor were bishops, abbots, or clerks to pronounce or countenance sentences of death or mutilation (London, 1075) (9). Lanfranc preferred to keep monks out of the public eye. But the latter council (2) ordered monks to observe their Rule, especially with regard to private property.

The second principal theme was episcopal government. Winchester (?1072) (5) enacted that no one was to put a priest in charge of a church without the authority of the bishop who would confer on the priest the cure of souls, and Windsor (?1072) framed the model. Bishops were to have fixed sees (9), appoint officials (5), hold councils twice a year (4), take action against apostate clerks and monks (8), and invite the laity to penitence (7). London (1075) looked at the re-siting of the sees (3). And Winchester (1076) (4) reinforced the bishops' jurisdiction over the laity accused of criminal sins, which had been referred to by Winchester (?1072) (8). All councils from Winchester (?1070) (3) to Winchester (1076) (2) condemned indiscriminate ordinations and the retention and ordination of foreign clerks and monks

ordinis quisquam canonicus uxorem accipiat, nec sortito antea, si presbyter aut diaconus est, nisi prebenda carere velit, habere ulterius liceat.' Lanfranc is, indeed, echoing the words of Norman legislation on this matter: cf. Lisieux (1064) cap. 3. But he makes no mention of the prohibition of marriage to the village clergy and does not reproduce the language of Winchester (1076), as it has been transmitted to us. It would seem, therefore, that the letter refers to the more limited decree of Winchester (?1072) and should be dated c. 1073 rather than 1076.

112. OV (Chibnall) ii. 200.
113. *Vita Wulfstani* 53–4.

without letters commendatory from their superiors. No doubt there was an influx of foreigners in search of spoils and perhaps a movement between dioceses determined by the severity with which the anti-marriage laws were enforced. Winchester (1076) also ordered that no such itinerant monk, even if accepted by the bishop, was to be put in public charge of a church. Changes in the calendar were enacted by Winchester (?1072) (11–14).

The laity, as was usual at the time, received the least attention. Windsor (?1072) (14), following Winchester (?1070) (14), ordered them to pay tithe, and forbade them to usurp ecclesiastical goods or deny due reverence to clerks and monks (13). Winchester (?1072) (1) indicated that infants could be baptized at any time. London (1075) condemned superstitious practices (8), and prohibited marriage within seven degrees (6), Winchester (1076) (5) returned to this last subject. This time, perhaps inspired by Rouen (1072) (14), it was decreed that no marriage was to be performed without the blessing of a priest, otherwise the union would be considered sinful. Here was a clear interference with Germanic marriage custom, but, of course, with a sound moral purpose. The priest would be able to investigate the relationship between the contracting parties. The enactment was the inevitable sequel to that of London (1075).

The last set of canons attributed to Lanfranc – the eight decrees of an unknown council – are best considered apart because the attribution is by no means certain. Although they fall within the Anglo-Norman family, they link better with Normandy than with England. There is the usual concern with letters dimissory (2), the giving of parishes to monks (5), penance (8), and the income of parish priests (3). The decree concerning marriage – that those petitioning for a divorce on the grounds of inability to consummate the marriage must prove in accordance with the law both that they cannot perform their conjugal duty and that their incapacity is not due to their own action – goes back to Rouen (1074) (10). The unknown council also breaks new ground. Ordinands are to fast before the ceremony (4) and must have reached the appropriate canonical age (6), and no one is to teach the people, for a fee or otherwise, unless licensed by the bishop (1).

Viewed as a whole Lanfranc's legislation, although fragmentary and unsystematic, does sketch the framework of a fairly comprehensive reform programme. The clergy and the monks were to observe their rules, especially chastity for the secular clergy and commonalty of possessions for the monks. All forms of simony were to disappear. The authority of the bishop was emphasized at every point: there was to be orderly diocesan administration and justice. The bishops' synods and courts were to enforce canon law, secure the blameless clergy which was required for the ministry, and supervise the morals, particularly the sexual morals, of the laity. The task was laid squarely on the shoulders of the diocesan bishop. He was given a programme and ordered to carry it out, and he was to be the master in his diocese. The novelties for the English church were not in the substance of the reforms. Although there were changes in emphasis, these were probably more characteristic of the age than of nationality. The real innovation was in ordering the creation of a new administrative machinery, purely ecclesiastical, which was to implement the reform. This policy, it cannot be said too often, reveals no hostility to the State. Norman custom was the model. The cooperation of the secular authorities was, quite rightly, assumed. And it was moral purpose rather than aggrandisement which dictated the course of action. Lanfranc's measures cannot be considered outside the context of the reform movement in the church at large, but they are almost completely independent of the narrower movement usually called 'Gregorian'.

It does not seem that Lanfranc's councils issued any general decrees after Winchester (1076). Rufus, who left Canterbury vacant from 1089 to 1093, would not allow Anselm to call a 'general council of bishops' according to the ancient custom, although the archbishop asked pressingly at least in 1094 and 1097.[114] In March 1094 at Dover Rufus inquired about Anselm's reasons, and the archbishop replied that he wanted to repress the most wicked sin of sodomy as well as incestuous marriages and other enormities, which, because of the lack of good government, were spreading widely in England. It was not until Henry I, who shared Anselm's moral principles, succeeded his brother in 1100 that the series of councils began again. Westminster (1102) resumed where Lanfranc had left off and London (1107) made the final settlement of the quarrel over investitures. The councils of Ralf d'Escures do not seem to have legislated. But at London (1125) the papal legate *a latere*, John of Crema, issued a notable set of canons, and William of Corbeil continued the practice at Westminster (1127) and London (1129).

Anselm's council of Westminster in 1102 had to deal with the abuses which had spread during Rufus's reign.[115] Nine abbots were deposed, six for simony and three for other sufficient causes. And thirty decrees, logically arranged as might be expected from Anselm, were designed to reform the morals of both clergy and laity. After the usual opening condemnation of simony, each order or rank was considered in turn. Bishops were not to be secular judges, were to dress appropriately and to have suitable companions, and were not to grant archdeaconries at farm (i.e. rent them out) (2-3). Archdeacons were to be in deacon's orders (4). These enactments acknowledge the emergence of archdeacons as a class, and were the first of a long series. The next five canons were aimed at clerical marriage and unchastity. The prohibition was sharpened by the order that priests who kept women were not to celebrate mass or, if they did, be listened to (7), and by the consequential prohibition of hereditary succession to benefices (9). Five more canons were concerned with other misdemeanours of the clergy: holding secular offices (10), attending 'drinkings' (11), wearing unsuitable clothes (12), and not showing a tonsure (14). Parish churches (15-18) were put under the control of the bishop (17-18) and were not to be impropriated to monasteries except through the bishop. After impropriation the incumbent was to retain an adequate share of the revenues (23). Among other monastic abuses condemned was the 'knightly' behaviour of abbots who did not live with their monks (19).

The morals of the laity then came under review. Marriage was regulated: secret weddings if subsequently denied by one party were to be annulled (24), and those who married within seven degrees of relationship

114. *HN* 48-9, 78.
115. *Chron.*; *HN* 141-4; *GP* 118; Florence; Hugh *HCY* 13; Wilkins i. 382; Mansi xx. 1149.

were to be separated (26). Men who wore their hair long were to be shorn so that their ears and eyes were visible (25). Corpses were to be buried within the parish (27). No one was to worship the bodies of the dead or springs and other such features without the bishop's permission (28). The slave trade was condemned (29) and so was sodomy (30). This last enactment was all the more severe because belated. All involved in the vice were to be under anathema until they confessed and did penance. Homosexual monks were not to be promoted and, if in a higher rank, were to be deposed. Homosexual laymen were to lose their law-worthiness throughout the kingdom. In future, except for those under a Rule, only a bishop could give absolution from the sin. This excommunication was to be published every Sunday in every church in England.

Anselm was prevented from waging a sustained campaign against the evils in the church by his renewed exile and worsening health. When he returned after the settlement of the investiture dispute, he once again at London (1108) made a great attempt to prevent priests cohabiting with women.[116] But William of Malmesbury, writing between 1118 and 1124, considered that the canons of 1102 had not been observed.[117] Simony was still practised, although covertly; bishops remained involved in the administration of the secular law, archdeacons were still farmers. Even the weekly excommunication of sodomites had been remitted by Anselm. Henry, hereditary archdeacon of Huntingdon, thought the prohibition of clerical marriage a novelty and most unwise: it could lead to quite horrible vices.[118]

After Anselm's death there was a lull until the papal legate, John of Crema, after a visitation of England in 1125, repeated and sometimes elaborated some of Anselm's decrees at a council in London.[119] Novelties were the prohibition of promotion to the priesthood or diaconate without a certain title (a benefice or other position) (8), holding two archdeaconries at the same time (12), clerical usury (14), and fortune telling (15). Some of Anselm's and John's legislation was repeated by Archbishop William of Corbeil at Westminster (1127 and 1129).[120] The decrees against clerical marriage were strengthened by the injunctions that archdeacons were to enforce the law (1127, cap. 5) and that the concubines of priests and canons were to be expelled from the parish unless they contracted a lawful marriage with someone free to marry (6), and by the more doubtful arrangement at one of the councils in 1129 that the king should have jurisdiction in this matter. Henry proceeded to fine (and in effect license) married clergy; and commentators thought that the measures were ineffective.[121] One of the few innovations was a sumptuary law against the wearing by nuns of furs richer than lamb or catskins (11).

116. *HN* 193–5; Florence ii. 59; Wilkins i. 387; Mansi xx. 1229.

117. *GP* 121 n.; cf. *HN* 144.

118. HH 234. There was indignation in Normandy in 1119 when Archbishop Geoffrey of Rouen tried to promulgate the conciliar decree made at Rheims against clerical marriage: OV (Chibnall) vi. 290–4.

119. *Chron.*; Florence; HH 245; *HR* 278; Wilkins i. 408; Mansi xxi. 327.

120. Florence; HH 247; Hugh *HCY* 130; Wilkins i. 410; Mansi xxi. 353. *Chron.*; John of Worcester; Wilkins i. 411; Mansi xxi. 383.

121. *Chron.*; HH 250–1.

In Stephen's reign there were both reactionary and revolutionary movements. As soon as the king had been accepted by Innocent II he obeyed the papal instructions and summoned a 'general council' of the magnates and clergy to London.[122] There were present the archbishops of Canterbury and Rouen, ten English and Welsh bishops, and two Norman bishops, one of whom was the brother of the absent archbishop of York. The main purpose was to persuade Stephen to repair the injuries which Henry I had done to the church. The prelates drew attention to the burden of royal pleas and litigation on bishops (*pastores*), to services arbitrarily required from them, to annual 'gifts' levied in the place of tribute (? danegeld), to Henry's simony, to his procurement of easy divorce, to his adultery and his toleration of it in others, to his enjoyment of *jus regale* (including gifts on the altars) during vacancies, and to his violence to those who withstood such actions by ecclesiastical measures. The prelates therefore asked Stephen to restore liberty to the church, give it back its own jurisdiction, and allow its institutions and decrees precedence over secular laws and unhindered operation. Stephen agreed, at least in general terms, and in April at Oxford, to which city the council was adjourned, issued a charter which redeemed his promises.[123] Here was the king behaving like his grandfather, the Conqueror. At the other extreme, his brother, Henry of Winchester, when papal legate, called ecclesiastical councils to deal with secular business.

The council held at Westminster in 1138 by the papal legate, Alberic of Ostia,[124] can be considered the last in the series which started in 1070. All the usual prohibitions and injunctions were made. But two new developments may be discerned which reveal the current and future preoccupations of the church. After a period of introspection, the church was beginning to concern itself with some of the evils in society at large. Its growing hostility to secular violence went beyond its interest in protecting its own persons and property from injury. And it was advancing beyond denunciation of the great evils to the correction of common administrative abuses. The details were beginning to be filled in. For example, episcopal fees and perquisites (3–4) and financial malpractices regarding cathedral schools (16)[125] were controlled.

The English legatine or general councils of the period 1139–51 developed the first more than the second of these themes. The councils held by Henry of Winchester as papal legate between 1139 and 1143 dealt with the social and political problems of the civil war, and Theobald's council of London (1151) with its last stages. At Winchester (1139) Henry attempted to try the king for his ill-treatment of the bishops and issued canons against those who injured clerks or usurped their possessions.[126] At Winchester (1141) he moved the church to recognize Matilda as ruler and then at Westminster (1141) swung

122. John of Hexham 288; *GSteph* 16–18. J. H. Round, *Geoffrey de Mandeville* (1892) 18 ff.

123. Below 304.

124. Gervase i. 107–8; Richard of Hexham iii. 173–6; John of Hexham 298; Wilkins i. 413; Mansi xxi. 507.

125. Below 225 f.

126. John of Worcester 55; *GSteph* 53; John of Hexham 301. Mansi xxi. 545. Below 305 f.

it back behind Stephen.[127] He held a number of councils in 1143 and at London in Lent issued seventeen drastic measures against disturbers of the peace of the church.[128] The deaths in the next year of some of the greatest offenders, such as Geoffrey of Mandeville and Robert Marmion, were ascribed to this action.[129] The eight canons of Theobald's legatine council at London (1151) show how far the church was prepared to go to defend its own property.[130] Churches and all ecclesiastical possessions were to be free from illegal exactions and tallages, although not from labour services owed to the king (1). Bishops were in future not to prosecute those who injured the church before the king's barons trying pleas of the crown, because losses were incurred in that way; instead the bishops were to proceed against them through ecclesiastical justice. Bishops who were remiss would be responsible for the losses (2). Those excommunicated for usurping church possessions were not to be absolved before they had either made full restitution or agreed to repay by instalments (3–4). Those still excommunicate after a year were to forfeit all standing in the lawcourts (5). Whenever booty was brought into a parish, all church services were to stop until an order was received from the bishop or archdeacon (7). No new tolls called *péages* were to be introduced anywhere on pain of anathema (8). All this is a far cry from the decrees of Winchester (1070). The church was taking over from a weak king responsibility for the peace and good order of his own lands. Henry II considered this a usurpation.

Beneath this superstructure of royal guidance and interference, papal diplomacy, and conciliar legislation at the several levels traditional church government in the parishes and dioceses changed only slowly. At the base of church government was the parish priest. Although there are no statistics, it can be inferred from the behaviour of reformers that the majority of the incumbents of simple village and urban churches in the eleventh century and most of the twelfth had obtained their office by hereditary succession and intended to pass their church on to a son or other heir.[131] Their position was therefore similar to that of the other tenants of their lord. It may be that the

---

127.   Below 306 f.

128.   HH 276; *Ann. Waverley* in *Annales Monastici* ii. 229; *HDE cont. i.* 149; John of Hexham 313; William of Newburgh i. 43; Alfred of Beverley: *Aluredi Beverlacensis Annales sive Historia de Gestis Regum Britanniae libris IX,* ed. Tho. Hearne (1716) 1–2. Lena Voss, *Heinrich von Blois* 47 ff. Canons assigned by Wilkins i. 417 to 1138 (Mansi xxi. 515) are attributed to this council by Böhmer *KuS* 346, n. 5 and Tillmann *Legaten* 44, n. 171. They were also, because associated in some MS with the canons of Rheims (1148) and hence conjoined in an early thirteenth-century collection of English twelfth-century canons, the *Sangermanensis,* attributed by later editors to Rheims (1148). C. N. L. Brooke, 'Canons of English church councils in the early decretal collections', *Traditio* xiii (1957) 471. It is most unlikely, as Professor Raymonde Foreville suggests, *Latran I, II, III, IV,* 102, that they were confirmed or reissued at Rheims.

129.   HH 277–8.

130.   HH 282; Mansi xxi. 749.

131.   For example, Thomas, monk of Norwich, writing about 1172–73 his account of the 'martyrdom' of the boy William, describes without surprise or censure the married priests in the boy's family, and relates that in 1144 the priest Godwin Stert in a general synod held by Bishop Everard, when denouncing the Jews for the murder of his nephew, stated publicly that the boy was the cousin of his own children: *Vita S. Willelmi Norwic. passim.* Likewise, as late as 1180–90 the Cistercian John of Ford, a theologian and sometimes papal judge, in his *Vita Beati Wulfrici anachoretae Haselbergiae* [*ob.* 1155], mentions without censure the exemplary married and hereditary village priests who come into his story. *Vita* ed. Maurice Bell, *Somerset Record Soc.* xlvii (1932).

owner of the church, whether lay or ecclesiastical, had to give his consent to the transfer and in certain circumstances could interfere in the succession; but hereditary descent, here as elsewhere, was basically acceptable to both lord and tenant. When there was no heir, the lord could make an appointment of his own choice. In theory the local bishop had an interest and should exercise control. According to the Norman council of Lillebonne (1080)[132] no layman should give a church to a priest, or deprive him of it, without the bishop's consent. But the bishop was not to reject a suitable candidate or accept an unsuitable one (11).

The main way in which the custom of hereditary succession was broken was by the impropriation of churches to monasteries and the provision of vicars. The council of Lillebonne's regulation of this business (15) is remarkably early. When a church is given to monks the tenure of the sitting priest is to be unharmed, but on his death or resignation the abbot, or prior of a canonry, shall present a candidate to the bishop, whom the bishop shall accept if suitable. If the new priest does not want to live with the monks, the abbot shall make proper provision for him out of the revenues of the church, and can be compelled to do so by the bishop. The priest shall be subject to the bishop and pay the episcopal dues. Any surplus revenue shall go to the monastery. In the course of the twelfth century the bishops consolidated their hold over the parish churches in their dioceses, the owners were reduced to patrons, and the bishop was able to insist on an orderly procedure when a vacancy occurred: presentation, examination, institution, and then induction into the church performed by an episcopal servant, usually the rural dean.[133]

One of the simplest expositions of the duties and rights of the various ranks in the church is in Gilbert bishop of Limerick's *De statu ecclesiae*, written 1107–11 to instruct the backward Irish church.[134] The priest, he wrote, had fourteen duties. He had to rule his parish and parishioners and impose penance on the sinful. He had to serve and obey his bishop.[135] He had to pray. He had to perform all the church services, including daily mass. He had to preach, baptize (normally in church), and instruct his flock, informing them of the eight deadly sins and which days in the following week were festivals and which fasts. He had to perform the various blessings, including solemnization of marriage and the blessing of the water or bread for the ordeal.[136] He had to excommunicate the wicked and reconcile the penitent. He had to administer the Eucharist to the faithful three times a year, at Easter, Whitsun, and Christmas, and when they were close to death. And finally he had to bury the

---

132. The text used here is in OV (Chibnall) iii. 26 ff., using the numeration of the canons in Mansi xx. 555 + 559, which follows the edition of G. Bessin.

133. For episcopal control of impropriation, see also Westminster (1102) (15–18), above 128. For the procedures, see Irene J. Churchill, *Canterbury Administration* (1933) i. 106 ff.

134. *Liber de statu ecclesiae* in *PL* clix, 1000. See above 33 f.

135. Lillebonne (1080) refers several times to episcopal dues owed by priests, and orders that once a year at Pentecost priests should go with their processions to the mother church and offer on the altar the candle-pennies due from every house for its illumination (5, 9, 15). For the episcopal customs, see Barlow, *Durham Jurisdictional Peculiars, passim*.

136. For the ordeal of consecrated bread, see *English Church 1000–1066*, 143. Cf. *VEdR* p. xxxvi and n.

bodies of the faithful and also maintain a suitable cemetery for those who perished through drowning or violence.

Gilbert then lists a priest's eight essential possessions: a parish composed of people who paid the various dues and tithe, an agricultural estate of at least one plough-land, a close with its buildings (*atrium*), a cemetery, a church, an altar, a chalice and patten, and the host (the body and blood). He also itemized the necessary equipment and furniture: a text of the gospels, a psalter, a missal, a book of hours, a service book (*manuale*), a book of synodal acts, and everything from a holy water sprinkler to a reading desk.

It is possibly because most of the village and urban parish priests in England continued throughout this period to be native born that we have less evidence than before about their activities and conduct. But since no new homiletic collections, penitential manuals, or other technical handbooks seem to have been published or taken into general circulation, probably because of the disappearance of Englishmen from the higher ranks of the clergy, we can assume that the lower clergy still followed the old customs, using Old-English manuals and conducting their ministry in English.[137] Towards the end of Henry I's reign Brihtric (Beohrtric), the parish priest of Haselbury Plucknett in Somerset, married to Godgifu and with a son Osbern who succeeded him in the benefice, spoke only English and so had to remain silent in the presence of the bishop and his archdeacon. He was ashamed of this, and was highly indignant with the anchorite Wulfric, whose cell was attached to the church, because he gave a dumb man the power to speak both English and French, something he had never deigned to do for his old friend and helper.[138] Wulfric himself, since he seems to have conversed with kings and nobles without the use of an interpreter, must have been bilingual. And it is likely that in the twelfth century complete monoglots at that level of society were becoming rare.

The domestic situation of the lower clergy changed considerably between 1066 and 1154. After Anselm's efforts at the beginning of the twelfth century they were less able to contract a lawful marriage or even live unmolested with a mistress.[139] And as a class they suffered economically by an increase in the services and dues required from them[140] and, more radically, by the replacement of parsons by vicars through the impropriation of churches to religious corporations.[141] On Domesday evidence the rural parish priest was at least as well off as the village farmers; and the composition of the typical village jury, the priest and reeve and four or six men of the vill (*villani*),[142] acknowledged his leading position under the lord and the gentry. A vicar, however, deprived of at least the greater tithes (those of corn), was not only poorer but had less kin. Nevertheless it is possible that on the whole his spiritual authority was strengthened. His partial withdrawal from the ordinary world, his celibacy,

137. *English Church 1000–1066*, 263 ff.
138. John of Ford, *Vita B. Wulfrici* 29.
139. Above 128 f.
140. Cf. Winchester (1076) can. 3; unknown council (1077–85) can. 3. Fore which see above 124 ff. Cf. also Lillebonne (1080) can. 4.
141. Above 51 ff.
142. *SSC* 101; *Leges Henrici Primi*, ed. and trans. L. J. Downer (1972) 7, 7b.

and, above all, his better education and professional skill, attracted the respect which illiterate societies pay to scholars. The aim of the authorities was that a clerk could be distinguished from a layman at a glance. The requirements are exemplified by the behaviour of Gilbert, parson of Sempringham, in the middle of Henry I's reign when he was still only in minor orders.[143] His clothes were never loose but always restrained and of clerical cut and hue. He was sober and sparing in food and drink. His haircut was appropriate and his tonsure clearly visible. He spoke modestly and was dignified in his gait. You would have thought him a canon regular rather than a secular clerk.

If village and urban priests were the rank and file of the *militia Christi,* bishops were commanding officers. The social and economic gap was immense. Parish priests never became bishops and there were few intermediaries between the princes of the church and those who worked among the people. Nor did the clergy at large elect the bishops, or indeed have any say in their selection. The main voice in the appointment to bishoprics was the king's, and if a strong king was in an arbitrary mood he simply had his way.

A bishop, Gilbert of Limerick explained, had all the duties and rights of a priest, and also seven functions peculiar to his rank. He had to confirm the baptized, give the various episcopal blessings, absolve the people from venial sins on Ash Wednesday and from the deadly sins on Maundy Thursday, hold a synod twice a year, in summer and in autumn, dedicate churches, altars and other fixtures, consecrate utensils, vestments and substances, including chrism and the iron used in the ordeal, and, finally, ordain abbots, abbesses, priests, and the lower orders.[144] A bishop's principal rights over the parish priests, especially those which were financially profitable – the holding of synods (*synodalia*), visitation (*procuratio* or *hospitium*), and jurisdiction (fines and amercements) – were called *episcopalia* or the episcopal customs. Some or all of the customs could be alienated to servants and immunists, but those inseparable from the bishop's order only to another prelate.[145]

Few bishops in practice regarded themselves as parish priests, and they had from the beginning of the Norman period a good number of helpers. These were found in the body of the clergy who were at the same time the bishop's clerks and the cathedral chapter, a society which cannot before the late twelfth century be divided sharply between the bishop's household, the cathedral chapter, and the archdeacons.[146] The archdeacons were often household clerks and usually members of the cathedral chapter; cathedral dignitaries served the bishop, and episcopal clerks were rewarded with canonries. The parochial duties and services in the cathedral church were normally performed by members of the chapter (or their vicars), who soon secured by custom a virtual monopoly of those responsibilities, leaving little more to the bishop than the Maundy Thursday ceremonies[147] and a place of honour on special occa-

143. *Vita S. Gileberti confessoris* in *Monasticon* vi. 2, p. viii*.

144. *De Statu Ecclesiae* in *PL* clix. 1002. Gilbert may have been following a pontifical.

145. Barlow, *Durham Jurisdictional Peculiars*, p. xv and *passim*.

146. Cf. H. Mayr-Harting, *The Acta of the Bishops of Chichester* (Cant. and York Soc. 1964) 3 ff.

147. For these, see *English Church 1000–1066*, 269–71. For Maundy Thursday as 'the day of absolution', see also *Vita S. Willelmi Norwic.* 26, 207.

sions. What is more, the bishop found in this body of clergy, especially the archdeacons, men who could also take much of the diocesan administration off his shoulders. The position was a little different where the cathedral had a monastic chapter, for, although William of St Calais bishop of Durham made the prior also archdeacon,[148] and monks could before the twelfth century be used quite freely in administrative duties, a clearer distinction occurred earlier here between the bishop's household and the chapter. Even so, and all the more so when the bishop was a monk, helpers could be found in the convent. With all this assistance bishops were able to find time not only for the general supervision of their dioceses but also for the running of their episcopal estates and their several royal and public duties. Bishops were members of the feudal nobility as well as princes of the church and had to make room for their various roles.

In both characters bishops were kept on the move. They travelled between their manors in order to feed their retinue[149] and they perambulated their diocese in order to carry out their pastoral duties. It was before the days of the legally defined and legally hazardous official visitation, and bishops seem to have behaved in a relatively informal and haphazard manner. They confirmed children at suitable places on their itinerary, dedicated churches and consecrated utensils when invited to do so, and called in at monasteries to enjoy the hospitality and take a look at the conditions. The early post-Conquest councils were much concerned about the proper conduct of ordinations;[150] but in the absence of episcopal registers we have no information about them. They were traditionally performed at the ember seasons, especially on the Sunday after 13 December,[151] and possibly wherever the bishop chose to be at those times. No ordination list from this period has survived. Wulfstan of Worcester and Ralf Luffa of Chichester were specially remembered for their assiduous visitation of their relatively small dioceses, and Gundulf of Rochester managed to perform the *episcopalia* in the diocese of Canterbury as well as his own.[152] The bishop riding along the road with his clerks, including a chaplain with a purse of alms and another with the *chrismatorium,* was how he was best known to the people.[153]

Ecclesiastical government was no more institutionalized in the eleventh century than royal or baronial government, and for all rulers the council, or meeting with their subordinates, was the main machinery. Lanfranc's council of Winchester–Windsor (?1072), can. 4, ordered bishops to hold councils twice a year,[154] and, although general diocesan synods have left

---

148. *Durham Jurisdictional Peculiars*, 3–4.

149. Eadmer explains clearly the economic reasons why Anselm could not remain with his beloved monks at Canterbury: *VA* 71.

150. See above 126 f.

151. See Claremont (1095) can. 24; Mansi xx. 815.

152. For Wulfstan see *English Church 1000–1066,* 92; for Ralf Luffa, above 68; for Gundulf, 65.

153. Cf. OV (Chibnall) iv. 194 on Hoel bishop of Le Mans, and Coleman on Wulfstan, *Vita Wulfstani* 36–7 (confirmations), 33 (alms).

154. Above 126.

little trace in the records, we can assume that they met from time to time.[155] More usual, perhaps, were assemblies held by archdeacons, which in this period are better viewed as episcopal synods than as archidiaconal chapters. The point is exemplified by a dispute between Archbishop Lanfranc and Bishop Stigand of Chichester.[156] Lanfranc had been allowing the clergy from the archiepiscopal manors within the diocese of Chichester (later the peculiar deaneries of Pagham and Tarring and of South Malling) to attend the local diocesan synods, but for instruction only, not for correction. Punishment for any fault found in them had to be reserved to the archbishop. But the archdeacons had been demanding and taking money from them (whether as penalties or as synodals is not stated). So Lanfranc stepped in, ordered the repayment of the money, and withdrew his clergy entirely from the jurisdiction of the bishop of Chichester and his servants. They would still be allowed, however, to obtain chrism from Chichester and pay for it. Lanfranc made no distinction in his letter between the bishop, his *ministri,* and his archdeacons. Episcopal authority alone was in question, and it had been abused by the bishop's servants.

The dispute also illustrates some of the business of a diocesan synod and throws light on the division of responsibility between the bishop and archdeacon. Lanfranc assumed that at a diocesan synod three things would happen. First, that there would be some sort of episcopal charge, 'instruction in the Christian religion', that is to say, a sermon. The commands of his own general councils had to be passed down. Second, that there would be an inquiry into the clergy's conduct and learning, and also, it seems, summary punishment of some faults. He had originally removed his own priests from the latter, if not entirely from the former. Now he reserved to himself their examination and punishment by pastoral authority when he visited his manors. And third, that dues and perhaps fines would be paid to the bishop. The Norman council of Lillebonne (1080),[157] cans. 5 and 15, confirmed, but restrained, payments which priests owed the bishop, and also listed among the faults for which priests incurred a money fine to the bishop non-attendance at a synod (22) and failure to pay synodal and visitation dues at the appointed time (23).

There is not much difference between local synods held by archdeacons and archidiaconal visitations. The council of Lillebonne (6) regulated these. Once a year the archdeacons were to inspect the vestments, altar vessels, and books of the priests under their authority. The bishops were to appoint three places in each archdeaconry to which the priests were to bring the items to be inspected, and the archdeacon could require from the priests hospitality for a party of five for up to three days. It is not known whether this precise procedure was introduced into England, but it helps to clarify the Chichester synods and the archdeacon's role. Basically he had a ministerial and inquisitorial office. He deputized for the bishop, collected his dues, investigated matters

---

155.   For example, Durham (1072–75), below 152; Hereford (1137), Wilkins i. 415, Mansi xxi. 507; Winchester (1150), J. H. Round, *Geoffrey de Mandeville* (1892) 127 n.; York (1153), Mansi xxi. 769.

156.   *HN* 21–2. I. J. Churchill, *Canterbury Administration*, i. 62 ff.

157.   See above 132, n. 32.

and reported his findings to the bishop for action to be taken. It is doubtful whether at this time he had power to punish in his own right (*ex officio*). But he could collect fines due to the bishop when a priest was found guilty of a fault in a synod or at a visitation, and this prepared the way for archidiaconal jurisdiction. Such fines were disliked by lay authorities: they preferred the church to impose penance or corporal punishment. There was a feeling that money penalties were a matter for the public courts. The Council of Lillebonne decreed (5) that priests were not to be punished by fines for keeping women.

The investigation of morals and learning was a feature of eleventh-century councils from papal to archidiaconal, and synods retained their disciplinary function throughout the Norman period. Gilbert of Limerick held that the main business of a diocesan synod was the investigation of the orders of the clergy.[158] In the early Norman period foreign bishops probably treated unsatisfactory native clergy ruthlessly. Ralf Luffa, bishop of Chichester (1091–1123), refers in a charter to Battle abbey quite casually to the position when the abbey's priests should die or be degraded, that is, be deprived of their holy orders.[159] The procedure in the synod was probably basically similar to that in the shire court, oral pleading with the production of witnesses and charters, followed by the judgment of the suitors, and the awarding of the method of proof. The correction of notorious faults in public must have had a deterrent effect and the settlement of disputes there allowed them to be determined in a wide context. The bishop's synod was still acting as a lawcourt in Stephen's reign.[160] But with the rise of the lawyers in the church and the establishment of a system of church courts in the late twelfth century synods lost their legal activity.[161]

When the bishop of Norwich's synod in 1144 decided to try some Jews for murder, the dean of Norwich was ordered to summon and produce them.[162] This official was probably the dean of Christianity, the urban version of the rural dean. These officials were the ecclesiastical counterpart to royal bailiffs, general servants on whom most executive duties ultimately devolved. They were not too grand to be ordered about, and, being resident in their deaneries, knew everything that went on. Rural deans drew their duties from several directions. As rectors of a mother church which, with its dependents, usually had a parish covering a hundred or wapentake they possibly had some inherent authority and most likely were, as in Normandy, responsible for the distribution of chrism and holy oils. They were also responsible to both the bishop and his archdeacon. They were required to watch over and correct the behaviour of the local clergy and also carry out all the administrative and judicial orders of their two superiors. They must have been most useful officials.[163]

158. *De Statu Ecclesiae* in *PL* clix. 1002.

159. H. Mayr-Harting, *The Acta of the Bishops of Chichester*, no. 5.

160. Cf. below 154, 170.

161. Cf. Colin Morris, 'From Synod to Consistory: the bishops' courts in England, 1150–1250', *JEH* xxii (1971) 115.

162. *Vita Willelmi Norwic.* 43ff., 92ff. See also below 154.

163. Cf. Rouen (1072) caps 3, 14: OV (Chibnall) ii. 286, 290; London (1108) cap. 8: Mansi xx. 1230. See also *English Church 1000—1066*, 179–82, 184.

If the bishop's first duty was the supervision of his clergy, his second was the government of his flock. It was accepted that he had not only authority over his priests but also the right to punish all men for infractions of the Christian code. The basic disciplinary institution in the church was, as it always had been, confession and penance. Two systems, one public and one private, existed side by side, and both are well documented.[164] Most sins, whether of the clergy or the laity, were punished in this way. And it was laid down by the Council of Lillebonne (42) that if anyone guilty of a sin or crime for which a penalty was due to the bishop came voluntarily to do penance, a suitable penance should be awarded and no fine taken. Episcopal jurisdiction exercised through more formal courts is examined in the next chapter.

The details of the penance imposed on a repentant sinner are sometimes mentioned by a chronicler. In 1075–76 Earl Waltheof, in Winchester gaol under sentence of death, confessed his sins and on the advice of the priests did penance for one year and recited daily the 150 psalms of David which he had learned as a child.[165] In 1093 Rufus, when he thought he was dying, accepted heavy penitential conditions imposed on him by the English bishops and augmented by Abbot Anselm.[166] In 1130 Henry I after his terrifying dreams was warned by his physician Grimbald to atone for his sins with alms, and when he was in danger of shipwreck vowed to God that he would remit Danegeld for seven years, go on a pilgrimage to Bury St Edmunds, and rule more justly in England.[167] Five years later he was seen out of the world by the pious and learned Cluniac, Hugh of Amiens, archbishop of Rouen and formerly abbot of Reading. Hugh wrote a most affecting letter to Pope Innocent II informing him of the king's death. Henry, he wrote, had confessed his sins, shown penitence, and promised to reform his ways. He had made provision for alms-giving by ordering that after all his debts had been paid the remainder of his wealth should be distributed among the poor.[168] Confession was obligatory before the final rites, and the deathbed was the occasion on which the priest had the upper hand. But promises *in articulo mortis* were not always carried out. Archbishop Hugh had to admit that the royal treasurers had not distributed Henry's wealth. Some great men even resisted what they considered unreasonable pressure. We are told that when that important royal counsellor, Robert of Beaumont, count of Meulan and earl of Leicester, confessed his sins when dying in June 1118, Archbishop Ralf d'Escures and the other priests in attendance demanded that he should restore all the lands which he had taken by force or stratagem from others. When the count asked what he would be able to leave his sons if he divided up into many parts all the lands he had gathered together, it was answered that his hereditary estates and those he had justly acquired should suffice for them, the rest he should give away. But Robert thought otherwise. He would give everything to his sons, and they would take

164. *English Church 1000–1066*, 258 ff. See also Cyrille Vogel, 'Les rites de la pénitence publique aux Xe et XIe siècles', in *Mélanges offerts à René Crozet* (Poitiers 1966) i. 137.

165. OV (Chibnall) ii. 320.

166. For the details, see above 26 f. And cf. Winchester annals re Newminster, Canterbury, Lincoln, Chertsey, and Winchester, *Annales Monastici* ii. 36, 37, 39.

167. John of Worcester 33–4.

168. *Hist. Nov.* 13–14. Cf. OV (Chibnall) vi. 448.

suitable action for the good of his soul.[169] Such men took, apparently with their eyes open, what seemed to contemporaries appalling risks.

A bishop, both as a prelate and as a baron, had much to do. He had the management of the episcopal estates and the performance of his feudal duties; often he held castles and sometimes, like the bishop of Durham,[170] a prison; he had usually family responsibilities, if not children, nephews to educate and place; he found it necessary, or had the ambition, to rebuild his cathedral church and found hospitals or other religious institutions in his diocese; and he had many rights and duties under the folk-law, by which he was still considered one of the principal justiciars in the shire. There were also his spiritual duties. For all these tasks he had all the help he needed.[171] He was wealthy and servants were cheap, although some skills were always in short supply. On the secular side he had the full complement of estate and domestic officers and, on the spiritual side, as we have seen, the aid of his archdeacons and cathedral chapter and of his more familiar clerks and chaplains. There may well have been much more specialization in the former than in the latter sphere, which was a more recent development.

Once definition set in, the bishop was in difficulty. The chapter concentrated on the cathedral church and its services and the archdeacons pursued their own ambitions. Archdeacons do not feature in Gilbert of Limerick's scheme. By 1135 they had greatly improved their status. Often episcopal *nipoti* and increasingly considered worthy of promotion to the bench, they were fast developing into a separate rank in the church. In 1141 at the council of Winchester, called to consider the situation after Stephen's capture, the papal legate, Henry of Blois, conferred secretly in turn with the bishops, abbots, and archdeacons.[172] And if these upstarts were also beginning to be regarded as arch-devils,[173] the reputation is proof of their new power. The bishop, therefore, had to create new servants to take the place of the old. He was prepared, and apparently allowed, to delegate any of his powers. Canterbury was fortunate in having the bishop of Rochester as a standing vicar.[174] In 1133 Nigel, the royal treasurer, on his consecration as bishop of Ely, appointed his clerk, master Ranulf of Salisbury, an 'ex-monk' of Glastonbury, 'his steward in all matters pertaining to his bishopric', an office which later would be called 'vicar-general'. Ranulf seems to have administered both spiritualities and

---

169. HH 307

170. Cf. Reginald of Durham *St Cuthbert*, cap. 95.

171. For Archbishop Anselm's household, see R. W. Southern, *St Anselm and his Biographer* 194 ff.

172. *Hist. Nov.* 52. Below 306 f.

173. Roger of Pont l'Evêque, archdeacon of Canterbury, who had some interesting adventures in courts, was so called, above 94, n. 175. For the subject, see F. Barlow, *The Letters of Arnulf of Lisieux* (Camden 3rd ser. lxi, 1939) p. xii.

174. An agreement made at Canterbury, dated 6 March, on the fees and perquisites due to the bishop of Rochester and his clerks and servants when he acted for the archbishop *sede plena* (either in the archbishop's company or on separate mission) and *sede vacante* is recorded in *Textus Roffensis*, ed. T. Hearne (1720) 227. At the end it is stated that when Canterbury was unable to act, or the see was vacant, Rochester should represent him both in consecrating the king and bishops and in all other duties pertaining to the archiepiscopal office.

temporalities, and was hated by the cathedral monks,[175] but his omnicompetence is, possibly, an extreme case. At the very time when a debate was taking place in the schools, in which theologians such as Peter Abelard, Hugh of St Victor, the masters of the school of Laon, and the Englishman Robert Pullen were engaged, on the sacraments of confession and absolution of sins and the nature of the keys entrusted by Christ to St Peter and through him to other members of the church,[176] we find English bishops delegating their powers of binding and loosing and of forgiving sins to a lowly deputy. Alexander bishop of Lincoln (1123–48) made his clerk, Gilbert of Sempringham, after his refusal of an archdeaconry, a priest, so that he could take cognizance of the sins of the whole people and judge them according to the law of the church. Although the words may mean that Gilbert was appointed the bishop's justiciar, the necessity for priestly orders makes it probable that Gilbert was also the bishop's penitentiary.[177] At Norwich Bishop William Turbe (1146–74), and probably his predecessor, Everard (1121–46), appointed a monk of the convent, Wickman, to hear the people's confessions in their place.[178]

The situation in 1154 seems to have been that bishops were delegating both general and specific powers and were experimenting with justiciars, stewards, and secretaries, but were not seen to have created new posts. They had not yet appointed an Official, Vicar-General, or Penitentiary General as such. Nor had they organized much of a secretariat under a personal chancellor. Although episcopal *acta,* the bishop's business documents, become increasingly common after 1100, they do not survive in large numbers until much later in the century.[179] Moreover, until the very end of our period they were written in royal chancery style, a feature which tells us a great deal about the English church. Not before Theobald of Canterbury, with John of Salisbury, and Gilbert Foliot did a more distinctly ecclesiastical structure, vocabulary, and *cursus* appear, imitated, no doubt, from papal letters.[180] In general, while it does not seem that at the end of the Norman period episcopal power was overall in decline, it was certainly being squeezed from both above and below, and bishops were for the time being without amenable officers. The formless administration in the arch-see shows how primitive conditions still remained. The archbishops had only a small diocese and were relieved of most diocesan duties by the bishops of Rochester. But, although Theobald was archbishop from 1139 to 1161, a period of most rapid growth in ecclesiastical business, it was not until John of Salisbury, after six years spent as a clerk in the papal curia, became his secretary in 1154, that the volume of correspondence markedly

175. *Liber Eliensis* 284–7, 294–7, 370.

176. Cf. F. Courtney, *Cardinal Robert Pullen* (*Analecta Gregoriana* lxiv, Rome 1945) 226ff.

177. 'Eo quod per sanctitatem posset et per discretionem nosset judicium ecclesiae rationabiliter exercere; voluitque illum tam suorum quam totius populi delictorum judicem ac conscium constituere; quod factum est.' *Vita S. Gileberti confessoris* in *Monasticon* vi. 2, p. viii*. See also below 155.

178. 'Episcopalium confessionum vicarius', *Vita S. Willelmi Norwic.* 30, 84. His description in the index as priest of St Nicholas is an error.

179. For all this, see C. R. Cheney, *English Bishops' Chanceries 1100–1250* (1950), and above 24.

180. Cf. F. M. Stenton, 'Acta episcoporum', *CambHJ* iii (1929) 11–12.

increased.[181] And there is no evidence for a specialized archiepiscopal staff until the age of the registers.

In Gilbert of Limerick's scheme the place of the metropolitan is simple: the archbishop ruled over from three to twenty bishops, and in his turn was, with his fellow archbishops, subject to a primate. The English situation inherited by Archbishops Lanfranc and Thomas I was confused through York's claim to some southern bishoprics and Stigand's long incapacity as metropolitan; and hardly had that disorder been righted when Canterbury's claim to a primacy troubled it once more. It was difficult for a clear provincial organization to develop when one metropolitan had at most two suffragan bishops and the other had at least seventeen, and, moreover, when the greater power claimed primatial rights over the smaller. York had hardly any metropolitan rights worth exercising, unless he could assert his authority over the Scottish bishops. And Canterbury confused its metropolitan and primatial powers, and later complicated the position still further with its papal legation. The archbishop of Canterbury, as the successor to St Augustine, was a great power, the one great power in the English church: and it is not always easy to see in what capacity he was acting, particularly when it is unlikely that he himself scrupulously separated his roles.

An archbishop's metropolitan powers were delegated, and were conferred by the pope through the grant of a pallium. But although most archbishops valued the filiation, it is likely that they viewed their dignity more as a special relationship than as a delegation, all the more since the ordinary powers of a metropolitan were small. Gilbert of Limerick awarded him only the right, aided by the other diocesan bishops, to ordain a bishop.[182] Even if we expand this to the right to examine the bishop-elect, take an oath of canonical obedience (profession) from him, and consecrate him with the help of his other suffragans,[183] we have not added much to his authority. Hugh, precentor of York, claimed that an archbishop had, besides the right of consecration of bishops, the right to crown the king and celebrate high mass before him at the crown-wearings at Christmas, Easter, and Whitsun, and precedence over other bishops within his province.[184] This last privilege included the right to have his cross borne before him in other dioceses.[185] But Hugh had a special interest in claiming the crowning of kings as a metropolitan rather than as a primatial right, and he was surely in error. Neither Gilbert nor Hugh mention metropolitan councils. And, although it would seem likely that archbishops had the right to summon them and with the help of their suffragans do justice and make reforms within their area of jurisdiction, there is no evidence that strictly metropolitan councils were held in either province in this period.[186] The

181. *Acta* printed Avrom Saltman, *Theobald archbishop of Canterbury* (1956) 233 ff. *The [early] Letters of John of Salisbury,* ed. W. J. Millor and H. E. Butler, revised by C. N. L. Brooke (Nelson's Medieval Texts, 1955).

182. *PL* clix. 1002.

183. Cf. *HN* 73–4, 76–7.

184. Hugh *HCY* 7.

185. Cf. *AEp*. 278, 227.

186. *Handbook of British Chronology* lists with reservations as Canterbury synods Windsor (April 1114), Gloucester (February 1123), and London (December 1152). Metropolitan councils

irreducible minimum of metropolitan authority would seem to be, besides consecration, the encouragement and correction of the suffragan bishops. But in the southern province this was inseparable from the archbishop's primatial and legatine powers.[187]

Rather surprisingly in view of the meagreness of his powers, the archbishop of Canterbury had a standing deputy in his province. It was accepted that the bishop of London was 'dean of the church of Canterbury'. And in this character he seems to have taken first place in consecrations when both archbishops were incapacitated and to have had a role in consecrating the archbishop of Canterbury even when York officiated. In 1093, when Thomas I of York consecrated Anselm, Walkelin bishop of Winchester read out the form of the election, but, according to Eadmer, at the request of Maurice bishop of London, whose duty it was.[188] In 1100, when Anselm was in exile and Thomas I at a distance, Maurice consecrated Henry I king.[189] Richard de Beaumais I of London consecrated Thomas II archbishop of York in 1109 while Canterbury was vacant.[190] He also consecrated, in person or by deputy, William of Corbeil archbishop of Canterbury in 1123, despite the complaints of Archbishop Thurstin, who was superseded because he would not make his profession to Canterbury.[191] During Becket's exile, Gilbert Foliot organized the collection and dispatch to Rome of Peter's Pence.[192] Decanal duties were hardly onerous.

Metropolitan authority, therefore, added little to the archbishop's ordinary powers as bishop. He was very much *primus inter pares*. The full potential of the office could not be realized before purely ecclesiastical government came into operation; and then, before the archbishops – or the primate – could consolidate their position on the appellate ladder, recognized as far as the archbishops by the constitutions of Clarendon (1164), the flood of appeals to the pope and the remittal of these to judges-delegate in England almost left the metropolitans stranded. In the early Norman period the archbishops were important largely because of their traditional closeness to the king. They had rank and places of honour and influence. The archbishops of Canterbury had in addition great wealth and were usually distinguished by their greater holiness and superior scholarship. But everything depended on the king. Although the archbishop was the spiritual father of his suffragans and had a claim to their support, loyalty, and counsel, there is little evidence before 1109 of either provincial fellowship or personal loyalty to the superior.

were, of course, held in Normandy, but only until 1118, when the custom fell generally into disuse. See Raymonde Foreville (see above 123, n. 94).

187. In 1106 Anselm, when rebuking Henry I for punishing married priests, claimed that such jurisdiction pertained only to the bishops within their dioceses, or, if they were negligent, to the archbishop and primate: *AEp* 391. Anselm was claiming to be a sort of universal ordinary in Great Britain.

188. *HN* 42.

189. *Chron. E*, Florence; but cf. *Liber Eliensis* 224–5, Hugh *HCY* 12.

190. Hugh *HCY* 29; *GP* 262.

191. He is named as the consecrator by *Chron E.* and Hugh *HCY* 109–11. According to Florence, William Giffard, bishop of Winchester, officiated, which was, Diceto i. 244 adds, because Richard was paralysed.

192. *The Letters and Charters of Gilbert Foliot*, ed. Adrian Morey and C. N. L. Brooke (1967), 203, 206–7, 255–6, 249–51.

Anselm's bishops were in general hostile, and when he most needed their advice it was usually withheld. At his trials his suffragans preferred to sit with the king.

During Henry I's reign, however, the royal court probably declined in importance as the centre of high ecclesiastical society. Not only the growing independence of the church and the increasing awareness of separateness, but also the frequent absences of the king in Normandy worked to this end. Instead, various ecclesiastical ceremonies, especially those associated with the making of a bishop, provided a series of festivities which encouraged a corporate feeling. By the 1120s new bishops were entering into a club of their own.

The ecclesiastical events of 1125 illustrate this very well.[193] Late in 1124 Archbishop William of Corbeil crossed to Normandy at the king's command, and at the end of Lent 1125 returned to England in company with Thurstin of York, Cardinal John of Crema, the papal legate, and two men who had just been elected to bishoprics in the royal court, Siegfried abbot of Glastonbury to Chichester, and Simon, the queen's chancellor, to Worcester. On 12 April at Lambeth, his London residence, Archbishop William consecrated Siegfried bishop in the presence of the cardinal, the archbishop of York, two other English bishops, Everard of Norwich and Richard of Hereford, the three Welsh bishops, Bernard of St David's, David of Bangor, and Urban of Llandaff, and John archdeacon of Canterbury and bishop-elect of Rochester. On Whit Sunday, 17 May, at Canterbury, the archbishop ordained Simon and John with the assistance of Richard of Hereford, David of Bangor, Godfrey of Bath, and Siegfried of Chichester. Richard, David, and Godfrey then returned with Simon to Worcester for his enthronement on 24 May and for his first episcopal act, the consecration of one of his own monks, Benedict, as abbot of Tewkesbury. Benedict, originally a child oblate at Tewkesbury, had received all his ecclesiastical orders from Wulfstan. For these ceremonies at Worcester the bishops were joined by the local monastic dignitaries, Abbots Guy of Pershore, William of Gloucester, and Godfrey of Winchelcombe. Dominic prior of Evesham, the historian, represented his sick abbot, and Walker prior of Malvern was there in his own right. In September all these prelates joined their brethren at Westminster for John of Crema's legatine council. The two archbishops, who were still in dispute over the primacy, then went with the legate back to the king in Normandy and took with them Alexander bishop of Lincoln, John bishop of Glasgow, Geoffrey de Gorron abbot of St Albans, and Thurstin abbot of Sherborne. In Normandy a novel compromise solution of the quarrel between the archbishops was with difficulty imposed on the contestants, and the two parties left for Rome, although with no intention of settling. York's company, which included his brother, the bishop of Evreux, and the papal legate, was ambushed, captured, and robbed on the way, possibly of Peter's pence, and arrived three weeks after Canterbury's. At Rome it was finally agreed that the compromise negotiated in Normandy should be dropped and that instead William of Canterbury should have a papal vicariate and legation over Britain for his life.

---

193.   See, especially, John of Worcester *s.a.*

Developments which were giving structure and cohesion to the whole Roman church were doing the same for the *ecclesia anglicana*. Within the kingdom the divisions caused by different nationalities and the lack of common activity and ideals were in decline. During Stephen's reign it looked at times as though the English church might become an almost autonomous self-directing body. But it was an illusion caused by the weakness of the royal power. Once Henry II discovered that he could not control the church as a whole by making his favourite archbishop of Canterbury, he quickly deprived it of its head and encouraged schism. If Thomas Becket would no longer serve the king, there were other prelates and officers who would. It was at the very end of the reign that Peter of Blois, by then archdeacon of Bath, wrote that there was something holy about serving the king, for the king was indeed holy and the anointed of the Lord. Unction at his coronation gave him power to banish the disease which attacked the groin and to cure scrofulas.[194] The pope was not going to have it all his own way. The king could not easily be pushed from his traditional place in the church.

194. *Ep*. 150, *PL* ccvii. 440.

Chapter IV

Justice

Government was supposed to be regulated by law and custom, and courts were required for the enforcement of the law and the dispensation of justice. The law of the church, canon law, had been transmitted as a series of collections, some genuine, some spurious, and some mixed.[1] In the tenth and eleventh centuries, although much attention was given to pruning the books of unacceptable passages, and some study to the improvement of the actual texts, a really critical approach was wanting, and the spurious was accepted without question. The antiquity of most of the excerpts discouraged criticism, and also, of course, limited their practical use. The early church, with its immense task of developing the Christian tradition and establishing orthodoxy, had produced the greatest and most authoritative corpus of Christian writing. Dionysius Exiguus compiled his influential collection of canon law at Rome about 514. But after this ecumenical councils had been few and important authors scarce. The revival of interest in law in the eleventh century gave rise to a few modern papal decretals. But the overwhelming tone of the collections remained ancient and Roman.

The larger English churches seem to have been adequately, in Worcester's case abundantly, supplied with canonical collections, mostly of Carolingian provenance, before the Conquest;[2] but these were regarded by the new foreign bishops as old fashioned. There was lacking, apparently, even a copy of the *Decretum* of Burchard of Worms, compiled between 1007 and 1015, and the most popular lawbook on the Continent. But why Cnut's bishops, when there had been such close ties with Germany, or the Edwardian bishops of Lotharingian origin or education, such as Herman of Ramsbury, Giso of Wells, Walter of Hereford, and Leofric of Crediton, had not introduced the *Decretum* is difficult to understand. Whatever the true position may have been, Lanfranc, on his appointment to Canterbury in 1070, compiled his own textbook of canon law for the English church out of two separate items:[3] first, a collection of papal decretals which was his own abridgement made at Bec of the ninth-century *Collectio Isidori Mercatoris* (Pseudo-Isidore, or 'the False

1.   P. Fournier and G. Le Bras, *Histoire des collections canoniques en Occident depuis les fausses décretales jusqu'au décret de Gratien* (Paris 1931–2). T. J. Gilchrist, 'Canon law aspects of the 11th century reform' in *JEH* xiii (1962) 21. A brief survey of the history of canon law and an interesting review of English canonistic scholarship is in Charles Duggan, *Twelfth Century Decretal Collections* (1963), chapter 1.

2.   *English Church 1000–1066*, 282 ff.

3.   Z. N. Brooke, *The English Church and the Papacy, from the Conquest to the Reign of John*, 47 ff. Robert Somerville, 'Lanfranc's canonical collection and Exeter', *Bulletin of the Institute of Historical Research* xlv (1972) 303.

Decretals');[4] and, second, a full collection of the decrees of the early church councils. His own copy still exists, so does the Durham copy, presumably the volume which William of St Calais brandished in his face when the bishop was on trial in 1089 in the king's court at Salisbury.[5] And it is likely that all bishops and important abbots were required to obtain copies.

In the early twelfth century Lanfranc's edition was generally superseded by the canonical collections of Ivo bishop of Chartres, especially the brief and well arranged *Panormia,* produced in 1095, which held the field until it in its turn was displaced at the very end of the Norman period by Gratian's *Concordantia Discordantium Canonum (Decretum),* published about 1140. By 1150 Christ Church, Canterbury, possessed at least six different editions of canon law: Lanfranc's volume, a complete copy of Pseudo-Isidore, Burchard's *Decretum,* the anonymous Italian *Collection in 74 Titles* (c. 1050), and the *Decretum* (1094) and *Panormia* of Ivo of Chartres. And it soon added Gratian.

The veneration in which these pioneer lawbooks were held obscures the fact that even the last (and standard, although unofficial) compilation of the *ius antiquum,* Gratian's *Decretum,* conveyed a set of rulings which had little relevance to actual conditions in the national churches of the West. True, they provided an encyclopedia far more liberal than is generally realized. A good education could be acquired by a study of the lawbooks alone. A few of them, particularly Ivo's collections, transmitted some useful parts of Roman law,[6] and advanced the understanding of jurisprudence. Gratian demonstrated the new scholastic method, *sic et non.*[7] But these collections presupposed social and legal conditions which no longer existed and dealt with problems many of which were stale. The churches of the texts were urban churches, holding property under Roman law. They were, moreover, select communities of the faithful, surrounded by the pagan or indifferent, concerned with maintaining the highest standards and in no wise afraid of using the penalty of expulsion. Hence, for example, the law concerning penance as stated in the collections was entirely unsuited to the eleventh-century church, where all men were considered to be Christian and discipline had been relaxed in order to hold the weakest brother within the community. Many folios of these compilations were devoted to the rules governing the marriages of priests, a subject which ceased to interest almost as soon as the study of law became popular again.

---

4. Horst Fuhrmann, *Einfluss und Verbreitung der pseudoisidorischen Fälschungen* (Stuttgart 1972–74); Schafer Williams, 'Pseudo-Isidore from the manuscripts', *The Catholic Historical Review* liii (1968) 58. It is interesting to note, however, that Lanfranc, when consulted by Thomas I of York on divorce law, quoted Christ according to Mark and Luke. 'There are', he wrote, 'many rulings of the holy Fathers on this matter; but when the sun shines there is no need to use a candle to shed light.': *LEp* 10. See also below 168.

5. Below 286. Brooke 109.

6. Jean Gaudemet, 'Le droit romain dans la practique et chez les docteurs aux XIe et XIIe siècles', *Cahiers de Civilisation Médiévale* viii (1965) 374 ff.

7. D. E. Luscombe, *The school of Peter Abelard* (1970) 214 ff. George Makdisi, 'The scholastic method in medieval education: an inquiry into its origins in law and theology', *Speculum* xlix (1974) 640.

On the practical side, the collections were inadequately organized and almost always without an index.[8] The books needed intensive study and required of the student a good memory. They could not be consulted casually in order to settle a point of law. They were not designed to serve as handbooks for those conducting or appearing before courts of law, which is some evidence that such courts did not exist. Indeed, the form in which law had been transmitted ensured that it would remain for long a purely academic study. The ordinary clergy could only hope to acquire a smattering of practical law from tradition, reinforced by the councils and injunctions of their bishops. The hereditary priesthood, which the eleventh-century reformers considered to be one of the greatest evils of the preceding age, was the only way in which clerical culture and skill could have been transmitted through that period. An hereditary caste was indispensable until schools became common. In the twelfth century with the greater provision of education the hereditary parsonage was successfully destroyed.

Gratian's *Decretum* marked the end of an era. The new age of canon law, which started effectively with the pontificate of Alexander III (1159–81), the canonist and former papal chancellor Roland Bandinelli, was the age of habitual appeals to Rome, remittal of cases back to judges-delegate, and the stream of papal decretals settling, on request, points of law. By 1174 those professionally involved in this activity realized that a *ius novum*, a new body of law, was being created in a haphazard manner, and began to collect and then organize editions of papal decretals. Mainly because Alexander III was at first recognized only in the West and his decretals were largely confined to England and France,[9] English canonists led the way, and letters to England bulk large in even the later collections. But little of this was manifest before 1154. The Anglo-Norman church, like the rest of western Christendom, lived under the *ius antiquum*.

Most disciplinary matters, whether concerning the laity or the clergy, were disposed of according to the law through the *forum internum*, the confessional, or some other kind of domestic action. Monasteries are a good example of an area where discipline was ideally completely internal. But the church also needed more formal and public procedures to deal with the unrepentant or recalcitrant sinner or criminal. These had to be forced to submit and make amends. In the early Middle Ages the church used mainly two methods of dealing with them: anathema of various kinds (excommunication), which involved deprivation of church services and social ostracism, and the secular arm. Before the Norman Conquest the bishop and his servants operated largely within the system of the folk-courts, the shire, hundred, and borough assemblies. The various orders of clerk were with other ranks of society subject to the various laws and, when accused either by their superior or a private person, or as a result of an inquisition, were tried according to the appropriate law and procedures by judges selected in accordance with that law.

---

8. For the gradual improvement in the layout of medieval books, see M. B. Parkes, 'The influence of the concepts of *Ordinatio* and *Compilatio* on the development of the book', *Medieval Learning and Literature: essays presented to R. W. Hunt* (1976) 115.

9. My review of Duggan in *History* xlviii (1963) 361.

This was probably true equally when a clerk or priest was accused of a sin like adultery or of a crime like theft, or when a layman was accused of fornication or of striking a priest. There were known and acceptable rules, many of which were contained in the royal codes, both ecclesiastical and lay. Also there were rules about the destination of the penalties. When the church had an interest, penalties could be divided between the king and bishop; royal could be added to the ecclesiastical penalties; or the church could take the lot.[10]

This mixed procedure would seem to have been the work of the church, and it was not repugnant to canon law, at least as understood at that time, for clerks were not being tried by laymen or by secular law, although the procedures were not purely ecclesiastical (if such existed) or the judges, the suitors to the court, always exclusively clerical. The set-up was typical of the period as well as of the English scene, and it is unlikely that the general position was greatly different in Normandy. Nevertheless there was some criticism of it after 1066 by the new foreign bishops, who seem to have felt that in England they did not have all the rights they enjoyed in Normandy and that therefore the situation was uncanonical.

We can get a good idea of what the Norman bishops were accustomed to from the canons of the council held at the royal vill of Lillebonne at Whitsun 1080, to which reference has already been made.[11] This council of the archbishop, bishops, abbots, counts, and barons of Normandy met under the presidency of the king-duke, and the occasion seems to have been William's desire to define and record the bishops' rights, possibly because of the debate over the matter in England and also, it seems, because of his dissatisfaction with the conduct and efficacy of episcopal jurisdiction in Normandy. The enactments imply that an inquest had been held (a precedent for the Clarendon inquest of 1164), and the findings, although issued as synodal decrees, are essentially royal precepts. The council produced a schedule of rights common to all the bishops of Normandy. It was also agreed that bishops would be allowed all other customs which they could justify by prescription or ducal grant within areas similarly delimited. But any claim by a bishop to have more than the norm, and any claim by a layman to have it reduced, had to be brought to the royal court and await its decision. The king stated pointedly that by publishing a list of episcopal jurisdictional rights (*leges*) he was not reducing in any way his own rights or those of any other layman. He intended to keep all that he had, and an aggrieved layman could bring a case before him.

Most of the rights or customs sanctioned by the council are the occasions on which a money penalty, or other profit, accrued to a bishop. To use Old English terminology, there is a list of those *bota* to which the bishop had a claim. This emphasis on the destination of judicial penalties rather than on jurisdiction is characteristic of the period and has no special significance. Courts are mentioned where there was innovation. Otherwise the normal system – whatever that may have been – is assumed. The *statuta* of the council are set out in a relatively orderly way and, apart from a bishop's duty to enforce

---

10. *English Church 1000–1066*, 137 ff. See also the views of Jean Scammell, 'The rural chapter in England from the eleventh to the fourteenth century', *EHR* lxxxvi (1971) 2 ff.

11. Above 123, 132, n. 132.

the Truce of God (1), three main categories of episcopal rights can be distinguished (16 ff.): rights within sacred places, the right to take penalties from criminous or offending clerks, and the similar, but far more restricted, right to punish the sinful laity. It is also implied that matrimonial disputes were subject to the bishop.

The first type of right protected the peace of the church, close (*atrium*),[12] and cemetery, and corresponds to the English church-grith. Permanent inhabitants of the close and cemetery were subject to the bishop's laws (12). The second type of right allowed the bishop to take a money penalty from all clerks, and probably a clerk's servant and an inhabitant of the close, guilty of crime (including robbery (*raptum*), theft, assaults, homicide, arson, and taking pledges or engaging in the *duellum* without the bishop's permission), or serious sin (such as adultery and incest), or serious dereliction of duty (such as non-attendance at synods, not wearing the tonsure, and unauthorized use of excommunication). It is expressly stated, however, that the bishop is to have nothing when a priest is guilty of a forest offence (8). The third category, actions by laymen which incur an ecclesiastical penalty, includes assaults on and slaying of priests, monks, and nuns, arson in the close, adultery, incest, the repudiation of husband or wife, divination and sorcery, perjury discovered by the ordeal of hot iron, and incurring excommunication for resisting the bishop's jurisdiction. Robbery (*raptum*) in the close incurred a penalty paid to the bishop, but elsewhere, however committed, was no concern of his (43).

All these penalties are those awarded by a court, not necessarily ecclesiastical, as Old English custom proves, but, since confession and penance halted the judicial procedure (42), the church was seized of the case. The *curia regis* is mentioned several times (46), the *curia episcopi* twice (3, 45); but since no penalties are specified for not attending the bishop's *curia*, this may well be a place, or a secular or general court. Ecclesiastical jurisdiction is described as *iudicium* (possibly the ordeal) (3, 37), *iusticia* (3, 44), and *iudicatio* (38), all words which have the sense of giving sentence or awarding a penalty. They could apply equally to the Old English scene. Little more can be inferred from the statutes of the council of Lillebonne about episcopal courts than that the bishop held synods, used archdeacons, and could judge and award penalties. The procedures for bringing sinners to justice are specified in two instances, probably because changes were being made.

With regard to priests and clerks who kept women (3), it is enacted that, if the prosecution is *ex officio* by the bishop's servants (probably his archdeacon or dean), the accused should purge himself of the charge (i.e. go to the ordeal) in the bishop's court (*curia*). But if it is a private prosecution by one of the priest's parishioners or lords, the accused could have respite in order to consult with his bishop; but if he chose to go to purgation, this should take place not in the bishop's court but in his own parish in the presence of his parishioners. The purpose was to strengthen the prosecution and prevent undue lenience

12. Gilbert of Limerick equated *atrium* with *cum domibus suis clausura, op. cit.* 1001. This meaning, the obvious sense in many eleventh- and twelfth-century passages, is omitted from *Dictionary of Medieval Latin from British Sources,* prepared by R. E. Latham (1975). But if it were accepted more often, it would reduce the number of people who are supposed to have lived in cemeteries.

on the part of the bishop or his justiciar. The bishop's servants were, however, to be present at the trial and administer the ordeal. If the accused failed in this, he was to lose his church. The removal of the hearing from the bishop's *curia*, which the king acknowledged was a curtailment of the bishop's rights, was to be a temporary innovation until the king was satisfied that the bishops had become more active in punishing clerical concubinage.

A similar injunction (37–40) concerned 'the crimes of parishioners which pertain to the bishop' (that is to say, our third category). Such crimes, when it is the custom, shall be examined by the judgment of the bishop (perhaps this means: in the bishop's *curia*, or by the bishop's ordeal). If his jurisdiction is denied, the objection shall be heard by him. After this there are alternatives: if the ordeal of hot iron is adjudged, the trial shall be held at the mother church (cathedral). But if compurgation (*plana lex*) is to be performed, that should take place where the plea started. With this injunction it is not clear whether the purpose was to reduce or increase the chances of the accused.

William of Poitiers wrote[13] that when Duke William heard of any terrible crime which a bishop or archdeacon had punished too lightly, he himself ordered the criminal, guilty of treason to God, to be imprisoned until the Lord's case had been determined with strict justice, and he also punished the bishop or archdeacon in the ducal court for opposing the divine cause. Although the panegyrist may have been making a principle out of a few occasions, as an archdeacon himself he knew what he was talking about. He accepts that a bishop (and archdeacon) had jurisdiction in cases 'against Christianity', and implies that they exercised it autonomously, perhaps in a synod. But we can see that though a bishop was allowed a substantial spiritual jurisdiction, it was nevertheless tightly hemmed in. It was not only restricted by the presence of competing jurisdictions, but could lapse through non-user, could be hampered or directed by the prince, and could be diminished by his arbitrary decision. As jurisdiction was broken down into particular cases, the possibility of a general conflict of laws was remote. A curious finding of the Council of Lillebonne (45) is that a priest who denied his lord's judgment in an ecclesiastical case, and unjustly harassed him by taking him into the bishop's court, should pay his lord a penalty of 10s; this suggests that at least some ecclesiastical cases were heard in seigneurial courts even if the penalties went to the bishop. However that may be, the general attitude expressed by the clause is that the king and the barons were not going to allow the nuisance of competing jurisdictions, and would not normally permit the bishop to interfere between a priest and his lord.

It is in the light not only of Old English practice but also of these enactments that the more fragmentary evidence for William's policy in England can best be examined. We learn from a royal writ, which can be dated 1072–76, the exact span of Lanfranc's reform councils, that in a council summoned by the king and attended by the archbishops, bishops, abbots, and all the magnates of the realm, there was a discussion about episcopal jurisdiction (*episcopales leges*); and it was decided that hitherto in England it had been exercised neither satisfactorily nor in accordance with canon law, and should be

13. *GG* 124–6.

reformed.[14] Up to a point the parallel with the council of Lillebonne is close. But unfortunately the English council cannot be identified with certainty, and no enactments on the pattern of the Norman were produced or have survived. At the council of Winchester in April 1072 Lanfranc 'decreed many things which were to be observed in the church',[15] and among the statutes which may be attributed to this council is one against the concealment of criminal sins from the bishop or his *minister* (8), and among those attributed to its adjourned session at Windsor are, (5) bishops are to ordain archdeacons and other clerical *ministri* in their churches, (6) bishops should have unrestrained authority (*libera facultas*) throughout their dioceses in respect of both clerks and laity, and (7) bishops and priests should summon the laity to penitence.[16] It appears from these canons that the council which produced them had discussed ecclesiastical jurisdiction and made provision for its better organization and better enforcement.

The royal writ, dispatched apparently to the earls, sheriffs, and royal vassals in the several dioceses, dealt with the *leges episcopales* in so far as they concerned the local popular courts and royal law officers. The king alleged that bishops and archdeacons had been administering episcopal jurisdiction in the hundred courts and bringing cases concerning the cure of souls to the judgment of laymen. These practices were to stop, and in future anyone accused of any matter or sin (*causa vel culpa*) which was subject to episcopal jurisdiction should be summoned to a place determined by the bishop and there tried, and should make amends to God and his bishop not according to the law of the hundred court but according to canon and episcopal law. A man summoned thrice and still contumacious should be excommunicated, and then the king or the sheriff would compel attendance. Amends[17] were due for each neglect of a summons. Also no sheriff, reeve, or other royal servant was to interfere with episcopal jurisdiction; no layman was to bring another to the ordeal except in the presence of the bishop's justiciar (*justitia*); and the ordeal was to be held only in the episcopal see or in some other place appointed by the bishop.

In language similar to that used at the council of Lillebonne, and in general harmony with its enactments, the writ conveyed explicit and almost unambiguous instructions. The king informs the shire and hundred courts that the bishops (and their archdeacons) are going to withdraw their ecclesiastical jurisdiction from the hundreds and hear all the cases to which they have a right in their own assemblies. The only ambiguity is the omission of reference to the shire at this point; but since it is not named, when the hundred is, it is straining

---

14. Liebermann *Gesetze* i. 485; *SSC* 99. Böhmer, *KuS*, 93, n.1. Curtis H. Walker, 'The date of the Conqueror's ordinance separating the ecclesiastical and lay courts', *EHR* xxxix (1924) 399. *English Church 1000–1066*, 275–6. Colin Morris, 'William I and the church courts', *EHR* lxxxii (1967) 449.

15. *Acta Lanfranci* 271.

16. M. Brett, 'A collection of Anglo-Norman councils', *JEH* xxvi (1975) 308. Wilkins i. 365 (dated 1076); Mansi xx. 459–60. For the councils see above 124 ff.

17. *Oferhyrnesse* or *lahslit* (Danelaw), according to Winchester (1076) cap. 4. See above 126. The triple summons leading to excommunication is well illustrated by Lanfranc's treatment of the rebellious Earl Roger of Hereford in 1075: *LEp* 39–41.

the sense to include it. The king also insists that there shall still be the fullest cooperation between all authorities: royal servants are to support and enforce episcopal jurisdiction and the church is to administer the ordeals for the lay courts. It is probably on the authority of this writ that the compiler of the *Leges Edwardi Confessoris,* a lawbook produced at the end of Henry I's reign, maintained (2, 9) that if anyone incurred a forfeiture to the bishop, the bishop should exercise the jurisdiction; and that if the accused would not submit to the bishop's justice and make amends the king would compel the law-breaker to make amends to those he had offended, that is to say, both the bishop and himself. 'Thus, and justly, one sword helps the other.'[18]

This description would fit the procedure followed in the diocese of Durham when Walker was bishop and Waltheof earl (1072–75). Because these two were so friendly, we are told, Waltheof sat with the bishop in the priests' synod, humbly and obediently prosecuting whatever the bishop required for the correction of religion in the earl's shire.[19] Here the bishop's synod and the shire court are as inextricably mixed as in the pre-Conquest period. And there seems to be nothing in the writ to upset this friendly relationship. If, however, the writ is regarded as an 'ordinance . . . separating the spiritual and temporal courts',[20] it must be judged to have been ineffective. The author of another lawbook written in Henry I's reign takes no notice of the writ and describes the Anglo-Norman legal scene as though Old English practices continued largely to be observed. Also there is no evidence that the church created new courts of its own, or shifted its legal business substantially from the folk-courts to the synods. There are some commentators, therefore, who prefer to interpret the writ in a much more limited way and suggest that it was aimed only at some minor abuses of the time.

The *Leges Henrici Primi*, written early in Henry I's reign by a 'French' clerk living in or around Winchester, who had had some connexion with Gerard bishop of Hereford and archbishop of York (died 1108), sheds much light on this problem.[21] The author, who had studied the Anglo-Saxon royal codes and legal treatises and also possessed a fair knowledge of canon law, drawn largely from Pseudo-Isidore and the writings of Ivo of Chartres, but had little acquaintance with Roman law, tried to describe the English legal system. The book is rather disorganized, theoretical (no actual cases are quoted), and possibly archaizing. But the treatise is not polemical, the author was acquainted with the courts, and he was clearly trying to do his best. It is, therefore, possible to argue also from his silences.

Primarily the author was attempting to reduce to order the law which had been declared in the Old English royal codes and which operated in the shire, hundred, and borough courts. Henry I had ordered about this time (1109–11), in a writ addressed to the shire courts, that the shire and hundred courts were to be held in the same way as they had been held in the time of King

18. Liebermann *Gesetze* i. 629. For the two swords, see below 270 n. 11.
19. *HR* 200.
20. As William Stubbs headed it, *SSC* 99.
21. Ed. and trans. L. J. Downer (1972).

Edward,[22] and this treatise may have been written as a consequence of that enactment. The author was also fully aware of the king's court, and of the courts of archbishops, bishops, earls, and other important people (20, 2). But on the whole he was only interested in their legal rights in so far as they affected the popular courts. He could draw a distinction between secular and ecclesiastical business, pleas, causes, procedures, and persons. He could state that a clerk in holy orders and a married clerk engaged in secular affairs would be subject to different procedures, 'for all cases have their own procedures' and much depends on the status of the parties (57, 9–9a). But he could also maintain that bishops had to attend the shire court and that the first business there was ecclesiastical, followed by the pleas of the crown and then private cases (7, 2–3; 31, 3).[23] He envisages a clerk answering a summons to a royal plea in the shire or hundred and, with the advice of his bishop, giving security for attendance (52, 2). In the case of priests who had committed homicide or some other most evil deed he relied on II Cnut 41, and believed that the guilty priest was sentenced to deprivation of his holy orders and a pilgrimage to Rome to be extended at the pope's discretion (66, 2). And he devotes a chapter to 'Ecclesiastical pleas which belong to the king' (11). This deals with those ecclesiastical cases, like homicide in a church, refusal to pay tithe, and adultery, from which the king took part of the penalty.

All this is familiar ground. It is governed by the *Laga Eadwardi* which Henry I had promised his subjects in his coronation charter. But he had prudently added, 'with those improvements which my father made with the advice of his barons'.[24] It must be asked whether the author of the *Leges* had taken those into account. He certainly knew of the *murdrum* fine and its ramifications (13, 2; 75, 6–6b, 91–2), but he does not seem to have noticed a writ separating ecclesiastical from the secular courts. Near the beginning of his treatise he takes a number of procedural rules from a treatise of canon law, Ivo's *Panormia* (5), but he thought that these were rules of jurisprudence rather than the distinctive features of purely ecclesiastical courts. He was probably aware that there was some conflict between canon and English folk-law; but it was not a subject which interested him, and it was not the matter in hand. And he gives the impression that by and large, although with occasional differences of procedure because of their status, clerks were tried and also conducted cases in the shire and hundred courts, as had always been the case.

Even if it is objected that the treatise is theoretical and that the author omitted ecclesiastical jurisdiction because it was not his theme, the *Leges* give no support to the view that revolutionary changes took place in the English legal scene between 1070 and 1118. Although the author does not mention the ecclesiastical synod or visitation, he notices the confessional (72–3). And he can write, 'A priest who is accused by his bishop or archdeacon shall swear an [exculpatory] oath with five other priests vested as though for mass' (64, 8c), without telling us that this must be done in a special place chosen

---

22. *SSC* 121–2.
23. Also in the slightly later *Leges Edwardi Confessoris*, cap. 3, Liebermann *Gesetze* i. 629.
24. Cap. 13, *SSC* 119. Cf. *Quadripartitus* in Liebermann *Gesetze* i. 535.

by the bishop and not in the hundred,[25] although to omit such a distinction in such a treatise would be grossly incompetent.

After Lillebonne (1080) the next royal pronouncement on ecclesiastical rights was in January 1164 at Clarendon, when, as a result of dissention between the clergy, the royal justices, and the barons over ecclesiastical jurisdiction, an inquest was held by a distinguished royal court into the customs and dignities possessed by the king's grandfather, Henry I, and his other ancestors and, less emphatically, into those possessed by the church and the barons.[26] Only a few of the findings – presumably those which were contentious – were summarized, and these are sometimes cryptic. As with William I's writ the cooperation of the various authorities is assumed, but by 1164 some of the warmth had gone out of the relationships, and whereas the writ told the church what it could do, the Constitutions largely tell it what it must not do. They are concerned almost exclusively with the frictional points of what were becoming competing jurisdictions, and, like William I's writ and the lawbooks of Henry I's reign, tell us little about purely ecclesiastical procedures. We can see, however, that a change has occurred. It is assumed by Henry's *curia* that it has a counterpart, the *curia ecclesiastica* or *curia sanctae ecclesiae*; and it accepts (3) that the royal justiciar's court and the ecclesiastical court will be in different places. The document also recognizes (8) the existence of three ecclesiastical courts in ascending dignity, with appeals lying from one to the other: the archdeacon's, the bishop's, and the archbishop's. Even though the *curia* is still more a place or an occasion than a tribunal, and the more ecclesiastical term *forum* is still missing, ecclesiastical jurisdiction would seem to have assumed by 1164, if not by 1135,[27] a more institutional form than it had possessed in the early years of Henry I.

The diocesan synod was still functioning as a lawcourt as late as Stephen's reign. For example, in April 1144, shortly after Easter, Bishop Everard of Norwich presided, probably in the cathedral, over a synod of all the priests of the diocese.[28] On the first day, after the sermon, a priest, Godwin Stert, possibly rector of Haveringland, rose and complained that his nephew, William, a skinner's apprentice, had been murdered by the Norwich Jews. It was decided that these should be summoned, through the dean of Norwich, to attend the synod on the morrow and make answer to the charge. The sheriff of Norwich, however, came to their rescue, agreed that they should not attend, and said that this sort of case was no concern of the bishop. Next day the matter was debated in full synod; it was agreed that Jews could be punished under ecclesiastical law; and it was decided to summon the Norwich Jews a second and third time. After some resistance the sheriff bowed to the bishop's threats and produced the accused. But after Godwin had repeated his charge, and offered to prove it by the ordeal, and the Jews had denied it, the wrangling over the nature of the proof judgment to be awarded was halted when the sheriff,

25. William I's writ, *SSC* 99.

26. *SSC* 161.

27. It is doubtful if the members of the court could in fact remember accurately the period before 1135. Of the bishops present only Henry Blois and Nigel of Ely held office under Henry I. The elderly Gilbert Foliot of London could also have helped.

28. *Vita S. Willelmi Norwic.* 43 ff.

without asking leave, departed with the accused and put them into the security of the royal castle. Subsequent action against the Jews included the murder of a Norwich Jew by one of the bishop's knights, and Bishop William Turbe's defence of this murderer in the king's court at London which took the form in part of countercharges against the Jews. In effect the bishop accepted that Jews were the king's own and outside his jurisdiction.

The synod, however, an annual or biennial general assembly, was incapable of handling the ordinary run of ecclesiastical cases. Some matters, no doubt, the bishop considered in his more domestic court or audience. But the general custom in the Middle Ages was to appoint a deputy to hold courts of law. After St Gilbert had refused an archdeaconry from Alexander of Lincoln, he reluctantly allowed the bishop to ordain him priest so that he could 'exercise the judgment of the church', that is serve as the bishop's justiciar. Alexander wanted him to take cognizance of and exercise jurisdiction over all the delicts of both the bishop's men and the whole populace.[29] It would seem that Gilbert was made presiding judge in the bishop's audience as well as his penitentiary. Perhaps at the time the two offices were indistinguishable. By the end of the century a more formal court, the consistory, split off from the bishop's *curia*, and was usually presided over by the bishop's Official.[30]

Nevertheless, it is likely that by Stephen's reign the bulk of the diocesan legal business was taken by the archdeacons' courts. It is clear from the Constitutions of Clarendon that the archdeacon has acquired his own court, subordinate to, but not comprehended within, the bishop's. The *Leges Edwardi Confessoris* (2, 8), of the end of Henry I's reign, awards the peace of God and the church to those going to synods and chapters, whether they have been summoned to attend or have their own business there. It is likely that the synods are episcopal and the chapters archidiaconal. This development corresponds to the establishment of many peculiars as archdeaconries.[31] Bishops have abandoned some petty jurisdiction to their servants and are in process of moving out of that sphere altogether, except in their own peculiars. And this jurisdiction was profitable. Archdeacons and rural deans (who seem here to have acted as the archdeacon's deputies) operated at a level where sin was notorious and, because of the censoriousness of neighbours, could easily be detected. St Gilbert of Sempringham, when refusing Bishop Alexander of Lincoln's offer of an archdeaconry (before 1131), said that it was difficult to hold that office without committing sin and that archdeacons brought more cases for the sake of money than for the saving of souls.[32] Henry II several times voiced the popular indignation at the depredations of archdeacons. And his 'Inquest of Sheriffs' of 1170 was concerned also with the unjust takings of archdeacons and deans (12).[33]

29.   See above 140, n. 177.

30.   For Exeter, cf. *The Registers of Walter Bronescombe and Peter Quivil*, ed. F. C. Hingeston-Randolph (Exeter 1889), 62 (*s.v.* Criditone, Gervase de), 323 (*s.v.* Dawlish); *The Register of John de Grandisson*, ed. the same (1894) i. 420, 481, 634–5.

31.   Barlow, *Durham Jurisdictional Peculiars*, 147.

32.   *Vita S. Gileberti confessoris* in *Monasticon* vi. 2, p. viii*.

33.   *SSC* 177.

It is difficult to see what went on in ecclesiastical courts in the Norman period, for two main reasons. There is no legislation on the matter or description of procedure; and the archdeacon's position was ambiguous: he was at the same time the bishop's main judicial officer and increasingly the holder of his own court. A change in the method of initiating prosecutions may also be a confusing factor.[34] Traditionally sinners were prosecuted in court, whether popular or ecclesiastical, as a result of private accusations or, possibly, of presentation by a body of neighbours. The latter procedure, under which sinners were accused before the bishop by 'synodal witnesses', was well known to canon law. But the Norman kings, as we can see from the council of Lillebonne and their creation of the office of local justiciar in the shires, favoured *ex officio* prosecutions. The bishops and their servants seem to have shared the royal enthusiasm. They were more effective and therefore more profitable.

Archdeacons and deans, accordingly, became prosecutors. They denounced and impleaded men and women in archidiaconal chapters. But some cases were outside their competence; and these they must have brought before the bishop or his *minister*. For example, after 1102 archdeacons and deans had the duty of investigating the sexual morals of the parish priests. But it is unlikely that these would be tried in an archidiaconal chapter, unless of course the archdeacon was acting as the bishop's justiciar.[35] Henry II in his legal reforms in this matter did not follow his Norman *antecessores*. He disliked *ex officio* prosecutions and substituted as far as possible accusations by juries of presentment. He had forbidden before 1158 unsupported prosecutions by archdeacons and deans; and at Falaise in 1159, repeating the ordinance already made in England, he decreed that no man of good reputation should be accused by a dean without the testimony of his neighbours. In other words, charges must be made by an accusing jury, which, in ecclesiastical terms, was a return to synodal witnesses.[36]

It was recognized that the change could lead to a loss of efficiency. There might be a conspiracy of silence through tolerance or fear. So in 1164, in the Constitutions of Clarendon (6),[37] Henry offered to the episcopal courts that if no trusty and lawful accusers and witnesses, through fear or otherwise, dared come forward to accuse a defamed man, the sheriff, at the bishop's request, would provide a presenting jury from the neighbourhood or vill to serve the same purpose. The sheriff was in some respects the secular counterpart to the archdeacon. Henry, who used archdeacons considerably in his own business, seems to have directed his measures more against their subordinates, the rural deans, than themselves. The jury offered in cap. 6 was not to be at the expense of archidiaconal rights (*ius*), nor was the archdeacon to lose anything on account of it. But what rights and dues he would be deprived of are unfortunately not clear.

---

34. Raoul C. van Caenegem, 'Public prosecution of crime in twelfth-century England', *Church and Government in the Middle Ages: essays presented to C. R. Cheney* (1976), especially 61–70.

35. Jean Scammell, 'The rural chapter in England from the eleventh to the fourteenth century', *EHR* lxxxvi (1971) 8, would give archdeacons and deans rather greater powers.

36. C. H. Haskins, *Norman Institutions* (1918) 329–33. van Caenegem, *loc. cit.*

37. *SSC* 165.

The pope is not mentioned in the Constitutions of Clarendon. But one decree (8) does reveal the king's interest in, and limitation of, appeals beyond the archbishop's court. It declares that a case may not proceed further than that without the king's assent. Although the pope in 1164 was little involved in the process of ecclesiastical justice in England, by 1154 appeals to him for advice or appeals from English ecclesiastical judges to his court by dissatisfied litigants or defendants were becoming not uncommon. But since they were still few, and there was usually a resident papal legate in England, it seems that such cases were heard either at Rome or by the legate. The system of judges delegate, in which the pope appointed a panel of suitable local bishops and others to hear a particular case and report its findings to him, was only in its infancy.[38] In Normandy the earliest extant report of Arnulf bishop of Lisieux, who often acted as a papal judge delegate, cannot be dated before 1159.[39] There is no need therefore to discuss this important development here.

The Constitutions of Clarendon are more concerned with limiting ecclesiastical jurisdiction than describing its competence.[40] It is only by studying the boundaries proposed that the two fields can be envisaged. Church courts are warned off disputes involving advowson (1), land held by feudal tenure (9), and debt (15); by implication they are allowed jurisdiction over the sinful laity (6, 7, 10, 13) and criminous clerks (3) and over land if held in free alms by a clerk (9). The discipline of the clergy and domestic litigation are ignored by the Constitutions because such jurisdiction was uncontested.

A principle which runs through the Constitutions, and one which made them offensive to the canonists in 1164, is the old Norman rule that the king and his council allow and control jurisdictional rights, and that whenever there was a conflict of laws the king or his justices should decide whether the case should go to the ecclesiastical court. This check appears in the Constitutions at every point where the church required the cooperation of the lay power. Clerks accused of crime in a secular court before a royal justiciar are not to be released automatically to the church, but the royal court will decide where the accused is to be tried (3). Especially there was restraint on the use of excommunication to force men to plead in the ecclesiastical court. No tenant-in-chief or demesne servant of the king could be excommunicated, or his lands put under an interdict, until the king or, in his absence overseas, his justiciar, had been requested to compel the accused to do the church justice, and the king or justiciar will decide whether the case should be heard in the royal or in the ecclesiastical court (7). If a baron forcibly prevented an archbishop, bishop, or archdeacon from doing justice on him or one of his men, it is the king who should compel him to satisfy the church. But similarly if one of the clergy deprived the king of any right then the ecclesiastical authorities were to compel the clerk (13). A man from the royal demesne who refused the summonses to an ecclesiastical court could be put under an interdict, but could not be excommunicated before the king's chief local official had been requested to

38. C. R. Cheney, *From Becket to Langton* (1956) 42 ff.
39. Frank Barlow, *The Letters of Arnulf of Lisieux*, Camden 3rd ser. lxi (1939) pp. xxi, xxiii, lxv.
40. *SSC* 163.

force him to attend; only when the official took no action could the bishop or archdeacon enforce attendance by excommunication (10).

These prohibitions seem, in part at least, to be aimed at preventing the church from using excommunication as a method of attracting a case into its courts. If a bishop or archdeacon excommunicated a man for a secular offence against the church – such as usurpation of land or rights – then the case would be heard in the lay court and the only aspect left to the church was the reconciliation of the excommunicate. And even in its treatment of excommunicates the church was restrained. An excommunicate could not be forced to give security or make an oath for his future good behaviour. He could only be required to give surety and pledge that he would submit to the church's judgment (5). It is also possible that, just as the king was using distraint on a man's chattels or lands as a punishment in itself instead of as a process to force a man to stand his trial (an abuse which, as we can see from Magna Carta, was resented), so the church was using excommunication and interdict in a similar way. It was difficult to correct the king. But the king believed that he had the right to reform the church.

From the evidence of the council of Lillebonne, the Constitutions of Clarendon, and other royal directives it is clear that the church possessed a large jurisdiction in the kingdom in the Norman period. The bishops claimed and were allowed a monopoly of the judicial ordeals, unrestricted disciplinary rights over the clergy, and extensive rights of punishing the sins of the laity, and its jurisdiction in matrimonial and bastardy cases was uncontested. All this is what we can call criminal or quasi-criminal jurisdiction. On the whole the kings encouraged this activity (except when royal interests or vassals were involved) and embarrassed the church only by offering what was sometimes unwelcome supplementary help, as with unchaste priests or criminous clerks. On the civil side the church was allowed to settle many domestic disputes, but the king's help was often solicited and he was also inclined to interfere especially if the litigation was over land or rights inextricably connected with land. Lawsuits over fiefs were reserved to a feudal court. On the other hand the church's jurisdiction over testamentary cases, for only chattels could be left by will, was undisputed. Contracts and other matters involving broken faith were border-line.

There are few detailed accounts of actual ecclesiastical cases in this period and no technical law reports by which the evidence of the councils and directives can be checked. All the *causes célèbres* of the earlier years, like the trials of William of St Calais and of Anselm, took place in the royal court. As the author of the *Leges Henrici Primi* wrote (20, 3), 'In the case of serious matters (*capitales questiones*) the king has jurisdiction (*socna*) over all barons and "senators", whether clerks or laymen, wherever they hold their land and whether this is within the king's soke or not.' After 1139 the princely papal legate, Henry bishop of Winchester, tried to reverse the situation, and the great 'trial' of King Stephen took place in the legate's council.[41] Some examples of all the branches of ecclesiastical jurisdiction can, however, be found, and these will be taken in the following order: the ordeals; internal discipline and crimin-

---

41. Below 305 ff.

ous clerks; punishment of the sinful laity (including matrimonial and bastardy cases); and ecclesiastical litigation.

The church's legal activity best illustrated in the Norman period is the administration of the various ordeals. They were awarded in both secular and ecclesiastical cases as 'proof judgments' and strictly speaking were not a part of ecclesiastical jurisdiction. They were God's judgment, and so under priestly control. The Conquest may have increased their use. As status was a fundamental strand in Old English law the popular courts probably preferred clearing oaths to the ecclesiastical ordeal as final proof, for the ordeals obliterated the advantages of birthright and degrees of law-worthiness. But William and his advisers inclined towards the ordeal. In the ordinance regulating the law of proof between Frenchmen and Englishmen[42] clearing oaths are in certain circumstances allowed to either party (1, 1; 2, 3), but the norm is the *duellum*, or judicial combat, with the ordeal for the English accused who would not fight. William may have thought that where there was racial tension English malefactors would not find it too difficult to swear their guilt away.

The Conqueror's writ put the ordeal – or possibly only the ordeal of hot iron[43] – under the exclusive control of the bishop. It was to be held either in the episcopal see or at a place appointed by the bishop, and his justiciar had always to attend the ceremony. At Canterbury trials by ordeal had customarily taken place in the ancient baptistery which stood as a detached building at the east end of the cathedral.[44] According to the *Leges Edwardi Confessoris* (9) ordeals, although under episcopal supervision, were still performed locally. When the ordeal of iron or water was awarded by a royal justiciar, the bishop's *minister* and his clerks should attend the ceremony together with the royal justiciar and the lawful men of the shire. When this method of proof was awarded by the court of a baron who did not have the privilege of holding the ordeal,[45] then the case was to be determined in the nearest church within the hundred which possessed the apparatus for the king's ordeal (9, 3). It was, therefore, believed that there was apparatus for the ordeals in each shire (which often corresponded to an archdeaconry) and in each hundred (or rural deanery), and the archdeacon and rural dean may ordinarily have been responsible for their administration. Certain churches claimed the exclusive right to some or all of the religious ceremonies. Robert of Chesney bishop of Lincoln (1148–66), notified William of St Clere archdeacon of Northampton,

---

42.   *Lad,* Lievermann *Gesetze* i. 483–4. For the subject in general, cf. Colin Morris, '*Judicium Dei*: the social and political significance of the ordeal in the eleventh century', *Studies in Church History*, ed. Derek Baker, xii (1975) 95.

43.   'Judicium vero in nullo loco *portetur* . . .', *SSC* 100, See also below, n. 45.

44.   Eadmer *Vita S. Bregwini* in Bernhard W. Scholz, 'Eadmer's life of Bregwine, archbishop of Canterbury 761–64', *Traditio* xxii (1966) 139–40; *PL* clix. 755, 'ut baptisteria et examinationes judiciorum pro diversis causis constitutorum, quae ad correctionem sceleratorum in ecclesia dei fieri solent, inibi celebrarentur'. For a plan, R. W. Southern, *St Anselm and his Biographer* 264.

45.   Laymen clearly had the right, and William I's writ possibly does not contradict, to hold at least the ordeal of cold water: they had a pit as well as gallows. The pit would be for the unfree or the 'law-unworthy'. A man, with the approval and confirmation of Bishop Ralf Luffa of Chichester, granted the *judicium aquae* he possessed to Battle abbey. Mayr-Harting, *Acta of the bishops of Chichester*, no. 5 (1107 x 23). Rouen (1096) can. 7 forbade laymen to have episcopal customs or jurisdiction which pertained to the cure of souls: Mansi xx. 921.

the (rural) dean, and the justiciars that he understood that St Peter's Northampton enjoyed the privilege that all who had to undergo the ordeal in
Northampton had to use the services of that church and also perform their vigil
and say their prayers within it.[46]

Gilbert of Limerick assigned consecration of water (and bread) to
the priest, and of iron to the bishop, and in the twelfth century it was thought
that the ordeal of cold water was for rustics, that of hot iron for the free and for
women of any condition, although in practice the rules were not always
observed.[47] Other ordeals of this type are also described in liturgical books,[48]
but their use is uncertain. The *duellum*, the judicial combat, was introduced by
the Normans and was probably the most honourable method of defence to a
charge. By the eleventh century all these ordeals had been given a completely
religious ceremonial. According to the full rite the accused was taken to a
church at Vespers on a Tuesday dressed in penitential garb and was kept there
fasting for three days. On the Saturday he attended mass, was abjured by the
priest not to communicate unless innocent, and, if he received communion, was
prepared religiously for the ordeal. If the man was to undergo the ordeal of cold
water, after mass he was stripped of his penitential clothes and led in a religious
procession to the pit. This was to be twelve feet deep, twenty feet in diameter,
and filled with water to the brim. Over a third of the pit was a platform on poles
strong enough to bear the priest, the judges, the man to enter the water, and the
men to put him in. The priest then blessed the water, and in prayers asked God
that if the man was innocent the water should receive him or, if guilty, reject
him. The man was then trussed with cords and lowered gently and smoothly on
a rope tied round his loins. On the rope was a knot, a long hair's length from the
point of attachment, and the man had to sink as far as the knot in order to
succeed.

When the ordeal was of hot iron, the bar, one pound in weight or
three pounds for the triple ordeal, was kept by the altar until the crucial mass
was to begin. The priest then lifted it in forceps and carried it with religious
ceremony to the fire. The form of the mass was similar to the other. There was
then a procession to the fire. At some point the iron was blessed and God was
entreated that it might be cold to the innocent and burning hot to the evil doer;
it was taken from the fire and placed on a log. The priest read the gospel,
asperged the iron with holy water, and made the sign of the cross. The accused
then took it and carried it for nine feet. His hand was bound up and sealed, and
examined after three days. If the iron had corrupted the hand the man was held
guilty, but if his hand was clean there was offered praise and glory to God. The
religious ceremonies of the *duellum* are less minutely described, but were
probably similar in essentials to the others. The main differences, of course,

---

46. F. M. Stenton, 'Acta episcoporum', *CambHJ* iii (1929) 12.

47. Glanvill, *De legibus et consuetudinibus Angliae*, ed. George E. Woodbine (New Haven 1932),
in his 'elementary and fragmentary' treatment of criminal procedure (Bk XIV), regards the ordeal
as one of the ordinary methods of proof; see especially p. 176 and Woodbine's notes, p. 296. Cf.
Assize of Clarendon (1166) caps. 2, 4, 12–14, *SSC* 170. See also Liebermann *Gesetze* ii. 385, 400,
530, *s.v. Eisenordal, Feuerordal* and *Kaltwasserordal*.

48. Liebermann *Gesetze* i. 401 ff.

were that two men were involved and the instruments to be blessed were the shields and the staves.[49]

A few anecdotes will illustrate the procedures. Reginald of Durham describes a rescued sailor hurrying to church still drenched as though just raised from the pit of justice.[50] Most stories, however, largely because they come mainly from books of miracles, are concerned with the ordeal of hot iron. One of the miracles of St Swithun probably displays English practice.[51] A royal justiciar, presumably at Winchester, sent the slave of Flodoard, a rich trader, to this ordeal on some charge or other, and repulsed all attempts at bribery. After the slave had carried the red-hot iron a huge burn appeared on the palm of his hand, which was then sealed in the usual way. Flodoard realized that his servant was condemned and guilty and, as he could not bear to see him executed, prepared to leave for home. But he prayed to God that through the intercession of St Swithun the man might be spared, and promised, if he were, to give him to the saint. At dawn on the third day the accused was led before the royal official for public inspection of his hand by the suitors, and to the amazement of his lord and companions his accusers declared him innocent. His supporters could see the burns and blistering but his accusers could see a hand as healthy as though it had never touched the iron. In Normandy, in 1080, William Pantolf when accused of treachery in connexion with the murder of Mabel countess of Shrewsbury, the wife of his lord, took sanctuary with his wife and sons in the monastery of St Evroul.[52] For some time he was not allowed to purge himself of the charge. But it was finally decided in the *curia regis* that he could undergo the ordeal of hot iron at Rouen in the presence of the clergy. The accused carried the red-hot iron in his bare hand, and, as by God's will he bore no sign of burning, was adjudged innocent; and the clergy with all the people there assembled praised God with a loud voice. He was indeed fortunate, for Orderic informs us that the man's enemies had come to the ceremony intending, if he failed in the ordeal, to cut off his head forthwith.

According to Henry archdeacon of Huntingdon[53] – and he was in a position to know – Bishop Remigius of Lincoln (1072–92), when accused of treason, was cleared by a servant (*famulus*) taking the ordeal. An equally remarkable story is told by Orderic.[54] Robert, after he had become duke of Normandy, was visited by the mistress he had had when he had been in rebellion against his father, the beautiful concubine of an old priest on the French border. She produced her two sons, Richard and William, and claimed that they were Robert's. When the duke hesitated to acknowledge them, she publicly carried the red-hot iron and came clean from the ordeal. Both were then educated as ducal bastards, Richard dying in a hunting accident in the New

---

49. *Ibid*. i. 430–1.
50. *St Cuthbert* cap. 32.
51. *Translatio S. Swithuni*, cap. 8: Paul Grosjean, 'De Codice Hagiographico Gothano', *AB* lviii (1940) 195; *PL* clv. 76–7.
52. OV (Chibnall) iii. 160–2.
53. HH 212. Cf. *LEp* 58.
54. OV (Chibnall) v. 202.

Forest, not long before his uncle the king met a similar fate.[55] Some Domesday entries show that men and women offered in 1086 to prove their right to land by the ordeal of hot iron.[56] And about 1114 Theodora of Huntingdon (Christina of Markyate) offered to the prior of Huntingdon this proof of the truth of her assertion.[57] Finally a Worcester story from 1130.[58] Two men and a woman accused of various crimes and judged to undergo the ordeal, carried the red-hot iron in accordance with ecclesiastical law on Saturday 25 January, and eye-witnesses declared that the woman's hand was badly burned by the fire both inside and out. But all the accused, trusting in God and the merits of Wulfstan, visited that bishop's tomb, knelt and asked for his help, and beat the palms of their hands on the stone. After mass, in the view of all the people, one after the other the accused showed their hands and each was found to be without stain. Whereupon *Te Deum* was chanted and all the bells were rung.

The crime to be cleared is given in most liturgical forms as theft. But once *maleficium*, perhaps sorcery, and *stuprum*, perhaps rape or adultery, are mentioned as crimes for which the water proof might be awarded.[59] It may be that the two most common ordeals, iron and water, gave little hope of escape except by a miracle or trickery. When granted to those who lacked standing in the court owing to forfeiture of rights or inability to secure oath-helpers the procedure is justifiable in the circumstances.[60] If they were awarded only to those who were seriously defamed then they conceded that remote sporting chance dear to medieval man. And men, as we have seen, did escape. Eadmer charged Rufus with not only an inclination towards Judaism but also a disbelief in the efficacy of the saints and God's direct intervention in the events of men.[61] For example, when about fifty fairly well-to-do Englishmen, who had been accused of poaching the king's deer and awarded the ordeal of hot iron, were all able to show unmarked hands on the third day, Rufus was indignant and made some typically profane remarks. 'What's this?', he exclaimed. 'You say that God is a just judge? Absolute nonsense! In future something that people can bend so easily must be subject to my justice and not the ordeal of God.' God was either ignorant of what went on or did not wish to judge men in this way.

The attitude of the clergy who administered these ordeals can only be surmised. Miracle stories usually reveal sympathy for the accused. Eadmer believed that the fifty Englishmen had been unjustly accused. The abbot and monks of St Evroul had been comforting Pantolf. The church of Winchester was interested in obtaining a slave, and the man's accusers, perhaps blinded by the money which the king's justiciar would not accept, could not see. Glastonbury abbey boasted in the twelfth century that it was so holy that within living memory all but one of those who had prayed there before undergoing the

55. Florence *s.a.* 1100; *GR* ii. 333.
56. *DB* ii. 110b (Breckles, Nf), 137 (Bittering Nf), 162 (Feltwell, Nf), 166 (Griston, Nf).
57. *The Life of Christina of Markyate*, ed. C. H. Talbot (1959) 62.
58. John of Worcester 30.
59. Liebermann *Gesetze* i. 423.
60. Cf. *Leges Henrici Primi* 18, 1.
61. *HN* 102.

ordeal of iron or water had been acquitted.[62] Escapes from condemnation must often have been with the connivance of the church. Failure to heat the iron to the correct temperature, heavy sprinking with holy water, or a protraction of the service while the metal cooled were obvious devices. Only clerks of the simplest faith, or cynically callous, could have supervised the ordeals without reservation or distaste.

The *duellum* had little except the call for divine intervention in common with the others. It reflects a completely different social attitude and has the fundamental distinguishing feature of not being deliberately weighted against the accused;[63] it was also the most beastly of the trials. Reginald of Durham tells us that once, when the *duellum* had been adjudged, one of the contestants went, as was the custom, to the church at Norham where he swore before the altar of St Cuthbert, holding the cross in his hand, that he was innocent. But because he thereby committed perjury, when he was taken to Midhop for the battle he could not see his adversary who promptly ran him through with his lance. This was witnessed by Swain, the priest of Fishwick.[64] At York an envious rustic maliciously accused a neighbour in one of the folk courts of arson. Despite his perjury he defeated his unwarlike defendant in the *duellum* and then exercised his right to tear out the conquered man's eyes and castrate him. But St William of York, to whose tomb the victim was carried, restored to him the parts he had lost, although the new eyes were of a different sort of colour.[65] Nor were the nobility and gentry immune from such savagery. In January 1096 William Rufus held his court at Salisbury and judged the rebels of the year before.[66] Robert of Mowbray, earl of Northumberland, was sentenced to perpetual imprisonment. Then Geoffrey Bainard accused William count of Eu of having been a party to the treason, and defeated him in the *duellum*. William was sentenced to have his eyes put out and to castration, and his cousin and steward, William of Aldery, was sentenced to be hanged. There was much sympathy for this fine-looking man who was thought to be innocent. He confessed his sins to aged Bishop Osmund of Salisbury and as penance was scourged at every church in the town. Afterwards he divided his clothes among the poor and went naked to the gallows, bloodying his knees with frequent kneeling. The bishop and people followed him to the place of execution, where he protested his complete innocence of the charge. Osmund commended his soul to God, asperged him with holy water and then went away. William died very bravely. The church did not shed blood, and clerks were forbidden to pass capital sentences; but there was no escaping from the slaughter.

Some of the theological implications of the clergy's part in the ordeals were considered by Robert Pullen, who not only taught theology in the cathedral school at Paris but also was the non-resident archdeacon of Roches-

62. William of Malmesbury, *De antiquitate Glastoniensis ecclesiae* in *Adami de Domerham historia de rebus gestis Glastoniensibus*, ed. T. Hearne (1727) i. 27: *PL* clxxix. 1692 (with a textual error).

63. Cf. V. H. Galbraith, 'The death of a champion (1287)', *Studies in Medieval History presented to F. M. Powicke* (1948) 282.

64. *St Cuthbert* cap. 57.

65. *Vita et miracula S. Willelmi Eborac. archiepiscopi*, B.M. MS Harl. 2, fos. 86v–87.

66. *Chron.*; Florence; *GR* 372–3.

ter.[67] In his *Sententiarum libri octo* (*c.* 1142–44), a theological textbook which antedates the more influential work of Peter Lombard, the 'Master of the Sentences', Pullen expresses the view that ordeals should be banished from the church of God, and prescribes rigorously what attitudes the confessor should adopt in the meantime. The defendant when preparing to undergo the ordeal was to be warned of the consequences of perjury. Better to suffer a corporal penalty on earth than everlasting punishment in hell, for 'God will not judge twice for the same offence' (Nahum 1: 7, Septuagint version). If the defendant confessed his guilt to the priest but still elected to undergo the ordeal, the confessor could take no public action on the perjury since he was bound to preserve the secrecy of the confession. But when the defendant failed in the ordeal and was thus shown to have committed perjury he was to be abandoned by his confessor. On conviction he was delivered to the secular judge, and should confess to him, for confession had to be made to him from whom the punishment was to be received. Even if the convict was repentant he was not to be given any sacraments by the church. (This refusal of the sacraments to a condemned man was a moot point. Pullen was rigorous. Gratian, XIII, q.2, c. 30, relying on Mainz (847) c. 27, where the same text from Nahum is used, took the opposite view.) There was also the position of the plaintiff when the defendant succeeded in the ordeal. Since he was manifestly guilty of perjury and attempted homicide, he should therefore do public penance (which was a matter for the bishop), or, if recalcitrant, be subject to ecclesiastical discipline. Pullen, by limiting his attention to perjury, which was not peculiar to these methods of proof, treated the subject inadequately. But the church's dislike of the ordeals grew during the century. And in 1215 the Fourth Lateran Council (c. 18), when tightening up the prohibition of the clergy's involvement in the shedding of blood, decreed that no clerk in major orders was to pronounce any kind of benediction or consecration in connexion with the ordeals of hot or cold water or red-hot iron.[68]

An area which, for obvious reasons, the *Leges Henrici Primi* neglects, internal discipline, is not well recorded because it was so usual. Subordinates were constantly being corrected. In monasteries the whipping of monks was a regular feature of daily chapter.[69] The irregularities of secular clerks, however, were usually treated more leniently. For example, Lanfranc wrote to Bishop Herfast of Elmham about a man who had confessed to him that, although he had possessed no orders, he had received the diaconate from Herfast, and also that he had a wife whom he did not intend to dismiss. The archbishop instructed Herfast that he was to take away the diaconate, promote the man to the several minor orders at fitting times, but not restore deacon's orders unless the man lived chastely and also swore that he would live chastely

67.   VI, 53–4: *PL* clxxxvi. 903–5. One of the fullest legal-theological considerations of ordeals is in Hincmar archbishop of Rheims's *De divortio Lotharii et Tetbergae* (*c.* 864) in *PL* cxxv. 659 ff.

68.   Cf. John W. Baldwin, 'The intellectual preparation for the canon of 1215 against ordeals', *Speculum* xxxvi (1961) 613.

69.   Besides the punishment of those guilty of faults were the penances of the sinful. Uhtred, Bishop Wulfstan's precentor at Worcester, who died in 1132, 'in a spirit of humility and for the remission of his sins', was in his last year, when semi-paralysed, severely beaten almost every day by two or three of the monks: John of Worcester 36.

in the future. If the orders were to be restored, the man was not to be re-ordained, but was to receive back the office through investiture by a book of the gospels either in a synod or in a large assembly of clerks.[70]

Rebellion was one of the most serious ecclesiastical crimes and its punishment can be illustrated by the celebrated revolt in 1088–89 by the monks of St Augustine's Canterbury against an abbot imposed upon them.[71] In July Lanfranc appointed a certain Guy (*Wido*), an attempt at domination which the monks, led by their English prior, Ælfwin, strongly resisted. The initial rebellion collapsed after the ringleaders and their followers had been imprisoned by the archbishop, some in Canterbury castle, some in Christ Church, and some in various churches throughout England, and one monk, Alfred, who confessed to intending the murder of Guy, had been sentenced by Lanfranc to be stripped naked, bound, and publicly flogged before the gates of the abbey, then 'unfrocked' and expelled from the city. After Lanfranc's death on 28 May 1089 the monks rebelled again and incited the citizens to break into the abbot's court. Guy barely escaped with his life, and some of his household were killed and wounded. As the see was vacant Rufus sent Walkelin of Winchester and Gundulf of Rochester with some barons to Canterbury. They listened to the monks' case, deemed it insufficient and sentenced the rebels to a public flogging; in the event, in order not to bring monasticism into disrepute, the sentence was commuted to a flogging within the church before a selected audience. Two monks of Christ Church carried out the sentence, and twenty-four Christ Church monks replaced the rebels, who were transported to the custody of distant churches. The citizens who aided them were put on trial, possibly in a secular court, and those who failed in the ordeal had their eyes torn out. Although Archbishop Theobald was a little more merciful in 1149, after St Augustine's had ignored the papal interdict on England, he had the prior and sacristan publicly flogged before the door of the church.[72] It is a mistake to think that ecclesiastical justice, whether exercised on clerks or the laity, whether in church or in popular courts, was usually mild and without the power to deter.

Normally the ecclesiastical and lay powers cooperated eagerly, especially in the earlier part of the period, in the repression of sin, crime, and rebellion, whether committed by layman or clerk. In 1106 Anselm, when he heard that Henry I was punishing with fines priests who kept women contrary to the council of Westminster (1102), asked the king to desist, since the sins of ecclesiastical ministers should be corrected by the bishops, not the lay authority; and Henry made a conciliatory reply.[73] But Anselm was over scrupulous. In general the bishops seem to have encouraged secular authorities to punish their criminal subjects, and such punishments caused no affront, especially since the penalties differed according to the order of the persons and the gravity of the crime. After the atrocities in Glastonbury abbey in 1083 the Conqueror sent

---

70. *LEp* 24.

71. *Acta Lanfranci* 273–5. The alleged presence of Odo of Bayeux at Canterbury where Guy was installed presents a chronological difficulty. He was in rebellion by Easter 1088.

72. *Hist. Pont.* 51–2.

73. *GP* 115. *AEp* 391–2.

the abbot back to Normandy and had many of the monks imprisoned in bishoprics and abbeys.[74] Orderic Vitalis, writing in 1133–35, tells the terrible story of how a clerk, who in Norway had been mutilated for the murder of a priest and fitted with iron fingers, with those hooks savagely killed the baby son of Earl David of Scots, and as punishment was tied to the tails of four wild horses and torn apart.[75] Sometimes the people were encouraged to punish an evil clerk. A northerner, Wimund, who could not afford much education, became a scribe in some monastery before entering the Cistercian abbey of Furness, founded in 1124, as a monk. After he had been elected bishop of the Isles he claimed to be a son of Angus earl of Moray (who had been killed in 1130), and turned pirate in order to conquer the earldom. Once he was defeated in battle by another bishop (possibly of Moray), but later he was able to extort from King David an estate in Cumbria which included Furness. His rule, however, was so oppressive that he was captured by some of his subjects who blinded and castrated him. He then retired to Byland abbey, which was ruled by a former monk of Furness.[76] William of Newburgh, who tells the story, obviously did not think that clerical immunity should have been respected in this case. After the discovery of the conspiracy at Ely in 1137, however, the laymen were hanged, the clerks condemned to exile for life.[77]

The English church was well represented at the council of Rheims in 1148.[78] One of its points of interest was the trial of the heretic, Eon de l'Étoile, and his disciples. Eon was condemned to imprisonment, but his followers, according to William of Newburgh, were delivered first to the secular court (*curiae traditi*, a technical term) and then to the flames, for they preferred to burn rather than amend their ways.[79] Reginald of Durham informs us that Robert, the son of Wulfmaer, the head cook in the monastic cookhouse, was educated on his father's orders as a clerk, but preferred a life of crime. One night he robbed the monks' kitchen, was arrested, and was condemned to be hanged. He confessed his crimes on the way to the gallows but was executed.[80] The bishop of Durham possessed every sort of jurisdiction, lay and ecclesiastical, and should have known what to do. In 1164 Henry II's court believed that in Henry I's reign clerks found guilty in an ecclesiastical court of serious crimes were as a rule deprived of their orders and handed over to the lay court for punishment.[81] Nothing can be put against this view.

The prosecution of sinful laymen is not well illustrated. In 1070 the bishop of Durham, probably for political reasons, declined to punish some laymen who had committed sacrilege. While the king had been ravaging the

74. Florence, *s.a.* 1083.
75. OV (Chibnall) iv. 274–5.
76. William of Newburgh 73 ff.
77. *Liber Eliensis* 298.
78. Above 114.
79. William of Newburgh 60 ff. Raymonde Foreville, *Latran I, II, III et Latran IV* (1965) 87, 101. Walter Map in one of his stories, *De Nugis curialium* IV, vi *ad fin.*, has a bishop of Beauvais standing by a great pyre which the civic judges had built outside the walls for the burning of a witch.
80. Reginald *St Cuthbert*, cap. 81.
81. Constitutions of Clarendon, *SSC* 164–5.

North, and the bishop and nobility of Durham had fled, all the treasures of the church, except the great cross which had been given by Earl Tostig and Judith and which was too heavy to remove, had been stolen. The indignant king ordered the looters to be arrested and delivered to the bishop and his priests for punishment. But they let the malefactors go free.[82] A little later Archbishop Lanfranc wrote to an Abbot T. that he had heard the case against the adulterers Godwin and Leofgifu at London (the woman was apparently deceased). After hearing the pleadings of both parties he had passed sentence on the pair and declared by common consent (presumably in a synod) that they were justly excommunicate. Nothing therefore remained except for the abbot to eject the adulteress from the cemetery until either her corruptor or someone else on her behalf made proper amends to the bishop.[83] Herbert Losinga bishop of Elmham-Thetford-Norwich (1090–1119), in a letter addressed to the royal sheriff and the people of his diocese (perhaps an early form of *Significavit*), announced that he had excommunicated those who had entered his deerpark at Homersfield and killed and eaten a stag he had there, and that he had imposed this anathema because he wanted evil-doers to repent, come to confession, and receive correction for their crime.[84] The purpose of this writ was to secure the arrest by the lay authorities of an excommunicate person in order to make him submit to episcopal justice.

The post-Conquest councils legislated against marriage within the prohibited degrees of kinship and affinity and also against fraudulent divorce. Matrimonial cases were the most difficult branch of ecclesiastical jurisdiction. The law was uncertain. St Augustine's *De adulterinis conjugiis,* to which many eleventh- and twelfth-century lawyers and theologians still referred, had been overlaid by a hotchpotch of penitential literature of doubtful authenticity.[85] What is more, at the end of our period the canonists of Bologna and the theologians of Paris held opposite views on the binding force of a betrothal.[86] Eventually Pope Alexander III decided for Paris, to the advantage of that persistent litigant, Richard of Anstey. But the church had still to wait for a useful and accepted compendium of matrimonial law. It even lacked a complete technical vocabulary. Although the distinction between an annulment of marriage and a divorce of the parties was even more important then than now, *divortium* was used indifferently and untechnically by most writers.

The matrimonial business of the courts was of two main kinds: the church's *motu proprio* processes against sinful marriages, and the hearing of petitions for annulment or divorce or other remedies, that is to say, cases *ad instantiam [partium]*. Robert Pullen, in his *Sententiarum libri octo,* recognized four major types of impediment to marriage:[87] lack of mutual consent; a contract with a Jew or gentile; a religious profession, public vow of chastity, or

---

82. Simeon *HDE* 101.

83. *LEp* 57.

84. *HEp* 36=35.

85. Ernulf (see below 168), when discussing a moot point, referred to the advice of the Fathers, penitentials, and the custom (perhaps practice) of the church; but in fact relied mostly on biblical texts. *PL* clxiii. 1458.

86. Cf. F. Courtney, *Cardinal Robert Pullen* 256–7.

87. VII, 28 ff.; *PL* clxxxvi. 945.

major orders; and consanguinity, affinity, or spiritual relationship. A marriage could be (and should be) annulled on any of these grounds, but even if the marriage was voided the divorced persons were not necessarily free to remarry. With category three this is, of course, obvious. In the Norman period the last category was the most important, and was drastic in its effect within small communities. A man was not only forbidden to marry his grandmother, but also his mistress, his mistress's sister, his deceased wife's cousin, and his nephew's godmother. It was almost impossible to contract an unassailable marriage. There were also causes for which a marriage could either be dissolved or allowed to stand. Pullen instances the cases when a freewoman has been deceived into marrying a serf and when one of the parties suffered from sexual impotence, whether physical or produced by sorcery. Oddly enough he does not consider bigamy (except with reference to betrothal) or the not uncommon case of several brothers sharing one wife. He does, however, when discussing the effect of ignorance, cite two interesting matrimonial adventures (VI, 6).

When a marriage was annulled because of a prohibited relationship, or Pullen's last two impediments, the parties, except for the impotent, were free to remarry. And the surest way to a radical divorce was to prove the existence of a pre-nuptual impediment. Actions which happened after the marriage, such as adultery, cruelty, or desertion, were usually ineffective. They could sometimes lead to judicial separation, but nothing more.[88] Pullen claimed that divorce had been abolished by Christ, with the only relief that in the case of adultery permanent separation could be allowed. But this led to no freedom. Both parties were obliged to continence and could not marry anyone else. They could, however, come together again.

Such, the archdeacon and professor of theology thought, was the law. It was, of course, often evaded. Illegal unions were not invalidated. Fraudulent and collusive annulments (especially by alleging pre-nuptual fornication with a relative of the wife or impotence) were not unknown. And many unhappy partners looked elsewhere for relief. There were political, social, and economic restraints on the legal termination of marriages. Property had to be restored and sometimes compensation paid. It is likely that throughout society repudiation of a wife, or the taking of a lover, mistress or concubine, were common alternatives. Above all, the frequency of early death considerably reduced the need for divorce. A succession of spouses was a characteristic feature of medieval social life.

Some of the main types of action can be illustrated, although no purely *motu proprio* action is available. Between 1089 and 1098 Walkelin bishop of Winchester consulted Ernulf monk of Beauvais/Bec/Canterbury and later abbot of Peterborough and bishop of Rochester on whether a woman who had committed adultery with her stepson could justly by episcopal authority be divorced from her husband.[89] Ernulf started by quoting St Augustine, *De adulterinis conjugiis* I, 25, 'I am aware that there are none more obscure or perplexing than matrimonial cases', and after writing several thousand words

---

88.   Cf. *AEp* 10; 'In his verbis dominicis (Mark 10: 11–12; Luke 16: 18) luce clarius liquet quia vivente viro vel uxore extraneam copulam quaerere nulli eorum licet.'
89.   *PL* clxiii. 1457.

on the matter in question cited a case which had come before Archbishop Lanfranc and some bishops. A mother had taken her daughter's husband away, and the wife complained. Lanfranc had ordered the husband to be removed from the mother. But this, Ernulf remarked, although it completed the action brought, was not enough. Since the daughter had complained of her mother's robbery (*rapina*) and her husband's injury (*fraus*), justice demanded that not only should the robber be deprived of her booty, but also that this should be restored to the victim. Lanfranc had not taken the case to its logical end because in his humility he had not wished to usurp the jurisdiction of the bishop to whom it pertained. Ernulf's answer seems to be that the errant wife, about whom he had been consulted, should not be divorced, but separated from her stepson and returned to her husband. Also in William I's reign William de Moulins was divorced from his wife Aubrée in the court of the bishop of Sées because of consanguinity, although there were two sons of the marriage. William then married again and founded a second family while Aubrée became a nun.[90] At about the same time an English case involved an appeal to the pope. Bishop Stigand of Chichester moved against a woman, presumably because of her uncanonical marriage, and she appealed to Rome. The pope ordered Lanfranc to hear and determine the case and in the meantime give her absolution and protect her from molestation. Whereupon Lanfranc ordered the bishop to allow the woman to live with her husband in peace until he could determine the case with the counsel of his fellow bishops.[91]

In the early twelfth century a man, after his wife had been crippled for five years and reduced to poverty, repudiated and deserted her. But after she had been cured by St Aldhelm at Malmesbury she brought a suit against the deserter, presumably for restitution of conjugal rights.[92] She won her case, and her husband accepted the judgment of the court and returned to her bed since neither poverty nor lust had caused her to be unchaste. Bishops were also asked for dispensations. One of Bishop Herbert Losinga's chaplains, William, pestered him on behalf of his sister, who wanted to remarry. But the bishop held to his view that this was impossible while her husband was alive. The chaplain was to pay more regard to the custom of holy church than to the desires of a woman.[93] The circumstances are not explained. It is possible that the woman's husband was in captivity, or disabled. But it may be that they had been divorced. There seems to have been a feeling that whereas the man could remarry, the woman should retire from the world.

The most celebrated Anglo-Norman matrimonial and bastardy case in the twelfth century was the marriage of Henry I and Edith-Matilda of Scotland and King Stephen's attempt to bastardize the surviving issue of that union, his cousin, Matilda the empress.[94] Edith-Matilda seems to have been simply a pawn in Anglo-Scottish diplomacy. The daughter of Malcolm king of

90. OV (Chibnall) iii. 132–4.
91. *LEp* 31.
92. *GP* 434–5.
93. *HEp* 3.
94. *HN* 121–6. R. W. Southern, *Saint Anselm and his Biographer* 183 ff.; *Chron. s.a.* 1100.

Scots and St Margaret, a member of the Old English royal family,[95] she had been educated as a child in the nunnery at Wilton where her aunt, Christina, Margaret's sister, was abbess. Also in the cloister was an older woman, Gunnhildr, the late King Harold's daughter. Malcolm of Scots negotiated a marriage for Matilda with one of the greatest Anglo-Breton barons of the north of England, Count Alan Rufus, lord of Richmond, a man in his fifties. But when Alan went to Wilton to inspect his future bride he fell in love with Gunnhildr, whom he abducted. Archbishop Anselm was outraged, but got some satisfaction when the count died before a marriage could take place (probably 4 August 1093). Alan Rufus's brother and heir, Alan Niger, then tried to inherit the woman. She, however, eventually returned to Wilton and made her peace with the church.

She did not find Edith-Matilda there. King William II had opposed her marriage to Count Alan Rufus on obvious political grounds, and had, apparently, by visiting Wilton, satisfied himself that she was a nun and so not free to marry. In this he was supported by Anselm. But her father in a fury 'tore the veil off her head', removed her to Scotland, and ignored Anselm's demand that she be restored to the cloister. In 1100, when Anselm returned from exile, he found the new king, Henry I, planning to marry Matilda, again for political reasons. As her earlier adventures were notorious, the king thought it prudent to get Anselm's consent. The archbishop was all too aware of the difficulties and, according to Eadmer, who was an eye-witness, proceeded in a completely regular way to deal with the case. First he interrogated Matilda, who protested that it was her aunt who had insisted that she wore a black cloth on her head in order to escape the lust of the Normans, but she had always trampled it under foot as soon as she was out of the abbess's sight. She was willing to prove this by the judgment of the whole English church. Anselm then convened a council of bishops, abbots, nobles, and other clerics to Lambeth. Witnesses gave evidence, including the archdeacons of Canterbury and Salisbury, whom Anselm had sent to Wilton to investigate the matter. Then Anselm withdrew and left the verdict to the others. After deliberation they declared that Lanfranc had given judgment on this problem in a general council: women who had fled to a monastery for fear of the Normans were free to go out into the world again.[96] They recommended a similar judgment in this case. Anselm acquiesced and called Matilda in. When informed of the court's decision she offered to affirm her case by oath or any other proof required by ecclesiastical law; she was told that this was unnecessary, and withdrew. The marriage was celebrated on 11 November 1100 at Westminster, and Anselm took the precaution of explaining to the congregation what steps he had already taken, before earnestly bidding anyone who knew of an impediment to declare it. But all pronounced that the matter had been settled justly, and Anselm blessed the marriage. Nevertheless, Eadmer informs us, quite a number of people believed that in this business Anselm had acted unjustly.[97] And it was because of this 'blasphemy' that Eadmer devoted so much space to the suit.

95. Barlow, *Edward the Confessor* 214 ff.
96. Cf. *LEp* 32.
97. *HN* 121. Cf. also Walter Map, *De Nugis curialium* V, vi.

Two children of the marriage survived infancy, the unfortunate William the Ætheling and the not much more fortunate Matilda, wife successively to the Emperor Henry V and Geoffrey count of Anjou. After Stephen had deprived her of the succession in 1135, he resisted the charge of perjury brought against him by the Angevins at the Lateran council of 1139 by pleading through his counsel, Arnulf, archdeacon of Sées, *inter alia* that Matilda was the daughter of a nun and so a bastard.[98] The pope did not deliver a definitive judgment, and the bastardy issue was allowed to drop.

Even more famous among modern historians is the Richard of Anstey case. This arose out of the matrimonial troubles of William of Sackville about 1138.[99] William, although he had promised marriage to Aubrée of Tresgoz, contracted and consummated a marriage with Adelicia de Vere. After Adelicia had borne him children he petitioned for the annulment of the marriage on the grounds of the impediment of the earlier contract. His case, pursued successively before the archdeacon of London, the synod of London, and Pope Innocent II, ended in success: Aubrée was declared to be his legal spouse, and to her he returned. When he died about 1140 he named as his heir his sister's son, Richard of Anstey, and between 1158 and 1163 Richard litigated in the royal and ecclesiastical courts to secure his inheritance against the claim of Mabel, the surviving child of his uncle and Adelicia. Richard claimed that she was a bastard (and so incapable of inheriting), and this issue he pursued in the courts of Archbishop Theobald and, after an appeal to Rome, before judges delegate in England. In the end Pope Alexander III confirmed the annulment of the marriage of Mabel's parents, thus following the theologians of Paris against the canonists of Bologna. She was, indeed, a bastard. Richard had succeeded where King Stephen had failed.

Finally, we come to ecclesiastical litigation. Litigants, when well advised, take their case to the court in which they expect to get good, cheap, and speedy justice; and the plaintiff tries to plead under that law which is most favourable to his cause. Since courts were profitable to their owners there must always have been some competition between tribunals, and the rivalry between episcopal and the various secular courts is attested by the decrees of the councils of Lillebonne and Clarendon. But in fact there is little evidence of conflict before 1154. Current practices must have been generally acceptable to the several authorities.

On the whole the church preferred – if only to avoid public scandal – to settle disputes between the clergy domestically. And its attitude was all the more defensible since in the early Middle Ages, and still in the twelfth century, the majority of cases which we would call civil also had a criminal aspect. Most litigation over rights between parties was given when possible a disciplinary gloss, a simple matter when the parties were of unequal status, with one enjoying a right to the obedience of the other. Defendants were usually also accused of various sins, largely in order to strengthen the plaintiff's case. And

---

98. See above 112 ff.

99. See Patricia M. Barnes, 'The Anstey case', *A Medieval Miscellany for Doris Mary Stenton*, ed. Patricia M. Barnes and C. F. Slade, Pipe Roll Soc. n.s. xxxvi (1962) 1; C. N. L. Brooke, 'Marriage law and the Anesty case', *The Letters of John of Salisbury* i. 267.

the loser in an action was *ipso facto* guilty of some wrongful act, such as illegal seizure or possession of the right in question, disobedience to the command to restore it, perjury, and so on. The hearing of disputes between members of the higher clergy was often willingly surrendered to the king, for sometimes his interest was paramount, and sometimes he was the only judge with the power to determine the case. For example, the great Kentish land pleas between Archbishop Lanfranc and Bishop Odo were heard in the public and royal courts.[100] In 1132–33 at meetings (*conventus*) held twice at London and once at Winchester, presumably sessions of the royal court, the boundary dispute (*placitum*) between the bishops of St David's and Llandaff was heard; and in 1134 Archbishop William of Corbeil and Bishop Alexander of Lincoln crossed to Normandy to litigate before the king over 'some customs of their dioceses', probably financial rights.[101] Also, as we know from later practice, clerks were often prepared to sue other clerks in the lay court, despite ecclesiastical condemnation, if they thought it advantageous. Litigation between clerks and laymen was always borderline, and the choice of court depended on the particular circumstances. The general picture, then, is the common desire on the part of the authorities, both ecclesiastical and lay, to preserve order and get cases settled in the most expedient way possible, and a social attitude among all ranks which would apportion cases according to their dominant nature: land cases to the lay court, spiritual matters to the church court.

The running dispute between the bishops of Elmham–Thetford–Norwich and the abbey of Bury St Edmunds, basically over subordination but soon widening, shows how all possible tribunals, episcopal, archiepiscopal, papal, and royal, could be invoked at one time or another without any conflict arising between the courts. The matter of principle does not seem to have been raised. A few episodes will illustrate the point. Bishop Herfast complained in a synod that Abbot Baldwin had gone to Rome without his permission; and Baldwin appealed from Herfast to the audience of Archbishop Lanfranc and the king.[102] Gregory VII wrote to Lanfranc to say that he had taken the monastery under his protection, that Lanfranc was to protect it and warn the king to do likewise and withstand Herfast's blandishments. And if Herfast would not desist, Lanfranc was to summon them both to Rome for the determination of their suit.[103] Meanwhile the king himself had taken cognizance of the matter, or of some part of it, and Lanfranc wrote to Herfast reminding him that the king had ordered him to drop the case concerning the abbot's clerks until he himself, or, if more convenient, Lanfranc, as his deputy, should hear it. As the king had now gone abroad Herfast was to absolve the clerks he had excommunicated and cease molesting them. Lanfranc would visit Herfast in a few days, would hear each party's case, and, as far as he could, saving his fealty to the king, put a just end to this protracted litigation.[104] Later Lanfranc informed

100. M. M. Bigelow, *Placita Anglo-Normannica* (Boston 1881; reprinted 1970) 4 ff.
101. HH 253.
102. *Heremanni archidiaconi miracula S. Eadmundi* in Liebermann *Ungedruckte* 250. Margaret Gibson, *Lanfranc of Bec* 148–50.
103. J-W 4803; *LEp* 20; *PL* cxlviii. 514; *Registrum Gregorii VII*, ed. E. Caspar, *MGH Ep. sel.* ii. 1, p. 51; to be dated 20 November 1073.
104. *LEp* 19.

the bishop that he would deal with his contempt of his instructions at the appropriate time and place. Meanwhile the bishop was not to molest the abbot's clerk before the case should come into the archbishop's audience where it would be properly and canonically terminated by his definitive sentence.[105] This is the type of case which increasingly in the course of the twelfth century went to the pope on appeal and was sent back to be heard by his judges delegate in England.

For an attempt to use rank we can cite another East Anglian case. Herfast's successor, Herbert Losinga (1090–1119), in a letter addressed to the priest Athselin provost of Thetford, accused him of not wearing the tonsure, not performing mass, generally neglecting his ecclesiastical duties on account of his secular office, and bringing suits against the church of Thetford. The bishop would come to Thetford and hear and determine the suits between Athselin and Bund, the bishop's dean (? of Thetford).[106] Here what was probably basically a 'civil' action was being given a disciplinary aspect by the injured bishop. We are not told whether Herbert intended to hear the case in an ecclesiastical synod or in a hundred or shire court. And it is possible that he did not make the distinction.

It is likely that most cases concerning land held by prelates in feudal tenure were heard in a temporal court.[107] It should be remembered that churchmen themselves possessed different kinds of secular courts. Bishops and most abbots were tenants-in-chief of the crown and were obliged, and probably thought it natural, to bring to the king's court any dispute concerning their fiefs. Their relations with their own feudal tenants were governed by the same rule, and they often possessed besides an 'honorial' court private hundreds. Moreover it would seem that there was no ecclesiastical land law. In the Norman period examples of litigation before bishops over what appears to be feudal land can be cited, but there is nothing to suggest that the king resented ecclesiastical behaviour in this field before the Constitutions of Clarendon of 1164.[108] In that declaration of rights, Henry II's court drew an important distinction between lands held in lay fee (feudal tenure) and those held in free alms (spiritual tenure), and established a procedure for determining the nature of the tenure should it be disputed. It was then decreed in which court cases should be heard. To the bishop's court should go all cases concerning land held in free alms, whatever the status of the litigants, and those cases concerning feudal land when both parties held of that bishop or called him to warranty (cap. 9). The king also stepped in to prevent a right appurtenant to land being treated by the church as a spirituality and so subject to the bishop's court. Cases of advowson and presentation to churches, it was declared (1), were for the

---

105. *LEp* 23. The addressee is given as Herbert [Losinga]. The initial H. has been wrongly extended.

106. *HEp* 35=36; cf. 37.

107. The largest franchise was probably held by Durham: its rights were a byword in Henry II's reign. Cf. Walter Map, *De Nugis curialium* V, vi, in his account of Henry I's offer to Gerard if he would accept Hereford: 'obtulit ei . . . et libertatem aeternam quantam habet Dunelmensis episcopatus, in quo nullus minister regius aliquid agere vel attentare potest; episcopi sunt omnes potestates et omnia jura.'

108. *SSC* 163.

king's court alone; here the king was withstanding an extension, however reasonable, of ecclesiastical jurisdiction.

Our first example of litigation over land before clerical judges reveals the power of Archbishop Lanfranc in Kent after the earl, Bishop Odo of Bayeux, had been thrown into prison. Between 1085 and Easter 1088, either in the last year of the Conqueror's reign, during his absence in Normandy, or at the very beginning of his son's, Lanfranc gave judgment in a case between his vassal, Bishop Gundulf of Rochester, and Gundulf's vassal, Gilbert of Tonbridge (Gilbert fitzRichard of Clare), an important baron who in 1088 was unsuccessfully to fortify his castle against Rufus. It was agreed that Gilbert should pay Gundulf 50s a year for the land he held of the church of Rochester until he gave the bishop another piece of land worth as much. Lanfranc ordered that the *conventio* should be recorded in writing, and it was witnessed by the archbishop, Bishop William of Durham (soon to join Gilbert in the rebellion), Abbots Gilbert Crispin of Westminster and Paul of St Albans (Lanfranc's nephew), Haimo sheriff of Canterbury, Bertram of Verdun, and the larger part of the archbishop's household.[109] It cannot be said in what capacity Lanfranc was acting, but his court, even if honorial, has a pronounced ecclesiastical appearance.

Four land cases from one decade in the latter part of Henry I's reign show different ways in which church courts could exercise jurisdiction. In the first example the monks of Durham started ineffectual proceedings for the recovery of the church of Tynemouth, which they claimed had been granted them by Waltheof earl of Northumberland and unjustly taken away and given to the abbey of St Albans by Earl Robert of Mowbray, because of his hatred of Bishop William of St Calais (probably about 1092–93). In mid-Lent 1121 (20 March) the monks instituted their suit (*querimonia*) in the cathedral church of York in the presence of Turgot, their former prior, then bishop-elect of St Andrews, their bishop, Ranulf Flambard, and Ouen bishop of Evreux (the brother and probably the surrogate of Archbishop Thurstin). This seems in fact to have been little more than a proclamation of their case, and no decision of the court, if court it was, is reported. Then in Easter week on 13 April the monks stated their grievance again (*replicatur:* probably not in its technical sense) before a great assembly of local nobles at Durham, who had apparently gathered for some other business. One of the barons gave evidence on their behalf. Then all declared that Durham had suffered an injustice. And they added that although the matter could not be corrected at that time it had been a wise provision for the future to have made the claim (*calumnia*) before so great a concourse.[110] It is possible that the monks were just manoeuvring for an advantageous legal position – establishing their objection and trying to weaken St Alban's possession. But such a case would not have been started in so muddled a way a generation later.

In the next example, although the bishop of Bath's curia has a very ecclesiastical look, it was acting simply as any tenant-in-chief's baronial

109.   *Textus Roffensis,* ed. T. Hearne (1720) 149.
110.   *HR* 261–2.

court.[111] A certain Modbert claimed that his father-in-law, Grenta, had made him his heir to some land in North Stoke, a few miles north-west of the episcopal city. The monks of Bath maintained that the land was theirs and that Grenta had only been a tenant for life. When they refused to give Modbert possession he sued out a writ from the regent, William the Ætheling, ordering the bishop of Bath to give Modbert seizin. The bishop was presumably the feudal lord of both litigants. The case was heard in the bishop's *curia* at Bath on the festival of St Peter and St Paul 1121, when Bishop John was attended by his friends and barons. The prior of Bath opened the convent's case, called witnesses in support from among those present, and produced a royal Anglo-Saxon charter granting the monastery the land. Modbert then denied the prior's case and stated his own. After these pleadings before the general concourse the bishop appointed a committee of men specially skilled in the law to discuss the matter and advise how the case should be determined (give the proof judgment). The committee after deliberation awarded the burden of proof to the complainant: he was to prove his case by two suitable witnesses, who were to be of the prior's *familia* (household, or perhaps in this context, tenants or vassals), or by a genuine charter. If he failed in this proof, he lost the case. The judgment was accepted by the whole assembly. And as Modbert had nothing to say for himself, he lost by default. Judgment was pronounced by the court under the presidency of John bishop of Bath and Maurice bishop 'of Ireland', sitting with three archdeacons and many clerks and chaplains. Seventeen laymen are then named, of whom the last twelve were witnesses. The judgment of the bishop's court was later confirmed by the king. Here we have a view of a secular court in the hands of the church. And since the archdeacons, who were the bishop's justiciars, seem to have played an important part in it, in some ways it was also an ecclesiastical tribunal.

We can compare a case in which the king appears to have played no part.[112] Walter of Hill Deverel in Wiltshire and the diocese of Salisbury, the lord of the manor, in 1129–30 disputed the claim of Roger of Ramsbury, canon of Salisbury, that the village church pertained to Roger's prebend of Heytesbury. Roger tried to bring the case before the Wiltshire archidiaconal chapter, but Walter appealed against this to the diocesan bishop, Roger, the king's justiciar, on the grounds that the archdeacon of Wiltshire, Azo, was Roger's brother. Whereupon the bishop appointed Adelelm, archdeacon of Dorset and probably his son, to act as his justiciar and preside over the chapter of Wiltshire. The chapter met in the disputed church; Canon Roger produced as witnesses in support three neighbouring parish priests, Edward of Norton Bavant, Ulward of Upton Lovell, and Azelin of Stockton, and Edward clerk of Warminster and Blanchard of Heytesbury; and the court gave judgment that the church of Hill Deverel did indeed pertain to Roger's prebend. Whereupon Walter's feudal lord, Elyas Giffard, granted the church in free alms to the church of Heytesbury. In this case, since the land in dispute was held in free alms, the king took

111. A detailed account, with English translation, printed T. Madox, *The History and Antiquities of the Exchequer* (1711) 74–7. See also *Regesta,* ii, nos. 1201, 1302; M.M. Bigelow, *Placita Anglo-Normannica* 114.

112. *Register of St Osmund* ed. W. H. Rich Jones (Rolls ser. 1883) i. 351–2, 349.

no part in the process. But the procedure followed by the bishop of Salisbury's court was similar to that used in the bishop of Bath's.

Finally, a feudal case concerning an abbot and his military vassal, which was terminated in an ecclesiastical court of some kind.[113] When Henry of Blois abbot of Glastonbury (after 1126), disputed with his baron, Ivan, over the knight service due from Ashcott and Pedwell in the Polden Hills, he first got a sentence of disinheritance against him in an unspecified court,[114] and then agreed to a composition which was made before Robert bishop of Bath and in the presence and with the consent of the whole convent of Glastonbury. The terms of the agreement were that Ivan should hold instead Milton Clevedon, less the church and its pertinencies which were reserved to the abbot, for the service of one knight only. Henry considered that he had done well for his abbey. He had also settled the matter without, apparently, involving the king.

The legal approach to the problem of the relationship between the *regnum* and the *sacerdotium* was the most useful. Law and custom govern, and reflect, the most fundamental and conservative social attitudes. And the various codes of law, even the ecclesiastical, took account of the world as it was. Lawyers are usually cool men, if not cynical, always prepared to compromise, and there were few medieval suits which did not end in an agreement. Moreover kings employed clerks as judges, and episcopal clerks kept one eye open to royal patronage. Clerks skilled in the law formed a professional class and could easily change from one side to the other. As pleaders this was their duty. By 1154 spheres of jurisdiction had been staked out, disputed, and sometimes agreed. The creation of an ecclesiastical judicial system in the twelfth century was an outstanding achievement by the church. But although it is possible that Thomas Becket became a martyr for the sake of a legal principle, it is this which made him exceptional. There remained ambiguities which everyone accepted, transgressions which both sides were willing to tolerate, common purposes to which all men held.

113. *Adami de Domerham historia* ii. 314–5.
114. 'tandem convenimus ubi publico ductus in exheredacionis sentenciam incidit', *loc. cit.* 314.

Chapter V

Monasteries

In 1070, when Lanfranc abbot of Caen was appointed archbishop of Canterbury, there were in his province between forty and fifty Benedictine abbeys, of which ten were for women.[1] North of the Humber, where recovery from the Viking conquests had been slower, there was still not a single monastery. The geographical imbalance was not the only unusual feature. Most of the communities had been reestablished in the second half of the tenth century by a group of determined bishops who, encouraged by the kings, especially Edgar, were able to use all available royal powers in order to recreate in England the best possible Benedictine monasticism.[2] At that time the new political unification of England, the desire of the church to be free from local secular domination, and the good repute of the West-Saxon royal dynasty produced conditions not unlike those which had existed in the Carolingian empire and legislation which may have owed something to Frankish precedent. The enactments of the council of Aachen of 817 were imitated when about 970 a council at Winchester, with the help of foreign monks, drew up a new set of monastic customs to apply to the whole kingdom, a code which was then promulgated by royal authority. All the reformed abbeys were put under royal patronage in order to thwart the influence of the earls and local landowners. But whereas Louis the Pious had nominated Benedict of Aniane, who had inspired the Aachen enactments, as arch-abbot in the empire, Edgar allowed the several bishops to control the houses they had reformed, refounded, or created. Hence in England all the important monasteries were royal *Eigenklöster*, but also under the disciplinary control of the diocesan or some other bishop. Sometimes the bishop functioned *de jure* or *de facto* as abbot. There were no ducal or baronial Benedictine monasteries. The office of advocate was unknown. There were no independent, purely monastic filiations, such as Cluny and her daughter houses; and no English abbey was subject directly to the Holy See. In general English was more like German than French monasticism.[3]

The wealth and the artistic treasures of the English houses greatly impressed the Normans; and some monasteries, Glastonbury, Ely, the two

1. The statistics with regard to England in this chapter are derived from David Knowles and R. Neville Hadcock, *Medieval Religious Houses in England and Wales* (1953). Cf. also David Knowles, *The Monastic Order in England, 943—1216* (1949) appendices V–VI. It should be noticed that Knowles sometimes disregards nunneries.

2. Barlow, *English Church 1000–1066* (1979) Appendix 2. Knowles *Monastic Order* 31 ff. The views of Eric John are also of interest. See especially, 'The king and the monks in the tenth-century reformation', *Orbis Britanniae and other studies* (1966) 154.

3. Cf. Kassius Hallinger, *Gorze-Kluny* (1950, reprinted Graz 1971). Few historians, however, would make the cleavage as sharp as Hallinger does.

Canterbury communities, Bury, the two Winchester abbeys for men, Westminster, and Abingdon, were indeed extremely rich.[4] Although their estates fell far short of those possessed by the earls, they surpassed those of the ordinary nobility. All the abbeys, both large and small, were very much a part of local society and only in one direction hostile to it. Their estates were of the ordinary pattern, and there is no evidence that they were receiving from the laity gifts of churches, episcopal customs, or tithes as separate items.[5] They recruited their monks largely from the children given by their noble parents to be brought up in the cloister (oblates), and the abbots were normally related to the higher aristocracy. The monasteries had a secure place in that 'feudal' world. But they resented interference from local powers and held to the alliance with the monarchy which had been forged in the tenth century. Possession by the greater houses of large tracts of hidated land and whole hundreds gave them important royal duties in the shires, both judicial and military. And there is everything to show that the monasteries served as local centres of royalism and patriotism and willingly performed their obligations. Their culture, despite the tradition of Bede and the efforts of the reformers, had a strong Germanic flavour. The monasteries were in general more outward than inward looking, neither influenced by the eremitical movements, nor sharing Cluny's preoccupation with the liturgy, and rising above the rural obscurity of most of the Norman convents. They had since the tenth century a strong craft tradition, and were renowned for their book production, metal work (including bell founding), and all church furnishings.

Considerable changes took place in the English monastic order between 970 and 1070. But many basic features remained. On the eve of the Conquest control over the monasteries was still shared between the king and the bishops. The king appointed the abbots, and some attended his councils. None of the great earls or landowners had subtracted abbeys from the royal estate. And the bishops remained in control. In Edward's reign Archbishops Stigand and Ealdred, and abbot Leofric of Peterborough, with royal connivance, subjected a number of monasteries to their rule. And there remained, in theory at least, but one monastic customary, and that distinctively English.[6] The *Regularis Concordia* of *c.* 970 was eclectic and admittedly borrowed customs from St Peter's, Ghent, and Fleury. The latter transmitted the pure traditions of Cluny; Ghent offered a mixture derived from Gorze and Brogne. And while all were derived from the *capitula* of Aachen (817), and ultimately from St Benedict's *regula*, each had its peculiarities. The English reformers had selected from the best available *consuetudines* what they considered most suitable to English conditions. There were, therefore, in the English monastic order in 1070 two quite distinct features which made change inevitable once

4. Knowles *Monastic Order* 702–3 lists the gross income (and military service) of the monasteries as recorded in Domesday Book (1086).

5. Cf. Hans-Erich Mager, 'Studien über das Verhältnis der Cluniacenser zum Eigenkirchenwesen' in G. Tellenbach, *Neue Forschungen über Cluny und die Cluniacenser* (1959) 169 ff.

6. *Regularis Concordia*, ed. and trans. Thomas Symons (Nelson's Medieval Classics 1953). The millenial conference held at the University of Leicester, 16–19 December 1970, was not only instructive but also served to remind us of how little we still know about the Rule itself – its authorship, ambience, and exact sources and antecedents.

the English church came under new management: its special customs and its common failings. The most usual meaning of 'reform' in monastic history is an enforced change in the customs, the substitution of the practices of the house from which the new abbot came or some other foreign usages. Such innovations were not necessarily an improvement, nor usually welcome. When Thurstin from Caen introduced the chant of Fécamp into Glastonbury, it needed the arrows of his soldiers to convince the English monks that the new liturgy was superior to their own variety of Gregorian plainsong.[7] A new calendar, from which many revered saints were excised and which commemorated saints to which there was no traditional attachment, was not demonstrably better. Nor did changes in the cut of the clothes automatically encourage more holy behaviour. Even new buildings did not always inspire new spiritual fervour.

This type of reform was far more common than reform in the purely disciplinary sense. Many abbots probably thought that the former was the means to the latter. And it was indeed sound practice when attempting to recover true Benedictine purposes to abrogate some of the old customs. It gave notice and had a symbolic value. The true moral condition of the English monasteries in 1070 is hard to discover. They had had no severe jolt for about a century, and it is therefore probable that the general standard had slipped. Many houses had become wealthy, and artistic patronage and activity are more in evidence than spirituality, asceticism, or intellectual and literary pursuits. Gross irregularities can be found. Worldly and immoral monks can be adduced. But so they can at all times. And it is quite as easy to point to well-conducted houses, like Worcester, which produced the saint, Wulfstan; seminaries of Latin prose, like Christ Church, Canterbury, which trained Osbern and Eadmer; centres of holiness like Evesham and Winchcombe from which went out missionaries to establish monasticism in the north of England and later in Denmark; and houses of wealth and distinction like Peterborough. Nevertheless the first four years of Norman rule, with the looting, the confiscations, and the uncertainties, cannot have improved the situation. It can hardly be doubted that most English abbeys were in need of some reform by 1070, and reform in one sense or another they were bound to receive.

Norman monasticism was in some respects different from English. In 1070 there were about thirty-three abbeys in the duchy, twenty-six male and seven female, as well as some dependent priories.[8] Ten or more were ancient

---

7. *Chron. s.a.* 1083; Florence ii. 16–17.

8. Ancient abbeys refounded are marked with an asterisk; nunneries are marked (F). Ducal foundations, before 1035: *dioc. Rouen*: St Ouen, Rouen*; Jumièges*; St Wandrille (Fontenelle)*; Fécamp*; Montivilliers*(F); *Lisieux*: Bernay; *Bayeux*: Cérisy-la-Forêt; *Avranches*: Mont St Michel. Ducal 1035–70: *Bayeux*, St Stephen, Caen; Holy Trinity, Caen (F). Ducal 1070–1100: *Coutances*: Montebourg. Baronial foundations, before 1035: *Rouen :* St Amand in Rouen (F); Holy Trinity (Mont de Sainte Catherine), outside Rouen (later, ducal); Bec; *Evreux:* St Taurin, Evreux*. Baronial 1035–70: *Rouen*: St Victor-l'Abbaye; Le Tréport; *Evreux :* St Sauveur, Evreux (F); La Croix-St-Leufroi; Conches; Lire; *Lisieux*: Notre Dame-du-Pré, Lisieux (F); St Peter, Préaux; St Léger, Préaux (F); St Evroul*; Grestain; Cormeilles; *Bayeux*: Fontenay*; Troarn; *Sées*: St Martin, Sées; St Pierre-sur-Dives; Almenèches*(F); *Coutances*: St Sauveur-le-Vicomte; Lessay. Baronial 1070–1100: *Rouen*: Pontoise; *Evreux :* Ivry; *Coutances*: St Séver-en-Côtentin. In addition, Longlé, near Domfront, founded by William Talvas in 1026, was in the diocese of Le Mans. For these monasteries, see A. du Monstier, *Neustria Pia* (Rouen 1563); Léchaudé d'Anisy, *Les*

foundations which had been restored after the Vikings had settled down and accepted Christianity. The dukes had led the way, but after 1035 there had been a wave of baronial restorations and foundations which had completely altered the picture. Despite the reconstructions and an interest in past history, there was still lacking the distinction which wealth and tradition give. There were, of course, no royal abbeys in Normandy, and, although ten or eleven, including six of the pre-Norman foundations, were ducal, the rest were baronial, of relatively low status.[9] There was also a striking difference in culture. In Norman monasticism, despite the Viking ancestry of the nobility and the presence of some German and Lotharingian monks, was to be found none of that Germanic idiom which was so noticeable in England. Indeed, the monastic way of life in the duchy, although enthusiastically embraced by the pious and penitent, was still in 1070 completely foreign in all its particulars. It is impossible to point to any Norman contribution to the ritual, learning, literature, art, or architecture. What the Normans gave was eagerness to learn and zeal to profess.

Missions from Lotharingia had had some effect on Norman monasticism in the late tenth century. But it was the arrival at Fécamp in 1001 of the Italian, William of Volpiano abbot of St Bénigne at Dijon, a house he had reformed from Cluny in 978, which was decisive. In 1015 William became abbot of Bernay as well; and he and his disciples also reformed, among many others, four monasteries which were to provide abbots for English houses, Jumièges, Mont St Michel, St Ouen at Rouen, and St Evroul. St Wandrille (Fontenelle) also was reformed rather later (after 1063) from Fécamp.[10] Although these monasteries formed a family, with remembered relationships, each was juridically independent of the others and also of Cluny. Moreover they probably developed individual customs. For example, St Evroul, refounded from Jumièges about 1050, with its daughters, St Martin, Sées, and Lire, looked also to the usages of the Lotharingian reformer, Richard of Verdun, and directly to Cluny.[11] This family was also unlike the Cluniac order in that, with the exception of Fécamp, which was subordinate to the metropolitan, they were subject to their diocesan bishop.[12] Nevertheless they were more Cluniac in observance and attitude than were English monasteries. These,

anciennes abbayes de Normandie (Caen 1834); Böhmer KuS 7n.; J-M. Besse, Abbayes et prieurés de l'ancienne France (Archives de la France monastique, xvii, Paris 1914); Knowles, Monastic Order, appendix V; Foreville GG 122–3.

9.   In Normandy, however, as in England, the office of lay advocate was missing. In a sense the duke was advocate-general of monasticism throughout the duchy. J. Yver, 'Autour de l'absence d'avouerie en Normandie', Bull de la soc. des antiquaires de Normandie lvii (1963–64) 194.

10.   Böhmer KuS 3 ff., Knowles Monastic Order 83 ff. For Fécamp, see also L'abbaye bénédictine de Fécamp, ouvrage scientifique du XIIIe centenaire, 658–1958 (Fécamp 1959–61), and Michel Bouard, L'abbaye bénédictine de Fécamp, conférance donnée à Fécamp le 5 juillet 1958, XIIIe centenaire de l'abbaye bénédictine (Fécamp 1959).

11.   OV (Chibnall) ii. 74.

12.   Jean-François Lemarignier, Etude sur les privilèges d'exemption et de juridiction écclesiastique des abbayes normandes depuis les origines jusqu'en 1140 (Paris 1937) 26 ff. Cf. the Norman Anonymous of c. 1100, J 27, Die Texte des normannischen Anonymus, ed. Karl Pellens (Wiesbaden 1966) 213. The Anonymous argues generally in Tract J 5, p. 45, that by God's ordinance every abbot is subject to his bishop.

although influenced by Fleury, had been no less indebted to Ghent. And England not only had had no William of Volpiano but also had continued, even under the Danish kings and Edward the Confessor, to provide almost all the abbots from its own cloisters. In contrast seven of the leading Norman monasteries in 1066 were under the rule of foreigners, three Italians, three Germans, and one from Anjou.

One of the earliest of the completely new foundations, Bec, with its daughters Lessay and St Stephen's Caen, stood rather apart. Established in the 1030s by Herlwin, one of Gilbert of Brionne's knights, who had not only been spurned by two monasteries, perhaps Rouen and Jumièges, but had also become a social outcast, it was typical of the new ascetic movement. Ruled by its illiterate founder, stocked with rustic monks, and incompetently sited, it would surely have sunk without trace had not Lanfranc of Pavia, seeking the ultimate abasement, about 1041 abandoned his successful career as a schoolmaster to enter this primitive and unusual community. Lanfranc, who became prior three years later, and was joined in 1060 by an even greater scholar, Anselm of Aosta, made Bec's reputation as a strict monastery with an excellent school.[13] Neither Herlwin nor Lanfranc, both monastic beginners, owed loyalty to any existing monastery or order, and they showed their independence of the dominant tradition in the duchy by devising a Rule which disregarded Cluniac customs and synthesised usages taken from many directions. Even St Dunstan was honoured at Bec. The result was idiosyncratic.[14] Herlwin, shortly before his death (1078) had a vision of 'the fruits' of the tree he had planted.[15] It had already lost Lanfranc to Caen (1063) and then Canterbury (1070), and William to Cormeilles (*ante* 1066). It was about to provide Henry to the deanery of Christ Church, Canterbury (*c.* 1074) and then to Battle (1096), Arnost and Gundulf to Rochester (1076, 1077), Gilbert Crispin, who wrote an elegant and moving Life of Herlwin, to Westminster (1085), and Anselm to Canterbury (1093). There were also the sons of the daughters.

In mainstream Norman monasticism the influence of Cluny worked towards cultivated piety and devoted service in the choir rather than scholarship of any kind. But the complicated liturgy could only be performed by *enutriti* who had been through a long musical and procedural training; and William of Dijon established an influential school at Fécamp. William, a son of Robert count of Volpiano in Piedmont, and nephew of Arduin marquis of Ivrea and king of Italy, although given as an oblate to the monastery of San Gennaro at Locedio, near Vercelli, had studied at Vercelli and Pavia before going with Abbot Mayeul to Cluny; he and his nephew, John of Ravenna, like Lanfranc later, had a *Latinitas* which was more liberal than strict Cluniac custom

---

13. For the early accounts of Bec's first years, see F. Barlow, 'A view of Archbishop Lanfranc', *JEH* xvi (1965) 164 ff. Gilbert Crispin's *Vita Herluini*, ed. J. Armitage Robinson, *Gilbert Crispin abbot of Westminster* (Notes and documents relating to Westminster Abbey 3, 1911) 87, is illuminating.

14. *Consuetudines Beccenses*, ed. Marie Pascal Dickson (*Corpus consuetudinum monasticarum*, ed. Kassius Hallinger IV, Sieburg 1967) pp. xxix ff.

15. *Vita Herluini* 100, 103.

required.[16] Fécamp had a school for the clergy as well as for the oblates and monks. And this may have set the pattern for Normandy. Herlwin, because illiterate, yearned after knowledge, honoured scholars, and prevented Lanfranc from renouncing his scholarship and pedagogic skills. The Norman monastic achievement in the arts, theology, philosphy, law, and medicine, although it was probably as high as the English in 1070, was not indisputably higher, and was largely confined to foreigners. Lanfranc had a European reputation and John of Ravenna was a distinguished master of spirituality.[17] But it is noticeable that most ambitious clerks went to schools outside the duchy,[18] and the most famous historical work of this period was written by an archdeacon who had studied at Poitiers. More imposing than the literary was the architectural achievement.[19] At Fécamp, Bernay, Avranches, Mont St Michel, Jumièges, among others, and in the episcopal cities, great churches were built in a romanesque style introduced in the wake of William of Dijon. Edward the Confessor's Westminster abbey was inspired by one or more of these, and was even larger.[20] But in 1070 it was the sole example of the new style in England.

The Norman monasteries, although completely under ducal control and entirely without revolutionary ambitions, were, if not more aware than English monasteries of the developments in the papal curia since 1049 and of recent intellectual and religious movements, at least more involved. The case of Berengar of Tours, for example, allowed 'Norman' monastic theologians, such as Durand of Troarn, a pupil of the German Isembert abbot of Holy Trinity, Rouen, and Lanfranc, both to demonstrate their rather old-fashioned orthodoxy and also for a moment to appear on the public stage.[21] Relations with Italy were exceptionally close: William of Volpiano always remained an

16.   He attracted to St Bénigne from Italy masters in arts, crafts, and agriculture, and sent John of Ravenna to study medicine. There were doctors at Fécamp when William died there in 1031. William was also interested in music. See Ralf Glaber, *Vita S. Guillelmi* in *PL* cxli. 856, 864, 868. For a description of the church he built at Dijon, *ibid.* 856 ff. For the present state of Cluniac studies and some of the problems, Noreen Hunt, *Cluny Under Saint Hugh, 1049–1109* (1967) 4 ff. For an extensive bibliography, Peter Segl, 'Zum Itinerar Abt Hugos I. von Cluny (1049–1109)', *Deutsches Archiv* xxix (1973) 206.

17.   Jean Leclercq and Jean-Paul Bonnes, *Un maître de la vie spirituelle au XIe siècle, Jean de Fécamp* (Paris 1946).

18.   For example, Odo bishop of Bayeux sent promising clerks to Liège 'and other cities where he knew that philosophic studies flourished', OV (Chibnall) iv. 118. Among these men was William of Rots, who succeeded John of Ravenna as abbot of Fécamp, *ibid.* ii. 292–4. See also Böhmer *KuS* 18.

19.   A. D. Clapham, *Romanesque Architecture in Western Europe* (1936) 27–8, 138 ff., *English Romanesque Architecture after the Conquest* (1934) 4 ff. K. J. Conant, *Carolingian and Romanesque Architecture 800—1200* (1959) 278 ff. Jean Taralon, *Jumièges* (Nefs et clochers 1955), with a useful list of the archaeological papers of Georges Lanfry, p. 40. Noreen Hunt, *op. cit.* 181–2. The origins of the Anglo-Norman style are still controversial. Clapham did not believe in an Italian origin via St Bénigne. But others do not believe in a 'Cluniac' style of architecture based on Cluny II (942–*c*. 964), of which the details are most uncertain, since there was great variety of architecture in the monasteries within the Cluniac order. Cf. René Crozet, 'A propos de Cluny', *Cahiers de civ. méd.* xiii (1970) 150.

20.   Barlow, *Edward the Confessor* 230–2.

21.   Böhmer *KuS* 20 ff. R. W. Southern, 'Lanfranc of Bec and Berengar of Tours', *Studies in Medieval History presented to F. M. Powicke* (1948) 27.

Italian at heart. He had also founded the monastery of Fruttuaria, near his birthplace, in which King Arduin, who had attended its dedication, chose to be buried, and Fruttuaria became head of a great Italian league. From St Bénigne, which he made a school for future abbots, William radiated Italian culture. Moreover, Norman conquests in Italy and Sicily opened up new lines of communication. The cult of St Nicholas of Myra and Rufus's oath by the Holy Face of Lucca[22] were products of this traffic.

William of Poitiers, who wrote his *apologia* for the Conqueror and eulogy of the duchy in 1073–74, compared Norman monasticism favourably with the blessed Egypt of old. This reflorescence he attributed largely to Duke William and his patronage of the order.[23] He thought that the duke, when he forced Lanfranc to become abbot of Caen, gave him a watchtower from which he could take care of the whole Norman church.[24] And it seems that in England the Conqueror shared with Lanfranc control of the monasteries in a way which was typical of both England and Normandy. The Anglo-Saxon Chronicle recorded in William's favour that 'in his days . . . this country was very full of monks, and they lived their lives under the Rule of St Benedict', and two years later remembered Lanfranc as 'the reverend father and consoler of monks'.[25] Both king and primate were by 1070 conservative in attitude, and their actions did not disturb the general situation existing in English monasticism. The monastic movement was slowing down in Normandy – only two monasteries, Ivry and St Leger, were founded between 1070 and 1100 – and the new lords in England founded no Benedictine abbey which could rival the best of the old establishments. The Conqueror's Battle (dedicated in 1094), presumably a penitential duty and richy endowed, Earl Roger of Montgomery's Shrewsbury (*c*. 1083–90), and Earl Hugh of Avranches' Chester (1093) never became first class. More distinguished were the new monastic chapters created by the bishops at Rochester (1080), Durham (1083), and Norwich (after 1094). Most important of all was the English-inspired monastic revival in the North: Jarrow (1074), Monkwearmouth (1075), Whitby (before 1077), Tynemouth (after 1083), St Mary's York (before 1086), and Melrose in Scotland (*c*. 1077), with Durham (1083) soon outpacing the rest.[26] No important nunneries were founded between 1066 and 1100, but the seven foundations, mostly independent priories, probably do show a greater interest in the religious vocation of women.

22. Marjorie Chibnall, OV, iv. 353–4. Bec compiled a book of the miracles of St Nicholas in 1125. See Barlow, 'A view of Archbishop Lanfranc', *JEH* xvi (1965) 165. For *il volto santo*, see René Herval, 'En marge de la légende du précieux-sang-Lucques-Fécamp-Glastonbury', *L'Abbaye bénédictine de Fécamp* (1959) ix, pp. 106 ff. It should be noticed that Bury St Edmunds claimed to have a rood copied exactly from the *volto santo*: Barlow, *English Church 1000–1066*, 20–1.

23. *GG* 124. Cf. *The Liber Vitae of Hyde abbey, Winchester*, ed. W. de Gray Birch (Hants. rec. soc. 1892) 7, where England at the end of the tenth century likewise was another Egypt. The phrase was commonplace.

24. *GG* 126; cf. 128.

25. *s.a.* 1087, 1089.

26. Knowles *Monastic Order* 159 ff. For Durham cf. also Bernard Meehan, 'Outsiders, insiders and property at Durham around 1100', *Studies in Church History*, ed. Derek Baker, xii (1975) 45.

All the great English Benedictine houses in the Norman period were therefore Old English foundations. They were strengthened economically by a novel development. The new aristocracy gave lands to existing monasteries, whether in England or Normandy or elsewhere in France, for the establishment of subordinate priories. Sometimes the initiative came from the mother house, which set up a cell on a remote estate. These priories and cells were administratively convenient, and also served as outposts to which difficult or disgraced monks could be sent. They seem never to have been popular with the monks, who feared boredom in exile. And although they widened the monastic impact on the country, they were usually undistinguished and liable to irregularity. Between 1066 and 1100 some thirty priories subordinated to Norman abbeys were established,[27] and about fourteen to abbeys neighbouring the duchy, while eighteen were in favour of English houses. A proportion of more than two to one shows where the religious interests of the aristocracy lay.

Direct Cluniac influence on England was no immediate effect of the Conquest.[28] Before 1075 William's monastic contacts seem to have extended no farther south than St Vincent in Maine and Marmoutier in Touraine. By then, however, both William and Lanfranc were beginning to look further afield. Lanfranc's customary for Christ Church, Canterbury, which was completed after that year, relied heavily on Cluniac practice;[29] about the same time William asked for confraternity with the chapter at Cluny, and received it through the hands of Abbot St Hugh's legate, Warmond, abbot of Déols in Berry, soon to be archbishop of Vienne. In return he and the queen sent to Cluny a cope of cloth of gold adorned with pearls and jewels and fringed with little gold bells, and a chasuble so stiff that it could not be folded.[30]

In 1076 one of the king's most important barons, William of Warenne, and his wife left on a pilgrimage to Rome and landed up at Cluny. They too entered into confraternity and started negotiating for the foundation of a priory in the church of St Pancras in the earl's town at Lewes, close to Battle.[31] St Hugh was far from enthusiastic, and soon after he had sent Lanzo and three monks to Lewes in 1077, Lanzo returned and was detained for a whole year at Cluny. William of Warenne, perhaps influenced by Battle, seriously considered transferring his foundation to Marmoutier. But at some point between 1078 and 1080 the king and his baron met Hugh in Normandy.

27.   See also Marjorie Morgan (Chibnall), *The English Lands of the Abbey of Bec* (1946), *Select Documents of the English Lands of the Abbey of Bec* (Camden 3rd ser. lxxiii, 1951). Donald Matthew, *The Norman Monasteries and their English Possessions* (1962).

28.   English historians, including Knowles, have usually ascribed William's overtures to Cluny to the very beginning of his reign. I hope to discuss this matter in more detail elsewhere.

29.   Below 189.

30.   Anonymous II, *Vita S. Hugonis* in Martin Marrier and André Du Chesne, *Bibliotheca Cluniacensis* (Paris 1614) 543–4; reprinted in part *Acta Sanctorum*, April III, 29 April, 660–1, whence *PL* clix. 923–5. Part of this story also occurs in Giles's Life of St Hugh, ed. A. L'Huillier, *Vie de Saint Hughes abbé de Cluny, 1024—1109* (Solesmes 1888) 588. For the career of Warmond, see D. N. Huyghebaert, 'Un légat de Gregoire VII en France: Warmond de Vienne', *RHE* xl (1944–45) 188, who for this episode relies on L'Huillier 334, who mistakenly refers to Raynald of Vézelay's Life of St Hugh, where it does not occur.

31.   Foundation chronicle in forged charter of William of Warenne: *Recueil des chartes de l'abbaye de Cluny*, by A. Bernard and A. Bruel, iv (Paris 1888) no. 3561, p. 689. *Monasticon* v. 13a.

The affairs of Lewes were straightened out, and the king, in a flush of enthusiasm, asked the abbot for a dozen, or at least half a dozen, of his monks to help him with the reform of the English church.[32] What he would have done with them at this late stage is not clear. Few episcopal vacancies could have been expected, or in fact occurred. Possibly he was thinking of expelling the last of the English abbots. But Hugh felt that he had done more than enough for England with Lewes. And when the king pressed him by letter, and offered to pay £100 per monk per annum as a friendly thanksgiving offering, Cluny considered this insulting and indeed simoniacal. Hugh replied angrily that his monks were not for sale, and he had no intention of selling them into perdition in a strange land.

According to the Cluniac source, the king was at first infuriated by this reply, but later felt admiration for Hugh's unworldliness and accepted his reasons as valid.[33] All the same, future negotiations were with Cluny's dependencies, and of the ten or so Cluniac priories established in the kingdom by 1100, half, including the important London house of Bermondsey, founded in 1089 by William Rufus and a London merchant of English extraction, Alwin Cild,[34] were dependent on La Charité-sur-Loire, Cluny's most distinguished and influential daughter, founded in 1056. It was the Conqueror's daughter, Adela countess of Blois, and his youngest son, Henry, who, with his wife Matilda, established really close relations with Cluny.[35]

Even greater impact was made on English monasticism by the reform of existing houses. Lanfranc was initially dismayed by English conditions[36] – the lax opulence of Christ Church agonized him after the simple austerity of Caen and Bec – but as immediate changes could be effected only by the substitution of new abbots, each supported by a number of helpers,[37] practical difficulties dictated a slow approach to the problem. There were not a few ambitious men anxious to get promotion in England, but both William and Lanfranc were probably averse to creaming the duchy for what might be an impossible task in England, and Lanfranc, who had seen Bec colonize Lessay and Caen, could not expect these to do more than provide him with monks for Canterbury and Rochester. William, when he needed inmates for St Martin's Battle looked outside Normandy to Marmoutier, on the Loire near Tours, a

---

32.   Anonymous II, *loc. cit.* Pseudo-charter of William of Warenne *loc. cit.*

33.   The abbot's answer, which has sometimes been considered tactful, is in fact highly indignant. Cf. also Noreen Hunt *op. cit.* 85, for Cluny's prodigality with colonists in some directions. At times Cluny was like a vast transit camp.

34.   Bermondsey annals in *Annales Monastici* iii. 427. Christopher Brooke and Gillian Keir, *London 800—1216* (1975) 321–3.

35.   See below n. 8. For the queen's gift of a magnificent copper gilt candelabrum for Cluny III, *Chronicon Cluniacense* in *Bibliotheca Cluniacensis* 1640. It is most unlikely, as M. F. Cucherat suggested, *Cluny au onzième siècle* (2nd ed. n.d., ?1873) 136, that this could be the wife of the Conqueror.

36.   *Ep.* 1. Cf. Eadmer, *Miracula S. Dunstani* in *Memorials of St Dunstan* ed. W. Stubbs (Rolls ser. 1874) 237–8.

37.   For example, Scotland, monk of Mont St Michel, when he came to St Augustine's as abbot in 1070, brought with him a large number of relatives, including two military nephews, who were killed by some Christ Church knights. Osbern, *Miracula S. Dunstani* in *Memorials of St Dunstan* 143. Cf. Eadmer *ibid.* 232–3.

monastery which he had for long held in high esteem, granting it for the salvation of the souls of himself and his family a whole whale's tongue to be rendered annually at Valognes.[38] It was also a house cited by the conservative monks of Molesme about this time as observing the best monastic customs.[39] For his abbots and monk-bishops William turned primarily to the Norman ducal houses: Jumièges (5), Fécamp (4), Mont St Michel (3), Caen (3), with single nominations from Bernay, St Ouen, and St Wandrille, eighteen out of thirty-one appointments.[40] Bec supplied three bishop-abbots and one abbot. From outside Normandy came two abbots from Marmoutier, and one from St Vincent in Maine. Rufus did not change the pattern, appointing one each from Jumièges, Mont St Michel, and St Evroul.

Both William I and Lanfranc were aware that in the new abbots holiness or learning would not be enough. Strength and determination and a good deal of worldly wisdom, *prudentia*, were required. In the event some of the new men were to prove themselves a little too strong. Although the new foreign abbots may have been as a whole more respectable than their Edwardian predecessors, it is difficult to hold that they were outstandingly more distinguished. If we cast our eyes over the lists of abbots 1070–1100 only three stand out: Lanfranc's nephew, Paul, monk of Caen, abbot of St Albans 1077–93; Gilbert Crispin, monk of Bec, abbot of Westminster 1085 (?) –1117/18; and Herbert Losinga, prior of Fécamp, abbot of Ramsey 1087–1090/1, and afterwards bishop of Thetford/Norwich. William of Malmesbury would certainly have omitted the last from any roll of honour and included Serlo canon of Avranches, monk of Mont St Michel, and abbot of Gloucester 1072–1104, and the Cluniac Lanzo, prior of Lewes 1077–1107.[41] Gilbert Crispin is perhaps the most outstanding of a not exceptionally impressive list.

When we come to consider the filiations of the English Benedictine houses after 1066,[42] the five cathedral priories stand apart. Their first foreign bishop usually imposed a foreign prior of his own choice; but after that the monks normally secured a prior elected *e gremio* and resisted changes forced on them by new bishops. They developed a strong sense of continuity. Worcester and Durham remained very English in tone; and Winchester, which had non-monastic bishops until 1129, and had to struggle to avoid disbandment, was not far behind. But they more than held their own against Christ Church and Rochester, both colonized from Bec and ruled by the primate. Although Lanfranc and Anselm were in a position to make their authority felt in the English monastic order as a whole, and Lanfranc had some success in getting the customs he created for Christ Church adopted in other houses,[43] Christ Church was not a school for abbots. It had to colonize St Augustine's after the

38.   *PL* cxlix. 1374. Marie Faroux, *Recueil des actes des ducs de Normandie de 911 à 1066* (Caen 1961) no. 160, cf. 141, 161–3, 228.

39.   OV (Chibnall) iv. 320.

40.   Knowles *Monastic Order*, app. VII. *The Heads of Religious Houses 940+1216*, ed. D. Knowles, C. N. L. Brooke, Vera London (1972).

41.   *GR* 512 ff.

42.   The following is based principally on *The Heads of Religious Houses*.

43.   Below 189.

rebellion there at the end of Lanfranc's pontificate,[44] and may have been considered too committed to archiepiscopal ambitions. Before 1100 only Battle took from it an abbot (Prior Henry in 1096), and only Peterborough (Prior Ernulf in 1107), Battle (Warner in 1125), St Benet of Hulme (Prior Conrad in 1126), Dunfermline (Geoffrey in 1128), Evesham (William in 1149), and Winchcombe (William in 1152) thereafter. Winchester was far more popular. It provided Burton with all its abbots between 1085 and 1154, Ely in 1083, Newminster in 1100, Tewkesbury in 1102, Malmesbury in 1106, Chertsey in 1107, and Abingdon in 1132.

Few Benedictine abbeys followed a steady course between 1070 and 1154. The pre-Conquest grouping into houses reformed by Dunstan, Æthelwold, and Oswald had collapsed; and Norman reform did not produce sharp divisions. It was rare after 1070 for an English monastery to take its abbots exclusively from either the Fécamp or the Bec group. Shrewsbury, because it was a Montgomery foundation, took its first two abbots from Sées. Malmesbury was consistently loyal to the Fécamp family; Abingdon turned to Jumièges whenever it could. St Albans, Bury, and Glastonbury clearly looked to Bec and its daughters, but only the first could remain constant. St Augustine's, Ely, Evesham, Peterborough, Ramsey, and Westminster took abbots from both groups. Royal patronage, archiepiscopal and episcopal influence, and claustral ambition produced kaleidoscopic changes in the superficial pattern. Underneath, regionalism was strong. In 1077 Bishop Wulfstan of Worcester, in a document written in Old English, announced that the communities of Evesham, Chertsey, Bath, Pershore, Winchcombe, Gloucester, and Worcester would in future be united, 'as if all the seven were one monastery', and each would recite two masses a week for all the brethren in the league, living and dead. They would be obedient to God, St Mary, and St Benedict, and to their bishop, loyal to their temporal lord King William and the lady Matilda. The abbots of Chertsey, Evesham, Bath, and Pershore and the bishop and prior of Worcester were the last Old English rulers of their houses, 'Rawulf' of Winchcombe and 'Saerle' of Gloucester, formerly canon of Avranches and monk of St Michel, were the first Norman incumbents. Unfortunately the document breaks off after reciting the names of the monks at Evesham, Chertsey, and Bath; but they at least are all English.[45]

Rather different principles underlie the network of some fourteen confraternity agreements made by the first bishop-abbot of Durham, William of St Calais (1080–96), recorded in the Lindisfarne-Durham *Liber Vitae*.[46] Lastingham/Hackness (Whitby), Selby, and St Mary's York were neighbours. William's old home, St Calais, appears, but apparently not St Vincent-des-

---

44. *Acta Lanfranci* in Earl, *Two of the Saxon Chronicles* (1865) 273–5.

45. B. Thorpe, *Diplomatarium Anglicum Ævi Saxonici* (1865) 615.

46. *Liber Vitae Ecclesiae Dunelmensis*, ed. A. Hamilton Thompson (Surtees soc. 1923) 136, fo. 21v unidentified (Clemens), Winchester (Gosfridus); fo. 22 Worcester (Wulstanus, Samson); fo. 33 St Augustine's (Abbot Wido); fo. 33v St Calais (as for Westminster), Chertsey, York, Gregory *scriptor* of Bermondsey, Wlfravenus canon of St Paul's; fo. 48 Vitalis abbot of Westminster, Gloucester, St Peter Lastingham, Walkelin of Winchester, William [of Rots] of Fécamp; fo. 48v St Stephen's Caen, Christ Church Canterbury, Malcolm and Margaret of Scots, Selby, Glastonbury, Hackness.

Prés, also in the diocese of Le Mans, of which he had been abbot. The two Norman abbeys in the list are Fécamp and Caen. With the two Canterbury monasteries and Westminster, Durham shared Lanfranc's customary. By his agreements with Worcester, Gloucester, and Chertsey, William joined Wulfstan's league. Winchester and Glastonbury complete the list of monasteries and extend it into all parts of the kingdom except East Anglia. The bishop also made an elaborate spiritual contract with Malcolm and the Scottish royal family and arrangements with a scribe of Cluniac Bermondsey and a canon of St Paul's. These Durham confraternity agreements no doubt witness to the popularity of St Cuthbert and indicate some of the personal allegiances and friendships of William of St Calais and his English prior, Turgot. They also show both how unsystematic (and probably mobile) such filiations could be and how ecumenic Durham's attitude was from the beginning. Within a short time it was ready to embrace even the new Cistercian abbeys and Augustinian priories of Northumbria.

Different again in pattern is the network of confraternities formed by the cathedral church of Rochester under its first four monk-bishops. Twenty-eight communities, all Benedictine, are listed geographically in the *Textus Roffensis,* compiled by Bishop Ernulf (1115–24).[47] At the head are the other three Kentish houses, Christ Church and St Augustine's Canterbury, and the nunnery at Malling, followed by Battle, Bermondsey, and Westminster. A large group from the East Midlands (possibly the interest of Ernulf, who had been abbot of Peterborough, although that church does not appear), St John's Colchester, Bury, Ely, Norwich, St Albans, and Eynsham, is balanced by a group of West country monasteries, Bath, Malmesbury, Gloucester, Winchcombe, Tewkesbury, Worcester, and Pershore. The latter is essentially the Worcester group, and Rochester may well have taken it on as a unit. Abingdon brings up the English rear. Finally there are eight French communities, led naturally by Bec, followed by six other Norman houses, Fécamp, Rouen (St Ouen), Sées (St Martin), Troarn, Préaux (St Peter) and Evreux (St Taurin), and finally Melun (? St Peter), probably the personal choice of Ernulf, who had been a monk at Beauvais. Here we have probably the intinerary to be followed round England and Normandy by the porter of the Rochester breve roll. We are also given a picture of the monastic world as seen from Canterbury and her daughter house, the leading Benedictine communities between the Humber and the Epte, with an outlier further up the Seine.

The aim of the Conqueror and Lanfranc in 1070 was to raise English monasticism to the best European standards.[48] But since neither had much experience of the monastic order in Christendom as a whole, what they had achieved in Normandy set the pattern. Lanfranc, who knew little about the English past, and cared less – ironically it was his successor Anselm who was more curious[49] – ignored English precedent and neither instigated royal legislation nor used his own general councils for detailed monastic reform. He decreed that monks were to observe their Rule, especially with regard to private

47. *Textus Roffensis*, ed. T. Hearne (1720) 321.
48. Böhmer *KuS* 106 ff., Knowles *Monastic Order* 100 ff.
49. *AEp* 39 (to Lanfranc), 42 (to Maurice, a Bec monk at Canterbury).

property, and condemned apostate and vagrant monks.[50] But the reforms were to be made by the individual abbots. By means of letters Lanfranc encouraged the zealous and reproved the slack, and protected the communities against outside interference.[51] He was inclined to regard all the English abbeys as subject to him rather than to the diocesan bishops. For his own monastery, Christ Church, he composed a new customary, which was soon adopted by at least nine other communities, St Albans (whence Crowland), Rochester, St Augustine's, Durham, Worcester, Evesham, Westminster, Battle, and Eynsham.[52] If Lanfranc had been responsible for the idiosyncratic customary of Bec, he now returned to the norm. Although a few of the usages of Bec and Caen were retained, he drew primarily on various Cluniac constitutions, especially the customary drawn up recently by Bernard.[53] The English *Regularis Concordia*, another idiosyncratic version, was ostentatiously ignored. The general effect was to increase the choir services and introduce the elaboration of ritual which Bec had avoided. The new Rule may be the result both of Lanfranc's greater experience of the monastic world and also his feeling that it would be better if English monks were kept more busily employed. Lanfranc's Constitutions, followed by Anselm's conservatism and admiration for Cluny,[54] confirmed that the life in the English Benedictine monasteries would remain primarily liturgical: a succession of common services, whether spoken prayers, singing, or ceremonies, which disregarded the daily time-table of the outside world and gave little time for either study or religious contemplation. It was a punishing life of action sustained by not more than two heavy meals a day.[55]

50.   Windsor (? 1072) 12 (Mansi xx. 460); London (1075) 2, 4 (Mansi xx. 451); Winchester (1076) 2–3 (Mansi xx. 462).

51.   To bishops, to aid monasteries: Walker of Durham, *Ep.* 26, Maurice (of London) 31, Geoffrey (of Coutances) 32; not to oppress them: Herfast (of Elmham) 19, 23, cf. 20, Robert (the MS has P=Peter) of Chester, 29. To abbots, mostly about unsettled monks: B (Baldwin of Bury) 42, Adelhelm (of Abingdon) 49, Thurstin (of Glastonbury) 53, R. (? Riwallon of New Minster, Winchester) 55, William (? of Cerne) 56, O. (? Odo of Chertsey) 57.

52.   *The Monastic Constitutions of Lanfranc,* ed. David Knowles (Nelson's Medieval Classics 1951). A revised and better version is in *Corpus consuetudinum monasticarum,* ed. K. Hallinger (Sieburg 1967) iii. For further observations on Lanfranc's *Decreta,* see Marie Pascal Dickson, *Consuetudines Beccenses, ibid.* iv, pp. xxix ff.

53.   For the customaries of Bernard and Ulrich, see Kassius Hallinger, 'Cluny's Bräuche zur Zeit Hugos des Grossen', *Zeitschrift der Savigny-Stiftung für Rechtsgeschichte, Kanonistische Abteilung,* xlv (Weimar 1959) 99–140, where it is suggested that Bernard's first edition should be dated *c.* 1075, Ulrich's *c.* 1083, and Bernard's second edition (the one in print) 1084–6. These dates are difficult to reconcile with Knowles's proposed dates, 1074/5–77, for *Decreta Lanfranci (CCM* p. xvi). See also Noreen Hunt, *Cluny under St Hugh* 12–13. Evidence is accumulating which suggests that Lanfranc's customary, in its transmitted form, is later than was thought. Margaret Gibson, *Lanfranc of Bec,* 240–1, would date it 1079–89.

54.   R. W. Southern, *St Anselm and his Biographer* 261. It was believed in Cluniac circles that Anselm, who died on 21 April 1109, and St Hugh of Cluny, who followed him eight days later, ascended to heaven at the same time, borne aloft on their couches by angelic hands. See the vision of the abbot of Affligem, in the diocese of Cambrai, in Giles, *Vita Sancti Hugonis,* ed. L'Huillier 616–17, followed by Hildebert and Raynald. The last also informs us that Anselm's *dispensator,* Baldwin of Tournai, while mourning his master's death, had a vision in England of Hugh's obsequies, which he related to Ralf d'Escures, bishop of Rochester, and later to Raynald, who was St Hugh's great nephew: *PL* clix. 905–6.

55.   Knowles *Monastic Order* 456 ff. Cf. Jean Leclercq, 'Pour une histoire de la vie à Cluny', *RHE* lvii (1962) 385. Noreen Hunt, *Cluny under St Hugh,* 99 ff. R. W. Southern, *St Anselm and his Biographer,* especially 349. Different views on the amount of time available for study, authorship,

The initial effect of the Norman conquest was greatly to disturb the monasteries. New direction, new constitutions, reorganization, and rebuilding at their worst upset monastic life, at their best gave renewed purpose and interest. In general the period 1070–1100 was a lively time in which the number of monks multiplied, the wealth of the houses increased, and complacency was banished. By the end of the first generation the majority of the monasteries were in a flourishing condition and had been raised to something approaching the best French standard. During that period two nations and two cultures existed side by side. In some places the English tradition showed great vitality. The Anglo-Saxon Chronicle was written at Peterborough until 1154. But about 1124 William of Malmesbury was asked by Worcester to translate Coleman's Old English Life of Wulfstan into Latin.[56] After the first bitterness, throughout the kingdom a *modus vivendi* was found which in the individual houses combined the two traditions in different proportions. Wulfstan, a pillar of the old order, quickly sent one of his favourite monks, Nicholas, an Englishman, to Canterbury to imbibe the new ideas.[57] Lanfranc himself became less intolerant. The spiritual leagues of confraternity which were formed disregarded race. That it was not all sweetness and light is shown by the troubled career and scornful remarks of the anglicized Goscelin of St Bertin. But even he found before 1100 a safe and congenial haven at St Augustine's.[58] There was nothing in England after the Norman conquest remotely like the situation in the Irish church after the English conquest of the twelfth century.[59]

Some glimpses of Christ Church, Canterbury, in transition can give us an idea of the strains and of the consolations. In his Monastic Constitutions Lanfranc cruelly settled an old score with Edward, the well-educated former archdeacon of London, who had taken the cowl at Canterbury after 1070 and was promoted sacristan a year later.

> Monks accused in Chapter [wrote Lanfranc] must be specified by their order or office. The accuser must not say, 'Dom Edward the archdeacon' or 'of London', or any surname he bore in the world. It should be 'Dom Edward the priest', or 'deacon', or 'subdeacon', . . . or 'sacristan', or 'master of the children or boys', or something of that sort.

private prayer, etc. depend basically on how strictly it is believed that the rules were enforced. Although, as in all communities at all times, most members could properly spend their whole life in common activities, it is quite clear on the evidence that zealous devotees of private prayer, devoted scholars, and enthusiastic authors, could, except perhaps in the most rigorous houses, always find adequate time for their pursuits. But these activities were naturally exceptional. For Cluny's defence of its diet against the initial surprise of the ascetic Peter Damiani, see Anonymous II, *Bibliotheca Cluniacensis* 460. St Hugh said that Peter, before criticizing, should attempt to perform the services on a more meagre diet.

56. *Vita Wulfstani* 1–2. Eadmer, however, in his letter to the monastery of Glastonbury (after 1112), assumed that there would still be monks there, who, like himself, could remember the pre-Conquest régime: *Memorials of St Dunstan* (Rolls ser.) 421.

57. *Vita Wulfstani* 56–7.

58. *VEdR* 100 ff.

59. For which see J. A. Watt, *The Church and the Two Nations in Medieval Ireland* (Cambridge studies in Medieval Life and Thought, 1970).

We learn from Osbern and Eadmer that Edward got tired of being corrected by men his inferior in learning and orders and planned to escape from the monastery with a clever young monk named Adrian. But St Dunstan appeared in order to bring them to their senses and both were fully repentant, Edward making a good end.[60] To judge by Lanfranc's punishment of him, Edward had been a real thorn in his flesh. On the other hand, apparently some time before this, when the young English monk, Æthelweard, went mad while serving at mass and threatened to expose widespread homosexual practices among the monks and, worst of all, to name one of the archbishop's youthful favourites, Lanfranc joined with the community to stop the delator's mouth and hush the business up. The archbishop was also able to prove that full and sincere confession gags the devil.[61]

Lanfranc, like many of the new Norman abbots, was sceptical of the Old English saints, partly because of their 'uncouth' names, partly because there were no Lives or Legends in Latin.[62] While making changes in the ritual – according to Eadmer, some reasonable, some simply arbitary – he cast doubt on the traditional calendar, suppressed some festivals, slighted St Dunstan, and was particularly worried about the presence of Ælfheah (Elphege), the archbishop 'martyred' by the Danes on 19 April 1012. Anselm, however, when visiting Canterbury in 1079 or 1081 removed his scruples, and Ælfheah occurs in Lanfranc's Constitutions sixth among the principal feasts of the church – in a quite astonishing position.[63]

The *prognosticon* at Lanfranc's consecration as archbishop was 'Give alms; and behold, all things are clean unto you',[64] and the archbishop gave generously from his revenues to the poor, the sick, and good causes. Eadmer tells a story which may be about himself.[65] Lanfranc made it his business to help the needy relations of his monks; and to one of the brethren he used to give 5s every two months to pass on to his mother. On one occasion the mother did not notice that her son had handed over the money tied up in cloth, and left it behind. When on her next visit she asked her son about it, and he realized that it had been lost, he sadly left her, thinking that Lanfranc would be offended. As it happened he found the archbishop, as was often the case, sitting in the cloister; and Lanfranc, noticing the monk's dejection, sent the other monks away and asked him what was wrong. And when he had heard the story,

60. *Decreta* (Nelson) 112, (*CCM*) 91. Osbern and Eadmer *Miracula S. Dunstani* 155, 241. Barlow, 'A view of Archbishop Lanfranc', *JEH* xvi (1965) 176–7. As Edward made his dying confessions to Prior Henry, to whom the *Decreta* are addressed, Lanfranc was probably writing before Edward's edifying death. But the exact date of the *Decreta* is problematical. See above, 189, n. 52–3 and below, n. 63. For subjective elements in the customaries of Bernard and Ulrich of Cluny, see Noreen Hunt, *op. cit.* 36–7.

61. Osbern and Eadmer, *Miracula S. Dunstani* 144–50, 234–7; *Vita Gundulfi* in *Anglia Sacra* ii. 277.

62. Cf. Barlow, *English Church 1000—1066*, 26.

63. *VA* 50–4; Miles Crispin *Vita Lanfranci* (ed. d'Achery 1548) cap. 16, p. 15b; Lanfranc *Decreta* (Nelson) 59, (*CCM*) 51. Marie Paschal Dickson, *Consuetudines Beccenses, CCM* iv, p. xxxiii. This is further evidence for a relatively late date for the customary. Cf. also R. W. Southern, *St Anselm and his Biographer* 248 ff., 291–2.

64. Luke 11:41. *GP* 68. *Vita Lanfranci* (ed. d'Achery) cap. 15, p. 15b.

65. *HN* 13–14.

he said, 'Cheer up. God has clearly intended that money for someone else, someone, perhaps, even more in need of it than your mother. Tell no one at all about this. And I will let you have seven shillings for the five which have been lost. But keep it a secret.'

Respected, even revered, though Lanfranc was at Canterbury, he was still more honoured at Bec. Gilbert Crispin abbot of Westminster describes the great occasions in October 1077 when the primate of All Britain visited Bec, the second time in order to dedicate their new church, a building which had been started while Lanfranc was still prior.[66] When Lanfranc arrived on his first visit there was a touching scene in which the archbishop and the abbot each tried to throw himself at the other's feet until their wrestling ended in embraces. Then Lanfranc sat with the brethren in the cloister, just as though he was one of them, speaking in turn to the seniors, juniors, and children. At table he shared the common dish and cup. And he went to talk to the children, inciting them to the love of God more by his benign comportment than by his words which they were not old enough to understand. He left great gifts behind for the community and promised to return for the dedication if the king would permit him. Although the king and queen could not be present on 23 October, there was a distinguished congregation of bishops and nobles on that bright autumn day, so great a throng that some of the older monks could not make their way into the church and were left outside in tears. Lanfranc consecrated the principal altar amid tumultuous rejoicing. A wedding feast followed the ceremony, with the aged abbot anxiously and wonderingly observing the arrangements, and, transported with joy, exclaiming again and again, 'What reward shall I give unto the Lord for all the benefits he hath done unto me?' (Ps. 116:11).

The next day Lanfranc left early in order to cut short the emotional scenes which he expected. Herlwin, who loved him above all other men and knew that he would never see him again in this world, rode with him for the first two miles. Later he sat alone in his chamber with the one whom after Lanfranc he loved best, perhaps Gilbert; and, allowing himself at last to weep, he raised his hands to heaven and prayed, 'Lord, now lettest thou thy servant depart in peace, for mine eyes have seen what I most desired to see before I die, and for which I have prayed to you continually.' Herlwin died on 19 August 1078 after a long illness.

Gilbert Crispin, who wrote so movingly of Herlwin in the most beautiful Latin, was a man of the new age. But he was not completely seduced by the achievements of Lanfranc nor even by the distinction of Anselm. For him the greatest *miles Christi* in their congregation was his fellow countryman, the old knight Herlwin. Lanfranc, although sent by heaven to save the tottering foundation, had come out of the blue and then left them for the purple. It was Herlwin who embodied the genuine spirit of reformed Benedictine monasticism: a mixture of goodness, simplicity, service, and eagerness to learn. Monks in flourishing houses often harked back to the good old primitive conditions.

In the Benedictine order, however, those were truly things of the past. The increase in the size and wealth of the monasteries caused after 1100 a

66. *Vita Herluini* 105–8.

growth in the administration which transformed the internal scene.[67] The abbot began to live apart from the community, and royal insistence on the custody of vacant monastic bishoprics and abbeys encouraged the division of the endowments between abbot and convent. Within the house the number of officials was increased, and to each was assigned his own estates and revenues. All officials had deputies and helpers. When most of these, together with the monks resident in the cells, those absent on business, and the sick, are subtracted from the total, the number of choir monks was much reduced. This 'obedientiary system' of administration was probably the best that could be devised short of relying almost completely on lay servants, and the number of these – perhaps usually equal to the monastic population – was already great.

The few new major foundations after 1100 also showed monasticism at its most elaborate. In 1121 Henry I founded Reading, and in 1148 Stephen imitated with Faversham. Both convents were Cluniac-inspired, but, because of their royal status, remained independent of that order.[68] Reading had as its first abbot the celebrated theologian Hugh of Amiens, monk of Cluny, prior of Limoges and of Lewes, who, after ruling Reading for seven years, was made archbishop of Rouen (1130–64). Faversham was colonized from Bermondsey. Stephen buried his uncle at Reading, and was himself interred with his wife and son at Faversham. At the humbler end of the scale the establishment of new priories and cells went on apace. But the former pattern was reversed: out of some eighty new foundations between 1100 and 1135 more than half were dependent on English houses, with the ratio between Norman and other French mother houses remaining at two to one.

The main new development in the old order was the proliferation of priories for women, chiefly in Stephen's reign. Some twenty-five Benedictine and three Cluniac nunneries were founded, mostly in the midlands and the north of England. The Gilbertine order was designed originally to cater for women. The problem was as much social as religious. It was not because Heloise had had a religious conversion that she became a nun at Argenteuil in 1119 and later deaconess and abbess of Abelard's Paraclete near Troyes. Nor was it primarily because of her piety that at about the same time

67. Knowles *Monastic Order* 395 ff. Noreen Hunt *Cluny under St Hugh* 46 ff. In Southern's view, *St Anselm and his Biographer* 261, Christ Church, Canterbury, under Anselm was moving closer to Cluny than to Cîteaux.

68. Liebermann *Ungedruckte* ii. 10–11; Bermondsey annals in *Annales Monastici* iii. 427, 438. Cf. Brian R. Kemp, 'The monastic dean of Leominster', *EHR* lxxxiii (1968) 505, *Reading Abbey* (1968); Denis Bethel, 'The making of a twelfth-century relic collection', *Studies in Church History* (1972) 61; K. Leyser, 'Frederick Barbarossa, Henry II and the hand of St James', *EHR* xc (1975) 491 ff. For the special form of profession made by Abbot Clarembald of Faversham to Theobald (11 October 1148), and the endorsement, see C. E. Woodruff, 'Some early professions of canonical obedience to the see of Canterbury by heads of religious houses', *Archaeologia Cantiana* xxxvii (1925) 64–6. For Cluny's gratitude to the kings of England for their gifts for the building of Cluny III, see letter of Peter the Venerable, *PL* clxxxix. 279. For the financial services of Henry of Winchester, including his loan of 1,000 oz of gold in 1149, see Bernard and Bruel v. 4012, 4142, vi. 4813; Lena Voss, *Heinrich von Blois, Bischof von Winchester,* Historische Studien, ccx (Berlin 1932) 108 ff. Peter the Venerable visited English monasteries in 1130: *Chron. E s.a.*; cf. *The Letters of Peter the Venerable,* ed. Giles Constable, Harvard Historical Studies 78 (1967), Peter to Henry of Blois, i. 150 (ep. 49). In his *De Miraculis* II, xxxii (*PL* clxxxix. 952) he refers to his second visit to England.

Theodora-Christina of Huntingdon was forced to lurk among the outskirts of religion in the English midlands.[69] There were always clerks and monks who for a variety of reasons regarded women as specially rewarding pupils. Theodora found protectors of every type. In 1080–82 Goscelin of St Bertin suggested to Eve, his protégée when she had been a nun at Wilton, that she furnish her cell at Angers, to which she had fled, perhaps from him, with a library of quite formidable weight.[70] The books were to include the commentaries and lives of the desert Fathers, in particular the Life of Saint Antony, the Confessions of St Augustine, the Ecclesiastical Histories of Cassiodorus and Eusebius, Orosius's History of the World, and Boethius On the Consolation of Philosophy. These would not have been entirely to the taste of Heloise. For her community Abelard not only saw to the organization but also wrote hymns of great beauty.[71] Archbishop Anselm was in correspondence with several religious women of high rank[72] and Gilbert of Sempringham was specially interested in Teaching girls.[73]

What most of these cases show is how great a need there was for safe refuges for widowed, abandoned, and persecuted women. The letters exchanged about 1132–35 by Heloise and Abelard give us a deep understanding of the problems of educated women and the special requirements of female communities. Archbishop Thurstin of York suggested once to Christina that she should enter the great Cluniac priory of Marcigny on the Loire, founded by St Hugh, to which Adela countess of Blois, the Conqueror's daughter, had recently retired, and to which Anselm, when in exile, was a not infrequent visitor. Or, if that was too grand, there was Fontevrault in Anjou. She chose to create her own convent in the familiar countryside near St Albans. The variety in the female monastic order was at least as great as in the male. At one extreme were the wealthy aristocratic houses, such as Wilton, at the other, the Gilbertine priories in their original severity. St Gilbert of Sempringham, because strongly attracted to women, thought them animal in their nature. Lust must be beaten out of them. Bathing was a danger to chastity, and only the most urgent reason could justify a bath, and then the patient must be shrouded in a sheet lest she see her own body. His nuns were not allowed to chant the psalms in church. And treated savagely, these brides of Christ could behave like beasts.[74]

---

69. See below 201 ff.

70. C. H. Talbot, 'The *liber confortatorius* of Goscelin of Saint Bertin', *Studia Anselmiana*, fasc. 37 = *Analecta Monastica* 3rd ser. (Rome 1955) 79–81.

71. The letters are printed *PL* clxxviii. 181 ff. and in translation, *The Letters of Abelard and Heloise*, trans. and introduced by Betty Radice (Penguin 1974). For an interesting essay on them, see R. W. Southern, 'The letters of Abelard and Heloise', *Medieval Humanism and Other Studies* (1970) 86. For the hymns, *Peter Abelard, Hymnarius paraclitensis* (2 vols), ed. Joseph Szövérffy (1975); and cf. his 'L'hymnologie médiévale: recherches et méthode', *Cahiers de civ. méd.* iv (1961) 403.

72. For example, Queen Matilda, Adela, countess of Blois, Ida, countess of Boulogne, and Gunnhildr, King Harold's daughter.

73. *Vita S. Gileberti confessoris* in *Monasticon* vi. 2, p. vi*. A turning point in his spiritual life was when he became physically attracted to the daughter of his landlord and dreamt that he put a hand into her bosom and could not withdraw it.

74. *Ibid.* pp. xv*, xciv*, lxxx*, and below 213 ff.

Not unconnected with the more enlightened side of this movement, the respect for educated and religious women, was the growth of the cult of the Virgin Mary, in which England played a large part.[75] The doctrine of the Immaculate Conception of the BVM – that she had been conceived free from the stain of original sin – had its roots in Greek Christianity and was formalized in the Feast of the Conception celebrated on 8 December. This festival had been introduced into England before the Conquest by Greek monks from Central Italy and was easily accepted, probably because many of the monasteries since their refoundation in the tenth century were dedicated to the Virgin. Lanfranc promptly suppressed the festival at Christ Church and other convents which followed his Rule. But its observance continued at Ramsey under Abbot Æthelsige (Ælfsige, Elsin) (1080–87), a former monk of St Swithun's, Winchester, and abbot of St Augustine's (1061–67); and when Ramsey passed under the rule of Herbert Losinga (1087–1090/91) the custom was transferred to Fécamp, where he had been prior, and so to its relations.[76] The feast was also restored by Abbot Anselm, former abbot of St Sabas in Rome, at Bury St Edmunds (1121–48), whence it spread to St Albans and other houses. At Christ Church Eadmer was an enthusiastic supporter and at Westminster Osbert of Clare. At Worcester the feast of St Anne, the Virgin's mother, was established at this time. The festival of the Conception was generally authorized by Archbishop William of Corbeil at his legatine council of London in 1129.[77] And Abbot Hugh of Reading, when he became archbishop of Rouen in the following year, would have done nothing to hinder the spread of the custom to Normandy. The one great voice which was raised against the cult was that of St Bernard. An interesting literary feature of this worship was the creation of a collection of the miracles of the Virgin, started apparently at Evesham by its prior and historian Dominic, and at Bury by Abbot Anselm, and consolidated by William of Malmesbury. Here was the nucleus of all later collections current in the Western Church.

By 1100 most of the immediate post-Conquest tensions had gone out of English Benedictine monasticism. The English and Norman traditions had fused. When Osbert of Clare, an 'English' monk of Westminster, rewrote in 1138 the commentary on Edward the Confessor's prophecy of the Green Tree and the servitude of the English race, he, unlike William of Malmesbury in 1124, did not include the non-existence of abbots of English blood as one of the proofs of the truth of the vision of doom. And when Ailred of Rievaulx, an

75. Knowles *Monastic Order* 510 ff. A. C. Baugh, 'Osbert of Clare and the Middle-English Saint Anne', *Speculum* vii (1932) 106. A. W. Burridge, 'L'Immaculée Conception dans la théologie de l'Angleterre médiévale', *RHE* xxxii (1936) 570. R. W. Southern, 'The English origins of the miracles of the Virgin', *MARS* iv (1958) 176. J. C. Jennings, 'The writings of Prior Dominic of Evesham', *EHR* lxxvii (1962) 298; 'The origins of the "elements series" of the miracles of the Virgin', *MARS* vi (1968) 84.

76. Jean Fournée, 'L'abbaye de Fécamp et les origines du culte de l'immaculée conception en Normandie', *L'abbaye bénédictine de Fécamp, ouvrage scientifique du XIIIe centenaire*, ii (Fécamp 1960) 163.

77. John of Worcester, MS G., *s.a.* 1129, repeated in *Winchcombe annals,* ed. R. R. Darlington, *Pipe Roll Soc.* n.s. xxxvi (1960) 126. For the council cf. *Chron. E, s.a.*, where it is said that the council was concerned solely with married clergy. Osbert of Clare's letter 7 on this matter was written just before the council met.

English Cistercian, revised the commentary for the last time in 1163, he was at pains to show that the impossible had been made possible, the severed tree had been rejoined, and as proof of this there were now abbots as well as nobles, bishops, and even a king of English stock.[78] The harmony was beneficial. Many of the monasteries recovered the renown of the past.[79] Bury St Edmunds under Anselm's nephew of the same name (1121–48), Glastonbury under the king's nephew, the Cluniac Henry of Blois (1126–71), and Gloucester under Gilbert Foliot (1139–48), another former prior of Cluny, showed different facets of Benedictine culture at its best. Faricius of Arezzo abbot of Abingdon (1100–17) was a celebrated physician; William of Malmesbury brought fame to his community; and Walker prior of Great Malvern (died 1125) was a major mathematical scholar.

All the intellectual and artistic activities of the monks were ancillary to their religious service. The monasteries inherited a great tradition of ecclesiastical craftsmanship from the English tenth-century reformation and much experience of rebuilding from Normandy. But the Anglo-Norman monasteries developed more as patrons of arts and crafts than as practitioners. The one field in which they continued to be directly involved was book production, and even here while the new libraries were being created, almost from scratch, professional scribes were employed. Nevertheless, all aspects of book making, authorship, editing of texts, copying, illuminating, and binding, engaged the attention of some monks at all times. By the twelfth century English decorated books were as highly prized throughout Europe as they had been in the late Old English period. The two great Bibles made at Winchester for Henry of Blois show the new art at its most splendid.[80] The literary achievement of monastic authors was at least respectable. If the Benedictines produced, except for Anselm (and he was hardly an English scholar), no original thinker in theology, philosophy, or any of the liberal arts, this cannot be put to their discredit for it was not their purpose.

Benedictine monasticism had not reached its peak in England by 1154 – the full blossoming of St Albans did not occur before the thirteenth century – but in some directions it was already, at least relatively, in decline.[81] It had never regained the place in the government of the kingdom which it had enjoyed in the late Old English period. Abbots as a class had lost importance. They played little part in the royal councils, and by Stephen's reign it is likely that archdeacons were almost as influential in church synods.[82] There was a strong movement in the English church to prevent monks getting bishoprics,

---

78. *VEdR*, appendix B.

79. Knowles, 'English monasteries under Henry I' in *Monastic Order* 172 ff., intended to paint the picture of a golden age, but listed at least as many failures as successes.

80. Cf. Margaret Rickert, *Painting in Britain in the Middle Ages* (Pelican History of Art, 1954) 79–84. For the making of books, see below 236 ff.

81. D. L. Bethel, 'English black monks and episcopal elections in the 1120s', *EHR* lxxxiv (1969) 693, argues that the Benedictines improved their position in the kingdom after the attacks on them in the 1120s, and that the real age of collapse was much later in the century.

82. In 1125 Archbishop William, on behalf of the papal legate, summoned his bishops to attend the forthcoming council of London. They were to attend with the archdeacons, abbots, and priors of their diocese: Wilkins i. 408.

and although some monks and abbots, like Faricius, might as individuals be close to the king, it was usually in a domestic character. Benedictine monasteries were also losing their cultural and moral pre-eminence. Peter Abelard, himself a monk who was to die at Cluny, writing to Abbess Heloise, criticized from his intellectual standpoint contemporary monasticism.[83] Some abbots, he claimed, in their recruitment policy aimed at quantity rather than quality, so that they could boast of their large numbers. Abelard did not think that more meant better. He complained that too much time was given to singing lessons (which were no more than uttering words without understanding them) at the expense of study into the meaning of the Scriptures. Here he was voicing the attitude of the cathedral schools toward Cluniac practice. And, he remarked scathingly, now that the monasteries had an abundance of books, no one read them. Abelard, suffering from the barbarity of the Breton abbey of St Gildas, had a vision of a more élitist and more intellectual monastic life, for both men and women, than ever found favour in the Middle Ages. The great increase in the monastic population in England between 1066 and 1154 is usually considered now, as then, a healthy sign.[84] And Abelard taught the monastic leaders how dangerous intellectual pursuits could be in their order. Already by 1100 no ambitious clerk was satisfied by a monastic school. Monastic teaching was becoming more domestic, and, with the decline in the custom of the oblation of children, much reduced in scope.

In the same letter Abelard remarked that a monastery should not be called irregular simply because irregularities occurred there, for no community could be faultless, but only if they remained uncorrected. In England there were some long-standing and glaring faults. At the beginning of our period Folcard of St Bertin ruled Thorney for about sixteen years without ever receiving the episcopal benediction before his deposition by Lanfranc in 1085.[85] Ely had a particularly troubled history. It was without an abbot for two periods of seven years (1075/76–1082; 1093–1100), was greatly disturbed by its transformation into an episcopal see in 1109, and badly affected by the East Anglian rebellion against Stephen in which Bishop Nigel was involved.[86] William of Malmesbury thought that Glastonbury had been most unfortunate in its abbots since the Conquest, and he saw faults elsewhere.[87] Peterborough had to suffer from 1127 to 1132 the imposed rule of a Cluniac adventurer, Henry of Poitou abbot of St Jean d'Angely.[88] Ranulf Flambard's financial operations on behalf of Rufus and himself were not usually conducive to monastic wellbeing. According to the Anglo-Saxon Chronicle Ranulf, at his master's death, held

83. *PL* clxxviii. 282, 303, 307–8, 308.

84. Cf. Knowles *Monastic Order* 126–7. But see also Noreen Hunt *Cluny under St Hugh* 86–7.

85. OV (le Prévost) iv. 281–2; *VEdR* pp. li ff., where the dates should be advanced to 1069–85, according to the late Helen Clover. See also Cyril Hart, 'The Ramsey Computus', *EHR* lxxxv (1970) 44, for the date.

86. *Liber Eliensis*, ed. E. O. Blake, Camden 3rd ser. xcii (1962).

87. *GP* 196–7; cf. 185–6, 254.

88. See especially *Chron E, s.a.* 1123, 1127–28, 1131–32. Cf. Cecily Clark, ' "This ecclesiastical adventurer": Henry of Saint-Jean d'Angely', *EHR* lxxxiv (1969) 548, where the chronicle account is discussed and amplified.

eleven abbacies in his own hands, all let out to 'farmers' at rent.[89] Because of the division of the revenues the monks did not necessarily suffer financial loss – and Durham, which he administered before he became bishop, was treated well[90] – but the lack of government must have weakened internal discipline. Anselm at the council of Westminster in 1102 deposed nine abbots, both English and French. In Henry I's reign the king's justiciar, Roger, bishop of Salisbury, accumulated monasteries,[91] and in Stephen's Henry of Blois, bishop of Winchester, was not guiltless of this practice.[92]

The characteristic literary productions of the twelfth century, the cartulary and the charter-chronicle, illustrate many of the typical Benedictine weaknesses of the period. They were the records of wealth. The charters, on which the narrative was based, were largely reconstructed or forged. Forgery of title deeds and privileges was a major monastic industry in the twelfth century because, in a more documentary-conscious age, it was discovered that the muniments had been destroyed by time or catastrophe, or did not fully support the rights which were claimed. At Canterbury, while Christ Church forged its various titles to lordship within the church of Great Britain, St Augustine's fabricated its privileges of exemption.[93] The priory of Durham produced an armoury to justify its possession of what would later be termed peculiars in the dioceses of Durham, York, and St Andrews.[94] Westminster in the time of Osbert of Clare manufactured its Edwardiana.[95] And so it was in most convents. It should be noticed that although some forgery was designed to justify spiritual rights, none of it was directed to true religious purposes. It was inspired by greed and ambition.

One later distraction which thrived on the manufacture of evidence – litigation – was, however, largely missing in this period. Most of the thirteenth-century facilities were lacking: the hierarchy of ecclesiastical courts with its system of appeals, the common law of the church against which claims could be measured, and the services of proctors, jurisconsults, and notaries public.[96] Also absent before the middle of the twelfth century was that purposeful ecclesiastical government of bishops and archdeacons, and their interference in what the monasteries considered their private affairs, which made it necessary for these to define and defend their rights and aspire to privileges of exemption. In the Norman period, as before, attempts by a bishop to annex a

---

89. *Chron. s.a.* 1100.

90. *HDE, cont.* i. in Simeon of Durham *Historical Works* i. 135 ff.

91. Edward J. Kealey, *Roger of Salisbury viceroy of England* (1972) 97 n. 44; but 104 ff. defends his behaviour against the charges of Knowles and D. Nicholl.

92. Lena Voss, *Heinrich von Blois, Bischof von Winchester*, 44–6, 100.

93. Margaret Gibson, *Lanfranc of Bec* 231 ff and above 44.

94. Frank Barlow *Durham Jurisdictional Peculiars* 149–51.

95. P. Chaplais, 'The original charters of Herbert and Gervase abbots of Westminster', in *A Medieval Miscellany for Doris Mary Stenton*, Pipe Roll Soc. (1962).

96. C. R. Cheney, *Notaries Public in England in the Thirteenth and Fourteenth Centuries* (1972) 12, quotes the papal legate Otto in 1237 on the non-existence in England at that date of public notaries. There were, of course, notaries. When Ranulf Flambard was abducted on the Thames, he threw his finger ring, and his notary his master's seal, overboard, lest their captors misused them: *HDE* 136.

monastery or encroach on its liberties could best be resisted by appealing to the archbishop or the king. When Bury St Edmunds obtained a splendid privilege from Alexander II, Lanfranc confiscated it. During Stephen's reign several monasteries put themselves under papal protection. But it was not until Henry II's reign that the history of monastic exemption from the local ordinary really begins.[97] And by then the tide had turned against the monasteries in favour of the bishops. The age of the Gregorian reformers, who had advanced monks as a spiritual force in a corrupt church and world, had passed away. The papacy even abandoned Cluny, its beloved and special daughter, in part to the ordinaries.[98] In fact before 1154 the monasteries experienced little interference in their control over the parish churches they owned. They could rely on the current attitudes to landownership to allow them all the rights they wanted: custody of vacant churches, nomination of incumbents, investiture of the new priest with the temporalities, imposition of pensions, appropriation at will, the taking of hospitality, jurisdiction over and within the parishes.[99] Typically the monastery of Ely, although it was its promotion into a bishopric in 1109 and the substitution of its own abbot-bishop and his servants for the traditional enemies, the bishop of Lincoln and the archdeacon of Cambridgeshire, Huntingdon, and Hertfordshire, which forced the monks to redefine their franchise, did not in fact go to law against the archdeacon of Ely until 1150.[100]

If litigation does not figure prominently in monastic chronicles before Henry II's reign, neither does religion nor any intellectual pursuits. The *Liber Eliensis*, the product of a distracted and unhappy community, which never in the century after the Conquest recovered the glories of the century which went before, records the miracles of St Etheldreda, for these were profitable. It also has a reference to scholarship. The inventory of 1143, after listing the splendid treasures of the church in detail, concludes, 'Bishop Nigel found these and many others in the church, and in a chest a good number of books, which if we stopped to list them would displease the reader'.[101] The chronicle is not only philistine but also parochial. National history is beyond its horizon; even the life of the diocese, not to say the events of the English church, is ignored. On the evidence of the charter-chronicles the monasteries were little more than selfish landowners. But this, of course, is only one side of the coin. The revenue was supposed to be put to spiritual ends.

At the beginning of the twelfth century there was a great debate in the monastic order about its proper role in the church. With the transformation of the intellectual climate in Christendom, the growth of government, and the opening of new opportunities for a ministry not only in the backward rural areas and thriving towns of Christian countries but also among the Jews and in

97.   Knowles *Monastic Order* 561 ff. J.-F. Lemarignier, *Etude sur les privilèges d'exemption et de juridiction ecclésiastique des abbayes normandes* (Paris 1937). Eleanor Searle, 'Battle abbey and exemption: the forged charters', *EHR* lxxxiii (1968) 449.

98.   Cf. Gerd Tellenbach, 'Der Sturz des Abtes Pontius von Cluny und seine geschichtliche Bedeutung', *Quellen und Forschungen* xlii (1963) 30 ff.

99.   Barlow, *Durham Jurisdictional Peculiars*, especially 146 ff.

100.   *Liber Eliensis* II, 127; II, 54; III, 37; III, 25; III, 101, 102, 107. Blake *ibid.* 402–4.

101.   *Liber Eliensis* III, 50.

the Muslim lands,[102] some monks began to question their traditional way of life and purpose. Those awakened to the challenge reexamined the concept of the *vita apostolica*, the apostolic life on which monasticism was supposed to be based, and were disturbed by their findings.[103] It was obvious that typical Benedictine and Cluniac monasteries lacked both the true poverty and the active ministry of the evangelical life as described in the Scriptures. But if a change in the latter direction was the more attractive, this proved the more difficult. Although there was agreement in the church that the state of the 'spoiled' secular clergy was a scandal, there was little inclination to welcome increased monastic encroachment in that field.[104] Monks were not well suited by tradition, training, or outlook for a general ministry. Their attempts to administer the sacraments to the laity, preach, and conduct schools were met with hostility from clerks.[105] And the monasteries were also faced with competition from other orders whose special purpose it was to engage in some of these activities, such as the canons regular, educated bodies of clerks, anxious to conduct a scholastic ministry in the towns, and the military and charitable orders designed to supplement the secular crusaders. Monasteries were, however, traditionally devoted to the distribution of alms and the relief of the poor, to hospitality, and, because of the acceptance of the aged and dying as monks, increasingly to the care of the sick.

One type of monastic evangelism was the begging mission dispatched by poverty-stricken houses. This could combine simple mendancy,

102.   At Pope Gregory VII's request Cluny sent a monk, Anastasius, to preach to the Moors in Spain; St Hugh visited Spain and returned with an ungrateful Moor; and later Abbot Peter the Venerable commissioned the first translation of the Koran into Latin. *Vita Gloriosi Anastasii* in *PL* cxlix 429; Giles, *Vita S. Hugonis*, ed. L'Huillier 585; J. Knitzeck, *Peter the Venerable and Islam* (Princeton 1964).

103.   See above 2 f. See also Jean Leclercq in *Analecta Monastica* iv (1957)= *Studia Anselmiana* 41; Valerie I. J. Flint, 'The original text of the *Elucidarium* of Honorius Augustodunensis from the twelfth century English manuscripts', *Scriptorium* xviii (1964) 91; M. O. Garrigues, 'A qui faut-il attribuer le *De vita vere apostolica*?', *Le Moyen Age* lxxix (1973) 421.

104.   Just as there was a great debate in the eleventh and twelfth centuries about the legality and expediency of monastic cure of souls, so in recent years there has been controversy over the extent to which the monks of that period were actually involved in such activities. A complication is the discrepancy between theory (the Rule and the customs) and practice. A general feature of the period is codification of the law, definition, and specialization. For some views, see U. Berlière, 'L'exercice du ministère paroissial par les moines dans le haut moyer-âge', *Revue Bénédictine* xxxviii (1927) 227; Charles Dereine, 'Le problème de la *cura animarum* chez Gratien', *Studia Gratiana* ii (1954) 309; M. Peuchmaurd, 'Le prêtre ministre de la parole, dans la théologie du XIIe siècle', *Recherches de théologie ancienne et médiévale* xxix (1962) 52; Giles Constable, *Monastic Tithes from their Origin to the Twelfth Century* (1964), 'The treatise "Hortatur nos" and accompanying canonical texts on the performance of pastoral work by monks', *Speculum Historiale* (Festschrift Johannes Spörl, Munich 1965) 567; Marjorie Chibnall, 'Monks and pastoral work: a problem in Anglo-Norman history', *JEH* xviii (1967) 165. C. N. L. Brooke is against the minimizers: see his review of Constable in *EHR* lxxxi (1966).

105.   For the debate in England see 'Un debat sur le sacerdoce des moines au XIIe siècle', *Studia Anselmiana* xli (Rome 1957) = *Analecta Monastica* iv. There was also a good deal of charity and moderation. Shortly after the death of Anselm in 1109 Bishop Herbert Losinga of Norwich declined the invitation of Abbot Richard (? of St Albans) to write a defence of the monastic order against 'its enemies, the secular clergy', and maintained that each had its proper place in the church, *epp.* 59–60. Likewise Godwin, precentor of Salisbury, perhaps a little later, expressed disapproval of the dispute, since all clerical orders were part of the same church: *Meditaciones Godwini cantoris Salesberie ad Rainilvam reclusam*, quoted Edward J. Kealey, *Roger of Salisbury* 110.

popular religion with miracles and cures, and moral exhortation in differing proportions. The ancient Flemish monastery of Marchiennes decided in the time of Abbot Alard (*c*. 1078–86) to send a party of monks on a preaching tour of England with the body of the blessed virgin Eusebia.[106] But although England had been chosen because of its reputation for great wealth and respect for indigent saints, the mission was a failure. People called to the preaching by the singing of hymns would not give a penny. The mendicants could not even cover their expenses, and, after disposing of their horses and all their gear, were forced to sell the silver tunic in which the virgin's body was displayed in her shrine. They attributed their lack of success to the refusal of the saint to work for them because of their avarice. More successful, perhaps, because more spiritual, was the visit to England of Andrew, founder and first abbot of the Vallombrosan community of Chézal-Benoît, between Issoudun and Bourges in Berry, who died in 1112.[107] He preached to clerks both rich and poor and to the laity, urging them to abandon the world and enter religion, and he returned with many ornaments and marks of silver, which he used for the decoration of his church and the maintenance of his poor monks. The next famous begging tour of England was that conducted by the canons of Laon in 1113.[108]

On the margins of the monastic orders was a more loosely textured fringe. Throughout the history of monasticism there was a demand for both the cenobitic and the eremitic ways of life. In the eleventh and twelfth centuries a good number of men and women, for a variety of reasons, abandoned organized society, ecclesiastical as well as secular, and trudged the roads or turned aside into waste lands. Some lived entirely solitary lives, but most joined up with a few others in free associations. Whenever a settlement became stable, it usually attached itself unofficially to a local church or monastery in order to get priestly services. Monasteries themselves, with their cells and other less formal detachments, tended to create similar bodies.[109] Most monastic chronicles of the period have references to such dependents and dependencies,[110] and we can get some interesting glimpses of the hermits who lived on, or just off, the twelve miles of Watling Street between St Albans and Dunstable from the life of

106. *Miracula S. Rictrudis* in *AB* xx (1901) 456.

107. *Rouleaux des morts du IXe et XVe siècle*, ed. Léopold Delisle (Soc. de l'histoire de France 1866) no. xxxiv. p. 170. Cf. OV (Chibnall) iv. 327.

108. See below 249 f.

109. Abbot Geoffrey de Gorron of St Albans (1119–46) turned the hermitage of Roger and Christina into the priory of Markyate; acquired the hermitage of *Modri* with its churches, tithes, and other things, and transferred there the monks of *Mulebroc*; and *c*. 1140 assumed responsibility for the hermitage built by two holy women in the wood of *Eywode*, and this developed into the priory of Sopwell. For the last two foundations, see *Gesta abbatum S. Albani*, ed. H. T. Riley (Rolls ser. 1867), i. 78, 80–2; *Monasticon* iii. 274, 362. About 1131 Gilbert enclosed seven of his former girl pupils in a building constructed against the north wall of his church at Sempringham – the beginning of his Order: *Monasticon* vi. 2, p. ix*.

110. Cf. *Gesta abbatum monasterii S. Albani*, i. 97 ff., 105, 148; *Vita Wulfstani* 65–7; William of Malmesbury *GP* 314; *The Life of Wulfric of Haselbury*, ed. M. Bell, Somerset record soc. xlvii (1933). Giraldus Cambrensis, *Descriptio Kambriae*, ed. J. F. Dimock (Rolls ser. 1868) vi. 204; Reginald of Durham, *St Godric*; *Cartularium monasterii de Rameseia*, ed. W. H. Hart and P. A. Lyons (Rolls ser. 1884) i. 162. Cf. H. Mayr–Harting, 'Functions of a twelfth-century recluse', *History* lx (1975) 337.

Theodora (Christina in religion), written by a monk of St Albans who knew her well.[111] (See map 3, below 321.)

Theodora was born at the end of the eleventh century into the Anglo-Danish urban patriciate of Huntingdon, a town on the Great North Road at the edge of the East-Anglian Danelaw. Her father with the Scandinavian name of Auti and her mother Beatrice, who had at least three other children, were leading members of the merchant gild, lived in a fine house, had their private chaplain, and entertained lavishly. Beatrice's sister, with the Old English name of Alveva (Ælfgifu), had been the mistress of the king's factotum, Ranulf Flambard, and had borne him children, and although Ranulf, when he became bishop of Durham in 1099, married her off to a citizen of Huntingdon, he still stayed with her on his journeys to and from London.[112] Theodora was always attractive to men. As a young girl she found a mentor in Sueno (Sveinn), a canon of the Austin priory of St Mary, who was reputed even in old age to be hot-blooded.[113] But it was probably Ranulf Flambard's attempts to seduce or rape her in her aunt's house about 1114 which made it impossible for her to accept the suitor whom Ranulf and her family then tried to force upon her, although Burhred (Burgraed), a young member of their circle, was considered by everyone, including the ecclesiastical authorities, an entirely suitable match.[114] Theodora claimed that some time before, on a visit with her parents to the abbey of St Albans, struck by the religious atmosphere, she had taken a private vow of chastity and therefore would marry no man; under immense pressure from all sides, she allowed herself to be formally betrothed (*desponsavit*) to Burhred but she would not consummate the marriage, and, although this hardly affected the legal position, there was no wedding.[115]

Whatever the exact teaching of canon law on this difficult matter, all the ecclesiastical persons involved – the family chaplain, the prior and canons of Huntingdon, the rural dean, the bishop of Lincoln (Robert Bloet), and the archbishop of Canterbury (Ralf d'Escures), although they sympathized with Theodora's desire to enter religion and supported her stand up to a point, were in the last resort unwilling to thwart her family, aided as it was by Ranulf of Durham. The bishop of Lincoln, 'bribed' by her father, gave formal judgment against her.[116] The result was an impasse: the girl would not accept her husband, and she could not become a nun without her husband's permission, which he withheld for about eight years. She was kept a prisoner in the family house for at least a year, while every method was tried to change her mind, and, when she realized that she was going to get no legal help, she decided to escape. If she

---

111. *The life of Christina of Markyate*, ed. and trans. C. H. Talbot (1959) [henceforth cited as Talbot]. See also *Gesta abbatum monasterii S. Albani* i. 97 ff. 148; *GP* 314 n.

112. Talbot 34 ff.

113. *Ibid*. 36 ff.

114. *Ibid*. 40 ff.

115. *Ibid*. 44 ff. For the law, see Gabriel LeBras, 'Le mariage dans la théologie et le droit de l'église du XIe au XIIIe siècle', *Cahiers de civ. méd.* xi (1968) 191, and E. W. Kemp, *Papal decretals relating to the diocese of Lincoln in the twelfth century*, ed. Walther Holtzmann and E. W. Kemp, Lincoln record soc. xlvii (1954) pp. xxvi–xxvii.

116. Talbot 68 ff.

were to fly the coop it could only be into the fastnesses of either an outlaw band or a hermit encampment, and the life of a Maid Marion was not without its perils. About 1115 she got secretly in touch with the hermit Edwin of Higney and his kinsman Roger, an old monk of St Albans in deacon's orders, who had been on a pilgrimage to Jerusalem and was allowed to live apart in a hermitage at Caddington.[117] Edwin, who went to Canterbury to consult the archbishop, spied out the land, and it was decided that Theodora, disguised as Christina, should be placed with an anchoress named Alfwen (Ælfwynn), who lived under Roger's direction at Flamstead, forty miles from Huntingdon, and so beyond the limits of her family's power. After two years Christina was moved to Caddington and remained there until Roger died in 1122, some four years later.

Towards the end of this period her husband released her from the marriage and she was taken to an interview with the archbishop of York, Thurstin, who undertook to clear up the remaining legal difficulties.[118] After Roger's death Thurstin put her under the care of one of his own friends, an important cleric whose identity the biographer prudently conceals, for the protector not only tried to seduce Christina and subjected her to some highly improper behaviour but also succeeded in arousing a sexual passion in her. Although she fled from the tempter back to the wilderness at Caddington, and eventually her desire cooled, she had doubts for a time whether she had preserved her virginity, perhaps even physically, intact. The death of Robert Bloet of Lincoln at the beginning of 1123 removed, however, the last obstacle to the regularizing of her position. In due course Thurstin made several suggestions: she could rule the community of women he had established at St Clement's York; or she could enter the French convents of Marcigny or Fontevrault; and there were other overtures. But she chose to remain attached to St Albans. She was consecrated a recluse by the new bishop of Lincoln, attracted converts to her hermitage, and began to exert an influence over the abbot, Geoffrey de Gorron, the former schoolmaster of Dunstable.[119] Ever since she had come into the open after Roger's death she had been the subject of scandal.[120] There can be no doubt that the abbot came to rely overmuch on her and that she made full use of his infatuation. Her detractors attributed her power to clairvoyance – the interpretation of dreams and spirits[121] – or to her business sense, or to using her physical charms. When Geoffrey thought that he had to go on a royal embassy to Rome in 1136 he asked Christina for two undervests (*interulae*), but not as a source of pleasure, merely to relieve the sweat and toil of the journey.[122] The pair disregarded the calumnies, and in the year of Geoffrey's death (1145) Christina's community was canonically estab-

117. *Ibid.* 80 ff.
118. *Ibid.* 106 ff.
119. *Ibid.* 112 ff. For Geoffrey, see also below 231.
120. Talbot 130, 172–4.
121. Talbot, 172–3, translates 'eam alii sompniatricem, alii animorum [*sic*] translatricem appel-labant' as 'some of them called her a dreamer, others a seducer of souls'.
122. *Ibid.* 160.

lished as a Benedictine priory for women on an estate at Markyate, near Caddington, which had belonged to St Paul's, London.[123]

Christina was a recluse for some thirty years and several other hermits come into her story. Although these, and others like them, were on the fringe of society, it is doubtful whether their lives can be interpreted simply and generally as a radical protest against institutionalized religion, still less as an English movement hostile to Norman discipline and privilege.[124] They followed an accepted alternative way of life. And most of the hermits were English only because most of the population was of Anglo-Danish extraction. If Theodora-Christina lived in a hermitage with English-speaking Roger – she was his Sunday's daughter ('myn sunendaege dohter') – her brother Gregory (perhaps christened Baldwin) became a monk at St Albans. Auti's family and circle were conscious of no social inferiority and were on the easiest terms with the foreign magnates of the church with whom they had dealings. One of the most remarkable features of Theodora's story is the complete absence of racial prejudice or tension. Even a Jewess makes a casual appearance.[125]

The life of a recluse could be ascetic and sordid in the extreme. Christina while hidden at Caddington, even from Roger's companions, was imprisoned in a small cell, from which she was released in order to eat and perform other bodily functions only in the hours of darkness. The effects on her health, although not permanent, were severe.[126] St Gilbert when he enclosed seven of his former girl pupils in a cell attached to his church at Sempringham, imposed bestial conditions on them.[127] Moreover, since most hermits were illiterate or semi-literate – Christina could recite the psalms, but perhaps only by heart (we are told nothing of her education) and Roger, a deacon and possibly a late convert, could probably do little more – they spent much of their time in reading the psalter, as a communal activity when possible, or in meditating upon it. We hear nothing of garden or craft work, or even of begging. Yet there were amenities. Few hermits lived completely solitary lives. But it comes as a surprise to learn from casual remarks how large some of the communities were. Five hermits, as well as Christina, lived with Roger, who also directed others who dwelt apart, and even an old married couple. Christina attracted a number of 'nuns' and sometimes had her sister, Margaret, with her. In addition most of the hermits had at least one servant. Edwin of Higney had a servant Loric (*O.G.* Luderic), who produced two horses when Theodora fled from her parents' house disguised as a man.[128] Roger had several. Christina once in command at Caddington recruited maids.[129] Nor were these communities completely isolated. There was much coming and going between

123. *Ibid.* 29–30.

124. Talbot's view, 12–13.

125. *Ibid.* 74. She seems to have been employed by Theodora's mother to work some spell to make her marry Burhred.

126. *Ibid.* 100 ff.

127. *Vita S. Gileberti confessoris* in *Monasticon* vi. 2, pp. ix*, xxix*.

128. Talbot 86 ff.

129. *Ibid.* 124, 128. The word *puellae* is ambiguous, and on the second occasion Talbot translates it as 'nuns'. Cf. 144, where *puellae* are also *virgines*. It is likely that in those early days the status of her household was equivocal.

Caddington and St Albans. Monks performed mass and other services. And, whenever a hermit got a reputation for holiness and – for this went easily with contemplation – the gift of prophecy, he received a stream of visitors, both clerical and lay. People came for cures, advice, solace, and to satisfy their curiosity.[130] As a result a complex of simple buildings had to be erected. Roger had a chapel at Caddington, and it is implied that each of the community had his own cell.[131] In Christina's time the abbot of St Albans assumed responsibility for the maintenance of the hermitage, and, although this may be a description of the priory at Markyate, there was a church, a dormitory and refectory, and a herb garden.[132]

In Normandy and other regions of France, perhaps because the best recorded eremitical movements were one or two generations earlier, the terrain seems even more primitive and inhospitable and the crop more vigorous and fruitful. It was about 1034 that the knight Herlwin took his mother and some of his tenants out of the world to form a simple religious community which developed into the abbey of Bec. Other leaders and organizers were often 'drop-out' monks or canons, sometimes with a mysterious past spent in vagabondage and false starts. Vitalis, born in 1050 in the region of Bayeux, became a wandering scholar before entering the service of the Conqueror's half-brother, Robert count of Mortain, and accepting a canonry in the college which Robert founded at Mortain (1082). He then followed the life of a wandering preacher, visiting Normandy, Brittany, and England. He preached before Anselm at the council of London (1102), and in between he lived with other hermits in the forests of Mortain.[133]

When such leaders organized a new community they usually tried to follow the primitive rule of St Benedict. But this could be variously interpreted. And it is characteristic of the age that the church authorities allowed much experiment and variety. Muret-Grandmont, near Limoges, an eremitical community similar to La Grande Chartreuse in the Alps, and one of the most extreme of the new orders, was formed towards the end of the eleventh century. Molesme-Cîteaux, south of Dijon in Burgundy, was organized *c*. 1075–99 out of dissidents by a monk Robert, and then by Stephen Harding, an English monk from Sherborne.[134] Out of settlements of hermits in the barren lands between Brittany and Maine arose not only Vitalis's monastery of Savigny, south-east of St Hilaire in the frontier region of the county of Mortain (1112–15),[135] but also the earlier Fontevrault, near Saumur (*c*. 1100), and

130. Reginald's *St Godric* gives a good account of visitors to Finchale, and *The Life of Wulfric* of visitors to Haselbury.

131. Talbot 102.

132. *Ibid.* 128 ff.

133. The best account of the origins of Savigny is in Bennet D. Hill, *English Cistercian Monasteries and their Patrons in the Twelfth Century* (Univ. of Illinois Press 1968) 80 ff. See also Knowles *Monastic Order* 191 ff.

134. Knowles *Monastic Order* 208 ff., 'The primitive documents of the Cistercian order', in *Great Historical Enterprizes and Problems in Monastic History* (1963) 199 ff. Jean-A. Lefèvre, 'Que savons-nous du Cîteaux primitif?', *RHE* li (1966) 5. Bennet D. Hill, *op. cit.* 5 ff. See also OV (Chibnall) iv. 310 ff.

135. See also OV (Chibnall) iv. 330–2.

Tiron, near Nogent-le-Rotrou, on the Norman border with Chartres (1107–09).[136] Norbert, the former canon of Xanten in Lotharingia, in 1120 organized his followers into a sort of Augustinian canonry at Prémontré in a forest near Laon.[137]

All these reformed French convents established offshoots in England. Savigniac houses were founded at Tulketh-Furness in Lancashire (1123–27), Neath in Glamorgan (1130), Quarr in the Isle of Wight (1132), Buckfast in Devon (1136), Byland in Yorkshire (1138), Coggeshall in Essex (1140), and at six other places before the order merged reluctantly with Cîteaux in 1147. Cistercian abbeys were established at Waverley in Surrey (1128), Tintern in the Wye Valley (1131), Rievaulx and Fountains in Yorkshire (1132), and at thirty-five other places scattered throughout the kingdom before 1154.[138] The other new centres made less impression. From Tiron came the abbey of St Dogmaels in South Wales, and the priories and cells at Mapledurwell and Hamble in Hampshire, St Cross on the Isle of Wight, and Titley in Herefordshire, all in Henry I's reign. But foundations from Fontevrault, La Grande Chartreuse, and Grandmont did not take place until the Angevin period. The one indigenous new order was that founded by the Lincolnshire parson and schoolmaster Gilbert of Sempringham, the son of a Norman knight and an Englishwoman, towards the end of Henry I's reign. By 1154 he was in control of six convents in the north-eastern regions of England. He died in 1189 at the age of 105 and was canonized by Innocent III in 1202.[139]

In the same period reformed canonical communities, societies of secular priests living under a rule, usually called Augustinian (Austin) or regular canons, were planted widely in England. And associated with this movement was the foundation in many towns of hospitals and almshouses of various kinds, often under the patronage of St Mary Magdalen, St Leonard, or St Giles. Houses for the care of the sick, especially lepers, and for the care of the poor and aged seem to have been founded in roughly equal numbers; there were also hospices for poor travellers and pilgrims.[140] Most original of all, in order to aid the Crusades, themselves an unprecedented religious activity, ancillary religious services of a completely novel type were devised, the Knights

---

136. See also *ibid*. 328–30.

137. Charles Dereine, 'Les origines de Prémontré', *RHE* xlii (1947) 352.

138. For the style of building, see Marcel Aubert, 'Existe-t-il une architecture cistercienne?', *Cahiers de civ. méd.* i (1958) 153. For a typical English house of this period, see W. H. St John Hope and J. Bilson, *Aechitectural description of Kirkstall abbey* (Thoresby soc. xvi, 1907).

139. *Monasticon* vi. 2, pp. v* ff. Rose Graham, *S. Gilbert of Sempringham and the Gilbertines* (1901). Raymonde Foreville, *Un procès de canonisation à l'aube du XIIIe siècle (1201–1202): Le livre de saint Gilbert de Sempringham* (Paris 1943), where the miracles (omitted in *Monasticon*) and other historical materials are printed.

140. For example, at Winchester, dependent on the cathedral but outside the walls, were the hospitals of St Cross (founded about 1136), St Mary Magdalen (founded before 1148), and the Sustren Spittal (founded possibly by 1110). The hospital of St John may also have been in existence by 1148. There were as well the charities of the citizens. By 1110 Osbert son of Thiard had built on his land outside West Gate five shacks to provide lodgings for poor men. See Frank Barlow, Martin Biddle, Olof von Feilitzen, and D. J. Keene, *Winchester in the Early Middle Ages*, Winchester Studies, ed. Martin Biddle, i (1976) 328–9.

Templars and the Knights Hospitallers.[141] The former established their English headquarters in London (the Old Temple at the Holborn end of Chancery Lane) about 1128, and the latter outside the walls at Clerkenwell about 1144; both created small preceptories at convenient points throughout the kingdom to serve as recruiting and collecting centres and to administer their estates. Stephen and his queen, both interested in the crusading movement, were generous to the Templars.

It will be seen that between 1130 and 1154 a monastic movement of the greatest magnitude occurred in England. Many more religious communities were founded than in the seventh or tenth centuries, and the contrast with the first sixty years of Norman rule is extreme. As it was part of a north European phenomenon it cannot be explained simply in terms of the 'anarchy' of Stephen's reign. The most important social and economic causes seem to be the increased wealth available for charitable purposes and the growing self-confidence, self-consciousness, and ambition of the propertied classes. Even the greatest of the Norman magnates were beginning to consider themselves Englishmen and to look to their English position. And if the high feudal baronage, busy with castle building, reorganizing their estates, and assuming armorial bearings, when deciding to add a monastery or two to their property favoured Savigny (a Norman foundation in Stephen's county of Mortain) or Cîteaux, the ministerial nobility, proud of their new status, and imitating their betters, patronized the more active orders, in particular reformed canons. It will also be noticed that suddenly there was much more variety in the religious landscape than ever before. By 1135 a man or woman wishing to abandon the world or make a donation for the good of his soul could pick and choose. There was something to everyone's taste. This diversification, these novelties, these 'schisms', would have been a scandal in the past and was still a matter for debate.[142] But it enriched society, ecclesiastical and secular alike.

Savigny was the most wayward of the new orders. Ruled by abbots of the greatest holiness, it remained loosely organized. Under Vitalis his own revivalist preaching missions and the various pastoral activities of his disciples kept alive some of their earlier ideals. His successor, Geoffrey of Bayeux, who had been a Benedictine monk at Cérisy, introduced more settled ways but provided no written constitution. And the congregation became so disorderly that the fourth abbot, Serlo, a great admirer of St Bernard, in the hope of using Cistercian discipline to reform his monasteries, in September 1147 put them all under the abbot of Cîteaux. This merger was resisted by the English houses led by Furness. But within two years the rebellion had been put down. The union seems to have been profitable to neither party: the Savigniac monasteries were not thoroughly reformed and the English Cistercian houses were corrupted by their weaker brethren.[143]

---

141. For the English Temples, see B. A. Lees, *Records of the Templars in England in the Twelfth Century* (1935). There is no useful study of the Hospitallers in England.

142. Cf. M. D. Chenu, 'Moins, clercs, laïcs au carrefour de la vie évangélique (XIIe siècle)', *RHE* xlix (1954) 70 ff.

143. Hill *op. cit.* 80 ff.

Cîteaux, despite its fairly rapid fall from grace after 1154, was by far the most influential of the reformed conventual orders. It owed its enormous impact on religious society in Western Christendom both to its challenging and uncompromising assertion of primitive asceticism and also to the early emergence from its ranks of a great spiritual leader, Bernard of Clairvaux. Its rule, which evolved out of the Cluniac with the spare *Carta Caritatis* (1119) and a few subsequent definitions, aimed at purging monasticism of all harmful accretions. To be avoided were wealth and ostentation of all kinds, the over-elaborate ritual, intellectual and artistic pursuits, everything that could come between a man and God. Endowments had to be unconditional; and originally undeveloped and remote tracts of land, which could be developed as private estates, were preferred. Manual work was expected of all the monks, but from the beginning the houses recruited their own labour force, illiterate estate workers, known as *conversi* or lay brothers, who were given a religious discipline suited to their station. The choice by the Cistercians of a new dress made out of undyed white cloth, in contrast to the black habits of the older Benedictines, proclaimed their difference. At first it was an order for the elite. No one could enter under the age of sixteen. A full year's novitiate was required. The life was hard and cushioned by no aesthetic pleasures. There was not only brutalizing physical work but also time appointed for spiritual reading and private prayer, pauses in which doubt, despair, and rejection could creep in. The constitution of the order was designed to preserve this fundamental harshness. A single customary and standard service books for the whole order established a uniformity which was enforced by a system of visitation and annual general chapters at Cîteaux. Even the abbot of Cîteaux was put under control so as to prevent decay at the top. And initially these humble communities were under the jurisdiction of their diocesan bishop.

The success of the new movement was extraordinary. It was soon apparent to all that the other monastic orders were further from the true ideal, were but second best. And the Cistercians could not deny that they were the only true professors. It was a challenge which idealists from all ranks of society hastened to accept. It appealed not only to the spiritual athletes who wanted to be tested to the limit of their endurance, but also to the refined, who wished to be purified even further. Its nurture of Bernard abbot of Clairvaux, who transcended all its limitations, gave the order a distinction which turned its advance into a flood. The success was, of course, fatal to the ideals. In England the miscellaneous nature of the endowments, the rapid increase in the number of monks, the necessary application of new drive and new methods to estate management, the literary and then the legal activities of some very gifted members, took the monasteries far from their beginnings in a few miserable wooden huts on marginal or completely useless land. But for a generation – roughly Stephen's reign – they were the purest of the pure, and fostered three saints, William and Ailred, abbots of Rievaulx, and Waldef abbot of Melrose, all true Englishmen, two with Old English names.

Although Cistercian monasteries were founded all over the kingdom, a northern group outshone the rest. These, straddling the border with Scotland and breathing the same air as Durham, formed, together with a group of Augustinian priories and some celebrated hermits, a particularly English society. Culturally Northumbria was as close to the kingdom of Scots as to southern England. The Scottish royal family regarded itself as being in succession to the monarchy of Edward the Confessor and was indeed very English in its tone. But the northern churches and people, although not unaffected by those features, never after 1073 allowed nostaligia to weaken their loyalty to the French kings of England.

Several first-rate Englishmen from the North, including Henry Murdac and a certain William, joined Bernard at Clairvaux and returned to be abbots of English houses. Other men of equal calibre were recruited from positions of importance at home. Maurice sub-prior of Durham chose the stricter life and succeeded William as abbot of Rievaulx in Yorkshire in 1145.[144] Ailred, a son of the last hereditary parson of Hexham, rose high in King David's court, becoming his steward and a friend of his son Henry and his stepson Waltheof or Waldef. But about 1134, when on a mission to the archbishop of York, he turned aside to visit Rievaulx and found it impossible to depart. We know Ailred best of all the English Cistercians of this period because we have, besides his own literary compositions, a sympathetic biography by his friend and disciple, Walter Daniel, a prolific author and perhaps the infirmarer of the house.[145] Ailred's books *The Mirror of Love (Speculum Caritatis)*, *On Spiritual Friendship*, and *On the Soul* are in the tradition of monastic mystical theology, and the first was written when he was novice-master at the command of St Bernard. The *Life of St Ninian*, the *Tract on the Battle of the Standard*, and his edition of the *Life of Edward the Confessor* reveal his interest in the traditions of the two kingdoms.[146] Ailred usually shows the brighter side of the Rule of Love.

In some ways even more interesting is the career of his friend Waldef.[147] Born after 1104, the second son of Matilda countess of Huntingdon and Northampton and her first husband, Simon of St Liz I, and so on the maternal side the grandson of Earl Waltheof and Judith the Conqueror's niece, he accompanied his widowed mother when she married after 1111 David, who became king of Scots in 1124. At the Scottish royal court he was brought up with his mother's second brood. His biographer claimed that Waldef always had a religious vocation – when children, his elder brother Simon used to play castles and knights while he played churches and priests – and there was talk of making him a bishop. But he fled from court to become a canon regular at St Oswald's Nostell in the West Riding of Yorkshire, where the prior was Aldulf, also bishop of Carlisle after 1133. Waldef rose to be sacrist, and before 1139 was elected prior of the canonry at Kirkham in the East Riding, a house which he made orderly and rich. It was in 1139 that he met at York St Malachy, the former bishop of Armagh and St Bernard's favourite Irishman. Malachy was

144.   For Maurice, see F. M. Powicke, 'Maurice of Rievaulx', *EHR* xxxvi (1921) 17.

145.   *Walter Daniel's Life of Ailred abbot of Rievaulx*, ed., trans. and introduced by F. M. Powicke (Nelson's Medieval Classics 1950).

146.   *PL* cxcv. See also R. Twysden, *Hist. Anglic. Script. X* (1652) 337 ff. *De anima* ed. C. H. Talbot (*MARS*, suppl. 1, 1952).

147.   Jocelin of Furness, *Vita S. Waltheni abbatis* in *Acta Sanctorum* Aug. I. 248, written about 1207. Cf. Powicke, *Walter Daniel's life of Ailred*, pp. xiii, lxxi ff.; Derek Baker, 'Legend and reality: the case of Waldef of Melrose', *Studies in Church History*, ed. Baker, xii (1975) 59.

going to Rome by way of Clairvaux and Waldef gave him his own horse. This was a strong, near-black cob, very rough to ride. But under the Irish saint it not only moved sweetly but also turned completely white, and served him well for the nine years he had still to live. Waldef, when he was abbot of Melrose, had a horse which he called Brother Dapple-Grey.[148] It was very intelligent and kind, once even kneeling down so that the enfeebled abbot could mount, and after its master's death it died of grief.

When Thurstin of York resigned in January 1140 Waldef's election was mooted; his kinsman, William of Aumale earl of York, offered to fix it at a price. But Waldef declined. In any case the king feared the Scottish connexion and vetoed the proposal. The result was the election of Stephen's nephew, William fitzHerbert, and the opposition of the Cistercian abbots.[149] Waldef's kinsmen disapproved strongly of his obscure ways of life. The count of Aumale rebuked him for dishonouring his family. As though to pique them even further, Waldef, after consulting his old friend Ailred, by then abbot of Rievaulx (1147–67), entered the daughter-house of Wardon in Bedfordshire as a novice monk. It was the beginning of a very troubled period of his life. Pressure on Wardon from his brother Simon, now recognized by Stephen as earl of Huntingdon and Northampton, forced him to transfer to Rievaulx; Kirkham brought a suit against him for deserting his post, and in the *probatorium* of Rievaulx he was assailed by doubts.[150] The tasteless food and drink, the cheap rough clothes, the hard manual work, and the burdensome choir services brought him to the conclusion that the Cistercian way of life was too hard for him. He began to feel that the more moderate Augustinian rule, being closer to the golden mean, was better designed for the saving of souls. But he overcame the temptation to desert, and in 1148, when the first abbot of reformed Melrose was, to King David's anger, deposed for tyranny, Waldef was substituted as a candidate acceptable to all. Eleven years later, when Robert bishop of St Andrews died, Waldef was elected in his place. Ailred, who was at Melrose at the time, ordered him to accept, but he refused on the grounds that he was ill and had not long to live. He died on 3 August 1159.

Ailred at Rievaulx was, at least on the personal side, easygoing. Waldef was moderate in all things except, perhaps, hospitality and the relief of the poor and sick. He aimed in his dress and deportment at simplicity and plainness, avoiding alike the extremes of ostentatious parsimony and worldly splendour. His noble birth and education freed him from the temptation to impress. On journeys he travelled with only one monk and one lay brother, each with a single servant. As we have seen, he did not go in for costly horse flesh; he rode like a poor squire with his baggage tied behind him, and often he and his companion carried their servants' boots and stockings on their horses'

---

148. *Frater Ferrandus*, p. 266a. It is agreed by lexicographers that *ferrandus* is a colour, comes from *ferrum* (iron), and is applied exclusively to horses. But there is no agreement on exactly what colour it is.

149. Above 96.

150. Cf. a story in *Walter Daniel's Life of Ailred*, 24–5, 31–2, 35–6.

cruppers.[151] In this state Waldef once approached King Stephen on some business, to the disgust of his brother who was in attendance. 'See, my lord king,' the earl remarked, 'how my brother, your kinsman, does us honour.' But Stephen, fixing his eye on the abbot, retorted, 'By God's birth! If we look at these things in the light of divine grace we shall judge that he honours us greatly. Just as a ruby embellishes the gold in which it is set, so he adorns our whole family.' When Waldef left, the king kissed his hands and asked for his blessing. Waldef, like Ailred, impressed men with his simple goodness. He often corrected his brother for his excesses, and in the end Simon repented and founded both Cluniac and Cistercian monasteries. Waldef also encouraged his half kin, the Scottish royal house, in their great religious works. His religion, like Ailred's, was unbigoted. Ailred's patron saint was St Cuthbert, the tutelary of Durham, and he admired St Gilbert of Sempringham and his order.[152] Waldef is found meditating on a saying of St Hugh of Cluny. But whereas Ailred acquired more than adequate learning and literary skill, the earl's son was probably not quite up to standard. His biographer claims that he was eloquent in both English and French and that his exposition of the Rule of St Benedict in French (*romane*)[153] gave his audience great pleasure. By implication he did not speak Latin easily. But he was probably closer than Ailred to the true Cistercian ideal.

Towards the end of the eleventh century the Cluniac Pope Urban II recognized that those who wished to pursue the apostolic life in a community had a choice between two main roads, the monastic and the canonical.[154] From the earliest Christian times communities of clerks serving churches, in particular episcopal households, had occasionally been put under a quasi-monastic rule. In 1066 the rule of St Chrodegang was in force at Exeter cathedral, and similar constitutions were observed at York, some of the other Yorkshire minsters, and Wells. But despite the interest of the Gregorian reformers in a celibate priesthood and the common life, Norman bishops in England broke up the common chests, refectories, and dormitories, and gave to their cathedral clergy individual prebends. It was not until the very end of the eleventh century that communities of clerks observing a rule, this time usually the Rule of St Augustine, were reintroduced into England. On the Continent the new movement had had various sources, including the eremitical and ascetic. But as the Austin canons usually served a church with cure of souls, the active life tended to dominate over the contemplative. In the twelfth century, however, regular canons allowed monks no superiority. Although without an equally emotive history, they felt that they trod the highway, while monks went increasingly off the beaten track. It is, indeed, permissible to express the difference in terms of

---

151. The text is not without difficulties: 'ipse vero more clientum sarcinulas in vectura retro ligatas gestare solebat sotulares aut caligas garcionum suorum, et aliquoties desuper equorum pediligulas, quas vulgo posturas vocant', 259b.

152. Below 215.

153. Cf. above 40.

154. Cf. Charles Dereine, 'L'élaboration du statut canonique des chanoines réguliers spécialement sous Urban II', *RHE* xlvi (1951) 546 ff. M. D. Chenu, 'Moins, clercs, laïcs au carrefour de la vie évangélique (XIIe siècle)', *RHE* xlix (1954) 71. For Urban II, see Alfons Becker, *Papst Urban II,* vol. i, Schriften der Monumenta Germaniae historica, 19/1 (Stuttgart 1964).

the sisters Martha and Mary (Luke 10), provided that the basic relationship and common purpose are not forgotten. Diocesan bishops, while they welcomed settlements of Cistercian monks as a regenerative spiritual force, an example of the Christian life as perfect as might be expected on earth, saw in the regular canons an auxiliary ministry. These brethren would establish schools, hospitals, alms houses and the like. Whereas the Cistercians in their way of life tried to go back to Christian beginnings and called on men to renounce the present, the reformed canons ministered more effectively to the new spiritual and cultural needs of twelfth-century society.[155]

During the reigns of Henry I and Stephen over a hundred Augustinian priories of all kinds were founded throughout England, with the greater part and the more important houses in the earlier period, when the royal court was interested. Towards the end of Stephen's reign the first Premonstratensian priories were introduced.[156] The black and the white canons, canons regular as they began to be called, competed with Savigny and Cîteaux for patrons and members. But there was room for both orders. The canons did not arouse the same sort of popular interest as the Cistercians – or the friars in the thirteenth century. Nor did they attract into their society men of quite the same calibre. They produced no English saint in this period. They had no Ailreds, nor even Henry Murdacs. They did, however, foster useful men. Merton priory in Surrey founded other communities and schools through its Italian schoolmaster, Guy.[157] Thomas Becket was educated there, and when archbishop he took one of the canons, Robert, as his confessor. Augustinian canons began to get bishoprics. William of Corbeil prior of St Osyth (Chich) in Essex became archbishop of Canterbury in 1123, Robert of Béthune prior of Llanthony obtained Hereford in 1131, and Aldulf prior of Nostell was made first bishop of Carlisle two years later. In Scotland Robert canon of Nostell and then prior of Scone was elected bishop of St Andrews in 1122.[158]

For the Templars St Bernard at the council of Troyes (1128) adapted the Cistercian rule; the Hospitallers made use of the Augustinian order. Gilbert of Sempringham was eclectic.[159] To a community of nuns, who followed the rule of St Benedict, he added at William of Rievaulx's suggestion lay sisters, and then lay brethren. Finally, after he had failed to put his experiment under the tutelage of Cîteaux (1147), he recruited priests into a canonical society to adminster to the others. In the end he became master of this composite community and then master general of the whole order. He composed a written constitution which took account also of the customs of Grandmont and Fontevrault, the former a congregation which made great use of lay brethren, the latter an order for nuns, lay sisters, and priests. It was, as his

155.   Charles Dereine, 'Vie commune, règle de Saint Augustin, et chanoins réguliers au XIe siècle', *RHE* xli (1964) 365. J. C. Dickinson, *The Origins of the Austin Canons and their Introduction into England* (1950). Caroline W. Bynum, 'The spirituality of Regular canons in the twelfth century: a new approach', *Medievalia et Humanistica* (North Texas State University) iv (1973) 3.

156.   H. M. Colvin, *The White Canons in England* (1951).

157.   See below 232 f.

158.   For Robert, see *DNB* xlviii. 366.

159.   Rose Graham, *S. Gilbert of Sempringham and the Gilbertines*; Knowles *Monastic Order* 205–7.

biographer claimed, a beautiful *florilegium*. The community itself, with the lay brothers and sisters recruited by Gilbert in a rather casual way from the ranks of the local peasants, fugitive serfs, and the riff-raff of towns, was (like Gratian's *Decretum*) 'concord made out of discord' (*discordantium concordia*).

> There the robber wolf lives with the lamb so meek and mild, and the spotted pard, the terror of the herds, lies down with the kid. In that place dwell together the calf, contrite in heart, the once harsh lion, and the sheep with its artless innocence. There the rhinoceros teaches the sheep to be tame and the unbroken bullock willingly submits its neck to the yoke. There the little doe hunts the hound, and the lark the hawk, while the tortoise ascends with the eagle to the stars. There the fox forgets its cunning and the crow disdains the body it has snatched.

But, as with all social experiments, there were dangers. A sexual scandal and a serious revolt of the lay brethren occurred in the 1160s.[160]

Gilbert's creation was popular because it was concerned with some urgent social problems of the age, the provision of a religious life for unmarried and widowed women and – a later development – the care of lepers and orphans. Since women could not be ordained priests and were considered unsuited to heavy manual work, men had to be organized to perform those services. In this lay danger, for, as Walter Map observed, 'too often the tricks of Venus pierce the walls of Minerva'.[161] It was a brutal age. Men and women involved in scandal were treated savagely. And extreme asceticism could have a brutalizing effect. Ailred of Rievaulx could write of spiritual friendship, but he could also relate with complacency an episode which, to our way of thinking, was discreditable to all concerned.[162]

About 1160 a scandal occurred in the Gilbertian house at Watton in the East Riding of Yorkshire some forty miles from Rievaulx. A girl whom the Cistercian archbishop of York, Henry Murdac (1147–53), had placed at the age of four in the monastery, on reaching puberty rebelled against the monastic life and began to show a keen interest in men. We are not told why she was not

---

160. For the rule (not in its primitive state), *Monasticon* vi. 2, p. viii*; rule printed pp. xxix* ff. For the recruitment, cf. p. x*. For the society, p. xiii*. For the rebellion, p. xviii* ff. and Foreville 83 ff., where she proves that it occurred 1165–67. The rebels, wishing to discredit their superiors, the nuns and canons, alleged scandals. But the Watton affair was successfully hushed up and no reference to it appears in the dossier of papal proceedings which followed and settled the disturbances. See especially the report of the papal commissioner, William bishop of Norwich, and the letter of Roger archbishop of York; Foreville 94, 97. All the same, the segregation of the sexes was made stricter. The severity of the discipline was undoubtedly one of the causes of the unrest, and two recalcitrant nuns and one canon appear in Gilbert's miracles: *ibid*. 76–7.

161. *De Nugis curialium,* ed. T. Wright, Camden soc. (1850), I, xxvii, about the early history of the order.

162. *De sanctimoniali de Wattun* in *PL* cxcv, 789. The date of the event is fixed roughly by the girl being four years old when placed in the convent by Archbishop Henry Murdac. Henry was not reconciled to Stephen and allowed to undertake his office until 1151, and died 14 October 1153. If the girl was born about 1148, she would be fifteen about 1163. Watton has been excavated, and some of the events of the scandal can be located on the plan. See W. H. St John Hope, 'The Gilbertine priory of Watton', *Archaeological Journal* lviii (1901) 1. The plan is reproduced in Rose Graham, *An Essay on English Monasteries* (Hist. Assoc. pamphlet no. 112, 1939).

expelled. Presumably she was an orphan.[163] Reproaches and chastisement had no effect, and it was not long before she had seduced the youngest and best looking of the canons who ministered to the community. The guilty pair used to meet at night outside her dormitory, after he had announced his arrival by throwing a stone against the wall or on to the roof. This method of signalling inevitably betrayed them. The man fled, the girl was roughly handled by the nuns. It was suggested that she should be burnt or flayed alive, or roasted on a spit, but the seniors moderated the fury of the younger nuns. She was stripped and beaten, and then, heavily fettered and chained, was imprisoned in a cell, where she was fed on insults and a diet of bread and water. The punishment was presumably imposed by the master of Watton, William. The one thing which surprised Ailred was that the adultery and its preliminaries should have gone so long undetected.

Although Gilbert's Rule dealt with this problem explicitly, and laid down that the guilty man should be unfrocked and then either imprisoned or expelled, and the guilty woman, to avoid scandal, condemned to perpetual imprisonment,[164] the community acted in a completely lawless way. When the nuns discovered that their prisoner was pregnant, there was further discussion about her fate. When one sister suggested that the wicked girl should be handed over to her lover, the girl exclaimed that that could easily be done, for the man would shortly be coming to a prearranged meeting. The master set a trap. One canon was disguised as the girl, others lay in wait. The lover was captured in secular dress, and, at the request of some of the nuns – 'who had a zeal for God, but not according to knowledge' (Rom. 10: 2) – was handed over to them for interrogation. They put a knife into the girl's hand, forced her to castrate the man, and then threw the bloody objects in her face. Ailred justifies at some length this punishment imposed for the insult to their chastity.

With vengeance satisfied, the man was returned to his brethren and the girl to her prison. When the girl was about to give birth she had a vision in her sleep of Archbishop Henry. He asked her why she cursed him daily, and she replied that it was because it was he who had forced her into that monastery where she had suffered so much. The prelate retorted that her misfortunes were due to her sins and lack of repentance, and instructed her in the penitential psalms she should recite. Next night he appeared to her again, this time accompanied by two beautiful women. As the girl knelt before him, he covered her face with his pallium and said, 'If you had cleansed yourself with a true confession you would understand clearly what is taking place. As it is, you will reap the benefit without knowing the extent or nature of the deed.' The girl then saw the women carrying a child away; and when she woke she found that she was no longer with child. Her gaolers naturally suspected her of infanticide. But no traces of a birth could be discovered and the most thorough physical

163.   According to Gilbert's Rule, *Monasticon* vi. 2, p. lxxxvi*, no girl should be admitted before the age of 12, become a novice before 15, and be professed a nun before she had made satisfactory educational progress. In this case the Rule was disregarded with disastrous results. No lay sister should be professed under the age of 20. Prospective canons could become novices at 15 and be professed at 20, *ibid.* p. xliii*.

164.   'De incestuosis et muliere includenda', *ibid.* p. lxxi*.

examination of the prisoner confirmed that she was completely restored to her pre-puerperal state.

The girl was retained in prison. But her chains began miraculously to disappear, removed each night, it was claimed, by two menservants of divine mercy. The master decided to go and consult Ailred. The abbot returned with him to Watton, interviewed the girl and all the witnesses, ordered that no new fetters be added to the single one which remained, commended himself to the prayers of the community, and left. Shortly afterwards he was informed by letter that the last pinion had disappeared and asked what should be done. The pith of his answer was, 'What God has cleansed, that call you not common (Acts 10: 15). And the woman he has loosed you are not to bind (cf. Matt. 16: 19; 18: 18).' Ailred showed compassion in the end, and he published this somewhat enigmatic miracle story to solace contemporaries, edify posterity, and incite all to devotion.

By 1154 the monastic revival was all but over. In 1152 the general chapter at Cîteaux had forbidden new foundations. The Gilbertine order was still expanding in England, but was hardly in the main stream. It was not until 1178 that the first English Charterhouse was with difficulty established, at Witham in Somerset, and in its third prior, Hugh of Avallon (c. 1180–86), later bishop of Lincoln in plurality (1186–1200), produced a saint; but only two more houses were founded before 1343. The propertied classes withdrew their patronage from both Benedictine and reformed monasticism. The next ascetic movement came in with the friars.

Attacks on monks and their behaviour, if not on their ideals, were not uncommon after 1100. Hugh the Chantor of York had, for obvious reasons, bitter things to say about monastic fraudulence; and the dignitaries of York told Pope Calixtus II (the former archbishop of Vienne) at Paris in 1119 how glad they were that at long last a clerk, and not a monk, was pope.[165] In 1135–36, when some of the novelty of the new orders had worn off, Orderic Vitalis, the English monk in the well-conducted, cultured, rich, and aristocratic monastery of St Evroul, took a sympathetic but not uncritical look at their early history.[166] He had nothing but praise for the religion and zeal of the founders of Cîteaux, Tiron, Chézal-Benoît, and Savigny, although he did not consider them superior to the monastic fathers of old. He clearly thought that they interpreted the monastic rule too literally – they did not, for example, take enough account of climate – but he set up the debate on this matter very fairly. He saw hypocrites and counterfeits among the most ascetic. He also thought their white garments ostentatious and in rather bad taste. By 1154 monasticism was far less fashionable than it had been a generation before, and it was no longer necessary in non-monastic circles to pay lip-service to the excellence even of the Cistercians.

Towards the end of the century that wit at the royal court, Walter Map, wrote entertaining, irreverent, and sometimes scurrilous pieces about monasticism in general and the origins of the Carthusians, the order of Grand-

---

165. *HCY* 70.
166. OV (Chibnall) iv. 310 ff.

mont, the Templars, the Hospitallers, the Cistercians, and the Gilbertines.[167] He satirized their wealth and avarice, their fraudulence, and their Pharisaism. His bitterest attack was on the Cistercians (the 'Hebrews') and he derided the stories of St Bernard's miracles. Map's contemporary, Gerald of Wales, wrote similar pieces in his *Speculum Ecclesiae* and told a story about the great Ranulf Glanvill, Henry II's justiciar.[168] Ranulf, who had decided to build two monasteries on his estates, discussed with his friends the various possibilities. The Cluniacs he thought too gluttonous, the Cistercians too covetous and too much on the make. In his long career on the bench no other order of monks had been so often convicted of forged charters, counterfeit seals, fraudulently moved landmarks, and other rapacious acts as the white monks. In contrast the canonical order seemed to him less inclined to excess than the others, and far less disposed to gluttony and covetousness. And so Ranulf established on his patrimony a house of Premonstratensian canons and on his acquisitions an Augustinian priory. When we have made full allowance for the satire it remains clear that in an age of greater spirituality material success had gravely harmed the reputation of the monastic order.

167.   *De Nugis curialium* I, xvi–xvii, xxiii–xxviii.

168.   Giraldus Cambrensis, *Opera omnia,* iv, ed. J. S. Brewer (Rolls ser. 1873) 244.

Chapter VI

Schools, Education, and Scholars

Schools are much more obscure than monasteries because they were less highly regarded, their population was transient, their activity and reputation were unstable, and their histories were not written. The anecdotes are naturally about the masters. The greatest school was the church itself, *schola Christi*, and other schools were more an activity than institutions.

Academic education in the medium of Latin was, at least in north-west Christendom, entirely a matter for the church.[1] Most laymen were educated through some sort of apprenticeship,[2] and, whether they were *bellatores* or *laboratores,* did not need the skills of reading or writing or a knowledge of Latin. The clergy had to be literate in order to train professionally for their various duties, and, since the language of the Western church was Latin, clerks had to be able to read, understand, and write that language.[3] It may be that, at some times and places, some use was made of French or English as an aid. Literacy in several languages is occasionally noted. We are told, for example, that Samson, born in 1135 in Norfolk and educated in the external school of Bury St Edmunds, where later he became abbot, was eloquent in French and Latin, read English perfectly, and used to preach to the people in English with a strong Norfolk accent.[4] But when we read of grammar without qualification we must understand the rudiments of Latin. Nor were the other ancient languages much studied. There were in this period no real Greek scholars in England and never more than one or two with even a smattering of Hebrew.[5] Arabists were on the eccentric fringe.

1. A useful introduction to twelfth-century advanced instruction, with special reference to dialectics and theology in French episcopal schools and universities is G. Paré, A. Brunet, P. Tremblay, *La renaissance du XIIe siècle: les écoles et l'enseignement* (Public. de l'Institut d'Etudes médiévales d'Ottawa: Paris and Ottawa 1933). See also L. Maître, *Les écoles épiscopales et monastiques en occident avant les universités* (768–1180) (Paris, 2nd ed, 1924). In Nicholas Orme, *English Schools in the Middle Ages* (1973), where most attention is given to the later period, there is a helpful list of English schools 1066–1530, pp. 293–325.

2. For example, William, nephew and grandson of village priests, was apprenticed in 1040–41 at the age of eight, to a master skinner of Norwich, and was completely separated from his family: *Vita S. Willelmi Norwic.* 14 ff.

3. Karl Strecker, *Introduction à l'étude de Latin médiévale* (Lille, 3rd ed, 1948), English translation (Berlin 1957). Cf. also Christine Mohrmann, 'Le latin médiévale', *Cahiers de Civilisation Médiévale Xe–XIIe siècles,* i (1957) 265–94. See also M. B. Ogle, 'Some aspects of mediaeval Latin style', *Speculum* i (1926) 170; W. B. Segwick, 'The style and vocabulary of the Latin arts of poetry of the twelfth and thirteenth centuries', *ibid* iii (1928) 349, 615.

4. *The chronicle of Joscelin of Brakelond*, ed. and trans. H. E. Butler (Nelson's Medieval Classics 1949) 40.

5. See below 247 f.

Not all clerks needed skill in Latin conversation, and the subjects studied beyond the basic requisites depended on the career which was to be followed. A boy who was intending to be a sheriff's clerk did not follow the same curriculum as one who wanted to search out all the secrets of heaven and earth. A boy destined to be an archdeacon and bishop had not the same requirements as an oblate monk. It should also be noticed that not all educated men became ministers of the church. A substantial number remained for most or all of their life in minor orders, which allowed them to live like laymen if they so desired. The Breton Peter Abelard tells us that his father, Berengar, had received some education before he became a soldier and intended all his sons to learn their letters before their military training. But Abelard renounced his military career.[6] Other men abandoned the clerical life for secular employment. One of the Conqueror's household knights, whom we find in conversation with an important royal clerk, Samson, had been to school. Later he rejoined the true road and became a monk.[7] Most commonly clerks proceeded no farther than the subdiaconate so that they remained free to marry, make war, and engage in other secular activities prohibited to those in major orders. In this way many royal clerks were enabled to establish a family before, in their graver years, aspiring to a bishopric.

It has to be emphasized that all literary education was ecclesiastical and that all the masters and pupils were clerks,[8] because the language of monastic writers has often been misunderstood.[9] When they wrote about the secular life from which they had fled and the secular studies which they had abandoned, they were not usually referring to a period when they had been laymen and never to a lay school, but simply to their life as clerks. Secular literature was, of course, the Latin classics as opposed to *sacra pagina*. A letter from an anonymous monk of Bec, written in the middle of the twelfth century to a certain Richard who was at school, displays the vocabulary very well.[10] Fifteen years, he writes, have now passed since he himself gave up secular studies (*studium saeculare*). He, being a monk, was a fugitive from the world (*de saeculo fugitivus*). Richard, being a clerk, was engaged in secular studies; and, although the monk was not trying to get Richard to assume the yoke of religion, he begged him after attending to the inventions of the poets (gram-

6. *Historia calamitatum*, in *PL* clxxviii. 114–15.

7. *Heremanni archidiaconi miracula S. Eadmundi* in Liebermann *Ungedruckte* 266.

8. Cf. Philippe Delhaye, 'L'organisation scolaire au XIIe siècle', *Traditio* v (1947) 211–3; Pierre Riche, 'Recherches sur l'instruction des laïcs du IXe au XIIe siècle', *Cahiers de civ. méd.* v (1962) 175. John of Salisbury, *Hist. Pont.* 9–10, discussed the practical effects of can. 13 of the Council of Rheims, 1148 (*Si quis suadente diabolo*), which reserved to the pope absolution of any one who laid violent hands on a clerk. He was of the opinion that it would not apply to a schoolmaster (*doctor in scolis*) who struck his pupil, nor to a pupil who struck another – for such actions were not done maliciously.

9. For example, A. J. Macdonald thought that Lanfranc, before entering the monastery at Bec, was a layman, F. Barlow, 'A view of Archbishop Lanfranc', *JEH* xvi (1965) 167. He was, as he told the abbot, a clerk and scholar. C. H. Talbot in his excellent book, *Medicine in Medieval England* (1967), has, however, some unfortunate remarks in this connexion, e.g. 'it is a gross error to imagine that education was limited to clerics' (pp. 52–3). There were, of course, exceptions. But most scholars were clerks. Cf. C. P. Wormald, 'The uses of literacy in Anglo-Saxon England and its neighbours', *TRHistS*, 5th ser. xxvii (1977) 95.

10. 'Les lettres familières d'un moine du Bec', ed. J. Leclercq, *Analecta Monastica* 2 = *Studia Anselmiana* xxxi (Rome 1953) 159–61.

mar), the eloquence of Cicero (rhetoric) and the disputes of logic (dialectic) to give some time to meditation on the psalms. For this monk of Bec and all other 'religious' the secular world was the world of clerks. Laymen were *laici illiterati*, the unlettered, *idiotae*, idiots. Lay schools did not exist. It was a contradiction in terms.

Although the identity between literate man and clerk was almost absolute, the position of educated women, since they were denied holy orders, was anomalous. Girls could easily obtain at least elementary education if their parents were willing. The daughters of priests must often have learned to read and write. Elviva, the daughter of Wulward the priest of Haveringland in the diocese of Norwich, seems to have given her son William, born in 1132–33 and 'martyred by the Jews' in 1144, some literary, or at least religious, education, before he was apprenticed at the age of eight to the Norwich skinners.[11] And by the twelfth century it was not unusual for girls to go to school. About 1120 Gilbert parson of Sempringham in south Lincolnshire, who had become a master in France, was teaching the local boys and girls in a sort of strict boarding school, and later organized seven girls into a monastic community attached to his church. One of the seven was the daughter of the village family with which Gilbert and his chaplain, Geoffrey, had lodged and who had so disturbed them with her ample charms that they had escaped from the temptation by withdrawing to a house they had built on the church's close or cemetery.[12] It is likely that the church did not encourage the taking of girl pupils. The schoolmaster was always exposed to moral danger.[13]

There was never any suggestion that educated women were clerks. But if a girl became a nun she acquired a special status in the church, equivalent to that of lay monks, a category which, until the introduction of lay brothers into some of the reformed monastic congregations, was becoming rare in the Benedictine houses. Helose, Abelard's pupil and wife, when abbess of Paraclete, usually described herself as 'deaconess', and both showed a lively interest in that almost obsolete office.[14] It is possible that sometimes lower educational standards were set for nuns than for monks and that French rather than Latin was considered the more suitable medium. But nuns were often enthusiastic Latin versifiers,[15] and there were some very learned ladies. If France had Helose, England had Eve and Nuriel.[16]

---

11. *Vita S. Willelmi Norwic.* 13–14.

12. *Vita S. Gileberti confessoris* in *Monasticon* vi. 2, p. vi*. Rose Graham, *S. Gilbert of Sempringham and the Gilbertines* (1901) inexplicably makes the girl Geoffrey's daughter.

13. Peter the Venerable, abbot of Cluny (1122–56), recounts the miracle of a monk in bed overhearing two devils disguised as men telling their adventures to a third disguised as a vulture. They boasted that they had gone through an (unidentified) monastery, where 'magistrum scholae cum uno puerorum fornicari fecimus', *Libri de miraculis*, I, xiv, *PL* clxxxix. 878.

14. They believed that the ancient equivalent of *abbatissa* was *diaconista*: Abelard in *PL* clxxviii. 238; cf. also 193, 239, 274.

15. For the breve roll of Matilda, abbess of Caen (who was not Henry I's sister), in 1113, the following English nunneries composed memorial verses: St Mary's Winchester, Amesbury, and Shaftesbury; for the breve roll of Vitalis, abbot of Savigny, in 1122, Wilton. These were the cream of the West-Saxon convents for women. Léopold Delisle, *Rouleaux des Morts du IXe au XVe siècle* (Soc. de l'histoire de France 1866), XXXVI, tituli 11, 13, 18; XXXVIII, tit. 153.

16. For Eve, Goscelin of St Bertin's muse, see C. H. Talbot, 'The *Liber confortatorius* of Goscelin of Saint Bertin', *Studia Anselmiana*, fasc. xxxvii = *Analecta Monastica*, 3rd ser. (Rome 1955) and

We should also notice the older students and their problems. To renounce the world and enter religion was a feature of the period. In the monasteries aged noblemen rubbed shoulders with old soldiers and retired merchants, in the nunneries were widows and abandoned wives, in the countryside hermits and recluses, and all had the same problem: to acquire enough elementary education to enable them to recite and understand the psalms.[17] Most of them found learning difficult, and it often needed a miracle to give them the knack.

Although the church was completely dependent on education, it made little official attempt in this period to devise a system, to establish a uniform network of schools, to control the schools which came into being (except in defending monopolies), to prescribe curricula, or to establish educational standards by means of examinations. Of the many legatine and provincial councils held in England between 1070 and 1151 (the statutes of diocesan synods have not survived) only one devoted a single enactment to schools and that is not very important.[18] The reasons for this neglect can be surmised. It was assumed that the responsibility for providing education lay with the diocesan bishop and that he would at least maintain a school in his cathedral city. It was also taken for granted that the number of scholars would be relatively small and that those wanting schooling would be willing to seek out a master.[19] The curriculum had been inherited from the classical world, and, although not entirely suited to an ecclesiastical purpose, was too sacrosanct to be subjected to effective criticism and reform.[20] Nor in the Norman period was it likely to be abused: the kingdom remained entirely orthodox. As for standards, the achievements were in general too modest to support any test more rigorous than the bishop's inquiry into the fitness of ordinands to undertake their duties.

Almost all schools were held in churches and conducted by an official or servant of that church. The itinerant master who lectured at the Petit Pont in Paris or who tried to set up an 'adulterine' school at Melun or in London was by no means unknown, especially in the twelfth century, but permanent schools were rarely founded in that way. The commonest elementary schoolmaster in England throughout this period, the man who taught boys and girls to read and write and the elements of Latin grammar, was the village or town priest. The schools held by religious communities were basically for their own members. The Benedictine monasteries usually provided for the education of

André Wilmart, 'Eve et Goscelin', *Revue Bénédictine* xlvi (1934) 414–38, 1 (1938) 42–83. For Muriel, see J. S. P. Tatlock, 'Muriel: the earliest English Poetess', *Publ. of the Mod. Lang. Assoc. of America* xlviii (1933) 317–21. Hildebert addressed a poem to her: *Carmina minora* (Teubner) no. 26. Both these ladies were at Wilton. When a party of canons of Laon visited the convent in 1113 they were shown the tomb of the *inclita versificatrix*, Muriel, which was next to that of the venerable Bede. She appeared in a dream to someone waiting to be cured at Bede's tomb and recommended the superior powers of the canons, Hermann, *De miraculis S. Mariae Laudunensis* in *PL* clvi. 983.

17.   Cf. the cases of Godric 'of Finchale' and Robert of St Martin, below 228 f., 238.

18.   Below 225 f.

19.   Robert Pullen, *Sententiarum libri octo* (c. 1142–44) vii. 22, *PL* clxxxvi. 935–6, included *discipuli* among the habitual travellers of the time.

20.   James A. Murphy, 'The arts of discourse, 1050–1400', *Mediaeval Studies*, xxiii (1961) 194; James A. Weisheipl, OP, 'Classification of the sciences in medieval thought', *ibid*. xxvii (1965) 54; Philippe Delhaye, 'L'enseignement de la philosophie morale au XIIe siècle', *ibid*. xi (1949) 77.

their child oblates and other novices in the cloister, and did not normally open their schoolroom to outsiders, although nunneries may have been less strict: Henry I, like Edgar before him, took a wife from Wilton abbey.[21] Similarly, the secular cathedrals and some of the great minsters held a song or music school for the choirboys and often a grammar school for the cathedral and city clergy, but these seem nearly always to have been open to some other scholars. Also, in the twelfth century, the priories of regular or Augustinian canons began to take over existing schools or establish new ones.

Although there is little specific evidence it seems likely on general grounds that most pupils were boarders.[22] The privileged, and occasionally the thruster, could get an advantageous place. A regular route to high ecclesiastical office in England was through the royal and episcopal households, sometimes through both. Ranulf Flambard, the son of a village priest in the diocese of Bayeux, rose to be Rufus's trusted and indispensable minister and bishop of Durham after an education started on the fringe of Odo of Bayeux's court and completed in the world of affairs.[23] From his household William of Corbeil went on to be archbishop of Canterbury.[24] Henry of Huntingdon, the son of an archdeacon in the bishopric of Lincoln, after attending the choir school was educated in the household of his bishop, Robert Bloet, formerly Rufus's chancellor, where, amid the splendour he later so graphically described, he had among his companions Richard, one of Henry I's bastards, who was drowned when the White Ship was wrecked in 1120, just two years before Robert's own sudden death in Woodstock park.[25] In that company Henry of Huntingdon learned some of the ways of the great world he was to chronicle and the lessons which caused him to write *De contemptu mundi*. Ranulf Flambard made his nephew, another Ranulf, archdeacon of Durham.[26] Many archdeacons were close kinsmen of their bishop and educated in his household; and in the twelfth century several archdeacons became bishops. These men were in effect educated by apprenticeship and received a professional training. This was the sycophantic world of patrons and clients, of connexions, of influence. It also enabled talented men of ambition to go far: Thomas Becket grasped one hand after another and learned some valuable trades. On the whole, this type of education was thought to produce the most useful bishops – men who knew the ways of both worlds, who were good administrators, had friends in the right places, and were likely to profit their see, the church, and the kingdom. Such a man was unlikely to be a great scholar or theologian, but he could be the patron of learning and was often a magnificent builder; and there was no reason why he should not be pious. Indeed, promotion to a bishopric after a career in administration was the heaven-sent opportunity for repentance. Thomas Becket also seized this chance, although belatedly. The children of kings and

21. Above 169 f.
22. Apprentices usually lived in the home of their master. Gilbert of Sempringham (above 219), Robert of Béthune (below 229), and Samson of Bury (below 222) took boarders, and Thomas Becket was boarded at Merton (below 232, n. 7).
23. OV (Chibnall) iv. 170–3.
24. Simeon, 'De mirac. et translat. S. Cuthberti', *HDE* 258; *HR* 269.
25. HH 299, 301, 304.
26. John of Hexham 312.

nobles usually had a private tutor, sometimes a well known master.[27] Boys could also be entrusted to a clerk when he went to a more advanced school for his own education, and in such schools were always to be found mature students willing to take private pupils.[28]

Although there were not equal opportunities for all, the church encouraged the able and rewarded the determined. Scholars had to be of free birth or licensed by their lord,[29] and, unless they came under some charitable provision, had to be able to pay for their maintenance and sometimes for tuition. At the external school maintained by the monastery of Bury St Edmunds scholars paid for lodgings in the later twelfth century a halfpenny or a penny twice a year, before Abbot Samson bought some stone houses for their accommodation. Samson recalled that when he was a boy towards the end of Stephen's reign a clerk needed five or six marks (£3–£4) a year to keep him at school (probably at Paris).[30] After that, in theory, all doors in the church were open to these masters. Hildebert of Lavardin, born of unfree parents near Le Mans about 1056, climbed to be schoolmaster, archdeacon, and bishop of that cathedral church and finally archbishop of Tours. He was the greatest poet of his time.[31] John of Salisbury and Nicholas Breakspear, neither of noble birth, rose the one to be bishop of Chartres and the other Pope Adrian IV. Samson, who became abbot of Bury, benefited from a free place at the abbey's school, and then was maintained at Paris by a clerk from the profits made from providing holy water.[32]

The Normans, who were a relatively indigent but very ambitious people, were well aware that not only the profession of arms but also education offered opportunities for advancement. A famous story told by Orderic Vitalis

---

27.   Henry I is said to have learned the rudiments of letters, *GR* 467, OV (Chibnall) iv. 120, vi. 50, and his sons and grandsons were literate. The future Henry II was tutored by Master Matthew and Adelard of Bath at Bristol and by William of Conches in Normandy. Gervase, i. 125; Charles H. Haskins, 'Adelard of Bath and Henry Plantagenet', *EHR* xxviii (1913) 515–16; *idem*, 'Normandy under Geoffrey Plantagenet', *EHR* xxvii (1912) 423, n. 28; J. de Ghellinck, *L'essor de la littérature latine au XIIe siècle* (Paris 1946) 65–7. Perhaps the most remarkable illustration of the spread of education among the nobility is the dialectical disputation which Henry I arranged when he met Pope Calixtus in 1119. He set up against the cardinals the young twin sons of Robert of Beaumont, count of Meulan and earl of Leicester, Waleran and Robert, whose subtlety of reasoning and liveliness of mind were irresistible. The cardinals were amazed at this evidence of culture in the West, *GR* 482. The boys, members of the highest nobility, were being educated in the king's household and their sister, Elizabeth, was his mistress. Cf. also Pierre Riche, 'Recherches sur l'instruction des laïcs du IXe au XIIe siècle', *Cahiers de Civ. Méd.* v (1962) 175.

28.   For tutors taking boys to advanced schools, see below 249 (William of Corbeil at Laon) and 266 (Baldwin at Ferentino) – both future archbishops of Canterbury. For a clerk keeping himself at school by teaching, see below 252 (John of Salisbury).

29.   'Filii rusticorum non debent ordinari abque assensu domini de cujus terra nati dignoscuntur', Constitutions of Clarendon (1164), cap. 16. Gilbert of Sempringham is said to have accepted as lay brethren, 'quosdam a dominis suis transfugas, quos nomen religionis emancipavit', *Monasticon* vi. 2, p. x*.

30.   *The chronicle of Joscelin of Brakelond* 45; 36.

31.   The standard biographies are, A. Dieudonné, *Hildebert de Lavardin* (Paris 1898) and F. X. Barth, *Hildebert von Lavardin* (Stuttgart 1906). For his poems, *PL* clxxi. and *Carmina minora*, ed. A. B. Scott (Teubner). For some aspects of his career, see Wolfram von den Steinen, 'Les sujets d'inspiration chez les poètes latins du XIIe siècle', *Cahiers de Civ. Méd.* ix (1966) 168.

32.   *The chronicle of Joscelin of Brakelond* 36–45.

incidentally makes this point.[33] On 1 January 1091 Walchelin, the priest of Bonneval in the diocese of Lisieux, when returning home at night from visiting a sick parishioner, met 'Hellequin's hunt', a great company of the dead who were suffering from the torments of purgatory or hell. The last rider in this ghastly rabble was Walchelin's brother, Robert, whom the priest at first refused to recognize. But Robert, a knight, plied him with proofs, and among other things said, 'I brought you up after both our parents died and loved you more dearly than any other human being. I sent you to school in France, kept you well provided with clothes and money, and advanced your career in many other ways.' Robert had then gone to England in some military capacity. After his death, Walchelin also had crossed the Channel and had been ordained priest in the kingdom, but, for reasons unstated, he had returned to Normandy and died as priest of Bonneval about 1106. An ambitious Norman clerk could look for the best schooling in France and for the best advancement in England. But, as can be seen from Walchelin's case, there were not plums for every visitor to England; and, obviously, not all clerks could go to school in France.

   A school was a kind of property, but what kind in this period is far from clear. What is abundantly plain is that the right to hold a school can be compared, on the secular side, with the right to hold a market or fair or any other liberty, and, on the ecclesiastical side, with the right to have a baptismal font or a cemetery. There were people, principally kings, earls, and bishops, who granted the right to hold a school. What they granted included a monopoly of teaching rights within a specified or understood area. And the monopoly would be protected by both ecclesiastical and royal power. The simplest explanation is that the 'owner' of the parish church, which usually in the beginning meant the owner of the manor, considered that a school was part of his property. Just as he could, with reservations, dispose of his church or its tithes, and found new chapels on his estates, so he could grant a school, or the right to hold a school, to any church. In other words, he possessed the sort of right which the church was beginning to define as a right of patronage, and this was an area of complete cooperation between laity and clergy.[34] The lay point of view was expressed by Henry I and the earl of Warwick when they disposed of their schools at Dunstable and Warwick respectively.[35] Henry claimed that he was conveying some of the 'liberties and free customs pertaining to the vill'. And when about 1123 he became involved in the earl's scheme, he confirmed to All Saints, Warwick, all its ancient customs, including the ordeals of iron and water, which it had possessed since the time of King Edward, and its school. The schools in question were no doubt 'alms', not lay fee; all the same, they were property in the gift of lay magnates.

33. OV (Chibnall) iv. 236.
34. Cf. Paré, Brunet, Tremblay 64 ff.; Orme 142 ff.
35. Inspeximus of Henry II of Henry I's charter [1131x5], *Monasticon* vi. 240a. Earl Roger's charter, *ibid*. 1326, no. 3. Henry I's confirmation of this, issued before the death of Theulf, bishop of Worcester (20 October 1123), *ibid*. 1327, no. 7. Henry's precept does not imply, as is stated *VCH Warwicks* ii. 299, that the school as well as the ordeals was possessed by the church T.R.E. Indeed, it is sharply distinguished from the ancient customs. It is not clear whether the king was aiding or impeding the earl's reorganization; but that is immaterial. See also below 232.

On the other hand, when Archbishop Lanfranc granted the Canterbury school to St Gregory's, although his action can be construed in the same way, it also has a strong ecclesiastical colouring. It could be argued that the archbishop regarded a school as an ecclesiastical benefice which could, like a church, be impropriated or burdened with a pension. When he endowed St Gregory's he gave it a portfolio of lucrative and useful rights so that the clerks would be able to perform their duties. He impropriated churches for its profit, granted tithe, the right of baptism and the explicitly unprofitable right of burial, gave the duty of ministering to the souls of the paupers cared for in the adjacent hospital, and put the local school under the control of St Gregory's servants.[36] It is not clear in the case of the school whether Lanfranc was conveying a duty, as with the hospital, or a lucrative right, as with the impropriated churches.[37] But that is unimportant: they were probably all to him, *spiritualia*. Moreover, schoolmasters, as clerks, were subject to ecclesiastical discipline and the church legislated about schools.

Since the church did not assert as a principle its exclusive right to the ownership, disposal, or control of schools, and laymen regarded the church's educational function as natural and welcome, the general position was entirely harmonious. Both powers accepted that a school was a property which, like a parish church or a market or fair, had to be protected against undue competition. Herbert Losinga, probably after he had transferred his see from Thetford to Norwich (*c.* 1091–1119), confirmed to Bund dean of Thetford his school there, and prohibited any other to be opened in the town without the dean's permission.[38] Between 1110 and 1123 Robert Bloet bishop of Lincoln sent a mandate to Henry archdeacon of Huntingdon and his deans, ordering them on the bishop's authority to impose silence on those who presumed to hold 'adulterine' schools to the detriment of the school of Huntingdon and without the licence of the (Austin) canons of Huntingdon, contrary to a papal privilege and the bishop's confirmation. The punishment for contempt of the order was to be suspension of the church in whose parish an illicit school was being held. One of the offenders, it seems, was archdeacon Henry himself, the historian, for he restored to the canons the song-school of Huntingdon, 'which was known to belong to them'.[39] In Stephen's reign Henry of Blois, administering the

36.   Böhmer, *Die Fälschungen* 174; *Cartulary of the priory of St Gregory, Canterbury,* ed. Audrey M. Woodcock (*now* Erskine), Camden 3rd ser. lxxxviii (1956) 1–3. 'Sed et intra septa sepedicte ecclesie scolas urbis et viculorum eius tam grammatice quam musice regi debere statuentes, earum regimen prepositis sacerdotum ipsius ecclesie et eorum dispositioni commisimus.' The meaning is not entirely clear. Who were the canons' provosts/reeves and what were they to do? As five knights, whose tithes were granted to the church, witness the document, it seems likely that the two witnessing masters are the schoolmasters, since their position, too, had been changed and their assent required. Margaret Gibson, *Lanfranc of Bec* 187, believes that Lanfranc assigned to St Gregory's much of the pastoral work of the cathedral.

37.   As he had been a wandering scholar, and the schoolmaster at Avranches, and had opened an external school at Bec in order to raise money for the poverty-stricken monastery, he knew everything about the profitability of schools.

38.   *Ep.* 37, correcting *promiserit* to *permiserit.* It is not known what sort of a dean Bund was; but the confirmation may have been connected with the conversion of St Mary's, Thetford, the former cathedral, into a Cluniac priory.

39.   Mary Bateson, 'The Huntingdon Song School and the School of St Gregory's Canterbury', *EHR* xviii (1903) 712–13, where she prints documents from the register of the priory, British

vacant bishopric of London, but before he became papal legate, 1138–39, ordered the chapter of St Paul's and Archdeacon William to excommunicate those who presumed to teach without the licence of Henry, master of the schools in the whole city of London.[40] At about the same time Roger bishop of Salisbury, in a writ addressed to the archdeacon of Berkshire, ordered that no one should conduct a school at Reading without the consent and goodwill of the abbot and convent.[41] At the beginning of Henry II's reign the famous Jordan Fantosme and John Joichel, both clerks of Henry bishop of Winchester who was then in exile at Cluny, disputed the mastership of the school in Winchester. The case went first before a (presumably diocesan) synod, then before the primate and papal legate, Archbishop Theobald, and finally on appeal to the pope.[42] It will be noticed that all these are ecclesiastical prohibitions and actions. It seems that a church which conducted a school normally looked in the first place to the diocesan bishop to protect its rights. But as the ultimate penalty was excommunication, the king would have come to its aid if the offender was contumacious.

The owner of a school, who was not usually the master, enjoyed a lucrative monopoly, a piece of property capable of being exploited in many ways. As there seems to have been no serious suggestion that the schoolmaster held a spiritual office, so that the laws against simony would apply,[43] or that he enjoyed a freehold, with all the protection afforded to that tenure, the owner probably could, in theory at least, have sold the appointment, leased the school, burdened it with a rent charge, mortgaged it, divided it up, and possibly sublet it in whole or in part. In cities such as Winchester there was a highly sophisticated property market by the twelfth century.[44] The one enactment which can be construed as a restriction on the exploitation of schools was decreed by the legatine council of Westminster, December 1138. The last of sixteen or seventeen canons has been transmitted in two discordant versions.[45] According to

Museum, Cotton MS Faust. C. 1, fo. 17a. A misleading translation is in William M. Noble, 'The cartulary of the priory of St Mary, Huntingdon', *Trans. of the Cambridge and Huntingdon Arch. Soc.* iv. 258–9.

40. *Early Charters of the Cathedral Church of St Paul, London*, ed. Marion Gibbs, R. Hist. Soc, Camden 3rd ser. lviii (1939) nos. 273–5. Henry of Blois was given by the pope control of the bishopric in 1138, Diceto, *Abbrev. chronic.* 252, and was not yet legate (1139) when he issued no. 275. The schoolmaster Henry may be the canon Henry of London who *c.* 1154 claimed the archdeaconry of Colchester from Bishop Richard of Beaumais II: John of Salisbury *Letters*, no. 5; *PL* cxcix no. 35, col. 22.

41. Edward J. Kealey, *Roger of Salisbury*, charter 22, p. 258.

42. John of Salisbury *Ep.* 56 (ed. Millor, Butler, and Brooke).

43. Gaines Post, 'Alexander III, the "Licentia docendi", and the rise of the universities', *Anniversary essays in medieval history by students of Charles Homer Haskins* (Boston, New York, 1929) 255–78, makes much of 'scholastic simony'. But he was mistaken, and his texts do not bear him out. In fact there is not a single reference to simony in the quoted texts. Cf. also Gaines Post, Kimon Giocarinis, and Richard Kay, 'The medieval heritage of a humanistic ideal: "Scientia donum dei est, unde vendi non potest" ', *Traditio* xi (1955) 195.

44. Frank Barlow in Barlow, Martin Biddle, Olof von Feilitzen, and D. J. Keene, *Winchester in the Early Middle Ages* (1976) 8.

45. Richard of Hexham 176: 'Sancimus praeterea, ut si magistri scholarum aliis scolas suas pro precio legendas [*sic*] locaverint, ecclesiasticae vindictae subiaceant.' Gervase i. 109: 'Magistri scolarum si aliis scolas regendas commiserint, prohibemus ne propter hoc quicquam ab eis exigant, quod si fecerint, ecclesiasticae vindictae subiaceant.'

Gervase of Canterbury, schoolmasters (*magistri scolarum*) who appointed others to rule their schools were not to take any payment from them in return; according to Richard of Hexham, they were not to hire out their schools to anyone for money. Both add that the guilty were to be subject to an ecclesiastical penalty. The Canterbury version (especially when construed in the light of canons 1, 3, and 4, which prohibit demanding any, or undue, fees for performing an ecclesiastical service) seems to envisage a single payment, the Hexham version a rent. Perhaps both actions were prohibited or discussed. They differ little in principle.

The enactment can be understood rather differently if it is considered in the light of a decree of the Third Lateran Council of 1179 (can. 18). This council, on the eve of the establishment of the first university, ordered that there should be no charge for the granting of the *licentia docendi* and no impost of any kind on teachers, and that the licence should not be refused to any suitable candidate. The subject of the ordinance is what we would call a Master's degree, the licence to teach. This is not to be sold. But the church distinguished between, on the one hand, exploitive and monopolistic exactions and, on the other, fees which paid the issuing official's expenses, for Peter Comestor, when he was chancellor of Notre Dame, Paris, was allowed by Pope Alexander III to take a reasonable fee for granting these licences.[46] If, therefore, as seems likely, the English decree of 1138, when regulating the conduct of *magistri scholarum* was referring to those cathedral dignitaries who had become too grand to teach and were about to turn themselves into 'chancellors',[47] it was concerned less with the exploitation of territorial monopolies than with financial abuses associated with the licensing of teachers.

The limitation of the right to teach to masters licensed by the church created a different kind of lucrative monopoly. In its attitude towards education the church was neither expansionist nor restrictive, simply cautious. The dominant feature of the educational scene was the competition of a restricted number of masters for a small number of pupils. The church was responsible for the instruction of the people and concerned that there should be no false teaching. It was, therefore, basically the bishop's responsibility (personally, or through officials) to license teachers, and there seems to have been a standing prohibition in the dioceses to teach without a valid *licentia docendi*.[48] What we do not know in this period is exactly how a man became a master, what curriculum he had to follow, what schools were qualified to prepare him, what examination was prescribed, who in fact issued the licence, and whether the licence was a standard written form. Our ignorance may be due to the informality of the whole process before the creation of universities. We must

---

46. 'Pro licentia vero docendi nullus pretium exigat vel sub obtentu alicujus consuetudinis ab eis qui docent aliquid quaerat, nec docere quempiam, petita licentia, qui sit idoneus interdicat. (Who does so is to be removed from his benefice.) Dignum quidem esse videtur ut in ecclesia dei fructum laboris sui non habeat qui cupiditate animi vendit licentiam docendi.' For Peter Comestor, see Gaines Post (as n. 43).

47. See below 234.

48. 'No one is to teach the people, for a fee or otherwise, unless licensed by the bishop', Anglo-Norman decrees (? late eleventh century), Mansi xx. 400, cap. 1. See above 127. Böhmer *KuS* 62, n. 2, attempts to date the enactment.

suppose that parish priests had a general licence to teach, at least at an elementary level, and were under the supervision of the rural deans and archdeacons. It is reasonable to think that any school would, for a fee, issue a certificate to a satisfactory student. And it is likely that the appointment to the mastership of a cathedral school and the issue of the licences to its pupils were the responsibility of the cathedral *magister scholarum*. It may even be that this dignitary had, under the bishop, responsibility for all schools in the diocese.

It should be noticed that possession of a *licentia docendi* was, in the twelfth century just as today, only a qualifying degree, and that a Master who wanted to teach had to seek employment. If successful, he became a regent master, one who ruled a school. It does not seem that there were usually assistant masters. A man took on if possible as many pupils as he could teach. It is also to be remarked that although the church authorities asserted that education, like all other aspects of religion, should be imparted gratis, and were fond of quoting in this context, 'freely ye have received, freely give' (Matt. 10: 8), in an imperfect world they were prepared to allow the taking of fees for all educational services, whether for teaching or for granting the *licentia docendi*. They intervened only to prevent undue restrictive or onerous practices on the part of the monopolists. The principle was general. The barons who forced King John to declare that he would not sell right or justice (*Magna Carta*, cap. 40) were not thinking to prevent his chancellor from charging a reasonable fee for the necessary writs.

Although masters differed greatly in their ability and training, it would not have been easy then, and it is even more difficult now, to classify the various schools according to scholastic standards. References to schools in the sources are few and casual, and rarely indicate the subjects taught, the level of instruction, or the size of the undertaking. The word *schola* (more usually in the plural *scholae*) often occurs without qualification.[49] The genus is obviously more important than the species, and the reader is supposed to be able to supply from his own experience the sort of school implied. The lack of precision is also fair warning that there were not at the time precise categories of institutions. Schoolmasters were not specialists. Even in the twelfth century the most famous masters were usually distinguished in several of the arts subjects.[50] And a schoolmaster also taught all forms, from the lowest to the highest. Obviously some masters did not presume to teach the more advanced subjects, and by the twelfth century there were masters who did no elementary work. By the later Middle Ages it is possible to distinguish between song-schools (usually considered elementary), grammar schools, and universities, as well as other more specialized schools – for example, of theology, of business studies – mostly of higher education. According to dictionaries, the earliest references to most of these occur in the course of the twelfth century, and the categories have little application to the Norman period.

---

49.   For a discussion of the scholastic terminology, see Paré, Brunet, Tremblay, 57 ff.

50.   Richard Hunt, 'Studies on Priscian in the eleventh and twelfth centuries', *MARS* i (1943) 223. When Hildebert of Le Mans recommended Guy of Etampes to Roger bishop of Salisbury early in the twelfth century, he claimed, 'Unus ille tibi pro multis erit, quoniam in illo uno multos magistros invenies.' Hildebert, *ep*. 12, *PL* clxxi. 219.

The first rung in the educational ladder was the reading school. Sometimes children may have learned their alphabet in a more important or advanced school, but there is good evidence that the most usual elementary teacher was the village priest.[51] As he was generally married, he had his own children to educate, and he took in paying pupils. In Rufus's reign, when the priest of Bury, an Englishman, Goding, was called to the deathbed of one of his parishioners, Wulfmaer, he hurried up accompanied, naturally enough, by his schoolchildren.[52] And towards the end of Henry I's reign the compiler of a law book included for the first time scholars among the clergy who, with their possessions, should enjoy the peace of God and of the church.[53] Early medieval authors, however, tell us little about their schooling, especially the first steps. It was probably a painful experience.[54] A valuable exception is the historian, Orderic Vitalis, who, writing in the second quarter of the twelfth century in the Norman monastery of St Evroul, relates that he was the son of an English mother and an immigrant priest, Odelerius of Orleans, to whom Earl Roger of Montgomery gave the church of St Peter, Shrewsbury. Born on 16 February 1075, baptized on 4 April at Atcham by the priest Orderic, he was entrusted five years later by his father to 'the noble priest', Siward, another of St Peter's clergy. For five years Orderic studied the first rudiments of letters under this master, and then, in 1085, he was given by his father as an oblate to St Evroul.[55] William of Malmesbury, at least ten years younger than Orderic, was like him of mixed parentage and also, perhaps, the son of a priest. He tells us that it was from his parents that he derived his great love of books, and, although his language is studiously vague, he gives the impression that he was taught letters by his father.[56] John of Salisbury in the early 1120s was sent as a child to a priest to learn the psalms, and he remembered some thirty years later, when writing about methods of divination in his *Policraticus*, a disturbing episode. In the presence of him and a slightly older boy the priest practised the sort of magic which operates through using a mirror in order to conjure up the dead. Although his companion thought he saw something or other mysterious, John saw nothing, and because of his scepticism was barred from later sessions.[57] But as he became one of the greatest Latin stylists of an age which cultivated style, he must have profited in other ways from the lessons of this dubious priest.

It is possible that both Siward and the Salisbury priest conducted schools, and similar establishments in the diocese of Durham are mentioned by Reginald of Durham in his hagiographical works. About 1110 Godric, having finished his pilgrimages and preparing to become a hermit, came to the epis-

---

51. In the Carolingian period parish priests or their clerks were to conduct a school: Theodulf, *Capitula ad presbyteros parochiae suae*, i. 19–20, *PL* cv. 196; *Ansegisi capitularium*, i. 68, *MGH Leges* i. 280; Hincmar of Rheims, *Capitula presbyteris data*, cap. 11, *PL* cxxv. 779. Theodulf's Capitularies were well known in England: Barlow, *English Church 1000—1066*, 285 and n. 3.

52. *Heremanni archidiaconi miracula S. Eadmundi* in Liebermann *Ungedruckte* 270.

53. *Leges Edwardi Confessoris* (1, 1), in Liebermann *Gesetze* i. 629.

54. For Anselm's abhorrence of excessive flogging in school, *VA* 37.

55. OV (Chibnall) iii. 6–8, 146, where Siward is called *liberalis didasculus;* vi. 552.

56. *GR* 103.

57. *PL* cxcix. 474; ed. Webb i. 164. As there was only one church at Old Sarum, the priest (canon) may have been the cathedral *scholasticus* or his deputy.

copal see. First he served as doorkeeper in the church of St Giles outside the walls, and then he migrated to the church of St Mary within the city so that he could attend the classes of boys learning their letters. He had been given a psalter at Carlisle, and at Durham he acquired a sufficient knowledge of the psalms, hymns, and prayers to serve his purpose when he established his hermitage at Finchale.[58] There was also the school conducted by the priest in his church at Norham, mentioned by Reginald in his *Miracles of St Cuthbert*. It was to get a holiday that a naughty schoolboy threw the key of the locked church into the River Tweed, a scheme frustrated by St Cuthbert who revealed that the key had been swallowed by a salmon which would be caught the following day. The reading school at Yarm on Tees, at the other extremity of the diocese, was conducted by a man who is not described as the village priest although he was a friend of the sacristan of Durham and had a brother who was a drinking companion of the priest of Kelloe. He was in any case a very sensible man, who dealt quickly and successfully with his brother's possession by the devil in the shape of a black dog.[59] *Delirium tremens*, of course, may have been a not uncommon event.

In the life of Robert of Béthune bishop of Hereford we are given a picture of the good elementary schoolmaster.[60] Robert, the youngest son of a knightly family, was educated by his eldest brother, a married man with children, towards the end of the eleventh century, but whether at Béthune or in England is not clear; he became a schoolmaster in turn, and is given by his biographer an excellent testimonial. He avoided all arrogance, ostentation, and desire for financial gain. He took nothing from the poor, accepted only freewill offerings from the rich, and, keeping little for himself, used his income for the common good. His dress and furnishings were modest and adequate. Although in the classroom he was the master, he was also the friend and companion of the boys. If on a holiday the children went out on a treat, he went with them to look after them and see that they did not play silly or unsuitable games (he may have remembered that St Wulfstan almost lost his chastity while playing hide and seek with the village boys and girls).[61] But Robert of Béthune's exemplary behaviour, his biographer remarks ominously, was a sign that he was destined to abandon the world for the monastic life.

By 1154 the existence of elementary education was taken for granted. That is to say there was basic education available for everyone who wanted and could afford it; and the clever poor would often be educated free. In the eleventh and twelfth centuries there was only one grade above this, but as with the elementary stage, of unequal standard. This education was provided

---

58.   Reginald of Durham, *St Godric* 59–60; 41. The church was either St Mary's the Great, alias St Mary le Bow, in the North Bailey, under the patronage of the archdeacon of Northumberland, or, less likely, St Mary in South Bailey, which had a lay patron. There is a further reference, 366, to the scholars *litteralibus studiis*, quarrelling over who was the better saint, Godric or Thomas of Canterbury (after 1070, ? after 1073); but the site of the school is not stated. Shortly before 1154 a priest of Norwich paid a man 3d. for a psalter which had in fact been written by the monk Thomas of Monmouth for his own use and 'lost': *Vita S. Willelmi Norwic.* 201–2.

59.   Reginald of Durham, *St Cuthbert* 34; 149.

60.   *Anglia Sacra* ii. 299–300.

61.   *Vita Wulfstani* 6–7.

by the larger churches: on the one hand, the Benedictine monasteries, and, on the other, the collegiate churches, especially the cathedral minsters. In the twelfth century the Augustinian priories also entered the field. All these churches were primarily catering for their own societies and most of them provided elementary as well as more advanced instruction.

The schools with the longest histories in England, but with little future in the old form, were those in the monastic sees and greater monasteries. In the mid sixth century Cassiodorus produced an educational programme for his monastery at *Vivarium* which established the pattern for the Middle Ages.[62] His monks were to acquire both divine and secular knowledge, and he divided his *Institutiones* into two books. Under the first heading he included not only the Bible, the great councils, and the Fathers, but also gardening, fishing, and the care of pilgrims and the poor. Medicine was to be practised as part of their ministry. They must grow herbs and know how to make drugs. They must read all the medical books he had placed in the library. In the second book he looked at each of the seven liberal arts and gave a reading-list for each. Rhetoric, of course, was still concerned largely with the courts and legal pleading. This balanced programme was for the education of the monks, for the *schola Christi*, but in the Carolingian period and thereafter many monasteries held also *scholae externae* for outside pupils, although in practice these may not always have been completely separate from the others. In the mid eleventh century Lanfranc had shown at Bec what even a poor and obscure house could do if it had a famous teacher.[63]

Already, however, opposition was growing to the pedagogic activities of monks. Available to the critics were some useful canonical texts derived from the period when monks were usually not even clerks. By the twelfth century a monk who taught publicly attracted criticism, as Peter Abelard was to discover. Accordingly those monasteries which maintained external schools began to employ clerks as masters. At the same time a growing dislike within the monastic order itself of the custom of parents offering their infant children to be brought up as monks led to the atrophy of the internal schools. In England after the Conquest the external schools conducted by Benedictine monasteries seem generally to have been ruled by a clerk, and there is evidence that even within the cloister clerks were sometimes employed. We do not know the name or status of the masters at Winchester[64] and Bath in 1113, when both schools provided verses in memory of Abbess Matilda,[65] but at Norwich, where Bishop Herbert Losinga's favourite pupil made a contribution, Herbert had appointed a Breton, who does not seem to have been a monk,

62. *Cassiodori Senatoris Institutiones*, ed. R. A. B. Mynors (1937).

63. Gilbert Crispin, *Vita domni Herluini abbatis Beccensis*, in J. Armitage Robinson, *Gilbert Crispin abbot of Westminster* (Notes and docs. relating to Westminster abbey, no. 3, 1911) 95–7.

64. A master, Osbert, perhaps of Inglesham, who may later have become a canon of Salisbury, had three properties in Winchester in 1138, *Winchester in the Early Middle Ages,* survey II, nos 715, 728, 941. For Master John Joichel and Jordan Fantosme, the historian, who were rival masters in the 1150s, see *The Early Letters of John of Salisbury* 95–6, and Winchester, survey II, no. 864 n.

65. Delisle, *Rouleaux des morts,* XXXVI, tituli 17 (Titulus Gui[n]toniensis scholae), 28 (Vox scolarium ejusdem urbis [Bath]), 40 (Norwich: Versus Othonis juvenis). In the roll of Vitalis of Savigny (1122) neither school appears and Norwich (97) offers no verse.

as his schoolmaster.[66] Even at Christ Church, Canterbury, in 1104 the grammar master in charge of Archbishop Anselm's nephew and namesake and some other monks was one 'who had recently joined himself to them'.[67] At St Albans early in the twelfth century Abbot Richard sent to Le Mans for Geoffrey de Gorron to come and rule his school, but he got tired of waiting, appointed someone else and when Geoffrey eventually arrived could only promise him the succession. Geoffrey went off to be schoolmaster at Dunstable, where there was an Austin priory. There he put on a miracle play of St Catharine, and the choristers' copes he had borrowed from the sacristan of St Albans for costumes were unfortunately destroyed, together with his books, when his house caught fire. In order to repay the monastery, Geoffrey became a monk, and in 1119 was elected abbot. He was commemorated at St Albans more as a great benefactor than as a scholar, and is now best known for his patronage of Christina of Markyate.[68] In Henry I's reign Abingdon abbey maintained an external school under a master, Richard,[69] and in Stephen's reign Bury St Edmunds had one under the master William of Diss, where, as we have already noticed, Samson was educated.[70]

Far more active in the general field of education were the various secular collegiate churches. It was expected of a college of clerks that it would provide, either through its own members or by the appointment of a school-master, some teaching for those wishing to take holy orders. It cannot be said how widely the expectation was satisfied. Although the capital requirements for a school at this level were small – a room (often part of the church), some forms, a few textbooks, and a birch – good and well qualified teachers in the arts were hard to come by in the eleventh century and had often to be recruited from the countries beyond Normandy. And when there was a scarcity, the less distinguished churches were at a disadvantage. St Oswald's, Gloucester, an old foundation, which had belonged to Archbishop Stigand and was then granted by the king to Thomas I of York, was endowed by Bishop Samson of Worcester (1092–1112), Thomas's brother, with 'the school(s) of the whole of Glouces-ter'. Possibly because St Oswald's ranked as a royal free chapel, Henry I confirmed the monopoly.[71] In the time of Bishop Hervey of Ely (1109–31) St Ætheldreda cured Ralf, the schoolmaster of Dunwich (Suffolk), a former

---

66. Below 241.

67. *AEp* 328 *ad. fin.*; cf. 290.

68. *Gesta Abbatum monasterii S. Albani*, ed. H. T. Riley (Rolls ser.) i. 72–3. 'quemdam ludum de sancta Katerina, quem Miracula vulgariter appellamus, fecit.' For this proud and authoritarian abbot and his relations with Christina, see *The life of Christina of Markyate*, ed. C. H. Talbot (1959) 134 ff. For miracle plays in London, see William fitzStephen, *MB*, iii. 9.

69. For Richard, in the time of Abbot Faricius, see *Chron. Abingdon* ii. 123. A. E. Preston, *The Church and Parish of St Nicholas, Abingdon,* Oxford Hist. Soc. xcix (1935), 274 ff. held that the school was attached to the parish church and that the rectors were its masters. But the evidence for this seems to be non-existent.

70. *The chronicle of Joscelin of Brakelond*, ed. and trans. H. E. Butler, 43, 138.

71. *Regesta*, ii. no. 1936 [1106–35]. The text, however, of this charter (in a fourteenth-century copy) is unreliable because of the late twelfth-century conflict between St Oswald's and Llanthony over the scolastic monopoly. For the minister, see Barlow, *English Church 1000–1066*, 75 n., J. H. Denton, *English Royal Free Chapels 1100–1300* (1970), 51–7. It was reforrmed by Archbishop Henry Murdac in 1152–53.

episcopal see, of quinzy, perhaps an occupational hazard. Ralf, a married clerk in the manner of Tobias and Sara, wrote a most pretentious Latin letter of thanks and described himself as 'monitor of the school', an early use of that title.[72]

Especially prominent were the reformed collegiate churches, those under one of the canonical Rules. The way was pointed early in the period. Archbishop Lanfranc, possibly in connexion with a policy of purifying his monastic chapter, concentrated all schooling, both grammar and music, within the precincts of the collegiate church of St Gregory he had founded outside North Gate, and put the school or schools under the control of the canons' provosts or reeves. Among the witnesses to Lanfranc's confirmation of his grant are Master Ebroin and Master Leofwine, clerks, probably the two schoolmasters, from their names a Lombard and an Englishman.[73] There was a school attached to Beverley minster in Henry I's reign.[74] The Austin canons of Huntingdon held a song-school before 1123.[75] At Warwick, where Roger the second earl founded an Austin priory about 1123, he granted a school which belonged to one of the churches to St Mary's as an act of piety, 'so that the service of God in that church might be improved by the concourse of scholars'. Henry I granted the Austin priory he had founded at Dunstable the manor, and with it the town's market and school.[76]

Merton priory, Surrey, founded in 1114, was one of the most influential houses of canons regular. It established daughter houses at Taunton, Bodmin, Canterbury, Christchurch in Hampshire (Twynham), Cirencester, and perhaps Dover. It also conducted a school of excellent repute where in the late 1120s Thomas Becket and possibly Nicholas Breakspear, the future pope, received some instruction.[77] Among the first canons of Merton and its first prior was Guy, an Italian who, according to his Life written between 1132 and 1151,[78] was already a famous schoolmaster. When William Giffard, bishop of Winchester, wanted to turn Taunton into a house of canons regular, he borrowed Guy for the purpose. But Guy showed indiscreet apostolic zeal there, was recalled, and about 1120 was sent to Bodmin, presumably at the request of William Warelwast bishop of Exeter, to found, with the help of Master Algar

---

72. *Liber Eliensis* 270–4. Dunwich, queried by the editor, is surely correct, because Ralf travelled to Ely via Kentford.

73. See above 224, n. 36.

74. See below 223 f.

75. See above 224.

76. For Warwick and Dunstable, see above 223.

77. William fitzStephen, *MB*, iii. 14, writes that Thomas was given to Prior Robert *nutriendum* and that he passed his childhood and boyhood in the city schools before going as a young man (*adolescens*) to Paris. The writer could have made the position clearer. For this passage in fitzStephen's work, see Mary Cheney, 'William FitzStephen and his life of Archbishop Thomas', in *Church and Government in the Middle Ages: Essays presented to C. R. Cheney*, ed. C. N. L. Brooke, D. E. Luscombe, G. H. Martin, and Dorothy Owen (1976) 151. For Nicholas, see R. L. Poole, 'The early lives of Robert Pullen and Nicholas Breakspear', *Essays in Medieval History presented to Thomas Frederick Tout* (1925) 66.

78. Guy's Life, in a letter from Rainald to his (perhaps carnal) son, Ralf, is printed from British Museum Royal MS 8 E ix ff. 91–8 by Martin L. Colker, 'The Life of Guy of Merton by Rainald of Merton', *Medieval Studies* xxxi (1969) 250 ff.

the *procurator*, a reformed priory. Algar, a future bishop of Coutances, was a pupil of the great Master Anselm of Laon. Guy died, from a riding accident, within a few months of his arrival at Bodmin. The career of this Italian schoolmaster suggests that bishops who patronized canons regular were interested in the furtherance not only of the *vita apostolica* but also of education.

The most famous schools in North France were in the episcopal sees. After the Conquest, as a result of changes which were often gradual, most secular (i.e. non-monastic) episcopal churches in England were served by a body of canons with some dignitaries at their head.[79] Although there was in this period much constitutional variety, there were always archdeacons, and sooner or later a precentor (*cantor*) and a schoolmaster (*magister scholarum* or *scholasticus*). Archdeacons had a general responsibility under the bishop for the conduct and education of the clergy.[80] The precentor (or his deputy, the succentor) had to train the choir. And the schoolmaster was obviously intended to teach grammar and anything else within his competence. Since the duties of these two dignitaries overlapped, the arrangements made in the cathedrals for teaching may have varied not only from place to place but also from time to time. The confusion is implied by the author of the history of the bishops of Le Mans in connexion with Guy of Etampes, who may have held both offices in that cathedral and who also was for a while schoolmaster at Salisbury: 'Precentors together with schoolmasters are established in the church to ensure that by their arrangement the canonical office is properly celebrated, and also that the young men are controlled by firm discipline, lest through the choir's negligence and indecorum irreverence and scandal should take root there.' But although it was Guy's 'external' school, attracting students to Le Mans from far and wide, which the chronicler emphasized,[81] it is possible that the importance of the precentor (or perhaps, more exactly, the choir) in the early history of education has been underestimated. Devotional singing was since the fourth century of the greatest importance in the liturgy. In Cluniac abbeys it was the precentor who was responsible for the liturgical education of the boys (a duty he delegated) and for the provision of books (he appointed the copyists).[82] So elaborate had the liturgy become by the eleventh century that the oblates needed long training in order to perform the changing time-table (*horarium*) of services. Collegiate churches also had choirs and the boys had to be trained. Thus the precentor was always the basic schoolmaster, or director of education, in a college.

We can see the educational importance of the precentor in some English churches. In Henry I's reign a young man who came to Beverley in search of a teaching post was put in charge both of the choir within the minster and also of the school outside it, and ruled both very well until he fell in love

79. Kathleen Edwards, *The English secular cathedrals in the Middle Ages . . . with special reference to the fourteenth century* (2nd ed 1967) 185 ff.

80. They often examined ordinands for the bishop. Cf. Archdeacon Robert Pullen, *Sententiarum libri octo* (c. 1142–44) vii, 10, *PL* clxxxvi. 922D.

81. J. Mabillon, *Vetera Analecta* (Paris 1723) 320. For Guy, cf. R. W. Hunt, 'Studies on Priscian in the twelfth century – II', *MARS* ii (1950) 17, 41.

82. Noreen Hunt, *Cluny under St Hugh* 22, 63.

with a beautiful girl. Fortunately St John of Beverley cured him of his infatuation, and all was well again.[83] At Lincoln Henry archdeacon of Huntingdon, the historian, remembered that it was Albin of Angers, the second precentor, who had been his master. Although he reviews all the Lincoln cathedral dignitaries he had known, he does not even list the *scholastici* as such.[84] At York, however, where Thomas I destroyed the old community and appointed canons with prebends and new dignitaries, he established a *magister scholarum* in advance of the main reform, and gave 100s annually to the school from the synodals levied by the archdeacons.[85] But the problem of whether the *scholasticus* ever taught in person is resolved when in the middle of the twelfth century in most churches he began to change his title to 'chancellor', perhaps formal recognition of his complete removal from the teaching scene.[86] It may be that from the beginning the men in the classrooms were usually the succentor and the hired professional schoolmaster.

In England grammar schools can be proved to have existed in three secular cathedrals – York, Salisbury, and St Paul's, London. But for the others – Lincoln, Lichfield, Hereford, Exeter,[87] Wells, and Chichester – evidence is either very sparse or completely lacking before 1154.[88] In 1113 the breve roll for the deceased abbess of Caen, Matilda, was taken to Salisbury, Exeter, York, Lincoln, London, and Chichester cathedrals, and verses were composed in her memory at Exeter, York, and Lincoln (the entry for Chichester is defective). In 1122 the breve roll of Vitalis abbot of Savigny went to York, Salisbury, and London. This time Salisbury produced 'the children's verses' and St Paul's the verses of Ralf, son of Fulchred of Caen, a man who may have migrated before 1129 to the court of William Warelwast, bishop of Exeter.[89] Verses produced in non-monastic communities can be regarded as some evidence for a school.

---

83. 'Scholasticus quidam a libidine carnis curatur': *Miracula S. Johannis episcopi Eboracensis*, in *HCY* i. 281–4.

84. *Epistola de contemptu mundi*, HH 301–2. He notices appreciatively three successive holders of an unnamed dignity, placed between the lists of treasurers and precentors – Hugh, Osbert, and William – and these may have been the *scholastici*. *Ibid.*

85. Hugh *HCY* 77. *Historians of the Church of York*, ed. J. Raine (Rolls ser. 1894) iii. 75. C. T. Clay, 'The early precentors of York', *Yorks. Arch. Journal* xxxv (1940–43) 116.

86. Edwards 178 ff. See also above 226.

87. For the lack of concrete evidence for Exeter before 1155, see David W. Blake, 'The Church of Exeter in the Norman Period' (unpublished Exeter University MA thesis, 1970) Appendix: 'Education at Exeter', pp. 218–20. The argument, accepted by Beryl Smalley, *The Becket Conflict and the Schools* 168, 175, that Robert Pullen taught at Exeter before Oxford, seems weak.

88. Paré, Brunet, Tremblay, *Les Ecoles* 22–3, insist that in view of later efforts of the church to make every bishop provide a school it is most unlikely that in the early twelfth century there was a stable and satisfactory school in every episcopal city. Most current lists, they suggest, could well be pruned.

89. Delisle, *Rouleaux des morts*, no. XXXVI, tit. 14 (Salisbury), 20 (Exeter), 42 (York), 43 (Lincoln), 51 (St Paul's), 233 (Chichester); no. XXXVIII, tit. 94 (York), 186 (Salisbury) 'pueriles versus', 204 (St Paul's) 'versus Radulfi filii Fulcredi Cadomensis'. A Radulfus filius Fulchard, who may be the last named, witnesses a charter printed J. H. Round, 'Bernard the king's scribe', *EHR* xiv (1899) 421. For the palaeographical interest of the Savigny roll, see N. R. Ker, *English manuscripts in the century after the Norman Conquest* (1960) 16.

If we may judge from the history of the better-known cathedral or episcopal schools in north France, repute depended on the fame of the master, and so fluctuated widely; a steady reputation could not be maintained by even Chartres, Laon, Rheims, or Liège. Salisbury once had a distinguished schoolmaster, but only for a short time. With the help of Bishop Hildebert, who had been exiled to England in Rufus's reign, Bishop Roger attracted from Le Mans its greatest star, Guy of Etampes, some time before 1124. Guy, a Breton and originally called Grumar, had studied before 1117 at Laon under Master Anselm. He is credited with a lost work, *De dialectica*, and was so successful as a teacher, according to his encomiast, that he held at the same time the office of *magister scholasticus* and a canonry in Salisbury, a canonry in Lincoln, and a canonry and archdeaconry in Rouen, while in the church of Le Mans he was canon, archpriest, master of the school, and precentor. In 1126, when Hildebert was translated to Tours, Guy succeeded him as bishop of Le Mans.[90] How long Guy stayed at Salisbury and what he achieved there are not known. There are the verses of 1122, when, it seems, an Ailwin was master.[91] In 1136 John of Salisbury decided to go to school in France.[92] The school at St Paul's, London, is the best documented. In Henry I's reign the succession of schoolmasters was Durand, Hugh, and Hugh's pupil, Henry; men, except for Durand,[93] apparently of no wide reputation. The bishop gave Hugh, as pertaining to the dignity, Durand's apartments in the corner of the tower. He put him in charge of all the books of the church, which were to be recalled from borrowers, listed, and handed over by a chirograph, and he consigned to him the cupboards near the altar which the bishop had had constructed as bookcases. Hugh built a house for himself in the close (*atrium*), which passed to his successor. Henry's monopoly in London (saving the rights of the schools of St Mary-le-Bow and St Martin-le-Grand) was confirmed in 1138–39 by Henry of Blois, when administering the vacant bishopric.[94] The public disputations and the pastimes of the scholars of these schools are vividly described by William fitzStephen in his life of St Thomas.[95]

It cannot be proved that the number of schools in England was greatly increased after the Conquest,[96] but it can hardly be doubted that a

---

90. *Acta episcoporum Cennomanensium*, J. Mabillon, *Vetera Analecta* (Paris 1723) 319–24. OV (Le Prévost) iv. 43; v. 78. Letter of Hildebert to Roger re Guy, *PL* clxxi. 219. Le Prévost identifies Master Anselm as Saint Anselm, 'the master of Anselm of Laon'. According to the *Acta*, Guy was born in Brittany at the village of St Armagilus (unidentified). For some aspects of Hildebert's life and works, see Wolfram von den Steinen, 'Les sujets d'inspiration chez les poètes latins du XIIe siècle', *Cahiers de Civ. Méd.* ix (1966) 168. His poem on his 'exile' at the court of William Rufus is *Carmina minora*, ed. A. B. Scott (Teubner, Leipzig 1969) no. 22.

91. He is the fifth witness after the dean to a charter of Bishop Roger which can be dated 1122: E. J. Kealey, *Roger of Salisbury* 238.

92. See below 251. In 1139 King Stephen gave the dean and chapter some of the disgraced Bishop Roger's churches for the benefit of the *magister scholae, Regesta* iii. no. 789.

93. The grammatical comments of a *Magister Durandus de Anglia* are noted among glosses on Priscian, R. W. Hunt, 'Studies on Priscian in the eleventh and twelfth centuries', *MARS* i (1943) 206, 208, 224–5.

94. See above 225, n. 40. Roger of Salisbury and Henry of Blois were successively deans in plurality of the collegiate church of St Martin-le-Grand.

95. William fitzStephen in *MB* iii. 4–11. See above 232, n. 77.

96. For schools in England before the Conquest, Barlow, *English Church 1000–1066*, 277 ff.

considerable expansion had occurred by 1154. Towards the end of Henry I's reign an anonymous monk, when refuting the claim of the Oxford master Theobald of Etampes that monks had only been allowed an external ministry because of a shortage of clerks, claimed, satirically and no doubt with some exaggeration, that to speak only of France, Germany, Normandy, and England, there were not only in towns and boroughs but also in villages at least as many schoolmasters as royal servants and tax collectors.[97] William fitzStephen tells us – but it is unfortunately not clear whether he is referring to the days of his and St Thomas's boyhood or to the time of writing – that in London besides the three great schools many others were licensed.[98] And Reginald of Durham, writing 1165–c. 1174, informs us that it was 'according to a pretty general custom nowadays' that the priest of Norham held a school in his church.[99] It can therefore hardly be doubted that by the end of the Norman period a network of schools of various kinds had been established by the church throughout the length and breadth of England. There are many indications that in the eleventh and twelfth centuries the population, and with it the number of clerks, increased considerably. New settlements were made, new chapels built. Greater opportunities for the employment of clerks arose in the royal and baronial households, in the cathedrals and prebendal churches, and even in business houses. And the Conquest itself may have given a new impetus to education. The first two archbishops of Canterbury were famous scholars, and Norman bishops were inclined to formalize activities such as justice and education.

Not immediately connected with elementary and secondary teaching, but part of the same cultural movement and a provision for further education, was the restocking of the churches with books. Many of the new prelates found their cathedral or monastic library unsatisfactory.[100] The contents were not what they were accustomed to and wanted, and sometimes the books were in an ancient script which they did not like. Consequently at most great centres there was, sooner or later, a spate of book production which lasted until the mid-twelfth century. Books were purchased or borrowed and copied. William of St Calais procured books for his cathedral church at Durham while he was in exile in Normandy 1088–91.[101] Some sixty-five extant manuscripts now or formerly at Salisbury, all written about 1100 in a very plain and utilitarian format, and the existing books and the library catalogue compiled shortly after 1122 at Rochester, show how purposefully and quickly some bishops acted. In contrast, the twelfth-century library catalogue of Lincoln cathedral is not very impressive.[102] At Abingdon Abbot Faricius (1100–17)

97. Raymonde Foreville and Jean Leclercq, 'Un débat sur le sacerdoce des moines au XIIe siècle', *Studia Anselmiana* xli (Rome 1957) = *Analecta Monastica* iv. 65.

98. *MB* iii. 4, in a rather corrupt passage.

99. See above 229.

100. N. R. Ker, *English manuscripts in the century after the Norman Conquest* (1960), 'The beginning of Salisbury cathedral library' in *Medieval Learning and Literature: essays presented to R. W. Hunt* (1976) 23; Jürgen Petersohn, 'Normannische Bildungsreform im Hochmittelalterlichen England', *HZ* ccxiii (1971) 282 ff.

101. Simeon *HDE* 128.

102. Giraldus Cambrensis *Opera*, ed. J. F. Dimock (Rolls ser.) vii (1877) 165–71.

employed six professional scribes to copy patristic manuscripts while leaving to the monks the production of service books. Abbot Paul (1077–93) did similarly at St Albans; and there are traces of the same policy elsewhere.[103] Both the English and the Norman eleventh-century scripts were varieties of the beautiful Carolingian minuscule, and the effect of the Conquest was, as in so many other spheres, to create variety in England. For a time English and Norman styles, modifications and mixtures of them, and entirely new developments existed side by side, sometimes even in the same *scriptorium*. In the second quarter of the twelfth century, when standardization reappeared, the handwriting was still in the basic English tradition, but within a generation that style gave way to a new angular Gothic script. There was also in the Norman period an attempt to improve the editions and correct faulty texts. Archbishop Lanfranc introduced a new text of the Vulgate and his own collection of canon law.[104]

What the better educated of the new prelates required in their church was, besides suitable service books, bibles, sermons, and homilies, a theological collection including at least Augustine, Jerome, Ambrose, and Gregory the Great, and the standard classical *auctores*. The development of the library at Bury St Edmunds, one of the last great monastic foundations before the Conquest, has been carefully charted.[105] Well equipped when established, but remaining small, basic, and insular throughout the eleventh century because Abbot Baldwin (1065–97/8), King Edward's foreign doctor, made few changes, it was transformed by Abbot Anselm (1121–48), the nephew of Archbishop Anselm. In his time it was rapidly expanded to become a large and comprehensive collection of patristic, classical, and late antique authors, on the same pattern, if not quite on the same scale, as some of the greatest monastic libraries north of the Alps, like Cluny, Corbie, or Christ Church, Canterbury.[106] Anselm's death marked the end of an era. Thereafter the library was expanded to take account of the current development in the schools, and the usual acquisitions were the schoolbooks written by contemporary authors. The purpose was becoming in a new sense educational as well as devotional.

Libraries are one thing, what is read is another. Peter Abelard's pessimism has already been noted.[107] The educational legacy of the Greco-Roman world to the Middle Ages was the *trivium* (grammar, rhetoric, and dialectics or logic) and the *quadrivium* (arithmetic, geometry, astronomy, and music), which together constituted the seven liberal arts. But the Roman scheme of education, under which the teaching of grammar and an elementary *quadrivium* was entrusted (at secondary level) to the grammar school, and rhetoric and dialectics to a more advanced school of rhetoric, was not generally

103. For Norwich, see below 241.

104. H. H. Glunz, *History of the Vulgate in England from Alcuin to Roger Bacon* (1933) 159 ff.; Raphael Loewe, 'The medieval history of the Latin Vulgate', *The Cambridge History of the Bible* ii (1969) 141–2. S. Harrison Thompson, 'Bishop Gundulph of Rochester and the Vulgate', *Speculum* vi (1931) 468. For canon law, see below 253 ff.

105. R. M. Thomson, 'The library of Bury St Edmunds abbey in the eleventh and twelfth centuries', *Speculum* xlvii (1972) 617.

106. For the library at Canterbury, see Margaret Gibson, *Lanfranc of Bec* 177 ff.

107. Above 197.

followed.[108] Such specialization was too sophisticated for the times. Moreover, the ancient curriculum did not meet the requirements of the post-classical age; and, although no new educational theories were produced or practical reforms advocated, medieval schoolmasters taught only what society at that time needed, or was thought to need. Thus throughout the centuries the emphasis must always have been altering, a process which, for lack of information, cannot be shown in detail. Rhetoric probably suffered the greatest change: because there was little demand for the art of public speaking, the subject became more Latin composition, especially the rules for letter writing. And the great school of rhetoric at Bologna shifted its emphasis from the art of pleading in the courts to the study of law.[109]

Since there were no treatises on education[110] and we have no school timetables, life in the classroom has to be reconstructed from scraps. At the elementary level we have seen how John of Salisbury was sent to a priest 'to learn the psalms', and as laymen who were converted to monasticism at a mature age were required to learn them, it is possible that the psalter was a common reader in the schools. In the later Middle Ages children learned reading by reciting from a book which contained the alphabet followed by familiar devotional texts, the basic prayers, the creed, and some liturgical pieces.[111] Something like that was used as a primer at Durham in the twelfth century. In the time of Bishop William of St Barbe (1143–54), a knight, Robert of St Martin, became a monk there, and was required to read and learn from a book the seven penitential psalms, the Lord's prayer, and the creed. For a long time he could not do this: each day he forgot what he had learned the day before. In his despair he threw the book under St Cuthbert's tomb; but then he had a change of heart, recovered the book, and found that he could read easily; and after that he could scarcely be parted from it.[112] Reading was never silent in the Middle Ages. It was a physical act of worship. The reader imbibed the nectar which flowed from the heavenly fountains, fed on the manna, chewed it over, masticated it, and digested its meaning.[113] It is possible, therefore, that not only in the choir or music schools but in all elementary schools reading was taught by chanting the devotional texts.[114] This would explain how it was that in

108. Murphy, *op. cit.* J. de Ghellinck, *Le mouvement théologique du XIIe siècle* (2nd ed, Bruges 1948) 9–16, 93–6.

109. But see also Richard Mckeon, 'Rhetoric in the Middle Ages', *Speculum* xvii (1942) 1.

110. There were, however, some grand programmes of study, in the tradition of Cassiodorus's *Institutiones*, e.g. Thierry of Chartres's *Epthatheucon* and Hugh of St Victor's *Didascalion* (*PL* clxxvi). See Paré, Brunet, and Tremblay, *Les Ecoles* 94 ff.; Berthe Widmer, 'Thierry von Chartres, ein Gelehrtenschicksal des 12. Jahrhunderts', *HZ* cc (1969) 556 ff. Cf. also Daniel D. McGarry, 'Educational theory in the *Metalogicon* of John of Salisbury', *Speculum* xxiii (1948) 659; Philippe Delhaye, 'L'enseignement de la philosophie morale au XIIe siècle', *Mediaeval Studies* xi (1949) 77.

111. Orme, pp. 62–3.

112. Reginald of Durham, *St Cuthbert* 158–60.

113. Jean Leclercq, *The Love of Learning and the Desire for God* (trans. Catharine Misrahi, Mentor Omega Books, 1961) 78–9.

114. Reginald of Durham, *St Godric* 60, says as much of Godric's elementary (and not very effective) schooling at St Mary's Durham: 'Ubi ea quae prius didicit arctius memoriae infixit et quaedam quae antea non cognoverat, ibi audiendo, legendo, atque psallendo apprehendit; nam ea quae pueris saepius eadem repetentibus audivit, tenacius memoriae infigere curavit; quae vero

the later Middle Ages all reading schools were known as song-schools. Writing was taught in the Norman period using wax tablets and stylos. Baudri of Bourgueil wrote a poem on his great grief at his broken style (154), and several on his tablets (47, 167, 206, 210).[115] From a letter which Bishop Herbert Losinga wrote to 'his only brother, G.' we learn that Archdeacon Richard had handed over G.'s tablets to a certain Eric for his school (*ludo suo*), and had given him some other boxwood tablets in compensation. Herbert asked for the loan of these.[116] Eric was probably an Anglo-Scandinavian native of the Danelaw and may well have been a village priest.

The grammar schools, when distinct from the reading or choir schools, carried on where they left off, and also switched to textbooks which were less exclusively religious. Although study of the Latin language (grammar) remained basic, most of the seven liberal arts were probably taught at some level, though not necessarily in separate lessons. One literary passage could serve several purposes and a good schoolmaster could draw many lessons from a single text. The scope of the instruction can be inferred from the literary productions of the age. It is clear that the master of a grammar school also taught rhetoric in all its seven branches[117] – the various forms of literary and oratorical composition – and possibly laid special emphasis on the art of letter writing. Epistolary composition was most important at this time not only because so many documents took the form of letters but also because letters were the main medium of communication. In the absence of the essay, the novel, the travel book, indeed most light literature, except for saints' lives and miracles, the letter could serve most of those purposes. It also made possible that farflung and intricate web of personal and spiritual relationships so characteristic of monastic society, and, by the twelfth century, of ecclesiastical society in general. The pleasure which men took in correspondence is shown by the passion with which letters were collected, largely to serve as models.[118] Epistolary composition was based on Cicero's *Rhetorica ad Herennium*, and by the mid-twelfth century the structure and style of the letter form was becoming stereotyped.[119] Grammar and rhetoric in the grammar schools were probably taken as far as most clerks wished to pursue those subjects, but logic and philosophy were taught only at an elementary level, and theology, law, and medicine not at all. For those subjects the ambitious scholar had to seek out the

---

recentius auditu fore sibi ignota persensit, his majorem recordandi, meditandi et ruminandi diligentiam adhibere curavit.' Godric preserved his psalter 'of St Jerome', given him at Carlisle, as his most precious possession.

115. *Les Oeuvres poétiques de Baudri de Bourgueil*, ed. Phyllis Abrahams (Paris 1926).

116. *Ep.* 54. For *tabellae* and *graphius* see also *VEdR* 2. Archdeacon Richard (of Beaufai) is said to have been the son of William of Beaufai, Herbert's predecessor as bishop (of Thetford) 1086–91, and his wife, Agnes; but the authority is elusive.

117. Murphy, *op. cit.*

118. For some interesting remarks on twelfth-century letter writing, see Jean Leclercq, *Analecta Monastica* ii = *Studia Anselmiana* xxxi (Rome 1953) 145–50; see also R. W. Southern, 'The letters of Abelard and Heloise', *Medieval Humanism and Other Studies* (1970) 86–8. It should be noticed as well that in all collections the youthful effusions, especially letters written before the author became a prelate, have been lost.

119. Murphy, *op. cit.* See also Mary Dickey, 'Some commentaries on the *De Inventione* and *Ad Herennium* of the eleventh and early twelfth centuries', *MARS* vi (1968) 1.

specialist master and schools of the highest standards, usually in this period abroad.

No description can be given of the schoolroom at St Paul's or at York. Something, however, can be told about the monastic schools. William of Malmesbury, it seems, was a child oblate, and he recalls that although literature was always his main interest he did study other subjects; he had given a little attention to logic, a subject which provided equipment for rhetoric, and rather more to medicine, ethics, and above all history, for the first served to preserve the health of the body, the second imparted the rules of conduct,[120] and the third taught salutary lessons.[121] It is a pity that William of Malmesbury does not tell us more. Of rather more interest in this connexion are the letters which Herbert Losinga, bishop of Norwich c. 1095–1119, wrote to his favourite pupils when he was absent on business from the cloister.[122] Herbert had been a monk at Fécamp under John of Ravenna, William of Dijon's nephew and one of the most distinguished Cluniac scholars of his time.[123] Herbert himself gave instruction when at Norwich and took his teaching duties very seriously. But there had to be some more stable arrangements, and glimpses of these can be obtained from the letters. The centre of erudition in the priory was probably the writing office, or *scriptorium*, for copying and composition were always closely connected.[124] Men who copied manuscripts became authors, and clerks who collected model letters also wrote them; in this sphere Norman the *aedituus* or sacristan possibly held a key role. In some monasteries this official was not only in charge of the church furniture and vestments, like the treasurer in a secular cathedral, but also had secretarial duties and sometimes was a scribe.[125] It was Norman who urged Herbert to collect his literary remains, and

120. It is possible that treatise 1 in Brit. Mus. MS Harleian 3969, 'De dictis et factis memorabilibus philosophorum', was compiled by William. See Stubbs *GR* i, pp. cxl–cxliii.

121. *GR* 103.

122. Herbert Losinga's letters were edited rather badly from the unique MS by Robert Anstruther (Brussels and London 1846). His own short *Errata* sheet is greatly extended by E. M. Goulburn and Henry Symonds, *The Life, Letters, and Sermons of Bishop Herbert de Losinga* (1878) i. 418–23. Goulburn and Symonds translate and comment on the letters. References to Anstruther's Latin text are given here by the number of the letter and to the translation by a page reference. It was also the custom of William of St Calais, bishop of Durham 1081–96, to write to his monks, Simeon *HDE* 125–6, but, apparently, on spiritual topics.

123. For the library at Fécamp, see Geneviève Nortier, 'Bibliothèque de Fécamp au moyen-âge', *L'abbaye bénédictine de Fécamp, ouvrage scientifique du XIIIe centenaire*, ii (Fécamp 1960) 221.

124. For the *scriptorium* at St Evroul, see Chibnall, *OV* ii, introduction. For William of Malmesbury's transition from book collector and transcriber to historian, see *GP* 431; *GR* 103–4. For the making of books and libraries in this period, see N. R. Ker, *English manuscripts in the century after the Norman Conquest* (1960). For the layout of the page, see M. B. Parkes, 'The influence of the concepts of *ordinatio* and *compilatio* on the development of the book', *Medieval Learning and Literature: essays presented to R. W. Hunt*, 115. For bindings, Graham Pollard, 'Describing medieval bookbindings', *ibid*. 50; H. M. Nixon, 'The binding', *Winchester in the Early Middle Ages*, 526.

125. The variety of titles under which the sacristan was known at different places and times shows the variety of his duties: *sacrista, aedituus, custos templi, secretarius, scriptor*. See also Paul Tombeur, 'Un nouveau nom de la littérature médiolatine: Gilbert de Saint-Trond', *Cahiers de Civ. Méd.* x (1967) 444–5. By the mid-twelfth century there was a *sacrista* at Norwich, Reginald of Durham, *St Cuthbert* 123. About the same time the terms *secretarius* and *sacrista* were used indifferently at Durham, *ibid*. 160, 164, 167. In 1113 or 1114 St Cuthbert accosted Bernard, the

probably made the extant collection of his letters.[126] Herbert treated this younger colleague with great respect and it is likely that Norman was engaged in creating the library at Norwich. Herbert also refers to a monk named Alexander, who had been wandering around making money by copying books, and who had promised to stay at Norwich and give his services in return for food and clothing only – an offer which Herbert after much deliberation agreed should be accepted.[127] Herbert attempted to provide a resident schoolmaster, not necessarily a monk. He dismissed one master in order to replace him with a Breton, G. This man became their fellow citizen and fellow member of the cloister, but later, completely forgetful of the philosophy he was to teach, or, of his intended way of life (*propositae philosophiae totus immemor*), had left the monastery to live feasting and drinking in the country. Herbert ordered him back under penalty of anathema.[128] He also took the opportunity to make a few remarks on the notorious fickleness of Bretons: great talkers, but great breakers of promises; quick to make an entry and as quick to take flight again. These stray indications, and the very fact that the bishop was so involved in the teaching, suggest that the priory's internal school was rather disorganized.

Ten letters of Herbert to the monks William and Otto, jointly or individually, and two or three to William *Turbo* (whirlwind), possibly the same man, have survived.[129] William became prior in 1121, two years after Herbert's death, and bishop in 1146. He was one of the inventors of the martyrdom of the boy William by the Jews in 1144, fostered his cult, and attacked the Jews. In this he was opposed by Elias, who succeeded him as prior. The monk Thomas of Monmouth, who wrote an account of the life and miracles of St William, dedicated it to his bishop, and praised his eloquence. In his book he gives some examples of this, but always devoted to an ignoble cause.[130]

Bishop Herbert in his letters to William and Otto reminded them that now they had reached boyhood (*adolescentia*), they were liable to all the temptations of that age, especially sexual impurity and restlessness.[131] It was, however, their laziness which pained Herbert most; and he complained in every letter about their slow progress and inadequate achievement. The basic study of these boys was the Latin language, grammar. And although Herbert mentions the *trivium* and *quadrivium*, the seven liberal arts, besides grammar only dialectic is referred to in the letters. The third part of the *trivium*, rhetoric, is undoubtedly taken for granted. The components of the *quadrivium* were obviously of less interest to Herbert, but could have been the responsibility of other masters.[132]

sacristan of Durham, when he was writing in the monastery, and told him that there was a woman in the church whom he must expel, *ibid*. 153.

126. *HEp*. no. 1.
127. No. 51.
128. No. 55.
129. Letters to William and Otto, nos. 9 (p. 19), 22 (p. 37), 24 (p. 20), 28 (p. 43), 32 (p. 29), 39 (p. 22), ?40 (p. 31), 47 (p. 22); to William, no. 49 (p. 35); to William *Turbo*, nos. 41 (p. 282), ?42a (p. 210), 42b (p. 282); to Otto, no. 30 (p. 24).
130. *Vita S. Willelmi Norwic*. cf. 104–8.
131. No. 22 (p. 37).
132. No. 49 (p. 35); cf. 53 (p. 53).

Herbert had spent a year 'sitting on the low form'[133] with William and Otto studying Donatus, with its declensions, conjugations, and voices, and 'our old friend Servius' (*Serviolus*), with its feet and all the other rules of grammar; and he informed the boys that they must know these books by heart – and he was going to examine them in it – before they proceeded to the study of the classical poets. The *Ars Minor* of Aelius Donatus, the mid fourth-century Roman rhetor and tutor of St Jerome, served as the standard elementary textbook of Latin grammar in all medieval schools. Marius or Maurus Servius Honoratus is best known as a commentator on Virgil, but in the Middle Ages some grammatical treatises also went under his name.[134]

When the boys had learned the rules of grammar they could go on to 'the flowery meads of the poets', in which they would acquire a polished style.[135] Especially were they to study Ovid.[136] Herbert exhibits the usual ambivalent attitude of educated monks to the heathen authors. He had been a great lover of the poets, including Ovid and Virgil, and had himself written much poetry. But recently, when reciting some elegiac verses in bed, he had had a conversion – he recalls the similar experiences of Jerome and Boethius[137] – and had renounced 'these obscenities'. He was an old priest who should be studying the Scriptures and the Fathers (in fact he seems to have turned to history).[138] It was not the office of a bishop to sit on the stage, but to preach in a church; it was not for him to take part in the infamy of the theatre or the cruelties of the circus, but to be concerned with the law of God and the words of the Gospels. For the young, however, it was quite another matter. It was in a dunghill that the cock in Æsop's fable found a pearl. Young men have to learn to write in Latin which will do them credit, and Herbert never doubted for a moment that the only acceptable models were the heathen writers. Boys may play; more serious things could come later.[139] Herbert was not at all pleased to hear that William and Otto were reading Sedulius. The fifth-century Christian poet and the Evangelists, whose treatment of the same matter was to be preferred, were, he declared, a heavy diet, suitable for more mature monks. Boys did better on the milk of much lighter literature.[140]

Herbert's letters to a monk, Felix, are likewise concerned with the problem of what scholastic activities a monk should follow. Herbert notes that Felix had spent his boyhood in honest studies,[141] and acknowledges that he was learned in the two different branches of learning (*doctrinae*), the old and the

---

133. Possibly the first form in the choir; but the church was not necessarily the schoolroom.

134. Cf. John of Salisbury *Metalogicon* I, 19 (ed. Webb) 47–8: 'Donatus, Servius, Priscianus, Isidorus, Cassiodorus, Beda noster et alii quamplures eam singuli tractant.'

135. No. 9 (p. 19).

136. No. 39 (p. 22).

137. However, as Gerald Bonner pointed out, 'Bede and medieval civilization', *Anglo-Saxon England* ii (1973) 83, although for the Fathers the classics were really dangerous – a temptation to apostasy, for the Middle Ages this was not so. Their paganism was Germanic heathenism.

138. He asked the abbot of Fécamp for a Suetonius (no. 5, p. 64) and another abbot for a Josephus (no. 10, p. 248). Cf. nos. 6 (p. 155) and 11 (p. 182).

139. Nos. 30 (p. 24), 32 (p. 29).

140. No. 9 (p. 19).

141. No. 43 (p. 196).

new.[142] As elsewhere the bishop calls Jerome, Augustine, Ambrose, and Gregory the 'modern fathers'; the doctors of the old learning are probably, as with Cassiodorus, the pagan authors.[143] Felix had become a scribe,[144] and recently had been copying out St Augustine. His labour was devotional and he enjoyed in the cloister the highest reputation for religion. But even if he was well versed in the classical authors, he had no higher education in grammar, and when he turned to this discipline, Herbert, although recognizing it as a praiseworthy pursuit, expressed some disappointment. His feeling of loss was naturally changed to anger when Felix began to neglect this study and started recording all the 'fatuities' of the monastery, copying martyrologies, psalters, little breviaries, and the 'secret writings of all'.[145] He was wasting his time. He should return, wrote the bishop, either to copying Augustine or to studying grammar. In a letter to William,[146] Herbert seems to make a slighting reference to Felix. William and the other pupils should get on with their studies: 'As for Felix, I want him to have plenty of vegetables and salads.' In this correspondence Herbert, although showing a preference for religious studies, is as scrupulous as Cassiodorus in advocating *utraeque doctrinae*.[147] More interesting is his apparent contempt not only for hack copying but also for the literary compositions which were being produced in his own monastery. Herbert was the kind of teacher who believed that everything had been done better in the past. There had been two great achievements, the classical and the patristic. Knowledge of the ancient wisdom was preferable to the inanities of the present.

Herbert required from his monastic pupils verses written in the style of Ovid. In one letter he complained that whereas William and Otto used to provide him with 400–500 lines every two or three days, now he got only twenty or thirty every two or three months, and the quality too was much worse.[148] On one occasion he criticized in detail the thirty-six lines sent by Otto. The boys teased him. Repeatedly they demanded that he too should write in verse,[149] no doubt so that they could get their own back and criticize his composition. And Otto in those thirty-six lines had reproved Herbert for sloth, somnolence, and greed. The bishop, immersed in the secular affairs of the church of Norwich and involved in various disputes with royal officials, replied tartly that it was only because of his unwearied defence of the cloister that Otto could study there in peace. It is no wonder that Herbert's criticism of the verses was sharp. From the same letter we learn that William had been hurt by Herbert's correction of his literary exercises and was sulking.[150] This tuition by

---

142. No. 23 (p. 192).

143. No. 32 (p. 30).

144. If the F. of no. 46 (p. 198) is Felix, Herbert paid him three shillings-worth of tablets and ink for a psalter.

145. Cf. letter of Archbishop Anselm to Hugh monk of Chester, *c.* 1102 (no. 232), 'Cum enim scribendi habeas scientiam, mavis aliud quod tibi melius videtur, quam scribere per oboedientiam.'

146. No. 49 (p. 36).

147. *Cassiodori Senatoris Institutiones*, ed. R. A. B. Mynors (1937), 6. He devoted Book I to *divinae lectiones* and Book II to *seculares lectiones*.

148. No. 39 (p. 22).

149. Nos. 32 (p. 30), 39 (p. 22), 47 (*ibid.*).

150. No. 30 (p. 24).

correspondence was not a great success. Herbert was, however, very proud of Otto. For the breve roll of Abbess Matilda in 1113 Otto wrote six elegiac couplets, which are ascribed to him – 'Versus Othonis Juvenis'.

> Commendant alii, commendant scripta Mathildam
>   Et vitae meritum justiciaeque modum,
> Scribere disposui tantae praeconia laudis;
>   Sed mihi verborum copia pauca fuit.
> Primitias Domino dum libat virginitatis,
>   Perpetua meruit virginitate frui.
> Virgo dicata Deo, rebus subtracta caducis,
>   Percepit merito praemia digna suo.
> In laudes gemitus redeant, in gaudia fletus:
>   Nil dignum lacrimis vita perennis habet.
> Transiit ad vitam felix et plena dierum,
>   Et meruit sponsi regna videre sui.

Otto was true to his reputation of being a boy of few words, if not downright lazy. He had some idea of how to write classical verse and could sometimes catch the Ovidian style, but the effect is vacuous. In the next surviving breve roll which went to Norwich, that of 1122, there are no verses, only a request for reciprocal prayers for 'dom Herbert, bishop, our patron and founder of our church, and for all the other deceased brethren of our congregation'.[151] William Turbe's reputation as a poet rested in later years on the first couplet of a quatrain he wrote on the death of St Thomas Becket, which, since it gives the date (29 December 1171=1170), was often quoted:[152]

> Annus millenus centenus septuagenus
>   Primus erat primas cum ruit ense Thomas.
> Quinta dies Natalis erat. Flos orbis ab orbe
>   Vellitur, et fructus incipit esse poli.

William was even more succint. But, although the scansion is weaker than Otto's, the verses are a tour de force and suggest that he was the more intelligent of the two.

Herbert also supervised the studies of his two clerks, Samson and Roger, whom he had sent away to school and whose course was basically similar, the *auctores* (probably the six authors: the poets Cato, Theodulus, Avianus, Maximian, Claudian, and Statius, who made up a common teaching anthology[153]), then the *trivium* and finally the *quadrivium*; and from them he asked for compositions in both verse and prose;[154] prose composition came after verses. In a letter to William Turbe, Herbert ordered him to get on with dialectic and write to him in prose.[155] Indeed prose was valued more highly than verse by the serious-minded. Archbishop Anselm in 1103–04 urged his

---

151. Delisle, *Rouleaux des morts*, XXXVI, tit. 40; XXXVIII, tit. 97.
152. J. F. Dimock in Giraldus Cambrensis, *Vita S. Remigii*, 56, n. 6.
153. Orme, 102–3. The poets, except the Carolingian Theodulus, were of the Silver Age.
154. No. 20 (p. 52).
155. No. 41 (p. 282).

nephew of the same name, the future abbot of Bury, to give full attention to grammar and practice *dictamen*, more in prose than in verses.[156]

Herbert recommended dialectic to some monks identified only by initials (W., G., W.). He wrote that he was getting tired of the fables of Ovid and would prefer his pupils to turn to a more useful subject. Logic was the door to the house of knowledge and solved all mysteries.[157] In another letter William was ordered to finish off Aristotle's Topics and start on his Categories.[158] Herbert hoped that his love of learning would burst into flame, and that he would hasten to the banquet of philosophy all the more quickly because from it he would serve God rather than men.[159] Herbert's enthusiasm for dialectic might a few years later, when the way that method was used in the schools aroused so much suspicion, have been considered in monastic circles almost indiscreet. But he followed in the steps of Lanfranc of Pavia and that even greater logician, Anselm,[160] and like them presupposed that dialectic would be used in the service of God, to provide theological understanding.

The study of the liberal arts as an aid to the monastic vocation led to characteristic monastic literary works[161] and produced abbots and bishops who were also scholars and divines, men who could speak fluently in Latin in ecclesiastical councils, men who were at home anywhere in the Western church. Anselm could move easily from Bec to Canterbury, and from Canterbury to Marcigny, Rome, Bari, and Lyons. It was an education for character, for a special life style. It presupposed a life to be spent in routine devotional services and meditation on religious themes, in commenting on the *sacra pagina* in the company of men of no great intellectual powers and with no ambition to shine as scholars, a society which cultivated humility and bowed to authority. Here was no training either for the eager scholar who wanted to make a career in the schools or for the clerk who had to make his way in the world.

By the twelfth century even bishop's protégés thought it necessary, or were sent, to get some higher education, and so joined for a time in the schools clerks without patrons and the true scholars. Those who missed out were always aware of their loss. Ailred abbot of Rievaulx (1147–67), who had no more than elementary education, used to say, once he had established his reputation as a preacher and writer, that he was but 'an ignorant and almost unlettered man'.[162] Future prelates usually studied law, scholars philosophy

---

156.   *AEp* 290, 328.

157.   No. 53 (p. 53).

158.   The Topics, with the Prior and Posterior Analytics, were the 'new logic', the Categories, presented by Boethius, were part of the 'old logic'.

159.   No. 49 (p. 35).

160.   R. W. Southern, 'Lanfranc of Bec and Berengar of Tours' *Studies in Medieval History presented to Frederick Maurice Powicke* (1948). Cf. S. Vanni Rovighi, 'Notices sur l'influence de saint Anselme au XIIe siècle', *Cahiers de Civ. Méd.* vii (1964) 423–37; viii (1965) 43–58.

161.   Jean Leclercq, *The Love of Learning and the Desire for God* (Mentor Omega Books), 153 ff.

162.   'Non sum sapiens, non sum legisperitus, sed homo idiota et fere sine litteris, piscatori quam oratori similior', quoted by C. H. Talbot, *Ailred of Rievaulx De Anima* (1952) 10n.

and theology.[163] A few clerks set off to acquire medical training and one or two went in search of Arabic mathematics and science. By the end of the twelfth century some centres of advanced learning can be identified in England, but there is hardly a trace of these before 1154.

Oxford beckons, but only to deceive.[164] Its school first rose to prominence soon after Robert Bloet became bishop of Lincoln (1094) and Walter Calenius archdeacon of Oxford and provost of the collegiate church of St George in the castle. After about forty years of distinction, it sank out of sight again for half a century. It seems that Walter, Geoffrey of Monmouth's patron, whom his fellow archdeacon, Henry of Huntingdon, called 'the superlative rhetorician',[165] encouraged the school attached to his church and also invited distinguished scholars to lecture there. The first schoolmaster to attract attention was the French clerk, Theobald of Etampes, who had previously been master at St Stephen's, Caen, William I's foundation where Lanfranc had been abbot.[166] Theobald corresponded with Queen Margaret of Scotland (d. 1093) on the possibility of becoming one of her chaplains, but how he got to Oxford is not known. Four of his five surviving letters are theological exercises. While still at Caen he wrote to his friend Philip on the sins of the flesh (he thought pride more deadly than lust); and as *magister Oxenefordiae* he gave his diocesan bishop (presumably Robert Bloet) his views on penitence and confession, defended himself against the misrepresentations of the neighbouring Abbot Faricius of Abingdon (1100–17) – he denied that he had ever taught that unbaptized infants would be saved, and opposed the thesis of the well-known and much-opposed dialectician, Roscelin of Compiègne, that the sons of priests and bastards should not be ordained. It seems from a remark of Archbishop Anselm that Roscelin had visited England some time between 1093 and 1097, after his condemnation by the council of Soissons, and unashamedly expounded his condemned views on the Trinity.[167] So it is just possible that this unpopular 'Nominalist', a protester against the dominant 'realism' of the period, was another who lectured at Oxford. Be that as it may, Theobald of Etampes must be considered a theologian of some note and worthy of a cathedral appointment. And his belittlement by an anonymous monk who attacked him for his views on the parochial rights of monks and called him 'an unimportant little clerk, who, although a nobody and one who had never

163.   A useful guide, with bibliography, to the methods of teaching theology in the schools of Laon and Paris, is John R. Williams, 'The twelfth-century theological "Questiones" of Carpentias MS 100', *Medieval Studies* xxviii (1966) 300 ff. For a contemporary description of the scholastic *lectio* (as opposed to monastic), see Abelard's introduction to his *Sic et Non*, in *PL* clxxviii. 1339.

164.   For the latest interpretation of the evidence, see R. W. Southern, 'Master Vacarius and the beginning of an English academic tradition', in *Medieval Learning and Literature: essays presented to R. W. Hunt* 257 ff. Southern, however, unnecessarily belittles the school under Theobald and Pullen. Cf. also H. E. Salter, 'Historical revisions: the medieval university of Oxford', *History* xiv (1930) 57–61. Raymonde Foreville, 'Le milieu oxfordien au début du XIIe siècle', *Studia Anselmiana* xli (Rome 1957) = *Analecta Monastica* iv, 16–19.

165.   HH, *De contemptu mundi* 302.

166.   'Un débat sur le sacerdoce des moines', *Studia Anselmiana* (as in n. 164) 54, 65. His letters are printed *PL* clxiii. 759.

167.   Anselm, *Epistola de incarnatione verbi prima* (ed. Schmitt) ii. 4. For Anselm and Roscelin see also *AEp* 128–9, 136, 147.

progressed beyond teaching grammar, was said to have at least a hundred pupils',[168] must not be taken too seriously. It is quite clear that he lectured in theology. Moreover, Robert Pullen, the English theologian,[169] taught there from about 1133 to 1137, and what may well have been the substance of his lectures, his *Sententiarum libri octo*, have survived; St Bernard approved of them wholeheartedly. As a further ornament to Oxford the inventive Geoffrey of Monmouth may have been a canon of St George between 1129 and 1151.[170] But Robert Pullen obtained the archdeaconry of Rochester and moved on to Paris and Rome. And Master Vacarius, the Roman lawyer, on whose presence so much has been built, has probably to be dismissed from the scene.[171] The school at Oxford is entirely obscure between 1137 and 1190. A promising start had not been maintained.

No less rare than acquaintance with Roman lawyers, and perhaps even less profitable, was contact with north European Jewry. It was not until Henry II's reign that the trickle of Jews which followed the Conquest became noticeable,[172] but the presence of these non-Christians in some of the cities and towns provoked a small but interesting theological interest. King William Rufus was believed to have organized a debate between Christian and Jewish apologists.[173] Gilbert Crispin monk of Bec, abbot of Westminster (*c.* 1085–1117/8), wrote a 'Dispute of a christian with a heathen touching the faith of Christ'.[174] A certain Maurice, described as prior of the Austin canonry of Kirkham (Yorks), who was connected with both Gerard and Roger, archbishops of York, claimed that he had spent three years as a young man in the study of Hebrew and had copied psalms from a Hebrew psalter owned by Gerard in a script which the Jews themselves had admired.[175] Master Vacarius, when he was studying at Northampton, became interested in the problem of the

---

168.   'Un débat sur le sacerdoce des moines' 8–16.

169.   For Robert see Southern, *loc. cit.* 267–9; Franz Pelster, 'Einige Angaben über Leben und Schriften des Robertus Pullus, Kardinals und Kanzlers der römischen Kirche', *Scholastik* xii (1937) 239; Francis Courtney, *Cardinal Robert Pullen* (*Analecta Gregoriana* lxiv Rome 1945); R. L. Poole, 'The early lives of Robert Pullen and Nicholas Breakspear' in *Essays in medieval history presented to Thomas Frederick Tout* (1925) 61; A. Saltman, 'John II, bishop of Rochester', *EHR* lxvi (1951) 71–3. His sentences are printed in *PL* clxxxvi. A pupil of Robert, apparently when teaching in England at Oxford (or Exeter, if that theory is accepted), was Gilbert Foliot, the future Cluniac monk, abbot of Gloucester (1139), bishop of Hereford (1148) and bishop of London (1163). See A. Morey and C. N. L. Brooke, *The Letters and Charters of Gilbert Foliot* (1967) 84–5; Beryl Smalley, *The Becket Conflict and the Schools*, 168, 175. Some good time before 1139 Foliot held a chair somewhere in N. France. For his scholastic career, see Smalley 167 ff.

170.   H. E. Salter, 'Geoffrey of Monmouth and Oxford', *EHR* xxxiv (1919) 382.

171.   Southern *loc. cit.* 273 ff.

172.   R. B. Dobson, *The Jews of medieval York and the massacre of March 1190* (Borthwick papers no. 45) 1 ff., casts a sceptical eye on the proliferation. In 1148 there were, apparently, only two Jewish families in Winchester: *Winchester in the Early Middle Ages*, 101 (nos. 443–4). For the small community at Norwich, which in 1144 was living in rented accommodation, and English Jewry at that time in general, see *Vita S. Willelmi Norwic.*

173.   Above 67.

174.   J. Armitage Robinson, *Gilbert Crispin abbot of Westminster* (1911) 60 ff. *Disputatio Judaei cum Christiano* printed in *PL* clix. 1007. Cf. also Clement C. J. Webb, 'Gilbert Crispin, abbot of Westminster: Dispute of a Christian with a heathen . . .', *MARS* iii (1954) 55. R. W. Southern, 'St Anselm and Gilbert Crispin, abbot of Westminster', *ibid.* 78.

175.   Dobson, *op. cit.* 3–4.

nature of the union of divine and human natures in Christ, and disputed with local Jews on the subject.[176] In April 1131, when Pope Innocent II visited the abbey of St Denis, near Paris, he was presented by the Jews of the Paris synagogue with a scroll containing the text of the Law, covered by a veil. The pontiff contented himself with echoing St Paul, 'May Almighty God take away the veil from your hearts' (2 Cor. 3: 15–16).[177] But Hebrew letters were used in magic, and the Cabbala was a forbidden subject. Moreover, between 1144 and 1150 some monks and citizens of Norwich, led by the prior, William Turbe, invented the martyrdom of the boy William by the local Jews and stirred up much racial hatred. Even the admission of a converted Jew as monk increased the misunderstanding.[178] Jewish learning was a dangerous field to enter.

The way in which English and Norman clerks went to France for their higher education, even in the twelfth century, is clear evidence of its scarcity in the kingdom. Laon and, a little later, Paris were the main resorts. In 1107 Henry I's chancellor, Waldric, a clerk in minor orders without any ecclesiastical benefice or office, whose main interests were warfare, hunting, and hawking, and who had indeed earlier in the year captured Duke Robert at Tinchebrai, was, rather surprisingly, elected bishop of Laon, but against the wishes of the regent of the cathedral school, Master Anselm.[179] It was Anselm, whom Guibert of Nogent considered 'the most brilliant exponent of the liberal arts in the whole of France, nay in the Latin world', and his brother Ralf, a mathematician and his successor as master (1117), who made the enormous and well-deserved reputation of the school.[180] After Ralf's death in 1131 the school declined.[181] In the five years of Waldric's episcopate the ties between England and Laon were exceptionally close. The bishop returned to England from time to time to raise money, and Master Anselm revisited the kingdom in order to see his friends. Waldric was considered a deplorable bishop by the learned men of his city and diocese and was accused by Guibert, a participator in these events, of cruelties and even murder. He had, it seems, perhaps as a result of the Crusade,[182] a moorish or Ethiopian servant named John, whom he used in these activities. In the spring of 1112 Waldric returned from England to

176. Southern, 'Master Vacarius' 261 ff.; Peter Stein, 'Vacarius and the civil law', in *Church and Government in the Middle Ages: Essays presented to C. R. Cheney,* 135, with bibliographies.

177. Suger, *Vie de Louis VI,* ed. and trans. H. Waquet (Paris 1964) 264.

178. *Vita S. Willelmi Norwic.* 93 and *passim.*

179. For Waldric's episcopate and these events, see Guibert abbot of Nogent, *De Vita Sua libri tres,* III, caps. 4–11, *PL* clvi. 911–36; cf. also Suger, *Vie de Louis VI, ed. cit.* 176–8. Alfons Becker, *Studien zum Investiturproblem in Frankreich* (Schriften der Universität des Saarlandes, Saarbrücken 1955) 120.

180. For these masters and their school, see Beryl Smalley, *The Study of the Bible in the Middle Ages* (2nd edn, 1952) 49–77; Manitius, iii. 238–9; J. de Ghellinck, *Le Mouvement théologique du XIIe siècle* (2nd edn, Bruges 1948) 133–48; *idem, L'Essor de la littérature latine au XIIe siècle* (Paris 1946) 41–3, bibliography 41 n.; and George Sarton, *Introduction to the History of Science* ii (1), 210. For their theological conservatism – refusing to go beyond the definitions of the Fathers, see John of Salisbury, *Hist. Pont.* 19. Probably because of this, John held them in the greatest respect, *Metalogicon* I. 5, ed. Webb, 17–18.

181. There were, however, Flemish students at Laon in 1127. See Galbert of Bruges, *Vita B. Caroli* in *ASS* March i. 184, 21; *PL* clxvi. 956.

182. But he refused to read Guibert's account of it, *Gesta Dei per Francos,* because it was dedicated to Lisiard, bishop of Soissons, *De Vita Sua,* 936.

find that the citizens of Laon had formed a commune and were in revolt. He failed to suppress the rebellion, was dragged by the hair from his hiding place in a cellar of his church, and then axed to death in the cloister. His ring finger was hacked off and his corpse was stripped and left naked, exposed to every indignity of the rioters. After the city had been burned, the mutilated body of the bishop was recognized only by means of some scars he had boasted of, the result of a joust with another knight in a tournament. Master Anselm, who had managed to avoid trouble, arranged for its burial.

Anselm and Ralf also took charge of the restoration of their church. In order to raise money they immediately sent out a party of canons with the most precious relics of their church on a tour of France, and in the following year, 1113, another party, including an English canon named Robert, visited England.[183] It is likely that the mendicants were given the addresses of the most important pupils of Laon to be found in the kingdom, and some of these are mentioned in the account of the mission. At Canterbury they were received by 'their old friend dom William, archbishop of Canterbury', who had stayed at Laon attending Anselm's lectures and tutoring the sons of King Henry's chancellor, Ralf. This is probably William of Corbeil, Ranulf Flambard's clerk, who became archbishop in 1123, but in 1113, when Canterbury was vacant, was probably a canon of St Martin's, Dover.[184] The royal chancellor, Ralf or Ranulf, was Waldric's successor, who died miserably (ridden over by a monk) and with a very bad reputation in 1123.[185] At Exeter they were welcomed by Archdeacon Robert, probably Bishop William Warelwast's nephew who succeeded to the bishopric in 1138, and who also had attended Anselm's lectures. At Salisbury the reputation of Anselm recommended them to the bishop, for Roger had sent his nephews Alexander (then possibly archdeacon of Salisbury; in 1123 bishop of Lincoln[186]) and Nigel (bishop of Ely in 1133) to school at Laon. At Bodmin in farthest Cornwall, on the edge of the moor, a clerk Algar, another student of Laon, later bishop of Coutances (and in 1113 *procurator* of the priory established by Bishop William of Exeter[187]), was not only pleased to see them but also protected them when they got into a dispute with the natives over whether Arthur was still alive. Since the account of the return journey is cut short, this may be an incomplete list of the distinguished *alumni* of Laon whom the canons visited in 1113. If they had gone to Llanthony, in the Vale of Ewias in the Black Mountains in Wales, they might have found among the canons Robert of Béthune, a future bishop of Hereford, who had abandoned his career as a schoolmaster to study theology under William of Champeaux (at

183. Herman, 'De miraculis S. Mariae Laudunensis', *PL* clvi. 961–88.
184. According to Hugh *HCY* 50, this was his position in 1116 when he accompanied the archbishop to Rome. Charles Johnson translated *Dorovernensis* as 'Canterbury'.
185. Florence, *s.a.* 1123; HH 244, *De contemptu mundi* 308.
186. Henry, archdeacon of Huntingdon in the bishopric of Lincoln, inserted into his *De contemptu mundi* an account of Thomas 'prince of Laon', which he could have taken from his own stay at Laon, from his bishop, Alexander, or from Guibert of Nogent's account: HH 308–10.
187. When Guy of Merton arrived at Bodmin *c.* 1120 to reform the church (see above 232 f.), Master Algar was *illus loci procurator*. Algar became a canon, visited the dying Guy at Exeter, and proposed taking the body back to Bodmin for burial. See Guy's Life in Marvin L. Colker, 'The life of Guy of Merton by Rainald of Merton', *Mediaeval Studies* xxxi (1969) 259–60.

St Victor, Paris, from 1108; bishop of Châlons-sur-Marne in 1113), and then under William's former master, Anselm of Laon, before taking the habit.[188]

At Laon was to be obtained a sound education in the arts and theology; and almost every schoolman of any theological consequence in the middle of the twelfth century, including the grateful Gilbert of la Porrée[189] and the ungrateful Peter Abelard,[190] had studied there. The educational background of Anselm and Ralf is unknown, but it is possible that Anselm had studied under Master Manegold, who taught at Paris and died as a canon of Lauterbach about 1110.[191] The brothers and their pupils played an important part in the composition of the medieval commentary on the Bible, the Gloss;[192] this work, systematic, comprehensive, and traditional, is, indeed, characteristic of the school of Laon. Abelard's contemptuous judgment on Anselm, 'smoke without fire', and, echoing Lucan, 'but the shadow of a great name', is the harsh censure of a brilliant and insolent pupil on a master in decline, the hostility of an individualist to an established authority and his circle. Abelard, who was not afraid to recognize that authorities were apparently in conflict,[193] was one of those who made the reputation of Paris.

It is possible that Englishmen and Normans were to be found from time to time in most of the episcopal schools in northern France. Odo of Bayeux sent the brothers Thomas and Samson, before their successful careers in England, to school at Liège.[194] About 1145 'Sir Richard', an Englishman at Sens, came to the aid of the satirical poet, Hugh, 'the Primate of Orleans'.[195] Earlier, in Henry I's reign there were English students at the cathedral school at Rheims, where the master was Alberic (*de porta veneris*) and the crowds of girls and the high living were a temptation to careless youths.[196] One Christmas,

188. *Vita domini Roberti de Betune* in *Anglia Sacra* ii. 300, reading *Campellensem* for *Capellensem*.

189. R. W. Southern, 'Humanism and the school of Chartres', *Medieval Humanism and Other Studies* 71.

190. *Historia Calamitatum*, PL clxxviii. 123; Lucan *Pharsalia* I, 135.

191. Smalley, *Study of the Bible* 49.

192. *Ibid.* 49–67.

193. Especially in his theological treatise, *Sic et Non* (Yes and No). But he was a reconciler. For the attitude of the civilians, see below, note 272.

194. OV (Chibnall) iv. 118.

195. 'Mais mis sire Richarz, quem misit Anglia, / super me commotus misericordia: / Non est, ait, virtus, sed est socordia; / nec habent hunc morem in nostra patria, / quod dives prebeat clerico prandia, / equus non habeat nocte cibaria. / Dona mei un fustainne et vadimonia / insuper redemit. / Cui sit gloria et gratia et copia / omnium bonorum per secula seculorum.' Poem XVI, lines 147–56. Wilhelm Meyer, 'Die Oxforder Gedichte des Primas', *Nachrichten von der Königl. Gesellschaft der Wissenschaften zu Göttingen; philologisch-historische Klasse*, 1907, p. 93. For the Primate, see J. H. Hanford, 'The progenitors of Golias', *Speculum* i (1926) 44–51; Berthe M. Marti, 'Hugh Primas and Arnulf of Orleans', *ibid.* xxx (1955) 233. For the macaronic poem XVI, see Heinrich Roos, 'Zu dem Oxforder Gedicht XVI des Primas', *Mittellateinisches Jahrbuch* iii (1966) 253.

196. *Anselmi Havelbergensis Vita Adalberti II Moguntini* in *Bibliotheca Rerum Germanicarum*, ed. Ph. Jaffé, iii (Berlin 1866) 577–88. The author was really Anselm, precentor of Mainz, Manitius, iii. 681–3. For Master Alberic, see below 251, n. 200. For the school at Rheims, see John R. Williams, 'Godfrey of Rheims, a humanist of the eleventh century', *Speculum* xxii (1947) 29, 'The cathedral school of Rheims in the eleventh century', *ibid.* xxix (1954) 661, 'The cathedral school of Rheims in the time of Master Alberic', *Traditio* xx (1964) 93. Abelard, *Hist. calam.* in *PL* clxxviii. 126, states pointedly that before seducing Heloise he had kept away from prostitutes.

about 1135, games in the snow, in which the French, the Germans, and the English were taking part, turned ugly when an English boy put a stone in his snowball and wounded a German in the face. To judge by the career of Adalbert of Saarbrücken (II), later archbishop of Mainz (1138–41), who brought this battle in the snow to an end, the teaching at Rheims was relatively elementary, for shortly after this incident he left for Paris to study the *trivium* and *quadrivium*, and to be boisterously greeted there by the French and English.

At Paris were not only the cathedral school (Notre Dame) but also the not far distant schools of the collegiate church of St Geneviève, on its hill south of the river, now replaced by the Pantheon, and of the Augustinian abbey of St Victor, on the south bank itself, a little to the east. Accordingly the number of masters teaching at any one time may well have reached double figures. The list of English *alumni* of Paris in the twelfth century is long and distinguished. Robert, born about 1100 at Gargrave (Yorks, W. Riding), and probably the son of the parson, for later he too possessed the church, went after elementary education to Paris to study the arts, and then, changing to the path which was to lead him to a Cistercian abbacy (Newminster, 1138/9–1159) and sanctity, switched to theology.[197] Ralf reached Paris before 1140, studied under Abelard, became a grammarian of note, and taught at Beauvais, after which city he was later called.[198] At about the same time as he and Adalbert of Saarbrücken found their way to Paris, arrived also John of Salisbury, who, when discussing the teaching of dialectics or logic in his book on the subject, *Metalogicon*, was reminded of his own experiences, and so produced one of the most detailed and liveliest accounts we have of the Parisian scene from 1136 until 1147. He went, he tells us, when quite a young man to school in France the year after Henry I, 'the lion of justice', died.[199] He made his way immediately to Mont St Geneviève, to hear the lectures of the 'peripatetic of Pallet' (Abelard), 'the famous scholar whom all admired', and from him eagerly imbibed such instruction in logic as he was capable of taking in. When Abelard left, 'all too soon', John turned to 'one of the most fashionable logicians', Master Alberic, 'a keen opponent of the nominalist party'.[200] He also heard Robert of Melun, an Englishman but called after the place where he had been a schoolmaster (bishop of Hereford in 1163). John regarded Alberic and Robert, whose

197.   Paul Grosjean, 'Vita S. Roberti Novi monasterii in Anglia abbatis', *AB* lvi (1938) 343–5.

198.   R. W. Hunt, 'Studies in Priscian in the eleventh and twelfth centuries II: the school of Ralph of Beauvais', *MARS* ii (1950) 11–16.

199.   *Metalogicon* II, 10; ed. Webb 77–83. For the masters, see R. L. Poole, 'The masters of the schools at Paris and Chartres', *EHR* xxxv (1920) 321–42; J. de Ghellinck, *Le Mouvement théologique du XIIe siècle* (2nd ed, Bruges 1948) 149 ff.; *idem, L'essor de la littérature latine au XIIe siècle* (Paris 1946) *passim*. J. O. Ward, 'The date of the commentary on Cicero's *De Inventione* by Thierry of Chartres and the Cornifician attack on the Liberal Arts', *Viator* iii (1972) 219–73. John F. Benton, 'Philology's search for Abelard in the *Metamorphosis Goliae*', *Speculum* l (1975), where there is a useful bibliography.

200.   As is shown by Wilhelm Mayer (*art. cit.* above 250, n. 195) 105–6, this is not the renowned Alberic of Rheims (1136–41 archbishop of Bourges), whom they called *de Porta Veneris*, which in the French tongue is Valois (*Valesia*) (John of Salisbury, *Ep.* 143, *PL* cxcix. 124), who possibly wrote a gloss on *Acts*, and who at Laon under Anselm was the fellow student of Abelard and Gilbert the Universal (Abelard, *Hist. Calam. PL* clxxviii. 125; Smalley, *Study of the Bible* 61).

abilities he analyses in detail, as the leading *disputatores* of the age. In two years he had mastered the elements of logic, and 'with the vanity of youth had learned all too well how to make his knowledge seem much greater than it really was'.

John then pulled himself together and turned to more serious matters, principally grammar. For three years he attended, possibly in the city of Paris,[201] the lectures of 'the grammarian of Conches' (William), a Norman, a decade later the tutor of Henry fitzEmpress, and he also profited from other masters teaching there. He studied the arts with Richard l'Evêque, a profound scholar although not a facile teacher (later archdeacon of Coutances and bishop of Avranches, and so perhaps likewise a Norman). Under him he applied himself again to some parts of the *quadrivium*, on which he had already made a start with the German Hardwin, and to rhetoric. He had also studied rhetoric before, listening rather inattentively to Master Thierry (of Chartres) and understanding little. Thierry, a Breton, was Adalbert of Saarbrücken's teacher at Paris and was highly regarded at Mainz as a teacher of the arts.[202] Later John was to pursue rhetoric more fruitfully under the guidance of Peter Helias.[203] Because of poverty John was forced to teach sprigs of the nobility (such as Adalbert) and pass on to them what he heard from his masters. So he took private lessons from the Englishman Master Adam of Balsham (Cambridge) (of the Little Bridge),[204] a man whom John greatly admired for his intelligence and knowledge of Aristotle, and himself taught the first elements of logic to William of Soissons, a great innovator whom John later opposed. He seems then to have taken the post of schoolmaster somewhere for three years.[205] In 1141 he returned to Paris and attended for a short time in 1141–42, probably at the cathedral school, the lectures of Master Gilbert (of la Porrée) on logic and theology,[206] and then (when Gilbert became bishop of Poitiers in 1142) those of his successor, Robert Pullen, in theology. He also studied theology with Simon of Poissy, a rather dull man.[207] In this way John spent almost twelve years in study.

201. The view of R. W. Southern, 'Humanism and the school of Chartres' 71–3. It has by no means been universally accepted. Ward and Benton (as in note 199) still favour Chartes, and cite their supporters.

202. *Vita Adalberti II*, 589–92. 'Donaque doctori dat magna set equa labori, / exule maiora, set nobilitate minora.' For Thierry, see Berthe Widmer, 'Thierry von Chartres, ein Gelehrtenschicksal des 12. Jahrhunderts', *HZ* cc (1965) 552.

203. R. W. Hunt, 'Studies in Priscian in the eleventh and twelfth centuries I: Petrus Helias and his predecessors', *MARS* i (1943) 194.

204. L. Minio-Paluello, 'The "Ars disserendi" of Adam of Balsham "Parvipontanus" ', *MARS* iii (1954) 116, proves that he was not the man who became bishop of St Asaph.

205. 'ut officium docentis aggrederer. Parui. Reversus itaque in fine triennii . . . ' It is possible that John is only saying that he spent three years in tutoring. But the 'return' and the 'triennium' do seem to indicate a sharp geographical and temporal break. It has been suggested that another of his pupils, perhaps in 1145–47, was Peter of Blois, then a schoolboy. Cf. *ep.* 240 in *PL* ccvii. 546. Carl Schaarschmidt, *Johannes saresberiensis nach Leben und Studien, Schriften und Philosophie* (Leipzig 1862) 59; R. W. Southern, *Medieval Humanism and Other Studies* (1970) 109.

206. John reports, *Hist. Pont.* 22, that when Gilbert's views were being attacked at second hand at the council of Rheims, 1148, Gilbert denounced some of his incomprehending pupils, including one choleric clerk who had since crossed over to England.

207. For John's study of theology under these masters, see Beryl Smalley, *The Becket Conflict and the Schools* 88–9.

To close his chapter John turned back to its beginning. Before leaving Paris he thought it would be nice to meet again the old friends he had known at St Geneviève, and found them still engaged in dialectics and disputation, still exactly where they were before. They had made no advances, solved no problems, made progress only in vanity and arrogance, so that one despaired of their reformation. 'I then realized', he concluded, 'what is plain for all to see, that while logic can be a help to all other disciplines, by itself it is sterile and anaemic. Nor can it bring the mind to yield the fruit of philosophy unless it takes its seed from another source.' In fact the only field of knowledge at this time to which logic could be profitably applied was theology.

In the space of twelve years, possibly from the age of sixteen to twenty-eight, John sat at the feet of at least twelve masters, some of them the most eminent of that period, in the schools of Paris. Three of these, it should be noticed, Robert of Melun, a logician, Adam, a philosopher and grammarian, and Robert Pullen archdeacon of Rochester, a theologian, were of English birth.[208] It was these numbers and facilities which made Paris without a rival north of the Alps as a place of learning. Abelard excelled in every branch of the arts and through his genius advanced them all. John, although aware of the limitations of the curriculum, in his own scholastic achievements exemplified them all too well. He was a graceful Latin stylist, and easily found employment as a secretary to the great. His letters were welcomed, admired, and collected. He wrote interesting near-contemporary memoirs of the papal court, *Historia Pontificalis*, and two books, *Policraticus* and *Metalogicon*, which were designed to display his erudition, wisdom, wit, and style. Today these last are pillaged for details rather than enjoyed as a whole.[209] John was without Abelard's creativeness, but he was at the very centre of the scholastic world, knew every scholar worth knowing, was aware of all the changing fashions and trends, and was deeply impressed by the 'new' logic. He can be regarded as both the crowning achievement and also the victim of a restricted literary education.[210]

Although John pursued liberal studies, they were utilitarian in that they qualified him to teach, to act as a secretary, and to be promoted bishop. Besides, from his study of theology he had gained some knowledge of canon law, and he knew at least some bits of Roman law. With an even sharper eye to the main chance were those who specialized in jurisprudence. Archbishop Theobald recruited Master Vacarius from Bologna as well as John of Salisbury from Paris. Jurists distinguished three main branches of law: the law of God, canon law; Roman or civil law; and the customary law of secular society and its

208.   In 1148 Robert of Melun, Adam of Balsham, and Hugh of Amiens (Reading) were with Peter Lombard, the future *Magister Sententiarum*, at the council of Rheims against Gilbert of la Porrée. For Robert, see Smalley, *Study of the Bible*, 73–4; *The Becket Conflict and the Schools*, 51 ff.; Manitius iii. 149–50; de Ghellinck, *L'essor* 55–7; for Adam, Manitius iii. 202–4; *L'essor* 76–8; for Robert Pullen, de Ghellinck, *Le mouvement théologique*, 162–3, 181–2; Smalley, *The Becket Conflict and the Schools* 39 ff. According to John of Hexham, 319, who gives an enthusiastic account of him *s.a.* 1147 = 1146, Robert Pullen refused the offer of a bishopric from Henry I. See also John of Salisbury *Metalogicon* I, 5; ed. Webb 19–20.

209.   And so they were in the twelfth century. For the borrowings of Peter of Blois, see R. W. Southern, *Medieval Humanism* 118–26.

210.   For a useful review of the literature 1947–57 see Heinrich Hohenleutner, 'Johannes von Salisbury in der Literatur der letzen zehn Jahre', *HJ* lxxvii (1958) 493.

courts. Only the first two were school subjects, and the civilians believed that their branch alone had true academic respectability. Both were taught by expounding or annotating the texts – producing glosses – so that the doctors in jurisprudence were known as glossators.[211] The civilians were convinced that their texts, the *Corpus Juris Civilis*, the Emperor Justinian's magnificent bequest to the Middle Ages, were more authoritative, homogeneous, concordant, and rational than the various unofficial collections of canon law, which were notorious for their discordance.[212]

The eleventh-century reform of the church owed much to a revival in canon law, and the progress of Gregorian reform encouraged its systematic presentation in the shape most useful to prelates of the new age. Gratian, a monk of San Felice at Bologna (the place is significant), with his *Concordia discordantium canonum*, produced about 1140, gave the subject academic respectability and provided the standard school text for the canonist glossators. By using all the logical devices available at the time he made a serious attempt to reconcile the discordant ecclesiastical authorities, and, even if the civilians thought him excessively timid, he gave the church a *Corpus Juris Canonici* which could be put beside that of Justinian. Scholastically speaking, canon law remained a branch of theology,[213] and lectures on ecclesiastical law were probably given in many cathedral schools. In 1126 Thurstin archbishop of York retained the Breton schoolmaster of Auxerre, the theologian Gilbert the Universal, best known as a glossator on the Old Testament, but in this context described as 'a wise clerk and famous advocate', to plead his case at Rome against the Scottish bishops and, if need be, Canterbury. In fact Gilbert transferred his services to the archbishop of Canterbury and incurred the taunt that he was like 'bold Curio with the venal tongue'. He got his reward in little more than a year, when he was given the bishopric of London.[214] Canon law was also studied in the monasteries – Lanfranc introduced into England his own compilation which soon became popular[215] – and litigation was to become one of the great monastic recreations.

In the early Norman period, however, customary law held its own very well against its competitor. When Bishop William of St Calais brandished in his defence in the royal court Lanfranc's collection no one took him seriously.[216] The new activity of church courts in Henry I's reign and the growing

---

211.   Useful summaries are H. F. Jolowicz, 'Revivals of Roman law', *Journal of the Warburg and Courtauld Institutes* xv (1952) 88 and H. Kantorowicz, 'Note on the development of the gloss to the Justinian and the canon law', in Beryl Smalley, *The Study of the Bible in the Middle Ages* (2nd edn, 1952) 52–5. See also Jean Gaudemet, 'Le droit romain dans la pratique et chez les docteurs aux XIe et XIIe siècles, *Cahiers de Civ. Méd.* viii (1965) 365.

212.   Joseph de Ghellinck, 'Master Vacarius: un juriste théologien peu aimable pour les canonistes', *RHE* xliv (1949) 173–8. Southern, 'Master Vacarius' 264, denies that Vacarius 'despised' canon law; but Peter Stein, 'Vacarius and the civil law', in *Church and Government in the Middle Ages: essays presented to C. R. Cheney* 125–7, is more judicious.

213.   J. de Ghellinck, *Le mouvement théologique* 58–60, 416–510.

214.   Hugh *HCY* 127; Lucan *Phars*. I, 269. For Gilbert see above 86 f.

215.   Z. N. Brooke, *The English Church and the Papacy* (1931) 57–83; see also above 145, n. 3.

216.   See below 286.

popularity of appeals was generally disapproved.[217] Semi-professional papal judges-delegate, pleaders, proctors, and notaries public all lay in the future. *Professores* of both laws, canon and civil, were hardly to be found. But, as with medicine, there were many men practising the law who, although they had had little academic instruction, had a good knowledge of the procedure of different types of courts and of the law which ran in them. Since most cases were compromised, it was of more practical use to pleaders to know their way round the court and to be familiar with all the tricks of the trade than to have a deep knowledge of the law.

Of even less practical use, at least in north-west Christendom, and outside the Roman Empire, was Roman law. In the eleventh century, and associated with the name of the jurist Irnerius, Bologna developed from a school of rhetoric into one of the leading centres of legal studies, and in the third and fourth decades of the twelfth century the influence of Bologna began to spread into Normandy and England. Arnulf,[218] born into a clerical family in Normandy in the first decade of the twelfth century and predestined to be an archdeacon and bishop, after schooling at Sées where his brother was arch-deacon and in 1124 bishop, seems to have studied the arts at perhaps both Chartres and Paris, and in 1133 went to Italy to study law. In 1141 he succeeded his uncle as bishop of Lisieux. He was a good poet, an eloquent orator, a master of the epistolary art, and a trusted papal judge-delegate. About 1143 Archbishop Theobald recruited Vacarius to help him with the administration of his church and province and in his disputes with Henry of Winchester.[219] This civilian, who was rather a large fish in the English pond, was born about 1120 and studied Roman law at Bologna, following Martinus, one of the Four Doctors who had been the pupils of Irnerius. Vacarius's career in England was in episcopal courts, not in the schools. He left Theobald to follow Roger of Pont l'Evêque to York, when the archdeacon of Canterbury was promoted to that see in 1154, and spent the last fifty years of his life in the northern province. Although Gervase of Canterbury was probably mistaken in claiming that Vacarius taught at Oxford, it is likely that the master did give some instruction in Roman law in England. His *Lectura* on Justinian's Institutes is evidence for this. Most likely he taught in Theobald's household or even at Northampton, where, probably towards the end of Stephen's reign, he went to study theology and specialize in canon law. He also had an important, but much delayed, influence on the later teaching of civil law in England. Early in his life, perhaps while he was still a master at Bologna, he produced an elementary compendium, known later as the *Liber Pauperum,* which consisted of extracts from the Digest and Code strung together by a commentary (glosses). At the end of the century this became a popular school book at Oxford, so that Vacarius was, if only in a remote way, one of the founders of a great law school in England. More immediate, no doubt, was the invigorating

---

217. HH 282.

218. *The Letters of Arnulf of Lisieux,* ed. Frank Barlow, Camden 3rd ser. lxi (1939), introduction.

219. The most recent accounts of Vacarius in England, and superseding all others, are R. W. Southern 'Master Vacarius', and Peter Stein, 'Vacarius and the civil law', *loc. cit.* If it is remembered that canon law was a branch of theology, the controversy over which of those subjects Vacarius studied at Northampton becomes almost meaningless.

influence his passionate belief in the superiority of civil law over all others must have had on ecclesiastical administration in the kingdom.

The backwardness of advanced studies in England at the end of our period and the paucity of legal instruction to be obtained in Archbishop Theobald's household, even while Vacarius was still there, is proved by the early career of Thomas Becket.[220] Thomas of London, after attending school at Merton priory and in the city, finished his education in the arts at Paris, studying possibly under Robert of Melun. After serving as a clerk in the office of a London merchant and sheriff, and then in the household of Theobald, he was prepared for a career in the church by being sent (before 1154) to study law at Bologna and Auxerre. Thomas tells us nothing about his studies and no contemporary remembered him in the schools. Clearly he was not a disinterested scholar. He was inferior in learning to the other clerks he found in Theobald's court, and it was alleged that he was unable in 1163, when archbishop, to make a speech in Latin at the papal council of Tours. His knowledge of canon law, even after his studies in exile at Pontigny, has never been rated very high. He owed his successful career in the church to other qualities, and he always studied the appropriate subject. Once he was made archbishop he recruited masters to coach him in theology, and, to his credit but to his grave temporal disadvantage, his viewpoint became much more theological than legal.[221] Also in the early 1150s at Bologna, in the school of Hubert Creveli, the future Pope Urban III, was Baldwin, later archdeacon of Totnes (in the diocese of Exeter), abbot of the Cistercian house of Ford, bishop of Worcester, and archbishop of Canterbury, who died on the Third Crusade. In England he was not only a heavily employed papal judge-delegate but also compiled one of the earliest and most influential collections of the new case law (the decretals), the Worcester Collection and its appendices, which with others of its kind put English canonists for a short time ahead of the Italians in this new field.[222]

Archdeacons and other episcopal law officers no doubt received some instruction in canon law and, at the very end of our period, in civil law, and also served a kind of apprenticeship. Even less is known about the training of those who worked in the courts of secular customary law. There were no inns of court. We have to imagine that royal justiciars, great men like Ranulf Flambard and Roger of Salisbury, and lower judges, like Geoffrey Ridel and Robert Bloet, probably building on some acquaintance with canon law, just picked up their knowledge of the secular law in the courts they presided over or served. The law of these courts, from the *curia regis* to the hundred, was declared when necessary by the suitors. Nevertheless, judges with great professional experience and forensic skill could influence the conduct and outcome of a case. Ranulf Flambard is said to have 'driven the courts'.[223] In this way clerks

220. William fitzStephen, *MB* iii. 14, 17.

221. Stephen of Rouen, *Draco Normannicus,* in *Chronicles of the reigns of Stephen, Henry II, and Richard,* ed. R. Howlett (Rolls ser. 1885) ii. 744, lines 997–8. For a view of Becket's education, see Smalley, *The Becket Conflict and the Schools* 109–11.

222. Peter of Blois, *Ep.* 211, *PL* ccvii. 494. For Baldwin as a decretalist, see Charles Duggan, *Twelfth-century Decretal Collections* (University of London Historical Studies, xii, 1963), especially 110–7.

223. Cf. Raoul C. van Caenegem, 'Public prosecution of crime in twelfth-century England', *Church and Government in the Middle Ages* (essays to C. R. Cheney) 55–6.

could modify traditional procedures. The need soon arose for textbooks and treatises. The state of legal scholarship in these circles in the middle of Henry I's reign can be seen from the *Quadripartitus* and the *Leges Henrici Primi*.[224] These are two parts of a rather disorderly treatise, the former being a collection of the source material (the corpus of Anglo-Saxon codes and some legal documents) and the latter an exposition of the law which ran in the courts at the time of writing. The anonymous author was an English clerk of Norman/ French descent, who had probably been in the service of Gerard, bishop of Hereford 1096–1101 and archbishop of York until his death in 1108, a royal clerk and ambassador and a nephew of Walkelin bishop of Winchester. He had then possibly entered royal service, for he greatly admired Henry I and his treatises seem to have been written in Wessex, perhaps at Winchester, and for the use primarily of those concerned with the customary courts. The deficiencies of the author are notorious. He had an imperfect knowledge of Old English, little theory, and small powers of analysis and presentation. He shows no acquaintance with Roman jurisprudence but knew his canon law, probably for the most part in the formulations of Ivo bishop of Chartres. Yet although the academically trained lawyers of the later twelfth century must have despised the artlessness of his work, it continued to be copied, for it remained of practical use.

The study of the various branches of science was equally utilitarian, although probably less lucrative. All the subjects of the *quadrivium* – arithmetic, geometry, astronomy, and music – were considered mathematical, with the first two serving the others, principally astronomy. Since astronomy was usually put to astrological ends, it is not surprising that in late-classical and medieval Latin *mathesis* and *mathematicus* more often meant 'astrology' and 'astrologer' than 'mathematics' and 'mathematician'.[225] John of Salisbury, who was fascinated by all forms of divination, sometimes employed *mathematicus* in the wide sense of 'soothsayer'.[226] It was, indeed, the belief in astrology in all civilized countries in this period which gave such an impetus to mathematical and astronomical studies, both theoretical and technological, and which sent most western scholars in pursuit of the lore of the East. The other science subjects, chemistry and medicine, were not ordinary school disciplines. The former, which was in the guise of alchemy, had few operatives.[227] The later was divided sharply by contemporaries into theoretical and practical, and it was recognized that most practitioners had little theoretical knowledge. In all these subjects the Muslim world, which had inherited Greek

224. The latest edition of the *Leges,* with a discussion of many of the problems concerning it and the *Quadripartitus*, is L. J. Downer, *Leges Henrici Primi* (1972).

225. Cassiodorus, however, treats in Book II of the *quadrivium* without mentioning the sinister aspects. It is only in his conclusion that he states that there are some who, under the study called *mathesis*, claim to foretell the future, a claim denied by all wise men.

226. *Policraticus*, II, caps. 18–29; (ed. Webb) i. 101–69. This book deals largely with the abuse of mathematics and science. 'Mathematici sunt, licet appellatio generaliter omnia complectatur, qui a positione stellarum situque firmamenti, et planetarum motu quae sint ventura conjiciunt.', i. 52–3. See further, Barbara Helbling-Gloor, *Natur und Aberglaube im Policraticus des Johannes von Salisbury*: Geist und Werk der Zeiten, i (Zurich 1956).

227. A rather more favourable view of twelfth-century chemistry, 'one of the neglected topics in the history of medieval science', is taken by Richard C. Dales, 'Marius "On the Elements" and the twelfth-century science of matter', *Viator* iii (1972) 191–218.

science and had studied its branches intensively over several centuries, was far in advance of Christendom. And to the conventional Christian mind there was something suspicious about them all. From Gerbert onwards, all who engaged in their study were in danger of being reputed in league with the devil and, for their unlawful profit, to be lusting after forbidden knowledge.[228]

At the end of the eleventh century, partly as a result of political events in Spain and southern Italy, partly inspired by the intellectual awakening, what had been the merest trickle of translations from Arabic into Latin became a flood. On a world map showing the medieval transmission of science the significant area is the crescent from Peking in the north-east to Cordoba in the west. England was on the fringe of the westerly tide, but, strangely enough, among the earliest translators of Muslim scientific treatises into Latin were two Englishmen, Adelard of Bath and Robert of Chester. Adelard studied at Laon, which was well known for its mathematics, and Tours, and in his western period wrote (before 1116) a philosophic treatise on Identity and Difference (*De eodem et diverso*), and books on the abacus and falconry. It was, it seems, in Sicily, Cilicia, and Syria that he became an Arabist, and translated some treatises of incalculable value to the west. His *Questiones naturales* expounded Arabic teaching on seventy-six scientific questions, but more basic were the mathematical works he made available: Euclid's Fifteen Books and Arabic trigonometry. He retired to England in his old age and in 1142–44 was appointed by Robert earl of Gloucester tutor to the earl's nephew, Henry, the future king, who was with him at Bristol. There Adelard wrote a book on the astrolabe which he dedicated to his ten-year-old pupil.[229]

Robert of Chester worked in Spain and became archdeacon of Pamplona in Navarre in 1143. He made the first translation into Latin of the Koran (1141–43); the first translation of the algebra of al-Khuwarizmi (Segovia 1135) thus introducing to Christendom a new mathematical subject; and one of the earliest translations of an important alchemical treatise (1144). He came to London in 1147 where he too wrote a book on the astrolabe and where he produced astronomical tables for the longitude of London (1149–50) based on Arabic tables.[230] The importance of these two men in the history of European knowledge can hardly be exaggerated.

The effect of their translations was not much felt in England before the middle of the twelfth century. English mathematical, scientific, and medical knowledge in the Norman period was probably mostly derived from the cathedral schools of northern France and Lorraine. Gerbert of Aurillac, Pope Silvester II, who died in 1003, had studied in Barcelona and taken his Spanish–Arabic mathematical knowledge to Rheims; he wrote on the abacus and

228. For this, and much of the following, see George Sarton, *Introduction to the History of Science*, i. *From Homer to Omar Khayyam* (Washington 1927), ii, pt I, *The Twelfth Century* (1931). C. H. Haskins, *Studies in the History of Medieval Science* (Harvard 1924), *Studies in Medieval Culture* (1929). A short summary with diagrams and a map is H. J. J. Winter, 'Mediaeval transmissions in science', *Endeavour* xxxii (1973) 134–8.

229. Sarton, ii. 167–9. de Ghellinck, *L'essor* 61–2. Haskins, 'Adelard of Bath and Henry Plantagenet', *EHR* xxviii (1913) 515–16. Abelard and Heloise called their son Astrolabe: *Hist. Calam.* in *PL* clxxviii. 129.

230. Sarton, ii. 175–7.

astrolabe and on various scientific problems.[231] From Lotharingia England continued to recruit prelates after the Conquest, reinforcing a native mathematical tradition going back to Bede and revived in the eleventh century. Robert of Lorraine bishop of Hereford (1079–95), who rebuilt his church on the model of Aachen, was skilled in the liberal arts, especially the *quadrivium*. He was an abacist, a computist, an astronomer, and a chronographer. He introduced the chronology of Marianus Scotus into England and typical western mathematics. He also put his knowledge of the stars to good use. He did not bother to set off for the dedication ceremony at Lincoln cathedral in 1095 because the stars foretold that it would not take place. As Bishop Remigius of Lincoln died only on the eve of the appointed day, Robert's predictions were extremely accurate. Robert was also apprised in a dream of the death of his friend, Wulfstan, bishop of Worcester, and hurried back from the royal court to conduct the burial.[232]

Robert's successor at Hereford, Gerard (1096–1101), another royal clerk and a nephew of Bishop Walkelin of Winchester, also inherited some of Robert's interests. But in him they were considered sinister. He owned a Hebrew psalter.[233] William of Malmesbury alleged that he was guilty of many crimes, including lust, and, because he read Julius Firmicus in the morning, was believed to have been engaged in sorcery. Firmicus Maternus, a Sicilian, wrote between 334 and 337, before his conversion to Christianity, *Matheseos Libri VIII* (*Mathematics in 8 Books*), a comprehensive textbook of astrology.[234] Gerard was promoted to York in 1101, and his death on 21 May 1108 was clouded with suspicion. When suffering from only a very minor illness, and reposing in an orchard near his house so as to enjoy the fresh air scented with flowers, he ordered his servants to leave him and go in and take their meal. When they returned they found him dead, and on a cushion by his side was 'a book of curious arts'. The canons of York refused at first to allow him to be buried with his predecessors within the church.[235] The study of astrology led easily to the black arts. John of Salisbury, as we have seen, was taught by a priest who tried to conjure up the dead.[236]

Some of the interests of the bishops of Hereford spread also to Worcester and Malvern. At the former church they led to the writing of Florence's chronicle.[237] At the latter the astronomer Walker was prior by 1120. Walker, according to his epitaph, was a Lotharingian and a learned and

---

231. Sarton, i. 669–71.

232. *GP* 300–3, 313; Florence *s.a.* 1095. For Robert as an abacist, see C. H. Haskins, 'The abacus and the king's curia', *EHR* xxvii (1912) 105–6.

233. R. B. Dobson, *The Jews of medieval York and the massacre of March 1190* (Borthwick papers no. 45, 1974) 3 ff.

234. Sarton, i. 354.

235. *GP* 259–60. Hugh the Chanter, *HCY* 12–14, although making a case for York and its archbishops against Canterbury, is discreetly silent about Gerard's virtues – and vices. Hugh of Flavigny heard in England the most scandalous stories: Gerard's brother, Peter, a royal chaplain, had been impregnated by another man, and had died of it; and Gerard had sacrificed a pig to the devil: *Chronicon Hugonis . . . abbatis Flaviniacensis*, ed. G. H. Pertz, *MGH SS* viii (1848) 496–7.

236. Above 228.

237. Above 18f.

religious man, a worthy philosopher, a good astrologer, a geometrician, and an abacist.[238] He was travelling, possibly to and from Sicily, in 1091–92, when in Italy he observed with an astrolabe the lunar eclipses of 30 October 1091 and 18 October 1092. He was an Arabist, about 1108 compiling a set of lunar tables from Arabic models, and in 1120 translating into Latin the astronomical treatise on the constellation the Dragon, written in Hebrew or Arabic by the Spanish Jew Pedro Alfonso.[239] Pedro, born Moses Sephardi in 1062, became physician to Alfonso VI, king of Castile, and was baptized in 1106. He may have visited the court of Henry I some time before his death in 1110.[240] William of Malmesbury recorded stories he had heard from Walker,[241] and William, as well as his fellow monks, Faricius and Gregory, studied medicine.

There seems to have been no dearth in England of people who practised medicine of a sort.[242] Many accounts of miraculous cures carefully state that every recourse to secular medicine had failed. Most practitioners were *medici rustici* or *practici*, those who had learned the secrets of their profession from either their father or a master. As medicine is an art, and, until quite recent times, lacked both a sound scientific basis and a useful technology, such physicians were no worse than the country doctor in most periods of history, and they were not necessarily worse than those contemporaries who had studied medicine as an academic subject. There was probably no insufficiency of diagnostic skill. Sickness and accidents were common and it was usually obvious what was wrong. In the third quarter of the twelfth century Reginald of Durham, in his account of 'recent' miracles of St Cuthbert and those of St Godric, often described the physical condition of the sufferers in minute and horrifying detail.[243] It is rarely stated in the miraculous stories what kind of doctor had been consulted, whether they were laymen (or women), clerks or monks, part-timers or professionals. For the hagiographers there was only the fundamental distinction between secular and spiritual medicine, and their claim that the latter was usually the more efficacious was, given the conditions, probably not entirely unjustified.

Medici practici may not always have been clerks, although evidence for this period is completely lacking. Clerks and monks in major orders who practised medicine had the advantage that both systems were at their disposal, that when they could not heal the body they could at least doctor the soul.[244] But lay practitioners may have been thought to have access to a body of

---

238. Quoted W. Stubbs, *GR* ii, p. xc.

239. Sarton, ii, 209–10; Stubbs, *loc. cit.*

240. Sarton, ii. 199–200; Manitius iii. 174–7. His visit to England, however, seems to rest on a marginal note in a fourteenth-century manuscript.

241. *GR* 346.

242. Cf. F. Vercauteren, 'Les médicins dans les principautés de la Belgique et du nord de la France, du VIIIe au XIIIe siècle', *Le Moyen Age* lvii (1951) 61. C. H. Talbot and E. A. Hammond, *The Medical Practitioners in Medieval England: a biographical register* (1965); Talbot, *Medicine in Medieval England* (1967).

243. Cf. *St Cuthbert* 221.

244. In the twelfth century, Master Ralf *medicus,* possibly a canon of Lincoln, gave to the cathedral only religious books, viz. a glossed Book of Kings and a glossed St Paul's Epistles: Giraldus Cambrensis *Opera* (Rolls ser. 1877) vii. 170.

knowledge prohibited to those in holy orders. Most sufferers with money seem to have tried every kind of doctor in turn. Before the twelfth century monasteries were probably the main centres of academic medicine. They had the books, inmates interested in the subject, and often a herb garden. The council of Rheims (1131) cap. 6, repeated by Lateran II (1139) cap. 9, forbade monks and canons regular to practise medicine (together with secular law) for money, but since monks normally gave advice in return for a free-will offering, the legislation was hardly restrictive. Lectures on medicine were probably given in most cathedral schools, and many clerical physicians may have received no further training. Among the medical treatises in the monasteries was the section in the popular encyclopedia, the *Etymologiae* or *Origines* of Isidore of Seville (died 636), which transmitted the purest Greco-Latin medical tradition,[245] and in the early post-Conquest period Anglo-Saxon medical lore was probably still available to English monks. There were the Old English translations of the possibly fourth-century authors, the herbalist Apuleius Platonicus (Ps.-Apuleius) and the animal druggist, Sextus Placitus Papyriensis, and compilations, such as the tenth-century 'Glastonbury' collection, which derived its recipes from a variety of late classical sources.[246] Although almost all the remedies listed are worthless, while some are dangerous and many disgusting, they were not in this different from those prescribed in the most advanced medical schools of the period.

Specialist teaching centres for practitioners were few. Salerno, south of Naples, became in the twelfth century the leading school of medicine in the west. It was carrying on, rather feebly, the tradition of Greek medicine when, after its conquest by the Normans in 1077, it was not only opened to Arabic influence, but also became more accessible to French and English students. Constantine, the African from Carthage who died at Monte Cassino in 1087, translated many important Arabic medical works into Latin; and ultimately Salernitan medicine inherited the entire body of Greek and Muslim knowledge.[247] The superiority of this over the existing European traditions, equally derived from the Greek, is not incontestable. But in any case it is unlikely that England was much affected by Salernitan medicine before 1150. Closer at hand was Montpellier in the south of France, Adalbert of Saarbrücken's next port of call after Paris and his last before becoming archbishop of Mainz on the death of his uncle of the same name in 1137. He went there to study 'physics', not in order to gain a professional qualification but because he was interested in natural science (*causae naturae*; *vis rerum*). At Montpellier he found physicians who not only offered advice to the healthy and cures to the sick but also taught the theory and rules of medicine.[248]

245. Ed. W. M. Lindsay (1910–11), book IV.

246. Printed in *Leechdoms, Wortcunning and Starcraft in Early England,* collected and ed. O. Cockayne (Rolls ser. 1864). Apuleius Platonicus, *Herbarius*; Sextus Placitus, *De medicina ex animalibus*, both in *Corpus Medicorum Latinorum* iv.

247. Sarton, ii. 63–95; Talbot 38–55.

248. *Vita Adalberti II,* 592–3. John of Salisbury, *Metalogicon* I, iv (ed. Webb) 13–14, satirizes those who give up logic to go to Salerno or Montpellier and emerge in no time as fully fledged doctors, quoting Hippocrates and Galen and speaking a strange jargon. They have also learned the maxims, Do not labour among the poor, and Present the bill while the patient is still in pain.

Medical teaching, increasingly divorced from clinical observation and practical anatomy, was based on the general theory of the four humours; for diagnosis doctors usually relied especially on inspection of urine and taking the pulse, and for cure they favoured blood-letting and purgation – allowing the bad influences to escape.[249] There was also a school of doctors who aimed to cure by regulating the diet. It does not seem that there were many, if any, specialized surgeons at this time, and most surgical operations likewise aimed at controlling the humours. The tendency to regard medicine as a theoretical, even philosophical system, had as effects the willingness of doctors to prescribe without even seeing the patient and their inclination to regard all the practical details of the treatment as beneath their dignity. They were not manual workers. When they were prepared to examine the sick, the faulty scientific basis of their knowledge could be influenced for the better by practical experience. But most treatments were influenced for the worse by the precepts of astrology. John of Salisbury at the end of Book II of his *Policraticus*, a section largely devoted to the misuse for magical purposes of mathematics and science, turned his attention to practising physicians. Since, he wrote, because of his sins, he fell all too often into their hands, he had to be careful what he said about them, lest they should treat him even worse than usual. They were, he admitted, when trustworthy and skilful, the most necessary and useful men in the world. But he also permitted himself to make some very old and very wry jokes about them.[250]

It is not known where most of those who practised medicine in Norman England had studied the subject. Forty-five names of *medici* in the period 1066–1154 have been collected, mainly from chronicles, letters, and witness lists to charters. Only one of those names is English, two or three are Italian, the rest are French. Eight of these physicians were monks, and the remainder, although rarely given a status, were probably clerks.[251] With this type of evidence we do not reach as low as *medici rustici*. Three of the monks became abbots. Edward the Confessor's doctor, Baldwin, a former prior of Leberau, a cell of St Denis, Paris, in German Alsace, north of Colmar, and with his typically Flemish name to be regarded as one of Edward's Lotharingian (not

249.   Sarton, i. 699–727, 769; ii. 63–95. Cf. 'Rex Ezechias egrotavit ad mortem (4 Reg. 20: 1: Is, 38: 1). An non credis regem Juda medicum invenisse, qui urinae et pulsus et multiplicium praenosticorum indicio morbi deprehenderet quantitatem?', John of Salisbury, *Policraticus*, II, 25 (ed. Webb) i. 136. William I's doctors, after inspecting his urine in 1087, predicted his certain death, *GR* 337. For another example of inspecting the urine, see *Hist. Pont.* 15. For taking the pulse, 'puer in quo consultae pollicibus venae proximum nuntiabant interitum', Hildebert, *Vita S. Hugonis abbatis Cluniac.* in *PL* clix. 877.

250.   *Policraticus*, II, 29 (ed. Webb) i. 168–9.

251.   Talbot and Hammond: *monks*: Albert of Bec, Aluric? of St Bertin, Baldwin of [Leberau] St Denis, Faricius, Gregory of Malmesbury, Hugh of Chertsey, Maurice of Bec, Peter de Quincy; *clerks*: Clarembald, Gilbert Maminot, Grimbald, John of Tours, Nigel, Ralf canon of Lincoln, Walter of York, William canon of London; *unknown status, but probably clerks*: Barnard of York, Cunbert, Ernulf of London, Eudo of Winchester, Gilbert of Falaise, Gilbert of London, Hugh of York, Hugh of Lewes, Hugh of Rouen, Iwod John of London, Lambert of York, Mark, Melbethe, Milo of Oxford, Nigel, Pagas [*recte* Pagan] of Winchester, Paul of York, Paulinus of York, Ralf of Huntingdon, Ranulf royal physician, Robert of Oxford, Robert of ?Nostell, Roland of Sussex, Theobald of Wiltshire, Walter of Sussex, William of Lincs, William of Winchester, William of Yorks.

French) recruits, survived the Conquest as abbot of Bury, specialized like his patron saint St Edmund in eye injuries, and was held in great repute by the newcomers.[252] Faricius from Arezzo in Tuscany was a monk of Malmesbury by 1078 and became abbot of Abingdon in 1100. He was so trusted by the royal family that Henry wanted to make him archbishop of Canterbury in 1114, but the bishops raised several objections, including the unsuitability for such a post of a man who spent his time examining women's urine.[253] When Faricius's successful competitor, Archbishop Ralf, went to the papal *curia* in 1116 with Bishop Herbert Losinga of Norwich, they took with them as physician Hugh abbot of Chertsey, and both needed his ministrations on the journey.[254]

The 'secular' doctors were mostly in the service of the royal family and other magnates. Henry I seems to have retained a good number in his household, and it has been noticed that the Spanish Jewish physician, Pedro Alfonso, may have visited his court. Many of the royal doctors were richly rewarded, two with bishoprics. The Conqueror was attended on his deathbed by Gilbert Maminot bishop of Lisieux and Gontard abbot of Jumièges, together with others unnamed.[255] In England he endowed his physician Nigel with large estates. Another of his doctors, John *de Villula*, who came from Tours, was rewarded by Rufus with the bishopric of Wells in 1088. William of Malmesbury claimed, perhaps jealously, that John had gained his medical skill only from practice and not from academic training. It is not surprising that John transferred his see into the abbey of Bath, adjacent to the hot springs. Although John was said by his detractor to be self-indulgent and addicted to the bottle, and indeed died from a sudden heart attack after his Christmas dinner, he lived to a ripe old age.[256] Another Italian in Henry I's household was Grimbald, possibly like Faricius from Arezzo. In 1130 he witnessed and interpreted his master's bad dreams and prescribed alms-giving.[257] A physician Clarembald passed from Henry's court to the service of the blind bishop of Exeter.[258]

These men were *medici et clerici* and could sometimes be described as chaplains. Bishops and secular magnates likewise retained such men; and their witness to charters shows them to have been part of the *familia*. There must also have been, at least in the cities, doctors in private practice. Traces of these can be seen in London, Winchester, and York, and some other places. At Winchester in 1138 three doctors, Pain, William, and Richard, all lived in the same suburb and were probably neighbours in the lane which ran west from Kingsgate Street to the road leading from South Gate, while the king's doctor,

252. Leberau is situated between Ste Marie aux Mines (Markirch) and Sélestat (Schlettstadt). For Baldwin, see *Heremanni archidiaconi mirac. S. Eadmundi* in Liebermann *Ungedruckte* 244 ff.; *LEp* 17–18.

253. *Chron. Abingdon* ii. 287.

254. Hugh *HCY* 50.

255. OV (Chibnall) iv. 80. The 'De obitu Willelmi' adds the name of John *de Villula*. This may be true, although the tract is now rather discredited; see L. J. Engels, 'De obitu Willelmi ducis Normannorum regisque Anglorum: Texte, modèles, valeur et origine', *Mélanges Christine Mohrmann* (Utrecht/Anvers 1973) 240–2.

256. Above 66 f.

257. Above 91.

258. D. W. Blake, 'Bishop William Warelwast', *Trans. Devonshire Assoc.* civ (1972) 28.

Grimbald, had had a house not very far away in St Thomas Street.[259] There were clearly sufficient doctors to meet the demand, and judging by their rewards, they were on the whole well-regarded. William of Malmesbury, however, had in general a poor opinion of them. He tells a story about a woman who, being paralysed for five years, used up most of her wealth unsuccessfully on doctors, and he claims that Bishop John of Bath made a lot of money out of his doubtful skill[260] – he thought his fellow monk, Gregory, at least more honest and less rapacious. The baron Ernulf of Hesding went to Malmesbury to consult Gregory, *probatissimus medicus*, about the loss of the use of his hands. Gregory, however, had to declare the disease incurable, and it was the abbot, with the aid of balm which had been found in St Aldhelm's tomb, who had to come to the rescue.[261]

Information about diagnosis and treatment is scanty. All doctors seem to have prescribed medicines, usually bitter concoctions, and mostly, no doubt, purgative. Much surgery was likewise designed to allow egress to the humours or evil spirits. In the north of England a woman suffering from headache had the top of her head incised in the form of a cross. Broken and weak limbs, swellings and tumours were treated by poulticing, cauterizing, and incisions. Even a woman suffering from some kind of heart disease was cauterized, scarified, and bled, as well as given various medicines. A Durham scholar living in Paris who fell ill of fever and consulted all the best doctors was finally sent home to eat the food he was used to as a boy.[262] Several cases recorded by English chroniclers concern the male genitals. One of the many human stories told by Eadmer about Anselm concerns his sympathetic treatment of a monk morbidly concerned with the state of his penis.[263] Two successive bishops of London, according to William of Malmesbury, received very different medical advice. Hugh of Orival (bishop 1075–85) became incurably ill of leprosy and covered with ulcers. He was advised by his doctors to be castrated, but the operation only added shame to his condition. Hugh's successor, Maurice (1086–1107), explained his unchastity as a means of preserving his health prescribed by his physicians.[264] A Durham monk, who suffered a crushed testicle when thrown from his horse, prudently declined to have the swollen organ surgically removed, and rightly preferred to offer a penny to St Cuthbert. Time and faith worked a cure.[265] Castration, practised in animal husbandry and as a legal punishment, was probably offered too readily as a panacea. It is some evidence, however, of surgical skill.

Mathematics was mostly applied to astronomy, and the movement of the stars was supposed to control or influence the destiny of men. Astrology had an application to medicine, indicating when herbs were best picked and

259. *Winchester in the early Middle Ages,* Survey II, 1023, 1028, 1044; 827.
260. *GP* 194, 434.
261. *GP* 437–8. Presumably Ernulf I who died after 1091: I. J. Sanders, *English Baronies* (1960) 124.
262. Reginald of Durham, *St Godric* 377, 385, 407, 441, 453.
263. *VA* 23–4.
264. *GP* 145 and n.
265. Reginald, *St Cuthbert* nos. 230–1.

when potions and other remedies were most efficaciously administered. It could also serve as an introduction to even more hermetic systems. Likewise chemistry can hardly be distinguished from alchemy. All sciences led into blind alleys. The one redeeming feature was the curiosity itself which led men on to these difficult and largely unrewarding paths. Men wanted to know the secrets of heaven and earth, and some of them coveted the power which would come from understanding. Men could still be very gullible. In 1118, according to Orderic Vitalis,[266] Bishop Hervey of Ely, a Breton with some reputation for learning, had a pregnant cow slaughtered, and there were found within, instead of the expected calf, three little pigs. A passing pilgrim told the bishop that this meant that three important persons of the realm would die within the year and that even greater tribulations would follow. Events, Orderic continued, proved the prophecy true, for within the year William count of Evreux, the queen, and Robert count of Meulan were dead. This was the usual sort of experimental nonsense, but there were also in England at this time, besides monstrous cows, some real exotics. Henry I collected wild animals. He emparked Woodstock and kept there lions, leopards, lynxes, camels, and a porcupine.[267] William of Malmesbury had examined at least this last creature, and in his Commentary on Lamentations mentions the ostrich which had been seen in England in the time of Henry I, 'who was very fond of collecting such foreign monstrosities'.[268] The king's nephew, Henry abbot of Glastonbury and bishop of Winchester, likewise had a zoo.[269] It was better to examine real animals in a zoological park than to study them in a bestiary. The day of experimental science had not yet arrived, but a movement in that direction is already perceptible.

Until the end of Henry I's reign there was a shortage of scholars in England.[270] And in the twelfth century, especially during the troubles of Stephen's reign, England seems to have been exporting more talent than it received in return. English scholars were not only attracted to foreign schools but also then became interested in posts abroad. Some of the famous English masters at Paris have already been noticed. There were others, less eminent. Serlo, an Englishman, born about 1110 at Wilton, studied at Paris and became a teacher of rhetoric. He attached himself to the Angevin cause and wrote an elegy on the death of Earl Robert of Gloucester in 1147. With the collapse of the Angevin hopes he returned to France and went to Antibes on the Mediterranean coast, which he claimed was full of Englishmen. Shortly after 1150 he was again teaching in Paris. About 1167 he visited Oxford. Later he became a Cluniac monk at La Charité-sur-Loire, and then a Cistercian, rising to be abbot of L'Aumône (about 1171). He wrote much light and erotic verse and compiled an interesting collection of Anglo-Norman proverbs, such as 'Chascun

---

266. OV (Chibnall) vi. 186–8.
267. *GR* 485; cf. HH 244.
268. Stubbs, *GR*, p. cxxiii.
269. Gerald of Wales, *Vita S. Remigii* in *Opera*, ed. J. F. Dimock, vii (Rolls ser. 1877) 45; cf. Wm of Newburgh i. 85.
270. Hugh the Chantor wrote before 1127 spitefully about Henry I's use of William Warelwast, bishop of Exeter, who was not only blind but *illiteratus*, as his regular ambassador to the pope, that when Rufus had used him and he could still see, 'Angliae imputatum est quod penuria litteratorum in ea legebatur', Hugh *HCY* 87.

prestre loe ses reliques' (Every priest praises his own relics).[271] Other English-men are found in high office abroad. Achard, a theologian, became abbot of St Victor, Paris, in 1155, was unsuccessfully elected to Sées in 1157, and success-fully to Avranches in 1161.[272] Isaac, another theologian and a metaphysician of some distinction, entered Cîteaux about 1145 and in 1147 became abbot of L'Étoile (*Stella*) in the diocese of Poitiers.[273]

        There were also the Englishmen at Rome. Robert Pullen was invited to the curia by Lucius II in 1144 and was papal chancellor for two years.[274] John of Salisbury was a papal clerk between 1149 and 1154; and Boso, the historian of the popes, who may have been on Robert's staff at the chancery and made his career in the papal service, has been claimed as an Englishman. Hilary, a clerk of Henry of Winchester, practised as an advocate in the papal court before he returned to England in 1145 and obtained in 1147 through papal influence the bishopric of Chichester.[275] In 1150–51 Baldwin, the future archbishop of Canterbury, met Pope Eugenius III at Ferentino, and was appointed tutor to Gratian, the nephew of an earlier pope, Innocent II.[276] The one who rose highest at Rome has one of the obscurest careers:[277] Pope Adrian IV was born at Abbot's Langley, Hertfordshire, Nicholas Breakspear, the son of Robert *de Camera*, a clerk in the king's chamber, who became a monk at St Albans. Nicholas, who may have received some education at Merton, about 1120 went to France to study, and became a canon of the Augustinian abbey of St Ruf, then on the outskirts of Avignon in Provence. In 1139 he probably went with Archbishop William of Arles on his legation to Barcelona, and later he was elected abbot of his house. As a result of quarrels with his canons he became known to the papal curia, where other Englishmen were to be found, and probably at Christmas 1149 he was made cardinal-bishop of Albano by Pope Eugenius III; in 1152–54 he undertook a mission to Scandinavia. Nicholas does not seem to have been a great scholar, and his career cannot now be explained. It does, however, demonstrate how far the talented and adven-

271. A. C. Friend, 'The proverbs of Serlo of Wilton', *Mediaeval Studies* xvi (1954) 179. Manitius, iii. 905–10. Serlo was one of the few medieval poets quoted by grammarians of the school of Ralph of Beauvais: R. W. Hunt, 'Studies in Priscian in the eleventh and twelfth centuries, II', *MARS* ii (1950) 30. See also John Öberg, 'Einige Bemerkungen zu dem Gedichten Serlos von Wilton', *Mittellateinisches Jahrbuch* vi (1971) 98.

272. For Achard's writings, see de Ghellinck, *L'essor* 58.

273. *Ibid.* 187n., 189. See also C. H. Talbot, *Ailred of Rievaulx De Anima* 48–9. His works are in *PL* cxciv.

274. R. L. Poole, 'The masters of the schools at Paris and Chartres' 335–6; 'The early lives of Robert Pullen and Nicholas Breakspear' 63–4. His elevation and death are noticed in the Waverly annals, in *Annales monastici* ii. 231–2. Pullen was at Rome by 18 November 1144; he signs as c.p. of St Martin's 4 January 1145, and by 31 January was papal chancellor. He was in office until 22 September 1146; and died between then and 17 December, when a new chancellor was at work: F. Courtney *Cardinal Robert Pullen* 14 ff.

275. For Boso, Hilary, and Baldwin, Poole, 'The early lives' 68–9. F. Geisthardt, *Der Kämmerer Boso*: Historische Studien ccxciii (Berlin 1936), argued that Boso was an Italian; but H. Mayr-Harting in *New Catholic Encyclopedia* keeps it an open question.

276. John of Salisbury, *Ep.* 292, *PL* cxix. 334.

277. R. L. Poole, 'The early lives of Robert Pullen and Nicholas Breakspear'; R. W. Southern 'Pope Adrian IV', *Medieval Humanism and Other Studies* (1970); W. Ullmann, 'The pontificate of Adrian IV', *Camb HJ* xi (1955) 233.

turous could go in the church. There was no sure place in England before 1154 for many of the cleverest and boldest spirits. In the sphere of education and the employment of the educated, the accession of Henry II was, as in so much else, a real turning point.[278]

278. According to William FitzStephen, *MB* iii. 24, Henry II, persuaded by his chancellor, Thomas Becket, recalled poor Englishmen of good repute who were living in France either as monks or schoolmasters, and established them in his own kingdom – for example, Robert of Melun, whom he made bishop of Hereford. For Robert see D. E. Luscombe, *The School of Peter Abelard* (1970) 281.

Church and State

In the early Middle Ages the Christian view of the world was monistic rather than dualistic:[1] Christ, the king of kings, ruled the world, which was also the church.[2] St Augustine's exposition of the City of God (*civitas dei*) was understood in the sense of unity and harmony, and the various powers were considered to differ in function rather than in nature: they were all agents of the sovereign Christ. There was therefore little inclination to distinguish sharply between the secular and ecclesiastical authorities (*imperium/regnum* and *sacerdotium*). And indeed confusion existed between the two spheres, for kings had assumed some of the functions and trappings of priests, and bishops the appearance of kings. Moreover, although Christ ruled, in a disturbed and dangerous world effective leadership fell to the secular powers. Kings, taking the title of *vicarius Christi* or *dei* (Christ's or God's representative), ordered the affairs of the church. But a persistent thread of dualism prevented the complete identification of Church and State and the complete absorption of the *sacerdotium* into the *regnum*. And in western Christendom, where there were many kingdoms, theocracy was always undermined by the obvious unsuitability of most kings to exercise spiritual authority.

To write of Church and State in this period is to use anachronistic terms and alien categories. Although the Latin word for church, *ecclesia*, had many meanings, it seldom if ever signified the body of the clergy and its institutions as opposed to the laity. Until the Gregorian reformers the distinction between laity and priests was not crucial. Laymen had an active role in the church, for example they had a part in the election of bishops, and could, in common with clerks, dispense some sacraments, such as baptism, marriage, and penance.[3] Even as late as 1100 the Norman Anonymous was, for certain

1.   For an introduction to medieval political ideas see Fritz Kern, *Kingship and Law in the Middle Ages*, trans. S. B. Chrimes (1939 etc.); G. Tellenbach, *Church, State, and Christian Society at the Time of the Investiture Contest*, trans. R. F. Bennett (1940); Ernst H. Kantorowicz, *The King's Two Bodies* (Princeton 1957); Walter Ullmann, *The Growth of Papal Government in the Middle Ages* (1955), *Principles of Government and Politics in the Middle Ages* (1961), *A History of Political Thought: the Middle Ages* (1965).

2.   The Norman Anonymous, *c*. 1100, when commenting on the Gelasian view of the two powers of the world, equates the world with the Christian people and the holy church on earth, NA 198, 222.

3.   Anselm's uncompromising attack on married and unchaste priests at the council of Westminster 1102, which led to their expulsion from their churches, produced such a shortage of officiating priests that the sacramental functions of the lower clergy and of the laity were reactivated. In 1102–04, when in exile, Anselm enjoined that the people, rather than going to such evil priests, must get the baptism of their children and penance, absolution, and burial of the dead from clerks

purposes, fighting against the Gregorian exaltation of priestly ordination and depreciation of the common bond of baptism.[4] In any case, a distinct clerical class within the church, hierarchically arranged, did not exist before the twelfth century. When *ecclesia* did not mean a physical building it usually referred to a body of Christians, from the whole world to a province or diocese. Those concerned with dualism within this world or church based themselves usually on the late fifth-century Pope Gelasius's statement to the Emperor Anastasius; 'For there are, august emperor, two things by which this world is primarily governed: the holy authority of the pontiffs and royal power. And the burden of the priests is the heavier, for it is they who have to render an account to the Lord for those very kings in the Last Judgment.'[5]

Gelasius's pair, *sacerdotalis auctoritas* and *regalis potestas*, or the ninth-century two persons, *sacerdotalis persona* and *regalis persona*,[6] lost ground in the eleventh century to *sacerdotium* and *regnum*, which can usually be understood as the priestly and royal areas of government. Since *sacerdotium* on its own could mean the priestly order, this last pair was closer than the others to Church and State; but it was still a long way off. It did not imply a fundamental dualism: at its most concrete it refers only to two political structures within the seamless garment of the church. The Norman Anonymous, who was neo-Gelasian, blurred the distinction by regarding kings as bishops and bishops as kings, and both as gods. In any case in the eleventh century there was lacking to the *sacerdotium* a machinery of government. The pope had no jurisdictional or coercive power. He had not even obedient subordinates. To implement ecclesiastical policies it was necessary to enlist the secular arm – if the emperor was unresponsive, then kings, or nobles, or even the people.[7]

As soon as the pope began to emerge as the true leader of the church, that is to say in the mid-eleventh century, many traditional royal functions, such as the investiture of bishops with their office, began to seem improper. But at first the call of the reformers was only for a redefinition of function within the one and only church. Both reformers and conservatives

or laymen: *Epp.* 254, 331. It must have been common for dying soldiers to confess to a comrade and receive absolution from him. For examples, see OV (Chibnall) iv. 51 on Richer of Laigle, and Walter Map's story of a former monk of Cluny in *De nugis curialium* I, xiv. The practice was authorized by a mid eleventh-century treatise, *Liber de vera et falsa poenitentia*, which was attributed to St Augustine: *PL* xl. 1122. And see the English theologian, Robert Pullen's *Sententiarum libri octo* VI. 51, *PL* clxxxvi. 897.

4.   A useful discussion is in Karl Pellens, 'Das christliche Volk in der Landeskirche', *Das Kirchendenken das Normannischen Anonymus* 134 ff.

5.   'Duo quippe sunt, imperator auguste, quibus principaliter mundus hic regitur: auctoritas sacra pontificum et regalis potestas. In quibus tanto gravius est pondus sacerdotum, quanto etiam pro ipsis regibus Domino in divino reddituri sunt examine rationem', *Ep.* 8, *PL* lix. 42.

6.   Jonas, bishop of Orleans, *De institutione regia*, in *PL* cvi, cf. c. 1 (col. 285), 'Sciendum omnibus fidelibus est quia universalis ecclesia corpus est Christi, et ejus caput idem est Christus, et in ea duae principaliter extant eximiae personae, sacerdotalis videlicet et regalis, tantoque est praestantior sacerdotalis, quanto pro ipsis regibus deo est rationem redditura.' He then quotes Gelasius, as above.

7.   After Anselm's Westminster council of 1102 (see above, 268, n. 3) he instructed Herbert, bishop of Thetford, who reported that he was unable to carry out the decree against unchaste clergy because of their resistance and the unavailability of chaste priests with whom to replace them, to order the laity to expel and persecute such rebels: *Ep.* 254.

argued from the same premises. Gregory VII expressed the unitary view clearly in his letter of 8 May 1080 to William I, in which, while restating the Gelasian doctrine, he likened the apostolic and royal powers, governing through their diverse offices, to the sun and the moon, the greatest lights in the world in their diverse seasons.[8] Royalists agreed. The Norman Anonymous opened his tract 'On the equality of the ecclesiastical provinces and the unity of the episcopal order within the one holy church' with the statement, 'We know on the authority of the Holy Fathers that the holy church, spread throughout the whole world, is one church, the one dove of the bridegroom (Cant. 9: 6), the one body of Christ, and, because it is joined unto the Lord, one spirit (1 Cor. 6: 17).'[9] The emphasis on unity was all the more marked because the church was sometimes divided by schism. For more than a quarter of the period 1066–1154 the German emperor had his own pope.

This antique view had not completely disappeared by 1154, but it was not so confidently held; and traditional expressions used by the papal curia concealed the considerable progress which had been made in marking out a boundary between ecclesiastical and secular affairs, in assigning to the *regnum* its own legitimate territory.[10] Reform ideas in the eleventh century were not necessarily fatal to the unitary world. Gregory VII, by claiming the ultimate authority, the superior power derived from St Peter, and by trying to subordinate kings as well as the other bishops to the *sancta Romana ecclesia*, even emphasized the unity. Kings had their place within the church and must use their inferior secular sword for moral ends and the protection of the church.[11] There were always men among the early reformers, usually monks, who gave the king this important role. Nevertheless Gregory's exaltation of the priestly office and his despair at the wickedness and unresponsiveness of secular rulers prepared the way for the expulsion of kings from the ecclesiastical structure. Given Roman primacy in the church, it was easy to construct a pyramidal design in which kings had no part, were, in fact, an awkward complication.[12] When Gregory VII proclaimed that kings and the emperor were lower in the church than an exorcist (one of the lowest clerical orders),[13] he was giving them a place which they could not accept. If that principle was to be pushed hard, practical needs required that not only had kings and the *regnum* to be taken out of the church (in its modern sense), but also they would have to be allowed their own legitimate status and function in Christendom. They could not be abolished; some of their ecclesiastical functions had to be tolerated, while

---

8.   *Registrum* VII, 25, ed. Caspar, *MG Epp. sel*. ii. 2, 505–7; *EHD* ii. 646.

9.   NA J 2, pp. 7–8; cf. also 43, 'Una enim est ecclesia, una columba, una Christi sponsa'; 67, 'At vero sancta ecclesia ubique terrarum diffusa una tamen est ecclesia, unum corpus Christi . . .'.

10.   Franz-Josef Schmale, 'Papstum und Kurie zwischen Gregor VII und Innocenz II', *HZ* cxciii (1961) 265 ff. Friedrich Kempf, 'Das Problem der Christianitas im 12. und 13. Jahrhundert', *HJ* lxxiv (1959) 104; 'Kanonistik und kuriale Politik im 12. Jahrhundert', *Archivum Historiae Pontificiae* i (1963) 11 ff.

11.   For the early history of 'the two swords', cf. Beryl Smalley, *The Becket conflict and the schools* (1973) 26 ff.; Hartmut Hoffmann, 'Die beiden Schwerter im Hochmittelalter', *Deutsches Archiv* xx (1964) 78.

12.   Cf. the scheme of Gilbert of Limerick, above 33 ff.

13.   *Registrum* VIII, 21, ed. Caspar, *MG Epp. sel*. ii. 2, 555. Pellens 115.

others, such as the protection of the church and the pursuit of heretics, were still required.

Gregory VII had, impetuously and intolerantly, opened a grand debate on the broad issue of the relationship between *sacerdotium* and *regnum*, had applied moral principles, and had made vast claims which were more a vision of a new world than a political programme. Inevitably the disputation began to narrow to particular problems. And when the post-Gregorians concentrated on the investiture of bishops and abbots, denied to the lay powers any rights over the church's temporalities, and, by prohibiting the performance of fealty or homage to the prince by prelates, tried to achieve the total independence of the *sacerdotium* from the *regnum*, by thus advancing too far in the one direction they made some retreat inevitable. The extreme position was reached at Paschal II's Lateran Council in 1102, and within four years a discreet withdrawal was being made. Because of the drama of the debate a good number of different and sometimes conflicting views of the proper world order came into circulation. Moreover, a growing intellectualism changed the tone of the debate. With the application of logic to the problems, elements could be distinguished, defined, and separated. Intellectuals could see ways in which problems could be solved, but their solution awaited a change in the moral climate of the papal curia and a movement in both *sacerdotium* and *regnum* towards new positions, tolerable to each other.

At the heart of the reform movement were legal studies.[14] The evil customs of the present had to be replaced by the sacred laws of the past. Men believed passionately that in the ancient traditions were to be found not only a programme for the abolition of abuses and the kindling of spiritual virtues but also, more widely, a blueprint for the re-ordering of Christian society. Every reform, whether in particular or in general, had to be based on the law. And in the eleventh century began that reassembly and publication of 'authentic' canons, followed by their interpretation and harmonization, which provided the church with more than a plan of action, with the very energy itself for a reform movement. This legal activity was not necessarily divisive of society. A great part of canon law was concerned with the rights and duties of all Christians, regulating the conduct of all members of the church from birth until death and making provision for their wellbeing from conception until the Day of Judgment. Yet because of the aims of some of the leading eleventh-century reformers there was an emphasis on those laws which enhanced priestly authority and separateness and emphasized the powers of the successor of St Peter.

The very recreation of a distinct corpus of ecclesiastical law produced a novel cleavage of society, and most planks in the reform programme had an economic significance which was unwelcome to the secular rulers.[15]

14.   A useful introduction to this subject is J. Joseph Ryan, *Saint Peter Damiani and his canonical sources* (Toronto: Pontifical Institute of Medieval Studies: Studies and Texts 2, 1956). Cf. also 'Report of a recent thesis defended at the Pont. Inst. of Med. Studies: Saint Peter Damiani and his canonical sources: A preliminary study in the antecedents to Gregorian reform: J. Joseph Ryan', *Mediaeval Studies* xvi (1954) 176. For the problems, see Stephen Kuttner, 'The scientific investigation of medieval canon law: the need and the opportunity', *Speculum* xxiv (1949) 493; 'Methodological problems concerning the history of canon law', *ibid.* xxx (1955) 539.

15.   Demetrius B. Zema, 'Reform legislation in the eleventh century and its economic import', *The Catholic Hist. Rev.* xxvii (1942) 16 ff.

Gregory VII, a prime mover in legal research and the codification of the law, was also much concerned with the economic position of the Roman church and of all the clergy. He wanted to re-endow the church by releasing ecclesiastical property from the control of the laity. His policies and actions led also to the creation of an ecclesiastical governmental machinery, but this, far from securing the triumph of his ideas, led to their abandonment. Hence the period 1124–54 has to be distinguished from its predecessor, and is now often termed 'post-Gregorian'. Papal primacy over the bishops and papal moral authority over the kings had been established by the time of Urban II at the end of the eleventh century.[16] Thereafter the construction of a papal government, based on the Roman curia and the college of cardinals, proceeded apace. *Sacerdotalis auctoritas* was given institutional form and changed into *sacerdotium*, an ecclesiastical body rather like 'the church' in its most usual modern sense. Concurrently, with the discarding of the heroic spirituality of the Gregorian period, a more accommodating spirit began to appear in the curia. 'Black' Italian attitudes, some associated with Benedictine renunciation, some with Italian and Roman political ambitions, lost ground to a more intellectual and 'rational' viewpoint associated with the educational developments in the cathedral schools north of the Alps, especially the French. On 1 October 1119 at Strasbourg, William of Champeaux bishop of Châlons-sur-Marne, who when a master at Paris and later a canon at St Victor had earned a great reputation as a logician and theologian, gave the Emperor Henry V some advice on how to end his dispute with the papacy. He is reported as saying:[17]

> If you really want to get a settlement, my lord king, you must renounce completely the investiture of bishoprics and abbeys. And you can learn from my case that by doing this you would suffer no loss of royal power. When I was elected bishop in the kingdom of the French [1113] I took nothing from the hands of the king either before or after my consecration. Yet, as regards tribute, military service, tolls, and all those things which originally belonged to the state (*respublica*) but were given to God's church by christian kings, I serve the king just as faithfully as the bishops in your realm serve you, those bishops for whose investiture you have incurred this dispute and, worse, this sentence of excommunication.

William of Champeaux was proclaiming both his freedom from the feudal relationship and also his eagerness to perform his secular duties. He was a responsible member of a *respublica*, not a feudal vassal.

In this transformation of the ideological scene, the election of Guy archbishop of Vienne, a Frenchman and a secular clerk outside the curia, as

16.   For a recent appreciation of Urban's policies, see Alfons Becker, *Papst Urban II,* vol. i, Schriften der Monumenta Germaniae historica xix. 1 (Stuttgart 1964). Cf. Charles Dereine, 'Une nouvelle biographe d'Urbain II', *RHE* lxvi (1971) 116.

17.   *Hessonis Scholastici relatio de concilio Remensi* or *Commentariolus* in *PL* clxiii. 1082–83; *MGH SS* xii. 423, *Lib. de Lite* iii. 21. Cf. Raymonde Foreville, *Latran I, II, III et Latran IV,* 35. An 'English' pupil of William was Robert of Béthune, above 393.

Pope Calixtus II in 1119 was the turning point.[18] Probably a compromise candidate, he finally supported the northerners and built on the settlement of the investiture dispute already made in England and France.[19] In 1122 the Concordat of Worms acknowledged the separation between *spiritualia* and *temporalia*, and in the following year the First Lateran Council recognized the primacy of the pope in the church, his universal episcopacy, and also accepted, though with reluctance, the concessions which Calixtus had made to the emperor. This marks the end of one era and the beginning of another. The history of the church as a hierarchically organized institution with its own laws starts from this point.

Calixtus, who followed five Benedictine popes, appointed men sympathetic to his views to the cardinalate, canons and men in touch with the new intellectual movements. In 1130, in the first schism occurring in the reform party itself, these new men resisted the counter-revolution led by Peter Pierleone (Pope Anacletus II), and secured the victory of Gregory cardinal deacon of St Angelo, one of the principal negotiators of the Concordat of Worms, as Pope Innocent II.[20] Of the next five popes only two were monks, and those were well-regarded in non-monastic circles. About 1140, during Innocent's pontificate, but independently of the curia, Gratian produced his *Concordia Discordantium Canonum* at Bologna. The author of the *Decretum*, as it is often called for short, was an unavowed dualist, who applied his attention unwaveringly to the autonomous *sacerdotium*. He produced a self-contained legal system for the church which took little account of the secular powers. It had, however, no political message for the papal curia, nor, in its codification of the old law, much influence on an institution which was beginning to change the law by means of decretals and even legislation.

The compromise of Bec and the Concordat of Worms were real compromises. Each side gave up something it greatly prized. The king and emperor conceded the investiture of bishops and abbots to the church and accepted a reduction of their ecclesiastical powers. The pope and curia abandoned the fiercely held but equally unrealistic position that the ecclesiastical office could not be separated from the ecclesiastical temporalities. Once it had been agreed that a bishopric could be split, the office could be assigned to the church, the proper interest of the secular authorities in the temporalities acknowledged, and the competing claims of both authorities on the man

18. For the various interpretations of Calixtus's pontificate, see Stanley A. Chodorow, 'Ecclesiastical politics and the ending of the investiture contest: the papal election of 1119 and the negotiations of Mouzon', *Speculum* xlvi (1971) 613.

19. There was never an open investiture quarrel in France, mainly because of the political weakness of King Philip I (1060–1108), accentuated by his excommunication (1095–1104) for his 'adulterous' marriage to Bertrada of Montfort, nor any concordat. After the king's absolution on 2 December 1104 a *modus vivendi* was achieved. Since the king had given up in practice investiture by ring and staff and feudal homage, the pope tolerated his interest in episcopal and abbatial elections and his royal authority over prelates. A political alliance between papacy and monarchy achieved a working compromise. See Alfons Becker, *Studien zum Investiturproblem in Frankreich* (Schriften der Universität des Saarlandes, Saarbrücken 1955), where there is a full bibliography.

20. Franz-Josef Schmale, *Studien zum Schisma des Jahres 1130* (Forsch. zur Kirchenrecht und zur kirchl. Rechtsgeschichte 3; Köln-Graz 1961), which, however, received critical reviews. J. W. Gray, 'The problem of papal power in the ecclesiology of St Bernard', *Trans. R. Hist. Soc.* 5th ser. xxiv (1974) 1.

allowed. *Sacerdotium* and *regnum* began to go their own ways. Nevertheless, the expulsion of the secular authorities proceeded slowly. Ancient attitudes could not be abandoned in a day, and the kings resisted the new tendency. Henry I and Stephen were pushed by a conquering church out of some of their traditional rights; Henry II, with fairly general support, tried to recover a part of them. In certain directions, such as royal powers of healing and the king's authority within the chapels royal, he even made new advances.[21] About 1168, according to John of Salisbury,[22] Henry boasted that he had at last recovered the privileges of his grandfather, who in his own land had been king, papal legate, patriarch, emperor, and whatever he desired. Be that as it may, few men really wanted a true divorce. Although in polemical writings, for example in the collection of correspondence concerning Henry II's quarrel with Becket, *regnum* and *sacerdotium* signified a dualism, they were in practice always *in copula*; and, indeed, given the political conditions, neither could be envisaged without the other.[23]

For the moral regeneration of the church the reformers could rely in general on the qualified support of the enlightened laity, especially noble-women. Feudal lords had some economic interest in most of the great evils under attack, simony, clerical unchastity, lay investiture, and abuse of the church's temporalities, and would suffer damage from their abolition. But only the king or duke had a vital interest in them, and most lords were willing to accept the financial loss in return for spiritual rewards. On one matter the laity seems to have felt more strongly than many of the clergy. The faithful preferred the clergy to be holy and chaste, and paid exaggerated respect to those, such as hermits, who clearly were. It does not seem, however, that the laity gave much heed to the precepts of the clergy except at times of danger. Alternations between contempt and passionate submission seem to have been common.

English kings, despite their authoritarian temper, set a relatively good example, for, although they protected their rights, they believed in the rule of law. Even Rufus was not quite a bandit. None insisted that all his clerical servants, even every bishop, should be unmarried; but all except Rufus were sympathetic to the moral aspects of the reform movement, provided this did not make royal servants too scrupulous. More problems were posed for the king by the attempt of the pope to rule the church, detach it from royal control, and aim not only to reform the clergy but also to impose God's commands, as interpreted by himself, on every sinner. England had been exceptionally loyal to Rome, and Normandy had felt its attraction. The king willingly allowed that the Roman pontiff had spiritual authority over all Christians and some limited jurisdiction over bishops and other prelates. He was usually ready to show him respect, but was never overawed. The Italian Normans became deeply involved with the papacy in the eleventh century and learned how to use the pontiffs for their own purposes. William I, with Lanfranc in his service and much traffic

21. For royal healing, see below 302 f. For the chapels royal, see J. H. Denton, *English Royal Free Chapels 1100–1300* (1970).

22. *Ep.* 239, *PL* cxcix. 271; *MB* vi. 160, 254, 416–17. See also Josef Deér, 'Der Anspruch der Herrscher des 12. Jahrhunderts auf die apostolische Legation', *Archivum Historiae Pontificiae* ii (1964) 168.

23. Cf. Frank Barlow, *The Letters of Arnulf of Lisieux*, Camden 3rd ser. lxi (1939) pp. xlii–xliii.

between the two communities, was apprised of the situation and knew what to do when the pope was unreasonable. He and his successors treated ecclesiastical principles as political problems which could be solved by diplomacy. The pope (or his agents), like the king of France, was a superior who could be ignored or defied, cajoled or bribed, according to the circumstances. English kings usually had three important cards up their sleeves: the threat to recognize the anti-pope and support the emperor, the threat to withhold payment of Peter's Pence,[24] and the threat to exert unfriendly influence on the Normans in Italy. These dangers encouraged a realistic spirit in the Roman curia and induced it likewise to use diplomatic means.

Even more important to the king was his own standing in the church, for unless he could rule his ecclesiastical as effectively as his lay subjects, his power would be much diminished. He was interested in securing the undivided allegiance of his bishops and abbots, maintaining his feudal and other fiscal rights in the bishoprics and abbeys, and assuring his control over both persons and properties by means of royal jurisdiction. There were other, mostly ceremonial, aspects of religious kingship which he valued, such as the custom of investing bishops- and abbots-elect by the ring and staff, his presidency over ecclesiastical councils, and the participation of the clergy in his own courts. He viewed himself as the ruler of the English and Norman churches, and, although he accepted that his power was not valid for all purposes, he was inclined to minimize that incapacity.

The clergy were put in a difficult position by the reformers. The secular clergy, often married, deeply involved in local society, and looking usually to lay patronage for advancement, saw their whole way of life threatened. The prelates were not only faced by a choice of loyalty, but also realized that they were in danger of acquiring a second master, and one as imperious as the other. Most of the clergy were affected in some way by the reform movement and the struggle for their allegiance. All clerks ambitious for benefices and ecclesiastical offices needed a patron, and a choice had to be made between a prelate and a lay lord, above all the king. All courts were thronged with jostling, intriguing, and backbiting clients. The tribulations of *curiales* were graphically described in the later twelfth century and were probably little different in the Norman period.

In theory the ecclesiastical ladder should have been the shorter and easier to climb. Bishops had parochial churches and cathedral prebends and dignities in their ownership or gift. But the most useful ecclesiastical step to a bishopric, an archdeaconry, was not simply for the asking: it was usually reserved for a *nipoto*, and the archdeacon who got a bishopric was usually specially well connected. Service in the royal court did not, of course, lead automatically to ecclesiastical wealth or high office in the church. Many royal clerks never obtained more than their livery and perquisites, and those who were given a bishopric were recommended by either outstanding services or the most distinguished connexions. Not every merchant's son, like Thomas Becket, could become, by switching patrons, sheriff's clerk, archdeacon of Canterbury,

---

24.   Even Alexander III (1159–81) greatly valued this revenue: W. E. Lunt, *Financial relations of the papacy with England to 1327* (Cambridge, Mass. 1939) 48–54.

royal chancellor, archbishop of Canterbury, and a saint and martyr. But, given modest ambition, a talented clerk probably did better with royal than with episcopal patronage. There was a greater variety of opportunity.

Clerks in royal service seem often by the twelfth century to have been a little troubled by their irregular position. They were the servants of rulers who sometimes oppressed the church, who were not even in appearance just kings. Their master might be excommunicated for his impiety, and an anathema raised practical problems of conduct. They were also employed in improper ways, such as taking legal action against clerks, administering sequestrated ecclesiastical benefices, or acting as royal judges, even in capital cases.[25] It is not surprising, therefore, that, threatened by Gregorian reformers, royal clerks clung to the idea of the anointed sacramental king. In England and Normandy the debate had to be conducted within the framework of traditional ecclesiastical thought, for there was no rival system to which royalists could turn. German publicists could call on Italian civilians for an alternative justification of the *imperium*. The Anglo-Norman church, protected by its geographical remoteness and tendency to follow France in its support of the non-imperial popes during the schisms, had no need to answer Gregorian stridencies with secular radicalism. The Norman Anonymous was not basically engaged in defending the *regnum*. He was much more disturbed by Gregorian attempts to refashion the *sacerdotium*.

On the whole, however, the 'victims' did not answer back. They were in no position to reply. The Gregorian reformers carried out considerable historical and legal research in order to find texts to support their theories. Hildebrand failed to persuade Peter Damian to produce a volume of ancient decretals, but at least four collections were started or completed in his time. These justified the reform programme. It was never, it seems, an embarrassment that there was little if any support for some key Gregorian positions in the Bible itself. Papal government, the inferiority of imperial and earthly power, and sacerdotal celibacy were hardly dominant themes in either the Acts or the Epistles. But so authoritative were the Fathers, the decrees of the early councils, and the letters of the popes that this weakness was not noticed. Even anti-Gregorian publicists did not make this point in a straightforward way.[26] They merely cited discordant texts. They did not in fact want to destroy the papacy; they merely wished to keep it in its traditional place.

Although no formal treatises of political theory of any merit were written in the eleventh and twelfth centuries, it was an age when several matters of interest to the political theorist were in frequent debate. New developments in government, both ecclesiastical and lay, could not hope to evade all application of principles: Archbishop Anselm made that quite clear to Rufus and Henry I and was painfully aware of it in the purely ecclesiastical sphere. Within both *regnum* and *sacerdotium* problems of government had to be discussed, and sometimes at a level above that of mere expediency. In both there was a

---

25. Cf. Ralph V. Turner, 'Clerical judges in English secular courts: the ideal versus the reality', *Medievalia et Humanistica* iii (1972) 75.

26. The NA, however, exceptionally pointed out that the marriage of priests was not condemned in the OT, NT, or the Epistles, and that therefore the prohibition was not divine or apostolic, but man-made, NA 204.

movement to free government from the shackles of custom and make the governor, within limits, not only a legislator but also an equitable force superior to the laws.[27] In the church, once the old law, suitably selected and presented, had been recovered, the question soon arose whether the pope could disregard it and likewise abrogate ancient privileges. The active force of government within a conservative society created strains and controversies, and the emergence of dynamic ecclesiastical and secular principalities led to clashes between them and a running debate on the proper place and function of each in God's scheme for the world. A livelier intellectual curiosity can be seen in the officeholders; when they had been trained in a cathedral school, as was increasingly the case, their attitude was often transformed.

The most dramatic conflicts were between the popes and the German emperors, the most interesting political speculation was in the papal curia and the schools of law. In this period no English king had his Canossa, no primate because he loved righteousness and hated iniquity died in exile. But Anselm and others were driven from the country; clerical rights were often in dispute. It was in the Anglo-Norman empire that the Norman Anonymous wrote, that the investiture dispute was first settled by concordat, and that the theocratic monarchy collapsed for a time, allowing us to see other possibilities and views which had usually been suppressed in the kingdom.

Most English chroniclers in the Norman period took an interest in papal affairs and the reform movement. As monks, most were sympathetic to the attack on notorious abuses, like simony, clerical marriage, and secular oppression. They were not, however, much concerned with the quarrel over lay investiture, and, although they could be critical of a king's behaviour, had no theoretical objection to royal power within the church. They knew, although they did not always state it in their notices, that the king appointed to bishoprics and abbeys and usually appointed his clerks and familiars, but they seem never to have thought that better men could be provided by any other method. And in their failure to distinguish clearly between royal courts and ecclesiastical councils they reveal their acceptance of the ambiguous conditions.

It was commonly held that the king owed his position in the church to his consecration and unction at his coronation. For some historians this is merely a christianizing of heathen kingship. Be that as it may, the initiative seems originally to have come in the main from the church. It was in the early Middle Ages in the church's interest to exert influence over a secular prince, and the affront caused by the exercise of his power in ecclesiastical affairs was reduced when he could be viewed as a sort of ecclesiastical person. By taking the king into its order the church preserved the decencies. Moreover, bishops and abbots had every reason to exalt royal power. Only a strong king could protect them from local tyrants.

The church's view of a sacramental king at the beginning of our period can be illustrated from the anonymous *Vita Ædwardi Regis*, written probably by a Flemish monk at about the time of Edward the Confessor's death.[28] In order to explain and legitimize Edward's tardy succession to the

---

27. Cf. *Dictatus pape,* VII, 'Quod illi soli licet pro temporis necessitate novas leges condere . . .', Gregory VII, *Registrum* II, 55a, ed. Caspar, *MG Epp. sel.* ii. 1, 203. J. W. Gray, *art. cit.* (n. 20).
28. *The Life of King Edward the Confessor,* ed. and trans. Frank Barlow (Nelson's Medieval

throne in 1042 and distinguish him from other less favoured claimants, God's special involvement in the events is stressed. The kingdom of the English was the kingdom of God. Although Edward was kept out of his rightful inheritance for a time owing to the sins of the people, he had been preelected to the kingdom by God and preconsecrated to the office by St Peter. It was in accordance with God's will that he was consecrated king in 1043 in Christ Church, Canterbury, and through the unction of chrism, became *christus dei*, God's anointed.[29] When he wore his crown he was Christ's standard-bearer.[30] He was prefigured by David, the stock type of the sacramental king, and by Solomon, but also by Saul, for in this last context David prefigures Earl Godwin, presumably to indicate that the earl was the founder of a new royal dynasty.[31]

Edward's powers in the church – mainly in connexion with the provision of ecclesiastical justice and the appointment of prelates – is fully recognized.[32] But there is a grudging note, because the Anonymous did not think that Edward always behaved wisely in these matters. In 1051 he had rejected the candidate who had been canonically elected to Canterbury and substituted his own nominee; the whole church had protested against this illegal act (*injuria*).[33] It is also implied that Edward had some responsibility for the bad state of the English church and had not heeded sufficiently the admonitions of 'the pope of Rome'.[34] Moreover, the author, when working from a completely different direction, emphasizes Edward's lowly status in the church. He was humble and devout at mass, and he always listened with great respect to the words of holy monks.[35] As a sinful man he was clearly lower than the lowest clerk. The Anonymous author, however, selects his principles to suit his case. In connexion with the theme of Edward's sanctity he wrote: 'Edward preserved with holy chastity the dignity of his consecration, and lived his whole life dedicated to God in true innocence.'[36] This suggestion that just as a priest after ordination, so also the king was obliged to a life of celibacy, was an unusual, rather particular, and most extreme development of the idea that unction at the coronation gave the king a special status. In the nature of things it could have no general application. But it shows how easy was the transition from an anointed king to a wonder-working saint. Edward's holy life, his patronage of the church, his love of monks, his succour of the poor and sick only brought out a potential which already existed: the power to work miracles.

The Anonymous, since he was writing with a political purpose and had an ambivalent and also changing attitude towards Edward, gives us a

Texts 1962) [*VEdR*]. For commentary, see also, 'The purpose of the *Vita Ædwardi Regis*', Frank Barlow, *Edward the Confessor* 291–300.

29. *VEdR* 9–10, 27, 29–30, 60–1.
30. *VEdR* 27.
31. *VEdR* 12, 77; 3; 28; 30.
32. *VEdR* 12–13, 17–19, 34.
33. *VEdR* 18–19.
34. *VEdR* 74 ff.
35. *VEdR* 40–2.
36. *VEdR* 60–1.

glimpse of various views of kingship which were current at the time. Although Edward's holy office is accepted, he can, at one moment, be seen as the master of the English church, even if an unjust master, at another as its lowest member. Both views were traditional, but their juxtaposition is characteristic of the mid-eleventh century monastic attitude: the king should be an obedient son of the church, observe its laws, carry out its orders, and further its aims.

Some of the charisma possessed by English kings was transferred to William I after his coronation; and William's view of the place of the church in his dominions was probably much the same as Edward's and hardly different from that of his bishops, whether English, French, or Italian. In the face of the papally directed reform movement his attitude seems to have been that although he was not prepared to reduce his own authority, jurisdiction, or revenue in any significant way, he was more than prepared to allow Lanfranc to inaugurate a moral reform and to suggest ways in which the organization of the English church could be improved.

William was determined to protect his *Eigenkirche* against papal aggression. He rejected or resisted any novel claims, such as Gregory VII's request for his fealty, his demand that English archbishops should regularly visit Rome, and his assumption that he could interfere in the domestic affairs of the English Church. But there was always the temptation to use the services of the pope when this was advantageous. The pope had many useful commodities for sale, and even Rufus was prepared to shop in the Roman market. The Conqueror had bishops deposed and himself crowned by Alexander II's vicars. He accepted that papal legates could impose penance on the army of conquest. He tolerated moral exhortation from the pope: but he drew the boundaries. He had two possible lines of defence, and, consciously or unconsciously, he used both. The first, which was also adopted in Sicily, and which culminated in Urban II's grant in 1098 of a papal legation to the ruler, Count Roger I,[37] was to channel all traffic between Rome and his dominions through his own hands, so that he was in effect the pope's viceregent. In the course of his reign William, by introducing Norman practices[38] and making rules, established precedents which were regarded by his successors as ancient customs, although by the more radical reformers as ancient abuses.[39] These were his prohibition that anyone in his dominions should recognize a bishop of Rome as pope except on his orders; his insistence that all papal letters should first be shown to him[40] and that no papal legate should enter his dominions without his permission; his denial of the right of egress to his prelates, especially to go to Rome or papal councils, without his licence; his restrictions on the right to appeal from the

37.   J-W no. 5706; *Hist. Pont.* 66. E. Jordan, 'La politique ecclésiastique de Roger I', *Le Moyen Age* xxxiv (1923) 48–9. Anselm was with Urban II at Capua in June 1098 when this concordat was negotiated. See Norman F. Cantor, *Church, Kingship and lay investiture in England 1089–1135*, 116–19.

38.   *HN* 9.

39.   *HN* 9–10; cf. also 29, 52–3, 58–60, 72, 78 ff., 93 f., 110 f., 116, 120 f., 131, 137, 140, 147, 152, 159, 162.

40.   Eadmer, *HN* 10, associates the receipt of papal letters with the recognition of a pope, and presumably means that no one is to accept instructions from a claimant before he has been recognized as pope. Later the prohibition was interpreted more widely. Cf. Hugh *HCY* 108.

courts within his dominions to the papal court; his control over ecclesiastical censures on his barons and officials; and his requirement that he should approve in advance all decrees promulgated by general councils of bishops held by the English primate.

These were all defensive moves, denials; and Rufus, unlike Roger of Sicily, was unable to turn them into anything as positive as a papal legation. Henry II seems to have thought that Henry I had enjoyed that right,[41] but it was not one which the papacy readily conceded. The king of Hungary too was disappointed. It should be noticed that William I was not prepared to make any significant gesture to the pope in order to reduce the offensiveness of his actions, or to create and nourish a special relationship. William of Poitiers believed that the duke fought under the papal flag at Hastings,[42] but the king would not swear fealty and become – like the counts of Sicily and some other rulers – the special son, the faithful knight, of the vicars of St Peter.

William's other defence, and the two positions were interrelated and mutually supporting, was the creation of a subservient domestic ecclesiastical agent. The German emperors appointed their own popes, at first apostolic and then schismatic. William chose an archbishop of Canterbury whom he trusted and could work with, and then sought to make Lanfranc into primate of All Britain. In 1086 England recognized the emperor's pope, Clement III, as legitimate, and moved into a position of neutrality between the contenders.[43] Later Anselm claimed that the archbishops of Canterbury had possessed a standing papal legation. This attempt to achieve autarky broke down partly because York would never willingly accept Canterbury's primacy and partly because in the twelfth century the usefulness, indeed indispensability, of the papal court could not be denied. Nevertheless, William I had successfully countered every measure of the 'demented' Gregory VII; he and Lanfranc were not to know that the world of their fathers was about to disappear.

William's readiness to allow moral and institutional reform within the kingdom also contributed to the defeat of the older order. Lanfranc arrived at Canterbury from Caen with the canonical collection he had made at Bec; and this law book was to be appealed to frequently during the Norman 'Conquest' of the church. Various reform measures, including the attack on clerical marriage and the tightening up of discipline in the monasteries, were designed to emphasize the distinction between the lay and clerical orders. And when William conceded to the church the monopoly of conducting ordeals and the right to hold its own courts, distinct from the folk courts,[44] he inaugurated a separate jurisdiction which later was to link with the papal curia and become part of an international legal system. But at the time he was merely recognizing the legitimate claim of various churches to hold courts, a claim not unlike that advanced by the barons or the towns. He was not intending to weaken his own power. Basically he regarded his bishops and abbots as rather special vassals

---

41. See above 274.

42. But Catherine Morton, 'Pope Alexander II and the Norman Conquest', *Latomus* xxxiv (1975) 362, casts reasonable doubt on this.

43. P. Kehr, 'Zur Geschichte Wiberts von Ravenna: Clemens III', *Abhandlungen der Preuss. Akad. der Wiss.*, Phil.-hist. Kl. 1921, 355–68.

44. See above 150 ff.

holding fiefs, for most ordinary purposes subject to the jurisdiction of his own court. Franchisal jurisdiction only operated at the next step down in the feudal ladder.

Since English kings put great trust in their prelates, their anger when betrayed was implacable. William I broke his half-brother, Odo of Bayeux, in 1082 for dereliction of duty, and in 1088 William Rufus attempted to try William of St Calais, a monk and bishop of Durham, for treason. Odo's attitude to his arrest is unknown. Bishop William refused to accept the jurisdiction of the king's court, and appealed from it to Rome for a canonical trial. The king and his court went, therefore, to great lengths to keep all the proceedings entirely secular. It was probably the same in 1082. In neither case was there any attempt legally to deprive the bishop of his office or order: his *episcopium* was never at risk, and the intention must have been to deny the pope any cause to interfere. But the protestations of the secular court in 1088 reveal the success the Gregorian reformers had had in publicizing their views, and it is possible that the proceedings in 1082 and 1088 played some part in the sharpening of the distinction between matters spiritual and temporal. However that may be, since Bishop William's stand was resolutely opposed by, among others, Archbishop Lanfranc, we have some clear expressions of opinion on the status of a bishop-baron, expressed in legal rather than philosophical terms, but revealing the attitudes which lay behind them.

It remains something of a mystery why Odo was broken in 1082;[45] and except for the citation of it as a precedent in 1088 little is known of the way in which he was tried. For William of St Calais's trial we have a *libellus*, drawn up apparently by one of the bishop's clerks, perhaps his scribe, who accompanied him to the hearing.[46] This, it hardly needs saying, is an *ex parte* account, completely sympathetic to the defendant.

In the spring of 1088, shortly after Rufus's succession, some of the Normans in England rebelled in favour of the king's elder brother, Robert duke of Normandy. Several bishops were closely involved in the warfare. Odo of Bayeux, the half-brother of Rufus and Robert, and earl of Kent, was one of the leading conspirators, and was supported by Geoffrey of Coutances, an English baron and the Conqueror's trusted captain. Archbishop Lanfranc, who had helped to put Rufus on the throne and detested Odo, was with the king's army, as was William of Durham, whose influence over the king Odo resented. Wulfstan of Worcester had a defensive command in the West. All these bishops were engaged in warfare, some of them physically. William of Durham, who was high in the king's favour and confidence and had been advising him to take

---

45. See Marjorie Chibnall, OV iv, pp. xxvii–xxx; David R. Bates, 'The character and career of Odo, bishop of Bayeux', *Speculum* l (1975) 15 ff.

46. *De injusta vexatione Willelmi episcopi primi* in Simeon *Historical Works* i. 171–94. Among the commentaries and evaluations are, G. B. Adams, *Council and Courts in Anglo-Norman England* (1965) 46–65; H. S. Offler, 'The Tractate "De I. V. W. episc. primi" ', *EHR* lxvi (1951) 321. Offler makes some useful points, but his attempt to discredit the authenticity of the report is unconvincing. The virtuosity of the account, the brilliance of the forensic repartee, the abundance of technical detail, the ignorance of the reporter of all that happened while the bishop was out of court rebut the argument that it was a later fabrication. Most of Offler's difficulties can be explained by the faulty transmission of the manuscript and the erroneous extension of names abbreviated to initials.

the offensive, had only a small contingent of seven knights with him, and, when ordered by Rufus to ride with him against the rebels, suddenly deserted and fled to Durham. The reason for the defection was never explained by the bishop, presumably because it was either cowardice or unwillingness to fight against Robert's supporters. But at no time did he plead that he had a conscientious objection to fighting or that the king had imposed on him duties contrary to his order. It was accepted by all the clerical actors in this drama, even the three monks, that as the king's vassals and barons they had military duties, even though they might prefer not to engage actively in the fighting.

On 12 March Rufus ordered the bishop of Durham to be dispossessed (disseised) of his lands and if possible captured. At the end of May Pevensey and Rochester surrendered and Odo of Bayeux was allowed to return to Normandy, having been deprived of all his English lands and honours. When he had been arrested in 1082 by the Conqueror, he had apparently been tried in the king's court before being sentenced to loss of his fiefs and imprisonment;[47] but there is no suggestion that in 1088 he was given a formal trial. It seems that, having been defeated in war, he was summarily punished. And it is probable that if Rufus could have laid hands on William of St Calais he would have treated him in the same way. But he could not, in fact, capture the city of Durham, and the bishop would not attend the royal court without a safe-conduct. It was these unusual circumstances which led to the unusual events and the, perhaps, abnormal trial which the *libellus* describes.

Rufus pardoned Geoffrey of Coutances, together with some other barons, for his part in the rebellion, but he was determined to break the bishop of Durham by trying him as a baron in his court on charges of perjury and infidelity (i.e. breaking his oath of fealty). In order to evade punishment the bishop relied not only on his constant assertion of injured innocence, but also on a series of appeals to canon law which clearly perplexed and sometimes angered the court. The one thing he would not do – and this may well have been his main offence in the eyes of many – was to submit and throw himself on the king's mercy. He was on the contrary defiant, and between his dispossession and his coming to trial wrote rather insolently to the king, using the royal chancery style and answering writ with counter-writ. He demanded first that before he was put on trial he be restored to possession of the lands of which he had been despoiled. This was a principle of canon law but was not usually observed in feudal courts. Next he required that he be tried as a bishop according to canon law in a place which accorded with the requirements of that law. He wanted a preliminary judgment on this issue by the king's court,[48] and offered that if he were awarded a canonical trial, he would plead to the charges and accept the judgment of the court even if he were sentenced to imprisonment or deprivation of his bishopric. But if he were adjudged a lay trial, he would offer the court no more than his purgation (his unsupported oath as a bishop that he was innocent – usually allowed only when there was a presumption of innocence or the court did not wish to press the case). From this

---

47. *De Injusta Vexatione* 184.
48. Cf. Constitutions of Clarendon (1164) cap. 3, *SSC* 164.

insistence on a canonical trial, however much he became involved in tactical manoeuvres and subsidiary issues, he never wavered.

If William of St Calais honestly meant that he would accept trial by the bishops in Rufus's court if they followed the procedures of canon law, it would have been simplest for the king to allow him to be condemned by the unsympathetic bench of bishops. But Rufus was eager to charge him as a baron with a feudal offence, and the whole court considered feudal law appropriate. In any case the king knew his man and would not bargain with him. In June or July he sent an army against Durham and on 8 September three earls made an agreement with William guaranteeing him safe-conduct to, and in certain events from, the royal court. He was to be conducted back to Durham and the safety of its castle if the king would not allow him a trial according to the law appropriate to a bishop and before the kind of judges who should rightly judge a bishop. But he was to surrender his castle and be conducted with his chattels into exile if the king offered him a canonical trial and he refused either to accept the judgment of the court or to plead to the charge. In the event, the king's court decided that the bishop had been offered a lawful trial (which, of course, is not the same thing as a canonical trial) and that, since he refused to plead, he could rightfully be condemned to forfeiture of lands and exile and could not invoke the first clause of the agreement with the earls.

On 2 November the bishop was conducted into the royal court in session at (old) Salisbury. We are not told where the court sat, but only two buildings would have been large enough, the castle and the cathedral, which were adjacent. The castle's dominance of the constricted site was denounced by Peter of Blois a century later when he congratulated the dean and chapter on their decision to move the church down to the plain. The castle was like that tower in Siloam (Luke 13: 4), and had at last inspired another Othniel to throw off its yoke (Joshua 15: 17). The church was held captive like the ark of the Lord taken by the Philistines on mount Gilboa (1 Sam. 31: 1); and the castle, in its insolence and outrage, was another house of Dagon (1 Sam. 5: 2). Nor was Noah's ark of any use once it had rested upon the mountains of Ararat (Gen. 8: 4).[49] It is most likely that in 1088 Rufus held his court in the castle and that to some present this symbolized royal control over the church. It may also be that some of the references to a canonical place of trial were to the cathedral. Present at the trial were the two archbishops, Lanfranc and Thomas, the English bishops and Geoffrey of Coutances, and earls, barons, and various lay officials and servants (such as sheriffs and huntsmen). Most, if not all, were hostile to the bishop of Durham. The bishops would neither speak to him nor give him the kiss of peace. Lanfranc, who during the preliminaries was the court's spokesman, was implacable until the bishop had been condemned. After that he prevented his further persecution.

William of St Calais immediately raised two preliminary matters: he asked that he and the other bishops should be dressed in vestments (a first move towards a canonical trial), and he required that he be restored to his

---

49. *Ep.* 104, *PL* ccvii. 326–7. For good photographs of the site, see C. N. L. Brooke and Gillian Keir, *London 800—1216*, pl. 4, Edward J. Kealey, *Roger of Salisbury*, pl. 2. Roger bishop of Salisbury held the castle and rebuilt it in Henry I's reign (Kealey 86); but it was not necessarily held by his predecessor, Bishop Osmund.

bishopric, of which he had been arbitrarily dispossessed, before being charged. Lanfranc drily dismissed the first request – 'We can deal perfectly well with the business between the king and you dressed like this: clothes do not hinder the truth' – and countered the second by denying that the bishop had been dispossessed of his bishopric, only of his lands or barony. He ended the argument over this by saying: 'You have been brought here to answer to the king, and you demand that first of all he make answer to you. First answer him, and then you can make a request.' Smartly came the rejoinder, 'Is this advice or a judgment?' 'It is not a judgment,' replied the archbishop. 'But if the king takes my advice he will quickly have it declared as a judgment.' The barons noisily approved of this course and made the required judgment.

Stung by their hostility the bishop told the barons and laity that he was just about to inform the king that he would reply only to the archbishops and bishops and that he had nothing to say to the others and would not accept their judgment. If the laity were allowed to stay they must remain silent. The king, tired of these diversions, said that he thought the bishop had come to answer his charges. The bishop's escorts testified that they had indeed brought him for that purpose. Whereupon the bishop declared that he was prepared to answer provided it was judged according to canon law that he ought to answer, even though he was dispossessed of his bishopric, 'for I do not intend in this case to transgress in any way the law appropriate to my order'.

The king was then advised by one of the barons to put his charges to the bishop. After the bishop had repeated his objections, Henry (in the manuscript, Hugh) of Beaumont rose and put the charge on behalf of the king – his desertion – asked him to plead to the charge, and indicated that later the king might prefer further charges. When the bishop maintained his objections, there was an uproar among the laity to which the bishop did not deign to reply. Geoffrey bishop of Coutances tried to break the impasse: 'My lord archbishops, we should not proceed further in this way. We should rise, take the bishops and abbots with us, and add a few earls and barons, and with them justly decide whether a bishop should be invested with his bishopric before he is bound to answer to the king's charges.' Lanfranc replied coolly, 'There is no need for us to rise. The bishop and his men can retire. We will remain, laymen as well as clerks, and consider what should be justly done in this matter.' 'I will go with pleasure', William of St Calais replied, 'But I tell you straight, archbishops and bishops, that you must do everything according to my [episcopal] order and the canons. Nor should those take part in your judgment who are banned from judging bishops by papal decrees and canons.' 'Off with you', Lanfranc answered, 'We will do whatever we have to do in accordance with justice.' And Henry of Beaumont added, 'If I cannot this day judge you and your order, in future I will not allow you and your order to judge me.' The bishop, after a final admonition to the court that it was to act canonically, then withdrew.

When the bishop was summoned back to court, the archbishop of York pronounced its judgment: he was to answer to the king before he was reinvested with his fief. When the bishop argued that he had never mentioned his fief, only his bishopric, Thomas said that it had been decided that there was no need to reinvest him with anything. The bishop then asked for the canonical authorities on which the judgment was based. He thought it was contrary to canon law and that he would be sinning against the holy priestly order and the holy church of God if he accepted an uncanonical judgment. Lanfranc replied that it was a just judgment and the bishop had either to accept it or make a formal answer. William of St Calais then tried unsuccessfully to get the advice of his brother bishops. Lanfranc said that they were the judges, and the king added, 'Consult your own men, you shan't consult mine.' Still protesting, the bishop retired for the second time.

On his return William of St Calais, addressing Lanfranc, rejected the court's judgment on the following grounds: the judgment had been made contrary to the canons and 'our law'. He had not been canonically summoned to the court but attended under duress. He was being compelled to plead his case despoiled of his bishopric, outside his province, in the absence of all the bishops of his province, in a lay assembly. They gave no heed to his words and judged him on what he had not said (a reference to the exchanges on fief and bishopric), and they were at the same time his accusers and judges. In his own law he found that he should not accept such a judgment, and his archbishop and his primate should have kept him from wrongdoing. And because he perceived that owing to the enmity of the king they were all his enemies, he appealed to the apostolic see, the holy Roman church, and St Peter and his vicar. He would accept a just sentence from the only one to whom the ancient authority of the apostles and their successor had reserved the more important ecclesiastical cases and judgments on bishops.

Since William of St Calais would not accept the judgment of the king's court as constituted and would not plead to the charge, only two courses remained open to the king: either to break down the bishop's resistance or to condemn him for contumacy. The court proceeded to follow both concurrently. First Lanfranc cited the case of Odo of Bayeux in 1082. Just as in that instance they were concerned with the accused's fief, not his bishopric. In that plea the king called him 'brother' and 'earl', not 'bishop'. When the bishop of Durham objected yet again that he had made no mention of his fief but only of his bishopric, Lanfranc said that even if that was so, 'I know all the same that you have a great fief, and so we judge you concerning it.' The bishop replied sarcastically and asked for the king's and the archbishop's licence to go to Rome in order to get a canonical judgment. He was ordered to retire while the court considered the point.

On the bishop's return Henry of Beaumont declared the court's judgment, which was in effect the final judgment and the technical end to the case.[50] The defendant was sentenced justly to forfeit his fief because he would not plead to the charges which the king had brought against him, but instead summoned him to Rome. The bishop replied, 'In any place where justice, not violence, rules, I am prepared to clear myself of the charge of perjury, and I will show in the court of Rome that what you have recited here as a judgment is a false and unjust declaration.' Since he had appealed to Rome for a canonical trial he would not enter a plea nor could he be judged at Salisbury. But Rufus said that as the bishop would not accept the judgment of his court he must

50. Adams 63–4.

surrender his castle. The bishop replied that it was contrary to the convention. Rufus blustered, 'By the face of Lucca, you will not escape from my hands until you return the castle.' And after further rejoinders from the bishop, Lanfranc said, 'If the bishop continues to deny you the castle, you can properly arrest him, because he has been the first to break the convention and so has put himself outside it.' 'Arrest him, arrest him,' cried the laity. And Ralf Peverel (Piperel) shouted, 'The old binder (*vetulus ligaminarius*)[51] has got it right.'

Nevertheless, the convention under which the bishop had attended the court could not be dismissed so lightly. The three earls who had guaranteed it were clearly of the opinion that they were being put in a dishonourable position. Lanfranc told them that the king would acquit them of all responsibility; Rufus had offered the bishop a full trial which the bishop had refused in their hearing and instead had unjustly summoned the king to Rome. 'Let the bishop recognize that we have made a just judgment which he will not accept, and then the king will allow him to go abroad.' But the bishop appealed to the three earls to conduct him back to Durham. Lanfranc cut the argument short. An end to prevarication. The judgment had been pronounced and the bishop must accept or reject it. Whereupon the bishop rejected it and appealed to Rome against it. 'And since none of you in your judgments or testifying dare say anything which would not please the king, since I may have no other witnesses, I invoke as evidence the Christian law, which I have here in this book. It declares that I should be allowed to go to Rome and that the final sentence should proceed from the authority of the pope.' The bishop was presumably holding a volume of canon law in his hands, in all probability the collection introduced into England by Lanfranc.[52] William of St Calais was a very clever pleader. Rufus, however, was unimpressed: 'You can say what you like. You will not escape from me before I have your castle.' Overcome by threats, the bishop submitted.

In the arguments which followed about the practical details of the surrender and exile Lanfranc referred to the injury the bishop was doing the king and the shame he was putting on them all by going to Rome, and began to suggest compromise solutions. If the bishop would make amends to the king in his court according to the judgment of his barons, he could remain and be restored to possession of all his bishopric less the city. Stung by the bishop's refusal Lanfranc exclaimed rashly, 'If you go to Rome without the king's permission I will tell him what to do about your bishopric.' All William of St Calais would offer was, as before, his purgation, and this Rufus would not accept. Lanfranc urged him to throw himself on the king's mercy. The bishop replied defiantly that if the king would see that the judgments which had been made to the harm of the holy church of God, the confusion of holy orders, and the shame of Christian law, were corrected, he would be willing to serve him again and even pay him a fine out of his own pocket. 'Throw yourself unreservedly on his mercy', Lanfranc reiterated; 'Stop denying the jurisdiction of his court.' But the bishop remained firm: 'God forbid that I accept a judgment

---

51. The stem is *ligamen*, a bond/tie/leash. Margaret Gibson, *Lanfranc of Bec* 161, translates it lyam-hound = bloodhound.

52. See above 145 f. It is Peterhouse, Cambridge, MS 74.

contrary to the canons.' On 14 November two royal sergeants received the surrender of Durham castle, and eventually William of St Calais, although harassed to the end, was allowed to sail from Southampton, the port of his choice. Before he left his destination was Rome. In the event he chose to remain in Normandy in the service of Duke Robert. In 1091, in return for some service performed during Rufus's campaign in Normandy, he was pardoned by the king and restored to his former position.

Rufus showed mercy, not a change of heart. And when he appointed Anselm to succeed Lanfranc at Canterbury, he came face to face with a man who was neither as amenable as Lanfranc nor as opportunist as William of St Calais. Anselm was not an impractical idealist: Eadmer exaggerated his other-worldliness.[53] A nobleman by birth and as abbot of Bec with considerable experience of the Norman feudal scene, he understood worldly affairs perfectly well.[54] It was his aristocratic fearlessness, his deep theological learning, the logical clarity of his thought, and his absolute obedience to moral principles and ecclesiastical superiors, together with his genuine lack of temporal ambition, which made him an uncomfortable man with whom to do business. And when he put his finger on what he considered to be the two moral cancers in English society, sodomy, and the marriage of priests, he aroused considerable ill will.

Anselm was forcibly invested by the 'dying' king through the ring and staff on 6 March 1093. Although he refused at first to recognize the investiture as valid, it was not because it had been done by a layman or by means of the spiritual symbols, but because it was done against his will; and once he agreed to take the archbishopric he tacitly accepted that the investiture was effective. In the late summer at Winchester he swore fealty and probably did homage to the king, 'according to the usage of the land', and was then put in possession of the archbishopric.[55] After he had heard the condemnation of lay investiture and the doing of homage by prelates to princes at the council of Rome in 1099 he felt he might have incurred the sentence of excommunication imposed on those who had accepted churches in this way, and was absolved by Pope Paschal on 23 March 1106 in the course of the general settlement of the investiture dispute.[56]

Throughout his prelacy Anselm subscribed to the Gelasian doctrine without ambiguity of any kind. On 6 March 1093, when the bishops were trying to force him to accept his investiture with Canterbury, in his desperation he answered them by a parable;[57] they were proposing to yoke to the same plough

53.   For a view of Eadmer's bias and evasions, see Norman F. Cantor, *Church, Kingship and Lay Investiture in England 1089–1135* (Princeton 1958) 52 ff. For the bibliography, see Fröhlich 7 ff.

54.   Cf. *ep.* 322 (Lyons 1104 x 5) to William Giffard, bishop-elect of Winchester, concerning conflicts of feudal duties. Cf. Fröhlich 150–2, and below 288.

55.   *HN* 41. 'Ille igitur, more et exemplo praedecessoris sui inductus, pro usu terrae homo regis factus est.' On later occasions Anselm frequently refers to the fealty he has sworn to, and owes the king, but never to homage. This is presumably because he learned in 1098 that homage was illegal, and Eadmer projects this illegality retrospectively. Since homage was the English custom we must presume that Anselm performed it; and it is implied by Eadmer's words.

56.   *AEp.* 397.

57.   *HN* 36.

a young and untamable bull and an old and feeble sheep, inevitably to the detriment of the sheep and its usefulness.

'The plough [he went on to explain] is the church. In England two oxen, superior to all the rest, I mean the king and the archbishop of Canterbury, drag the plough, that is to say, rule the church, the former by means of secular justice and authority, the latter by divine learning and instruction. One of these oxen, Lanfranc, has died, and the other, who is still young and has the ferocity of an unbroken bull, rushes on with the plough; and in place of the dead man, you want to join me, an old and feeble sheep, to the untamable bull.'

Anselm was not denying the king's place in the government of the church; indeed he was emphasizing it. He was merely drawing attention to his own unsuitability and the disastrous effects of making him the king's partner. In fact, the royal charter he attested at Gloucester at Christmas 1093 is the last he witnessed in Rufus's reign.[58] In February 1094, after his consecration as archbishop, he asked the king at Hastings for permission to summon a general council of bishops for the reform of morals. Especially he wanted to attack sodomy. He thought that if both the king and the prelates threatened the sinners with judicial penalties, the king using royal power, the archbishop pontifical authority, the evil could be destroyed.

Rufus's outlook, however, was hardly Gelasian. It was at this same meeting that he and his archbishop disputed over the nature of the king's ownership of churches.[59] Anselm asked him to appoint abbots to the vacant abbeys, according to the will of God. Rufus was incensed. 'What has it to do with you? Aren't they my abbeys? You do what you like with your manors; and you say I can't do what I like with my abbeys?' Anselm replied that they were indeed the king's as an advocate to defend and preserve, but not his to attack and destroy. They belonged to God, and were a provision for the servants of God, not for Rufus's wars. The king had manors and other revenues for that purpose. He should release to the churches their own property. Rufus stormed, 'Your predecessor would never have dared to speak to my father like that, and I will not do anything for you.' Rufus seems to be not only claiming extreme proprietary rights but also arguing that if the church could own lay property, he could own ecclesiastical property. Anselm's view was that the king had a proper role in the government of the church, but must not abuse it. Even Rufus, if he interpreted God's will, could appoint abbots (and bishops). But he must act in accordance with the will of God, and he must not put God's property to secular uses.

Anselm in his writings, and particularly in his reported conversation, was much given to feudal imagery. He spoke much of lords and their vassals and servants, and of their various duties and attitudes.[60] On several occasions, according to Eadmer, Anselm defined his relationship to his various superiors. When a reluctant archbishop-elect, he said that as abbot of Bec he

58. *Regesta* i. 338; Fröhlich 20n.
59. *HN* 49–50.
60. R. W. Southern, *Saint Anselm and his Biographer* 107 ff.

owed the archbishop of Rouen obedience and the duke of Normandy subjection.[61] In 1094, after he had quarrelled with Rufus, he told the bishops, who were trying to mediate, that he owed the king fealty (*fides*) and honour. The king should love him as his spiritual father, and Anselm would make sure that he put himself and his possessions at the king's service and disposal, insofar as he was bound to do.[62] In 1095 he declared that he owed the pope subjection and obedience.[63] The distinction which Anselm made between his ecclesiastical and secular superiors is clear and was frequently and unambiguously repeated during the debate on his obligations. He owed the pope obedience, the king fealty and some limited secular duties. It is also clear which obligation had precedence. It was this logical separation, this clarity of attitude, and this directness of speech which distinguished him from Lanfranc and his suffragan bishops. The latter said to him in 1097,

> 'We know, lord and father, that you are a religious and holy man and dwell in Heaven. But we, who are hampered by the kinsmen we have to support and by all the things of this world which we love, have to confess that we cannot rise to the lofty heights on which you live nor join with you in despising this world. But if you should care to descend to our level and travel with us along our road, we will advise you just as though you were one of us; and we will aid you in your affairs, whatever they may be and whenever there is need, just as though they were ours. But if you should choose to continue as you have started and hold solely to God, as far as we are concerned you will have to travel alone. As it has been, so it shall be. We will not withdraw the fealty we owe the king.'[64]

The bishops, probably through the mouth of the renegade William of St Calais, spoke clearly too, but only to advocate ambiguity and compromise. Once again we must remember that we are dependent on an *ex parte* account: Eadmer was completely committed to the defence of his lord.

Rival claims on a man's loyalty were a feature of feudal society. The problems were in general well understood and usually regulated by the growing body of customary law. The rise of the papacy in the eleventh and twelfth centuries, with its intrusion into this sphere and its claim to the first loyalty of prelates, was extremely disturbing, and the problems it raised could not easily be solved. One of these novel conflicts arose in 1095, when Anselm, who as abbot of Bec had recognized Urban II as pope, asked Rufus, who had recognized neither of the contenders, for permission to go to Urban for his pallium.[65] Rufus cited his father's custom about the recognition of popes and declared that if Anselm attempted to usurp his power in this respect, he was breaking the oath of fealty he had made him, and it was as though he were trying to deprive him of his crown and kingdom. Anselm simply repeated that he had already,

61. *HN* 33.
62. *HN* 51.
63. *HN* 53.
64. *HN* 82. See below 291.
65. *HN* 52 ff.

when abbot in another kingdom, recognized Urban, that Rufus had been aware of the fact, and that it was out of the question for him to renounce the obedience and subjection he owed Urban. This being so, he had to consider whether in the circumstances he could maintain his fealty to his earthly king. If the two obligations were incompatible he would like to go into exile until Rufus recognized Urban.

Rufus summoned Anselm to a court at Rockingham in February. And what seems to have started as a discussion was turned by the king into a trial (*placitum*) of the archbishop.[66] Anselm stated his dilemma quite simply: could he, saving his fealty to the king, preserve the obedience he owed the apostolic see? When the prudent bishops refused to support him or give him advice, he turned from them to 'the angel of great counsel', the Messiah, and the Petrine text.[67] Like William of St Calais in 1088 he appealed to the true law, but pitched his appeal rather higher. He did not rely on a book of canons, but on the law of God itself as declared by the Gospels. Christ, he said, gave the keys of the Kingdom of Heaven to St Peter and the other apostles, and so to the vicar of St Peter and through him to all bishops who were the vicegerents of the apostles, but not to any emperor, king, duke, or earl. 'In so far as we ought to be subject to and serve the princes of this world, the angel of great counsel instructed us to "Render unto Caesar the things which are Caesar's; and unto God the things that are God's."'[68] This is the advice of God, and this counsel I accept.' The bishop of Durham put the charge: 'You unjustly take away as far as you can that superiority which your lord and ours has in all his dominions, and in which he excels all other kings; and by taking it away you violate the fealty you have sworn to him.' Anselm replied that if anyone wished to put the charge that by declining to renounce the obedience he owed the pope he was violating the fealty he had sworn his earthly king, he was ready to answer it 'in the proper manner and at the proper place'. This was understood by the bishops to refer to the claim that the archbishop of Canterbury could not be judged or condemned by any one except the pope, nor could he be compelled by anyone, except the pope, to answer any charge against his will.[69]

Unlike the Salisbury court in 1088, sympathy at Rockingham was with the accused, especially among the laity, for all could see the unfortunate position in which Anselm had been placed. But no one could suggest an honourable solution. When the court refused to declare a judgment or condemnation, Rufus turned his fury on the bishops who had led him into this impasse. Since the dispute was over obedience, he forced them to renounce their obedience to Anselm. Some did this unreservedly; some limited their disobedience to orders given by him on behalf of Urban II,[70] and were immediately disgraced by the king for this evasion. The barons refused to do anything

66. *HN* 53 ff.; Adams 65; Cantor 79–87; Fröhlich 96–8.

67. Isa. 9: 6 (Septuagint and Old Latin), quoted in the Introit for the third mass on Christmas Day; Matt. 16:18–19. Oddly enough, William of St Calais is called '[vir] magni consilii', in Simeon *HDE* 133.

68. Matt. 22: 21.

69. *HN* 61; Cantor 83; cf. *Dictatus Pape* III, XX, XXI, Gregory VII, *Registrum* II, 55a, ed. Caspar, *MG Epp. sel.* ii. 1, 202–6.

70. *VA* 86 makes the matter clear.

against their archbishop. The trial was a fiasco, and the problem was resolved when Rufus recognized Urban. The papal legate who negotiated Rufus's submission brought a pallium for Anselm, and it was suggested that in recognition of the special dignity of the royal majesty the archbishop should take it from the king's hands.[71] This seems to be a suggestion that Rufus possessed, or had been granted, a papal legation (perhaps the dignity in which Rufus surpassed all other kings). Anselm declined: the gift of the pallium, he said, did not pertain to royal dignity but to the unique authority of St Peter. The king gave way. It was decided that the papal messenger should put the pallium on the high altar at Canterbury and that Anselm should take it from there, as though from the hand of St Peter.

So far, at the cost of much personal suffering, Anselm had been successful in defining some boundaries between the affairs of Caesar and the affairs of God. But it seems that the complaisant pope had made a concordat with the king by which he recognized the ancestral customs,[72] and it is possible that Anselm too was a party to the agreement. In 1097 Rufus claimed that Anselm in the previous year had agreed to accept all the customs.[73] The king was a man of honour; he was supported by the witness of the lay magnates, and Anselm was driven to what sounds like prevarication. It is possible that it was this awkwardness in his position which made him so anxious to leave England for Rome.

A quarrel in 1097 arose out of the archbishop's feudal obligations, and Anselm thought the king's charge trumped up.[74] Rufus charged him with providing him with unsatisfactory soldiers for the Welsh campaign he had just fought. Anselm was completely disheartened. He was in despair at the state of the English church. He was receiving little cooperation from his bishops. There were disagreements with his monks. He expected this time to be condemned in the royal court. His ministry was going to be thwarted by a minor failure in his obligations to his earthly lord. At the Whitsun court Anselm asked permission to go to Rome and get the pope's advice. Rufus refused, but dropped the charge. He refused again in August and October. Anselm in his desperation said to the bishops, who forecast that the king would never let him go, 'If he will not give permission, I shall take it upon myself, for it is written, "We ought to obey God rather than man",'[75] When the bishops begged him to come down to earth and told him straight that they were not going to abandon the king,[76] Anselm replied, 'You go to your lord, I will hold fast to God'.

Anselm's threat to leave England without the royal licence provoked Rufus to remind him that he had promised after Rockingham (probably during the mission of the legate Walter of Albano) to observe all the king's usages and laws and faithfully defend them in the king's interests against all

71. *HN* 71. Tillmann 19–21.

72. Hugh of Flavigny *Chronicon*, ed. G. H. Pertz, *MGH SS* vii (1848) 475; Cantor 89 ff.; Fröhlich 98–104.

73. *HN* 83–5.

74. *VA* 91–3.

75. Acts 5: 29.

76. See above 289.

other men, and that now he was threatening to break one of them.[77] Rufus was tired of all these complaints and difficulties. He offered Anselm a choice: he could either undertake never again to appeal to the pope when charged by the king on any matter, or go immediately into exile.[78] If he chose the former he would have to make amends in the king's court for his persistence in making his request. Anselm claimed that he had only agreed to observe the royal customs under the formula that he would observe according to the will of God those customs which the king possessed justly and according to the will of God in his kingdom, and that he would defend them as far as he could in the way of justice against all men. This version was denied by the king and the magnates. Anselm then declared that even if his opponents were right, such a reservation was inherent in his stand. How could any Christian be expected to observe or protect laws or customs which were known to run counter to God and justice? In any case he now pronounced this restraint on his going to the pope contrary to justice and therefore invalid and ineffective. In preserving his faith to God he was not harming the fealty which he should owe the king, for the oath of fealty ran, 'Through the faith I owe God, I will be faithful to you.'

When Anselm made it abundantly clear that his first duty was to God and so to the vicar of St Peter, and that these obligations overrode his duties to the king, he entirely lost the sympathy of the barons.[79] When he further observed that to renounce his right to appeal to the pope was to abjure St Peter, and so Jesus Christ, he was ordered to leave the country. This end to his tribulations caused his spirits to rise. Joyfully he offered the king his blessing, which Rufus grudgingly accepted. They parted, never to meet again. Anselm crossed to St Bertin's at St Omer, spent Christmas at Cluny, and then accepted an invitation to stay with the archbishop of Lyons in his native Burgundy. From Lyons he went to Rome, and remained largely with the pope or the archbishop until recalled to England after Rufus's death by the new king. He had championed the law of God when it was, according to his view, in conflict with evil earthly customs. He had tried to define the boundary between his two persons, as a baron and as an archbishop. He had been logically dualistic. This simplicity was embarrassing to most men of the time. It was contrary to the rules of gentlemanly behaviour. But after Anselm's debates with Rufus, things could never be the same again in England. Although Rufus had a case and was not out-debated, Anselm's arguments in support of an autonomous spiritual hierarchy were left to sink in and have their effect. The clergy were the intelligentsia and always responded to shifts in ideas and attitudes prevailing within educated opinion. Anselm had prepared the way for Henry I's defeat.

It was about this time that the theologian known as the Norman Anonymous was at work.[80] A collection of tracts, drafts, notes, and supporting

77.   *HN* 83; cf. also Anselm to Pope Urban, *ep.* 206.

78.   *VA* 91–3.

79.   *HN* 85–6.

80.   Heinrich Böhmer, *KuS*; George H. Williams, *The Norman Anonymous of 1100 A. D.* (Harvard Theological Studies xviii, Cambridge, Mass. 1951); Ruth Nineham, 'The so-called Anonymous of York' *JEH* xiv (1963) 31; Karl Pellens, *Die Texte des normannischen Anonymus* (Wiesbaden 1966); Pellens. *Das Kirchendenken des normannischen Anonymus* (Wiesbaden

texts in a Corpus Christi College, Cambridge, manuscript (no. 415) appears to be the literary remains of a single Anglo-Norman theologian, writing about 1100. The author would seem to be a clerk rather than a monk, a canon or cathedral dignitary, perhaps a *scholasticus*, rather than a bishop, and connected with the church of Rouen. The evidence will support nothing more and is insufficient to warrant an attribution of the work to any historical character. The collection is a miscellany of pieces which vary widely in theme, length, finish, and importance; the more complete are possibly sermons or lectures, in the form of primitive *questiones*,[81] and these are supported by alternative versions, drafts, notes and *pièces justificatives*. The 'tractates' are concerned mostly with the powers of a priest or prelate (*sacerdotalis auctoritas*),[82] and occasionally with some controversial matter of the time, such as the denial of holy orders to priests' sons, and legal disputes involving the church of Rouen and once York. In one exceptionally long treatise and a few scraps the position of the secular powers within the church is examined. The author was well versed in all the intellectual disciplines of his day. He had had a good education in the arts and delighted in the use of logic; indeed, some of his pieces may be no more than dialectical exercises. He was a good theologian and knew Origen, Ambrose, Augustine, Jerome, and Gregory the Great, and, among his contemporaries, Anselm of Bec. He was also abreast of the latest canonical research, quoting from the *Decretum* and *Panormia* of Ivo of Chartres, published in 1094–95. His method was very much that of the school of Laon, and he was obviously aware of all that was happening in learned circles in northern France. His views are not to be regarded as unorthodox.

The Norman Anonymous was in general against papal power and sovereignty and all other primacies, for example, Lyons over Rouen, Sens, and Tours, and Canterbury over York. He stresses the equality of all bishops under Christ and the apostles, and, although he usually had the province of Rouen in mind, he never discusses archiepiscopal or metropolitan powers. He disapproved of monastic exemptions from episcopal authority created by papal privileges. He looked at royal power, secular laws and justice, through clerical eyes. Even though he balanced his view that the king was the son of the holy church not a ruler (*praesul*), a disciple not a master, a subject not a lord,[83] with an occasionally reckless exaltation of royal authority, he probably still agreed with Gelasius that ecclesiastical jurisdiction was superior to lay.[84] It should be

---

1973); Wilfrid Hartmann, 'Beziehungen des Normannischen Anonymus zu frühscholastischen Bildungszentren', *Deutsches Archiv* xxxi (1975) 108. References (NA) are to Pellens's edition. Fröhlich 103n gives additional bibliography.

81. Cf. J 14: 'Si queritur . . . Illud quoque inquirendum est . . .' For the *questio* see above 246, n. 163.

82. The NA, possibly because of his anti-hierarchical temper, possibly because of the comprehensiveness of the word *sacerdotium*, possibly because *episcopus* is rare in the texts he relies on, never differentiates between sacerdotal and episcopal authority, and in fact under cloak of *sacerdotalis auctoritas* is usually referring to the latter. This ambiguity tends to make his treatise on the *regnum* and *sacerdotium* (J 24) strikingly academic. It is also convincing evidence that the author was not a bishop.

83. J 10. This short tract is usually considered Gregorian and contrary to the NA's normal views. But this line can be pushed too far. He was prepared to explore in various directions. For a discussion of it, see Pellens *Das Kirchendenken des NA* 30–31.

84. J 9.

noticed that in his most royalist thesis there are several hesitations, safeguards, and losses of nerve.[85] Moreover, here the treatment is at its most academic: the piece smells of the schoolroom. The Norman Anonymous debates with skill, but he uses authorities arbitrarily, interprets allegorical themes with literal crudity, and often builds up a large edifice on a single word wrenched from its context. Some of his arguments are clearly specious and he tends to avoid awkward objections, however obvious they may be. It should not, of course, be assumed that he had the same interest or sincerity in defending royal authority as in protecting the rights of the church of Rouen.

The long treatise (J 24), which has been given the modern title, 'On the consecration of pontiffs and kings and their rule in the holy church', occurs in two versions. The first has a unique appendix of supporting documents and texts, the second a unique introduction. In the *Exordium* the Anonymous treats of the marriage of the church: Christ is the church's bridegroom, Christ who is both a true king and priest, but only as king married to the church. In this church of God are instituted and ordained the two principles described by Pope Gelasius, priestly authority and royal power. Kings, ordained by divine authority and instituted by the bishops, are co-rulers with Christ. The episcopal order shares with the kings the government of the holy church. Some say that the priest has authority over the souls, the king over the bodies, but this is nonsense, for body and soul are inseparable. Kings have authority over priests and should not be excluded from the government of the church, for exclusion would cause division, desolation, and lack of protection. Kings have been consecrated for the protection of holy church and defence of the catholic faith, especially against the infidel and heretic. The priest and the king are two persons, vicegerents and images of Christ. This introduction may originally have been an independent piece.

The body of the tractate is divided into six parts. In Part I the author investigates the evidence of the Old Testament. With the anointing of Saul kings as well as priests were consecrated for the government of the people. Henceforth priest and king had in common the unction of holy oil and the spirit of holiness, and both were in the image and figure of Christ. But whereas the priest prefigured Christ as man, the king prefigured Christ as God. It was, therefore, just that the king should have authority over priests. In Part II the Anonymous turns to the New Testament, St Augustine, and Gelasius. The New Testament, he thought, fully confirmed the old dispensation.[86] It is the *kingdom* of heaven, not the *sacerdotium* of heaven, which is offered to all the faithful. There are, therefore, some who claim that among men the king and his authority are superior (*praestantior*)[87] to the priest and his authority. Since royal power is the power of God, in that God acts through his representative on earth (*vicarius suus*), it can be claimed that it is not contrary to God's justice if priestly dignity is instituted by royal authority, and is subject to it. For what

---

85.   Cf. Williams 181–2, who underemphasizes this point.

86.   As Pellens 235 points out, the NA's inability to show the anointing of any king in the NT is a weakness in his case.

87.   An echo, and reversal, of Gelasius's view. See above 269, nn. 5–6.

does the king confer by the grant of the pastoral staff? Not the priestly order or jurisdiction (*ius*), but those things which pertain to earthly authority and rule – rule over the temporalities (*rerum dominatio*), tutelage of the church, and the power to rule the people of God.[88] The king is passing on to the bishop-elect prerogatives given to him by God. St Augustine acknowledged that priests held secular possessions from the king and saw nothing wrong in it. Gelasius recognized the two powers; king and priest have an equal share in holy government. Because government is something holy, only holy men can exercise it.

In Part III the roles to be played by the king and pontiff in the government of the people are further considered. All sanctified rulers should live holy lives: their heads should be in heaven even if their feet are on earth. Both kings and priests have the same grace to teach holy church and instruct the people of the Lord by precept and example and to remove the heretics and schismatics in order to keep the church apostolic, chaste, and free from sin. Obedience to king and priest is a foretaste of heavenly liberty. Although there are kings who cannot be called holy, St Paul said that tribute was paid not to the person but to the authority: Tiberius might have been unjust, but Caesar was good. Royal power is superior to priestly; God has given kings power to rule not only over knights and laymen but even over the priests of the Lord. In Part IV the Anonymous points out that bishops and kings receive at ordination a similar symbol of power, the staff, and therefore it can be said that a priest is also a king, and a king in this respect (*in hac parte*) a priest. It is accordingly not improper for an emperor or king to summon and preside over ecclesiastical councils, and it is not against the rule of holiness if the king grants bishops the symbols (*signa*) of their holy rule, that is to say the ring and staff. This may well be the point to which all the arguments and proofs are directed.[89] In Part V he examines the royal coronation *ordo* and points out that in the number of blessings it is superior to the ordination of a bishop. After such treatment a king should not be called a layman: he is the Lord's anointed (*christus domini*), by God's grace he is God, the supreme ruler, shepherd, master, defender, and instructor of holy church. He should be adored by all because he is the principal and highest ruler (*presul*). Nor because he is consecrated by a pontiff should he be considered inferior to him, for it is common for superiors to be consecrated by inferiors – the pope by cardinals, a metropolitan by his suffragan bishops. The author concludes this section with the remark, 'Nor should the lord pope be offended by the things I have said about the king, since he himself is the highest bishop inasmuch as he is a king.' The Anonymous then gives the orders for the consecration of a bishop and of a king, and finishes with a few scraps and texts on royal power (VI).

This defence of the royal position is probably as good as could be devised on the basis of texts acceptable to all, although his arbitrary selection and strained interpretation of these would not have escaped notice. The Anonymous also refers to royal power in a tract (J 28) in which he attacks papal encroachments. The pope, he claims, can only be regarded as apostolic when he

---

88. Presumably the other powers are conferred by consecration: cf. Pellens 168.
89. Cf. Pellens 252–3.

seeks to perform the will of Christ. And he gives four examples of unapostolic behaviour by the pope: the attempt to force archbishops and bishops to visit Rome every year or as often as possible; the encouragement of abbots to be disobedient to bishops by conferring privileges of exemption on them; the excommunication of his fellow bishops; and, lastly, the attempt to remove royal power from the government of the church, to the greatest possible harm to the whole church. Such behaviour is contrary to the Gelasian view of the two powers in the world, that is to say the Christian people or holy church. Each authority has its proper role. The priestly authority protects us from invisible enemies, royal power from visible foes, against whom priestly authority is not allowed to proceed.

The Anonymous cites Pope Gregory the Great in support of the legitimacy of royal power. The emperor has been invested by God and it is just that he should pass on part of this investiture to those priests who have been entrusted to him by God. He is investing the priest with his own governmental powers over the people and with earthly possessions, not with the priesthood or priestly powers (*gratiae*). 'I have never heard the word "investiture" used in these latter cases.' The king performing this investiture is not a layman, but by grace the Lord's anointed and co-ruler with him who is the Lord's anointed by nature. Whoever tries to make a division between these two powers harms Christ's kingdom. It is not against the rule of justice that kings should institute laws for the protection of the holy church. Nor should the saints fear to invoke royal laws when Paul did not hesitate to call himself a Roman citizen and appeal to Roman law. In conclusion, royal power is needed so that the church when in peril may be freed from danger and enjoy peace, and so that priestly authority may be strengthened. For priestly authority cannot stand by itself: it needs the support of royal power. Whosoever tries to make schism between these two powers[90] is working towards the destruction of priestly authority.

The Norman Anonymous is a defender of the old order, but, forced to devise arguments acceptable to the late eleventh century in defence of conditions which had been tolerated rather than rationally displayed, he sometimes seems revolutionary. With regard to the pope he is egalitarian, and favours a decentralized church composed of equal bishoprics grouped under kings (or dukes). He is therefore opposed, sometimes eccentrically, to many of the governmental and jurisdictional innovations of his time. But he is very clerically minded, and although, as a last resort, he would rely in defence of royal power in the church on Melchisedech, who was both priest and king,[91] he is happier with Saul, David, and Solomon, who had been anointed to rule. It is precisely because the king is not a layman that he has an important role in the government of the church. But this great part is far more restrained than the arguments which support it. The Anonymous contents himself with awarding the king a general defence of the church and entitlement to the highest reverence, and mentions only two concrete functions: the summoning of and

90. The pope is probably meant: Pellens 179.
91. Cf. Williams 167–8.

presiding over synods, and the choosing and investiture of priests (= bishops).[92] Moreover, with regard to royal investiture of bishops he stops well short of what his arguments would allow. Except that he would permit the king to invest using the symbols of ring and staff, his position, with its clear distinction between *temporalia* and *spiritualia* and sharp reminder that the king conveys only the former, is close to the compromises which ended this conflict, and the Anonymous may well have been one of those who through his views prepared the way for the settlement. The Norman theologian was not merely a defender of the past or even of contemporary usage, he was helping to take sacramental kingship into the post-Gregorian age.

The foundation charters of this age are the compromises of 1105–06 and (for Germany) 1122. In England the political situation facilitated a relatively quick end to the sudden and unexpected dispute over lay investitures. Archbishop Anselm had been forced into exile in 1098 by Rufus's brutal treatment of the English church, his encouragement of sodomy and hostility to moral reform, and the extreme contrast between the characters and policies of the two men.[93] Rufus exemplified lay oppression at its worst, and his accidental death was therefore regarded by all reformers as God's punishment for his sins.[94] The accession of Henry I and his coronation charter, in which he promised that the church should be free and renounced the unjust oppressions of his brother, raised the hopes of the reformers. Anselm, soon after his return in September 1100 at the king's invitation, received instructions from the new pope, Paschal II (1099–1118), to reform the English church according to the decrees of the Roman church, secure the payment of Peter's Pence, and help the crusader Count Robert of Normandy, who claimed that Henry by seizing England had broken his oath.[95]

Anselm, however, had already collided head on with the king, the barons (including Henry's principal adviser, Robert count of Meulan), and the prelates. By refusing to do homage to, and receive investiture from, his new king, he further weakened Henry's parlous position. And when he made it clear that, although he would consecrate William Giffard to Winchester, for that clerk had been invested by Henry while Anselm was still abroad, there could be no further toleration of this abuse since these things had been prohibited by the council of Rome held by Pope Urban II in 1099, at which he had been present, the king and his counsellors were greatly upset.[96] Henry wrote to Paschal.[97] He

---

92.   The selection (*electio*) of the candidate by the king, although certainly implied by NA, is not much considered. Pellens 257 observes rightly that NA does not distinguish sufficiently between election, investiture, and consecration. It should also be noticed that the English 'investiture dispute' was little concerned with election. Paschal introduced the theme once, merely in order to be nasty.

93.   Cf. *AEp.* 210. All the following references to letters are to the Anselm collection, ed. Schmitt.

94.   Paschal to Henry, 15 April 1102, *ep.* 224; cf. 222.

95.   *Ep.* 213. For Anselm and Henry I, see R. W. Southern, *Saint Anselm and his Biographer* 163 ff.

96.   *Epp.* 214, 217, 229; *HN* 120. Fröhlich 177 ff. It is one of the oddities of this conflict that only Anselm and Eadmer remembered the anathemas pronounced against investiture and homage at this council: cf. Southern *op. cit.* 165. Those more in touch probably took them for granted.

97.   *Ep.* 215.

congratulated him on his election and hoped that the traditional friendship between England and Rome would be restored. As the first move towards this he was sending Peter's Pence and confirmed to the pope those honours and that obedience which popes had had in England in the time of his father. This was on condition that he, the king, should likewise enjoy those dignities, usages, and customs which his father had enjoyed in the kingdom. (These, his envoys intimated, included the investiture of bishops and abbots.[98]) He was not going to surrender any of them, and his stand would be supported by the whole kingdom. If Paschal was obdurate Henry would consider withdrawing his obedience. The pope replied with a long and conciliatory letter, which William Warelwast brought back in August–September 1101.[99] He could not allow investitures to Henry. For the Lord said, 'I am the door: by me if any man enter in, he shall be saved' (John 10: 9). The entry to the sheepfold, the church, must be by way of the good shepherd, Christ. It was wrong for a king or prince to make himself that door. Paschal added a number of other texts, but it was on this from St John's Gospel that he usually relied in later letters. If its relevance to the matter in dispute was accepted, it was a neat and unanswerable formulation of the reformers' attitude. In his arbitrary, and to his way of thinking irrefutable, application of a biblical text, the pope was at one with the Norman Anonymous. Paschal concluded his letter with the placatory remarks that he had no wish to reduce Henry's royal power and was claiming no more than investiture in the promotion of bishops (i.e. he was not questioning Henry's patronage; nor in fact did he refer to homage). If Henry would renounce investitures Paschal would help him all he could. Moreover, the surrender of this wicked usurpation would not weaken Henry's power; on the contrary, when he ruled in accordance with the laws of God, his authority would be all the greater in his kingdom.

None of the parties moved publicly from the position taken up in 1101 until 1105. Paschal simplified his attitude to a defence of the law of the church, which was the law of God. Lay investiture of bishops and abbots, the doing of homage by clerks to laymen, and the consecration of those who had accepted investiture or done homage had been condemned by a succession of councils and most recently at Rome in 1099; he himself renewed these decrees at the Lateran Council of 1102;[100] and he could not allow Henry dispensation, for, if he did, every prince would want it.[101] Henry stood on his rights and rested his case on the customs which admittedly had been those of William I and Lanfranc, both religious men. According to Eadmer, he said, 'What my ancestors owned in this kingdom belong to me. What have mine to do with the pope?'[102] which was not much different from Rufus's views. Anselm entered, at least in public, into no theological or legal arguments. He was personally bound by prohibitions which with his own ears he had heard decreed and he was an

---

98. *Ep.* 216.

99. *Ep.* 216; cf. 224, 305; *HN* 128–31.

100. As he informed Anselm, 15 April 1102, *ep.* 222.

101. Dispensations *pro temporum necessitate et pro personarum qualitate* were being discussed at this time: A. Becker, *Papst Urban II* 143 ff.

102. *HN* 147.

obedient son of the church.[103] At an early stage he was wounded when the pope negotiated over his head,[104] but later he probably preferred to leave it to his masters. In his letters he usually greeted the king with 'faithful service and faithful prayers'. This spiritual fealty was his substitute for feudal homage.

All parties wanted a settlement. The quarrel was inconvenient to Henry, who not only had problems in the kingdom but also wished to deprive his brother of Normandy. He did not care to appear as an irreligious tyrant, ill-treating a saintly monk. For the church could switch its support to Duke Robert, where no doubt it would have been had Robert not had an even worse reputation than Henry. Nevertheless, the king stood firmly on his traditional rights and adjusted his stance according to the political circumstances. By 1103 he was prepared to allow Anselm to go into exile again and by 1104 even to deprive him of the temporalities of his archbishopric for not returning. On the whole things went well for him. He defeated Robert in England and made some progress in Normandy, and Queen Matilda produced a son and heir. Anselm in this period is inscrutable, but he may well have preferred to return to England and Canterbury, however uncomfortable his position there might be, and despite the storm raised by his attack in 1102 on married priests, rather than to live abroad on charity. He was getting old and by 1106 his health was poor. But, although he knew that his voluntary exile was deplored even by his own monks and his trusted friend and vicar, Gundulf bishop of Rochester, and could easily be misrepresented, he never preferred convenience to principle. He had the most scrupulous conscience. Paschal, although not in an impregnable position, would seem to have had the diplomatic advantage over Henry, but clearly valued Anglo-Norman support and never allowed the dispute to get out of hand. All the extant letters of the king, pope, and archbishop are affectionate and respectful. Equally important, most of the negotiations were carried out secretly through agents trusted by all. The king used his clerk, William Warel-wast, and Anselm the monks Baldwin (of Tournai) of Bec and Alexander of Canterbury.

There were as well important intermediaries. Queen Matilda loved and revered Anselm and ardently desired a settlement.[105] The king's sister, Adela countess of Blois, possibly advised by the great canonist Ivo bishop of Chartres, was also involved.[106] Anselm's views went privately to many leading churchmen, including Hugh archbishop of Lyons. It is likely that all possible compromises were given an airing at one time or another, although the actual terms on which the conflict was settled cannot as yet be shown to have originated with any particular canonist or political thinker. In 1102 Gerard of York, Herbert of Thetford, and Robert of Chester returned from Rome with the story that the pope had told them privately that although he could make no

---

103. Cf. *epp.* 308, 315, 319, 329, 338. Eadmer believed that Anselm himself was opposed to lay investiture, *HN* 153.

104. *Ep.* 220.

105. Cf. especially *epp.* 317, 323.

106. *HN* 151, 164–5. Hugh the Chanter *HCY* 13–14 associated Ivo with the settlement. Modern commentators are less confident, see H. Hoffmann, 'Ivo von Chartres und die Lösung des Investiturproblems', *Deutsches Archiv* xv (1959) 401–3, 438–40; R. Sprandel, *Ivo von Chartres und seine Stellung in der Kirchengeschichte*: Pariser historische Studien i (Stuttgart 1962) 175.

concessions in public, he would in fact tolerate Henry's investitures provided the king appointed good men. On the strength of this Henry invested two of his clerks with bishoprics using the ring and staff, and, when Anselm refused to consecrate, hoped to use the services of the archbishop of York. Whatever the truth of the matter, the pope denied the story.[107] And Henry's attempt to employ York antagonized many bishops.

By the end of 1104 Paschal's patience was wearing thin and he began to put pressure on Henry. Sentences of interdict were passed at the General Council held at the Lateran in Lent 1105 against the count of Meulan and others who had encouraged Henry to retain investitures and those who had accepted investiture. Sentence on the king had been suspended, the pope informed Anselm, only because an embassy from Henry was expected.[108] These sentences broke the deadlock. Through the good offices of the countess of Blois Anselm travelled to Normandy, and on 21 and 22 July met Henry at L'Aigle, not far from Bec, to ratify an agreement which doubtless had already been negotiated. Henry reinvested Anselm with his archbishopric (the form this ceremony took is not described) and promised to repay everything he had taken from it. A royal legation would be sent to Rome to offer a settlement of the dispute over investiture and homage in time to return before Christmas with the pope's response. In the meantime Anselm, although restored to his position in England, would remain abroad.[109] The king's offer was, as Anselm explained to Archbishop Hugh of Lyons,[110] that he would accept the prohibition of investitures provided he could retain the homage of prelates. Included in the reconciliation of L'Aigle was the count of Meulan, whom the pope released from interdict on condition that he encouraged the king to favour the liberty of the church. Excluded were those who had accepted investiture and those who had consecrated them.

Anselm's various references to the count of Meulan at this time would allow it to be thought that he was the author of the scheme.[111] It was his conversion which made these events possible, and when there were hitches Anselm appealed to him. Even if the idea originated elsewhere (and it could have occurred to several people), it was a practical solution to an intractable problem. It is doubtful if it was based on any theoretical argument. It was a straightforward compromise, involving a separation of *temporalia* (if not *regalia*) from *spiritualia*,[112] which made sense in the historical context. Anselm, a Gelasian, clearly had no personal objection on principle. But he could conjure up difficulties. What if the pope agreed, and then some religious prelate-elect declined to become the king's vassal? What should he do in the circumstances, he asked the archbishop of Lyons. Hugh, who had returned from a visit to the Holy Land less rigorous in his attitude, thought this too much

107. *Epp.* 250, 253, 280, 281; *HN* 137 ff. Fröhlich 162.
108. *Epp.* 348, 351, 353, 354, 361.
109. *Epp.* 364, 369; *HN* 164–7.
110. *Ep.* 389.
111. Cantor 234 ff.
112. See below 302 and n. 121.

and advised Anselm to accept the papal decision and not raise further scruples.[113]

There was time for reflection, for it was not until after Michaelmas that the legation began to move. It was agreed that Henry should send William Warelwast and Anselm the monk Baldwin.[114] Anselm refused to send a copy of the letter the king had written to the pope for registration at Canterbury, for he did not think that it should be preserved.[115] Anselm's own letter explains the circumstances in neutral tones, and states that he saw no reason to dissent from the settlement proposed.[116] The pope's answer to Anselm (his reply to the king has not survived) dated 23 March 1106, arrived in Normandy in May.[117] Paschal gave thanks to God for moving Henry to obey the apostolic see and to Anselm who also had used his influence. To pick up a prostrate man it was necessary to bend a little in his direction, and the pope was willing to make that inclination. He absolved Anselm, who thought that he might have incurred the interdiction or excommunication pronounced by Urban II against those involved in lay investitures and homage to laymen. Anselm in his turn was to absolve those who had accepted investiture from the king and those who had done homage, together with those who had blessed such prelates, provided they accepted the penance which the ambassadors, William and Baldwin, would transmit orally. The abbot of Ely alone was left out of the reconciliation. Then came the crucial papal surrender: 'In future those who accept prelacies of churches without [lay] investiture, even if they have done homage to the king, are not on this account to be deprived of benediction, until through the grace of Almighty God the heart of the king shall be softened by the sweet showers of your preaching and abandon this requirement.' Other categories of delinquents were also to be pardoned. Although Paschal was very angry with those bishops who had reported him falsely in 1102, at the intercession of the king they were to be restored to communion until they were summoned to appear before the pope. Anselm was to absolve from their penances and their sins the king, the queen, and certain barons who had used their endeavours to get this treaty, and on his return to England was to settle everything with mercy and wisdom.

On 15 August 1106 the king and archbishop met at Bec, were reconciled, accepted the compromise, and settled some subsidiary matters. Anselm crossed to England; and late in September Henry defeated and captured Robert, and so won Normandy, at the battle of Tinchebrai. There were some who thought that this victory was Henry's reward for his agreement with Anselm. The king himself attributed the victory to God and assured Anselm that he intended to defend the liberty of the church.[118] It was proposed by the king that a council should be held in England at Easter 1107 to give effect to the

113. *Epp.* 389–90.
114. *Epp.* 370–1, 377–8.
115. *Ep.* 379.
116. *Ep.* 388.
117. *Ep.* 397.
118. *Epp.* 401–2; *HN* 181–4.

compromise. But the pope's arrival in France,[119] which aroused Henry's hope of even better terms, and then Anselm's renewed illness, which could have been mortal, caused the council to be postponed until Whitsun and finally to 1 August. When the council eventually met in Westminster Hall, Henry resisted those who urged him to preserve the customs of his brother and father and decreed that in future no one should be invested with a bishopric or abbey by the king or any other layman by grant of the pastoral staff and ring. In return Anselm conceded that no prelate-elect should be deprived of consecration to his honour on account of homage that he had done the king. Almost all the vacant English and Norman bishoprics and abbeys were then filled without royal investiture by ring and staff. On 11 August at Canterbury five bishops, including William Warelwast, who had been rewarded with Exeter for his services, were consecrated by Anselm and seven others. Anselm wrote to the pope that Henry was now obedient to the pope's command and had entirely surrendered investitures, although many had tried to prevent him.[120]

This compromise, which significantly was never put into writing, was a defeat for both parties. Henry had had to surrender investiture of prelates, Paschal had had to concede their homage, but, in the papal view, only for the *regalia*.[121] It was the first decisive check to the English sacramental monarchy, the first retreat from the full Gregorian position. Each party felt its defeat keenly. In one way Henry had come off worse, for he gave up something he had inherited in return for the temporary and provisional withdrawal of a speculative claim. But he had done better than the Capetian monarchy. By retaining (implicitly) the power to nominate bishops and abbots and (explicitly) their homage, he surrendered in fact no more than a cherished ceremony and one that he personally had never with clear conscience performed. Paschal had not been merely specious when he had argued that if Henry were to put himself in the right with the church, even at some cost, his authority and influence would be strengthened. As Anselm frequently pointed out to Henry, times had changed; and the compromise also helped to change them. It was a settlement in the spirit of a more pragmatic, accommodating age. It was the precedent for the Concordat of Worms. And in the end it received general acceptance.

If Paschal was proved right about Henry's improved esteem, the cause was probably more the king's greater piety after the death of his son (1120) than his surrender of investitures. Be that as it may, in compensation for the loss of ecclesiastical character which Henry suffered in 1107, there arose a new cult of sacramental kingship. The cult of Edward the Confessor began to be developed at Westminster abbey, and the influential west-country historian, William of Malmesbury, helped to popularize his reputation for sanctity and for possessing the power to cure the sick.[122] Although on available evidence it

119. Paschal confirmed the settlement at the Council of Troyes on 30 May, *Ep.* 422.

120. *Ep.* 430; *HN* 185–7.

121. Cf. Johannes Fried, 'Der Regalienbegriff im 11. and 12. Jahrhundert', *Deutsches Archiv* xxix (1973) 450.

122. Frank Barlow, *VEdR*, Appendix D; *Edward the Confessor* (1970) 256 ff. As late as 1142 William of Malmesbury, in his *Hist. Nov.* 4, referred to Edward as the last and most illustrious of his race.

seems that the custom of touching sufferers from the King's Evil (*regius morbus*), or scrofulas, was not institutionalized until the thirteenth century, probably in England by Henry III, there are hints that these miraculous powers had been attributed, in rivalry with the French but apparently with little success, to both Henry I and Henry II.[123] Some rise in the religious reputation of the monarchy after the death of Rufus was, of course, inevitable, and Henry's behaviour ensured that it would climb high. Even Stephen, for all his weakness, was not to lose all the increment. Durham writers particularly, because their church was attacked by a Scottish faction, were great admirers of their distant king. For Reginald of Durham Stephen was *piissimus*.[124]

Henry I's control over the English and Norman churches was as effective as his father's had been. Stephen's power was much reduced. The disputed succession, the new king's character, his lower standing as the son of a count, the inevitable reaction against strong and arbitrary royal government, and some unusual features in the church, especially the position of Stephen's brother, Henry bishop of Winchester, abbot of Glastonbury, and papal legate, and the rise of a Cistercian party, all these sapped his authority. The English church was able to stake out its claims to liberty and in some fields seize it precipitately. Indeed, occasionally it advanced rather more rashly that the Roman curia would have advised. The papacy itself resisted the temptation to take advantage of Stephen's weakness and upset seriously the understanding on which the compromise of Bec was founded. Even when the hostile Eugenius III was prompted by the hostile St Bernard, decent restraint was shown.[125]

Henry of Blois, as papal legate from 1 March 1139 until 24 September 1143, and also as the king's brother, probably the stronger character, and a very ambitious man, had an unusual position in the English church and used it or abused it, according to the point of view. He certainly assumed the direction of the English church and treated his brother almost as an equal. In August 1139 Henry claimed that Stephen owed his succession to the support of the church and therefore was under an obligation to repay the debt.[126] In 1141, after Stephen's capture, Henry asserted that he had in 1135 warranted to God his brother's promises to honour and promote the church, and claimed that the right to elect and consecrate a ruler pertained principally to the clergy of the kingdom.[127] It may be that Henry was the architect of Stephen's fortune, that he intended to manipulate him in the church's and his own interests, and that his fluctuations in allegiance were influenced by his concern for ecclesiastical liberty (until 1153 Stephen was the lesser of the two evils). But the king, after he had paid his debts, was ungrateful; he was urged to recover and maintain his uncle's rights; he resented the unusual claims which his brother advanced; he had to take account of the implication of the bishops in the civil war; and

123. For Henry I, cf. *GR* 273; *VEdR* 61–2. For Henry II, see Peter of Blois, *ep.* 150, *PL* ccvii. 440.
124. Reginald, *St Cuthbert* 134. There is a panegyric of him in c. 64.
125. Cf. Friedrich Kempf, 'Kanonistik und kuriale Politik im 12. Jahrhundert', *Archivum Historiae Pontificiae* i (1963) 22 ff.
126. *Hist. Nov.* 30.
127. *Ibid.* 53–4.

inevitably he became involved in a new debate on the respective positions of *regnum* and *sacerdotium*. He had to fight a defensive action. The most obvious contrast with the old order is seen in the astonishing reversal of the jurisdictional situation. Whereas William I and his sons had successfully tried bishops in the royal court according to feudal law, Henry of Winchester attempted to try Stephen in an ecclesiastical council according to canon law. But Stephen never willingly capitulated. He was a determined though erratic fighter for his rights. It should not be overlooked that the ability of his successor, Henry II, to recover most of the traditional royal position in the church was due to Stephen's tenacious defence.

At his coronation Stephen renewed Henry I's initial promises, and so confirmed that the church should be free. This freedom was defined in more detail in the king's Oxford charter of April 1136.[128] He allowed himself to be styled, 'by the grace of God elected king of the English with the assent of the clergy and people, consecrated by William archbishop of Canterbury and legate of the holy Roman church, and confirmed by Innocent pontiff of the holy Roman church'. This formula, although again only an elaboration of one already used by Henry I,[129] is entirely ecclesiastical, and, especially in its reference to the participation of the clergy and people, would seem more appropriate to the election of a bishop than of a king. The church was, indeed, as Henry of Blois reminded the bishops in 1139,[130] 'embracing Stephen within its bosom'. In return Stephen gave the church almost everything it asked for. He renounced simony. He gave the bishops jurisdiction and authority over all ecclesiastical persons and clerks and their possessions, and also the arrangement of the church's endowments. He confirmed all the churches' dignities, privileges, and ancient customs. He conceded that the churches should have all the property which they possessed at the time of the Conqueror's death and all benefactions made since. But the line drawn at 1087 was an important limitation. He promised to maintain peace and justice. He restored to the church and kingdom the afforestations of Henry I. He allowed bishops and abbots to dispose of their chattels at death. He agreed that vacant sees should be adminstered by clerks or trusted men of the church until the vacancy was filled. Although the exact import of some of these concessions is open to dispute, and it is doubtful whether free elections, the renunciation of royal custody over vacant bishoprics and abbeys, or the complete abolition of royal jurisdiction over ecclesiastical persons and possessions can be read into them, Stephen's surrender was abject. There is, however, a final saving clause. 'All these things I grant and confirm, saving my royal and rightful dignity.' It could be argued that this takes back most of what had been given away; even if it was no more than a sop to the royal dignity, it did give the king a possible means of escape.

In fact, after 'buying the crown', Stephen attempted to keep in force the ancient customs and rights of his predecessors. In 1141 Henry of Blois, when justifying his transfer of allegiance from the captive king to the trium-

---

128. *SSC* 142–4. See also above 91, 130.

129. Henry, immediately after his coronation, to Anselm, 'et ego nutu dei a clero et a populo Angliae electus', *SSC* 120; *AEp.* 212.

130. *Hist. Nov.* 30.

phant Matilda, claimed that Stephen had broken all the promises for which Henry had stood surety. He had not maintained peace and justice, he had sold abbeys, pillaged churches of their treasures, and taken the advice of the wicked, and he had arrested bishops and deprived them of their possessions. The last charge was a reference to Stephen's actions in June 1139, when, fearing an invasion from Matilda, he had put under arrest the justiciar, Roger bishop of Salisbury, and Roger's nephew, Alexander bishop of Lincoln, because they refused to surrender their castles. He had then through the use of rather rough actions and threats forced Roger's family to hand over Salisbury, Sherborne, Devizes, and Malmesbury, and Alexander's Newark and Sleaford. The surrendered castles he entrusted to his lay friends, the bishops he released.

There were churchmen of the highest repute who saw nothing wrong in this old-fashioned behaviour. But although Hugh of Amiens, archbishop of Rouen, a monk and theologian of distinction, was prepared to defend this royal action on the grounds that the building of castles by bishops was contrary to canon law and that the king could properly repress such an abuse, Henry of Blois maintained that if the bishops had done wrong they should be tried not by the king but according to canon law and that they should not be deprived of the possession of any property, especially buildings constructed at their own expense on church lands, except in a general ecclesiastical council. The legate therefore summoned Stephen to attend a council to be held at Winchester on 29 August. Henry, who himself held castles, no doubt feared for his own. But his assertion that castles were *spiritualia* was worldly in the extreme, an extraordinary paradox; his refusal to recognize the baronial character of bishops at a time when civil war was about to break out was perverse, and his attempt to put a king publicly on trial was outrageous by contemporary ways of thinking. At the council the legate acted like a king, putting the charges and requiring the archbishop of Canterbury and bishops to give judgment.[131] The prince-bishop, himself a chimaera,[132] was introducing a new sort of confusion into the relations between the two powers.

Stephen made no reply to the summons, but sent earls to the council, not as his proxies or counsel but more as intermediaries. In fact, rather like William of St Calais in 1088, he never accepted the jurisdiction of the court nor stood to judgment. The legate charged him with the arrest, imprisonment, and humiliation of the bishops and the spoliation of church property. The king should make amends for the sin he had committed. He told the earls that the king should either justify his deed or submit to the court's judgment. The king then sent his chamberlain, Aubrey de Vere, to justify his actions. Aubrey gave political and feudal reasons for the arrest and stated that Roger of Salisbury (Alexander was not present) had been arrested not as a bishop but as a royal servant (*serviens*) who carried out the king's business and received his pay (he was referring to his office as justiciar). The bishops had willingly surrendered their castles to avoid a secular charge against them. Money found in the castles was royal treasure that had been embezzled, and was willingly given up by

---

131. *Hist. Nov.* 30.
132. 'qui futurus est novum quoddam monstrum ex integro et corrupto compositum, scilicet monachus et miles', HH *De contemptu mundi* 315.

Roger. The matter was closed, and the king wished it to remain closed. Bishop Roger interjected that he had never been Stephen's servant (*minister*) nor taken his pay, and if he could not get justice in that court he would appeal to one of higher jurisdiction (presumably the papal court). The legate probably thought these were rash statements, for he tried to bring the council back to the question of how accused bishops should be tried. These he said had been sentenced without trial, contrary to canon law. It was contrary to the law of nations and the procedure of even lay tribunals (*forensibus iudiciis*) to require men to plead when dispossessed of their property, so the king should first reinvest them. We are reminded of the plea made by William of St Calais in 1088.

The court was adjourned until 1 September to await the arrival of the archbishop of Rouen. Hugh stated quite simply that it was contrary to canon law for bishops to hold castles, and even if permitted as an act of grace, it was general custom for a king to have the disposal of all castles in time of danger. Hence the bishops had no case at all against the king. Aubrey de Vere added that the king had heard that some of the bishops were preparing to go to Rome to act against him. 'He advises none of you to do this, for if one of you should go anywhere out of England against his wish and the dignity of the kingdom, it would be very difficult for him to return. Moreover, as he sees that he is being injured, of his own accord he takes this case on appeal to Rome.'[133] It is not clear whether the arguments of the archbishop or the threats of the chamberlain made the greater impression; but the council broke up without taking action. Instead, the legate and the archbishop fell at the king's feet in his chamber and begged him not to allow discord to exist between *regnum* and *sacerdotium*. Stephen seems to have given affable assurances. He had withstood and overcome this outrageous threat to his dignity. It must have given him much pleasure to see the legate and the archbishop on their knees before him.

The expected invasion took place shortly after the council closed, and most of the bishops were caught up in the civil war and behaved not unlike the barons. On 2 February 1141 Stephen was captured before Lincoln and handed over to Matilda. A month later the legate recognized Matilda as his lady, after she had made him assurances similar to those he had extorted from Stephen in 1136. And on 7 April Henry held a legatine council at Winchester.[134] The chronicler William of Malmesbury was present and has given us a lively account of the proceedings. After separate secret meetings with the bishops, abbots, and archdeacons, the legate addressed the assembly. He explained and excused the repudiation of Henry I's true heir in 1135 and the

---

133.   In an interesting account of this council, for which Geoffrey de Gorron, abbot of St Albans, was ultimately responsible, contained in the life of Theodora (Christina) of Markyate, ed. C. H. Talbot (1959) 166 ff., the king appeals to Rome to prevent the council excommunicating him, and both sides arrange to send representatives to the papal curia (Geoffrey was to represent 'the church'). The point of the story is that, since the king threatened anyone who proceeded to Rome against him with the loss of all his property, Geoffrey was anxious to evade the duty – and did so. It is not stated, but can be inferred, that the appeals and counter-appeals were dropped.

134.   *Hist. Nov.* 50 ff. Cf. Karl Schnith, '*Regni et pacis inquietatrix*: Zur Rolle der Kaiserin Mathilde in der "Anarchie" ', *Journal of Med. Hist.* ii (1976) 135.

substitution of Stephen. He listed Stephen's misdeeds against the church and pointed to God's punishment of his sins. Since the kingdom needed a ruler, he had consulted the majority of the clergy, and with the help of God it had been decided that they should elect as lady of England and Normandy the daughter of that great king, Henry I. Although the proposal was opposed by the commune of London, by various barons and by a clerk of the queen, who read a letter from his mistress, the legate had his way. The council had in fact little choice but to accept the *fait accompli*.

Within seven months, however, the legate had quarrelled with Matilda, Robert earl of Gloucester had been captured and exchanged for Stephen, and it became necessary for the legate to revoke his earlier measures. Another legatine council was called for 7 December, this time at Westminster. Unfortunately William of Malmesbury was not present and relied for his report on hearsay. Sympathy was with Stephen, who complained in person of the treatment he had received, and inevitably Henry incurred odium for having deserted his brother's cause and backed the loser. But the legate pleaded necessity: with Stephen captured and his military forces dispersed, there was nothing else he could have done. But, he continued, as Matilda had broken her undertaking to observe the rights of the church, God had ordered things in such a way that he, the legate, had been able to escape from the danger which had threatened him and also to rescue his brother from his bondage. Therefore, in the name of God and the pope he ordered them to aid the king with all their might, a king who had been anointed by the will of the people with the approval of the apostolic see. He excommunicated Matilda's supporters, but spared the person of their cousin.[135]

An unusual situation in England and Normandy had produced unusual claims and events. Henry of Blois had become not only a king-maker (in 1153 he was negotiating in the same way with Matilda's son, Henry[136]) but also a sort of royal ecclesiastical person. In his control of the English church, his orders to the archbishop of Canterbury and the suffragan bishops, his disposal of what had been royal patronage, his advancement of *nipoti* and dependents, and his interference in the affairs of the kingdom, he had taken over a large part of his brother's authority. But the reasons he advanced to justify his behaviour were not well founded in contemporary English political attitudes or in papal policies. It was not difficult to regard him as an adventurer and his justifications as cloaks for his own ambition. His authority was unpopular with the archbishop of Canterbury and the suffragan bishops who naturally preferred the old order, and his aims were suspect to many spiritual men, such as Hugh of Amiens. St Bernard and Eugenius III were not his greatest admirers. Although he helped the church in England to escape from many of the fetters imposed on it by his uncles and grandfather, he introduced an instability and incoherence which were resented. When Henry II succeeded on Stephen's death in 1154, many leading men, both lay and ecclesiastical, were ready for a return, if not exactly to the old order, at least to a polity in which *regnum* and *sacerdotium*

---

135. Cf. also the account in the Waverley annals in *Annales Monastici* ii. 229, where it is stated that Stephen's perfidious vassals were banned on the order of Pope Innocent II.

136. John of Hexham 331.

were properly distinguished and existed in reasonable harmony. Men wanted neither a Henry I nor a Henry of Blois.

Nevertheless, if a choice had to be made, they would probably have preferred a 'good' king. An eminent theologian of this time was Robert Pullen. Born near Sherborne, he may have studied under William of Champeaux in Paris. He became archdeacon of Rochester under Bishop John II, and in a teaching career at Oxford and Paris, which extended from about 1133 to 1142, he had gifted pupils, including Gilbert Foliot and John of Salisbury, and distinguished contemporaries – Peter Abelard, Hugh of St Victor, Gilbert of la Porrée, Walter of Mortagne, and Peter Lombard, the 'Master of the Sentences', to mention only the greatest. Although Pullen was not quite in the first class, he was in no way provincial or unaware of the most advanced teaching of the leading masters. St Bernard was an enthusiastic patron and dear friend, and Lucius II almost immediately after his election as pope called him to Rome, made him a cardinal, and appointed him chancellor. In 1145 Bernard, in a most flattering letter, asked him to keep his eye on the new Cistercian pope, Eugenius III (whom the abbot thought a bit of a simpleton), and see that he was not deceived or misled. It is interesting to find, therefore, that Pullen in his theological compendium, *Sententiarium libri octo*, written probably in 1142–44, expresses very clearly moderate Gelasian views on *regnum* and *sacerdotium*.[137]

According to Pullen (VI, 56), the two powers, the priestly dignity (*sacerdotalis dignitas*) and the secular or royal power (*saecularis/regia potestas*), each wields its own sword in the church. Jesus Christ considered that in his own struggle two swords were enough (Luke 23: 38); and holy church, the body of which Christ is the head, likewise needs two swords in its struggle against the world (=the devil), swords in the form of the Cross. One is entrusted to the clergy, the other to the laity, and this is an expedient division of function, since the one power rules the body, the other the soul (*spiritus*), the one strikes the recalcitrant a physical, the other a spiritual blow. The common and sole purpose of both powers is that their subjects, after correction, should live in peace. They seek not revenge but emendation; they are like schoolmasters whipping their pupils, parents their children, masters their slaves, inflicting punishment only in order to correct their faults. Neither power should sell its services, neglect its own rights, or usurp the other's; each should come to the other's aid. The one punishes with imprisonment, mutilation, or, if necessary, death; the other with St Peter's sword cuts off the ear of its opponents (cf. John

---

137. For Pullen see F. Pelster, 'Einige Angaben über Leben und Schriften des Robertus Pullus', *Scholastik* xii (1937) 239; F. Courtney, *Cardinal Robert Pullen (Analecta Gregoriana* lxiv Rome 1945); Hartmut Hoffmann, 'Die beiden Schwerter im Hochmittelalter', *Deutsches Archiv* xx (1964) 93–4. His *Sententiarum libri octo* is in *PL* clxxxvi. 625. He had a nephew named Parisius. His connexion with Lucius II, who had been Innocent II's chancellor, is not clear. But *c.* 1141 St Bernard, when writing on Pullen's behalf to Bishop Ascelin of Rochester, referred to the archdeacon's important friends in the Roman curia (*ep.* 205), and in this and the letter he wrote to Pullen in 1145 (*ep.* 342) he expressed the warmest friendship and also praised his erudition, wisdom, and sound teaching (*sana doctrina*). St Bernard may well have been behind him in his career; but how he attracted the abbot's attention is not known. To have spoken against Abelard would have been enough.

18: 10) when it deprives them of hearing the word of God either by suspension or by anathema. Both swords are committed to the maintenance of discipline in the church.

Pullen returns to the subject later in his treatise (VII, 7). All powers in this world are established by God and should cooperate in order to further his purpose. Since the priestly power, wielding the sword of St Peter, is unable to cut off all the evils in the church, evils which renew themselves incessantly, it needs the help of the other sword which has been entrusted to the royal power. If the priest could bring about the correction and peace of the church solely by using the spiritual sword, he would have no need of the corporal sword of the king, but because the church may not shed blood royal power is necessary. The king, however, must act with justice, keep to his own role, and assist the church. If he does so, he is truly a king; if not, he is a tyrant. Since the body is inferior to the soul, and the body goes astray if not ruled by the soul, so kingdoms will collapse unless supported by the direction of priests. The *sacerdotium* therefore excels the *regnum* in those matters which pertain to God, the *regnum* excels the *sacerdotium* in those which pertain to the world. Accordingly they should pay their due debts to one another. The king should obey the priest in God's commands, and the prelate should know that he is subject to the king in the business of the world. In this way are rendered 'to Caesar the things which are Caesar's, and unto God the things that are God's (Matt. 22: 21). Pullen even pays some attention to royal servants and their proper conduct (VII, 8–9), additional proof that he gave the secular sword an important role in church affairs.

There is much to suggest that Pullen's views were not out of line with the general attitude of the English church at the time. And it would seem that, despite the anarchy, by Henry II's reign the underlying positions established by the Compromise of Bec had been established. Men were anxious to define the frontiers on the terms which had been indicated. The intellectuals and policy-makers in the church were mostly men whose background was the cathedral chapter and the bishop's school and whose main interest was in law.[138] Pope Alexander III (1159–81), a distinguished canonist, experienced in administration, and a man of reason, set the tone. The Becket dispute, despite the unusual passions generated and its tragic outcome, on one level was always regarded by the pope as a demarcation dispute within an undefined area of jurisdiction. *Regnum* and *sacerdotium* learned to live with such skirmishing on the frontiers. The kings had been waging a losing battle. Henry I had been unable to recover all the customs of his father and Lanfranc, Henry II all those of his grandfather. They had, however, fought tenaciously, restabilized the position, and, as it turned out, made certain that the *regnum* would not be seriously weakened in the future. Moreover, they had not lost all charisma. Henry II's clerical servants believed that they served someone who was no ordinary layman, someone who, although as a sinful man he could be flogged at

---

138. Cf. Hans Liebeschütz, 'Das 12. Jahrhundert und die Antike', *Archiv für Kulturgeschichte* xxxv (1953) 247–71; Heinrich Hohenleutner, 'Johannes von Salisbury in der Literatur der letzten zehn Jahre', *HJ* lxxvii (1958) 497 ff.

Becket's tomb, had himself miraculous powers of healing, the sign that, king by the grace of God,[139] he still had some special part to play in the government of the English church.[140]

139. Henry inserted *dei gratia* into his charter style at some point between 1172 and 1173, after his reconciliation with the church, cf. R. L. Poole, 'The dates of Henry II's charters', *EHR* xxiii (1908) 79, supporting the hypothesis of L. Delisle.

140. Cf. *Dialogus de Scaccario* (1177-79) (ed. Johnson), preface, 1-2; Peter of Blois, *Epp.* 150, cf. 6, 14; *PL* ccvii. 16, 42, 440. Even John of Salisbury, although not adulatory, regarded the king as God's vicar on earth and his duties patriarchal. Cf. John Dickinson, 'The medieval conception of kingship as developed in the *Policraticus* of John of Salisbury', *Speculum* i (1926) 308.

Conclusion

An evaluation of the Norman achievement in the English church should not be particularly difficult. The changes made between 1066 and 1154 are adequately documented; most of the leading actors in church and state are well known and scarcely controversial figures; and the several biases which have to be taken into account are obvious. There were the conquerors and the conquered. The residual biases are most easily identified in ecclesiastical historians of those nations which consider themselves particularly the victims of Norman, or Anglo-Norman, imperialism, that is to say the Welsh, Irish, and Scots. The major temptations are to claim that the conditions in the native church in the pre-Norman period were not as bad as portrayed by the conquerors; that the reforms were inspired, inaugurated, approved, or made by the natives themselves; and that in any case the changes were inevitable and would have come about in the long run, Norman conquest or no Norman conquest. All these views are valid up to a point, and can be applied to the English church, but they should not be pressed too hard.

The Norman treatment of the national churches was clearly imperialistic, and most of the features associated with imperialism can be seen. The conquerors removed from the English church its leaders and possible trouble-makers, favoured the few English prelates who were willing to collaborate, and treated the lower clergy like the agricultural classes to which it belonged. The attitude of the parish clergy is not on record. They were, however, the natural leaders of their flocks,[1] and it may be thought that they were deeply involved in the insurrections which followed William's coronation and the start of the Norman settlement, and suffered with their fellow countrymen. But they were not generally replaced by foreigners; and the traditional social cleavage in the church between prelates and parish priests was further sharpened by a difference in race. In this respect the position had changed little by 1154: the bishops and the majority of the abbots were of French ancestry, the lower clergy of Anglo-Danish. Nevertheless, acute racial tension disappeared relatively quickly in England. There was still some sensitivity after a century of foreign rule. The boasts of those who claimed Norman lineage prove that race remained a factor in the social structure and class feelings. But there had been a good deal of intermarriage, even at the highest

---

1. Cf. above 133. In 1138, when the Scots invaded across the Tees, Archbishop Thurstin of York ordered the men of every parish, led by their priests and carrying the Cross and the banners and relics of their saints, to join him and the barons, who were flying the royal standard at Northallerton: Ailred of Rievaulx, *Relatio Standardi* in *Chronicles of the reigns of Stephen, Henry II, and Richard I*, ed. R. Howlett (Rolls ser. 1886) iii. 182.

levels, and hostility had been reduced to tolerable dimensions. It may be doubted whether there was more racial antagonism than is found in twentieth-century 'Western' industrial states with their mixed populations.

The situation in 'the Celtic fringe' was rather different. The Welsh, Scottish, and Irish churches were in 1066 far more idiosyncratic than the English, and the people had easily recognizable national characteristics. If the English were considered 'boorish' by the Normans, the Celts were 'savages', several degrees lower on the scale. Until 1070 the moderately idiosyncratic English church had served as a buffer between the Celtic and the Italo-Frankish churches. After 1070 not only was there a drive towards greater uniformity on the Continent but also the English church was reformed on this model and thereafter kept up to date. The peculiarities of the Celtic churches were revealed for all to see, and were indeed perceived not only by the Anglo-Normans and the directing powers in the Roman church but also by the 'backward areas' themselves. A native reform movement similar to that which had taken place after the Synod of Whitby in 664, became inevitable. But it took widely different courses, and produced distinctive results, in the three main areas.

Wales suffered piecemeal military conquest, and although acknowledged to be a geographical entity (*Wallia*) was allowed no political or ecclesiastical unity or independence. The bishops who were appointed in the twelfth century with the connivance of the local church and secular powers, whether Norman barons or Welsh princes, and with the approval of the English king and primate, were mostly Welshmen and members of the church to which they were appointed, but also clerks sympathetic to reform of the Norman type and seldom averse to working with the archbishop of Canterbury and his other suffragans. Indeed they created a Welsh church on the English pattern. Typically Llandaff was recognized as pertaining to the local Llancarfan family, although the descent of the bishopric within the kin was a matter for negotiation. But no less typical, the bishop whom Welsh historians regard as the greatest upholder of the interests of the Welsh church and nation, Bernard bishop of St David's (1115–48), was by birth a Frenchman and by training a royal clerk. His struggle to make St David's the metropolitan of a Welsh province had in fact little connexion with Welsh nationalism: its real driving force was Norman ambition. Bernard's model was the archbishop of York, although he himself would undoubtedly have accepted Canterbury's primatial authority. He wanted to create his own empire within a Norman-directed British church, and his ambitions for St David's only came so near to success because he was a familiar and popular colleague in the *regnum Angliae*. The next champion of St David's claims to metropolitan status, Gerald 'the Welshman', was more ambiguous and volatile in his allegiances, but again hardly a Welsh patriot. It may be thought that the Norman conquerors treated the Welsh church less brutally than they treated the English, if only perforce. There were usually negotiations with the chapter of the episcopal church; the local views were often taken into account; and control was maintained more by veto than by nomination. This was no more, and probably much less than a native prince would have done. It is true that candidates were chosen who would reform the Welsh church on the Anglo-Norman model; but at the time this was generally considered a laudable aim. Canterbury had the entire backing of Rome.

Although a similar process took place in Scotland in the same period, it followed a different course because that country was mediatized under the Anglo-Scottish monarchy.[2] Malcolm Canmore and his sons, based on an anglicized Lothian, in direct imitation of, and helped by, the reformed English church, created a Scottish church on the English pattern and one which, like the Welsh, could easily have formed part of a church of Great Britain, had there not been political obstacles. Rome backed York's claim to metropolitan authority in Scotland almost unreservedly throughout this period. But the Scottish monarchy resisted English ecclesiastical as well as temporal imperialism, and was strong and persistent enough to struggle through to independence. The direct power of the English crown and church over the *ecclesia scotticana* was negligible, its indirect influence far-reaching.

Unlike Wales and Scotland, Ireland came under no military or political pressure from Anglo-Normans before 1154, and the considerable changes which took place in the Irish church in the first half of the twelfth century were purely the result of an awareness of, and discontent with, Irish peculiarities which arose within some sections of the inhabitants of Erin. Bishops who had been consecrated at Canterbury, and more so those who had been educated in England or Normandy, prepared the ground for reform. But, because of the slenderness of the connexion and distrust of the seaports and their bishops who had contrived and maintained the link, recourse was had direct to Rome. And it was papal legates, the first, it is true, a resident bishop of Norman extraction (Gilbert of Limerick), who refashioned the Irish structure on the English model and made preparations for a reform on the general western pattern. If this opened the way to English political and clerical imperialism, that had not been in the minds of any of the parties concerned. Nor did reform of this kind usually lead to subjection. Indeed, as the Welsh and Scottish cases show, reform prepared a national church for self-sufficiency and independence within the common framework of western Christendom. It was the relative failure of the reform movement in Ireland – the reluctance entirely to destroy Irish idiosyncracies and extirpate notorious abuses – which left it in a vulnerable position. Henry II's agents at the papal curia made charges against the Irish church and people which they would not have made against the Welsh and could not have levelled against the Scottish.

Even though Canterbury's patriarchate within Great Britain began to disintegrate in the twelfth century, this itself was partly the result of the reforms which had been introduced into the Celtic lands either directly or indirectly from the Anglo-Norman church. The magnitude of the influence proves the excellence and vitality of the church the Normans created in England and warns us not to underrate their achievement. At the same time the failure to inspire a lasting affection and maintain a permanent cultural hold points to the unpleasant features of Norman behaviour. The greater success of France in all cultural matters in the twelfth century can be compared. The Normans, still in some ways Vikings, were only parvenu French and English.

2.   R. L. G. Ritchie, *The Normans in Scotland* (1954).

But at first they were the sole colporteurs of this superior civilization operating in the northern lands, barbarians carrying gifts of great value.

It is generally acknowledged that one of the effects of the Norman conquest on the English church was to give it greater structural coherence. The diocesan and metropolitan boundaries were redefined and the cathedrals rebuilt in a fairly standard style; the government was reanimated and the several competencies were debated and decreed. There was an attempt to bring all English institutions, primarily the cathedral chapters and the monasteries, up to the best Norman standards. It may be argued that most of the results would have occurred in the English church sooner or later without the help of a Norman conquest. The history of the Scottish and Irish churches shows how independent churches could in different ways be quite drastically remodelled without military compulsion. And reform, it should be noticed, whether made by foreign rulers or native, was just as painful for the victims of the changes. But, although the English church would have accepted in time all the new movements in the church at large, it would, for better or for worse, have kept more of its Anglo-Saxon past and probably retained a more disorderly constitution. The Normans were at first positively hostile to English tradition and so could be ruthless reformers. No tears were shed by them over the hallowed places and customs of the natives as they were cast down or torn out. Anything irregular, inconvenient, or strange could be destroyed. In this they earned the praise of the radicals at Rome. They were agents of righteousness, wielding the sword of justice.

The Normans took over the English church as one of the spoils of victory. Its wealth and offices were at their disposal. But, as we have already remarked, a reformed national church was prepared for a life of its own, and it is quite clear that the new *ecclesia anglicana* soon had an identity as distinct as its predecessor's. The kingdom itself was a heavy appendage to the duchy. And the church of Great Britain, *alter orbis*, a great patriarchate at the edge of the world, could never be in any way subject to a mere metropolitan church, and one subordinate, if ineffectually, to the primacy of Lyons. Canterbury was in every particular superior to Rouen, and from Lanfranc's pontificate onwards the rivalry between the two mother churches, although sometimes perhaps encouraging the pretensions of York, helped to give a sense of oneness, continuity, and individuality to the English church. Just as Thomas of Bayeux took up the cause of York, and, later, Bernard that of St David's, so Lanfranc and even Anselm championed the rights and privileges not only of Canterbury but also of the whole *ecclesia anglicana*. Thus the Norman conquest of the English church did not in at least one respect lead to national shame. For some Englishmen, like Eadmer at Canterbury, it led to glor . Not for centuries had Canterbury been more powerful and influential, or ruled by such holy men. These *novi Angli* had revived the greatness of the English past.

Those prelates who had been deposed and their clientèle, and those Englishmen who were kept from high office because of the royal policy, obviously viewed the situation differently. Englishmen were largely excluded from the highest governmental circles and overlooked for the highest posts. It may be that owing to the destruction and depression of the old Anglo-Danish nobility the entry of natives of high birth into the church was reduced, but racial prejudice also must have operated against their prospects. It was only in Scotland that Englishmen were offered bishoprics.[3] The recruitment of foreigners by reforming kings was nothing new; Cnut and Edward the Confessor had appointed foreigners to bishoprics and abbeys; William I's abbots in the duchy were in part foreign. An influx of Normans and other strangers into the English church after 1066 would have been considered usual and justifiable, but the totality of the ban on Englishmen hurt. Almost a century of racial discrimination was a great injustice and was not overlooked. Clerks of mixed parentage, like Orderic Vitalis and William of Malmesbury, were aware of it. It was, however, accepted with resignation, and simple justifications were to hand: God had punished the English for their sins, or for the sins of their ruler.[4] Moreover, in this world all plagues came eventually to their end.

The imposition of a new aristocracy, both secular and ecclesiastical, on the general population was, indeed, an added burden. The baronage and prelacy was a rentier class, and tribute when exacted for strangers is even more resented. The exactions of the church were heavy. Tithe, the various customary dues, the penances and judicial penalties, and finally the mortuary, reduced the income of the primary producers of wealth. But most of these taxes went to either the local clergy or familiar bodies; the church remained decentralized; and it would seem that the ordinary villager was not much affected by the Norman conquest of the church. In the local church the same priest officiated, the language was unchanged, no image was overthrown. Newfangled practices came in slowly, if at all.

The new prelates at first probably felt as insecure as the new barons and needed their own foreign households and military escorts. They were solidly allied with the king and barons in a common enterprise, and there is nothing to suggest that the sense of fellowship had weakened much by 1154. The bishops and abbots, because of their estates, military duties, governmental responsibilities, and feudal relationship with the king and other landowners, were barons of a sort and shared many interests with the lay magnates. Despite some rough passages and the strains of Stephen's reign they still looked to the king as the effective head of the church and their real master. The bishops had never conspired with the people, the barons, or the pope against the king. Anselm, who committed several 'treasons', inciting the people against married priests and maintaining that his obedience to the pope came before his duties to the king, was greatly blamed in England for these; and he himself, much disturbed by competing loyalties, had to invoke the highest moral justifications for his anti-social behaviour. Henry of Blois was likewise blamed for his changes in allegiance. The English church developed its own institutions and corporate spirit not in opposition to the baronage or the crown but because the growth of such 'orders' was a feature of the time – the baronage and the towns also became more self-conscious – and it suffered little interference from any direction in its internal affairs. It had secured a near monopoly of the adminis-

---

3. For example Turgot (1107), Eadmer (1120) (ineffective), and Waldef (?1159) (ineffective) to St Andrews.

4. Cf. the remarks in *VEdR* v. 77–9. William of Poitiers justified the Conquest as punishment for the sins and crimes of Earl Godwin and his son, *GG* 10–12, 166, 204, 206–8, 224, 230, *etc.*

tration of the sacraments and of a religious ministry; and hardly any of its practices or claims were disputed, overtly at least. If it put a price on most of its services (the prohibition of simony notwithstanding), it was a price almost all men were willing to pay, sooner or later.

The Norman prelates swept away in their own churches most of the peculiar Old English customs and traditions, and, although they came gradually to accept the English past, their achievements and failures were their own. It does not seem that the remnants of the Old English prelacy or the lower clergy made much contribution after 1070 to the way in which the church developed. The achievement of the new foreign hierarchy was considerable. By 1154 the reform programme laid down under Lanfranc had been carried out. The grosser forms of simony had disappeared. The marriage of priests and deacons had been invalidated, if not abolished, and hereditary succession to benefices checked. An ecclesiastical administration had been established and professional administrators and judges produced. The clergy as a whole was, because much more professionally trained and governed, far more distinct as a class and aware of its differences than had been the case in pre-Conquest England. Also its rule had become much more effective. The Anglo-Norman church not only disciplined the clergy but also increased its control over the laity, notably in the field of sexual morals and matrimonial business. Paganism had disappeared and heresy was absent. And the church had become stricter in everyday affairs. In an economic sense the whole church depended on the sins of the people, and when guilt gave out police action could take over. Archdeacons rose to power on their prosecution of vice. Habitual and distinctive activity generated power. By the later years of Henry I the church had advanced beyond the programme of Lanfranc and achieved a good measure of freedom and independence from lay control. But this was almost always at the cost of greater papal interference, and the substitution of the one master for the other was not a universally welcomed innovation in the English church.

Most of these changes were European movements rather than specifically Norman designs. But the Normans, with a wide network of communications and receptive to new ideas, implemented them without undue delay. The barrier which the Norman kings maintained against outside interference in their church could not prevent the spread of new ways of thinking among the intelligentsia. The effect of the barrier was merely to smooth out minor oscillations in papal policy and distinguish between the ephemeral and the serious changes. As can be seen from the reign of Henry I, none of the major European movements could be arrested. It was only beyond the frontiers of the English kingdom, in the poorer and more remote areas, that these lost their momentum.

The Anglo-Norman church was not at first conspicuously holier than the Anglo-Saxon. Each had its saints and sinners. Each was worldly, if in rather different ways. But since the church set ever higher standards in this period, and the English church always passed muster, it is likely that the average level of behaviour improved. This again may have been a general European phenomenon, a product of greater prosperity, better education, and more effective government. The church's teaching probably reached further down into lay society, and was more compelling than before. There may have been at least more seemliness, if not more spirituality, among the secular clergy. And in the latter part of the period, with the renewed interest in the ascetic life and the wave of new monasteries, it can hardly be doubted that there was more piety in the English church than at any time since the seventh century.

The Norman intellectual achievement in England was at least respectable. Although the greatest luminaries, Lanfranc and Anselm, were Italians, they would not have come to England except for the Conquest. And the re-establishment of Latin as the language of the church and of scholarship, with French as the auxiliary venacular, opened new roads for English scholars. The careers of men like Adelard of Bath, Robert Pullen, and John of Salisbury were a new phenomenon; and although these men, and others like them, caught a European tide, it was the Normans who caused it to flow around England. The kingdom in 1154 was not an originating centre of ideas, art, or piety any more than it had been in 1066. Its schools were inferior to those in northern France. It had had no Anselm of Laon or Peter Abelard. It produced no monastic saint of the stature of Bernard. It had no great shrine to serve as an attraction to pilgrims. Its main reputation was for wealth and beer, a beverage which dulls the intellect. But the Normans had at least raised its potential. All that was lacking in 1154 was a king who could exploit the riches, who could use his wealth to give satisfying and creative employment to talented Englishmen and attract to the kingdom a new wave of distinguished foreigners. These things Henry II did. And he also, inadvertently and to his disgrace, played a part in the establishment of one of the greatest shrines in Christendom. Although in reaction against the spirit of Stephen's reign, Henry in many ways summed up, and then magnified, the Norman achievement. In his aim to restore order to the *regnum* and *sacerdotium* he referred back to the golden age of his grandfather. But in his pursuit of the ancient laws and customs of the kingdom he not only completed one age, he also inaugurated another. Some growths which had become rank and disorderly he cut back; others which had been neglected and overshadowed he encouraged. He contrived a *renovatio imperii*, and within the empire was a proper place for the national church. What was proper had, of course, to be defined anew.

The literary relationship between some of the sources.

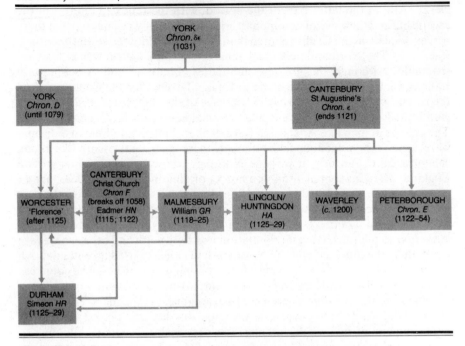

The Anglo-Welsh Episcopate 1066–1154: its composition
(percentages of the total number of bishops calculated on 5 year averages)

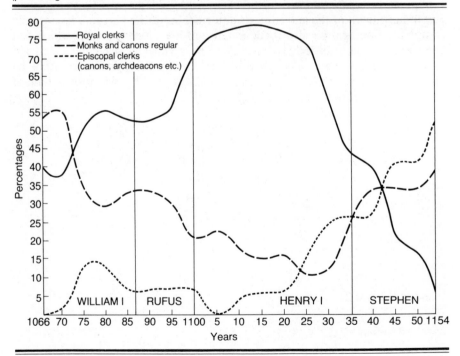

Map 1   Some of the more important centres

319

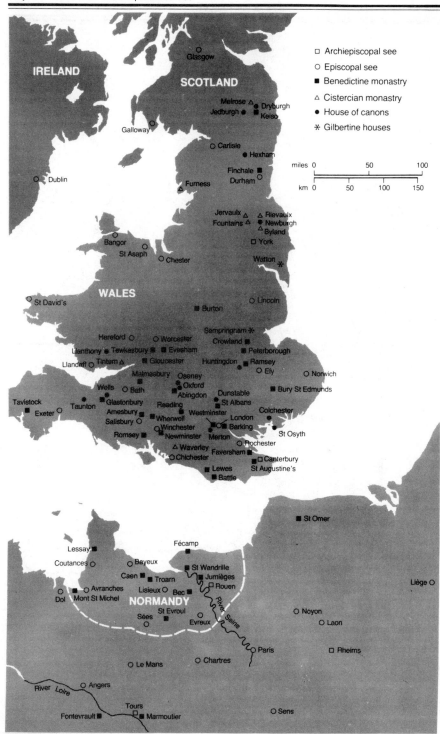

Archiepiscopal see □
Episcopal see ○
Benedictine monastery ■
Cistercian monastery △
House of canons ●
Gilbertine houses ✳

IRELAND

SCOTLAND

○ Glasgow

Melrose △ ● Dryburgh
Jedburgh ● ■ Kelso

Galloway

○ Carlisle
● Hexham

Finchale ■
Furness △ Durham ○

miles 0   50   100
km 0   50   100   150

Jervaulx △   △ Rievaulx
Fountains △ ● Newburgh
             △ Byland
             □ York

○ Bangor
St Asaph ○ ○ Chester

Watton ✳

○ Dublin

WALES

○ St David's

○ Lincoln

■ Burton

Sempringham ✳
Hereford ○   ○ Worcester   Crowland ■
Llanthony ● Tewkesbury ■ ■ Evesham   ■ Peterborough
Llandaff ○ Tintern △ ■ Gloucester Huntingdon ● ■ Ramsey
           Malmesbury ■   ○ Ely   ○ Norwich
           Oseney ●
Wells ● ○ Oxford   ■ Bury St Edmunds
Tavistock ■ Taunton ○ Bath Abingdon ● Dunstable ●
Exeter ○ Glastonbury ■ Reading ■ ● St Albans Colchester ●
         Amesbury ●   Westminster ■ ● St Osyth
         Salisbury ○ Wherwell ■ London □
         Romsey ■ Winchester ■ Barking ●
                  Newminster ■ Merton ● ○ Rochester
                  △ Waverley Faversham ■
                  ○ Chichester □ Canterbury
                  Lewes ■   St Augustine's ■
                  ■ Battle

■ St Omer

Fécamp ●

Lessay ■
Coutances ○ ○ Bayeux   ■ St Wandrille
         Caen ■ Troarn ■ ■ Jumièges   Liège ○
Avranches ■ Lisieux ○ Bec ■ □ Rouen
○ Dol Mont St Michel ■ NORMANDY   River Seine
         Sées   St Evroul ■   ○ Noyon
         ○   Evreux ○   ○ Laon

□ Rheims

○ Le Mans ○ Chartres   Paris ●

River Loire ○ Angers

Tours
□ ■ Marmoutier
Fontevrault ■   ○ Sens

Map 2   Parish Churches in Winchester and its suburbs

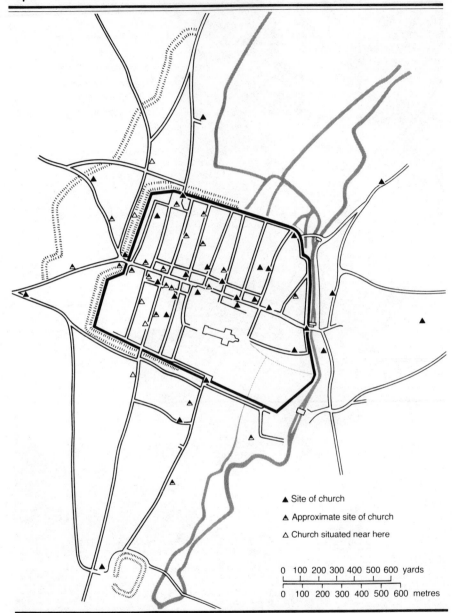

▲ Site of church

▲ Approximate site of church

△ Church situated near here

0   100 200 300 400 500 600   yards

0   100 200 300 400 500 600   metres

Winchester Studies Vol 1: Winchester in the Middle Ages by Barlow, Biddle, von Feilitzen and Keene. Edited by M. Biddle. © Oxford University Press 1976.

Map 3 The Hermits of Watling St

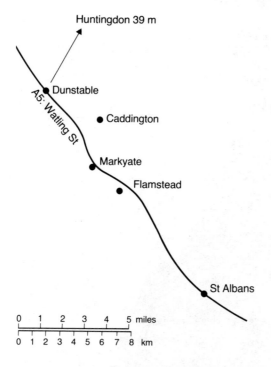

Huntingdon 39 m

A5: Watling St

Dunstable

Caddington

Markyate

Flamstead

St Albans

0   1   2   3   4   5 miles
0 1 2 3 4 5 6 7 8 km

Map 4   The Dioceses, Shires and Episcopal Sees

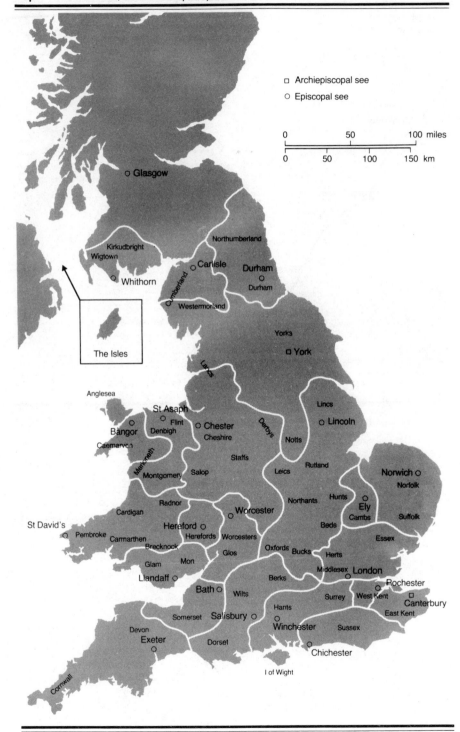

□ Archiepiscopal see

○ Episcopal see

0   50   100 miles

0   50   100   150 km

○ Glasgow

Northumberland

Kirkudbright

Wigtown

○ Carlisle   Durham
Whithorn   ○
Cumberland   Durham

Westermorland

The Isles

Yorks

□ York

Anglesea

Lancs

St Asaph
Flint   Lincs
Bangor   ○   ○ Chester   ○ Lincoln
Denbigh   Cheshire
Caernarvon   Notts
Merioneth   Staffs
Montgomery   Salop   Leics   Rutland

Radnor   Norwich ○
Cardigan   Northants   Hunts   Norfolk
St David's   Worcester ○   Ely
Pembroke   Hereford ○   Cambs   Suffolk
Carmarthen   Herefords   Worcesters   Beds
Brecknock   Glos   Oxfords   Bucks   Essex
Glam   Mon   Herts
Llandaff ○   Middlesex   London
Berks   Rochester
Bath ○   Wilts   West Kent   □
Surrey   Canterbury
Somerset   Salisbury ○   Hants   East Kent
Devon   Winchester   Sussex
Exeter   Dorset
○   Chichester ○
I of Wight
Cornwall

Map 5 Normandy: The Dioceses and Episcopal Sees

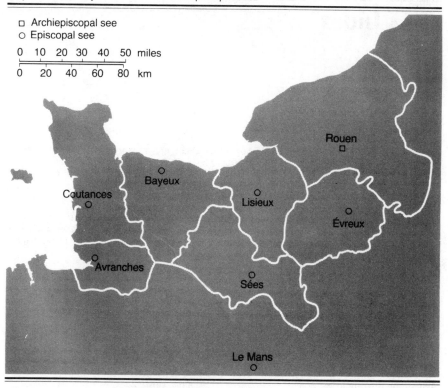

☐ Archiepiscopal see
○ Episcopal see

0 10 20 30 40 50 miles
0 20 40 60 80 km

Rouen ☐

Bayeux ○

Coutances ○

Lisieux ○

Évreux ○

Avranches ○

Sées ○

Le Mans ○

Index

Abbreviations: abp = archbishop; abt = abbot; archd. = archdeacon; bp = bishop;
card. = cardinal; cath. = cathedral; c.b. = cardinal bishop; ccl = council;
ch. = church; Cist. = Cistercian; Cl. = Cluniac; c.p. = cardinal priest; ct = count;
ctess = countess; d. = died; dioc. = diocese; Gilbert. = Gilbertine; k. = king;
pr. = prior; Sav. = Savigniac

Order of entries: persons are indexed under their Christian name. The clergy precede
the laity; the order is then according to rank, i.e. abps, bps, abts etc., then according
to the alphabetical order of the office, e.g. William of St Calais, bp of Durham
precedes William of Beaufi, bp of Elmham.